English Silver

in the
Museum of Fine Arts
Boston

VOLUME II

English Silver

in the

Museum of Fine Arts, Boston

VOLUME II • SILVER FROM 1697

including Irish and Scottish Silver

Catalogue by Ellenor M. Alcorn

with contributions on Irish silver by Thomas Sinsteden

MFA Publications

a division of the

Museum of Fine Arts, Boston

MFA Publications
a division of the Museum of Fine Arts, Boston
295 Huntington Avenue
Boston, MA 02115

This catalogue was made possible by the generous
support of the Andrew W. Mellon Publications Fund
and the National Endowment for the Arts.

NATIONAL
ENDOWMENT
FOR THE ARTS

COVER: 99. Sugar Box (detail). London, 1747/8.
Silver. 1991.3
FRONTISPIECE: 187. Salt cellar. London, 1824/5.
Silver gilt. 1989.313

PHOTOGRAPH CREDITS: All photographs except
those listed below are by the Museum of Fine Arts,
Boston, Department of Photographic Services:
fig. 1 courtesy of the Society of Antiquaries, London;
fig. 2–5 courtesy of Sir John Soane's Museum, London;
fig. 6 courtesy of the Victoria and Albert Museum,
London; fig. 8 courtesy of the Public Record Office,
National Archives, England; fig. 9 courtesy of the
Stevens and Williams Archive, Royal Breirley Crystal

Designed and produced by Cynthia Rockwell Randall
Edited by Fronia W. Simpson
Printed and bound at Sfera International Srl, Milan,
Italy

Available through D.A.P./Distributed Art Publishers
155 Sixth Avenue, 2nd floor
New York, NY 10013
Tel. (212) 627-1999 Fax (212) 627-9484

First edition
PRINTED IN ITALY

Table of Contents

7   Preface

8   Acknowledgments

10   Introduction

16   Abbreviations

20   Color Plates

49   Use of Catalogue

50   Catalogue

    ENGLISH OBJECTS, 50

    ENGLISH SPOONS, 305

    SCOTTISH SILVER, 327

    IRISH SILVER with Thomas Sinsteden, 332

    DOUBTFUL AUTHENTICITY, 358

365   Concordance

369   Index

Preface

AMONG ITS MANY TREASURES, the Museum of Fine Arts, Boston, is fortunate to possess a distinguished collection of English silver. The Museum's founda-
tions rest firmly on the excellence of its permanent collections, and the curatorial
staff is constantly refining and expanding our understanding of this material. It has been
a particular pleasure for me to witness and support the progress of this second volume
of the catalogue of the collection, which encourages us to scrutinize our holdings with
the greatest precision and critical acuity. The findings are intensely rewarding, and occasionally unexpected. This process is central to scholarship, and central to the life of our great
museums.

An initial grant from the National Endowment for the Arts supported much of the
research for this project, and the cost of the publication was underwritten by the Andrew
W. Mellon Publications Fund, Mrs. Jerome T. Gans, and many other private contributors
who are acknowledged in the following pages. I would like to express my gratitude to
those supporters and to the many members of the staff whose dedication and commitment
to excellence are evident in this volume. Above all we are indebted to Ellenor Alcorn,
whose profound scholarship and passion for her subject are evident in every page.

MALCOLM ROGERS
Ann and Graham Gund Director

Acknowledgments

THIS VOLUME IS THE RESULT of a long collaboration with a group of truly splendid colleagues. I wish to thank each of them for sharing their high standards, ideas, and, perhaps more important than anything, great good humor. Anne Poulet's commitment to the research and publication of the Museum's collection provided the essential framework for this project; her steadfastness and encouragement were unwavering. My fellow staff members, particularly Jeffrey Munger and Joellen Secondo, gave me intellectual stimulation, moral support, and friendship over many years. They also absorbed many of my regular responsibilities, allowing me liberty to devote myself to the book. Titanic contributions were made by my two research assistants, Kristina Wilson and Taryn Zarrillo, whose productivity and dedication were astounding. Kristina worked for nearly two years in the early stages of the undertaking, recording the vital statistics, zealously unraveling the history of each object, and organizing the photographic requests. Taryn took over in the final two years, meticulously correcting and molding the manuscript, taming my unruly references, and overseeing the photography. There would be no book without their dedication. George T. M. Shackelford was very supportive in the final stages of the manuscript preparation and production, and ensured that the production schedule was honored. Cynthia Randall was responsible for the handsome design of the book. Not only was she sensitive to the objects, she was a pleasure to work with. Cynthia Purvis and Dacey Sartor, also in the Department of Scholarly Publications, were key players in the production of the book. Over the course of several years many departmental interns and volunteers were enlisted to organize or pursue information. I thank Fran Altvater, Mathilde de Bellescize, Anne Cuniholm, and Irit Kerstein, for their contributions. Photographers Gary Ruuska, John Woolf, Greg Heins, and Chester Brummel guided by Tom Lang with support from Jennifer Riley, ensured that the objects are represented by informative, beautiful images. I acknowledge the many members of the Department of Objects Conservation and Scientific Research who cleaned the silver in preparation for photography, and the staff of the William Morris Hunt Library, particularly Joanne Donovan and Nicole Salamone, for the patient assistance they offered tracking obscure references. Jeannine Falino, who is completing a catalogue of the Museum's American silver, shared many insights and offered encouragement.

I had several key collaborators outside the Museum. I acknowledge gratefully the wise influence of my editor, Fronia W. Simpson, who played the role of a witty Virgil to my dispirited Dante. Thomas Sinsteden coauthored the entries on Irish silver, patiently illuminating what was new territory for me; he was a stimulating and generous contributor. Gale Glynn identified and provided biographical material on the engraved coats of arms, a crucial component of the book. Rob Butler spent many days reviewing with me the condition and construction of each object, so that the description of each was accurate and the terminology consistent.

I benefited greatly from the expertise and enthusiasm of colleagues in the field of silver, who responded to my inquiries, offered opinions and references, and allowed access to the collections under their care. I have tried to recognize individual assistance in the footnotes, but I would like to mention here the names of several who were chronically helpful. Christopher Hartop, Ubaldo Vitali, Amelia Fearn, and Beth Carver Wees were unstinting in their encouragement and support. Among my associates in England, Philippa Glanville was a tremendous source of motivation. I am also grateful to Robert Barker, David Beasley, Helen Clifford, John Culme, Anne Eatwell, Amelia Fearn, Eileen Goodway, Titus Kendall, James Lomax, Lucy Morton, Anthony Phillips, Hugh Roberts, Timothy Schroder, Pippa Shirley, Eric Smith, Peter Waldron, Harry Williams-Bulkeley, and Timothy Wilson. Closer to home, I acknowledge the assistance of Roger Berkowitz, Fred Bridge, Alexander Yale Goriansky, John Hyman, Ian Irving, Jeanne Sloane, and Kevin Tierney.

The preparation of the manuscript was made possible by a grant from the National Endowment for the Arts and by the contributions of Edith I. Welch. It was Edith's unwavering dedication to the project and her steady friendship and interest that enabled me to carry it through to completion. The publication was funded by the Andrew W. Mellon Publications Fund, Mrs. Jerome T. Gans, Mr. and Mrs. David Firestone, Simone and Alan Hartman, Edith I. Welch and Robert A. Radloff and Ann Macy Beha. I wish to thank these individuals for placing their confidence in me and for recognizing the great merit of the Museum's collection.

ELLENOR M. ALCORN
Boston, 2000

Introduction

THIS VOLUME IS THE SECOND of a two-part series covering the British silver in the Museum of Fine Arts, Boston. The entries are arranged chronologically, with the year 1697—when the higher Britannia standard silver was introduced—marking the division between volumes one and two. This collection includes more than 450 objects ranging in date from the mid-sixteenth to the early twentieth century. The great majority of them are domestic pieces produced in London. Irish and Scottish examples have been included in separate chapters. A few English-made objects with long histories of American ownership are housed in the department of The Art of the Americas and will be included in Jeannine Falino's forthcoming catalogue of American silver.[1] Notwithstanding these exceptions, this catalogue presents a complete record of the known history of each object in the collection, with a brief discussion when warranted regarding its historical, stylistic, or technical significance. Many of the pieces have never been published, and although a few are known to scholars, it is hoped that this volume will make available new primary material that may be woven into broader studies of the field.

The Trustees of the Museum of Fine Arts, which was founded in 1870, did not set out to build a comprehensive collection of English silver. They had in mind, like the founders of the Victoria and Albert Museum, the general elevation of public taste through exposure to works of quality. The preservation movement in America had been stimulated by the centennial celebrations of 1876, which cultivated a patriotic and nostalgic image of the eighteenth century. Interest in domestic interiors was encouraged by women's voluntary organizations, which arranged reconstructions of colonial kitchens and parlors as fund-raising components of historical fairs. The popular image of colonial New England as a tightly knit community of virtuous patriots living in tastefully elegant moderation was well established by the 1870s.

The silver first methodically studied and exhibited in Boston, nearly all of it made in New England during the colonial period, was lent to the Museum of Fine Arts by the area's churches. A major exhibition of church silver in 1909, and the subsequent publication in 1913 of *Old Silver of American Churches* by E. Alfred Jones, launched the formal study and public appreciation in America of antique silver. Following the example set by English researchers, American scholars and collectors were interested mainly in an object's original owners and its marks. Although the greatest enthusiasm was reserved for locally made objects, families in possession of English silver that had been passed down from the colonial period celebrated the historical associations of their treasures. The Hancock Cup (cat. 45), a London-made two-handled cup and cover marked by George Wickes, is a case in point. The cup descended in the May family with the tradition that it had belonged to the patriot John Hancock. It was believed to have been presented to the family by Hancock's widow, "full of ice cream, then considered a rare and very elegant delicacy." The novelist Louisa May Alcott allowed it to be exhibited during the centennial celebrations in Concord, Massachusetts, in 1875 but wrote that letting the precious piece out of her sight had caused her great anxiety. In 1914 the cup was placed on long-term loan to the Museum of Fine Arts, just when Orchard House, Alcott's family home in Concord, was established as a museum. The founders of the Orchard House Museum wished to preserve not only the memory of the novelist but also the moral standards of her generation, which were felt to be threatened by the encroachment of immigrants, entrepreneurs, and urban sprawl. By defining a vision of a genteel past, the historic preservation movement sought to provide for a more civilized future.

It was against this backdrop that the two benefactors who established the MFA's collection, Frank Brewer Bemis (1861–1935) and Theodora Wilbour (1861–1947), must have begun acquiring English silver. Bemis was a Boston banker with a fairly conventional range of interests. In addition to English silver, which he bought in New York and London, he collected Chinese export porcelain and books. His first silver purchases were made about 1911, and in 1929 the Museum of Fine Arts exhibited his collection in the newly constructed Decorative Arts Wing. Bemis seems to have been particularly smitten by objects with stories associated with them (for example, see the tontine cup, cat. 13) and by plain forms of modest size, praised by the curator at the time for their "enriched simplicity."

Theodora Wilbour was considerably more eccentric. She was the daughter of Charles Edwin Wilbour (1833–1896), a businessman and adventurer who became involved with the Tweed Gang in New York. He managed to avoid prosecution and protect his fortune by taking his family to Paris, where he took up Egyptology. Theodora's mother, Charlotte Beebe Wilbour (1833–1914), was a Massachusetts native and an active suffragette. It was apparently Charlotte's interest in English silver that encouraged her daughter, Theodora, to collect, and Theodora's gifts and later her bequests were made to the Museum of Fine Arts in memory of her mother. Charles Edwin Wilbour made annual visits from Paris to the Nile, often with members of his family, and there he developed an international reputation as a scholar and, to a lesser extent, a collector. His collection was presented to the Brooklyn Museum in 1916, two years after the death of his widow, and their daughter, Theodora, watched carefully over it. She also allowed the Brooklyn Museum to exhibit her collection of English silver. According to tradition, Miss Wilbour was visiting the museum one day in 1928, accompanied by her lawyer, the museum's curator, and members of the administration. When she pointed out with pride an eighteenth-century cucumber slicer, the curator questioned some aspect of the object. A debate ensued, with the administrators siding with the curator. Miss Wilbour was indignant and withdrew her collection immediately. A few years later she made her first gifts to the Museum of Fine Arts, Boston. Miss Wilbour's other collecting interests included clocks, furniture, and, particularly, coins and medals. She bequeathed a large group of Byzantine coins to the MFA as well as two endowment funds to support further acquisitions of English silver and antique coins.

In the field of English silver, Miss Wilbour's tastes were generally consistent with those of Frank Brewer Bemis and the generation of collectors who began collecting in the 1920s. Clean lines, sturdy construction, and recognizable, domestic forms were admired. The pendulum of taste swings steadily between "plain" and "fancy," but in Boston, the balance clearly favored "plain" silver until at least 1950. The traditionally austere New England aesthetic continued to guide acquisitions, and when, in 1965, the purchase of the fully rococo Bolton centerpiece (cat. 115) was proposed, one member of the staff objected that Miss Wilbour would never have approved.

Every generation asks new questions of the past. Traditional decorative arts scholarship has focused on the primary evidence of surviving objects. The language of connoisseurship, deeply rooted in the tradition of art appreciation and collecting, has encouraged the admiration of technical and stylistic innovation. The first studies of many areas of the decorative arts quite correctly examined the history of the guilds, and the field has generally been divided by materials, emphasizing the history of technology. In the last few decades, scholars have used a more holistic approach, borrowing the methods of social and economic historians to address the larger issues of the climate in which these objects were produced. There is an unresolved tension between the two traditions. Modern decorative arts historians, in an effort to defend their territory, have been reluctant to admit the distinction between art and artifact. It is important to acknowledge, however, that although a large proportion of the surviving decorative arts may be interesting as evidence of social history, the objects were made as production pieces. They cannot be assessed as objects of art any more than a newspaper should be interpreted as literature.

What is the role of a museum collection in the study of such a field? Through the gifts and bequests of generous benefactors, the Museum of Fine Arts is fortunate to have silver holdings that are both broad and deep. A significant proportion of the collection consists of modest pieces made in multiples for middle- or upper-middle-class consumption. Some of these pieces are of interest for the history of their ownership, for their armorials, marks, or technique, or simply as representatives of a common or influential form. These objects provide the landscape against which the more ambitious and innovative object may be seen. Though many of these pieces are rarely, if ever, on public view, they are available to specialists for study and remain extremely important to our growing understanding of the goldsmiths' trade. (The term *goldsmith* denoted a worker using gold or silver.) In New England, the strong awareness of British cultural and historical roots has motivated collectors of English silver, but it has also inhibited the appreciation of a range of styles that are only now being acknowledged. It is the role of a museum collection such as Boston's to describe the whole achievement of the goldsmiths' tradition, and to offer a broad context for the appreciation of the exceptional masterpiece.

Silver—which was fashioned for wealthy people who wanted to demonstrate their prosperity—is one of the most extensively studied areas of the decorative arts. Because of its intrinsic value, it has long enjoyed an exalted status among collectors. However, in spite of relatively abundant documentation and the very useful presence of hallmarks on most objects, there are many fundamental questions that remain unanswered. Who contributed to the design of an object? How much of a role did the purchaser play? How did new models pass from one goldsmith to another? Who were the great modelers, and did they work anonymously for several shops? One impediment to a clear understanding of the history of English silver has been the image of the artist-craftsman, a survival of the teachings of the Arts and Crafts movement of the late nineteenth century, which has limited modern perceptions of the eighteenth-century goldsmith. Particularly problematic is the notion that because an object is made by hand, in the artisanal tradition, it must be assessed as the unique artistic production of a single individual. The London goldsmiths' trade in the eighteenth century was a sophisticated industry that generated production pieces in enormous quantity. A large proportion of the silver objects produced were conceived as functional domestic wares and as a secure form in which their purchasers might store spare capital. Relatively few surviving pieces represent the rare collaboration of great designers and craftsmen working for an ambitious patron. The traditional language associated with the study of the crafts, which venerates the creator, has made it awkward to differentiate frankly between the mass-produced object, however handsome, and the groundbreaking masterpiece. A great museum collection must include both. The decorative arts are a window into the world that produced them, and a piece of silver may be of interest as evidence of the history of taste, as a representative of change in social habits, or as an illustration of an innovative form or technique. Only infrequently can an object stand alone, as a great creation of a maker working at the limits of his experience.

The unbroken stewardship of the Worshipful Company of Goldsmiths from the thirteenth century gave the London trade an unparalleled stability. The company kept a watchful eye on the training of apprentices, defended the field from foreign competition, and monitored the quality of the silver alloy used by assaying, or sampling, each piece of silver. The reputation of the business as a whole depended on the confidence consumers could place in the value of their purchases, so enforcing a consistent standard of silver purity was essential. A goldsmith took his finished, or nearly finished, wares to the Assay Office for sampling. Once tested, they were marked with a standard mark, a town mark, and a date letter. The sterling standard (92.5 percent pure silver) is indicated by the lion passant mark. For the period between 1697 and 1720, a higher standard (98.5 percent pure silver) was introduced to discourage the melting or clipping of silver coins. The higher standard was indicated by the Britannia mark. The usual London town mark, a leopard's head crowned, was replaced during this period with the lion's head erased. The date letter, used to identify the warden responsible for the testing, was changed yearly on St. Dunstan's Day in May, and thus refers to two calendar years. The fourth mark, the maker's or sponsor's mark, was struck to indicate the individual who presented the piece for assay and who guaranteed the purity of the metal. This mark does not necessarily indicate the shop in which the object was produced. Convenient as the marks may be for modern collectors in establishing a chronology or identifying a maker, they were intended to protect the consumer by preventing fraud. A goldsmith whose mark appeared on a piece of substandard silver would be fined, and a warden who had been persuaded to mark a piece of silver improperly could be traced by the date mark and required to face the company's court. The records of the Goldsmiths' Company offer an insight into the issues faced by the trade—the threats posed by imported goods or foreign workers, members' abuses of the regulations regarding apprentices, and a sense of the volume of silver produced during a given period. The best-studied records of the company, of course, are the registers in which, after 1697, all makers were required to enter their marks.

The presence of marks on English silver has reinforced the temptation to focus on the craftsman as artist. It is only in the last few decades that the limitations of this approach have been challenged. It has long been understood that many London goldsmiths functioned as bankers, while others operated only as retailers and had no manufacturing capabilities at all. In trying to sort out the character of a given goldsmith's business, evidence must be assembled from disparate fragments. There are few documentary resources equal to the ledgers of the royal goldsmith, George Wickes and his successors, known as the Garrard Ledgers. These accounts, which have been meticulously studied, reveal a great deal about the working methods of a major London shop. Wickes's relations to his partners, suppliers, outworkers, and journeymen can be sketched, and the ongoing accounts of individual clients are recorded in the Gentlemen's Ledgers. Tracing these records over a period of years reveals much about the way silver was used in an aristocratic household. A client might order a silver service to mark a marriage or the elevation to the peerage or might return silver to the goldsmith for refashioning, engraving, gilding, or repair. The Garrard Ledgers, however, are a remarkable exception, and in general terms the London goldsmiths are poorly represented by such documents.

Nonetheless, in recent years scholars have begun to exploit other, more tangential documentary evidence to help define the complex system of business and family connections within the London goldsmiths' trade in the eighteenth century. Probate inventories, tax records, and insurance records can help establish the size of a maker's shop and the extent of his personal property. Marriage and baptismal records or wills indicate the personal connections within a family, which are often carried into business dealings. The chance discovery of a court case involving a goldsmith can uncover unexpected glimpses of an overly ambitious business speculation and its consequences. A rough picture of a large and complex network is beginning to emerge. It is clear that the goldsmiths' business was highly specialized, with modelers, mold makers, chasers, and engravers sometimes working for many masters. Some makers devoted their shop to the production of a single form—such as candlesticks—or had a limited range of wares that might be sold finished and then marked by a retailing goldsmith. Some goldsmiths almost certainly employed unregistered foreign craftsmen, who offered special skills and were willing to work at lower wages.

If the maker's mark or, as it is sometimes called, the sponsor's mark does not indicate the author of a piece of silver, is it possible or even worthwhile to speculate about the production or personal style of an individual shop or maker? For a large part of the conventional domestic silver produced, the effort may be futile. The evidence from scattered documents is much too sparse to begin to draw useful conclusions. Surprisingly little is known from contemporaneous written sources about a shop as prolific and famous, even in its own time, as that of Paul de Lamerie. Here, however, a broad resource like a museum collection can be useful. By close comparison of the details of objects—cast handles, engraved armorials, or chased ornament—workshop groups can tentatively be suggested. The modeler who worked for Paul de Lamerie, not yet known by name, contributed his distinctive fat-cheeked putti and lion's masks to works marked by James Schruder and Charles Kandler. His background and relationship to this group of makers remain uncertain, but identifying his hand is the first step in establishing his existence. For the great masterpieces, the traditional methods of art history can be useful. Future generations will mingle the methods of social historians and art historians to resolve the tantalizing question of this modeler's identity. Using both visual and documentary evidence, it will eventually be possible to group together the products of a single "hand" and to characterize the methods of the eighteenth-century goldsmith's shop practices. The first step is to make readily available a broad number of works in public collections.

1. Similarly, a small group of silver owned by the Newport collector, Forsyth Wickes, is published in the 1992 catalogue of that collection and therefore is not included here.

Abbreviations

BOOKS AND ARTICLES

Akre 1983
Akre, Nancy, ed., *Miniatures* (New York, 1983).

Barr 1980
Barr, Elaine, *George Wickes 1698–1761, Royal Goldsmith* (London, 1980).

Baxter 1945
Baxter, W. T., *The House of Hancock* (Cambridge, Mass., 1945).

Bennett 1972
Bennett, Douglas, *Irish Georgian Silver* (London, 1972).

Bennett 1984
Bennett, Douglas, *Collecting Irish Silver, 1637–1900* (London, 1984).

Bigelow 1917
Bigelow, Francis Hill, *Historic Silver of the Colonies and Its Makers* (New York, 1917).

Bliss 1992
Bliss, Joseph, *The Jerome and Rita Gans Collection of English Silver on Loan to the Virginia Museum of Fine Arts* (New York, 1992).

Brett 1986
Brett, Vanessa, *The Sotheby's Directory of Silver, 1600–1940* (London, 1986).

Buhler 1972
Buhler, Kathryn C., *American Silver 1655–1825 in the Museum of Fine Arts, Boston* 1 (Boston, 1972).

Clayton 1971/1985a
Clayton, Michael, *The Collector's Dictionary of the Silver and Gold of Great Britain and North America* (New York 1971, rev. ed. 1985).

Clayton 1985b
Clayton, Michael, *Christie's Pictorial History of English and American Silver* (Oxford, 1985).

Clifford 1993
Clifford, Helen M., "The Richmond Cup," *Apollo* 137, no. 372 (1993), pp. 102–6.

Cornforth 1996
Cornforth, John, "A Splendid Unity of Arts,"
Country Life 190, no. 24 (June 13, 1996), pp. 128–31.

Culme 1977
Culme, John, *Nineteenth Century Silver* (London, 1977).

Culme 1987
Culme, John, *The Dictionary of Gold and Silversmiths, Jewellers, and Allied Traders, 1838–1914,* 2 vols. (Woodbridge, Suffolk, 1987).

Davis 1976
Davis, John D., *English Silver at Williamsburg* (Williamsburg, 1976).

Fergusson 1974
Fergusson, Frances, "Wyatt Silver," *Burlington Magazine* 116, no. 61 (December 1974), pp. 751–55.

Finlay 1956
Finlay, Ian, *Scottish Gold and Silver Work* (London, 1956).

Gardner 1938
Gardner, Bellamy, "Sprimont as Silversmith: A Set of Tea Caddies by the Founder of the Chelsea Porcelain Factory," *Antique Collector* (August 1938), pp. 206–8.

Gilbert 1896
Gilbert, Sir John T., *Calendar of Ancient Records of Dublin* 6 (Dublin, 1896).

Gillen 1976
Gillen, Mollie, *Royal Duke: Augustus Frederick, Duke of Sussex (1773–1843)* (Dublin, 1896).

Glynn 1996
Glynn, Gale, "Some Tontines Commemorated on English Plate," *Silver Society Journal* (Autumn 1996), pp. 445–61.

Grimwade 1969
Grimwade, Arthur, "Crespin or Sprimont: An Unsolved Problem of Rococo Silver," *Apollo* 90, no. 90 (August 1969), pp. 126–28.

Grimwade 1974
Grimwade, Arthur, *Rococo Silver: 1727–1765* (London, 1974).

Grimwade 1988
Grimwade, Arthur, "The Master of George Vertu," *Apollo* 127, no. 312 (February 1988), pp. 83–89.

Grimwade 1990
Grimwade, Arthur, *London Goldsmiths, 1697–1837: Their Marks and Lives* (London, 1990).

Gruber 1982
Gruber, Alain, *Silverware* (New York, 1982).

Hackenbroch 1969
Hackenbroch, Yvonne, *English and Other Silver in the Irwin Untermyer Collection* (New York, 1969).

Halén 1990
Halén, Widar, *Christopher Dresser* (Oxford, 1990).

Hartop 1996
Hartop, Christopher, *The Huguenot Legacy* (London, 1996).

Hatfield 1981
Hatfield, Leslie Campbell, "A Set of English Silver Condiment Vases from Kedleston Hall," *Bulletin of the Museum of Fine Arts, Boston* 79 (1981), pp. 4–19.

Hayward 1959
Hayward, John F., *Huguenot Silver in England, 1688–1727* (London, 1959).

Hayward 1978
Hayward, John F., "The Earl of Warrington's Plate," *Apollo* 10, no. 197 (1978), pp. 32–39.

Hipkiss 1941
Hipkiss, Edwin J., *Eighteenth-Century American Arts of the M. and M. Karolik Collection* (Cambridge, Mass., 1941).

Jackson 1911
Jackson, Charles James, Sir, *An Illustrated History of English Plate* 2, vols. (London, 1911).

Jackson 1989
Pickford, Ian, ed., *Jackson's Silver and Gold Marks of England, Scotland, and Ireland* (Woodbridge, Suffolk, 1989).

Jones 1981
Jones, Kenneth Crisp, ed., *The Silversmiths of Birmingham and Their Marks, 1750–1980* (London, 1981).

Kenin 1979
Kenin, Richard, *Return to Albion: Americans in England 1760–1940* (Washington, D.C., 1979).

Lee 1909
Lee, Sidney, ed., *Dictionary of National Biography* (London, 1909).

Lomax 1992
Lomax, James, *British Silver at Temple Newsam and Lotherton Hall: A Catalogue of the Leeds Collection* (Leeds, 1992).

Mallet 1996
Mallet, John, in *The Dictionary of Art* (London, 1996).

Miles 1976
Miles, Elizabeth B., *English Silver: The Elizabeth B. Miles Collection* (Hartford, 1976).

Oman 1965
Oman, Charles, *English Silversmith's Work, Civil and Domestic: An Introduction* (London, 1965).

Oman 1966
Oman, Charles, "A Problem of Artistic Responsibility: The Firm of Rundell, Bridge & Rundell," *Apollo* 3, no. 49 (March 1966), pp. 174–83.

Phillips 1997
Phillips, Anthony, and Jeanne Sloane, *English and French Silver-gilt from the Collection of Audrey Love* (New York, 1997).

Puig 1989
Puig, Francis J., et al., *English and American Silver in the Collection of the Minneapolis Institute of Arts* (Minneapolis, 1989).

Quickenden 1980
Quickenden, Kenneth, "Boulton and Fothergill Silver: Business Plans and Miscalculations," *Art History* 3, no. 3 (September 1980), pp. 274–94.

Rowe 1965
Rowe, Robert, *Adam Silver: 1765–1795* (London, 1965).

Sargent 1856
[Lucius Manlius Sargent] A Sexton of the Old School, *Dealings with the Dead* (Boston, 1856).

Schroder 1988a
Schroder, Timothy, *The National Trust Book of English Domestic Silver, 1500–1900* (Harmondsworth, Middlesex, 1988).

Schroder 1988b
Schroder, Timothy, *The Gilbert Collection of Gold and Silver* (Los Angeles, 1988).

Shipton 1968
Shipton, Clifford K., *Sibley's Harvard Graduates* 14 (Boston, 1968).

Sinsteden 1999
Sinsteden, Thomas, "Four Selected Assay Records of the Dublin Goldsmiths Company," *Proceedings of the Silver Society* 11 (1999), pp. 143–57.

Snodin 1997
Snodin, Michael, "Adam Silver Reassessed," *Burlington Magazine* 139 (1997), pp. 17–25.

Truman 1993
Truman, Charles, ed., *Sotheby's Concise Encyclopedia of Silver* (London, 1993).

Wark 1978
Wark, Robert R., *British Silver in the Huntington Collection* (San Marino, 1978).

Watson 1969
Watson, Colonel S. J., *Between the Flags* (Dublin, 1969).

Wees 1997
Wees, Beth Carver, *English, Irish, & Scottish Silver at the Sterling and Francine Clark Art Institute* (New York, 1997).

EXHIBITIONS

Austin, Texas, The University Art Museum, *One Hundred Years of English Silver: 1660–1760*, 1969.

Birmingham, City Museum and Art Gallery, *Birmingham Gold and Silver, 1773–1973: An Exhibition Celebrating the Bicentenary of the Assay Office*, 1973.

Boston, Museum of Fine Arts, *An Exhibition of English Silver, 1571–1800: The Charlotte Beebe Wilbour Collection*, 1933 (no catalogue).

Boston, Museum of Fine Arts, *The Folger's Coffee Collection of Antique English Silver Coffee Pots and Accessories*, 1968.

Boston, Museum of Fine Arts, *Paul Revere's Boston: 1735–1818*, 1975.

Boston, Museum of Fine Arts, *The Taste for Luxury: English Furniture, Silver and Ceramics, 1690–1790*, 1994 (no catalogue).

Cambridge, Fitzwilliam Museum, *Cambridge Plate*, 1975.

Houston, Texas, Museum of Fine Arts, *Silver by Paul de Lamerie in America*, 1956.

London, Christie's, *The Glory of the Goldsmith: Magnificent Gold and Silver from the Al-Tajiir Collection*, 1989.

London, Goldsmiths' Hall, *Paul de Lamerie, At the Sign of the Golden Ball*, 1990.

London, Queen's Gallery, *Carlton House: the Past Glories of George IV's Palace*, 1991.

London, Victoria & Albert Museum, *Rococo: Art and Design in Hogarth's England*, 1984.

Minneapolis, The Minneapolis Institute of Arts, *The American Craftsman and the European Tradition, 1620–1820*, 1989.

New York, Cooper Hewitt, *Courts and Colonies: The William and Mary Style in Holland, England, and America*, 1988.

New York, The Metropolitan Museum of Art, *American Rococo, 1750–1775: Elegance in Ornament*, 1992.

Springfield, Massachusetts, Springfield Museum of Fine Arts, *25th Anniversary Exhibition*, 1958 (no catalogue).

Toronto, George R. Gardiner Museum of Ceramic Art, *Your Presence is Requested: the Art of Dining in Eighteenth-Century Europe*, 1998 (no catalogue).

Washington, D.C., National Gallery, *The Eye of Thomas Jefferson*, 1976.

Color Plates

PLATE 1. Cat. 7. Set of casters. Unmarked.
London, ca. 1700

PLATE II. Cat. 10. Brazier. Marked by Anthony
Nelme. London, 1701/2

PLATE III. Cat. 20. Fountain. Marked by David
Willaume (I). London, 1707/8

PLATE IV. Cat. 20. Cistern. Marked by David
Willaume (1). London, 1707/8

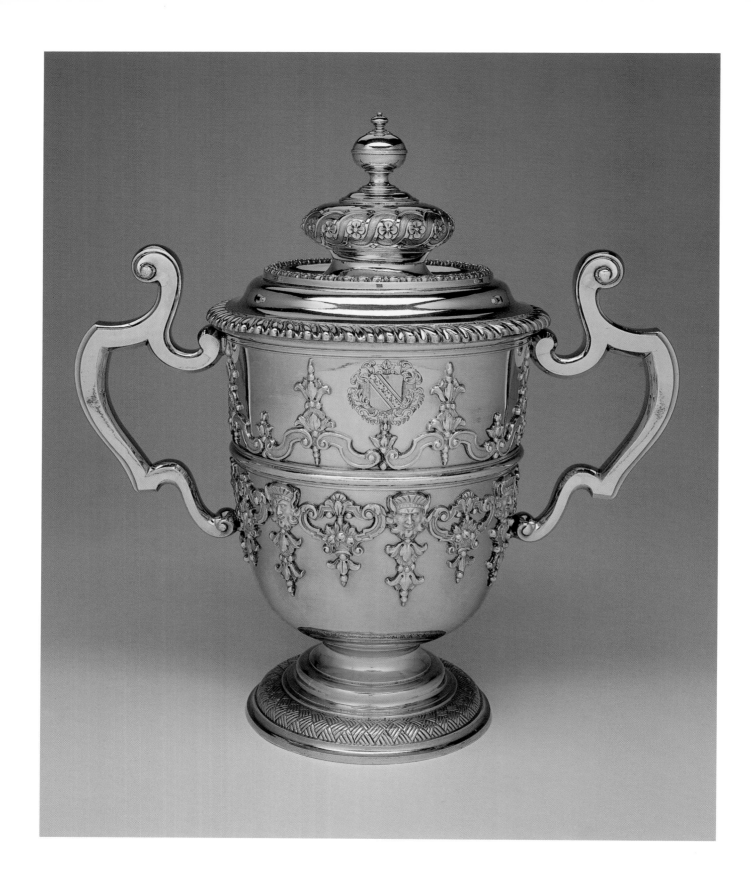

PLATE V. Cat. 44. Two-handled cup and cover.
Marked by Samuel Margas. London, 1721/2

PLATE VI. Cat. 68. Salver. Marked by Thomas
Farren. London, ca. 1730

PLATE VII. Cat. 74. Tureen. Marked by Charles
Kandler. London, 1732/3

PLATE VIII. Cat. 76. Two-handled cup and cover.
Marked by Paul Crespin. London, 1733/4

PLATE IX. Cat. 82. Basket. Marked by
Benjamin Godfrey. London, 1738/9

PLATE X. Cat. 91. Two tea canisters and a sugar box.
Marked by Nicholas Sprimont. London, 1744/5

PLATE XI. Cat. 99. Pair of tea canisters and a sugar
box. Marked by Samuel Taylor. London, 1747/8

PLATE XII. Cat. 115. Epergne. Marked by John
Parker and Edward Wakelin. London, ca. 1760

PLATE XIII. Cat. 119. Salver. Marked by Thomas
Pitts. London, 1763/4

PLATE XIV. Cat. 121. Richmond Race Cup.
Designed by Robert Adam, marked by Daniel
Smith and Robert Sharp. London, 1764/5

PLATE XV. Cat. 132. Three condiment vases.
Marked by Louisa Courtauld and George Cowles.
London, 1771/2

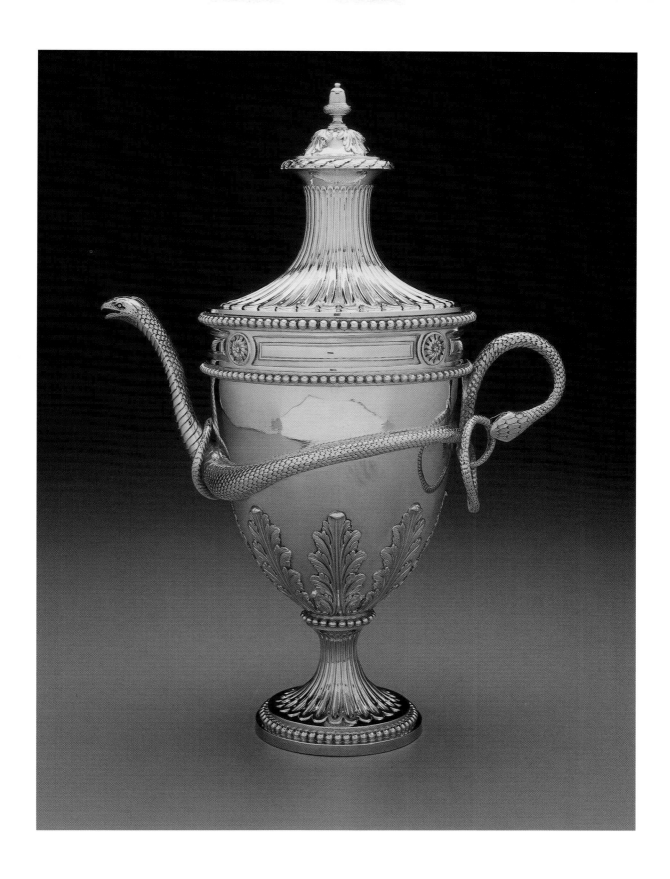

PLATE XVI. Cat. 133. Argyll. Marked by Louisa
Courtauld and George Cowles. London, 1772/3

PLATE XVII. Cat. 139. Nanny. Marked by
Charles Frederick Kandler. London, 1777/8

PLATE XVIII. Cat. 163. Tureen and stand.
Marked by John Scofield. London, 1791/2

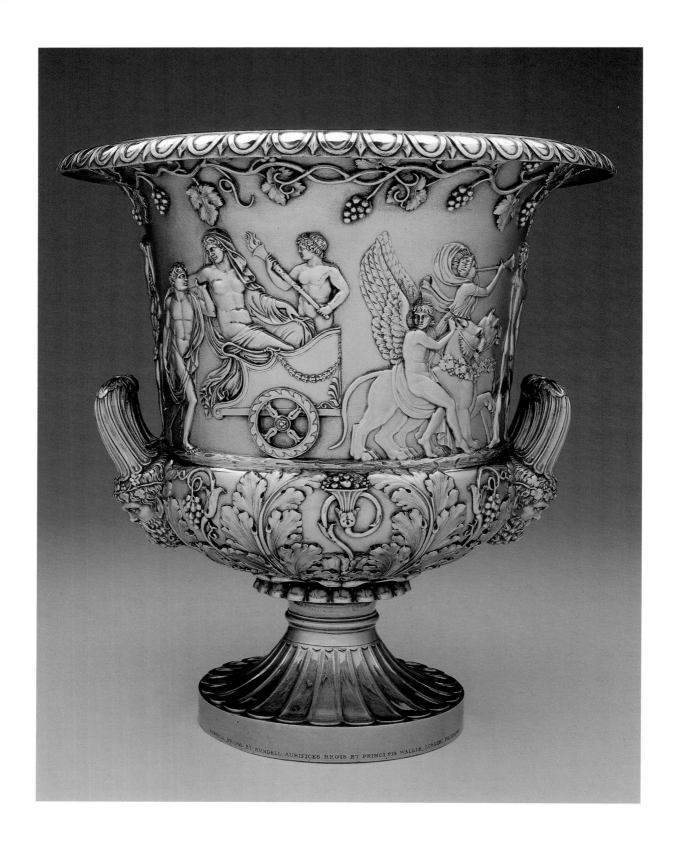

PLATE XIX. Cat. 179. Wine cooler, one of a
pair. Marked by Paul Storr. London, 1808/9

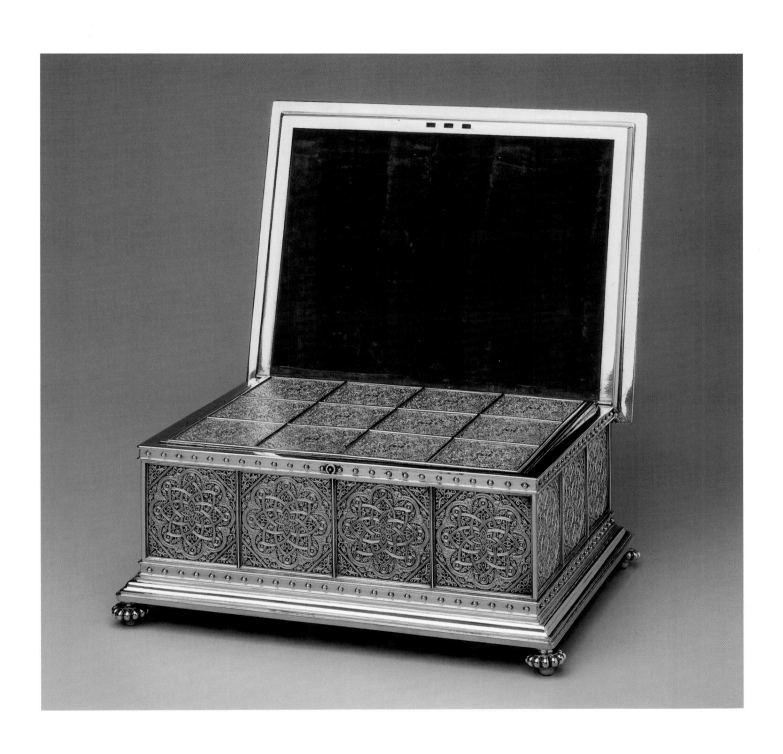

PLATE XX. Cat. 184. Casket. Marked by John
Harris. London, 1820/1

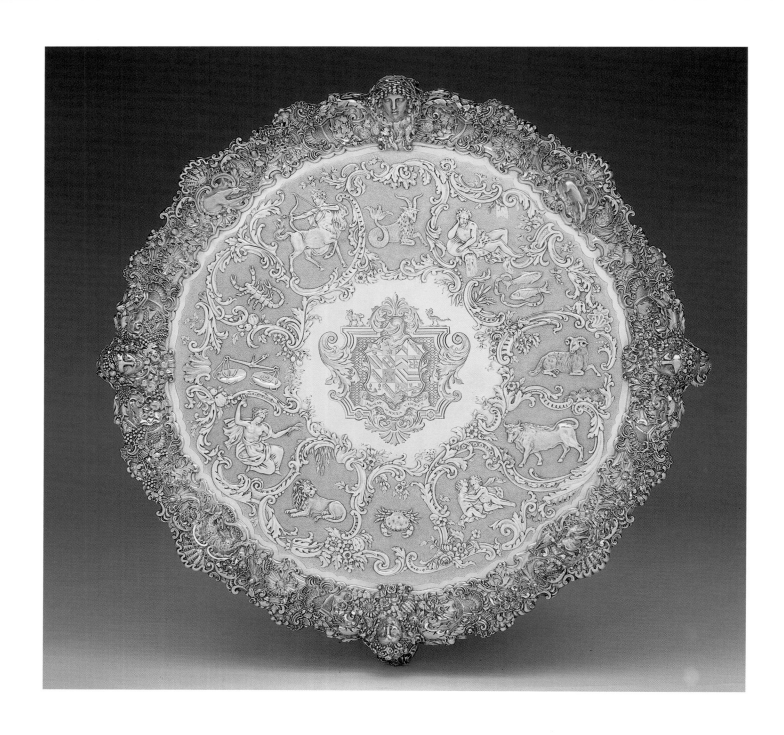

PLATE XXI. Cat. 185. Salver. Marked by Paul
Storr. London, 1823/4

PLATE XXII. Cat. 187. Pair of salts. Marked by
Edward Farrell. London, 1824/5

PLATE XXIII. Cat. 191. Game dish. Marked by
John Samuel Hunt. London, 1846/7

PLATE XXIV. Cat. 202. Claret jug. Marked by
Elkington & Co. London, 1897/8

PLATE XXV. Cat. 206. Rose bowl. Marked by
Bernard Cuzner. Birmingham, 1911/2

PLATE XXVI. Cat. 255. Two-handled cup and
cover. Marked by Thomas Bolton. Dublin, 1694/6

PLATE XXVII. Cat. 257. Ewer. Marked by
Thomas Bolton. Dublin, 1699/1700

PLATE XXVIII. Cat. 258. Dish. Marked by
Thomas Bolton. Dublin, 1702/3

Use of Catalogue

The objects are catalogued in chronological order within chapters. The conventional term "maker's mark" has been used in place of the less familiar "sponsor's mark." Marks are recorded as they appear on the object, from left to right or clockwise. Dimensions are listed in centimeters followed by inch equivalents. Unless otherwise indicated, the maximum dimension is recorded. The following abbreviations are used: H.=height; w.= width; d.=depth; diam.=diameter; l.=length. Weights are listed in grams followed by Troy equivalents.

Provenance cited is limited to documented owners; engraved armorials are not taken as evidence of previous ownership, but are identified separately. The Museum's acquisition of an object is recorded on the date of the vote of the Trustees. A dealer bidding on behalf of the Museum of Fine Arts at auction is listed in square brackets following the sale date. A comma between the names of two former owners indicates that the piece passed directly from the first to the second; a semicolon indicates a gap in documentation.

Notes on construction and condition are incorporated into the section headed "Description."

References in the notes to objects in other collections include the accession number whenever possible. Unless otherwise indicated, objects referred to in the notes were made in London, and the material is silver.

Identifications of maker's marks referenced in the Marks section of the entries are from the following sources: (Bennett) Douglas Bennett, *Irish Georgian Silver* (London, 1972); (Culme) John Culme, *The Dictionary of Gold and Silversmiths, Jewellers, and Allied Traders, 1838–1914,* 2 vols. (Woodbridge, Suffolk, 1987); (Grimwade) Arthur Grimwade, *London Goldsmiths, 1697–1837: Their Marks and Lives* (London, 1990); (Jackson) Ian Pickford, ed., *Jackson's Silver and Gold Marks of England, Scotland, and Ireland* (Woodbridge, Suffolk, 1989); (Jones) Kenneth Crisp Jones, ed., *The Silversmiths of Birmingham and Their Marks, 1750–1980* (London, 1981).

1

• I •

TWO-HANDLED CUP

Marked by John Cory (free 1687)
London, 1697/8
Silver
35.1574

MARKS: near handle, maker's mark *CO* (Grimwade 382); Britannia; lion's head erased; date letter *B*

INSCRIPTIONS: engraved on underside, *B/R⋆E*

H. 7.4 cm (2¹⁵⁄₁₆ in.); w. 13.4 cm (5¼ in.); diam. of rim 5.7 cm (2¼ in.)

WEIGHT: 119.1 gm (3 oz 16 dwt)

PROVENANCE: Brooks Reed Gallery, Inc., Boston, purchased by Frank Brewer Bemis, April 1, 1921, Bequest of Frank Brewer Bemis, November 7, 1935

DESCRIPTION: The bell-shaped body, raised from sheet, is chased on the lower third with spiral fluting framed by semicircular and star punches. A band of gadrooning encircles the body at its midsection. The two cast ear-shaped handles have beaded foliate scrolls.

The design of this cup, with its simple construction and light gauge, had a remarkably long life, appearing constantly from about 1690 until the 1720s.[1] A slightly grander version, with a roughly chased baroque cartouche centered on one side, was preferred for presentations.[2]

1. For other examples, see cats. 25 and 35; Lomax 1992, pp. 62–63, cat. 43; Christie's, New York, April 19, 1990, lot 313.

2. See the cup in the Victoria and Albert Museum inscribed *The Company of Porters*, illus. W. W. Watts, *Victoria and Albert Museum, Catalogue of English Silversmiths' Work* (London, 1929), pl. 36, fig. 88.

• 2 •

PAIR OF CANDLESTICKS

Marked by Richard Syng (free 1687, first mark entered before 1697)
London, 1698/9
Silver
33.82-83

MARKS: on corners under each base, maker's mark *Sy* (Grimwade 2673); lion's head erased; Britannia; date letter *c*

ARMORIALS: engraved on each base, the crest and motto of Hazlerigg or Hesilrig, possibly for Sir Thomas Hesilrige, fourth baronet of Noseley Hall, co. Leicester (1664–1700); an unidentified crest and motto (a demiwoman nude; motto: *Vivat solum post funera virtu*)

INSCRIPTIONS: scratched on underside of each base, *1698* and *c 200/2*

33.82: H. 20.8 cm (8³⁄₁₆ in.); w. 14.3 cm (5⅝ in.); d. 14.1 cm (5½ in.)

33.83: H. 20.7 cm (8⅛ in.); w. 14 cm (5½ in.); d. 14 cm (5½ in.)

WEIGHT: 33.82: 343 gm (11 oz). 33.83: 340.2 gm (10 oz 18 dwt)

PROVENANCE: Anonymous Gift in Memory of Charlotte Beebe Wilbour (1833–1914), March 2, 1933

EXHIBITED: Boston, Museum of Fine Arts, 1933; Boston, Museum of Fine Arts, 1994

PUBLISHED: Gruber 1982, p. 237

DESCRIPTION: The stepped, octagonal, gadrooned base supports a tapering spool form surmounted by an octagonal, gadrooned flange. The bases are formed from raised, chased sheet, rising to a plain spool-shaped midsection with an applied wire rim around the edge. The stem, in the form of a fluted column, rises from the knop. It is formed from seamed, chased sheet. The nozzles, made from chased sheet, are in the form of capitals and are surmounted by attached octagonal waxpans with a circle of gadrooning.

2

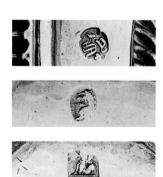

Candlesticks in the form of a classical column, fluted to add rigidity to the sheet, have survived in some quantity.[1] Lighter and presumably somewhat cheaper than the alternatives with cast bases and stems, they must have seemed impressive in size nonetheless. Syng seems to have specialized in the form.[2]

1. For example, see a pair at Colonial Williamsburg marked by William Denny and John Bache, illus. Davis 1976, p. 22, cat. 6; a pair marked by *DB*, sold Sotheby's, London, October 25, 1973, lot 34; a pair marked by John Bache, illus. Hayward 1959, pl. 73C.

2. For other examples marked by Syng, see Christie's, London, June 13, 1911, lot 92; Sotheby's, London, February 20, 1975, lot 188; Christie's, London, November 28, 1979, lot 110; Brett 1986, p. 150, fig. 561.

3

• 3 •

COVERED BOWL

Marked by William Keatt (free 1689, d. ca. 1735)
London, 1698/9
Silver
33.89

MARKS: below rim, maker's mark *KE* (Grimwade 1868) (repeated on top of cover); Britannia; lion's head erased; date letter *c*

H. 10 cm (3¹⁵⁄₁₆ in.); diam. of cover 13.5 cm (5⁵⁄₁₆ in.)

WEIGHT: 317.5 gm (10 oz 4 dwt)

PROVENANCE: Anonymous Gift in Memory of Charlotte Beebe Wilbour (1833–1914), March 2, 1933

EXHIBITED: Boston, Museum of Fine Arts, 1933

PUBLISHED: Edwin J. Hipkiss, "The Charlotte Beebe Wilbour Collection of English Silver," *Bulletin of the Museum of Fine Arts* 31, no. 184 (1933), p. 29

DESCRIPTION: The raised circular bowl rests on a cast gadrooned foot. The lower half of the body is chased with spiraling fluting and punched with semicircles, fleur-de-lys, and acorns. The slightly domed cover, formed from sheet, has a molded rim and a band of chased gadrooning around the rim. Surrounding the gadrooned baluster finial is a chased design of spiral fluting and punching. The finial has been reattached, and there are file marks on the rim. The shadow of a removed coat of arms is visible on the rim.

File marks on the rim of this covered bowl suggest that a pair of handles has been removed. It was probably part of a toilet service, which might have included two such bowls, as well as sets of boxes (see cat. 12), candlesticks, a pincushion, mirror, and salvers.[1] Similar bowls, often slightly smaller, are sometimes called sugar bowls,[2] and one, marked 1700 by Joseph Ward, was engraved in 1742 with an unusual inscription in which it is named as a sugar bowl.[3]

1. See a partial service of 1691 sold Christie's, London, December 14, 1938, lot 68.
2. For example, see Brett 1986, p. 151, fig. 568.
3. Ibid., p. 152, fig. 572.

4

· 4 ·

TOY TWO-HANDLED CUP
Marked by Alexander Roode (free 1676, first
mark entered 1697)
London, 1698/9
Silver
33.469

MARKS: near rim, maker's mark *RO* (Grimwade
2388); Britannia; lion's head erased; date letter *c*

INSCRIPTIONS: engraved near rim, *R★P*; scratched
on underside, *No 276*

H. 4 cm (1⁹⁄₁₆ in.); w. 8.9 cm (3½ in.); diam. of rim
5.5 cm (2³⁄₁₆ in.)

WEIGHT: 31.2 gm (1 oz)

PROVENANCE: Gift of Mrs. Charles Gaston Smith's
Group, May 4, 1933

PUBLISHED: Edwin J. Hipkiss, "Some Additions to
the Collections of Decorative Arts," *Bulletin of the
Museum of Fine Arts* 31, no. 188 (December 1933), pp.
92–93

DESCRIPTION: The cup is formed from thin sheet,
raised and chased around the lower half with spiraling fluting. A plain wire foot and two molded wire
ear-shaped handles are applied.

5

· 5 ·

PAIR OF TRENCHER SALTS
Marked by Benjamin Bentley (first mark entered
1698)
London, 1699/1700
Silver
35.1577–1578

MARKS: in bowl of each salt, maker's mark *BE*
(Grimwade 155); Britannia; date letter, possibly *d*;
lion's head erased

INSCRIPTIONS: engraved on underside of each
base, *F/G S*

35.1577: H. 6.3 cm (2⁷⁄₁₆ in.); diam. of foot 7.8 cm
(3¹⁄₁₆ in.)

35.1578: H. 6.1 cm (2⅜ in.); diam. of foot 7.9 cm (3⅛
in.)

WEIGHT: 35.1577: 45.4 gm (1 oz 9 dwt). 35.1578:
42.5 gm (1 oz 7 dwt)

PROVENANCE: Walter H. Willson, Ltd., London,
purchased by Frank Brewer Bemis, May 27, 1929,
Bequest of Frank Brewer Bemis, November 7, 1935

DESCRIPTION: Each spool-shaped body, raised
from a single piece of thin sheet, has a spreading
base and a band of chased gadrooning around the
foot. The circular well at the top is surrounded by a
similar band of chased gadrooning. The salts are
worn overall, and several cracks have been repaired.

· 6 ·

TOY PORRINGER
London, ca. 1700
Silver
55.976

MARKS: on underside, Britannia; maker's mark *D* with a pellet between and a crown above (unrecorded)

INSCRIPTIONS: engraved on handle, *MO/to/MK*

H. 2 cm (¾ in.); w. 6.8 cm (2¹¹⁄₁₆ in.); diam. of rim 4.3 cm (1¹¹⁄₁₆ in.)

WEIGHT: 17 gm (11 dwt)

PROVENANCE: James S. Barnet, Shreve, Crump, and Low, Co., purchased December 8, 1955, Theodora Wilbour Fund in Memory of Charlotte Beebe Wilbour

PUBLISHED: Nancy Akre, ed., *Miniatures* (New York, 1983), p. 74, fig. 64

DESCRIPTION: The circular bowl is raised and has a flat base and curved walls. A shaped handle, formed from cut sheet, is applied to the rim.

6

· 7 ·

SET OF CASTERS
London, ca. 1700
Silver gilt
1992.433.1a-b–3a-b

Unmarked

ARMORIALS: engraved on front of each, the arms of Offley impaling Crewe for Anne, daughter and heir of John Crewe (d. 1684) of Crewe Hall, Cheshire, who married John Offley, Esq., of Madeley, co. Stafford

INSCRIPTIONS: 1992.433.1 (large caster): scratched on underside of base, *18oz13*. 1993.433.2 (small caster): scratched on underside of base, *9on8*. 1993.433.3 (small caster): scratched on underside of base, *9on*

1992.433.1a-b: H. 22 cm (8¹¹⁄₁₆ in.); diam. of base 7.6 cm (3 in.)
1992.433.2a-b: H. 16.5 cm (6½ in.); diam. of base 5.6 cm (2³⁄₁₆ in.)
1992.433.3a-b: H. 16.3 cm (6⁷⁄₁₆ in.); diam. of base 5.5 cm (2³⁄₁₆ in.)

WEIGHT: 1992.433.1a-b: 584 gm (18 oz 16 dwt). 1992.433.2a-b: 280 gm (9 oz). 1992.433.3a-b: 283.5 gm (9 oz 2 dwt)

PROVENANCE: lord and lady Walston; purchased from How (of Edinburgh), London, September 23, 1992, Theodora Wilbour Fund in Memory of Charlotte Beebe Wilbour

PUBLISHED: Clayton 1971, p. 50, fig. 106; Clayton 1985a, p. 75, fig. 106; Ellenor Alcorn, "Acquisitions," *The Museum Year 1992–93, The One Hundred Seventeenth Annual Report of the Museum of Fine Arts, Boston* (Boston, 1993), p. 29

EXHIBITED: San Marino, California, Henry E. Huntington Library and Art Gallery, *English Domestic Silver, Elizabeth I to Anne: 1558–1714*, 1963, pp. 28–29, cat. 63; London, How (of Edinburgh), *An Exhibition of English and Scottish Domestic Silver from the 17th and Early 18th Centuries with a Loan Collection of Early English Silver Toys and Miniatures*, 1992, p. 8, cat. 28

DESCRIPTION: Each caster has a pear-shaped body that rests on a cast foot with a gadrooned border. The body is formed from two raised parts, with two wires, a molded and a crimped, covering the join at the midsection. The lower part of the body is ornamented with an applied foliate cut-card pattern. The upper section of the body is engraved overall with intertwined foliage enclosing birds and at the center a winged demifigure. Below the rim is an applied cut-card trefoil border. The domed cover, which is

7 (Color Plate 1)

raised, has a cast gadrooned flange and a molded rim. The cover is ornamented with an engraved and pierced design representing swags, vases of flowers, and birds. The fluted cast finial is centered on a cut-card quatrefoil.

These casters are distinguished by the richness of their decoration and the quality of its execution. A single caster, identical to the large one in this set and engraved with the same arms, survives in a private collection.[1] It is fully marked for 1700/1 and bears the maker's mark of David Willaume I. This suggests that the original group included at least six such casters, and it is possible that they were part of a table centerpiece or epergne.[2]

Engraved scrolling foliage appears on a group of about twenty objects of the highest quality ranging in date from about 1690 to 1705. Most of the pieces are marked by French-trained makers, many by the unidentified maker FS over s and David Willaume.[3] A subset of this group, associated by Arthur

Grimwade with the engraver Blaise Gentot, has borders of acanthus leaves and pinecones.[4] The engraver of these casters seems to have had as a model ornament prints by a seventeenth-century engraver such as Henri Le Roy (1579–1631).[5]

As with candlesticks, the making of casters seems to have been largely the work of specialists. A special order such as this set from Willaume, one of the leading Huguenot goldsmiths, was perhaps executed in-house. However, the pierced and engraved pattern of the cover, with its fanciful birds, swags, and stylized flowers, seems to be executed by the same hand that decorated casters marked by other makers. It may be that the piercing, a particularly delicate task, was contracted out to a piercer. In the years around 1700, the plain straight-sided "lighthouse" caster of the 1680s[6] was still in production, but the influence of the French immigrant makers is evident. Some English-born makers, such as Charles Adam,

who specialized in casters, added the characteristically Huguenot cut-card ornament and a more decorative pierced cover to accommodate a changing sensibility.[7] The more robust pear-shaped body with dense geometric ornament was favored by the Huguenot makers including David Willaume, Pierre Harache,[8] and Phillip Rollos.[9] Willaume's mark appears on a small group of particularly grand sets of casters.[10]

1. Exh. London, Victoria and Albert Museum, *The British Antique Dealers' Association Golden Jubilee Exhibition,* 1968, cat. 44.

2. The earliest surviving English epergne (sold Sotheby's, New York, October 19, 1995, lot 545) is dated 1730, but it is clear from inventories and engravings that epergnes were in use by 1700.

3. See a teapot in this collection, illus. Ellenor M. Alcorn, *English Silver in the Museum of Fine Arts, Boston, Volume I* (Boston, 1993), pp. 181–82, cat. 89, and the discussion by James Lomax of a pair of cups at Temple Newsam, Lomax 1992, pp. 169–70, cat. 192.

4. Grimwade 1988.

5. I am grateful to Edith I. Welch for this suggestion. Examples of Le Roy's work may be seen in the Print Room of the Victoria and Albert Museum, VA-2537-1913.

6. For example, see Wees 1997, pp. 208–10, cats. 122–23.

7. For example, see a set of three casters sold Sotheby's, New York, October 16, 1996, lot 333.

8. See the silver-mounted glass casters in the Clark Art Institute, illus. Wees 1997, pp. 212–13, cat. 125.

9. See the set of 1705 in the Al-Tajiir collection, exh. London, Christie's, *The Glory of the Goldsmith: Magnificent Gold and Silver from the Al-Tajiir Collection,* 1989, p. 74, cat. 49.

10. Set of 1706 sold Sotheby's, New York, April 23, 1993, lot 506; another set of 1707 sold Christie's, London, June 15, 1966, lot 63, and another set of 1704 sold Sotheby's, London, February 11, 1999, lot 24.

· 8 ·

CASTER
Marked by William Gamble (free 1688)
London, 1700/1
Silver
15.915

MARKS: near rim, maker's mark *GA* (similar to Grimwade 738)[1] (repeated on cover); Britannia (repeated on cover); lion's head erased; date letter *e*

INSCRIPTIONS: engraved on base, *F/I★S*

H. 16.1 cm (6⁵⁄₁₆ in.); diam. of base 6.7 cm (2⅝ in.)

WEIGHT: 175.8 gm (5 oz 13 dwt)

PROVENANCE: according to tradition, John Foye of Boston, who married Sarah (1672–1721), daughter of Simon Lynde of Boston, then by descent to their son, John Foye (1706–1778) who married in 1729 Sarah Boucher (b. 1706), daughter of Louis Boucher of Boston, to their daughter, Elizabeth (b. 1735) who married David Munroe of Lexington, Massachusetts, to their daughter, Abigail (b. 1771) who married Willard Brigham of Marlborough, Massachusetts, to their daughter, Abigail (b. 1807) who married in 1836 Joseph Hill of West Cambridge, to their daughter, Harriet A. Hill, Gift of Miss Harriet A. Hill in Memory of her mother, Abigail Brigham Hill, July 15, 1915

PUBLISHED: Bigelow 1917, pp. 315–17

DESCRIPTION: The cylindrical body, formed from seamed sheet, rests on a domed foot with a chased gadrooned rim. Its plain surface has three horizontal bands of applied molded wire: one above the foot, one just below the midsection, and one along the rim, which has a notch cut in it to match a bayonet fitting on the caster cover. The high domed cover is formed from a seamed, cylindrical lower section soldered to the raised domed top. It is pierced and engraved overall with stylized flowers, vases, and birds. The rim is strengthened with a molded wire and a gadrooned flange. A cut-card collar is applied to the top of the cover, and a cast baluster finial is at the center.

The pair to this caster is in the collection of the Minneapolis Institute of Arts.[2] The casters probably belonged to a set of three, including two of this smaller size for pepper and mustard, and a larger caster for sugar. Along with a pair of London snuffers of 1700 (cat. 9) and several pieces of early-eighteenth-century American silver,[3] it is said to have descended in the Boston family of John Foye, a ship's captain.

8

Correspondence in the Museum's file from a descendant describes the preparations for the wedding in 1729 of John Foye to Sarah Boucher, the daughter of Louis Boucher (b. Paris, d. 1715) and Sarah Middlecott (1678–1728). "They sent to Paris for orange damask curtains for their bridal chamber, and the hangings and furnishings were of that color, which they chose on account of their great admiration for the Prince of Orange. . . . At the time of the Battle of Bunker Hill their house [in Charlestown] was burned to the ground and all of their silver . . . and a part of their furniture was thrown down the well."[4]

1. The mark has an additional pellet beneath the initials not shown in Grimwade.

2. Puig 1989, p. 31, cat. 23.

3. MFA acc. no. 15.912, 57.701, 15.913, illus. Kathryn C. Buhler, *American Silver, 1655–1825, in the Museum of Fine Arts, Boston, Vol. 1* (Boston, 1972), pp. 55–56, 68–69, 81.

4. Transcript of a letter from the donor, Harriet A. Hill, in the curatorial file.

9

· 9 ·

SNUFFERS
Marked by John Laughton (II) (d. 1703)
London, 1700/1
Silver
15.916

MARKS: on flat sheet of snuffer, date letter *e*; lion's head erased (repeated on dish of snuffer and below handle rings); Britannia; maker's mark *LA* (Grimwade 1898) (repeated on dish of snuffer)

INSCRIPTIONS: engraved on handle side of dish, *F/I★S*

L. 13.5 cm (5⅜ in.); W. 3 cm (1³⁄₁₆ in.)

WEIGHT: 82.2 gm (2 oz 13 dwt)

PROVENANCE: according to tradition, John Foye of Boston, who married Sarah (1672–1721), daughter of Simon Lynde of Boston, then by descent to their son, John Foye (1706–1778) who married in 1729 Sarah Boucher (b. 1706), daughter of Louis Boucher of Boston, to their daughter, Elizabeth (b. 1735) who married David Munroe of Lexington, Massachusetts, to their daughter, Abigail (b. 1771) who married

Willard Brigham of Marlborough, Massachusetts, to their daughter, Abigail (b. 1807) who married in 1836 Joseph Hill of West Cambridge, to their daughter, Harriet A. Hill, Gift of Miss Harriet A. Hill in Memory of her mother, Abigail Brigham Hill, July 15, 1915

DESCRIPTION: The scissor-style snuffers have small oval rings for handles. The cast arms are riveted at the point of crossing. One arm has a curved shallow pan with a deep rim attached to one blade and a shaped, pointed tip. The opposite arm is fitted with a flat blade that matches the pan opposite. The snuffers are assembled from cast and fabricated parts. The steel cutting edge has been lost.

This pair of snuffers, like the caster marked in the same year (cat. 8) descended in the family of John Foye of Boston, a ship's captain who married Sarah Boucher in 1729.

The snuffers have lost the sharp steel blades that would have made them useful for trimming the candlewick. The pointed end of the snuffers could be used for cleaning or manipulating the wick in the hot wax. Such snuffers were often supplied on a tray or in a stand, sometimes with a matching set of candlesticks.[1] The tray would have had a practical function, to protect the tabletop from the waxy snuffers, which were in constant use to maintain the wicks.

1. For example, see a set in the Clark Art Institute, illus. Wees 1997, pp. 531–32, cat. 395.

· 10 ·

CHAFING DISH
Marked by Anthony Nelme (free 1679)
London, 1701/2
Silver
39.20

MARKS: on rim between piercings, maker's mark *Ne* (repeated on base of burner); Britannia; lion's head erased; date letter *f*

ARMORIALS: engraved on cover of burner and on rim of body, the arms and crest of Grenville impaling Temple, possibly for Richard Grenville of Wotton, co. Buckinghamshire (d. 1719), who married Eleanor, daughter of Sir Peter Temple of Stanton Barry, co. Buckinghamshire

H. 12.8 cm (5 1/16 in.); w. 22.6 cm (8 7/8 in.); diam. of rim 20 cm (7 7/8 in.)

WEIGHT: 1,757.7 gm (56 oz 10 dwt)

PROVENANCE: Tiffany & Co., New York, purchased by Theodora Wilbour, January 5, 1939, Anonymous Gift in Memory of Charlotte Beebe Wilbour (1833–1914), January 12, 1939

EXHIBITED: Boston, Museum of Fine Arts, 1994

PUBLISHED: Gruber 1982, p. 229, fig. 328

DESCRIPTION: The dish is supported by three scrolled legs of complex outline, with beading applied to the center ridge. They are cast in two pieces and seamed vertically. The body of the dish is hemispherical, with a pierced and gadrooned fitting to contain the lamp at the center of the base. It is raised from heavy sheet, with applied cut-card work in an arcaded pattern on the underside. In several areas the surface is unevenly adhered. The upper rim is a separate seamed section with an applied wire rim, pierced with an arcaded pattern. The gadrooned fitting for the lamp protrudes below the dish with a finial on its underside and a band of circular piercing connecting it to the dish. The circular lamp with cylindrical base has a gadrooned rim. It has a flat cover with deep bezel, wire rim, and cut-card decoration around a molded hole; a screw with a scallop collar fits in the hole. The scrolled cast triangular frame is suspended across the dish from the three scrolled legs.

The highly sophisticated design and construction of this chafing dish, or brazier, reflects the internationalism of London silver in the years around 1700. The strength of the design depends on the complex planes of the cast legs, which are almost architectural in character.

10 (Color Plate II)

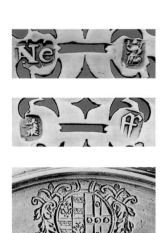

Anthony Nelme, who is most often mentioned as a signatory to the 1682 petition against admitting aliens to the freedom of the Goldsmiths' Company, nonetheless supplied his clients with silver in the French style.[1] On one occasion in 1706 he was charged with having employed the services of a foreign journeyman, described as German, who was not free of the city.[2] There were doubtless many such unreported infractions in the trade, which would explain the rapid assimilation of Continental styles. The chafing dish is fitted with a lamp for burning spirits and might have been used at table to warm a dish of food.[3] It may once have had a matching hot water kettle,[4] a form produced in some quantity by Nelme,[5] and it is close in design to a Dutch example with ornament inspired by the designs of Daniel Marot (1661–1752) in the Gemeentemuseum, The Hague.[6]

1. For example, see the candelabrum of ca. 1670–90 at the Art Institute of Chicago, illus. Philippa Glanville, *Silver in England* (London, 1987), p. 71, fig. 26, and the Bridgeman toilet service of 1691, illus. Schroder 1988a, p. 139, fig. 37.

2. Grimwade 1990, p. 760.

3. As illustrated in an engraving by Abraham Bosse, illus. Gruber 1982, p. 228, fig. 326.

4. Other roughly contemporaneous examples of braziers with kettles include a set of 1715 by Gabriel Sleath, illus. Clayton 1985b, p. 127, fig. 4; another of 1720 marked by Ambrose Stevenson, sold Sotheby's, New York, June 17, 1981, lot 43.

5. See an example of 1715, illus. Clayton 1985b, p. 124, fig. 6. A smaller brazier of 1700 marked by Nelme, considerably simpler than the present example, was sold at Sotheby's, New York, November 6, 1980, lot 355.

6. Exh. New York, Cooper-Hewitt Museum, *Courts and Colonies: The William and Mary Style in Holland, England, and America*, 1988, p. 127, cat. 62.

11

· 11 ·

FOUR SALTS

Marked by David Willaume (I) (1658–ca. 1741)
London, 1701/2
Silver
42.84–87

MARKS: 42.84–86, on underside of each, maker's mark *WI* (Grimwade 3192); date letter *f*; lion's head erased; Britannia. 42.87: unmarked

ARMORIALS: engraved on underside of 42.84–86, an unidentified coat of arms (three cocks)

42.84: H. 2.6 cm (1 1/16 in.); w. 7.1 cm (2 13/16 in.); d. 7.1 cm (2 13/16 in.)

42.85: H. 2.6 cm (1 1/16 in.); w. 7.3 cm (2 7/8 in.); d. 7.3 cm (2 7/8 in.)

42.86: H. 2.6 cm (1 1/16 in.); w. 7.2 cm (2 13/16 in.); d. 7.2 cm (2 13/16 in.)

42.87: H. 2.4 cm (15/16 in.); w. 7.1 cm (2 13/16 in.); d. 7.1 cm (2 13/16 in.)

WEIGHT: 42.84: 113.4 gm (3 oz 13 dwt). 42.85: 104.9 gm (3 oz 7 dwt). 42.86: 107.7 gm (3 oz 9 dwt). 42.87: 85 gm (2 oz 14 dwt)

PROVENANCE: Anonymous Gift in Memory of Charlotte Beebe Wilbour (1833–1914), February 9, 1942

DESCRIPTION: Each round salt has a low molded foot, lobed and fluted sides, and a hemispherical bowl. The salts are assembled from cast sections. The fourth, unmarked salt, is a copy.

12

• 12 •

PAIR OF BOXES

Marked by Benjamin Pyne (free 1676)
London, 1702/3
Silver
33.92–93

MARKS: on underside of each, maker's mark *PY* (repeated on inside of cover); Britannia; lion's head erased (repeated on inside of cover); date letter *G*

ARMORIALS: engraved on covers of each, the crest of Hobson

33.92: H. 4.9 cm (1¹⁵⁄₁₆ in.); diam. of base 8.8 cm (3⁷⁄₁₆ in.)

33.93: H. 5.1 cm (2 in.); diam. of base 8.7 cm (3⁷⁄₁₆ in.)

WEIGHT: 33.92: 195.6 gm (6 oz 6 dwt). 33.93: 195.6 gm (6 oz 6 dwt)

PROVENANCE: Anonymous Gift in Memory of Charlotte Beebe Wilbour (1833–1914), March 2, 1933

EXHIBITED: Boston, Museum of Fine Arts, 1933

DESCRIPTION: The low cylindrical boxes are formed of seamed sheet with an applied base. The gadrooned foot and base are chased, and there is an applied wire on the foot rim. The covers are formed of chased sheet, with an applied wire rim with chased gadrooning, and a bezel. A molded wire encircles the plain section of the cover. The original engraving on the covers has been removed and hammer marks are visible on the underside.

Toilet services of the 1690s generally included a mirror, a pincushion, candlesticks, large and small boxes, salvers, jars or pots, and brushes. More elaborate sets, particularly those made in the French style, might also include an ecuelle and a ewer and basin. Though toilet services were restricted mainly to aristocratic households, there was nonetheless a range of quality available. At one extreme was the finely chased figural work such as that on the Calverley service,[1] and at the other extreme, a simply chased, light-gauge service such as that represented by these boxes. As the influence of the French court took hold in the years around 1700, chased ornament was replaced by crisply cast moldings.[2]

1. Victoria and Albert Museum, acc. no. 240–240m-1879, illus. Oman 1965, pl. 81a.

2. See, for example, the service in the Gilbert collection attributed to Philip Rollos, illus. Schroder 1988a, pp. 141–47, cat. 34.

· 13 ·

TONTINE CUP

Marked by Peter Harache (first mark entered
1698)
London, 1702/3
Gold
35.1546

MARKS: on rim, maker's mark *HA* (Grimwade 936);
leopard's head crowned; lion passant; date
letter *g*

ARMORIALS: engraved on side, the arms of
Winstanley of Braunton, co. Leistershire

INSCRIPTIONS: engraved on underside, a skull and
crossbones within a circle, series of names, initials,
and dates, surrounded by the inscription: *I was your
friend unto my end: Your friend I was and so did
dy.★Gratia Regis floret Lex: Imperium & Libertas*

H: 5.4 cm (2⅛ in.); diam. of rim 7.5 cm (3 in.)

WEIGHT: 146.2 gm (4 oz 14 dwt)

PROVENANCE: sold Christie's, London, January 19,
1921, lot 11, purchased by Caldicott; Frederick
Bradbury, [William E. Godfrey, New York], purchased by Frank Brewer Bemis, 1925, Gift of Frank
Brewer Bemis, November 7, 1935

PUBLISHED: "The 'Tontine' Cup," *Boston Evening
Transcript,* July 11, 1936; Kathryn C. Buhler, "English
Silver in the Bemis Collection," *The Connoisseur* 130
(December 1952), pp. 226–31; Clayton 1971, p. 331;
Clayton 1985a, p. 448; Gale Glynn, "Some Tontines
Commemorated on English Plate," *Silver Society
Journal* 8 (Autumn 1996), pp. 445–61

DESCRIPTION: The plain cup, raised from sheet,
has a rounded base.

This gold cup and other English objects commemorating tontines have been discussed by
Gale Glynn in a recent article.[1] A tontine is
described as "an annuity shared by subscribers
to a loan, the shares increasing as subscribers
die until the last survivor gets all, or until a
specified date when the remaining survivors
share the proceeds."[2] Named for and promoted
by a Neapolitan banker, Lorenzo Tonti (ca.
1620–ca. 1684), such schemes were undertaken
throughout Europe from the late seventeenth
century, both among private subscribers, as in
the case of this gold cup, and by governments
seeking to raise funds. In England and Ireland
state tontines were set up by an act of Parliament, and the interest paid was based on the

age of the individual whose life was nominated. Private tontines were established with varying guidelines, but the essential structure called
for interest to be paid to the participants and
for the capital to be distributed to survivors.
The original investor might name another life
on which the tontine would run, and yet
another individual to whom the benefits would
be paid. Objects made as mementos of private
tontines include salvers, an etui, an inkstand, a
mug, a pair of asparagus tongs, and snuffboxes.
Most are made of silver, but it is clear that the
value of the object itself is not related to the
amount invested in the tontine.

This cup commemorates the earliest known
English tontine. The specific terms of the
agreement are not recorded, but Glynn has
successfully identified nearly all the members
of the group by the initials and death dates
engraved on the base of the cup and traced
their relationships to each other. The subscribers were a group of wealthy friends, many
of them members of the Winstanley and
Willoughby families. The arrangement was
probably conceived about 1667 or 1668. Sir
Francis Willoughby (d. 1672), an ornithologist
and a founding member of the Royal Society,
married Emma Barnard in 1667, and the following year his sister Katherine married
Clement Winstanley, who died in 1672.
Winstanley's sister, Katherine, and a niece by
another sister also subscribed to the tontine.
Other members of the Willoughby family who
subscribed include Sir Francis's oldest son, his
two sisters, and his father-in-law. One of the
Willoughby sisters, Letticia, married Sir
Thomas Wendy, of Hasingfield, Cambridgeshire, whose uncle, Sir Peter Wentworth, was
also a member. A transcription of the engraving
on the underside of the base, with Glynn's proposed identifications, follows:

1. F: Will:by 3: July 72 [Sir Francis Willoughby Knt]
2. Cl: Wins:tly ob: aug 72 [Clement Winstanley]
3. J: L: ap 73
4. T: Wendy: 17: nov 73 [Sir Thomas Wendy Knt]
5. S:r P: W: ob 1 de [Sir Paul Wentworth Knt]
6. A: W: [?Lady (Anne) Wentworth]
7. H: B: 25 ap 80 [Henry Barnard]
8. G: M: Æ 64, ob 9M 81
9. P: P: ob 12: June 81

13

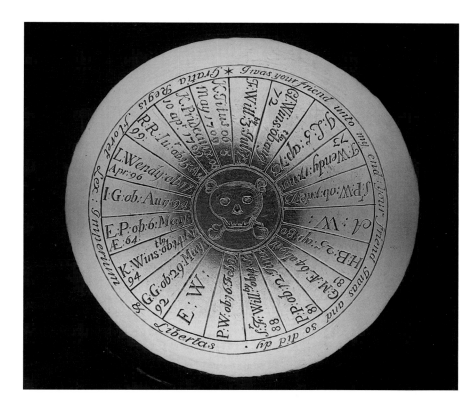

10. S:r: F. Will:by ob 14 Se 88 [Sir Francis
Willoughby Bt.]

11. P:W: ob 16: Feb 89 [Peter Wentworth]

12. E: W: [?Lady (Emma Barnard) Child]

13. G: G: ob: 29 May 92

14. K:Wins:tly ob: 14 Ap 94 [Katherine
Winstanley]

15. E: P: ob: 6: May: Æ 64

16. I:G: ob: Aug 94

17. L:Wendy: ob 17 Apr:96 [Lady Letticia Wendy]

18. R: R: Iu:r ob: 15 Au 99

19. K. Prideaux ob: 10 Ap.r 1709 [Katherine
Prideaux]

20. K. Titus ob 5 May 1709 [Lady (Katherine)
Titus]

The first member of the tontine to die was
Sir Francis Willoughby in 1672, and the last was
Lady Katherine Titus in 1709. Precisely how
the tontine was dispersed remains uncertain.
The cup bears the engraved arms of James
Winstanley, whose parents, Clement and
Katherine, and aunt, Letticia Wendy, had been
members. Letticia, who died in 1696, had given
James a gift of gold sometime before drawing
up her will in which she left him an additional
one thousand pounds. Winstanley probably did
not come into a great fortune from his father,
Clement, however, who died in 1672. The year
in which the cup was made—1702—does not
correspond to any significant date in the
Winstanley family, although James Winstanley
was elected a member of Parliament for
Leicester in 1701 and may have bought the cup
to mark this event. It seems most likely that
Winstanley bought the cup secondhand sometime after 1709 when the last member of the
tontine died and had it engraved to reflect the
membership and history of his parents' associations.

1. Glynn 1996, pp. 445–61. The following entry
summarizes her research.

2. R. E. Allen, ed., *Concise Oxford Dictionary* (Oxford,
1990), quoted by Glynn 1996, p. 445.

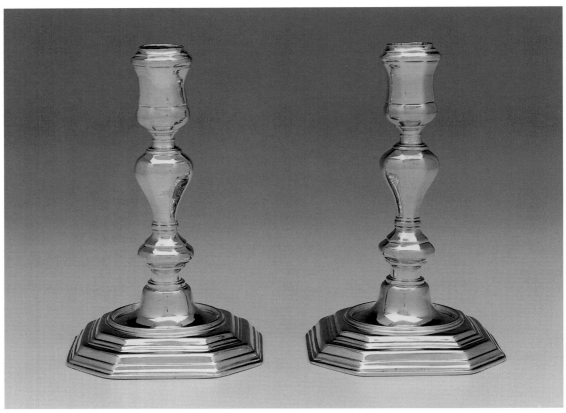

14

· 14 ·

PAIR OF CANDLESTICKS

Marked by John Barnard (I) (free 1685)
London, 1704/5
Silver
37.1166–1167

MARKS: 37.1166: on underside, maker's mark *Ba* (Grimwade 112); date letter *j*; lion's head erased; Britannia. 37.1167: on underside, maker's mark *Ba* (Grimwade 112); date letter *j*; Britannia; lion's head erased

37.1166: H. 18.6 cm (7⁵⁄₁₆ in.); W. 11.6 (4⁹⁄₁₆ in.); D. 11.4 cm (4½ in.)

37.1167: H. 18.8 cm (7⅜ in.); W. 11.5 cm (4½ in.); D. 11.4 cm (4½ in.)

WEIGHT: 37.1166: 541.5 gm (17 oz 8 dwt). 37.1167: 521.6 gm (16 oz 15 dwt)

PROVENANCE: Walter H. Willson, Ltd., London, purchased by Theodora Wilbour, October 6, 1937, Anonymous Gift in Memory of Charlotte Beebe Wilbour (1833–1914), November 10, 1937

DESCRIPTION: Each candlestick has a stepped square base with cut corners and a molded profile.

The base is cast in one piece, with a notched wire applied to the edge of the foot and a molded wire applied around the base of the stem. The baluster stem is octagonal, with a faceted knop rising to a flaring octagonal midsection and an octagonal, vase-shaped nozzle. The stem and nozzle are cast in two pieces, seamed vertically.

Eighteenth-century baluster-stem candlesticks survive in enormous quantity.[1] This is a reflection of their durable construction and continuing popularity among collectors. In a grand household, midsized candlesticks such as these would probably have been used with beeswax candles in all of the public and private rooms—on card tables, dining tables, writing desks, and dressing tables.

1. Examples similar in design to the present pair include a pair of 1707 marked by Richard Syng, sold Christie's, London, June 27, 1979, lot 127; a pair of 1705 marked by Thomas Pritchard, sold Sotheby's, New York, April 12, 1995, lot 330; and a pair of 1713 marked by Anthony Nelme, sold Christie's, New York, October 17, 1996, lot 353.

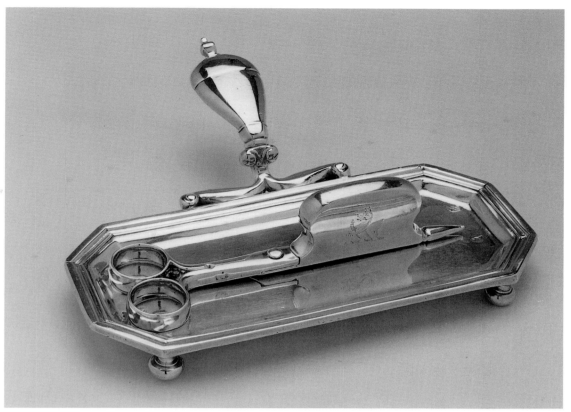

15

· 15 ·

TRAY AND SNUFFERS

Marked by Anthony Nelme (free 1679) and
Joseph Bird (fourth mark entered 1724, d. 1735)
London, 1706/7
Silver, steel
33.95a–b

MARKS: 33.95a (tray): on top, Britannia; date letter *l*;
lion's head erased; maker's mark *ANe* (Grimwade
68). 33.95b (snuffers): inside pan, maker's mark *Bi*
(Grimwade 177); lion's head erased. Outside pan,
date letter *l*; lion's head erased; Britannia; maker's
mark *Bi* (Grimwade 177)

ARMORIALS: engraved on each, an unidentified
crest (a demiwolf rampant)

INSCRIPTIONS: engraved on underside of 33.95a,
10=8=0, scratched *1840*
33.95a: H. 4.8 cm (1⅞ in.); w. 28.2 cm (11⅛ in.);
d. 17 cm (6¹¹⁄₁₆ in.)
33.95b: L. 14.4 cm (5¹¹⁄₁₆ in.); w. 3.2 cm (1¼ in.)

WEIGHT: 33.95a: 313.7 gm (10 oz). 33.95b:
118.2 gm (3 oz 16 dwt)

PROVENANCE: Anonymous Gift in Memory of
Charlotte Beebe Wilbour (1833–1914), March 2, 1933

EXHIBITED: Boston, Museum of Fine Arts, 1933

DESCRIPTION: The tray is rectangular with
mitered corners. It is formed of sheet, with cut
molded wire applied to the rim. The tray rests on
four ball feet that have been reattached. Centered
on one side is a drop-shaped handle, hollow-formed
with a sheet applied to form a smooth back. It is
soldered to a cast scrolled bracket that laps over the
edge of the tray. The snuffers are of scissors form,
riveted where the two arms cross, and with small
oval rings for handles. One arm has a curved shallow pan with a deep rim attached to one blade and
a shaped, pointed tip. The opposite arm is fitted
with a flat blade that matches the pan opposite. A
thin wedge of steel is inset to form an edge on each
blade. The snuffers are assembled from cast and fabricated parts.

The manufacture of candlesticks and related
implements such as snuffers was the province
of specialist makers. Joseph Bird, who marked
this pair of snuffers, was one such specialist
whose marks appears mainly on candlesticks.[1]
The remarkable continuity of the trade is
reflected in the transfer of skills from master to
apprentice. Bird seems to have fostered a suc-

cession of extremely successful candlestick makers, having trained David Green, who in turn trained James Gould, who trained his brother William Gould.[2] Anthony Nelme's mark appears on some of the grandest plate of the early eighteenth century but also frequently on production pieces, such as candlesticks or this snuffer tray.[3] He may have employed a candlestick maker in his shop or bought finished pieces for marking and retail sale.

1. For example, see Christie's, New York, October 17, 1996, lots 355, 359.
2. Grimwade 1990, pp. 441, 526–25, 528.
3. For candlesticks marked by Nelme, see Elizabeth B. Miles, *English Silver: The Elizabeth B. Miles Collection* (Hartford, 1976), p. 120, cat. 151; Wees 1997, pp. 506–7, cat. 373; Christie's, New York, October 17, 1996, lot 353. Nelme's son Francis also marked such wares, for example a snuffer tray in the Wadsworth Atheneum, Hartford, illus. Miles, *English Silver*, p. 127, cat. 158.

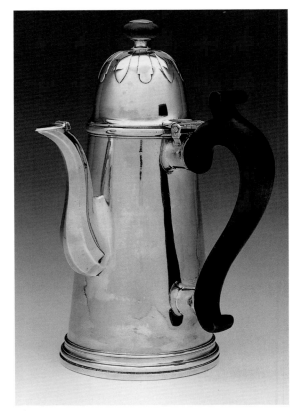

16

· 16 ·

COFFEEPOT

Marked by Simon Pantin (I) (ca. 1680–1728)

London, 1706/7

Silver, wood

35.1585

MARKS: to right of handle, Britannia; maker's mark *PA* (Grimwade 2124) (repeated on bezel of cover); lion's head erased (repeated on bezel of cover); date letter *l*

ARMORIALS: engraved on side, the arms of Craven quartering Craven (ancient), possibly for William Craven, second baron Craven of Hampsted Marshall (1688–1711)

H. 19.6 cm (7¾ in.); w. 13.8 cm (5⁷⁄₁₆ in.); d. 11.7 cm (4⅝ in.)

WEIGHT: 490 gm (15 oz 15 dwt)

PROVENANCE: Crichton Brothers, London, purchased by Frank Brewer Bemis, May 2, 1932, Bequest of Frank Brewer Bemis, November 7, 1935

DESCRIPTION: The tapering cylindrical pot is formed from sheet that is seamed behind the handle. The base is inset, with a molded wire foot and rim. A faceted curved spout, cast in two pieces and seamed vertically, has a hinged cap, and the wooden scrolled handle, at a right angle to the spout, has cylindrical, slightly tapered mounts. The high domed cover is raised, with a slightly flaring rim and an interior wire bezel. Radiating from the wooden finial is a cut-card design of alternating notched and smooth lobes. The finial is secured by a screw and wing nut threaded through the top of the cover. Patches of firescale on the highly polished body show that the piece has been repaired, particularly in the area of a small patch near the lower handle socket.

The eccentric format of the engraved arms, for which the Craven supporter, a griffin, is used in place of mantling, may not be contemporaneous with the manufacture of the coffeepot. However, after 1801, the Cravens were granted an earldom, so the baron's coronet shown here suggests an earlier date. If the engraving was done at the time of manufacture, the arms are those of William Craven, second baron Craven, of Combe Abbey, co. Warwick, who succeeded his father in 1695. He held the posts of lord lieutenant of Berkshire (1702), lord proprietor of the province of Carolina (1705/6), and lord palatine (1708).

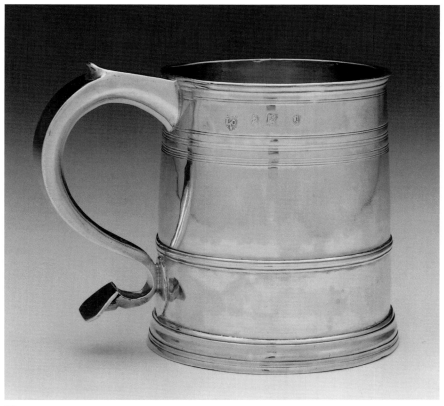

17

the body, leaving patches at the upper and lower junctures.

Plain mugs such as this half-pint example were sometimes purchased in pairs or sets as gifts to colleges or livery companies.[1] Half-pint mugs were also produced in pottery, which was less durable and not as appropriate for presentation.[2]

1. A half-pint mug was part of the equipage required at Rugby School in the early eighteenth century, where a new student was also required to bring sheets and a spoon. See exh. London, Goldsmiths' Hall, 1990, p. 100.

2. For other examples of this form, see a pair marked by Benjamin Pyne and J. Read, sold Christie's, Geneva, May 15, 1985, lot 84; another in the Huntington collection marked by John Cole for 1701, illus. Wark 1978, p. 25, cat. 75; another at Colonial Williamsburg of 1716/7 marked by Timbrell and Bell, illus. Davis 1976, p. 68, cat. 57.

· 17 ·

MUG

Marked by Nathaniel Lock (free 1687, d. ca. 1749)

London, 1707/8

Silver

33.98

MARKS: to right of handle, maker's mark *LO* (Grimwade 1948) (repeated on handle); Britannia; lion's head erased; date letter *m*

INSCRIPTIONS: engraved on underside, *B/H★E*; scratched on underside, *Revd. S. Sneade/Brand Lane Ludlow 1786, M-S/72842/A.D 1707*

H. 10.7 cm (4¼ in.); w. 13.3 cm (5¼ in.); diam. of rim 8.6 cm (3⅜ in.)

WEIGHT: 319 gm (10 oz 5 dwt)

PROVENANCE: Anonymous Gift in Memory of Charlotte Beebe Wilbour (1833–1914), March 2, 1933

DESCRIPTION: The cylindrical tapering body rests on a molded base. It is formed of raised sheet. An applied molded wire and a series of incised lines divide the body horizontally into thirds. The rim is thickened with applied wire. The ear-shaped handle, fabricated from four pieces, has been reattached to

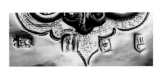

· 18 ·

MONTEITH
Marked by John Leach (free 1682, d. 1713)
London, 1707/8
Silver
40.191

MARKS: below rim, maker's mark *LE* (Grimwade 1916); Britannia; lion's head erased; date letter *m*

ARMORIALS: engraved within a cartouche on each side, an unidentified coat of arms (vair a fess, impaling three annulets)

H. 21.2 cm (8⅜ in.); w. 34.5 cm (13⅝ in.); diam. of rim 31.7 cm (12½ in.)

WEIGHT: 1,995.8 gm (64 oz 3 dwt)

PROVENANCE: Tiffany & Co., New York,[1] purchased by Theodora Wilbour, May 30, 1940, Anonymous Gift in Memory of Charlotte Beebe Wilbour (1833–1914), April 15, 1940

EXHIBITED: Boston, Museum of Fine Arts, 1994

PUBLISHED: Gruber 1982, p. 224

DESCRIPTION: The circular bowl, raised from sheet, rests on a fluted, domed foot. The bowl is chased with vertical fluting and has punched foliate motifs below and above. The scalloped rim is formed of applied cast scrolls, outlined with chased and matted panels. On each side of the bowl is a chased cartouche with a scale ground. A cast lion's mask is applied to a matted panel on each side of the bowl and holds in its mouth a cast faceted drop handle with gadrooned ball.

The monteith, a vessel with a notched rim used for cooling wineglasses, was an innovation of the 1680s.[2] The design of the present example, with fluted body, attached rim outlined with scrolls, and bail handles secured to lion's masks, became a standard formula.[3] The monteith is presumed to be English in origin, and it is often observed that Huguenot makers seem not to have taken up the model. The motifs, however, show the somewhat dissipated influence of French ornament, particularly in the scrolls of the border, which echo Daniel Marot's (1661–1752) designs, and the lion's masks, which are a feature of seventeenth-century French silver.[4] John Leach seems to have made something of a speciality of monteiths, and Georgina Lee records seven with his mark ranging in date from 1698 to 1707.[5]

1. The monteith may have been part of the estate of Louis Huth, Esq., Possingworth, Hawkhust, and London, sold Christie's, London, May 26, 1905, lot 42, where the catalogue describes it as 66 oz 15 dwt.

2. Georgina E. Lee, *British Silver Monteith Bowls* (Byfleet, Surrey, 1978), pp. 9–15. The diarist Anthony Wood recorded in 1683 that a new vessel had appeared with a notched rim like the border of the coat worn by a "fantastical Scot called Monsieur Monteigh," after whom the bowl was named.

3. See an example of 1713 marked by William Penstone, sold Christie's, London, July 17, 1959, lot 80; another of 1701 marked by Thomas Parr, sold Christie's, London, March 26, 1975, lot 179; another of 1702 marked by William Denny, sold Christie's, London, November 28, 1979, lot 109.

4. See the title page from Marot's *Nouveaux Livre d'Orfevrerie* in exh. New York, Cooper-Hewitt Museum, *Courts and Colonies: The William and Mary Style in Holland, England, and America*, 1988, p. 116, cat. 41. Also see the lion's mask on the Kedleston fountain, illus. Gillian Wilson, "The Kedleston Fountain: Its Development from a Seventeenth Century Vase," *The J. Paul Getty Museum Journal* 11 (1983), pp. 1–12.

5. Lee, *Monteith Bowls*, pp. 74, 75, 79, 85, 90, 93. To this list should be added a bowl of 1703 sold Christie's, London, November 28, 1985, lot 47, and another of 1704 sold Christie's, New York, October 30, 1990, lot 342.

18

· 19 ·

PAIR OF SCONCES
Marked by John Jackson (I) (free 1681)
London, 1707/8
Silver
63.784–785

MARKS: on each backplate, maker's mark *Ja* (Grimwade 1092) (repeated on 63.785 waxpan); Britannia; lion's head erased; date letter *m*

INSCRIPTIONS: 63.784, on back, *N9.* 63.785, on back, *N10*

63.784: H. 32 cm (12⁹⁄₁₆ in.); w. 21.2 cm (8⅜ in.); d. 18.9 cm (7⁷⁄₁₆ in.)

63.785: H. 32 cm (12⁹⁄₁₆ in.); w. 21.2 cm (8⅜ in.); d. 18.6 cm (7⁵⁄₁₆ in.)

WEIGHT: 63.784: 1,207.7 gm (38 oz 16 dwt). 63.785: 1,165.2 gm (37 oz 9 dwt)

PROVENANCE: lord Brownlow, Belton House, Grantham, sold Christie's, London, May 29, 1963, lot 16, purchased from Spink and Sons, Ltd., London, June 19, 1963, Theodora Wilbour Fund in Memory of Charlotte Beebe Wilbour

EXHIBITED: London, Seaford House, *Queen Charlotte's Loan Exhibition of Old Silver,* 1929, cat. 338; London, 25 Park Lane, *Catalogue of a Loan Exhibition of Old English Plate and Decorations and Orders,* 1929, cat. 779

PUBLISHED: *Christie's Review of the Year, 1962–1963* (London, 1963), p. 58; Clayton 1971, p. 248, fig. 502; Gruber 1982, fig. 366; Clayton 1985a, p. 332, fig. 502

DESCRIPTION: The sconces are composed of a richly chased cartouche-shaped backplate supporting a scrolled bracket with nozzle. The backplate, formed from a single sheet, is chased with a figure of a putto flanked by swags of fruit against a crisply matted ground. Above is a chased concave shell, and at the base of the bracket is a chased grotesque mask. The backplates are cracked and repaired in many places. Some of the repairs, consisting of patches of silver applied over weak areas in the chasing, are contemporaneous with the manufacture. The arm, formed of complex scrolls and square in section, is cast in two pieces and seamed vertically. The waxpan has molded wire edges and pierced hearts on its underside and surrounding the nozzle. The nozzle, cast in two vertical pieces, is urn-shaped.

These sconces were acquired from the 1963 sale of plate from Belton House, Lincolnshire.[1] The Belton silver, an important group of

which remains in the house, was acquired by the Brownlows in several stages. The family's wealth was established in the sixteenth century by Richard Brownlow (1553–1638), who had a successful and lucrative career in law. He purchased the Belton estates in 1603, but it was not until 1684 that his great-grandson, Sir John Brownlow, third baronet (1659–1697), embarked on the construction of an ambitious house in the classical style. The two-storied house with projecting wings at either end and four great chambers clustered in the main block was richly embellished with plasterwork and carved ornament and hung with tapestries and a series of portraits of the kings and queens of England.[2]

At Belton and in nearly every other country or town house of equal pretension, large sets of wall sconces were an essential element of the decoration since they (along with chandeliers) provided whatever ambient light was available for late afternoon or evening occasions. This pair of sconces must have been part of a set of at least twelve, for they are engraved with the numbers *9* and *10.* Although large sets would have been the norm in a grand household, few have survived intact, because in the nineteenth century sconces were replaced by the much cheaper and more effective argand and gas lamps. This pair was modified by the addition of a fitting on the branch for a hurricane lamp. The shield-shaped backplate crested with a shell, outlined with scrolls, and embellished with swags of fruit and foliage is a reminder of the far-reaching influence of the French court style, disseminated in part through the printed designs of Daniel Marot.[3] The basic design formula had a long life, ranging from the sets made for Charles II[4] to the set of 1730 made for the earl of Warrington.[5] The present sconces, which are chased, not cast, were a more modest purchase, and the design might have been repeated by hammering the sheet into a wooden die.[6] Other sconces with a similar combination of motifs are known, some, presumably costlier, with pierced backplates.[7]

It is uncertain when these sconces were acquired for Belton. Inventories of 1754 and 1810 list pairs of silver sconces, but without weights.[8] A bill from Rundell, Bridge & Rundell of 1821 to the first earl Brownlow lists "two large heart shaped sconces" at 76 oz 9 dwt that may refer to the present pair.[9] Rundell's had, since 1808, kept in reserve items

19

of plate from the Jewel Office (the division of the royal household responsible for plate) that had been brought in for melting and offered them to their better customers as antiques.[10] A set of four large sconces with the cipher of William and Mary were certainly purchased for Belton through Rundell's in this period.

1. See cat. 68, which also came from Belton House.

2. Adrian Tinniswood, *Belton House* (London, 1992), pp. 8–15.

3. See exh. New York, Cooper-Hewitt Museum, *Courts and Colonies: The William and Mary Style in Holland, England, and America*, 1988, pp. 116, 188.

4. See the set of eight at Colonial Williamsburg (acc. no. 1938-34, 1-8), illus. Davis 1976, pp. 15–17, cat. 2. These are almost twice the size of the present pair, with backplates made of cast, not chased, elements.

5. Two are at the Clark Art Institute, illus. Wees 1997, pp. 501–4, cat. 371.

6. The other examples of this design also show the putto with his right arm raised, though there is a variation in the shell crest, which is convex on some, concave on others. See Christie's, London, November 24, 1971, lot 85.

7. See a pair of 1702/3 at the Metropolitan Museum, in exh. New York, Cooper-Hewitt Museum, *Courts and Colonies: The William and Mary Style in Holland, England, and America*, 1988, p. 170, cat. 128. A similar pair is in the Victoria and Albert Museum (acc. no. 816,816a-1890), illus. W. W. Watts, *Catalogue of English Silversmiths' Work* (London, 1920), p. 44, pl. 37.

8. Lincolnshire Archives, BNLW 2/2/5/25; BNLW 2/2/5/29. I am grateful to Christopher Hartop, Christie's, New York, and Adrian Wilkinson, archivist, Lincolnshire Archives, for providing these references.

9. Lincolnshire Archives, BNLW 2/2/5/10.

10. See the note preceding the sale of plate from Belton, Christie's, London, May 29, 1963.

· 20 ·

CISTERN AND FOUNTAIN

Marked by David Willaume (I) (1658–1741)
London, 1707/8
Silver
1999.98.1–2a-b

MARKS: 1999.1 (cistern): on rim of foot, date letter *n*; lion's head erased; Britannia; maker's mark *WI* (repeated on body to left of each handle). 1999.2a-b (fountain): on body to left of spout, maker's mark *WI* (Grimwade 3192) (repeated inside cover); Britannia; lion's head erased (repeated inside cover); date letter *n*. On front molding above lion, date letter *n*; lion's head erased; Britannia; maker's mark *WI*

ARMORIALS: engraved on both cistern and fountain, the badge and motto of George, Prince of Wales, later George II, king of England (r. 1727–60); handles of the cistern and cover of the fountain modeled as the supporters and crest of the earls of Meath

1999.1: H. 66 cm (26 in.); w. 114.3 cm (45 in.); d. 68.6 cm (27 in.)
1999.2a-b: H. 108 cm (42½ in.); diam. of base 33.5 cm (13³⁄₁₆ in.)

WEIGHT: 1999.1: 1,775 oz 15 dwt (scratch weight, unverified). 1999.2a: 1,049 oz 18 dwt (scratch weight, unverified); 1999.2b: 38 oz 8 dwt (scratch weight, unverified)

PROVENANCE: Chambre Brabazon (ca. 1645–1715), fifth earl of Meath; purchased by the Prince of Wales (later George II) (1683–1760), by descent to Ernst August IV, prince of Hanover and duke of Brunswick and Lüneburg (1914–1987); private collection; Museum purchase with funds provided anonymously and other funds to be determined, June 23, 1999

PUBLISHED: Sir Charles James Jackson, *An Illustrated History of English Plate*, 2 vols. (London, 1911), vol. 2, p. 709, figs. 1024, 1025; L. L. G. Ramsey, "Treasures of the House of Brunswick," *Connoisseur* 130 (October 1952), pp. 91–93, figs. 3, 4; Norman M. Penzer, "The Great Wine Coolers, II," *Apollo* 66, no. 391 (September 1957), p. 45; Hayward 1959, pls. 23, 27; Walter de Sager, "Our Atlantic Heritage," *Connoisseur* 165 (June 1967), p. 87

EXHIBITED: London, Victoria and Albert Museum, *Exhibition of the Brunswick Treasures*, 1952; Toronto, Royal Ontario Museum, *English Silver: Seven Centuries of English Domestic Silver*, 1958, p. 43, cat. F44.b.1–2

DESCRIPTION: The cistern rests on a domed spreading foot assembled of three raised sections chased with two horizontal bands of gadrooning, and above, a chased band of pendant, stylized leaves below a molded arcade. The bombé body of the vessel is raised from heavy sheet, with a chased border of stylized leaves decorating the upper edge. The applied heavy rim is formed of a broad band of gadrooning. The handles are suspended from two brackets in the form of wyverns, cast in several pieces and heavily chased, applied at either end of the body. The urn-shaped fountain rests on a domed spreading foot that is chased with a broad gadrooned band. The spool-shaped stem, formed of several chased sections, has applied vertical brackets and cast gadrooned borders. It supports the baluster body of the vessel, which is formed of seven sections of raised sheet with a gadrooned underside, and four applied cast vertical brackets with rosettes. Four cast lion's heads are applied to the shoulder of the vessel, each holding a cast shaped handle in its mouth. The removable cover is surmounted by a cast and chased figure in the form of a falcon.

Of all the goldsmiths working in London in the first half of the eighteenth century, David Willaume I seems to have secured the patronage of the loftiest clients, both private and institutional. This monumental cistern and fountain, with its complex registers of gadrooned work, boldly rendered architectural motifs, and fine chasing, is among the most ambitious of his pieces to have survived.

The cistern and fountain is believed to have been supplied in 1707 to Chambre Brabazon, fifth earl of Meath, whose supporters and crest form the handles of the cistern and the finial of the fountain. Brabazon may have made the purchase to mark his succession to the peerage that same year on the death of his brother, Edward. The Brabazon family had considerable estates in Ireland and in England, and the fifth earl served as paymaster of Ireland and as a privy councillor to Queen Anne and George I. He married Juliana, the daughter of Patrick, second viscount Chaworth of Armagh, a granddaughter of the eighth earl of Rutland. The engraved arms on the applied shield were removed and replaced by the motto and badge of George Augustus, Prince of Wales (crowned George II in 1727).

20 (Color Plates III and IV)

A cistern and fountain was the centerpiece of a magnificent buffet of the late seventeenth and eighteenth centuries, which might also include ewers, dishes, pilgrim bottles, and two-handled cups. Although its main role was display rather than utility, the cistern and fountain would certainly have been used during a grand banquet. Glass bottles or silver flagons of wine were cooled in the cistern, which sat on the floor. The fountain, which rested on a table above, was filled with water. In the early part of the eighteenth century, wineglasses were not laid out on the dining table, and a guest wishing to have a glass of wine would summon a footman, who filled a glass at the sideboard and delivered it on a salver. When the glass had been drained, the footman returned it to the buffet and rinsed it in water from the fountain so that it could be used again as needed. Smaller versions of the form were also made, and at least occasionally, a single set might include both a grand cistern and a smaller cooler, with matching fountain, as represented by the extraordinary set made by Anthony Nelme in 1719 for Thomas Parker, first earl of Macclesfield (1666–1732) now in the Victoria and Albert Museum. As dining customs began to change in the early years of the eighteenth century, individual bottle coolers which were placed on the table became fashionable, allowing the diner more autonomy and privacy.

Compared with other contemporary European monarchs, the Hanoverian kings were not voracious consumers of plate, but a clearer picture of George II's purchases for the Hanover residences is beginning to emerge that suggests an attachment to magnificent display. The precise circumstances under which George Augustus, as Prince of Wales, bought the cistern and fountain remain to be shown,[1] but it may have been bought in 1717 when he commissioned a set of forty-eight knives and forks, twenty-four spoons, twenty-four salts, four casters, four mustard pots, a pair of sauceboats, and three sideboard dishes from Pierre Platel. This service, like the present cistern and fountain, was engraved with the feathers of the Prince of Wales and the motto *Ich Dien*.[2] The Prince of Wales continued to add to his plate, and a group of wares described in contemporary documents as "English style" made in Celle in 1722/3 bears the same engraved initials and badge.[3] The service was listed in the Hanover records as Service F, and known as the English service. Accounts describing the celebrations marking the queen's birthday in 1788 and 1789 record the use of two cisterns and fountains from the service called Service D and the large cistern and fountain from the English service,[4] presumably the present example. The three may be seen in an 1868 photograph taken in Vienna, where the dukes of Brunswick resided after the Prussians sacked Hanover in 1866.[5]

After his accession, George II bought even grander silver for the Hanover court. In 1731, at the death of August Wilhelm, duke of Brunswick-Wolfenbüttel (1662–1731), he seized the opportunity to buy from his debt-ridden relatives the set of silver furniture made in Augsburg between 1725 and 1730.[6] Included in the group were two monumental mirrors, two tables, four gueridons, and five chairs. In 1736 and 1737, encouraged by the Oberhofmarschall von Reden, the king commissioned a set of five silver chandeliers to a design by William Kent, executed by the Hanover court goldsmith, Balthasar Friedrich Behrens.[7] In 1739 and 1745 he ordered a set of twelve silver girandoles to be made up after a design by Kent. George II visited Hanover twelve times during his reign, where he was usually installed at Herren-hausen, the sprawling summer residence outside the city. His arrival was sometimes commemorated with a display of fireworks, and the entertainments, in addition to hunting, theater, and music, often included a fountain display, an illumination, or a masked ball. For such festivities, the silver was installed on one or sometimes two buffets, of unequal size, which might also be left in place for a second event the following day.

1. The cistern and fountain is not listed in the 1747 inventory of plate at Hanover but was apparently among the group of silver brought from England to Hanover in 1738 that is mentioned, but not inventoried (British Museum Add. 42,227, p. 154).

2. Niedersächsisches Hauptstaatsarchiv Hannover Dep. 103, XXI, nr. 719.

3. The casters and a set of salts were sold Christie's, Geneva, November 19, 1996, lot 56.

4. Niedersächsisches Hauptstaatsarchiv Hannover, Dep. 103, XXIV, nr. 2959. I am extremely grateful to Ulriche Mathies for undertaking research. One of the smaller sets must be that offered for sale by Christie's, New York, October 20, 1997.

5. Alheidis von Rohr, *Eldes Tafelgerät* (Hanover, 1993), p. 53.

6. Exh. Munich, Bayerisches National Museum, *Silber und Gold: Augsburger Goldschmiedekunst für die Höfe Europas*, 1994, cat. by Lorenz Seelig, pp. 354–73, cats. 83–87.

7. One is in the Museum of Fine Arts, acc. no. 1985.854, see Ellenor M. Alcorn, "'A Chandelier for the King': William Kent, George II, and Hanover," *Burlington Magazine* 139, no. 1126 (January 1997), pp. 40–43. A pair of chandeliers is at Anglesey Abbey, Cambridge, and a fourth was sold by Christie's, Monaco, December 4, 1993, lot 95.

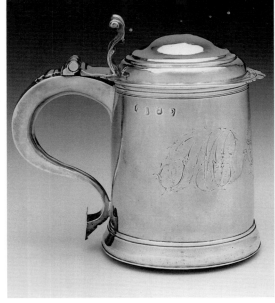

21

· 21 ·

TANKARD

Marked by Thomas Folkingham (first mark entered 1707, d. 1729)
London, 1708/9
Silver
37.242

MARKS: to right of handle, maker's mark, *FO* (Grimwade 703) (repeated twice on handle); Britannia (repeated inside cover); lion's head erased (repeated inside cover); date letter *n* (repeated inside cover)

ARMORIALS: engraved on front, the arms and crest of Abbot

INSCRIPTIONS: engraved to either side of the coat of arms the monograms *THP, IMP*

H. 19.6 cm (7¾ in.); w. 20.6 cm (8⅛ in.); diam. of base 12.9 cm (5⅛ in.)

WEIGHT: 989.4 gm (31 oz 16 dwt)

PROVENANCE: Given in Memory of Dr. William Hewson Baltzell by his wife, Alice Cheney Baltzell, February 4, 1937

DESCRIPTION: The body of the tankard has tapering sides and is raised, with an applied molding at the foot and a caulked rim. The ear-shaped handle is fabricated from several pieces. It has a heart-shaped terminus and a hinge with a shaped drop and a scrolled thumbpiece. The domed, stepped cover is raised, with an applied bezel. The tankard shows considerable wear, and the cover has been patched

and coarsely soldered in the area of the hinge. There is a brass disk soldered to the center of the base, possibly an early museum mount.

The engraved arms on this tankard are probably about twenty years later in date than the tankard itself. The cover, which may be a replacement, lacks the maker's mark and has been rehammered in the area of the marks.

· 22 ·

TEA CANISTER

Marked by John Wisdome (first mark entered 1704)
London, 1709/10
Silver
40.192

MARKS: on lower edge of back, Britannia; date letter *O*; maker's mark *WI* (Grimwade 3187) (repeated on base); lion's head erased (repeated on base, neck, and rim of cover)

ARMORIALS: engraved on side, arms and crest of Ayde, co. Norfolk

INSCRIPTIONS: scratched on base, *oz : dwt / 11 : 15; 12192*

H. 14.9 cm (5⅞ in.); w. 8.4 cm (3⁵⁄₁₆ in.); d. 6 cm (2⅜ in.)

WEIGHT: 360 gm (11 oz 11 dwt)

PROVENANCE: Tiffany & Co., New York, purchased by Theodora Wilbour, March 30, 1940, Anonymous Gift in Memory of Charlotte Beebe Wilbour (1833–1914), April 11, 1940

EXHIBITED: Austin, Texas, University Art Museum, *One Hundred Years of English Silver: 1660–1760*, 1969, cat. 45

DESCRIPTION: The straight-sided rectangular canister, formed from five pieces of seamed sheet, has a slightly curved upper edge. The cover is a flat sliding panel with a circular opening and high lip that fits into the raised domed cap. The surface has been highly polished.

This generously sized tea canister has a sliding cover to permit refilling, while the removable domed cap can be used for measuring the leaves. It seems to have formed part of a service engraved with the same arms that included a teapot marked by Gabriel Sleath,[1] and a kettle

22

23

and stand in this collection marked by Frances Garthorne.[2] Wisdome's mark appears on plain, undecorated tea and coffee wares like the present canister.[3]

1. Formerly in the collection of Mrs. R. M. Robertson, sold Christie's, New York, October 27, 1987, lot 440.

2. See cat. 33.

3. For example, see a bowl of 1713/4, illus. Puig 1989, cat. 35, and a chocolate pot of 1708/9 at Colonial Williamsburg, illus. Davis 1976, pp. 84–85, cat. 80.

· 23 ·

STANDING CUP

Marked by William Pearson (first mark entered 1704)
London, 1711/2
Silver
42.8

MARKS: on side, maker's mark *PE* (probably Grimwade 2166); Britannia; lion's head erased (repeated on underside of base); date letter *Q*

INSCRIPTIONS: engraved on side, *S/W★I/S+SHOVE*; engraved on underside, *S/W+I*

H. 17.4 cm (6⅞ in.); diam. of rim 9.4 cm (3¹¹/₁₆ in.)

WEIGHT: 320.4 gm (10 oz 6 dwt)

PROVENANCE: Anonymous Gift in Memory of Charlotte Beebe Wilbour (1833–1914), January 8, 1942

DESCRIPTION: The raised body of the cup has straight sides and a slightly flaring lip. It is supported by a circular spreading foot that rises to a round baluster-form stem. The foot of the cup is raised, with a square wire added to the rim. The baluster stem is cast in two pieces, seamed vertically.

Plain silver wine cups on baluster stems were a standard feature of the mid-seventeenth century, but by the early eighteenth century, glass, which had become more widely available, was preferred.[1]

1. See two silver wine cups of 1641/2 and 1667/8 at Colonial Williamsburg, illus. Davis 1976, pp. 53–54, cats. 42–43.

24

Spout cups are generally thought to have been used for syllabub or posset, drinks made from sweetened milk or cream curdled with wine.[1] The low position of the spout allowed the clear beverage to be drunk freely, separated from the solids, or curds, floating above. It has also been suggested that they may have been used for feeding infants or invalids.[2] The form has stronger associations with Colonial America than with England. This modest example is badly worn, but representative of the form.

1. Philippa Glanville, *Silver in Tudor and Early Stuart England* (London, 1990), p. 269.
2. John Salter, "Silver in East Anglia," *Silver Society Proceedings* 3 (1985–87), p. 196.

· 24 ·

SPOUT CUP

Marked by John East (first mark entered 1697)
London, 1712/3
Silver
51.2

MARKS: below rim, maker's mark *EA* (Grimwade 525) (repeated on bezel of cover); Britannia; lion's head erased (repeated on bezel of cover); date letter *R*

INSCRIPTIONS: engraved on underside, *D/M · G*; engraved on cover, *DG*

H. 11 cm (4⁵⁄₁₆ in.); w. 14.3 cm (5⁵⁄₁₆ in.); d. 13.4 cm (5¼ in.)

WEIGHT: 232.5 gm (7 oz 9 dwt)

PROVENANCE: Robert Ensko, New York, purchased January 11, 1951, Theodora Wilbour Fund in Memory of Charlotte Beebe Wilbour

DESCRIPTION: The bell-shaped cup is formed from thin raised sheet and rests on a plain foot. A curved spout, formed from seamed sheet, is joined to the vessel's center base. There are two ear-shaped handles, formed from molded wire. The removable, stepped, domed cover has a bezel and an applied wire ring at the center of the cover. The cup has been rehammered and polished.

· 25 ·

TWO-HANDLED CUP

Marked by Gabriel Sleath (1674–1756)
London, 1713/4
Silver
35.1587

MARKS: near rim, maker's mark *SL* (Grimwade 2569); Britannia; lion's head erased; date letter *s*

INSCRIPTIONS: engraved on underside, *1713*; scratched, *No-288; aa–s/62743; No-287; R4=*

H. 12.4 cm (4⅞ in.); w. 20.9 cm (8¼ in.); diam. of rim 12.3 cm (4¹³⁄₁₆ in.)

WEIGHT: 354.4 gm (11 oz 8 dwt)

PROVENANCE: Walter H. Willson, Ltd., London, purchased by Frank Brewer Bemis, March 29, 1923, Bequest of Frank Brewer Bemis, November 7, 1935

DESCRIPTION: The bell-shaped body, raised from sheet, is chased on the lower third with spiral fluting and foliate punches. A band of chased gadrooning around the shoulder of the cup is framed above and below with foliate punches. A scrolled and foliate cartouche with a ground of scales is chased on the front of the cup. The two cast handles are ear-shaped with scrolling termini.

Two-handled cups with rudimentary chasing in this pattern were produced in many sizes, of which this is the largest (see cats. 1 and 35). Engraving has been removed from the central cartouche on this cup.

25

DREDGER
Marked by William Fleming (free 1695)
London, 1713/4
Silver
37.1168

MARKS: on underside, maker's mark *FL*
(Grimwade 694) (repeated on underside of cover);
Britannia; lion's head erased (repeated on underside
of cover); date letter *s*

INSCRIPTIONS: engraved on underside, *.M.P.*

H. 7.3 cm (2⅞ in.); W. 6.4 cm (2⁹⁄₁₆ in.); diam. of base
4.9 cm (1¹⁵⁄₁₆ in.)

WEIGHT: 65.2 gm (2 oz 2 dwt)

PROVENANCE: Walter H. Willson, Ltd., London,
purchased by Theodora Wilbour, October 6, 1937,
Anonymous Gift in Memory of Charlotte Beebe
Wilbour (1833–1914), November 17, 1937

DESCRIPTION: The cylindrical body rests on a
molded, stepped foot. Applied to the side of the
body is an ear-shaped handle. The detachable,
molded, domed lid is pierced in its center and in a
ring of the molding.

For another example of this form, see cat. 56.

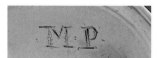

26

27

· 27 ·

COMMUNION CUP AND PATEN/COVER

Marked by John Fawdery (free 1695, d. 1724)
London, 1714/5
Silver gilt
33.102

MARKS: near rim and repeated on paten, date letter *t*; Britannia; lion's head erased; maker's mark *FA* (Grimwade 662)

INSCRIPTIONS: engraved on side of cup and on paten, the sacred monogram; engraved around the foot of the cup and around the paten, *Ex Dono Rollandi Williams in Templum Diva Maria in Antegua*; scratched on inside of foot, *1107*

H. 25 cm (9¹³⁄₁₆ in.); diam. of rim 13.8 cm (5⁷⁄₁₆ in.)

WEIGHT: 802 gm (25 oz 16 dwt)

PROVENANCE: Anonymous Gift in Memory of Charlotte Beebe Wilbour (1833–1914), March 2, 1933

EXHIBITED: Boston, Museum of Fine Arts, 1933

DESCRIPTION: The raised bell-shaped cup has a slightly flared rim and rests on a cylindrical stem on a domed, stepped foot. The stem is formed of two raised sections with a molded midband. The circular paten/cover has a molded raised rim and a molded ring at the center.

The form of the standard English communion cup was well established by the mid-sixteenth century and was not subject to changes of fashion. This heavily proportioned cup, substantial in weight and with decoration limited to the sacred monogram within the rays of glory, with a cross above and nails below, exemplifies the Anglican plate of the early eighteenth century.

The engraved inscription around the foot of this cup indicates that it was presented by Colonel Rowland Williams to the church of St. Mary, Antigua. Rowland Williams (ca. 1632–1713) had a distinguished career in the governance of Antigua, an island that was prized as a base for sugar plantations. Williams's father was believed to have been the first Englishman to have set foot on the island, and Rowland Williams was reputed to have been the first white male child born there. In 1668 he was granted a patent for three hundred acres, and in 1675 he was appointed lieutenant governor.[1] He married first Elizabeth, daughter of Samuel Winthrop, a former deputy governor of the island and granddaughter of Governor John Winthrop.[2] In his will, proved May 21, 1714, he left cash bequests to his daughters and grandchildren and specified that his natural daughter should receive six slaves, who were to be turned over to the girl's mother. The will does not specify a gift of plate to the church, and the cup may have been bought in Williams's memory by his son and chief heir, Thomas.

1. [Mrs. Lenerghan], *Antigua and the Antiguans* (London, 1844), p. 49. The position at that time was titled deputy governor.

2. Vere Langford Oliver, *History of the Island of Antigua* (London, 1898), vol. 3, p. 231.

28

· 28 ·

TOY TANKARD
Marked by George Manjoy (free 1685)
London, 1714/5
Silver
56.138

MARKS: to right of handle, maker's mark *MA* (Grimwade 3731) (repeated on underside of cover); lion's head erased (repeated on underside of cover); Britannia; date letter *t*

INSCRIPTIONS: scratched on underside, *A✶B*

H. 5.2 cm (2⅟₁₆ in.); w. 5.1 cm (2 in.); d. 3.2 cm (1¼ in.)

WEIGHT: 23.3 gm (15 dwt)

PROVENANCE: Robert Ensko, New York, purchased March 8, 1956, Theodora Wilbour Fund in Memory of Charlotte Beebe Wilbour

DESCRIPTION: The cylindrical tankard has slightly tapering sides. It is formed from seamed sheet, with an inset base and a molded wire around the foot. A flat cover, hinged to the C-shaped handle, has a shaped thumbpiece.

29

· 29 ·

COFFEEPOT

Marked by Robert Timbrell and Joseph Bell (I)
(entered into partnership 1707)
London, 1714/5
Silver, wood
1974.564

MARKS: near rim, maker's mark *TB*, *i* above, *e*
below (Grimwade 2707); lion's head erased (repeated on bezel of cover); Britannia; date letter *t*

ARMORIALS: on body, the arms of Hawkins, proba-
bly for Elizabeth, daughter and co-heir of Philip
Hawkins of Pennans who married in 1715, Thomas
Carlyon of Tregrehan, co. Cornwall

INSCRIPTIONS: engraved on underside, *28 14*

H. 27.6 cm (10⅞ in.); w. 17.4 cm (6⅞ in.); d. 15.9 cm
(6¼ in.)

WEIGHT: 929.9 gm (29 oz 18 dwt)

PROVENANCE: T. R. G. Carlyon, Esq., sold
Sotheby's, London, February 8, 1962, lot 150;
Garrard & Co., Ltd., London; Jennings family sold
Sotheby's, London, December 12, 1974, lot 126

[How of Edinburgh, London], purchased January 8,
1975, Theodora Wilbour Fund in Memory of
Charlotte Beebe Wilbour

EXHIBITED: Bath, Assembly Rooms, *International
Art Treasures Exhibition*, 1973, cat. 192; Boston,
Museum of Fine Arts, 1994

PUBLISHED: Brett 1986, p. 157, no. 609

DESCRIPTION: The plain octagonal body rests on a
molded base and tapers to a molded rim. It is
formed from a single seamed sheet with panels
scored on the interior, folded and soldered. The
base, formed from sheet, is applied and finished with
a heavy molded wire rim. The domed octagonal lid
is raised and joined to the body by a hinge. It is surmounted by an octagonal baluster finial. The curved
eight-faceted spout, cast in two pieces, is joined to
the body at a right angle to the handle. The sockets
for the wooden ear-shaped handle also have eight
sides.

This coffeepot is distinguished from other
examples of the form by its elongated proportions, precise workmanship, and uncompro-
mised surface.[1] The geometric profile of hexagonal tea and coffee wares was probably inspired
by imported Japanese Arita porcelain forms and
was not, as has often been proposed, the pur-
view of Huguenot makers.[2] Robert Timbrell,
who entered into partnership with his former
apprentice, Joseph Bell, is known to have acted
as a banker, lending money to merchants as
early as 1694.[3] The partnership seems to have
made a speciality of hexagonal tea and coffee
wares.[4]

1. For other examples, see a coffeepot marked by
Anthony Nelme for 1712/3, sold Sotheby's, New
York, April 6, 1989, lot 233; another marked by
Humphrey Payne for 1716/7, sold Christie's,
London, November 28, 1990, lot 140; another
marked by Richard Bayley for 1713/4, illus. Hartop
1996, p. 285, cat. 65.

2. For examples of Arita porcelain, see Ulrich
Pietsch, *Meissner Porzellan und seine ostasiatischen
Vorbilder* (Leipzig, 1996), pp. 75, 77, 81; also see
Hartop 1996, pp. 284–86.

3. Grimwade 1990, p. 682.

4. See a coffeepot of 1712/3, illus. Hackenbroch
1969, p. 61, no. 117; another of 1714/5, exh. Boston,
Museum of Fine Arts, *The Folger's Coffee Collection of
Antique English Silver Coffee Pots and Accesories*, 1968,
p. 19.

· 30 ·

PAIR OF TEA CANISTERS

Marked by William Truss (free 1713)
London, ca. 1715
Silver
1977.812–813

MARKS: 1977.812: on underside, maker's mark *TR* (Grimwade 2896); maker's mark (obscured), possibly *RO* (Grimwade 2393); lion's head erased (repeated on inside of cover). 1977.813; on underside, maker's mark *TR* (Grimwade 2896) (struck twice); lion's head erased (repeated on inside of cover)

ARMORIALS: engraved on sides of each, the arms of Wilson impaling an unidentified coat of arms (a wolf rampant and in chief three estoiles, impaling on a fess a lion passant)

INSCRIPTIONS: on underside of each, engraved *T/I★E*. 1977.812: engraved below rim, *B*. 1977.813: engraved below rim, *G*

1977.812: H. 13 cm (5⅛ in.); w. 7.1 cm (2¹³⁄₁₆ in.); d. 5.2 cm (2¹⁄₁₆ in.)
1977.813: H. 13 cm (5⅛ in.); w. 7.8 cm (3¹⁄₁₆ in.); d. 5.4 cm (2⅛ in.)

WEIGHT: 1977.812: 200.5 gm (6 oz 9 dwt).
1977.813: 201.3 gm (6 oz 9 dwt)

PROVENANCE: Firestone & Parson, Inc., Boston, purchased by Mrs. Harding Greene, Gift of Mrs. Harding Greene, December 14, 1977

DESCRIPTION: The bombé canisters are eight-sided, with broad panels in the front and back. They are constructed of eight formed sections, seamed vertically, with an inset base. The covers are similarly constructed. The finial is cast. Several dents have been removed and resoldering has been done, particularly on the interior of the cover.

The engraved initials *G* and *B* on the sides of these canisters indicate that they were intended to hold green and bohea (black) tea, respectively. There may have been a third container of a similar design in the set to hold sugar.[1] The complex construction of the canisters, which are not cast, but assembled from panels of sheet, involved precise soldering and suggests the work of a specialist. They are not fully marked, but it appears that William Truss may have struck over the mark of Ebenezer Roe, whose mark appears on other similarly constructed canisters.[2]

1. A similar set, marked for 1718/9, is illustrated by Sir Charles James Jackson, *An Illustrated History of English Plate*, 2 vols. (London, 1911), vol. 2, p. 965, figs. 1293–95.

2. See a single canister, 1721/2, sold Christie's, London, July 11, 1990, lot 180, and another, 1714/5, sold Sotheby's, London, November 17, 1988, lot 81.

30

31

· 31 ·

TOBACCO BOX

Marked by Edward Cornock (first mark entered
1707)
London, 1715/6
Silver
35.1589

MARKS: on side of box, maker's mark *CO*
(Grimwade 390a) (repeated on inside of cover);
lion's head erased (repeated on inside of cover); date
letter *u*

ARMORIALS: engraved on top of cover, in cartouche, the coat of arms and crest of Lucas of
Rathealy and Ricksfordtown, co. Cork, Ireland

H. 2.7 cm (1¹⁄₁₆ in.); w. 7.9 cm (3⅛ in.); d. 9.9 cm
(3⅞ in.)

WEIGHT: 138.9 gm (4 oz 9 dwt)

PROVENANCE: Walter H. Willson, Ltd., London,
purchased by Frank Brewer Bemis, June 2, 1924,
Bequest of Frank Brewer Bemis, November 7, 1935

DESCRIPTION: The flat, oval box has a removable
cover. Around the base and the edge of the cover is
a chased molded ridge. Each piece is formed of
sheet.

· 32 ·

PORRINGER

Marked by Henry Penstone (free 1689)
London, 1715/6
Silver
63.1419

MARKS: on underside, maker's mark *PE*
(Grimwade 2159 or 2158); lion's head erased (repeated on underside of handle); Britannia; date letter *v*

INSCRIPTIONS: engraved on underside, *The Gift of
H. Trecothick/to her Grandaughter Hannah Ivers/1760*;
engraved on top of handle, *T/MH/1721*

H. 5 cm (1¹⁵⁄₁₆ in.); w. 18.5 cm (7¼ in.); d. 12.7 cm
(5 in.)

WEIGHT: 187.1 gm (6 oz)

PROVENANCE: according to tradition, Mark
Trecothick (d. ca. 1733), Hannah Trecothick Ivers
(1728–1807) by 1760, Hannah Ivers, by descent to
Mark Trecothick de Silva, Gift of Mrs. Mark
Trecothick de Silva in Memory of Mark Trecothick
de Silva, September 18, 1963

DESCRIPTION: The low round bowl, raised from
sheet, has in-curved sides and a straight rim. The
cast handle has a geometric openwork pattern. It
has been broken in several places and crudely
repaired. The body of the bowl is dented and
roughly hammered overall.

The initials and date, 1721, engraved on the
handle of this modest porringer suggest that it
may have been brought to Boston by Mark
Trecothick, a mariner believed to have been
born in England. With his wife, Hannah
(1683–1766), he had at least one daughter,
Hannah, who in 1753 married James Ivers.[1]
First of four children, their son James (b. 1754),
a loyalist, became an associate to his uncle
Barlow Trecothick, who served as lord mayor
of London and procured weapons and provi-
sions for William Shirley, governor of
Massachusetts.[2] Their second child, Hannah
Ivers (b. 1756), was given this porringer, a traditional gift for a child, by her grandmother in
1760.

32

1. Massachusetts Historical Society Thwing Index; "The James Ivers Family Bible," *New England Historical and Genealogical Register* 140 (1986), pp. 332–33.

2. Wendell Garrett, *Apthorp House, 1760–1960* (Cambridge, Mass., 1960), p. 6. James Ivers was compelled to adopt his mother's maiden name, Trecothick, when he fled Boston.

· 33 ·

KETTLE AND STAND

Marked by Francis Garthorne (first mark entered before 1697)

London, 1716/7

Silver, wood

40.193

MARKS: on underside of kettle and on scrolls of stand, maker's mark *GA* (Grimwade 736)[1] (repeated three times on underside of lamp); Britannia (repeated on bezel of cover); lion's head erased; date letter *A*

ARMORIALS: engraved on side of kettle, the arms of Ayde

H. 35.6 cm (14 in.); w. 26.3 cm (10⅜ in.); d. 30.5 cm (12 in.)

WEIGHT: 2,806.7 gm (90 oz 5 dwt)

PROVENANCE: Tiffany & Co., New York, purchased by Theodora Wilbour, March 30, 1940, Anonymous Gift in Memory of Charlotte Beebe Wilbour (1833–1914), April 11, 1940

DESCRIPTION: The flattened pear-shaped kettle, resting on a three-legged stand, is formed from raised sheet, joined at the base of the spool-shaped neck to a second raised section. The kettle has a curved, faceted spout terminating in a duck's head that is cast in two pieces and seamed vertically. Cast scrolled brackets support the hinges for the bail handle. Both ends of the handle are cast double-scrolls, giving way to the central wooden baluster-shaped section. The removable stepped, domed cover is raised and has a bezel formed of seamed sheet. It is surmounted by a baluster finial with a wooden knop. The cast, circular molded rim of the stand is supported by three legs in the form of double scrolls, cast and seamed vertically. A hemispherical lamp is supported between the three legs by scrolled bracket extensions. The raised lamp has a hinged domed cap that covers the flame outlet.

Although in the first few decades of the eighteenth century tea kettles were sometimes made en suite with a teapot, canister, lampstand, and other accoutrements for the tea table, they were quite often purchased as single items.[2] In this case, a service was clearly assembled piece by piece. The arms on this kettle appear on a tea canister by John Wisdome of 1709/10 in this collection (cat. 22) and on a

33

teapot marked by Gabriel Sleath for 1713.[3] The engraving on all three, while not necessarily by the same hand, follows the same design. The present kettle is more modest in size and complexity than other contemporaneous examples. It lacks handles on the frame or the hinges and pins that appear on some models (cat. 260) that allow them to be carried as a unit. Francis Garthorne, one of the subordinate goldsmiths to the king and queen, economized on the manufacture by avoiding the duty he would have owed for the assay of the lamp, which is struck three times with the maker's mark only, instead of hallmarks.

1. The mark differs from Grimwade's representation by the addition of a pellet.

2. For references to early tea kettles, see Wees 1997, p. 353, nn. 1–2.

3. Formerly in the collection of Mrs. R. M. Robinson, sold Christie's, New York, October 27, 1987, lot 440.

· 34 ·

KETTLE AND STAND
Marked by Ambrose Stevenson (first mark entered 1707)
London, 1717/8
Silver, wood
33.107

MARKS: on underside of kettle and of stand, maker's mark *St* (Grimwade 2638); Britannia (repeated on handle); lion's head erased (repeated on handle); date letter *B*. On kettle handle, to right of hinge, on underside, on rim of stand, on leg of stand, and on bezel of lamp cover, French import mark used from July 1, 1893

ARMORIALS: engraved on each side, the coat of arms, crest, and motto of Grove impaling O'Grady, for Sir Thomas-Fraser Grove (1823–1897) and Katherine-Grace O'Grady (d. 1879) whom he married in 1847

INSCRIPTIONS: scratched on underside of kettle, *Geo I/1717/A Stevenson/9102 10/R[?]W 2 44/1HTuTu*

H. 36.3 cm (14⁵⁄₁₆ in.); w. 25.9 cm (10¾₆ in.); d. 21 cm (8¼ in.)

WEIGHT: 2,849.2 gm (91 oz 12 dwt)

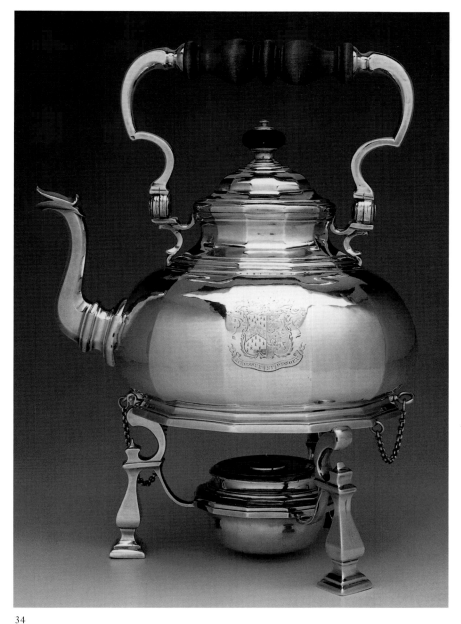

34

PROVENANCE: sold Christie's, London, June 18, 1902, lot 29, purchased by S. J. Phillips, London; J. H. Fitzhenry, Esq., sold Christie's, London, November 17, 1913, lot 59, purchased by Crichton Brothers, London; Anonymous Gift in Memory of Charlotte Beebe Wilbour (1833–1914), March 2, 1933

EXHIBITED: Boston, Museum of Fine Arts, 1933; Springfield, Massachusetts, Museum of Fine Arts, 1958; Boston, Museum of Fine Arts, 1994

DESCRIPTION: The pear-shaped faceted body rests on an open three-legged stand. The lower section of the body is raised, and the faceted neck is cast in two sections, joined vertically. The foot of the kettle is formed by a strip of sheet. The domed, stepped cover is cast in one piece and surmounted by a wooden finial. The curved, faceted spout is cast in two pieces. The handle, joined to the body with heavy hinges, has a wooden baluster section between two curved, faceted silver segments. A lamp, with a molded, faceted rim, is suspended between the three legs. The legs, hollow-cast in sections and seamed vertically, are of faceted baluster shape surmounted by scrolls, on top of which rests the faceted rim. The kettle fastens with a hinge in front and a peg in back, secured with removable pins.

A kettle such as this might originally have had a silver tripod stand, only a few examples of which survive. The Bowes kettle and stand in the Metropolitan Museum suggest the full effect of such a set.[1] The engraved arms on this kettle may have been added at the time of the marriage of Sir Thomas-Fraser Grove in 1847.

1. Hackenbroch 1969, p. 72, pl. 138.

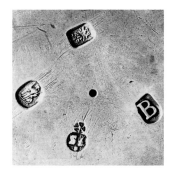

35

TWO-HANDLED CUP
Marked by William Fleming (free 1695)
London, 1717/8
Silver
1984.185

MARKS: on underside, maker's mark *FL* (Grimwade 694); date letter *B*; lion's head erased; Britannia

INSCRIPTIONS: engraved on underside, *In Recognition of Her Fruitful Devotion to the Art of American Goldsmiths. Kathryn C. Buhler. Museum of Fine Arts Boston 1966*

H. 8.1 cm (3⁵⁄₁₆ in.); w. 15.5 cm (6⅛ in.); diam. of rim 9.2 cm (3⅝ in.)

WEIGHT: 181.4 gm (5 oz 17 dwt)

PROVENANCE: Gift of the Museum of Fine Arts, Boston, to Kathryn C. Buhler, 1966, Gift of Mrs. Yves Henry Buhler, May 9, 1984

DESCRIPTION: The bell-shaped body, raised from sheet, is chased on the lower half with spiral fluting and pellet punches. Around the midsection is a band of chased gadrooning, with rows of pellet, half-circle, and foliate punches below and above. On the front is a chased cartouche of foliate scrolls and scales. The two cast ear-shaped handles have beading along the edges and scrolling termini.

This cup, a form used commonly from about 1690 and as late as 1720,[1] was presented by the Museum of Fine Arts to Kathryn C. Buhler (d. 1986), distinguished specialist and a pioneer in the study of American silver, on her retirement from the Museum in 1966.

1. Also see cats. 1 and 25. For other examples of the form, see Christie's, New York, April 19, 1990, lot 313; Christie's, New York, November 2, 1977, lot 217; Sotheby's, London, June 3, 1976, lot 168; Lomax 1992, p. 63, cat. 43.

36

· 36 ·

TOBACCO BOX

Marked by Edward Cornock (first mark entered
1707)
London, 1718/9
Silver
39.183

MARKS: on rim of base, maker's mark *CO*
(Grimwade 390a) (repeated on inside of cover);
Britannia; lion's head erased (repeated on inside of
cover); date letter *C*

INSCRIPTIONS: engraved on underside, *Benjin.
Pickman 1780*; engraved in cartouche on cover,
SAMEBG; engraved on inside of cover, *I*B/1719*

H. 2.5 cm (1 in.); w. 7.6 cm (3 in.); d. 9.8 cm
(3⅞ in.)

WEIGHT: 110.6 gm (3 oz 11 dwt)

PROVENANCE: according to tradition, Benjamin
Pickman II (1740–1819) who married Mary, daugh-
ter of Bezaleel Toppan, to their son Benjamin III
(1763–1843) who married Anstiss Derby
(1769–1836), to their daughter Anstiss Derby
Pickman (1793–1856) who married John W. Rogers
(1787–1872), to their daughter Martha Pickman
Rogers (1829–1905) who married John Amory
Codman (1824–1886), to their daughter Martha
Catherine (1858–1948) who married Maxim Karolik
(1893–1963), The M. and M. Karolik Collection of
Eighteenth-Century American Arts, January 12, 1939

PUBLISHED: Hipkiss 1941, cat. 177

DESCRIPTION: The flat oval box has a removable
cover. Around the base and the edge of the cover is a
chased molded ridge. Each piece is formed of sheet.
The base may have had previous engraving removed,
since the silver is thin and slightly uneven.

The large number of boxes surviving bearing
Edward Cornock's mark doubtless reflects the
large output of a specialized shop as well as the
popularity of snuff.[1] Women and men were subject to the addictive habit, and the proper han-
dling of snuff was a mark of cultivation. The
box must have been bought secondhand, for the
inscription of 1780 and the monogram seem to
replace earlier engraving. This box is believed to
have belonged to Benjamin Pickman II, son of
Colonel Benjamin Pickman, a successful Salem,
Massachusetts, merchant.[2] Colonel Pickman,
who claimed to have made his fortune in cod
fishing, decorated the stair risers of his mansion
with carved and gilt codfish.[3] In 1762 he married Mary, daughter of Bezaleel Toppan of
Salem, and he expanded his father's fishing
enterprise into the field of mercantile insurance.
Because of his loyalist sympathies, he fled to
England in 1775 and maintained his business
connections to America while profiting from
the war. He was among the loyalists in exile
who met weekly for dinner at the Adelphi in
London.[4] He found the dirt and crowds of
London distasteful but wrote, "when I am in
Town and hear Leoni sing and see Garrick act
young Hamlet, or Mrs. Barry play Violante, I
am surprised that the whole World does not
flock to London."[5] After the war he eventually
returned to Salem, where he served as town
treasurer and justice of the peace. His son,
Benjamin, married Anstiss Derby, a daughter of
Salem's most prosperous mercantile family.

1. For examples, see two at Colonial Williamsburg,
illus. Davis 1976, pp. 207–9, and others sold
Sotheby's, New York, December 13, 1984, lots
159–60, and Sotheby's, London, October 16, 1986, lot
55.

2. For other silver that descended in the Pickman
family, see Kathryn C. Buhler, *American Silver,
1655–1825, in the Museum of Fine Arts, Boston, Vol. 1*
(Boston, 1972), pp. 51–52, 339–40.

3. Clifford K. Shipton, *Sibley's Harvard Graduates*
(Boston, 1968), vol. 14, p. 485.

4. E. Alfred Jones, *The Loyalists of Massachusetts*
(London, 1930), p. 236.

5. Quoted in Shipton, *Sibley's Harvard Graduates*,
p. 488.

· 37 ·

SALVER

Marked by David Willaume (I) (1658–ca. 1741)

London, 1718/9

Silver

40.545

MARKS: on underside, maker's mark *WI* (Grimwade 3192); Britannia; lion's head erased (repeated on foot); date letter *C*

ARMORIALS: engraved on center of salver, the arms of Bowes of Streatlam quartering Trayne, Delahay, Conyers, Aske, or Blakiston

INSCRIPTIONS: engraved on underside, *84-13*

H. (with foot) 8 cm (3⅛ in.); diam. of rim 37.5 cm (14¾ in.)

WEIGHT: 2,202.8 gm (70 oz 16 dwt)

PROVENANCE: purchased from Tiffany & Co., New York, by Theodora Wilbour, June 24, 1940, Anonymous Gift in Memory of Charlotte Beebe Wilbour (1833–1914), October 10, 1940

EXHIBITED: Minneapolis, The Minneapolis Institute of Arts, *French, English and American Silver: A Loan Exhibition in Honor of Russell A. Plimpton*, 1956, cat. 160, fig. 23

DESCRIPTION: The salver is circular with a heavy gadrooned edge. It is formed of sheet, with the rim, cast in sections, applied. Three cast shaped feet, a later addition, are riveted to the edge. The underside of the salver has a cut-card pattern radiating from a screw, which is used to join a gadrooned trumpet foot to the salver. The surface has been heavily buffed in the plain area around the engraving. Slight texture and color to the engraved area suggest that the salver might once have been gilt.

The extraordinary engraving on this footed salver represents the arms of Bowes of Streatlam.[1] A ewer and basin of the same year also marked by David Willaume belonging to Her Majesty Queen Elizabeth the Queen Mother is similarly engraved.[2] The silver was almost certainly commissioned by William Blakiston Bowes (1697–1721) while he was rebuilding and furnishing Streatlam Castle.[3]

The Bowes family had been established at Streatlam Castle, co. Durham, since the fourteenth century. Though their fortunes had fluctuated, the marriage of Sir William Bowes (1656–1706) in 1693 to Elizabeth Blakiston (d. 1736) marked a prosperous period.[4] Their properties included Streatlam Castle (no longer standing), which was rebuilt by William Blakiston Bowes between 1717 and 1718, and Gibside, where William's younger brother and heir, George Bowes, began an extensive building program in the late 1720s. This salver and the ewer and basin, doubtless part of a large order of sideboard plate, must have been ordered by William for Streatlam, although he wrote to his mother from London in 1718: "Surely you don't think me such a fool to prefer the Charms of a stupid, dull, Country Life, to the pleasure of the Town."[5] He was actively searching for a suitable wife and may have had this in mind when he undertook the renovations. A salver of this size was more likely decorative than functional. At some later date, the three rather awkwardly applied bracket feet were added, presumably to make the piece more useful when the trumpet foot was unscrewed.[6] The young William Blakiston Bowes traveled to Rome in 1714 and the following year visited France, Switzerland, Naples, and Rome. William Bowes died in 1721, shortly after the completion of the renovation and was succeeded by his younger brother George. Other silver made for the family includes a Newcastle punch bowl of 1725, now in the Bowes Museum,[7] a hexagonal coffeepot of 1724 by John Bache,[8] the Bowes Gold Cup, of 1675 by Jacob Bodendick, now in the Victoria and Albert Museum,[9] and the magnificent teakettle and stand of 1724 by Simon of Pantin in the Metropolitan Museum.[10] George Bowes's only daughter and heir, Mary-Eleanor (1749–1800) married in 1767 John, ninth earl

37

of Strathmore, who took the name Bowes. Their grandson John Bowes built the Bowes Museum, which opened in 1892. It is uncertain when the salver left the family. The present salver was purchased by Miss Wilbour in 1940, and some additional silver was sold by the family in 1948.[11]

David Willaume was well established by 1718 when this salver was made. He was tightly connected by both marriage and business to the Huguenot community that supplied some of the grandest plate to England's wealthiest clients. The engravers available to this circle of goldsmiths worked to a very high standard. This engraver, active almost a generation later than the Frenchman identified as Blaise Gentot,[12] had nonetheless inherited a few of Gentot's innovations, such as the architectural ledge supported by a bracket and mask. In this case, since the arms have no supporters or coronet, the engraver has filled the ground with scrolls and flowers against a scale ground and, unusually, enclosed the whole in a circle. The engraving style has features in common with that on a plateau made by John White in 1728.[13]

1. There is a variation, however, in the representation of the motto. The usual motto used by Bowes of Streatlam is *Sans Variance Terme de Vie*, whereas the engraving here reads, *Virtute Non Sanguine*.

2. Collection of the Queen Mother. Formerly in the collection of William Randolph Hearst, sold Christie's, London, December 14, 1938, lot 41.

3. I am indebted to John Cornforth, London, and Howard Coutts, ceramics officer, Bowes Museum, for generously offering material on the Bowes family. See the article by Coutts, "The Bowes Family of Streatlam Castle and Gibside and Its Collections," *Metropolitan Museum Journal* 34 (1999), pp. 3–15.

4. Margaret Wills, *Gibside and the Bowes Family* (Newcastle upon Tyne, 1995), pp. 1–2.

5. Ibid., p. 2.

6. The salver has warped and the feet no longer reach beyond the protruding level of the threaded mount for the foot.

7. Acc. no. Sil.1984.5. The bowl was a gift of George Bowes to the Company of Bakers and Brewers of Newcastle upon Tyne. Howard Coutts kindly provided this and the following references.

8. Sold Christie's, London, July 12, 1989, lot 197.

9. Philippa Glanville, "The Bowes Cup: A Stuart Race Prize?" *Burlington Magazine* 137 (1995), pp. 387–90.

10. Illus. Hackenbroch 1969, pp. 72–73, cat. 138, pl. 138.

11. Christie's, London, December 8, 1948.

12. Grimwade 1988, pp. 83–89.

13. Sold Sotheby's, London, June 8, 1995, lot 117. See the discussion about White's engravers in A. J. H. Sale and Vanessa Brett, "John White: Some Recent Research," *Silver Society Journal* 8 (Autumn 1996), pp. 472–73.

38

· 38 ·

THREE TOY SAUCEPANS

Marked by David Clayton (free 1689, first mark entered 1697)

London, ca. 1720

Silver, wood, ivory

55.975, 55.974, 55.973

MARKS: 55.975: on underside, maker's mark *DC* (Grimwade 452); lion passant (struck twice). 55.974, 55.973: on underside, maker's mark *DC* (Grimwade 452); lion passant

ARMORIALS: 55.973, engraved on side, the arms of Rockley, Tirrell, or Tyrell

55.975: H. 3 cm (1³⁄₁₆ in.); w. 9.3 cm (3¹¹⁄₁₆ in.); d. 4.6 cm (1¹³⁄₁₆ in.)

55.974: H. 3.6 cm (1⁷⁄₁₆ in.); w. 7.7 cm (3 in.); d. 3.7 cm (1⁷⁄₁₆ in.)

55.973: H. 4 cm (1⁹⁄₁₆ in.); w. 7.8 cm (3¹⁄₁₆ in.); d. 4.2 cm (1⅝ in.)

WEIGHT: 55.975: 17 gm (11 dwt). 55.974: 14.2 gm (9 dwt). 55.973: 19.8 gm (13 dwt)

PROVENANCE: John S. Barnet, Shreve, Crump, and Low, Co., purchased December 8, 1955, Theodora Wilbour Fund in Memory of Charlotte Beebe Wilbour

PUBLISHED: 55.973: Nancy Akre, ed., *Miniatures* (New York, 1983), p. 74, fig. 64

DESCRIPTION: 56.975: The saucepan has a flat base and a flaring rim. It is formed from seamed sheet with an applied wire around the foot. The turned wooden handle is mounted on a cylindrical socket.

55.974: The bulbous pan, formed from two pieces of sheet, has a narrow crimped rim and turned wooden handle mounted on a cylindrical socket. 55.973: The bulbous pan, formed from two pieces of sheet, has a narrow crimped rim and turned wooden handle mounted on a cylindrical socket.

A large percentage of the eighteenth-century silver toys that survive bear the mark of the specialist maker David Clayton II, a member of a large family of goldsmiths.[1] The manufacture and collecting of silver toys was a tradition that flourished particularly in the Netherlands and became popular in England in the years around 1700. Made to furnish dollhouses, the toys were collected by women and children, and their forms included tea and table wares, candlesticks, braziers, and warming pans.

1. The Clayton family has been studied by Peter Kaellgren, "The Clayton Family of Goldsmiths and Jewellers circa 1658–1743," *Silver Society Journal* 9 (Autumn 1997), pp. 590–600.

39

· 39 ·

TOY KETTLE, TWO TEAPOTS, AND COFFEEPOT

Marked by David Clayton (free 1689, first mark entered 1697)

London, ca. 1720

Silver, wood

55.972, 55.977a–b, 55.971, 55.980

MARKS: 55.972 (teapot): on underside, maker's mark *DC* (Grimwade 452). On rim, lion passant (repeated on bezel of cover). 55.977 (kettle): on underside, maker's mark *DC* (Grimwade 452) (repeated on each side of handle). On body, lion passant. 55.971 (teapot): on underside, maker's mark *DC* (Grimwade 452). On rim, lion passant. 55.980 (coffeepot): on underside, maker's mark *IC* (unrecorded)

55.972 (teapot): H. 4.4 cm (1¾ in.); w. 5 cm (1 15/16 in.); d. 3.3 cm (1 5/16 in.)

55.977 (kettle): H. 6.9 cm (2¾ in.); w. 6.2 cm (2 7/16 in.); d. 4 cm (1½ in.)

55.971 (teapot): H. 4.3 cm (1 11/16 in.); w. 5.2 cm (2 1/16 in.); d. 3.2 cm (1¼ in.)

55.980 (coffeepot): H. 5.9 cm (2 5/16 in.); w. 7.8 cm (3 1/16 in.); d. 2.7 cm (1 1/16 in.)

WEIGHT: 55.972: 17 gm (11 dwt). 55.977: 31.2 gm (1 oz). 55.971: 17 gm (11 dwt). 55.980: 22.6 gm (15 dwt)

PROVENANCE: John S. Barnet, Shreve, Crump, & Low, purchased December 8, 1955, Theodora Wilbour Fund in Memory of Charlotte Beebe Wilbour

PUBLISHED: 55.980: Nancy Akre, ed., *Miniatures* (New York, 1983), p. 74, fig. 64

DESCRIPTION: 55.977: The squat pear-shaped kettle is formed from two pieces of sheet. It has a straight, tapering spout and a wooden handle mounted on hinged brackets. 55.972, 55.971: Each pear-shaped teapot is formed from two pieces of sheet, with a straight, tapering spout and a scrolled handle formed of wire. The removable cover is domed with a ball finial. 55.980: The coffeepot, formed from seamed sheet, has tapering sides, an inset base, and a straight, tapering spout. A turned wooden handle is mounted on a cylindrical socket.

40

· 40 ·

TOY PLATE RACK AND MUG

Marked by David Clayton (free 1689, first mark
entered 1697)
London, ca. 1720
Silver
55.979, 56.507

MARKS: 55.979 (plate rack): on legs, maker's mark
DC (Grimwade 452) (repeated on prongs); lion passant. 56.507 (mug): on side, lion passant; on underside, maker's mark *DC* (Grimwade 452)

55.979: H. 8.4 cm (3⁵⁄₁₆ in.); w. 3.6 cm (1⁷⁄₁₆ in.);
d. 3.6 cm (1⁷⁄₁₆ in.)
56.507: H. 4.1 cm (1⅝ in.); w. 4.2 cm (1⅝ in.); diam.
of base 3 cm (1³⁄₁₆ in.)

WEIGHT: 55.979: 14.2 gm (9 dwt). 56.507: 17 gm
(11 dwt)

PROVENANCE: 55.979: John S. Barnet, Shreve,
Crump, and Low, Co., purchased December 8, 1955,
Theodora Wilbour Fund in Memory of Charlotte
Beebe Wilbour. 56.507: John S. Barnet, Shreve,
Crump, and Low, Co., purchased October 11, 1956,
Theodora Wilbour Fund in Memory of Charlotte
Beebe Wilbour

PUBLISHED: 55.979: Nancy Akre, ed., *Miniatures*
(New York, 1983), p. 74, fig. 64

DESCRIPTION: 55.979: The plate rack consists of a
four-pronged bracket on a baluster stem rising from
a three-legged stand. It is fabricated from wire and
cut sheet. 56.507: The mug is formed from seamed
sheet with an inset base. It has tapering sides, a
scrolled handle formed from wire, and applied wire
on the rim and foot.

· 41 ·

DISH

Marked by David Willaume (I) (1658–ca. 1741)
London, 1720/1
Silver
35.1599

MARKS: on underside near rim, maker's mark *WI*
(Grimwade 3192); Britannia; lion's head erased; date
letter *E*

ARMORIALS: engraved on the center of the dish,
the arms of Sylvestre or Sylvester impaling Evans,
Gwyn, Lloyd, Morgan, Stormyn, or Story

41

INSCRIPTIONS: engraved on underside of dish, *6,10*

H. 1.9 cm (¾ in.); diam. of rim 14.2 cm (5⁹⁄₁₆ in.)

WEIGHT: 201.3 gm (6 oz 9 dwt)

PROVENANCE: Crichton Brothers, New York, purchased by Frank Brewer Bemis, March 7, 1918,
Bequest of Frank Brewer Bemis, November 7, 1935

DESCRIPTION: The circular dish is raised with low
sides divided into sixteen flutes and a scalloped border. A plain wire foot rim is applied to the underside.

This small dish was probably part of a large
surtout. On the underside, which is fitted with
a plain wire rim, the silversmith marked the
divisions of the sixteen flutes with a lightly
engraved line. A slight disturbance in the
engraving marks the removal of a fitting, probably a threaded socket, designed to secure the
dish on the end of a branch. Dishes like this,
albeit with scrolled feet rather than a wire foot,
may be seen on the Williams centerpiece[1] and
the Kirkleatham centerpiece.[2] They were
optional components of the surtout and could
be used to display fruit as part of the centerpiece or freestanding on the table.

1. Now in the National Museum of Wales. Sold
Sotheby's, New York, October 19, 1995, lot 454.
2. Lomax 1992, pp. 87–91.

42

In discussing a set of four similarly sized dishes in the Clark Art Institute, Beth Wees has reviewed their possible uses.[1] The ledgers of George Wickes, royal goldsmith, indicate that sets of fluted dishes, usually on low feet, were called salad dishes. Two from a set of eight made by George Wickes for lord Montford have been identified.[2] They are deeper than the present example and rest on three scrolled feet. This dish lacks feet, like the four marked for 1700 in the Clark, but as Wees points out, the Wickes ledgers record that clients sometimes returned plain dishes to have feet added. This simple dish is likely to have served a variety of functions.

1. Wees 1997, pp. 129–30, cat. 60.
2. Barr 1980, p. 201.

· 42 ·

DISH

Marked by Edmund Pearce (first mark entered 1705)
London, 1720/1
Silver
35.1600

MARKS: on the underside of the dish, maker's mark *PE* (Grimwade 2169); lion's head erased; Britannia; date letter *E*

ARMORIALS: engraved in the center of the dish, the arms of Vincent impaling an unidentified coat of arms (three quartrefoils, two and one, impaling a chevron engrailed between three escallops)

INSCRIPTIONS: engraved on underside, *17:18:0*

H. 1.9 cm (¾ in.); diam. of rim 17.6 cm (6¹⁵⁄₁₆ in.)

WEIGHT: 235.3 gm (7 oz 11 dwt)

PROVENANCE: Crichton Brothers, New York, purchased by Frank Brewer Bemis, May 1, 1918, Bequest of Frank Brewer Bemis, November 7, 1935

DESCRIPTION: The circular dish is raised, with a scalloped rim and low sides divided into sixteen flutes.

· 43 ·

CASTER

Marked by Isaac Liger (first mark entered 1704)
London, 1721/2
Silver
37.1170

MARKS: on underside, maker's mark *LI* (Grimwade 1931) (repeated on bezel of cover); date letter *F;* Britannia; lion's head erased (repeated on bezel of cover).

ARMORIALS: engraved on body, an unidentified coat of arms and motto (quarterly 1 and 4, sable a cross engrailed and in sinister chief a rose, 2 and 3, a fess gules between a demilion rampant in chief and three mullets in base; motto: *Nil Volentibus Ardum)*

H. 17.7 cm (6¹⁵⁄₁₆ in.); diam. of foot 6.2 cm (2⁷⁄₁₆ in.)

WEIGHT: 357.2 gm (11 oz 10 dwt)

PROVENANCE: Walter H. Willson, Ltd., London, purchased by Theodora Wilbour, October 6, 1937, Anonymous Gift in Memory of Charlotte Beebe Wilbour (1833–1914), November 17, 1937

DESCRIPTION: The pear-shaped body rests on a cast domed foot. The body is formed of two raised

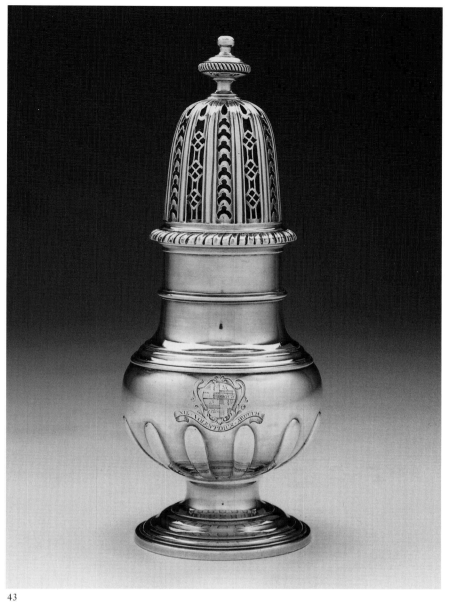

43

sections, joined horizontally. Around the base are applied ribs of ninepin form, and at the middle of the plain neck is an applied molded wire band. The high domed cover has a cast gadrooned flange and is assembled from six cast vertical panels with a complex pierced pattern and molded ribs between. It is surmounted by a baluster finial.

Liger's mark appears on a range of well-made domestic wares in the French taste. Among his clients was George Booth, earl of Warrington, for whom he supplied a richly ornamented toilet service and the extraordinary chapel plate engraved by Simon Gribelin.[1] This caster and a set of three of the same design in the Minneapolis Institute of Arts are plain but nonetheless expertly made, with finely cast panels assembled to form the pierced covers.[2] The form was produced in some quantity, and also as part of a cruet stand.[3] Like Lamerie, Liger continued to use the Britannia standard when it was no longer mandatory.

1. Hayward 1978, pp. 34–36; Charles Oman, *English Engraved Silver* (London, 1978), pp. 78–79; Brett 1986, p. 117, fig. 689.

2. Puig 1989, p. 666, cat. 49.

3. See a caster of 1721 sold Sotheby's, London, December 12, 1974, lot 112, and another of 1722 sold Sotheby's, New York, October 31, 1991, lot 396. For the cruet stand marked by Liger, see Davis 1976, p. 153, cat. 158.

· 44 ·

TWO-HANDLED CUP AND COVER
Marked by Samuel Margas (first mark entered
1715)
London, 1721/2
Silver gilt
1975.361a–b

MARKS: on underside of foot, maker's mark *SM*
(Grimwade 2588); leopard's head crowned (repeated
on underside of cover); lion passant (repeated on
underside of cover); date letter *F* (repeated on
underside of cover)

ARMORIALS: on one side, royal arms and cipher of
George I; on other side, arms of Edgcumbe differ-
enced with a crescent for George Edgcumbe
(1720–1795), second surviving son of Richard, first
baron Edgcumbe of Mount Edgcumbe (1680–1758)

H. 33.5 cm (13³⁄₁₆ in.); w. 32.2 cm (12¹¹⁄₁₆ in.);
d. 18 cm (7¹⁄₁₆ in.)

WEIGHT: 2,579.9 gm (82 oz 19 dwt)

PROVENANCE: HRH duke of Kent, sold Sotheby's,
London, June 26, 1975, lot 63; S. J. Shrubsole, Corp.,
New York, purchased September 10, 1975, Theodora
Wilbour Fund in Memory of Charlotte Beebe
Wilbour

EXHIBITED: Boston, Museum of Fine Arts, 1994

PUBLISHED: Brett 1986, p. 172, fig. 694

DESCRIPTION: The raised bell-shaped body rests
on a domed, stepped foot. The foot is raised in several sections and chased with a broad band of basket
weave. There is a heavy wire foot rim. The smooth
body of the cup is divided at the middle by a horizontal molded wire. Above it are applied cast lambrequins, and beneath it alternating lambrequins and
satyr's masks. A coat of arms is engraved in the central cartouche on each side. The harp-shaped handles, cast in two pieces and seamed vertically, are
surmounted by scrolls. The domed, stepped cover is
assembled from three raised sections joined by cast
wires and moldings. There is a cast band of
gadrooning around the rim, a row of bellflowers
around the midsection, and a dome decorated with
chased guilloche above. The whole is surmounted
by a spherical finial cast in two vertical sections.
There is a crack in the cover where two sections
were joined. The dark gilding covers the inside of
the foot and has presumably been renewed, but the
surface is otherwise in excellent condition, and the
burnishing marks and engraver's scribings are still
visible.

This cup was presented by George I as a christening gift to George Edgcumbe, second surviving son of Richard, first baron Edgcumbe of
Mount Edgcumbe by his wife, Mathilde,
daughter of Sir Henry Furnese. The warrant,
signed by the lord chamberlain, allowed for
eighty ounces of gilt plate "as a gift from His
Majesty at the christening of his child to be
made into such vessels and after such fashion as
he shall direct." The warrant was issued on
August 11, executed on October 18, and the
cup, described as "knurled," was delivered
December 21.[1] Compared with other royal
christening gifts of the period, this one was relatively modest. The duke of Portland was
allowed 130 ounces, Monsieur Duyvenvoides
was given 150 ounces, and the marquis of
Annendale received a gilt tea table weighing
161 ounces.[2]

Richard Edgcumbe was a valued member of
Robert Walpole's circle and served as a lord of
the treasury, vice treasurer, receiver general, and
treasurer of war and paymaster general of the
king's revenues in Ireland. He was elevated to
the peerage in 1742 when Walpole fell from
power so that he could not be investigated by
the secret committee assigned to examine the
records of the Cornish borough, which
Edgcumbe had managed. Horace Walpole
called him "one of the honestest and steadiest
men in the world," although John Hervey
claimed that his popularity with George II was
due to the fact that he was shorter than the
king.[3] This cup, offered as a christening gift to
his second son, George, was presented by the
king in the early stages of Edgcumbe's career.
George Edgcumbe succeeded his brother
Richard as baron Edgcumbe in 1761. He
embarked on a career in the Royal Navy and
served as a Whig member of Parliament for
Fowey from 1746 to 1761, and as clerk of the
council of Cornwall from 1761 until his death.
He held several positions in the royal household, including treasurer of the household
(1765–66).[4]

The design of the cup was a standard one
supplied by the royal goldsmith during the
reign of George I. The robust strapwork and
masks, cast and applied to the plain cup, reflect
the lasting influence of the court designer
Daniel Marot. At least seven such cups or sets

44 (Color Plate v)

issued from the Jewel House between 1712 and 1725 have survived.[5] Some are paired with footed salvers, while others, such as the present example, were intended to stand alone. Samuel Smythin, who held the position of royal goldsmith, was not a practicing maker, but he relied on a network of subordinates to execute the Jewel House commissions. One of these was Samuel Margas. Margas had been apprenticed to his brother, Jacob, also a subordinate goldsmith to the crown, who was born in Rouen before the family immigrated to London about 1688. Their father and grandfather, both named Samuel, had worked as goldsmiths in Rouen, and it is clear that in London the brothers were well connected in the community of Huguenot goldsmiths active in the area of their shops on St. Martin's Lane. Their marks appear more often on domestic than on royal plate, but the present cup, a cup marked by Jacob Margas in 1725, and a ewer and basin marked by Samuel suggest that the Jewel Office supplied some of their most important commissions.[6]

1. London, PRO, LC5/109, 278; LC9/44, 253.

2. London, PRO, LC5/109, 222, 227, 246; LC9/44, 253. The tea table is illus. Clayton 1985a, p. 419, fig. 649.

3. Sidney Lee, ed., *Dictionary of National Biography* (London, 1908), vol. 6, p. 377.

4. Other silver from the family was sold by Sotheby's, London, February 28, 1991, lot 222, and May 24, 1956.

5. Pair of cups by Phillip Rollos, 1714, The Toledo Museum of Art (acc. nos. 65.171–172), illus. Hayward 1959, pl. 9; cup with Wentworth arms by Phillip Rollos, 1712, The Toledo Museum of Art (acc. no. 63.21), sold Sotheby's, London, June, 27, 1963, lot 53; pair of cups with salvers made for the use of baron Bingley as ambassador to Spain, returned to the Jewel House by 1725, by Phillip Rollos, 1714, collection Sir Phillip Sassoon sold Christie's, London, May 18, 1988, lot 195; two cups made as a christening gift for George Townsend (second marquess of Townsend), one unmarked, the other marked by Matthew Cooper, ca. 1725, sold Sotheby's, London, February 5, 1970, lots 105–6; cup and salver made as a christening gift for George Seymour, viscount Beauchamp, by Jacob Margas and Edmund Pearce, 1725/6, sold Sotheby's, London, May 3, 1984, lot 54.

6. The Metropolitan Museum of Art, New York, illus. Hackenbroch 1969, p. 76, cat. 145.

· 45 ·

TWO-HANDLED CUP WITH COVER

Marked by George Wickes (1698–1761)
London, after 1722
Silver
30.437a-b

MARKS: on a disk inserted into underside of foot, maker's mark, *G* with a *W* inside (Grimwade 918) (struck twice); lion passant; leopard's head crowned

ARMORIALS: engraved on front and on cover, the arms and crest of Hancock impaling Henchman for Thomas Hancock who married Lydia Henchman in 1731

INSCRIPTIONS: scratched on underside, *55-170*

H. 28.5 cm (11¼ in.); w. 27.5 cm (10¹³⁄₁₆ in.); d. 17.8 cm (7 in.)

WEIGHT: 1,729.4 gm (55 oz 10 dwt)

PROVENANCE: according to tradition, Thomas Hancock (1702–1764), by descent to his wife, Lydia Henchman Hancock (1714–1777), to their nephew John Hancock (1736–1793), to his widow, Dorothy Hancock Scott, given in 1825 to her nephew-in-law Joseph May (1760–1841), by descent to Samuel Joseph May (1776–1870), to his son Frederick Warren Goddard May (1821–1904), to his son Frederick Goddard May (1861–1954), Gift of the heirs of Samuel May (1723–1794), May 10, 1972

EXHIBITED: Jamestown, Virginia, Hampton Roads, *The Massachusetts Colonial Loan Exhibit*, 1907, cat. 494; Boston, Museum of Fine Arts, 1975, pp. 52–53; Boston, Museum of Fine Arts, *John Singleton Copley in America*, 1995 (not in catalogue)

PUBLISHED: Bigelow 1917, pp. 194–95; Kathryn C. Buhler, "The Hancock Cup," *Bulletin of the Museum of Fine Arts* 168, no. 28 (1930), pp. 70–71

DESCRIPTION: The raised body of the cup is in the form of an inverted bell. It rests on a domed, stepped foot. An applied wire circles the midsection of the cup. Above it, an engraved coat of arms is centered on the plain surface. The rim has a slightly flared lip, and the insides of the cup and cover are gilt. The two ear-shaped handles have leaves at the shoulder and terminate in scrolls. They are hollow-cast in halves and seamed vertically. The domed, stepped cover is raised, with an applied bezel formed of seamed sheet. It has an engraved crest on the dome and is topped with a baluster finial, which has a banded knop. The marks are struck on a separate disk that is let into the foot; the solder is uneven and pitted, and the underside of the foot was subsequently turned on a lathe, partly defacing one of the maker's marks. A vent hole is visible next to the center punch.

45

The early history of this cup has been the subject of some discussion. According to a tradition first recorded in the 1870s by Abigail May Alcott, mother of the novelist Louisa May Alcott, it belonged to Thomas Hutchinson, provincial governor of Massachusetts from 1771 to 1774. Hutchinson presided over the colony and tried, unsuccessfully, to quell the discontent provoked by the Stamp Act. His home in the North End of Boston was burned on August 26, 1765, and his possessions looted. Family history indicated that the cup was "selected [from his confiscated property] as a grateful memorial to the first Governor of Massachusetts, for John Hancock."[1] The engraved arms on the cup, however, are those of Hancock impaling Henchman for Thomas Hancock, not the arms used by the patriot John.[2] Although the Hutchinson association must be considered tenuous, the subsequent history of the cup is better documented.

The arms of Thomas Hancock are shown with those of his wife, Lydia Henchman, whom he married in 1731. There are signs that the center of the cartouche has been erased and the Hancock-Henchman arms engraved within the existing surround. It is entirely possible that the original purchaser returned the cup to George Wickes or sold it to another London goldsmith sometime before 1731. Thomas Hancock, a prosperous Boston merchant, married the daughter of Daniel Henchman, a bookseller and the builder of the first paper mill in New England. In 1739 he had written to his agent in London "to look into the Herald's office and take out my armes."[3] Thomas Hancock died in 1764, and his widow specified in her will proved November 21, 1777, that all her silver plate should go to her mother, Elizabeth Henchman, "excepting a silver bowl, a silver spout cup, and a large two-handled silver cup which I give to my nephew, John Hancock."[4] She also bequeathed a pair of standing cups to the First Church, Boston, and a silver tankard to the Old South Church. John Hancock died intestate in 1793, and the distribution of his holdings, much diminished by unskilled management, was so contentious that some matters were still unresolved in 1902.[5] His widow, Dorothy, was appointed administratrix.[6] According to the account written in the 1870s by Abigail May Alcott, the widow's right to her late husband's estate was challenged by a nephew. The chronicler's father, Joseph May, is said to have worked with another family member, John Galliyn, to defend her in court, and in recompense she presented him with this cup in 1825.[7] She eventually agreed with Hancock's siblings and mother to accept only about one-sixth of the value of the entire estate.

The historical tradition of the cup was quickly honored by the family. Abigail Alcott described how it had been presented to her mother by Madam Hancock (Scott) in 1824 "full of ice cream, then considered a rare and very elegant delicacy." It was exhibited during the centennial celebrations in Concord in 1875.[8] Abigail's daughter, the novelist Louisa May Alcott, wrote a letter to Frederick Warren Goddard May in 1875 on behalf of her mother, who was too frail to write: "[Mother] enjoyed showing off the jolly old bowl immensely, and I shall enjoy getting it off my hands still more, for I have had it on my mind ever since it

came and stood guard over it as if my salvation depended on its safety."[9] In 1907 it was exhibited at the Jamestown Tercentenary exhibition, and in 1914 it was placed on long-term loan at the Museum of Fine Arts.

The cup is an unusual duty dodger. The marks are struck on a disk inserted into the stem of the foot, but they are incomplete. Instead of a date letter, the maker's mark is struck twice.[10] Thomas Hancock is not listed as a client of George Wickes in the Gentlemen's Ledgers of 1735–40 or 1740–48, which record his business with individual clients,[11] and since the arms have been reengraved it appears that Hancock's agent must have bought it for him secondhand.

1. Transcript of a letter from Abigail Alcott to the Reverend Samuel May, January 1873, in the curatorial files. The location of the original is unknown, but there is a draft of part of the text at Houghton Library, Harvard University, Cambridge, Mass., bMSAM 1817(44).

2. For other silver associated with John Hancock, see cats. 114 and 117.

3. Quoted in Baxter 1945, p. 69.

4. E. Alfred Jones, *The Old Silver of the American Churches* (Letchworth, 1913), p. 27.

5. Baxter 1945, p. 292.

6. In 1796 she married a shipmaster, Captain Scott. By the time of his death in 1809, her resources were limited.

7. Joseph May's wife, Dorothy Quincy Sewall, was the niece of the widow Hancock, thus explaining her choice of legal representation.

8. The proceedings were lavish, attended by President Grant. The towns of Lexington and Concord competed to stage the largest celebration. In a dinner tent in Concord, which seated 4,400 people, there was a display of historic weapons, but no silver is mentioned. See David B. Little, *America's First Centennial Celebration* (Boston, 1961).

9. Typescript of a letter in the curatorial file. See n. 1.

10. For a similar duty dodger by George Wickes, see Partridge Fine Arts PLC, *Silver at Partridge: Recent Acquisitions* (London, 1992), p. 24, cat. 11.

11. Victoria and Albert Museum, Garrard Ledgers, Gentlemen's Ledgers 1 and 3. I am very grateful to Helen Clifford for providing this information.

46

· 46 ·

SAUCEPAN

George Greenhill Jones (first mark entered 1719)
London, 1722/3
Silver, wood
33.118

MARKS: on underside, maker's mark *IO* (Grimwade 1563); lion's head erased; date letter *G*; Britannia

INSCRIPTIONS: scratched, *No 267, oz 2=18, 2133*

H. 9.7 cm (3¹³⁄₁₆ in.); w. 15.9 cm (6¼ in.); d. 7.7 cm (3¹⁄₁₆ in.)

WEIGHT: 96.4 gm (3 oz 2 dwt)

PROVENANCE: Anonymous Gift in Memory of Charlotte Beebe Wilbour (1833–1914), March 2, 1933

EXHIBITED: Boston, Museum of Fine Arts, 1933

DESCRIPTION: The baluster body has a slightly flaring rim and a small shaped pouring spout. The body is raised from sheet, and the cylindrical mount for the wooden handle, at a right angle to the spout, is formed from seamed sheet. The body has been rehammered.

Designed to be used with a spirit burner for warming sauce or brandy, plain saucepans like this example were made in a range of sizes. The baluster shape is the most common, but a variant form with a molded foot rim and flaring sides was also widely used. An example by the same maker who marked this example is in the Clark Art Institute.[1]

1. Illus. Wees 1997, p. 241, cat. 153.

47

This handsome and substantial tea canister is engraved with the arms of the dukes of Hamilton surrounded by the Order of the Thistle. The engraving and form seem to match an unusual rectangular teapot at Brodick Castle that was marked by George Fenwick in 1809.[1] It is possible that the teapot was made to match the earlier tea canister, and that the canister was freshly engraved to make a set, although 1809 is an early date for such an improvisation. The ninth duke of Hamilton (1740–1819) succeeded in 1799, but neither he nor his son Alexander, tenth duke, who married Susan, daughter of William Beckford, held the Order of the Thistle.

1. Exh. London, Spink & Son, Ltd., *Beckford and Hamilton Silver from Brodick Castle*, 1980, cat. by Malcolm Baker, Timothy Schroder, E. Laird Clowes, cat. H 47. I thank W. J. Cowell, custodian, Brodick Castle, and Christopher Hartley, assistant curator, National Trust for Scotland, for their assistance.

· 47 ·

TEA CANISTER
Marked by John Pero (first mark entered 1717)
London, 1722/3
Silver
35.1604

MARKS: on underside, lion's head erased; Britannia; date letter *G*; maker's mark *PE* (Grimwade 2171)

ARMORIALS: engraved on front of canister, the arms of Hamilton quartering Douglas for the dukes of Hamilton, surrounded by the Order of the Thistle

INSCRIPTIONS: engraved on underside, *14 = 16*

H. 11.8 cm (4⅝ in.); w. 8.9 cm (3½ in.); d. 5.9 cm (2⁵/₁₆ in.)

WEIGHT: 447.9 gm (14 oz 8 dwt)

PROVENANCE: William E. Godfrey, New York, purchased by Frank Brewer Bemis, January 18, 1922, Bequest of Frank Brewer Bemis, November 7, 1935

DESCRIPTION: The rectangular body has a molded base and a stepped lid hinged on the short side. It is constructed of scored, seamed sheet with an inset base. The foot rim consists of a thick molded wire. The cover is cast, with an applied molded wire rim.

· 48 ·

PAIR OF CANDLESTICKS
Marked by Thomas Folkingham (first mark entered 1707, d. 1729)
London, 1722/3
Silver
35.1606–1607

MARKS: on the underside of each base (in two corners), maker's mark *FO* (Grimwade 703); date letter *G*; lion's head erased; Britannia

INSCRIPTIONS: 35.1606, engraved on underside, *13=16*. 35.1607, engraved on underside, *12=11*

35.1606: H. 15.2 cm (6 in.); w. 9.9 cm (3⅞ in.); d. 9.9 cm (3⅞ in.)

35.1607: H. 15.2 cm (6 in.); w. 9.9 cm (3⅞ in.); d. 9.9 cm (3⅞ in.)

WEIGHT: 35.1606: 411 gm (13 oz 4 dwt). 35.1607: 374.2 gm (12 oz)

PROVENANCE: Crichton Brothers, London, purchased by Frank Brewer Bemis, December 4, 1917, Bequest of Frank Brewer Bemis, November 7, 1935

DESCRIPTION: The candlesticks have a square stepped base with incurved corners rising to a circular, sunken center. The baluster stem rises first to a

48

flattened knop, surmounted by a flaring, shaped, square midsection. The nozzle is urn-shaped. The base of the candlestick is heavily cast in one piece. The stem is hollow-cast in two vertically seamed pieces. The surface is considerably rubbed, obscuring whatever crispness the molding might have had.

From about 1690 to 1725 designs for baluster candlesticks were remarkably consistent, varying only slightly in proportion, the shape of the base, or the profile of the stem or nozzle.[1] One explanation must be that the specialist makers who supplied many retailers had a limited range of molds and, with a relatively small fashioning charge per ounce, little financial incentive to devise new ones. Thomas Folkingham seems to have had a highly successful retail business, leaving an estate of thirty thousand pounds on his death in 1729. Grimwade suggested that he must have employed Huguenot journeymen because of the French character of much work bearing his mark.[2] Typical of this work is a pair of candlesticks similar in outline to the present pair, embellished with cast and chased strapwork panels.[3]

1. Examples similar to the present candlesticks include a set of four of 1732 marked by William Gould, sold Christie's, London, February 14, 1979, lot 94; a pair of 1686 marked *IL* sold Sotheby's, London, March 2, 1995, lot 172; a pair of 1726 marked by Arnet and Pocock, sold Christie's, London, October 24, 1979, lot 118.

2. Grimwade 1990, p. 511.

3. Illus. Brett 1986, p. 172, fig. 696.

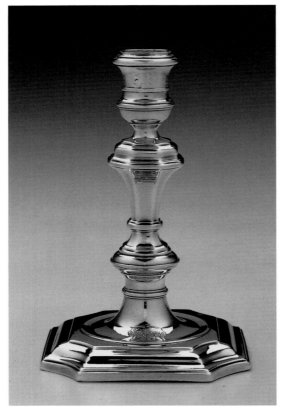

49

DESCRIPTION: The stick has a stepped square base with incurved corners. The faceted baluster stem rises from a circular base to an octagonal knop. The nozzle is urn-shaped. The base is cast in a single piece, and the stem is cast in vertical halves.

Paul de Lamerie sold a range of plate for the writing table, both plain and richly fashioned.[2] A standish might include a tray, inkpot, pounce pot, and bell. Tapersticks were sometimes, but not always, included in the set[3] and were used to hold the thin wax candle that was lit briefly to melt sealing wax. This example is identical in design to a full-size stick, but reduced in scale. They were occasionally produced in pairs.

1. Exh. London, Goldsmiths' Hall, 1990, p. 29, mark 3, used from about 1720–32.

2. The Walpole inkstand (illus. London, Goldsmiths' Hall, 1990, p. 96, cat. 51) represents one extreme, while the duke of Marlborough's inkstand represents the other (illus. ibid., p. 145, cat. 94).

3. A Lamerie standish of 1745 in the Gans Collection, illus. Bliss 1992, pp. 70–71, cat. 22, includes a taperstick.

· 49 ·

TAPERSTICK

Marked by Paul de Lamerie (1688–1751)
London, 1723/4
Silver
35.1612

MARKS: on underside, one mark in each corner, maker's mark *LA* (unregistered);[1] lion's head erased; Britannia; date letter *H*

ARMORIALS: engraved on base, an unidentified coat of arms (a chevron or between three birds within a bordure or charged with eight roundels, impaling, or three crescents)

H. 10.3 cm (4 1/16 in.); w. 6.7 cm (2 5/8 in.); d. 6.7 cm (2 5/8 in.)

WEIGHT: 158.8 gm (5 oz 2 dwt)

PROVENANCE: Crichton Brothers, London, purchased by Frank Brewer Bemis, September 29, 1930, Bequest of Frank Brewer Bemis, November 7, 1935

EXHIBITED: Houston, Texas, Museum of Fine Arts, 1956, cat. 5

· 50 ·

TANKARD

Marked by Edward Feline (free 1721)
London, 1723/4
Silver
63.488

MARKS: on underside and on bezel of cover, maker's mark *Fe* (Grimwade 679); date letter *H*; Britannia; lion's head erased

INSCRIPTIONS: engraved on the underside of the body, *A* with an earl's coronet above, scratched on the underside, *no 2682, oz 53-2*

H. 24.2 cm (9½ in.); w. 20.4 cm (8 in.); diam. of base 14.1 cm (5⁹⁄₁₆ in.)

WEIGHT: 1,647.1 gm (52 oz 19 dwt)

PROVENANCE: property of Bertram, fifth earl of Ashburnham, sold by his executors, Christie's, London, March 24, 1914, lot 89, purchased Tessier, Ltd., London; property of Mrs. Pamela J. Combemale, New York, sold Christie's, London, March 20, 1963, lot 91 [Garrard & Co., London], purchased May 8, 1963, Theodora Wilbour Fund in Memory of Charlotte Beebe Wilbour

DESCRIPTION: The tankard, raised from heavy sheet, has a rounded base and slightly everted rim. It rests on a stepped base formed from several cast sections. The plain surface of the body is ornamented with applied alternating ribs. At the midsection is a molded wire band. The C-shaped handle, cast in two pieces, has a baluster drop at the top and bottom. The raised domed cover is attached with a hinge to the handle. The dome is decorated with applied ribs similar to those on the base of the tankard, and at the center is a baluster finial, cast in halves and seamed vertically.

This massive tankard is decorated with a distinctive pattern of applied ribs that was used more commonly on two-handled cups and covers. A similar tankard of 1730 and a large group of two-handled cups with similar straps, ranging in date from 1721 to 1730, are marked by various makers including Augustine Courtauld, John White, Bowles Nash, Paul Crespin, David Willaume II, and Edward Feline.[1] Most of these are made of Britannia standard silver, which was no longer mandatory. Feline, the maker of this tankard, was apprenticed to Augustine Courtauld, so it seems likely that several of these objects were

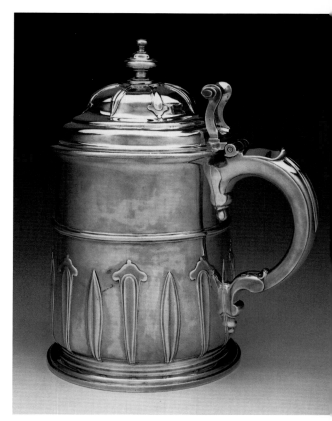

50

manufactured in a single shop. The high polish may have been given to the tankard and the engraved coat of arms removed when the tankard was owned by the fifth earl of Ashburnham, who added an engraved initial on the underside of the base.

1. See a tankard, 1730/1, Britannia standard, marked by Augustine Courtauld, sold Sotheby's, London, February 6, 1947, lot 165; a cup, 1723/4, marked by Augustine Courtauld, sold Sotheby's, London, October 17, 1985, lot 386; a cup, 1725/6, Britannia standard, marked by Augustine Courtauld, sold Sotheby's, London, December 13, 1973, lot 118; a cup, 1721/2, Britannia standard, marked by Bowles Nash, sold Sotheby's, London, April 24, 1986, lot 202; a cup, 1728/9, marked by John White, sold Christie's, London, October 14, 1987, lot 218; a cup, Britannia standard, 1726/7, marked by Paul Crespin, exh. New Haven, Yale Center for British Art, *British Art Treasures from Russian Imperial Collections*, 1996, p. 237, cat. 62, cat. ed. Brian Allen and Larissa Dukelskaya; a cup, 1732/3, sterling standard, marked by David Willaume II, illus. *Silver at Partridge* (October 1993), p. 16, cat. 11.

· 51 ·

KETTLE AND STAND
Marked by Gabriel Sleath (1674–1756)
London, 1724/5
Silver, rattan, ivory
35.1613

MARKS: on underside of kettle, maker's mark *GS* (Grimwade 890) (repeated on inside of cover and four times inside lamp); leopard's head crowned; date letter *I*; lion passant (repeated on inside of cover)

ARMORIALS: engraved on side of kettle, an unidentified coat of arms and crest (quarterly 1 and 4, a lion rampant, two ten roundels, four, three, two, and one, three, two chrevonelles; in pretence, 1 and 4, on a chevron five between three saltires; 2 and 3, a lion rampant and in chief three escallops; crest: a leopard's head)

INSCRIPTIONS: engraved on underside of lamp, *69=0*

H. 31.7 cm (12½ in.); w. 23.8 cm (9⅜ in.); d. 18.8 cm (7⅜ in.)

WEIGHT: 2,103.6 gm (67 oz 13 dwt)

PROVENANCE: Crichton Brothers, New York, purchased by Frank Brewer Bemis, December 2, 1918, Bequest of Frank Brewer Bemis, November 7, 1935

DESCRIPTION: The plain kettle, raised from sheet, is in the form of a compressed globe. It sits on a circular open stand supported by three scrolled legs with pad feet, assembled from cast components. Suspended between the three legs by scrolling supports is a circular molded lamp, with a removable flat top and a hinged, rounded cap. The spout of the kettle, cast in two vertically seamed pieces, is curved and has a circular drop. The plain bail handle is covered with rattan. The cover, formed from sheet, fits flush with the rim of the kettle, and its baluster finial has an ivory knop. The rim around the cover is engraved with a geometric pattern and scrolls, and on the center of one side of the kettle is an engraved cartouche enclosing a coat of arms. Although the surface of this kettle has suffered, the plain, rather rough workmanship is evident.

Teakettles in the form of a compressed sphere, common from about 1720, echoed the shape of the silver or porcelain teapots with which they were used. This kettle, with an undecorated spout, simple handle, and plain legs, is a modest example of the form. Gabriel Sleath seems to have specialized in tea and coffee wares (see

51

cats. 62 and 78). By striking his sponsor's mark four times on the interior of the spirit burner in imitation of hallmarks, Sleath avoided paying the required duty of sixpence per ounce. The engraved arms appear to replace an earlier engraving within the original mantling.

· 52 ·

PAIR OF TRENCHER SALTS
Marked by Mary Rood (only mark entered 1721)
London, 1724/5
Silver
35.1614–1615

MARKS: on the underside of each, maker's mark *MR* (Grimwade 2060); leopard's head crowned; lion passant; date letter *I*

INSCRIPTIONS: scratched on underside of each, *I★S*
35.1614: H. 3 cm (1³⁄₁₆ in.); w. 8.1 cm (3³⁄₁₆ in.); d. 6.8 cm (2¹¹⁄₁₆ in.)

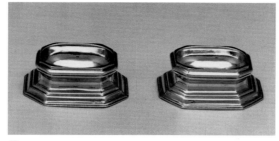

52

35.1615: H. 2.9 cm (1⅛ in.); W. 8 cm (3⅛ in.);
d. 6.7 cm (2⅝ in.)

WEIGHT: 35.1614: 82.2 gm (2 oz 13 dwt). 35.1615:
82.2 gm (2 oz 13 dwt)

PROVENANCE: Crichton Brothers, New York, purchased by Frank Brewer Bemis, May 1, 1918,
Bequest of Frank Brewer Bemis, November 7, 1935

DESCRIPTION: Each salt is rectangular, with cut
corners, on a spreading, stepped foot. The oval well
for salt is raised and let into the molded rim, which
is assembled from eight fabricated panels. A wire is
applied to the bottom edge. The salts have been
extensively repaired and patched in the area of the
marks.

· 53 ·

SAUCEPAN
Marked by William Fleming (free 1695)
London, 1725/6
Silver, wood
33.124

MARKS: on underside of pan, maker's mark *FL*
(Grimwade 694, see note); lion's head erased;
Britannia; date letter *K*

ARMORIALS: engraved on side, the arms of
Hooker, alias Vowell, or Downing, co. Essex, possibly
with Hillary, co. Norfolk, Masculer, or Berge in pretence

INSCRIPTIONS: on underside, engraved 5=3

H. 9.9 cm (3⅞ in.); W. 19.1 cm (7½ in.); d. 9 cm
(3⁹⁄₁₆ in.)

WEIGHT: 175.8 gm (5 oz 13 dwt)

PROVENANCE: Anonymous Gift in Memory of
Charlotte Beebe Wilbour (1833–1914), March 2,
1933

EXHIBITED: Boston, Museum of Fine Arts, 1933;
Springfield, Massachusetts, Museum of Fine Arts,
1958

DESCRIPTION: The baluster body has a slightly
flaring rim and a shaped triangular pouring spout.
The body is raised from sheet, and the cylindrical
mount for the wooden handle, at a right angle to
the spout, is formed from seamed sheet. The body
has been rehammered.

53

54

· 54 ·

SALVER

Marked by Isaac Ribouleau (first mark entered 1724)
London, 1725/6
Silver
33.123

MARKS: on underside, maker's mark *IR* (Grimwade 1610) (struck twice); lion passant; leopard's head crowned; date letter *K*

ARMORIALS: engraved in the center, the arms of Horn, Horne, Mathews, Matthews, Montfichett, or St. Owen impaling Hebden or Winchingam

INSCRIPTIONS: engraved on underside, *52=10*

H. 3.3 cm (1⁵⁄₁₆ in.); w. 38.4 cm (15⅛ in.); d. 31.7 cm (12½ in.)

WEIGHT: 1,559.3 gm (50 oz 3 dwt)

PROVENANCE: Anonymous Gift in Memory of Charlotte Beebe Wilbour (1833–1914), March 2, 1933

EXHIBITED: Boston, Museum of Fine Arts, 1933

DESCRIPTION: The rectangular salver has a shaped rim and incurved corners. It is formed from sheet, with an applied rim, cast in four parts. The four faceted scrolled feet are cast.

Shaped rectangular salvers, usually somewhat larger than this, were called "tea tables" in the eighteenth century. A grander example, made as a christening gift from George I for the marquess of Annendale, retains its matching teapot, canister, sugar bowl, and milk jug.[1] The surface of this salver has been buffed and the coat of arms reengraved, although the mantling appears to be original.[2]

1. Illus. Clayton 1985a, p. 419, fig. 649.
2. For a square version of the form marked by Riboleau in 1725, see Christie's, London, March 1, 1979, lot 189.

55

· 55 ·

WAITER

Marked by Francis Nelme (first mark entered
1723)
London, 1725/6
Silver
35.1617

MARKS: on underside, date letter *K*; Britannia;
maker's mark *Ane* (Grimwade 68) (partially obliterated); lion's head erased

ARMORIALS: engraved in center, the crest of
Osborne beneath a ducal coronet for the dukes of
Leeds

INSCRIPTIONS: engraved on the underside, *8=12=*;
scratched, *Date 1725*; *7x13*; *10402 t/γ/s B/CC/–*

H. 2.1 cm (¹³⁄₁₆ in.); w. 13.3 cm (5¼ in.); d. 13.3 cm
(5¼ in.)

WEIGHT: 238.1 gm (7 oz 13 dwt)

PROVENANCE: Crichton Brothers, New York, purchased by Frank Brewer Bemis, May 1, 1918,
Bequest of Frank Brewer Bemis, November 7, 1935

EXHIBITED: Springfield, Massachusetts, Museum of
Fine Arts, 1958

DESCRIPTION: The square waiter has incurved
corners, a cast molded rim, and four bracket feet.

This waiter of 1725/6 bears the mark first used
by Anthony Nelme, who died in 1723. Nelme's
son Francis took over the same mark shortly
after his father's death and did not register a
distinct mark until 1739.[1] The original arms
have been removed and replaced with the crest
of the duke of Leeds, in a nineteenth-century
style.

1. Grimwade 1990, p. 606.

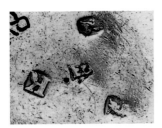

56

· 56 ·

DREDGER

Possibly by William Fleming (free 1695)
London, 1725/6
Silver
35.1618

MARKS: on underside, maker's mark *FL* (similar to
Grimwade 694) (repeated on underside of cover);
Britannia; lion's head erased; date letter *K*

H. 8.2 cm (3¼ in.); w. 5.2 cm (2⅛ in.); diam. of base
5.1 cm (2 in.)

WEIGHT: 82.2 gm (2 oz 13 dwt)

PROVENANCE: Bequest of Frank Brewer Bemis,
November 7, 1935

DESCRIPTION: The cylindrical dredger is formed
from sheet with an inset base and a molded fabricated foot. An ear-shaped handle, formed from flat,
molded wire, is applied to one side. The removable
domed cover, formed from sheet with a molded
wire rim, is pierced with plain small holes in a geometric pattern.

A distinction is sometimes made between the
function of plain straight-sided casters such as
this (often referred to as spice casters) and the
early shaped or faceted dredgers (sometimes

called pepper casters) (see cat. 64).[1] It seems
likely that the dredger could have been used
for any dry spice, such as mustard, as well as for
cayenne or black pepper.[2]

1. See Miles 1976, p. 116. Also see G. Bernard
Hughes, "Silver-Spice Dredgers," *Country Life* 110
(September 28, 1951), pp. 974–75.

2. For other examples of the form, see cat. 26; a
dredger of 1708 marked by Charles Adam, sold
Sotheby's, New York, October 22, 1993, lot 56; and
several in the Clark Art Institute, illus. Wees 1997,
pp. 220–23, cats. 133–37.

· 57 ·

DISH

Marked by Paul de Lamerie (1688–1751)
London, 1725/6
Silver
55.460

MARKS: on underside, maker's mark *LA* (Grimwade
1892); lion's head erased; Britannia; date letter *K*

ARMORIALS: engraved in center the arms of Yorke
impaling Cocks, for Philip Yorke (1690–1764), baron
Hardwicke of Hardwicke

H. 7.2 cm (2¹³⁄₁₆ in.); diam. of rim 28.8 cm (11⅜ in.)

WEIGHT: 1,805.9 gm (58 oz 1 dwt)

PROVENANCE: Philip Yorke, first earl of Hardwicke,
by descent through the family, sold Christie's,
London, April 4, 1895, lot 92; collection of the Rt.
Hon. lord Swathling (Samuel Montagu), sold
Christie's, London, July 17, 1946, lot 110; property of
William H. Green, Esq., sold Christie's, London,
May 19, 1955, lot 115, [Garrard & Co., London],
purchased September 15, 1955, Theodora Wilbour
Fund in Memory of Charlotte Beebe Wilbour

EXHIBITED: London, St. James's Court, *Old Silver
Work, Chiefly English, from the XVth to XVIIIth
Centuries*, 1902, cat. case C, no. 29, pl. 113, fig. 2

PUBLISHED: Philip A. S. Phillips, *Paul de Lamerie,
Citizen and Goldsmith of London: A Study of His Life
and Work, A.D. 1688–1751* (London, 1935), pl. XLV;
Richard P. Came, *Silver* (New York, 1961), fig. 66;
Gruber 1982, fig. 323

DESCRIPTION: The dish is circular with the sides
divided into twenty fluted panels; each panel terminates in a scroll, creating a flaring, scalloped rim.
There is a plain circular foot rim. On the outside of
the dish, the panels are alternately ornamented with

57

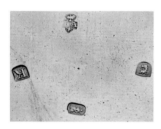

female heads surmounted by lion's masks and pendents of flowers and fruit against a matted ground. Around the inside rim the scrolls are chased with shell motifs. The dish was raised from heavy sheet. The alternating motifs of female heads and flowers beneath a scroll were cast and applied. The chased shells on the interior of the rim obscure the join at the rim of the bowl.

This dish, marked for 1725, may represent the earliest appearance of the unidentified modeler employed by Paul de Lamerie and others whose work is the fullest expression of the rococo in English silver. The dish is part of a large group of plate made by Lamerie for Philip Yorke, first earl of Hardwicke. Born in Dover, the only son of a solicitor, Yorke embarked on a distinguished career, skillfully managing the delicate Whig political machine. In 1725, the year this dish was marked, he bought the manor and estates of Hardwicke, co. Gloucester, for about twenty-four thousand pounds. By that date, he had already been appointed attorney general, a position he held until 1733, when he was elevated to the bench and peerage as lord chief justice of England and baron Hardwicke of Hardwicke. From 1736 he served as lord high chancellor of

Great Britain. In 1740 he purchased the estate Wimpole Hall from its impoverished owner, Edward Harley, earl of Oxford. There he employed Henry Flitcroft to update both the exterior and the interior, which had been designed by Gibbs for lord Harley.[1] In 1754 he was created viscount Royston and earl of Hardwicke. He married Margaret, widow of John Lygon and daughter of Charles Cocks of Worcester, in 1719. His professional and public accomplishments were generally admired by his contemporaries, with the exception of Horace Walpole, who was a lifelong detractor. Among his many vituperative remarks about Yorke, Walpole accused him of ill humor, avarice, and obsequiousness.[2]

There is an error in the engraving of the arms, which lack a bezante in the middle of the saltire for Yorke. This may represent an error on the part of the engraver. On the other hand, Yorke had not yet been elevated to the peerage when this piece was made, and it is possible that he used this variation on the family arms in error until corrected by the College of Arms at the time of his elevation.[3]

A large group of Yorke's silver by Paul de

Lamerie was sold at auction from Wimpole Hall in 1895.[4] He was clearly a loyal patron over an extended period—the objects range in date from 1723 to 1741.[5] The only objects earlier than this dish sold from Wimpole in 1895 are a pair of cups of 1723.[6] A large circular sideboard dish is marked 1725, the same year as the present dish; they were probably ordered by the ambitious attorney general for his newly purchased house, Hardwicke. Yorke's son-in-law, lord Anson, also patronized Lamerie in the same period.[7]

The dish is an unusual size and weight.[8] The fluted form, commonly called a strawberry dish, is generally a smaller size,[9] whereas salad dishes are usually fitted with feet.[10] A closely related dish of 1724 in the Ashmolean Museum is similar in size and weight.[11] It has a molded foot ring, however, unlike the plain thick wire applied to the foot of the present dish, which may have been designed to fit into a footed stand as part of an epergne, as, for example, the Brobinsky centerpiece.[12] Indeed, when sold from Wimpole Hall in 1895, the dish was fitted with a plated stand, perhaps a replacement for a lost epergne base.[13]

Comparison with the Ashmolean dish reveals an important aspect of the Yorke dish. Divided into twenty-four, not twenty, flutes, it has applied female masks around the rim beneath a cresting of scallop shells. One year earlier in date than the Yorke dish, it is perfectly symmetrical in design. On the Yorke dish, by contrast, the female heads are asymmetrical in

composition and alternate with floral clusters. The scrolls above the rim curl in opposing directions. Above the female heads, beneath the scrolls, are the lion's heads that characterize so many of Lamerie's important pieces in the rococo style. These details, undeniably rococo in intention, predate by at least ten years the full-blown rococo style in Lamerie's silver and invite a reassessment of Lamerie's innovations.[14]

1. Nicholas Pevsner, *The Buildings of England: Cambridgeshire* (Harmondsworth, 1954), pp. 490–91; Royal Commission on Historical Monuments, *An Inventory of Historical Monuments in the County of Cambridgeshire, West Cambridgeshire* (London, 1968), vol. 1, pp. 214–16; Christopher Hussey, "Wimpole Hall, Cambridgeshire II," *Country Life* 142 (December 7, 1967), pp. 1466–71.

2. Mrs. Paget Toynbee, ed., *The Letters of Horace Walpole* (Oxford, 1903), vol. 2, p. 216.

3. I am grateful to Gale Glynn for her remarks regarding this, and for the biographical information she supplied.

4. Christie's, London, April 4, 1895, lot 92, property of the Rt. Hon. the earl of Hardwicke.

5. Among the Hardwicke silver is a salver in the Clark Art Institute, see Wees 1997, p. 433 n. 4, where the author lists the present locations for many of the objects in the 1895 sale. To this list should be added a beer jug, 1729, sold Christie's, London, November 28, 1990, lot 129; a pair of footed salvers, 1736, sold Sotheby's, New York, June 6, 1980, lot 31. See also Christie's, New York, October 27, 1987, lot 431.

6. Phillips, *Paul de Lamerie*, p. 80, pl. 30.

7. London, Goldsmiths' Hall, 1990, pp. 113–17.

8. For example, a fluted dish by Lamerie, without foot and of approximately the same dimensions, is recorded at 28 oz 15 dwt, nearly half the weight of the present dish. See Sotheby's, London, July 18, 1974, lot 265.

9. See, for example, London, Goldsmiths' Hall, 1990, pp. 122–23, cat. 77.

10. See Schroder 1988a, p. 155, cat. 37.

11. See London, Goldsmiths' Hall, 1990, p. 85, cat. 44.

12. Grimwade 1974, pl. 44.

13. Christie's, London, April 4, 1895, lot 92.

14. See the discussions of the advent of rococo motifs in Michael Snodin, "Paul de Lamerie's Rococo," *Paul de Lamerie at the Sign of the Golden Ball* (London, 1990), pp. 16–23, and Elaine Barr, "Rococo Silver: Design," in *Rococo: Art and Design in Hogarth's England* (London, 1984), pp. 100–102. The significance of this was suggested to me by Ubaldo Vitali.

58

The distinction between waiters (small trays used for the service of a single glass) and salvers (larger trays used both at the tea table and in the dining room) is sometimes unclear even in eighteenth-century documents.[2] This piece, originally one of a pair,[3] falls between the two categories. It was probably used as needed in the dining room for the service of wine or on the sideboard as well as in the drawing room under a teakettle or teapot. It is somewhat smaller in size and weight than most other hexafoil or octafoil salvers.[4] It exemplifies the clean construction and simple design so admired by American collectors of English silver.

1. Garrard's identified the arms as those of Seckford following their correspondence in 1957 with the College of Arms, which houses records regarding the right to bear arms administered by thirteen officers of arms. The arms might also be associated with the families of Loder, Ingram, Sackford, Whatton, Cotes, or Cotys.

2. Hartop 1996, p. 358; Clayton 1985a, pp. 317–23.

3. The Museum purchased the pair in 1957 and sold one in 1979.

4. For example, see a salver marked by Gabriel Sleath, 1719, diam. 12¼ in., 30 oz, sold Sotheby's, London, February 20, 1975; a pair marked by Simon Pantin, 1729, diam. 12 in., 69 oz (combined weight) in the Metropolitan Museum, illus. Hackenbroch 1969, cat. 140; another marked by William Darker, 1728, diam. 10 in., 19 oz, at Colonial Williamsburg, illus. Davis 1976, pp. 127–28, cat. 128; another marked by John East, 1720, diam. 11 in., illus. Clayton 1985a, p. 320, fig. 463; another marked by Peter Archambo, 1722, diam. 12¼ in., 41 oz, illus. Brett 1986, p. 189, fig. 790.

· 58 ·

HEXAFOIL SALVER
Marked by David Green (first mark entered 1701)
London, 1725/6
Silver
57.101

MARKS: on underside, maker's mark *DG* (Grimwade 465); lion passant; date letter *K*; leopard's head crowned

ARMORIALS: engraved in center, the arms of Sekford, co. Suffolk[1]

H. 2.6 cm (1 in.); w. 24.4 cm (9⅝ in.); d. 24.4 cm (9⅝ in.)

WEIGHT: 419.6 gm (13 oz 10 dwt)

PROVENANCE: Garrard & Co., Ltd., London, purchased February 14, 1957, Theodora Wilbour Fund in Memory of Charlotte Beebe Wilbour

DESCRIPTION: The six-lobed salver has three cast panel feet and a simple raised border. It is formed from a single piece of sheet, with swaged corners and a curved rim. The feet are fabricated in two pieces.

59

COFFEEPOT

Marked by Joseph Collier (mark entered 1713)
Exeter, 1727/8
Silver, wood
33.126

MARKS: on underside, maker's mark *JC* (Jackson
1989, p. 293); date letter *c*; leopard's head crowned;
lion passant; castle

INSCRIPTIONS: scratched *12943/J Collier/London/
1727*

H. 24.1 cm (9½ in.); w. 16.1 cm (6⁵⁄₁₆ in.); d. 15.5 cm
(6⅛ in.)

WEIGHT: 674.7 gm (21 oz 14 dwt)

PROVENANCE: Anonymous Gift in Memory of
Charlotte Beebe Wilbour (1833–1914), March 2,
1933

DESCRIPTION: The cylindrical, tapering body is
formed from sheet and seamed behind the handle.
The inset base has a molded foot and rim. The
faceted curved spout, cast in two pieces and seamed
vertically, has a baluster drop. A high domed cover
has a baluster finial and a bezel. The wooden handle
is mounted on cast, scrolled brackets at a right angle
to the spout.

Joseph Collier was one of a group of Plymouth
goldsmiths who entered their marks in the
Exeter assay office soon after it was opened in
1701. In addition to the substantial trade in
Exeter, the assay office served goldsmiths from
Plymouth, Falmouth, Bristol, and Barnstaple,
who produced a large quantity of church and
domestic plate for local consumption. As was
the case in London, the trade included manufacturing goldsmiths as well as retailers.
Collier's mark sometimes appears overstriking
that of the working goldsmith Samuel
Willmott, who mentioned Collier in a letter to
the assay master complaining that he had been
unjustly charged with hallmarking violations.[1]
The form of this coffeepot, current in London
by 1700, had a long survival both in London
and in the provincial centers.[2]

1. T. A. Kent, "The Great Days of Exeter Silver,
1700 to 1750," *Silver Society Proceedings* 3, no. 3
(1983), p. 62.

2. An Exeter chocolate pot marked by Pentecost
Symonds similar in form was sold Sotheby's, New
York, April 12, 1994, lot 307.

· 59 ·

PAIR OF WAITERS

Marked by Thomas Farren (first mark entered
1707, d. 1743)
London, 1726/7
Silver
42.10–11

MARKS: on the underside of each, maker's mark *TF*
(Grimwade 2749); lion passant; leopard's head
crowned; date letter *L*

ARMORIALS: engraved on the center of each, the
crest of Barham, Barnardston, or Pert

42.10: H. 1.9 cm (¾ in.); w. 13.3 cm (5¼ in.);
d. 13.6 cm (5⅜ in.)
42.11: H. 2 cm (¹³⁄₁₆ in.); w. 13.2 cm (5³⁄₁₆ in.);
d. 13.3 cm (5¼ in.)

WEIGHT: 42.10: 204 gm (6 oz 11 dwt). 42.11:
204 gm (6 oz 11 dwt)

PROVENANCE: Anonymous Gift in Memory of
Charlotte Beebe Wilbour (1833–1914), January 8,
1942

DESCRIPTION: Each square waiter has incurved
corners, a cast molded rim, and four bracket feet.

Somewhat smaller and lighter than many such
waiters by marked Lamerie (see cat. 77), this
pair has had its original engraving removed and
a later crest added.

60

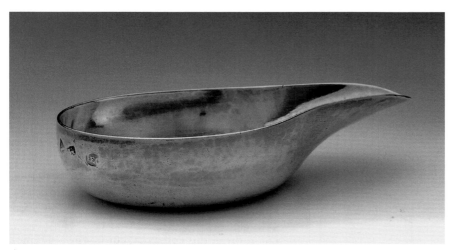

61

· 61 ·

PAP BOAT
Marked by Edward Cornock (first mark entered
1707)
London, 1728/9
Silver
18.658

MARKS: just below the rim at the back, leopard's head crowned; date letter *N* (1728/9); lion passant; maker's mark *EC* (Grimwade 546) (struck twice)

INSCRIPTIONS: engraved on underside, *HS/1770*

H. 3 cm (1³⁄₁₆ in.); w. 12.1 cm (4¾ in.); d. 7.1 cm (2¹³⁄₁₆ in.)

WEIGHT: 76.5 gm (2 oz 9 dwt)

PROVENANCE: by tradition, the property of Henry Sargent (1770–1845), by descent to his granddaughter, Mrs. Winthrop Sargent, lent to the Museum by Mrs. Winthrop Sargent, 1917, Gift of Mrs. Horatio A. Lamb in Memory of Mrs. Winthrop Sargent, December 5, 1918

DESCRIPTION: The low oval vessel, raised from sheet, has a broad spout drawn out on one side. There are several small dents on the lower edge.

A pap boat is a vessel for feeding an infant or invalid. This example, first lent to the Museum in 1917 by Mrs. Winthrop Sargent, bears the engraved initials *HS* and was believed to have belonged to her grandfather Henry Sargent. The engraved date of 1770 suggests that it may have been a christening gift to him. His father, Daniel, was a successful Boston merchant, and Henry, with the support of his mother, chose to become an artist. In 1793 he went to London and studied under Benjamin West, who was enjoying enormous success. When Sargent returned to America in 1799, he was discouraged by the few opportunities available to a history and genre painter and entered the military. He had a long association with the Massachusetts militia and also served in the state senate. He returned to painting later in life and achieved moderate recognition.[1]

1. Dumas Malone, ed., *Dictionary of American Biography* (New York, 1935), vol. 16, pp. 360–61. For examples of his work see Carol Troyen et al., *American Paintings in the Museum of Fine Arts, Boston* (Boston, 1997), p. 236. I am grateful to Carol Troyen for her help with the family history.

62

KETTLE AND STAND
Marked by Gabriel Sleath (1674–1756)
London, 1728/9
Silver, rattan, wood
33.127

MARKS: on underside of kettle and underside of
lamp, maker's mark *GS* (Grimwade 890); date letter
N (repeated on frame); leopard's head crowned
(repeated on frame); lion passant (repeated inside
cover and on cover of lamp)

H. 37.6 cm (14¹³⁄₁₆ in.); W. 27.6 cm (10⅞ in.);
D. 20.2 cm (7¹⁵⁄₁₆ in.)

WEIGHT: 3,132.7 gm (100 oz 14 dwt)

PROVENANCE: Anonymous Gift in Memory of
Charlotte Beebe Wilbour (1833–1914), March 2,
1933

EXHIBITED: Boston, Museum of Fine Arts, 1933

PUBLISHED: Edward Wenham, "Georgian Silver in
American Collections," *International Studio* 88 (1927),
p. 39

DESCRIPTION: The plain, octagonal, globular body,
raised from sheet, sits on an octagonal open stand
and is held in place by two removable pins on
chains. Its faceted spout is formed from two
vertically seamed halves and has a scalloped base and
a molded leaf at its tip. The cover has a raised hinge
on one side and sits flush with the rim of the kettle.
A wooden finial is mounted on a hexagonal base
and secured with a silver nut and bolt. The shaped
bail handle, cast and covered in rattan, has lobed
mounts securing the hinges to the body of the kettle. The stand, assembled from cast components, rests
on four double-scrolled legs with cushion feet. They
hold between them a faceted octagonal lamp with a
molded midsection, a raised thimble-shaped liner,
and a flat, octagonal cover.

This capacious kettle is grander than the slightly earlier example marked by Sleath in this collection (cat. 51). Though it lacks carrying handles on the stand, its weight, boldly modeled
spout, and faceted lamp suggest that it was part
of an exceptional tea service. An engraved coat
of arms has been removed from the front face
of the kettle.

63

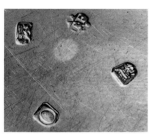

· 63 ·

ECUELLE

Marked by Thomas Farren (first mark entered 1707, d. 1743)

London, 1729/30

Silver

33.128

MARKS: on underside, maker's mark *TF* (Grimwade 2749); leopard's head crowned; date letter *O*; lion passant (repeated on underside of one handle)

ARMORIALS: engraved on each handle, crest of Fellowes

INSCRIPTIONS: engraved on underside, *30=16; 15=4* (crossed out), a later engraving, *R Ford to JR*; engraved on handle, *No48=29-19*; engraved under cover, *No48=29-19, 15-8-1/2*

H. 9.7 cm (3¹³⁄₁₆ in.); w. 29.9 cm (11¼ in.); d. 18.2 cm (7³⁄₁₆ in.)

WEIGHT: 927 gm (29 oz 16 dwt)

PROVENANCE: sold Christie's, London, May 21, 1930, lot 83; Anonymous Gift in Memory of Charlotte Beebe Wilbour (1833–1914), March 2, 1933

EXHIBITED: Boston, Museum of Fine Arts, 1933

PUBLISHED: Edwin J. Hipkiss, "The Charlotte Beebe Wilbour Collection of English Silver," *Bulletin of the Museum of Fine Arts* 31, no. 184 (1933), p. 28; Clayton 1971, p. 115; Clayton 1985a, p. 164

DESCRIPTION: The shallow bowl of circular form, raised from sheet, has two flat cast handles of geometric openwork design. The raised domed cover has an applied gadrooned rim and a cut-card foliate pattern radiating from the center, where a cast gadrooned finial is placed.

Though ecuelles were a standard form in France, where they were often presented to women in childbed, they seem not to have become fashionable in England. Only a few of this plain form are known, most dating from the years around 1700.[1] This very late example has skillfully applied cut-card work and a substantial weight. The crest engraved on the handles was probably added in the early nineteenth century and replaces early engraving. The absence of any mark on the cover is troubling, although there is one area of repair near the cut-card that might be a trace of an obliterated mark.

1. See an example marked by Daniel Garnier of 1694 in the Untermeyer collection, illus. Hackenbroch 1969, cat. 83; another marked by Pierre Platel for 1706, sold Christie's, New York, September 27, 1978, lot 95; another by the same maker marked for 1704, illus. Hayward 1959, pl. 69A.

64

sheet, with applied wire at the lower and upper sections. The dome is formed from sheet and is set onto the faceted lower section. It has an applied wire at its rim; the lower section of the cover continues the tapering of the panels of the body. The scrolled handle is formed of molded wire.

A large number of the dredgers made in this design are marked by Glover Johnson, who seems to have specialized in such small faceted forms.[1] The earliest of these examples is marked 1708, and the present piece is a particularly late version of the model. It is consistent, however, with the sound, if conservative work of Augustine Courtauld, who continued to use Britannia standard until 1729, the year this dredger was made. Though often called kitchen peppers, it is unlikely that they would have been relegated to the kitchen. In the dining room they would have been used for casting pepper, mustard, or other dry spices.

1. For example, see Christie's, London, October 15, 1985, lot 14; Sotheby's, New York, June 16, 1988, lots 201–2; Sotheby's, London, March 24, 1960, lot 24.

· 64 ·

PAIR OF DREDGERS

Marked by Augustine Courtauld (ca. 1686–1751)
London, 1729/30
Silver
33.131–132

MARKS: on underside of each, maker's mark *CO* (Grimwade 385) (repeated on front panel of cover); lion's head erased; Britannia; date letter *O*

INSCRIPTIONS: engraved on each, ★*C*★/*G*★*M*. 33.131: scratched on base, *10566, 1730, No.2*. 33.132: scratched on base, *10566, 1730, No. 1*

33.131: H. 9.2 cm (3⅝ in.); w. 6.1 cm (2⅜ in.); d. 4.7 cm (1⅞ in.)
33.132: H. 9.1 cm (3⅝ in.); w. 6 cm (2⅜ in.); d. 4.8 cm (1⅞ in.)

WEIGHT: 33.131: 124.7 gm (4 oz). 33.132: 121.9 gm (3 oz 18 dwt)

PROVENANCE: Anonymous Gift in Memory of Charlotte Beebe Wilbour (1833–1914), March 2, 1933

EXHIBITED: Boston, Museum of Fine Arts, 1933

DESCRIPTION: Each octagonal tapering body rests on a molded stepped foot. The paneled sides of the caster are formed from heavy seamed sheet, joined to the cast lower section with a horizontal seam. The flat base is inset. The octagonal cover rises to a faceted dome, pierced with a fleur-de-lys and surmounted by a small baluster finial. It is formed from

· 65 ·

CANN

Marked by Thomas Farren (first mark entered 1707, d. 1743)
London, 1729/30
Silver
53.2083

MARKS: on underside, maker's mark *TF* (Grimwade 2749); date letter *O*; leopard's head crowned; lion passant

ARMORIALS: engraved on front, the arms of Faneuil

INSCRIPTIONS: scratched on underside, *12 oz 11 p*

H. 11.7 cm (4⅝ in.); w. 13 cm (5⅛ in.); d. 9.5 cm (3¾ in.)

WEIGHT: 385.6 gm (12 oz 8 dwt)

PROVENANCE: Gift of Mrs. Anna R. Briggs, September 10, 1953

DESCRIPTION: The raised bulbous vessel rests on a cast stepped foot and has a flaring, thickened rim. The leaf-capped handle, cast in two pieces and seamed vertically, has a scrolled terminus.

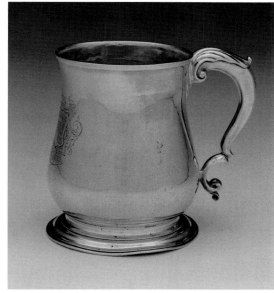

65

66

67

This mug, a standard London form of the 1730s, is engraved with the Faneuil arms.[1] For the silver associated with Peter and Benjamin Faneuil, see cats. 94 and 103.

1. The surface, particularly on the front of the mug, has been buffed, and the date of the engraving, which is otherwise relatively crisp, is unclear.

· 66 ·

TOY SUGAR SCISSORS
London, ca. 1730
Silver
39.819

MARKS: on inside of each tong, maker's mark *IG* (unrecorded)

L. 5.6 cm (2³⁄₁₆ in.); w. 2.5 cm (1 in.)

WEIGHT: 5.7 gm (4 dwt)

PROVENANCE: Anonymous Gift in Memory of Charlotte Beebe Wilbour (1833–1914), December 14, 1939

DESCRIPTION: The fabricated cross-shaped scissors have ring handles and shaped blades with a disk-shaped terminus.

· 67 ·

TOY KETTLE AND STAND
London, ca. 1730
Silver
55.978a-c

MARKS: on underside of kettle, maker's mark *IG* (unrecorded) (repeated under lamp)

H. 9.7 cm (3¹³⁄₁₆ in.); w. 7 cm (2¾ in.); d. 4.8 cm (1⅞ in.)

WEIGHT: 93.5 gm (3 oz)

PROVENANCE: John S. Barnet, Shreve, Crump, and Low, Co., Boston, purchased December 8, 1955, Theodora Wilbour Fund in Memory of Charlotte Beebe Wilbour

DESCRIPTION: The globular kettle is formed from two pieces of sheet, seamed horizontally. It has a shaped spout and a bracket handle. The removable cover has a baluster finial. The kettle rests on a tall stand with three scrolled bracket legs supporting a molded ring. Suspended below is a lamp with a removable cover and reeded rim.

· 68 ·

SALVER

Marked by Thomas Farren (first mark entered 1707, d. 1743)

London, ca. 1730

Silver gilt

61.107

MARKS: struck twice on underside, maker's mark *TF* (Grimwade 2749)

ARMORIALS: engraved on the center of the salver, royal arms of George I

INSCRIPTIONS: scratched on underside, *44=0; 2331*

H. 5.5 cm (2³⁄₁₆ in.); w. 33.8 cm (13⁵⁄₁₆ in.); d. 23.3 cm (9³⁄₁₆ in.)

WEIGHT: 1,366.5 gm (43 oz 19 dwt)

PROVENANCE: property of the Rt. Hon. lord Brownlow, Belton House, Grantham, sold Christie's, London, March 13, 1929, lot 57, purchased Crichton Brothers, London; S. J. Phillips, London, purchased January 11, 1961, Theodora Wilbour Fund in Memory of Charlotte Beebe Wilbour

EXHIBITED: Austin, Texas, University Art Museum, *One Hundred Years of English Silver: 1660–1760*, 1969, cat. 63

PUBLISHED: Edward Wenham, "The Dispersal of the Belton Plate," *International Studio* 93, no. 384 (May 1929), p. 28

DESCRIPTION: The oblong tray has a molded stepped rim with a gadrooned border and an applied mask on each of the four sides. It is formed from heavy sheet and the border is cast, chased, and applied. The surface of the tray is decorated with a

broad border of engraved and chased strapwork and engraved floral patterns. At the center of the tray, the royal coat of arms is engraved. The tray is supported by four scrolled feet in the form of dolphins, cast in halves. The gilding, which covers the underside of the tray and feet, has presumably been renewed.

This rectangular salver, engraved with the royal arms, is one of a pair; its mate is at Colonial Williamsburg.[1] The complex geometry of the heavy cast border and the extraordinary quality of the chased ornament represent the best capabilities of the London trade. The salver is also distinguished by its excellent condition and offers a rare opportunity to appreciate the sparkling effect of the chasing on French and English silver that in most cases has been worn to dullness.

Thomas Farren was subordinate goldsmith to the king from 1723 to 1742 under the principal goldsmiths John Tysoe and Thomas Minors.[2] In this capacity, he carried out orders from the lord chamberlain for plate to be made up for the Jewel House and also had authority to sign for plate from one of the royal residences that had been delivered for repair, cleaning, or engraving. This salver bears only the maker's mark, which is, unusually, struck twice on opposite ends of the underside. The chased decoration on the face may be compared with that on a salver marked by Farren in the Victoria and Albert Museum with similar ornament and full marks for 1733/4.[3] A pair of candlesticks, marked for 1728/9 in the Alan and Simone Hartman collection, have a similar border ornament with masks and, like the present salver, an unusual dense richness.[4]

The salvers were removed from Belton House[5] in 1929 and sold by lord Brownlow. The Brownlow silver, much of which remains in the house, included a large group of royal plate that had come into the family on two occasions, but it is unclear when these salvers were acquired. The first, and certainly larger, group was issued by the Jewel House to Sir John Cust (1718–1770) on his appointment to speaker of the House of Commons in 1761. The lord chamberlain's warrant book for 1762 records that 4,000 ounces of white plate was delivered to Speaker Cust. Included are twenty-eight oval dishes, an epergne, tureens, sauceboats, candlesticks, and salts. Four waiters, described as "large," weighed 383 oz 11 dwt, much larger than the current pair. In 1769, when reelected, the speaker received an addi-

68 (Color Plate VI)

tional 4,000 ounces of plate, including bottle stands, tea wares, and one waiter at 58 ounces (15 ounces heavier than the present example), but not including the present salver. Plate issued by the Jewel House was expected to be returned, but often the debt was cleared or paid back and the silver kept by the recipient. Both lots were discharged in 1770 and remained in the family.[6]

On the second occasion, in 1808, John Cust, baron Brownlow (1779–1853; created earl Brownlow in 1815), purchased plate and jewels from Rundell, Bridge & Rundell. Rundell's, in their dealings with the crown, had begun to reserve silver from the Jewel House that was brought in as a credit against new purchases.[7] Rundell's, recognizing the silver's antiquarian interest, was able to resell it at a higher value, while the crown was credited with its melt value. While some of Rundell's bills to lord Brownlow survive from the 1720s, the salvers do not appear in them.[8]

1. Acc. no. 1961-1, see Davis 1976, pp. 127–28, cat. 129.

2. H. D. W. Sitwell, "The Jewel House and the Royal Goldsmiths," *The Archaeological Journal* 117 (1960), pp. 154–55.

3. Acc. no. M.3-1926, illus. Oman 1965, pls. 125–26.

4. Illus. Hartop 1996, p. 376, cat. 98.

5. See Adrian Tinniswood, *Belton House* (London, 1992), for a concise history of the house and the Cust family, and the chapter by Philippa Glanville on the history of the plate.

6. PRO LC9/44, p. 181r (1762) and 257 (1769). These pieces also appear in a Belton inventory of 1772, where they are listed without weights but described as having the king's arms. Lincolnshire Archives, BNLW 2/2/5/27. Christopher Hartop was extremely kind to have shared this information.

7. See the note preceding the sale of plate from Belton, Christie's, London, May 29, 1963.

8. I am grateful to Adrian Wilkinson, archivist, Lincolnshire Archives, for his assistance.

69

In the years around 1730 most tea tables seem to have been set with a combination of silver, porcelain, and stoneware. Although silver services composed of matching teapot, sugar bowl, waste bowl, and cream jug were made—presumably infrequently—in the first decade of the eighteenth century,[1] mixed services were more usual. Interior views of the 1730s and 1740s show silver teakettles with stands, teapots, spoons, and tongs being used with porcelain cups and saucers, and porcelain or Yixing stoneware teapots.[2] This sugar bowl, modeled after a Chinese or Japanese bowl, has a cover that may be inverted to stand on a molded foot, possibly for use as a spoon tray. The advent in the 1730s and 1740s of European-made porcelain broadened even further the range of wares available for the fashionable tea table. Although the surface of this bowl has been buffed, the engraved armorials have not been worn. The brickwork background may be compared with the engraving on a mug of 1729 marked by the same maker.[3]

1. See Clayton 1985a, pp. 418–20.

2. See paintings by Joseph van Aken, Charles Phillips, William Hogarth, and Gawen Hamilton, illus. Charles Saumarez Smith, *Eighteenth-Century Decoration* (London, 1993), figs. 69, 73, 74, 75, 81.

3. Sold Sotheby's, New York, March 2, 1995, lot 173.

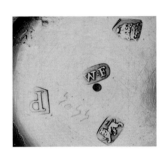

· 69 ·

SUGAR BOWL

Possibly by William Fordham (first mark entered 1707)

London, 1730/1

Silver

33.133

MARKS: on underside of bowl and cover, maker's mark *WF* (Grimwade 3874); lion passant; date letter *P*; leopard's head crowned

ARMORIALS: engraved on side, the coat of arms and crest of Cooke, Gildea Hall, co. Essex, and Gloucestershire, with Bruers, Powell, Powis, or Sutton in pretence

INSCRIPTIONS: scratched on underside, 5505

H. 9.7 cm (3¹³/₁₆ in.); diam. of cover 11.1 cm (4⅜ in.)

WEIGHT: 280.7 gm (9 oz)

PROVENANCE: Anonymous Gift in Memory of Charlotte Beebe Wilbour (1833–1914), March 2, 1933

EXHIBITED: Boston, Museum of Fine Arts, 1933; Boston, Museum of Fine Arts, 1994

DESCRIPTION: The covered bowl forms a flattened sphere resting on a raised stepped foot. The body is raised from sheet, with an applied wire rim. The raised cover has a molded wire rim and at the center a circular applied wire that serves as a handle or, when inverted, as a foot.

· 70 ·

BASKET

Marked by David Willaume (II) (1693–1761)

London, 1731/2

Silver

57.715

MARKS: on underside, leopard's head crowned; date letter *Q*; maker's mark *DW* (Grimwade 514); lion passant (repeated on underside of handle)

ARMORIALS: engraved on top of handle, arms of Hunt impaling Robartes for Thomas Hunt of Mollington Hall, co. Chester, and his wife, Mary, daughter of the Hon. Russell Robartes

H. 21.2 cm (8⅜ in.); w. 31.7 cm (12½ in.); d. 30.6 cm (12¹/₁₆ in.)

WEIGHT: 1,885.3 gm (60 oz 12 dwt)

PROVENANCE: purchased from Thomas Lumley, Ltd., London, November 14, 1957, Anonymous Gift in Memory of Charlotte Beebe Wilbour (1833–1914), by exchange

70

EXHIBITED: New York, James Robinson, Inc., *The Thomas Lumley Collection of Old English Silver*, 1957, cat. 20

DESCRIPTION: The oval basket has flaring sides formed of sheet in a diaper pattern to suggest an open basket weave. The outside surface is engraved at the straps' crossings with rosettes. The base of the basket, a flat sheet, is inset. Two borders of half-round molding are applied to the outer rim, and between them, the walls of the basket are pierced in a pattern of alternating diamonds and panels. The fixed handle is mounted on cast trefoils soldered to the sides of the rim. The handle, which is fabricated and cast, is engraved on its top with diaper and block patterns and a coat of arms.

David Willaume II was connected through his family, his marriage, and his business dealings to a large group of manufacturing goldsmiths flourishing in London in the 1730s. It is likely that, although his father had run his own very productive workshops, David Willaume II was mainly a retailer and banker. Grimwade proposed that many of his suppliers were English, rather than Huguenot manufacturers.[1] This basket belongs to a group of similar models,

almost certainly manufactured in the same shop, but marked by Willaume II, Peter Archambo, and Paul Crespin.[2] One nearly identical basket, marked by Peter Archambo for 1730, was among the purchases of George Booth, earl of Warrington, for Dunham Massey.[3] Archambo was the earl's chief supplier of plate in the 1730s, but by about 1740, Willaume II seems to have received some of his business. The arms engraved on this basket are those of Hunt impaling Robartes for Thomas Hunt, of Mollington Hall, co. Chester, one of the tellers of the Exchequer.

1. Grimwade 1990, p. 704.

2. Two other closely related examples marked by Willaume II are known. One, marked for 1731, was exhibited by Thomas Lumley (New York, James Robinson, Inc., *The Thomas Lumley Collection of Old English Silver*, 1957, cat. 21). The second, marked for 1730, was sold Christie's, London, March 27, 1985, lot 172. A similar basket marked by Crespin for 1727 was sold by Sotheby's, London, July 19, 1982, lot 99.

3. Hayward 1978, fig. 11.

71

· 71 ·

PAIR OF TUMBLERS

Marked by Paul de Lamerie (1688–1751)

London, ca. 1732–39

Silver

35.1619–1620

MARKS: on underside of each, maker's mark *PL* (Grimwade 2203)

ARMORIALS: engraved on side of each, the crest of Graham, probably for James Graham, third duke of Montrose

INSCRIPTIONS: engraved on side of each, a double cipher of the initials *LR*

35.1619: H. 6.9 cm (2¹¹⁄₁₆ in.); diam. of rim 8.9 cm (3½ in.)

35.1620: H. 7 cm (2¾ in.); diam. of rim 8.9 cm (3½ in.)

WEIGHT: 35.1619: 172.9 gm (5 oz 11 dwt). 35.1620: 164.4 gm (5 oz 6 dwt)

PROVENANCE: Crichton Brothers, London, purchased by Frank Brewer Bemis, September 29, 1930, Bequest of Frank Brewer Bemis, November 7, 1935

EXHIBITED: Houston, Texas, Museum of Fine Arts, 1956, cat. 26

DESCRIPTION: The cups, raised from sheet, have straight sides and rounded bases.

Paul de Lamerie continued to use Britannia standard silver long after it ceased to be mandatory in 1720, a sign of the prosperity of his clients. This pair of tumblers bears the first mark that Lamerie entered for sterling silver on March 27, 1732. He continued to use this mark until the Statute of 1738/9 required all goldsmiths to register new punches.[1]

The tumblers bear the monogram *LR*, probably contemporary with their manufacture in the mid-1730s, and the slightly later crest of the dukes of Montrose, probably for James Graham, third duke of Montrose (1755–1836). He held the positions of lord of the Treasury (1783–89), joint paymaster (1789–92), vice president of the Board of Trade (1789), lord justice general (1795–1836), and served as member of Parliament for Richmond (1780–84) and for Great Bedwyn (1784–90). He also held several positions in the royal household, the last of which was lord chamberlain of the household (1821–30).

1. London, Goldsmiths' Hall, 1990, p. 29.

72

· 72 ·

SET OF FOUR TRENCHER SALTS

Marked by James Smith (I) (first mark entered 1718)

London, 1732/3

Silver, parcel gilt

33.134–137

MARKS: on underside of each, lion passant; leopard's head crowned; date letter *R*; maker's mark *IS* (Grimwade 1643)

ARMORIALS: engraved on side of each, crest of Morshead of Trennant Park, co. Cornwall

INSCRIPTIONS: engraved on underside of each, *H/I H* (defaced)

33.134: H. 2.8 cm (1⅛ in.); w. 7.7 cm (3 in.); d. 6 cm (2⅜ in.)

33.135: H. 2.8 cm (1⅛ in.); w. 7.5 cm (2¹⁵⁄₁₆ in.); d. 6.1 cm (2⅜ in.)

33.136: H. 2.8 cm (1⅛ in.); w. 7.6 cm (3 in.); d. 6 cm (2⅜ in.)

33.137: H. 2.8 cm (1⅛ in.); w. 7.6 cm (3 in.); d. 6.1 cm (2⅜ in.)

WEIGHT: 33.134: 56.7 gm (1 oz 16 dwt). 33.135: 56.7 gm (1 oz 16 dwt). 33.136: 56.7 gm (1 oz 16 dwt). 33.137: 56.7 gm (1 oz 16 dwt)

PROVENANCE: Anonymous Gift in Memory of Charlotte Beebe Wilbour (1833–1914), March 2, 1933

EXHIBITED: Boston, Museum of Fine Arts, 1933

DESCRIPTION: Each salt is rectangular, with incurved corners, on a spreading, stepped foot. The gilt oval well for salt is raised and let into the molded rim, which is assembled from eight fabricated panels. A wire is applied to the bottom edge.

· 73 ·

TWO-HANDLED CUP AND COVER

Marked by John Hugh Le Sage (free 1718)
London, 1732/3
Silver
55.462a-b

MARKS: on underside of cup and on bezel of cover, lion passant; maker's mark *IS* (Grimwade 1646); leopard's head crowned; date letter *R*

ARMORIALS: engraved on front, the arms of Conolly impaling Wentworth, for Rt. Hon. William Conolly (d. 1760), co. Castletown, co. Kildare, who married Lady Anne Wentworth

INSCRIPTIONS: engraved on the underside of the cup, 95-5

H. 32.1 cm (12⅝ in.); w. 29.6 cm (11⅝ in.); d. 17.8 cm (7 in.)

WEIGHT: 2,934.2 gm (94 oz 7 dwt)

PROVENANCE: sold Christie's, London, July 4, 1894, lot 188; Edward Steinkopff, sold Christie's, London, July 10, 1935, lot 115; property of Miss Mary Blackwell and J. G. Blackwell, Esq., sold Christie's, London, June 29, 1955, lot 135, [Garrard and Co.] purchased September 15, 1955, Theodora Wilbour Fund in Memory of Charlotte Beebe Wilbour

DESCRIPTION: The bell-shaped body rests on a raised stepped foot. It is raised from heavy sheet, with a thickened rim embellished with an incised line. The lower half of the cup is decorated with applied cast straps incorporating scallops, rosettes, and bellflowers. At the midsection of the cup is a molded wire. The double-scroll handles, cast in two pieces and seamed vertically, are surmounted by leaves. The stepped, domed cover is raised and has applied straps similar to those on the cup. It is surmounted by a baluster finial, cast in sections and seamed horizontally.

John Hugh Le Sage's mark appears on some of the most ambitious plate of the 1720s and 1730s, such as the ewer of 1725 in the Toledo Museum of Art.[1] As a subordinate gold smith to the king he contributed to the ambassadorial service supplied to the fourth earl of Chesterfield, along with his fellow Huguenots David Willaume and Paul Crespin.[2] More conventional domestic plate bearing his mark, such as this cup and a series of baskets,[3] suggests that his business circle included Paul de Lamerie and John White. The cast straps decorating the lower section of this cup appear on a cup of 1736 at Brasenose College and a punch bowl of 1735 marked by John White at Oriel College.[4] The duplication of cast ornament or such elements as handles and spouts on plate was widespread. Workshops may have shared castings or molds, but it seems more likely that pieces with such similar elements were fabricated in a single shop and supplied to goldsmiths finished to be marked as required.

The cup bears the arms of William Conolly impaling those of his wife, Lady Anne Wentworth, daughter of Thomas, first earl of Strafford. Conolly served as speaker of the House of Commons in Ireland. He inherited a fortune, estimated at seventeen thousand pounds a year, from his uncle, also named William "Speaker" Conolly (d. 1729), the son of an innkeeper who became the richest man in Ireland. "Speaker" Conolly had profited from the forfeiture of lands by the Jacobites, and he was appointed a lord justice ten times. Eventually he became speaker of the Irish House of Commons. He acquired vast properties in the north and west of Ireland, as well as his principal residence, Castletown, a massive house designed in the 1720s by the Italian architect Alessandro Galilei. William Conolly and Anne Wentworth had four daughters and one son who in 1758 married Lady Louisa Lennox, third daughter of the second duke of Richmond.

1. Illus. Brett 1986, fig. 763. Also see the covered bowl with the arms of Henry Vane, baron Barnard, sold Christie's, London, December 8, 1994, lot 99, and the pair of candelabra after Thomas Germain's model, now in the Hartman collection, illus. Hartop 1996, pp. 126–31.

2. See the salver of 1737 in the Victoria and Albert Museum, illus. Hayward 1959, pl. 39, and Hartop 1996, pp. 98–101.

3. See Wees 1997, pp. 181–83, cat. 100; Hackenbroch 1969, p. 84, cat. 163.

4. Exh. Oxford, Ashmolean Museum, *A Loan Exhibition of Silver Plate Belonging to the Colleges of the University of Oxford*, 1928, p. 47, cat. 240, fig. 68; p. 46, cat. 232, fig. 64.

73

74

TUREEN

Marked by Charles Kandler (b. 1695, first mark
entered 1727)
London, 1732/3
Silver
65.397a-b

MARKS: on underside and repeated on bezel of
cover; date letter *R;* leopard's head crowned; lion
passant; maker's mark *CK* (Grimwade 341)

ARMORIALS: engraved on both sides of tureen, the
arms and crest of Howard quartering Brotherton,
Warren, and Fitzalan, impaling Gower quartering
Leveson, for Henry Charles Howard, thirteenth
duke of Norfolk (1791–1814)

INSCRIPTIONS: engraved on underside, *144★15;*
scratched, *D7265*

H. 27.8 cm (10¹⁵⁄₁₆ in.); w. 42.7 cm (16¹³⁄₁₆ in.);
d. 25 cm (9¹³⁄₁₆ in.)

WEIGHT: 4,564.4 gm (146 oz 15 dwt)

PROVENANCE: Firestone and Parson Inc., Boston,
purchased March 10, 1965, Theodora Wilbour Fund
in Memory of Charlotte Beebe Wilbour

DESCRIPTION: The oval tureen rests on four feet
modeled as couchant lions that are cast and seamed
vertically. The vessel has a bombé body with chased
vertical fluting in alternating panels. It is formed of
raised sheet, chased around the base, with a second
raised section applied to form the incurved rim. The
domed cover is similarly fluted, with a horizontal
band of chased gadrooning, a cast gadrooned border
forming the rim, and a finial of cast and chased arti-
chokes. The handles, each cast in two pieces, are in
the form of winged griffins. The surfaces of the
tureen and cover are engraved and chased overall
with a fine pattern of shells and clusters of vegetables against a diaper ground. There have been substantial repairs to the base of the tureen.

It has long been recognized that Charles
Kandler was one of the most innovative and
stylistically adventurous makers working in
London in the 1730s, but the details of his
biography and marks remained uncertain.[1]
Recent research has resolved some key questions about his identity and training. The distinctly German character of Kandler's work,
often observed, has been borne out by the discovery that he was indeed the older brother of
Johann Joachim Kändler (1706–1775), the great
modeler for the Meissen porcelain factory. In

1710 he was apprenticed in Dresden to the
court goldsmith Johann Jacob Irminger
(d. 1726), who that year had been appointed
artistic director of Meissen.[2] Kandler entered
his first mark in London in 1727 and for a time
was in partnership with James Murray, about
whom little is known. Sometime in the late
1730s Kandler may have left London, for in
1735 his business was taken over by another
member of the family, Charles Frederick
Kandler.[3]

This tureen, an awkward marriage of
heraldic motifs applied to a baroque carcass,
exemplifies the un-English nature of Charles
Kandler's work. The bombé profile with vertical panels of reverse ribs was a feature of both
German silver[4] and porcelain.[5] Kandler produced many variations of the form, with and
without figural feet or finials, from about 1728.[6]
The panels of engraved and chased ornament
on the body, filled with shells and symmetrical
scrolls, clusters of game, vegetables, and fruit
against a diaper ground, appear on a large
number of Kandler's pieces and were probably
decorated by a specialist within Kandler's shop.[7]
Most of the other examples of this type of decoration, however, consist only of symmetrical
panels of scrolls and shells (similar to the *Laub
und Bandelwerk* ornament on Meissen porcelain
in the early period). The panels of the present
tureen are filled with softly rendered organic
forms—rabbits, ducks, and vegetables—possibly
after a printed source.

The handles and feet of the tureen are modeled in the form of the supporters of the earls
of Rockingham: a lion and a griffin ducally
gorged. The tureen must have been made for
Lewis Watson (ca. 1714–1745), second earl of
Rockingham, who succeeded his grandfather
in 1724. He took his seat in the House of
Lords in 1736 and the following year was
appointed lord lieutenant of Kent. His marriage in 1736 to a cousin, Catharine, sister and
co-heir of Sir Henry Furnese, brought a fortune of two hundred thousand pounds. He was
succeeded in 1745 by his brother Thomas (b.
ca. 1715) who died the same year, only three
months after his succession. With his death the
earldom of Rockingham became extinct, and
the succes-sion passed to a cousin, Thomas
Watson-Wentworth (ca. 1690–1750), who had

74. (Color Plate VII)

inherited through his mother vast estates in Yorkshire. The marquess of Rockingham, a title he assumed in 1746, bought a prodigious quantity of plate (see also cat. 96), including a tureen by George Wickes, now at Colonial Williamsburg,[8] with handles modeled as griffins, analogous to the present tureen.[9] The heraldic ornament is carried one step further on the Wickes tureen, which has a finial in the form of the family crest, a griffin passant. The Wickes tureen invites the question as to whether the Kandler tureen might also have originally had a heraldic finial. The artichoke and cauliflower finial is an interruption of the iconographic scheme and seems to be modeled and chased by a different hand.[10] At some point the tureen may have been returned by the family to a silversmith,[11] and it was subsequently owned by the Howards, another family that patronized the Kandlers throughout the eighteenth century.[12] Probably about 1814 it was engraved with the arms of Henry Charles Howard, thirteenth duke of Norfolk (1791–1856), and it may be that a heraldic finial was replaced at that time.[13]

1. See Norman M. Penzer, "The Jerningham-Kandler Wine Cooler, Part I," *Apollo* 64, no. 379 (September 1956), pp. 80–82, and Norman M. Penzer, "The Jerningham-Kandler Wine Cooler, Part II," *Apollo* 64, no. 380 (September 1956), pp. 111–15; Grimwade 1990, p. 567; Phillipa Glanville, "Silver Torah Scrolls by Kandler," *National Arts Collections Fund: Annual Review* (London, 1992), pp. 27–28; Peter Cameron, "Henry Jerningham, the Kandlers, and the Client Who Changed His Mind," *Silver Society Journal* 8 (1996), pp. 495–99; Hartop 1996,

pp. 52–53.

2. Glanville, "Silver Torah Scrolls," p. 28, referring to research by Rainer Rückert.

3. Christopher Hartop (Hartop 1996, p. 55 n. 37) proposes that Charles Frederick Kandler may be the younger brother of Charles Kandler. For works by Frederick Kandler, see cat. 139.

4. For example, a tureen by Johann Ludwig Biller (II), Augsburg, 1731, Berlin, Kunstgewerbemuseum, illus. Stefan Bursche, *Tafelzier des Barok* (Munich, 1974), pl. 157; a pair of tureens by Nicholas Ostertag, Augsburg, ca. 1730, sold Christie's, Geneva, November 19, 1991, lot 128.

5. See models by Johann Joachim Kändler, illus. Bursche, *Tafelzier*, pls. 170–71.

6. For plain examples, see a tureen of 1728, illus. Brett 1986, fig. 827; another of 1728, sold Christie's, London, October 28, 1964, lot 95; another of 1729, illus. Clayton 1985b, fig. 2. For an example with figural handles, see the Meynell tureens, ca. 1735, sold Sotheby's, New York, June 16, 1982, lot 77.

7. For example, see the coffeepot in the Clark Art Institute, illus. Wees 1997, pp. 289–91, cat. 194. Beth Wees (p. 290 nn. 2–4) lists other examples of this category of decoration on Kandler's work.

8. Acc. no. 1972-245, illus. Davis 1976, pp. 120–21, cat. 123.

9. Some of the plate was sold Christie's, London, June 9, 1948.

10. The current weight is 2 ounces more than the scratch weight.

11. Charles Kandler's successor, Frederick Kandler, supplied considerable plate to the marquesses of Rockingham; see the examples sold by the earl of Fitzwilliam, Christie's, London, June 9, 1948, lots 87, 104, 107, 108, 126, 129, 131.

12. See cat. 139. The engraving appears to date from the early part of the nineteenth century, possibly from the marriage of Henry Charles Howard to Charlotte Sophia, daughter of George Granville, first duke of Sutherland, in 1814. It was certainly engraved before Howard succeeded to the dukedom in 1842.

13. For the thirteenth duke of Norfolk, see John Martin Robinson, *The Dukes of Norfolk* (Oxford, 1982), pp. 195–202.

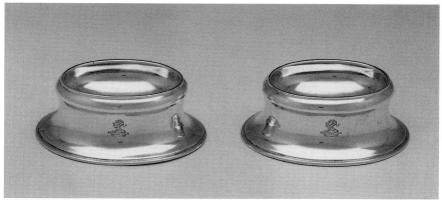

75

· 75 ·

PAIR OF TRENCHER SALTS

Probably marked by James Smith (I) (first mark entered 1718)[1]

London, 1733/4

Silver

42.12a-b

MARKS: on underside of each, leopard's head crowned; date letter *S*; lion passant; maker's mark *IS* (Grimwade 1643)

ARMORIALS: engraved on the side of each, the crest of Moore, of Ireland

42.12a: H. 3.2 cm (1¼ in.); w. 8.3 cm (3¼ in.); d. 6.6 cm (2⅝ in.)

42.12b: H. 3.2 cm (1¼ in.); w. 8.2 cm (3¼ in.); d. 6.6 cm (2⅝ in.)

WEIGHT: 42.12a: 70.9 gm (2 oz 6 dwt). 42.12b: 73.7 gm (2 oz 7 dwt)

PROVENANCE: Anonymous Gift in Memory of Charlotte Beebe Wilbour (1833–1914), January 8, 1942

DESCRIPTION: The oval bowl of each salt rests on a plain oval spreading foot. The bowl is raised and inset into the base, which is fabricated in two sections, seamed vertically.

1. The mark might also be interpreted as that of James Stone (first mark entered 1726) (Grimwade 1649).

· 76 ·

TWO-HANDLED CUP AND COVER

Marked by Paul Crespin (1694–1770)

London, 1733/4

Silver

1978.177a-b

MARKS: on underside of cup, maker's mark *PC* (similar to Grimwade 2143a);[1] lion passant (repeated on bezel of cover); leopard's head crowned (repeated on bezel of cover); date letter *S* (repeated on bezel of cover)

INSCRIPTIONS: engraved in cartouche on one side, initials *HF* in double cipher; engraved in cartouche on other side, *The TRUSTEES in Acknowledgment of the Judgment Integrity & Conduct of Mr. H Flitcroft in Designing and Building the Parish Church of St GILES'S in the Fields have Presented him with this Cup. 1734*; scratched on under side of base, *138=2*

H. 37.1 cm (14⅝ in.); w. 34.9 cm (13¾ in.); d. 21.3 cm (8⅜ in.)

WEIGHT: 4,280.8 gm (137 oz 13 dwt)

PROVENANCE: presented to Henry Flitcroft in 1734; purchased by Ogden Mills Bishop by descent to his great-nephew, James Peabody, Theodora Wilbour Fund in Memory of Charlotte Beebe Wilbour and Gift of Mrs. James Peabody, May 10, 1978

EXHIBITED: Boston, Museum of Fine Arts, 1994

DESCRIPTION: The bell-shaped body rests on a domed, stepped foot with a gadrooned rim that is constructed of cast and raised sections. The body was raised from heavy sheet. A molded wire divides the body at the midsection. The lower half is decorated with cast and chased straps against a matted ground. The straps incorporate portrait medallions in the antique style, shells, and bellflowers. On the upper half of the body an applied cast cartouche, contained in a matted ground and composed of scrolls, fruit, and foliage, encases an inscription on one side and a monogram on the other. The ear-shaped handles, cast in two pieces, terminate in scrolls below the wire and have acanthus caps. The domed, stepped lid has a baluster finial, cast in two vertical pieces. It is raised in a single piece with an applied bezel and cast gadrooned rim. The dome is decorated with cast alternating straps similar in design to those on the body of the cup, but smaller in scale. They are set against a richly matted ground.

This cup was presented by the trustees of the church of St. Giles in the Fields to the architect

Henry Flitcroft (1697–1769) in 1734. Flitcroft was a protégé of lord Burlington, for whom he was working as a journeyman carpenter at Burlington House when he is said to have fallen from a scaffold and broken his leg.[2] The earl paid particular attention to Flitcroft's recovery and, impressed by his drawing skills, employed him. "Burlington Harry," as he became known, held a series of positions in the Office of Works, following William Kent in 1748 as master mason and deputy surveyor.

The construction of St. Giles was part of a broad program authorized in 1711 to build fifty new parish churches at public expense. Flitcroft competed with James Gibbs, Edward Shepherd, and Nicholas Hawksmoor for the commission.[3] In 1731 he signed a contract for the project, for which he was both designer and builder. The building, almost certainly influenced by the design of St. Martins in the Fields, rigidly follows the Palladian formula, and the facade, almost devoid of ornament, is austere. While extensive drawings, notes, and even Flitcroft's model for the building survive,[4] there is no mention in the vestry minutes of the decision to commission this cup.[5]

The cup is one of a large group of closely related examples that suggests the interdependence of the London goldsmiths. Cups of 1732 marked by Peter Archambo,[6] Benjamin Godfrey,[7] and Bowles Nash[8] appear to have the same cast strapwork design of the cover and body of the cup and vary slightly in proportion, size, and weight. Cups of 1731 and 1736 marked by Simon Pantin[9] and Charles Hatfield[10] have an alternative design in one strapwork panel, and two others of 1732 and 1734 by John Tuite[11] and Edward Feline[12] have more elaborate faces incorporated into the straps. Only the present cup has the applied molded surround for the cartouche on the body. Although the motifs of this embellishment are asymmetrical, the style is not truly rococo.[13] It seems likely that these groups were executed in the same workshop, and that the business was divided between English and Huguenot makers.

1. The mark lacks the pellet shown in Grimwade 2143a.

2. H. M. Colvin, *A Biographical Dictionary of British Architects* (London, 1954), pp. 309–10.

3. H. M. Colvin, "Fifty New Churches," *The Architectural Review* 107, no. 639 (March 1950), p. 192. See also John Parton, *Some Account of the Hospital and Parish of St. Giles-in-the-Fields, Middlesex* (London, 1822).

4. I am grateful for the help of Tim Knox at the British Architectural Library, where several designs are housed. The model is kept at the church.

5. The Reverend Gordon Taylor, rector, generously provided information on the history of the church and its documentation and searched the vestry minutes on my behalf.

6. Sold Christie's, London, February 1, 1978, lot 181.

7. Sold Christie's, New York, April 15, 1997, lot 334.

8. St. John's College, Cambridge, exh. Cambridge, Fitzwilliam Museum, *Cambridge Plate*, 1975, cat. by R. A. Crighton, p. 42, cat. 2H8.

9. Sold Christie's, London, November 24, 1976, lot 54.

10. Sold Sotheby's, London, October 25, 1973, lot 170.

11. Sold Sotheby's, London, October 25, 1973, lot 160.

12. Sold Christie's, London, July 5, 1972, lot 77.

13. The applied scrolls and grapevines might be compared with those on the Jerningham-Kandler wine cistern. Peter Cameron, "Henry Jerninghan, Charles Frederick Kandler, and the Client Who Changed His Mind," *Silver Society Journal* 8 (Autumn 1996), pp. 487–501.

76 (Color Plate VIII)

135

77

· 77 ·

WAITER

Marked by Paul de Lamerie (1688–1751)
London, 1734/5
Silver
1988.282

MARKS: on underside, leopard's head crowned; date letter *T*; maker's mark *PL* (Grimwade 2203); lion passant

ARMORIALS: engraved in center, the arms of Sir Theodore Janssen (ca. 1658–1748), and his wife, Williamsa, daughter of Sir Robert Henley, of the Grange, Hampshire. Engraved in four corners, the crest of Janssen

H. 2.2 cm (⅞ in.); w. 14.6 cm (5¼ in.); d. 14.5 cm (5¼ in.)

WEIGHT: 343 gm (11 oz)

PROVENANCE: Bequest of S. Sydney DeYoung, April 27, 1988

DESCRIPTION: The square waiter rests on four scrolled feet and has a molded, flared rim with shaped corners. The body and rim are engraved with strapwork, scrolls, and flowers. The waiter is formed from sheet with an applied, cast rim and cast feet.

Small square waiters (also called salvers) such as this one were used for serving drinks. They were often supplied as part of a toilet service[1] or for use in the dining room, sometimes with a matching, larger salver.[2] The form seems to have been a speciality of Lamerie's shop and a large number survive, ranging in date from about 1720 to 1735.[3]

This waiter is one of two (see cat. 81) given to the Museum in 1988 with a group of American silver, all traditionally said to have belonged to John Quincy Adams. It is engraved with the arms of Janssen, probably for one of the sons of Theodore Janssen, a Dutch-born merchant and director of the South Seas Company who was created baronet in 1714. His oldest son, Abraham Janssen (d. 1765), was member of Parliament for Dorchester from 1720 to 1722, died unmarried, and was succeeded by his brother Henry (d. 1766). Henry and his younger brother, Robert, established themselves in Paris, where they are recorded as having owned a large and important collection of plate, now identified as the Orléans-Penthièvre service.[4] Another son, Stephen Theodore (d. 1777), served as lord mayor of London and was the owner of York House, the Battersea enamel factory.

As Beth Wees has commented, the design of the engraved cartouches on many of these waiters follows a standard formula.[5] The Treby toilet service in the Ashmolean represents the very finest engraving produced by Lamerie's shop.[6] This cartouche, though small in scale and greatly simplified, includes a baroque surround with a rusticated background, flanked by winged figures trailing a laurel garland. Though not necessarily by the same hand as the Treby engraving, it certainly follows a design that remained in circulation for more than a decade.

1. See, for example, the Treby service, by Lamerie, illus. London, Goldsmiths' Hall, 1990, pp. 57–63, cat. 27.
2. See the set in the Hartman collection, illus. Hartop 1996, pp. 340–41, cat. 84.
3. Wees (1997, p. 423 n. 3) lists many. See also

Houston, Texas, Museum of Fine Arts, 1956, cat. 6; Christie's, London, July 11, 1960, lot 128; Christie's, London, November 29, 1961, lots 57 and 111; Christie's, London, February 15, 1967, lot 45; Sotheby's, New York, February 28, 1991, lot 221; Sotheby's, New York, October 28, 1992, lot 309.

4. See Sotheby's, New York, November 13, 1996, pp. 38–41.

5. Wees 1997, p. 423.

6. See n. 1.

1758, there are small variations in the form of the spout, the profile of the cover, or the size.[1] This example is smaller than most.

1. James Lomax (Lomax 1992, pp. 121–28) recorded several versions relating to two coffeepots at Temple Newsam. Other examples include a pot of 1727, illus. Mary L. Kennedy, *The Esther Thomas Hoblitzelle Collection of English Silver* (Austin, 1957), p. 121, pl. 21; another of 1737 sold Christie's, New York, October 18, 1989, lot 126; another of 1728, sold Christie's, London, December 6, 1989, lot 217.

· 78 ·

COFFEEPOT

Marked by Gabriel Sleath (1674–1756)7

London, 1735/6

Silver, ivory

35.1626

MARKS: on underside, maker's mark *GS* (Grimwade 890) (repeated on underside of cover); leopard's head crowned; date letter *V*; lion passant (repeated on underside of cover)

ARMORIALS: engraved on side, the arms of Polhill impaling Shelley, for Charles Polhill who married (ca. 1760) Tryphena, fifth and youngest daughter of Sir John Shelley, fourth baronet of Michaelgrove, co. Sussex

INSCRIPTIONS: engraved on underside, *18=14*

H. 19.3 cm (7⅝ in.); w. 18.7 cm (7⅜ in.); d. 9.6 cm (3¾ in.)

WEIGHT: 589.7 gm (18 oz 19 dwt)

PROVENANCE: Arthur S. Vernay, Inc., New York, purchased by Frank Brewer Bemis, December 1, 1919, Bequest of Frank Brewer Bemis, November 7, 1935

DESCRIPTION: The tapering cylindrical pot is formed from sheet, seamed behind the handle. The inset base has an applied molded rim. The curved spout, cast in two vertical halves, has a bell-shaped drop. The ivory handle, presumably a replacement for the original, is mounted on cast scrolled sockets opposite the spout. The hinged, domed cover, which is cast, has a baluster finial. The surface has been highly polished.

Gabriel Sleath seems to have specialized in plain coffeepots with a tapering profile. Among many examples ranging in date from 1723 to

78

· 79 ·

BASKET

Marked by Peter Archambo (I) (first mark entered
1721, d. 1767)
London, 1735/6
Silver
58.1010

MARKS: on underside, maker's mark *PA* (Grimwade
2127); lion passant; date letter *V*; leopard's head
crowned

ARMORIALS: engraved in the center of the base,
surrounded by the motto and ribbon of the Garter,
the arms and motto of the dukes of Argyll, for John
Campell, second duke (1678–1743), and behind the
arms, two honorable badges, one for the office of
hereditary great master of the household in
Scotland, the other for the office of lord justice general of Scotland. The Garter motto and a monogram
are engraved on the handle.

H. 25.3 cm (9¹⁵⁄₁₆ in.); w. 37.1 cm (14⅝ in.);
d. 31.1 cm (12/in.)

WEIGHT: 2,565.7 gm (82 oz 10 dwt)

PROVENANCE: Miss Lucy Hope, sold Christie's,
London, August 20, 1941, lot 81, purchased by
Thomas Lumley, Ltd., London; Dr. Christophe
Bernoulli, Basel, Switzerland, purchased
November 13, 1958, Theodora Wilbour Fund in
Memory of Charlotte Beebe Wilbour

DESCRIPTION: The oval basket has flaring pierced
sides imitating woven wicker. It rests on a plain
molded foot formed from seamed sheet. The base of
the basket, formed from sheet, is plain, and an
applied wire covers its juncture with the sides. The
interlacing straps forming the sides of the basket are
formed from sheet, pierced and engraved. The flaring rim is bound with a thick applied band imitating wrapped wicker, and the edge of the basket is
finished with applied twisted wire. The bail handle,
cast and fabricated, is attached by two circular
hinges supported on cast trefoils. The top of the
handle is engraved with a basketweave pattern and
encloses a cartouche. The join of the hinges to the
rim has been damaged and reinforced with large
patches on the underside of the rim.

Peter Archambo's mark appears on a wide
range of plate that is generally sound in its
construction if conservative in design. Among
Archambo's loyal clients was George Booth,
earl of Warrington, whose purchases for

Dunham Massey are known in part through
their remarkable survival and in part through
the earl's meticulous inventory.[1] A basket of
1730 at Dunham Massey that is marked by
Archambo does not relate in design to the present basket but follows almost precisely the
design of a basket in this collection marked by
David Willaume II (see cat. 70).[2] Pierced baskets imitating wickerwork much closer to the
duke of Argyll's basket bear the marks of many
different Huguenot makers, including Paul
de Lamerie,[3] John Hugh Le Sage,[4] David
Willaume,[5] and Aymé Videau.[6] One shop may
have specialized in fabricating certain models,
which were subsequently marked by various
members of the trade.

The second duke of Argyll had a long and
turbulent career in the military, a calling to
which he is said to have been drawn as a
youth. He succeeded his father as duke in 1703
and in 1705 was nominated lord high commissioner to the Scottish Parliament, where he was
a passionate advocate of the union with
England and a supporter of the Protestant line.
He served during the War of Spanish Succession in Flanders in the campaign of 1706 with
the duke of Marlborough, a bitter rival. In 1712
he was appointed commander in chief of the
forces of Scotland and was credited with a vic-
tory in 1715 against the Jacobite armies at
Sherriffmuir, which greatly outnumbered him.
In 1719 he was created first duke of Greenwich. His favor at court was variable, but he
was admired for his rhetorical powers and sin-
cerity. His first wife, Mary, daughter of Thomas
Browne, died in 1717, and he subsequently
married Jane, daughter of Thomas Warburton,
by whom he had five daughters. Argyll died in
1743, and the duchess commissioned a grand
monument to him for West-minster Abbey.
Both John Michael Rysbrack and Louis-
François Roubiliac submitted drawings and
models for the project, which was awarded to
Roubiliac; it was one of his first major commissions.[7]

1. Hayward 1978, pp. 32–39.
2. Ibid., p. 37, fig. 11.
3. Exh. London, Goldsmiths' Hall, 1990, p. 101,
cat. 57.

79

4. The Metropolitan Museum of Art, illus.
Hackenbrock 1969, p. 84, cat. 163.

5. Sold Christie's, London, March 6, 1991, lot 136.

6. Sold Sotheby's, London, June 2, 1992, lot 187; see
also Brett 1986, p. 204, fig. 877.

7. A maquette by Rysbrack is in the collection of
the Museum of Fine Arts (acc. no. 1997.142). See
Katherine Eustace, *Michael Rysbrack, Sculptor
1694–1770* (Bristol, 1982), and Malcolm Baker,
"Roubiliac's Argyll Monument and the
Interpretation of Eighteenth-Century Sculptors'
Designs," *Burlington Magazine* 134 (December 1992),
pp. 785–97.

· 80 ·

PAIR OF SAUCEBOATS

Marked by Phillips Garden (first mark entered 1738) and Richard Pargeter (first mark entered 1730)

London, 1736/7 and 1753/4

Silver

19.1384–1385

MARKS: 19.1384: on underside, leopard's head crowned; lion passant; maker's mark *PG* (Grimwade 2181); date letter *s*. 19.1385: on underside, maker's mark *RP* (Grimwade 2405); lion passant; leopard's head crowned; date letter *a*

INSCRIPTIONS: engraved on the underside of each, *From/Mrs. Anna Winslow,/To her Nephew/Joshua Green/1802*

19.1384: H. 10 cm (3¹⁵⁄₁₆ in.); w. 20.9 cm (8¼ in.); d. 10.8 cm (4¼ in.)

19.1385: H. 9.8 cm (3⅞ in.); w. 20.4 cm (8 in.); d. 12.2 cm (4¹³⁄₁₆ in.)

WEIGHT: 19.1384: 340.2 gm (10 oz 19 dwt). 19.1385: 354.4 gm (11 oz 8 dwt)

PROVENANCE: Anna Winslow (1728–1816) by 1802, Joshua Green (1764–1847), by descent to Samuel Abbott Green (1830–1918), Bequest of Samuel A. Green, December 4, 1919

DESCRIPTION: Each sauceboat has a low oval body, raised from sheet, a cut, shaped rim, and a broad curved pouring lip. The body rests on three cast legs with shell mounts and applied shell feet. The cast handle is formed of a series of leaf-capped scrolls.

These modest sauceboats, separated by seventeen years in date and marked by different makers, were paired sometime before 1802. Anna Green married her cousin, Joshua Winslow, a Boston merchant in 1758.[1] The Green family had come to New England in 1635 and in the mid-eighteenth century was established in Boston on Hanover Street. Joshua Green, to whom Anna Winslow presented the sauceboats in 1802, graduated from Harvard in 1784 and was a judge of the county court. By his first wife, Mary, daughter of David Moseley of Westfield, Massachusetts, he had a son, Joshua (1797–1875), who in 1824 married Eliza Lawrence of Groton, Massachusetts.[2] Their son, Samuel Abbott Green, a medical doctor and genealogist, bequeathed the sauceboats to the Museum of Fine Arts.

1. Anna Winslow is recorded on a deed of October 20, 1772, with Joshua Green (merchant) and his wife, Hannah, Edward Green (mariner) and his wife, Mary, Ebenezer Storer (merchant) and his wife, Elizabeth, Frances Green (merchant) and his wife, Susanna, and Joshua Winslow and his wife, Anna. The deed was transferred to John Hancock (Massachusetts Historical Society Thwing Index).

2. G. Andrews Moriarty, "Hon. Samuel Abbott Green," *New England Historical and Genealogical Register* 74 (1920), pp. 243–45.

80

81

· 81 ·

WAITER
Marked by Paul de Lamerie (1688–1751)
London, 1736/7
Silver
1988.283

MARKS: on underside, leopard's head crowned; date letter *a*; maker's mark *PL* (Grimwade 2203); lion passant

ARMORIALS: engraved on center of salver, the arms of a son of Sir Theodore Janssen (ca. 1658–1748), probably Stephen (d. 1777) and his wife, Catherine, daughter of Col. Soulgere of Antigua (married before 1757); engraved in four corners, the crest of Janssen

H. 2.3 cm (⅞ in.); w. 14.6 cm (5¾ in.); d. 14.5 cm (5¾ in.)

WEIGHT: 297.7 gm (9 oz 11 dwt)

PROVENANCE: Bequest of S. Sydney DeYoung, April 27, 1988

DESCRIPTION: The square waiter rests on four scrolled feet and has a molded flared rim with shaped corners. The body and rim are engraved with strapwork, scrolls, and flowers. The waiter is formed from sheet with an applied, cast rim and cast feet.

For comments, see cat. 77.

· 82 ·

BASKET
Marked by Benjamin Godfrey (first mark entered 1732, d. ca. 1741)
London, 1738/9
Silver gilt
60.946

MARKS: on underside, lion passant (repeated on underside of handle); maker's mark *BG* (Grimwade 170) (repeated on underside of handle); date letter *c*; leopard's head crowned

ARMORIALS: engraved in cartouche in center of basket, arms of Harley impaling Archer for Edward Harley, fourth earl of Oxford (1726–1790), who married Susanna, daughter of William Archer of Welford, co. Berkshire

H. 31.8 cm (12½ in.); w. 37.1 cm (14⅝ in.); d. 38.4 cm (15⅛ in.)

WEIGHT: 3,019 gm (97 oz)

PROVENANCE: Thomas Lumley, Ltd., London, purchased September 21, 1960, Theodora Wilbour Fund in Memory of Charlotte Beebe Wilbour

EXHIBITED: London, Victoria and Albert Museum, 1984, cat. G8; Boston, Museum of Fine Arts, 1994

PUBLISHED: Kathryn C. Buhler, "Some Recent Accessions," *Bulletin of the Museum of Fine Arts* 58, nos. 313–14 (1960), pp. 94–95; Gruber 1982, p. 218

DESCRIPTION: The oval basket rests on a base of cast foliate openwork, the larger leaves of which form four feet. The body of the basket is formed from sheet, and the base and rim are cast in sections and were pinned to the body before soldering. The bottom of the interior is covered in an engraved and chased cartouche of foliate-and-scroll pattern with a matted ground at its edges. The sides of the basket are pierced with trellis, foliate, and shell patterns. The flaring rim has cast foliate openwork that includes shells, rockwork, and flowers, with the head of a winged putto at either end. The curved swing handle is supported by cast caryatid figures and decorated on the top with an engraved and flat-chased cartouche. The gilding has been renewed.

Benjamin Godfrey is one of many sparsely documented goldsmiths who seems to have been intimately tied to the group of foreign craftsmen in the London trade through personal and professional relationships. Although there is no record of his apprenticeship,[1] he was working in 1724 for the jeweler John Craig, George Wickes's early partner.[2] He is presumed

to have worked for Elizabeth Buteux (widow of Abraham, and probably the daughter of Simon Pantin), whom he married in 1732, the same year he entered his first mark. The work bearing his mark ranges from purely conventional to the eccentric.[3]

This basket is distinguished by its size and weight—roughly twice that of average baskets of the late 1730s. The substantial weight of this basket is accounted for by the heavy, dense design of the cast foot and border, with its lively scrolls suggesting seaweed. By the late 1730s the vocabulary of rococo silver design was fully developed, and there are half a dozen distinctive "shop styles" that can readily be classified; this basket does not fit neatly into any one group. The agitated, abstract foliage with its rippling border is without precise parallel. Its affinity to German sources has been noted by Philippa Glanville,[4] but there seems to be a precise parallel neither among English or German objects nor among published design books. The chaser has been particularly ambitious in the interpretation of the gnarled shell-like passages and the coral (or waterfalls?) at the base of the handle mounts, using different tools to ensure the dynamic movement. Most unusually, there are engraved details in the midst of the chased passages, in which the edges of simple scrolls are outlined. A kettle of 1739 marked by Eliza Godfrey shares some of this dense ornament and a similar sensibility.[5] Its richly modeled cartouche is taken from a design by Jacques de Lajoüe.[6]

The engraving of the coat of arms on this basket was added after Edward Harley's succession to the peerage; he was created earl of Oxford in 1755. The basket may have been returned by its first owner to Godfrey who would have sent it to his engraver when he sold it as secondhand plate to Edward Harley. The engraver made a particular effort to integrate the inserted arms into the chased rocaille ornament on the base of the basket, repeating the shell scrolls under the motto, for example. The cartouche at the center of the handle has had engraving removed and does not bear the Harley arms. The same hand must have engraved the arms of the earl of Anglsey on a cup and cover of 1738 by Benjamin

Godfrey in the Gilbert collection,[7] as well as the arms on a group of other pieces marked by Eliza Godfrey as late as 1753.[8] This group may have been engraved by Stent, who signed a trade card for Thomas Payne, a tallow chandler, that shows similar conventions in the format and the treatment of drapery and scrolls.[9]

Edward Harley, fourth earl of Oxford, inherited a diminished estate. His father's cousin, the second earl and great bibliophile, was so profligate a collector that he was reduced to selling Wimpole Hall in 1738 to Phillip Yorke, first earl of Hardwick.[10]

1. Grimwade 1990, p. 524.

2. Barr 1980, pp. 24–25.

3. See a pair of candelabra with stems in the form of kneeling blackamoors (marked by Benjamin Godfrey, London, 1739), illus. Clayton 1985a, p. 143, fig. 3.

4. Exh. London, Victoria and Albert Museum, *Rococo: Art and Design in Hogarth's England*, 1984, p. 110.

5. Sold Sotheby's, New York, December 13, 1984, lot 178.

6. I am grateful to Kevin Tierney for this suggestion. See Marianne Roland Michel, *Lajoüe et l'art rocaille* (Paris, 1984), fig. 338.

7. Illus. Schroder 1988a, p. 235, cat. 59.

8. See a cup, maker's mark only of Eliza Godfrey, exh. London, Timothy Schroder, Ltd., *An Inaugural Exhibition*, 1989, p. 31, cat. 20; an epergne, 1753/4, marked by Eliza Godfrey, exh. London, Partridge Fine Arts, *Recent Acquisitions*, 1998, cat. by Lucy Morton, p. 21, cat. 6.

9. Illus. Ambrose Heal, *London Tradesmen's Cards of the XVIII Century* (London, 1925), pl. 89.

10. James Lees-Milne, *Earls of Creation* (London, 1962), pp. 212–18.

82 (Color Plate IX)

· 83 ·

COFFEEPOT

Marked by Edward Feline (free 1721)
London, 1739/40
Silver, wood
33.142

MARKS: on underside, maker's mark *EF* (Grimwade 587) (repeated inside cover); lion passant (repeated inside cover); leopard's head crowned; date letter *d*

ARMORIALS: engraved on one side, the arms of a spinster member of the Hickes family of Shipston-on-Stour, co. Worcester; engraved on other side the crest of the same; engraved on cover, an unidentified later crest (a wyvern with wings addorsed)

INSCRIPTIONS: on underside, *27=18*

H. 24.9 cm (9¹³⁄₁₆ in.); w. 20.4 cm (8 in.); diam. of base 10.1 cm (4 in.)

WEIGHT: 898.7 gm (28 oz 18 dwt)

PROVENANCE: Anonymous Gift in Memory of Charlotte Beebe Wilbour (1833–1914), March 2, 1933

EXHIBITED: Boston, Museum of Fine Arts, 1933

DESCRIPTION: The raised pear-shaped body rests on a spreading, domed circular foot. The foot is constructed of a cast base joined to a raised midsection. The curved spout, cast in two pieces and seamed vertically, has an acanthus leaf at the tip and a molded drop at the base. A band of engraving encircles the neck of the pot just below the applied wire rim. The double-scrolled wooden handle has faceted mounts, the upper of scrolled foliage and the terminus of scroll form covered by a leaf. The hinged, stepped, domed lid has a baluster finial. The hinge is set into the molding wire.

By the late 1730s a client in the market for a coffeepot had a broad range of designs from which to choose, ranging from highly sculptural models with elaborate chasing or casting to plainer and less costly pots, such as this one. The purchaser of this pot opted for a distinctive engraved cartouche to contain her arms and, unusually for a woman, included a crest on the reverse. The soft rendering of the shells, bent reeds, and inclusion of flowing water appear in the engraved decoration of pieces marked by Lamerie during the same period.[1] Among the printed sources available to engravers that showed these motifs were the designs of Jacques de Lajoüe (1687–1761).[2] The band of Régence engraving around the neck,

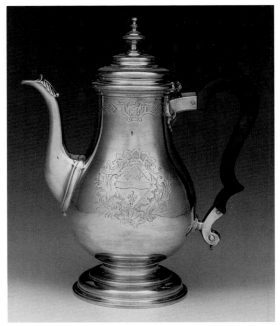

83

more characteristic of the late 1720s, is not in keeping with the rococo cartouche.

1. For example, see the Newdigate centerpiece, Victoria and Albert Museum, acc. no. 149-1919, illus. Oman 1965, fig. 134; a salver in the Hartman collection, illus. Hartop 1996, p. 361, cat. 92; a salver in the Gilbert collection, illus. Schroder 1988a, p. 243, cat. 62.

2. See Marianne Roland Michel, *Lajoüe et l'art rocaille* (Paris, 1984), figs. 211, 214.

· 84 ·

MUG

Marked by John Gamon (first mark entered 1727)
London, ca. 1740
Silver
42.218

MARKS: on underside, maker's mark partially obliterated, probably *IG* (similar to Grimwade 1323)

ARMORIALS: engraved on front, an unidentified coat of arms (a lion rampant, impaling, three tuns) impaling those of Orleton, or possibly Athull, Brickman, or Crowner

H. 9.6 cm (3¾ in.); diam. of rim 6.8 cm (2¹¹⁄₁₆ in.)

WEIGHT: 206.9 gm (6 oz 13 dwt)

PROVENANCE: The Philip Leffingwell Spalding Collection, given in his Memory by Katherine

Ames Spalding and Philip Spalding, Oakes Ames Spalding, Hobart Ames Spalding, April 9 and 16, 1942

PUBLISHED: Edwin J. Hipkiss, *The Philip Leffingwell Spalding Collection of Early American Silver* (Cambridge, Mass., 1943), pp. 32–33

DESCRIPTION: The raised baluster mug has a slightly flared rim and rests on a cast, molded foot. The ear-shaped handle, cast in two vertical halves, has a scrolled terminus.

This small mug, bearing only a maker's mark, was acquired by Philip Leffingwell Spalding for his important collection of American silver. The mark does not appear on other American silver, however, and it seems likely that it is a conventional example of a London mug of the 1730s that is, unusually, lacking hallmarks. The arms appear to replace earlier engraving.

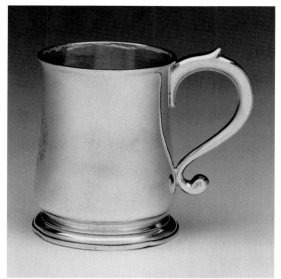

84

85

· 85 ·

PAIR OF CANDLESTICKS
Marked by George Wickes (1698–1761)
London, 1743/4
Silver
33.144, 146

MARKS: one mark under each corner of base, maker's mark *GW* (similar to Grimwade 927); lion passant; leopard's head crowned; date letter *h*

ARMORIALS: engraved on each base and waxpan, an unidentified crest (out of a ducal coronet an elephant's head), apparently later, replacing previous engraving

INSCRIPTIONS: 33.144, engraved on underside, *No. 2, 19=2*; on the bezel of waxpan, *No2*. 33.146, engraved on underside, *No. 4, 18=12*; on bezel of waxpan, *No1*

33.144: H. 21 cm (8¼ in.); w. 11.6 cm (4%₆ in.); d. 11.7 cm (4⅝ in.)
33.146: H. 20.6 cm (8⅛ in.); w. 11.8 cm (4⅝ in.); d. 11.8 cm (4⅝ in.)

WEIGHT: 33.144: 581.2 gm (18 oz 14 dwt). 33.146: 564.2 gm (18 oz 3 dwt)

PROVENANCE: Anonymous Gift in Memory of Charlotte Beebe Wilbour (1833–1914), March 2, 1933

EXHIBITED: Boston, Musuem of Fine Arts, 1933; Springfield, Massachusetts, Museum of Fine Arts, 1958

DESCRIPTION: The candlesticks have a square base with rounded corners, incurved sides with leaf ornaments, and a complex molded profile. The base is cast

86

in a single heavy piece, and the stem is cast in two pieces, seamed vertically. The baluster stem has a flattened knop rising to a flared octagonal midsection with leaf ornament at the top of the shoulder. The vase-shaped nozzle is surmounted by a detachable waxpan with a fluted border. The waxpans are fabricated from cut sheet, with applied wire moldings. The present crests are engraved over earlier engraving.

Although leading goldsmiths such as George Wickes were producing more monumental candlesticks in the French taste by the 1730s,[1] they also continued to supply simpler, more conservative plate. The crisply modeled moldings of these candlesticks and the even casting of their bases place them in a category above much of the production work of the period. This pair was orginally part of a set of at least four.[2] The record of Wickes's client sales (the Gentlemen's Ledger of 1740–48) lists several references to "two pairs" of candlesticks. This pair may have been part of a large dinner service delivered to George Pitt, Esq., in 1743/4 that included two pairs of candlesticks with weights totaling 73 oz 13 dwt.[3]

1. See a pair of 1737 with heavy square baluster stems and rococo cartouches modeled on the base, illus. Barr 1980, p. 34, fig. 34.
2. Two were sold by the Museum in 1979.
3. Victoria and Albert Museum, Garrard Ledgers, Gentlemen's Ledgers, VAM2, p. 30. I am very grateful to Helen Clifford for having offered this information.

· 86 ·

PAIR OF SAUCEBOATS
Marked by John Pollock (first mark entered 1734)
London, 1743/4
Silver
Res.65.32–33

MARKS: on underside of each, maker's mark *IP* (Grimwade 1596); lion passant; leopard's head crowned; date letter *h*

ARMORIALS: engraved on side of each, the arms of Fithie or Fythie impaling an unidentified coat of arms (azure a crane impaling quarterly 1 and 4, a chevron between three spear heads, 2 and 3, three scythes and on a chief an ox statant)

Res.65.32: H. 10.5 cm (4⅛ in.); w. 18.2 cm (7³⁄₁₆ in.); d. 9.8 cm (3⅞ in.)
Res.65.33: H. 10.6 cm (4³⁄₁₆ in.); w. 18 cm (7¹⁄₁₆ in.); d. 9.7 cm (3¹³⁄₁₆ in.)

WEIGHT: Res.65.32: 309 gm (9 oz 19 dwt). Res.65.33: 309 gm (9 oz 19 dwt)

PROVENANCE: Bequest of Maxim Karolik, April 14, 1965

DESCRIPTION: The low oval boat, formed from sheet, has a broad pouring lip, fluted body, and shaped edge. It rests on three cast scrolled legs with simple shell chasing at the join to the body, and shell feet. A cast handle in the form of a C-scroll is mounted opposite the pouring lip.

87

87

· 87 ·

PAIR OF BRAZIERS
Marked by Richard Gurney & Co. (company mark 1734)
London, 1743/4
Silver, wood
1973.138–139

MARKS: on underside of each and on underside of each removable plate, leopard's head crowned; date letter *h*; maker's mark *RG* with *T* above and *C* below (Grimwade 2325); lion passant

ARMORIALS: engraved on each handle, an unidentified crest (a ship in full sail)

1973.138: H. 10.7 cm (4¼ in.); w. 32.1 cm (12⅝ in.); d. 20.5 cm (8¹⁄₁₆ in.)
1973.139: H. 10.7 cm (4¼ in.); w. 32.3 cm (12¾ in.); d. 20.4 cm (8 in.)

WEIGHT: 1973.138: 861.8 gm (27 oz 14 dwt).
1973.139: 861.8 gm (27 oz 14 dwt)

PROVENANCE: estate of Mrs. Theodore Lyman, Lent by Mrs. Henry Lyman in 1931, Gift of Mrs. Henry Lyman, February 14, 1973

PUBLISHED: Bigelow 1917, pp. 326–29

DESCRIPTION: Each brazier rests on three scrolled legs with flared scallop feet that are cast in several sections. The raised circular bowl has a broad flaring rim and a sunken well at the base, at the top of which is a pierced gallery. The rim is pierced and chased on the outside with C-scrolls and shells. At the center of the bowl is a removable pierced disk formed of sheet, threaded through the base of the bowl with a silver bolt and nut. A turned wooden handle is attached to a horizontal silver nozzle at the top of one leg.

This handsome pair of braziers, or chafing dishes, is a late example of a form that by the middle of the eighteenth century had been largely superseded by the dish cross, with a spirit lamp as a heater instead of charcoal embers.

88

1. Davis 1976, p. 100; Clayton 1971, p. 81.

2. The service supplied by George Wickes to the duke of Leinster, for example, included sauceboats in two sizes. See Barr 1980, pp. 197–205.

3. See the set of four sauceboats, 1735/6 in the Hartman collection, illus. Hartop 1996, p. 183, cat. 32, and a single sauceboat, ca. 1735, illus. Brett 1986, p. 188, fig. 784.

4. See a pair of sauceboats, marked 1734/5, sold Sotheby's, London, February 6, 1986, lot 174.

· 88 ·

PAIR OF SAUCEBOATS

Marked by Paul Crespin (1694–1770)
London, 1744/5
Silver
35.1630–1631

MARKS: on underside of each, maker's mark *PC* (Grimwade 2149); lion passant; date letter *i*; leopard's head crowned

INSCRIPTIONS: 35.1630: engraved on underside, *No 1 5 = 1*. 35.1631: engraved on underside, *No 2 5 = 3½*

35.1630: H. 7.8 cm (3⅟₁₆ in.); w. 12.6 cm (4¹⁵⁄₁₆ in.); d. 6.9 cm (2¾ in.)

35.1631: H. 7.6 cm (3 in.); w. 12.8 cm (5⅟₁₆ in.); d. 6.8 cm (2¹¹⁄₁₆ in.)

WEIGHT: 35.1630: 155.9 gm (5 oz). 35.1631: 158.8 gm (5 oz 2 dwt)

PROVENANCE: Crichton Brothers, New York, purchased by Frank Brewer Bemis, February 2, 1920, Bequest of Frank Brewer Bemis, November 7, 1935

DESCRIPTION: The raised oval body with a cut and shaped rim is supported by three cast legs with lion's mask mounts and claw-and-ball feet. The cast handle is composed of a series of leaf-capped scrolls. Engraving has been removed from the area under the lip.

Though often presumed to be intended for a coffee or tea table,[1] small cream boats like this pair may have been supplied with matching full-size sauceboats as part of a service.[2] The model, with its stiffly rendered lion's masks, was produced in a richer version, with applied castings of floral swags between the masks and engraved diaperwork borders. For the larger model marked by Crespin,[3] the lion's tail is wrapped around the legs, a conceit also used by Lamerie.[4]

· 89 ·

CHAFING DISH

Marked by Paul Crespin (1694–1770)
London, 1744/5
Silver, wood
42.14

MARKS: on underside, leopard's head crowned; maker's mark *PC* (Grimwade 2149) (repeated on underside of frame and lamp); lion passant (repeated on underside of frame and lamp); date letter *i*

ARMORIALS: engraved on one foot, the frame, the side of the lamp, and the lamp cover, the crest of Fitzroy, for Charles Fitzroy, second duke of Grafton (1683–1757)

INSCRIPTIONS: scratched on underside of body, *39=1*; scratched on underside of frame, *4=17*; scratched on underside of lamp, *8 =2*; *8223*, *H374LU/WS/L*

H. 9 cm (3⅟₁₆ in.); diam. of rim 21.7 cm (8⅟₁₆ in.)

WEIGHT: 1,610 gm (51 oz 15 dwt)

PROVENANCE: Anonymous Gift in Memory of Charlotte Beebe Wilbour (1833–1914), January 8, 1942

DESCRIPTION: The chafing dish has straight pierced sides and rests on three shaped cast feet. The pierced panel forming the main section of the dish is formed of raised sheet, joined to a heavy cast gadrooned border and flaring cast rim at the base. Hinged to either side are double-scroll handles with wooden baluster insets, each formed of two pieces of silver, cast and seamed. The cylindrical, flat-bottomed lamp is raised and supported by an open-work frame that rests inside the cylinder of the stand. The frame is assembled from shaped strips of flat sheet. The lamp has a detachable flat cover with a molded rim and tubes for three wicks. These appear to replace an original single opening for a

89

wick, which has been plugged at the center of the cover.

Chafing dishes or braziers served the important function of warming food in the dining room. Early examples held charcoal, but by the early eighteenth century the form was modified to accommodate a spirit lamp (see also cat. 10). In addition, some dishes were prepared at the table, as described in recipes from the early seventeenth century. Sometimes fitted with a saucepan or a bracket for a kettle, the form is similar to a dish ring, which was used only to elevate a dish on the table. This example lacks a trivet or bracket to support the cooking vessel.[1]

The engraved crest is that of Charles Fitzroy, second duke of Grafton, who succeeded to the peerage on the death of his father in 1690. As a young man he served in the army in the War of Spanish Succession, and at the coronation of George I he was lord high steward and bearer of St. Edward's crown. He served in Ireland as lord justice and later as viceroy and lord lieutenant, and during the absences of the king, he acted as a lord justice of the realm. Under George I and George II, he was lord chamberlain of the household. In 1713 he married

Henrietta, daughter of Charles Somerset, styled marquis of Worcester. His reputation was that of an ineffectual courtier, rather than a serious politician.[2]

1. Two braziers marked by Benjamin Pyne, dated 1713 and 1720, are similar in design to the present example. See Christie's, London, July 15, 1998, lot 251, and Christie's, London, March 4, 1992, lot 195. An example with a saucepan marked by Archambo and Meure is illustrated in Clayton 1985a, p. 331, fig. 493. There are several marked by Paul de Lamerie; see Davis 1976, pp. 160–61, cat. 167.

2. Other plate bearing his arms include a dish in the Clark Art Institute (Wees 1997, p. 130, cat. 61) and a pair of salvers sold Sotheby's, New York, April 19, 1991, lot 274.

· 90 ·

SALVER

Marked by Nicholas Sprimont (1716–1770)
London, 1744/5
Silver
1975.733

MARKS: on underside, date letter *i*; leopard's head crowned; lion passant; maker's mark *NS* (Grimwade 2102)

ARMORIALS: engraved on salver in a large radiating floral cartouche, the arms and crest of Norreys

INSCRIPTIONS: engraved on underside, *190=12*

H. 8.8 cm (3⁷⁄₁₆ in.); diam. 65.4 cm (25¾ in.)

WEIGHT: 5,698.4 gm (183 oz 4 dwt)

PROVENANCE: sold Christie's, London, June 26, 1956, lot 28; Lent by Mrs. S. J. Katz, the Jessie and Sigmund Katz Collection, 1970, Gift of Mrs. Sigmund J. Katz, January 14, 1975

PUBLISHED: Richard Ormond, "Silver Shapes in Chelsea Porcelain," *Country Life* 143, no. 370 (February 1, 1968), p. 226, fig. 8; Zorka Hodgson, "Survey of the Sources of Inspiration for the Goat and Bee Jug and Some Other Noted Chelsea Creations," *English Ceramic Circle Transactions* 14 (1990), p. 37

DESCRIPTION: The circular salver rests on four scrolled feet surmounted by the heads of a Chinese, an African, a Turk, and a Hungarian. Between the heads, the rim is modeled with foliage: tea, sugar cane, coffee, and peppers. The heavy rim is cast in sections, and each head is inset. The center of the salver, formed from sheet, is soldered onto the cast border and has been distorted and discolored through repair. The center of the salver is engraved with a flowing symmetrical medallion incorporating leaves of the plants on the border and enclosing a coat of arms.

Of the approximately thirty pieces bearing Nicholas Sprimont's mark, a distinct group of them, including this salver, is characterized by peculiarly whimsical and softly modeled figures, fine engraving, and somewhat imprecise construction. The group includes the set of tea canisters and sugar box in this collection (cat. 91) and a pair of baskets—one in the Gilbert collection and the other in the Ashmolean Museum.[1] A kettle and stand in the Hermitage, certainly the most eccentric and original piece marked by Sprimont, is the centerpiece of this stylistic group.[2] The kettle has a densely ornamented surface with cast panels depicting

scenes of tea drinking and a spout in the form of a highly animated dragon, whose tail wraps around the kettle. It rests on a frame formed entirely of foliage and a stand with exotic heads at each foot that match the heads on the present salver.[3]

Because of his importance for the history of English porcelain, Sprimont's artistic personality and his association with Paul Crespin continue to inspire debate.[4] While scholars in the field of silver have generally accepted the impossiblity of defining an individual goldsmith's precise role in the design and execution of a particular object, Sprimont remains a tantalizing exception. Two drawings survive that are attributed to his hand, and he is described by contemporary accounts as an accomplished modeler. The short period of his activity as a silversmith and the idiosyncratic nature of several of the pieces that bear his mark suggest that he may have personally designed and modeled some of these pieces. The originality and whimsy of the figures on certain pieces of silver in this group may also be seen in some of the early Chelsea wares, lending strength to the possibility that it is Sprimont's sensibility at work in both media.

The kettle and stand in the Hermitage, marked one year later than the salver, must have been designed to sit on this salver, or another of the same model. Not only are the four heads similar on each, but the feet of the kettle rest symmetrically in the engraved panels in the center of the salver. The heads, representing an African, a Turk, a Chinese, and a Hungarian, emerge from a border of plants, each keyed to the head it surrounds—sugar cane, coffee, tea, and pepper. On the kettle, the appropriate plants extend above the heads into the frame.

The salver is engraved with the arms of Sir John Norris (ca. 1660–1749), a distinguished naval commander. The third son of Thomas Norris of Speke, co. Lancashire, John Norris served off the coast of Ireland, off Lagos, in Hudson's Bay, in Malagar, and in Barcelona. He was named admiral of the blue in 1707 and vice admiral of the white in 1708, when he was posted to the Mediterranean. In 1711 Archduke Charles of Austria granted him a pension and the title of duke, which he was to keep secret until it was deemed appropriate to

make it public, but Norris seems not to have claimed this privilege. The most significant missions of his career were in the Baltic, where he was first sent in 1715 to protect the Anglo-Dutch trade from Swedish privateers. In this capacity he first encountered Tsar Peter the Great (1682–1725), who is said to have held him in high regard. He was entertained in Copenha-gen by the king of Denmark with the tsar in 1716. Norris played a key role in negotiating the independence of Sweden, and in 1734 he was named admiral and commander in chief. He continued to see active service in the 1740s, though he was in his eighties. The date of the salver coincides with his retirement from service.

It cannot be confirmed that the kettle and stand in St. Petersburg were ever associated with Norris. It is considered part of the Oranienbaum service, a group of apparently later matched tea wares marked by Fuller White and Thomas Heming that is believed to have been in the Russian royal household from the mid-eighteenth century.[5] Oranienbaum was built for Prince Menshikov (1663?–1729) and later confiscated for the crown. It was given in 1743 to Prince Peter Fedorovich, later Peter III, and in 1792 his wife, Catherine the Great, removed the contents of the palace, including the silver service, before presenting the estate to the Naval Cadet Corps. The exotic themes of the silver service suggest that it may have furnished the Chinese Palace, a chinoiserie confection built at Oranienbaum between 1762 and 1768. It is possible that the kettle and stand were sold sometime after Sir John Norris's death in 1749 and acquired for the Chinese Palace.

1. Schroder 1988a, pp. 284–87, cat. 74.

2. Exh. New Haven, Yale Center for British Art, *British Art Treasures from Russian Imperial Collections in the Hermitage*, 1996, p. 241, cat. 65.

3. I thank Mrs. Lopato of the State Hermitage Museum, St. Petersburg, Timothy Goodhue, Yale University Art Gallery, who allowed me to examine the piece, and Christine Mack, The Toledo Museum of Art, for providing me with additional information.

4. See summary in Mallet 1996, vol. 29, p. 432. Also see cats. 91, 95, 96.

5. E. Alfred Jones, *The Old English Plate of the Emperor of Russia* (London, 1909), p. 100, pl. 49.

· 91 ·

TWO TEA CANISTERS AND A SUGAR BOX

Marked by Nicholas Sprimont (1716–1770)
London, 1744/5
Silver
1988.1075a-b—1077a-b

MARKS: on each, on inside rim of foot, lion passant (repeated on bezel of cover); maker's mark *NS* (Grimwade 2102) (repeated on bezel of cover); leopard's head crowned; date letter *i*

1988.1075: H. 17.2 cm (6¾ in.); diam. of foot 7.5 cm (3 in.)
1988.1076: H. 14.9 cm (5⅞ in.); diam. of foot 6.1 cm (2⅜ in.)
1988.1077: H. 14.9 cm (5⅞ in.); diam. of foot 6.1 cm (2⅜ in.)

WEIGHT: 1988.1075: 402.6 gm (12 oz 19 dwt).
1988.1076: 558.5 gm (17 oz 19 dwt). 1988.1077: 377 gm (12 oz 2 dwt)

PROVENANCE: estate of Victor George Henry Francis, fifth marquess Conyngham, sold Christie's, London, February 10, 1938, lot 36, purchased by Thomas Lumley, London; collection of Maj. W. M. Tapp by August 1938; A. G. Lewis collection, New York, by 1951; Lent by Mrs. S. J. Katz, 1973, The Jessie and Sigmund Katz collection, November 30, 1988

EXHIBITED: London, Brompton Square, *English Ceramics Circle*, 1938, p. 98 (loaned by Maj. W. H. Tapp); London, The Royal Hospital, *Loan Exhibition of Chelsea China*, 1951, cat. 174

PUBLISHED: Gardner 1938, p. 206

DESCRIPTION: Each canister is of inverted pear form resting on a spreading base. The foot is raised and chased with an abstract undulating motif. Between the top of the raised section and the base of the body is a cast spacer of C-scrolls that is crudely soldered to both. The body of the vessel is raised and has three applied cast vertical ribs terminating in leaves. In the plain panels between them are applied stalks of plants: tea on the two smaller canisters, sugar cane on the larger. The rim, modeled with an undulating motif, is cast and applied. The raised cover is domed and chased with vertical fluting and surmounted with a cast finial—tea blossoms and berries on the smaller canisters, strawberries on the larger. The surface has suffered from overpolishing.

91 (Color Plate x)

Only about thirty pieces or sets of silver marked by Nicholas Sprimont survive, all hall-marked between 1743 and 1747, by which time Sprimont had turned his attention exclusively to the manufacture of porcelain at Chelsea.[1] Although he was born in Liège into a family of silversmiths, the extraordinarily original character of some pieces bearing his mark suggests that he must have received his training and considerable experience in another European center. He was settled in London by 1742 and seems to have readily established close connections to the French-speaking group of artists and artisans centered in Soho.

There is evidence that Sprimont was an accomplished draftsman and modeler, skills also required by the porcelain manufactory. As is the case with any of the London goldsmiths, his precise role in the manufacture of the silver bearing his mark remains uncertain. A few pieces are conventional London models of the period, suggesting that he collaborated with other makers in supplying or marking standard wares.[2] Much discussion has centered on the marine centerpiece in the queen's collection, which is marked for 1741 by Paul Crespin but attributed by many to the hand of Sprimont, whose mark appears on a set of sauceboats and salts made to match.[3] This group, clearly influenced by Parisian models, is characterized by clusters of coral and other naturalistic motifs that are cast and finished with extreme precision. A third group, which includes this set of canisters, shares distinctive qualities in conception and manufacture and appears to be the work of a single hand, possibly Sprimont himself. These pieces are fanciful in conception, and the modeling for the cast components is freely rendered and rather eccentrically adapted to the whole. Among the objects in this third group are a salver of 1744/5 (see cat. 90), a kettle and stand in the Hermitage,[4] and a pair of

baskets divided between the Gilbert collection[5] and the Ashmolean Museum. The heavy construction of these canisters is characteristic of the group. The raised inverted-pear shape with applied naturalistic plants and flowers and rather loosely defined abstract scrolls is without parallel in London silver of the period. Though the surface has been badly rubbed, there is evidence that the leaves were once defined by quite fine chasing. The decoration of each vessel reflects its contents and use, with sugar cane and a strawberry finial on the larger pot, and tea plants (blooming and bearing fruit) on the smaller canisters.

1. The literature on Sprimont is extensive. For a summary, see Mallet 1996, vol. 29, p. 432. Also see Grimwade 1969, pp. 126–28; John Mallet, "A Chelsea Greyhound and Retrieving Setter," *The Connoisseur* 196, no. 789 (November 1977), pp. 222–25; John Mallet, "A Painting of Nicholas Sprimont, His Family and His Chelsea Vases," *Les Cahiers de Mariemont* 24–25 (1996), pp. 77–95; Bernard Dragesco, *English Ceramics in French Archives* (London, 1993).

2. For example, see the silver dishes of 1743, one pair sold Sotheby's, London, June 4, 1998, lot 215, and another in the Gilbert collection, illus. Schroder 1988a, p. 273, cat. 70. The cataloguer for Sotheby's points out that Sprimont's shop in Compton Street adjoined that of William Cripps and suggests that the two are likely to have done business together.

3. See cat. 96 for further discussion of this group.

4. Exh. New Haven, Yale Center for British Art, *British Art Treasures from Russian Imperial Collections in the Hermitage*, 1996, p. 241, cat. 65.

5. Illus. Schroder 1988a, p. 285, cat. 74, and fig. 71.

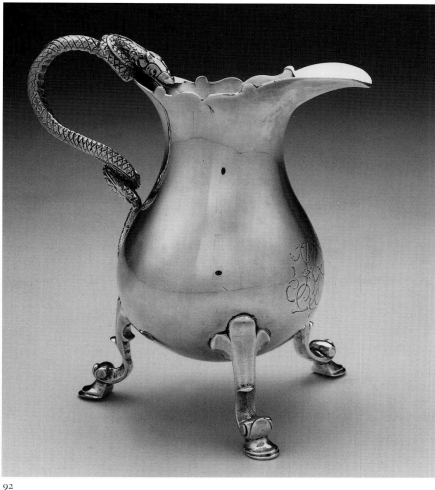

92

CREAM JUG

Marked by Eliza Godfrey (first mark entered 1741)

London, ca. 1745

Silver

1975.19

MARKS: on underside, maker's mark *EG* (Grimwade 591)

INSCRIPTIONS: engraved on body, *KG* in cipher

H. 11.3 cm (4⁷⁄₁₆ in.); w. 7.9 cm (3⅛ in.); d. 10.4 cm (4⅛ in.)

WEIGHT: 164.4 gm (5 oz 6 dwt)

PROVENANCE: property of H. Warhurst, Esq., sold Sotheby's, London, October 17, 1978, lot 167; Thomas Lumley, Ltd., London, purchased February 25, 1975, Theodora Wilbour Fund in Memory of Charlotte Beebe Wilbour

EXHIBITED: Boston, Museum of Fine Arts, 1994

PUBLISHED: Brett 1986, p. 213, fig. 930

DESCRIPTION: The raised pear-shaped body rests on three cast hooved feet. The cast handle is in the form of a snake with its head resting on the cut and shaped rim.

At the death of Benjamin Godfrey, probably in 1741, Eliza Godfrey took over a prospering business, which she continued to manage until about 1758. She had married Benjamin Godfrey after the death of her first husband, Abraham Buteux, and she had extensive connections through her family and business to the Huguenot community. It seems likely that her trade was primarily for retail goods, and among her many distinguished clients was the duke of Cumberland.[1] The snake handle on this elegantly proportioned milk jug is an apparent innovation; it does not appear on other silver for the tea table made in the 1740s.

1. See Grimwade 1990, pp. 524, 750; Philippa Glanville and Jennifer Faulds Goldsborough, *Women Silversmiths, 1685–1845* (Washington, D.C., 1990), pp. 93, 139.

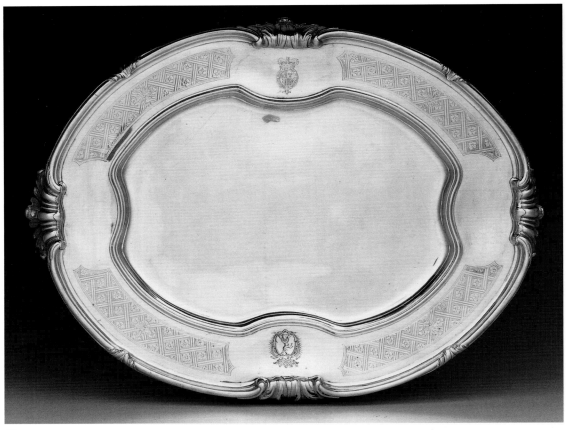

93

· 93 ·

STAND FOR A TUREEN

Marked by Nicholas Sprimont (1716–1770)
London, 1745
Silver
1996.269

MARKS: on underside of rim, leopard's head crowned; date letter *k*, maker's mark *NS* (Grimwade 2102); lion passant

ARMORIALS: engraved on rim within the Garter, the English royal arms prior to 1801. Opposite, an unidentified set of Continental arms

INSCRIPTIONS: engraved on underside, *N.1; 84=12; 83=13; N1; 83=8*

H. 3.6 cm (1⁷⁄₁₆ in.); w. 52 cm (20½ in.); d. 39 cm (15⅜ in.)

WEIGHT: 7,098.9 gm (82 oz 8 dwt)

PROVENANCE: Gift of Alan and Simone Hartman, November 20, 1996

DESCRIPTION: The oval stand has a molded border, a broad shaped rim, and four foliate feet. The border is engraved with panels of diaperwork and rosettes. The stand is hammered from a single piece, and the border and feet, cast in sections, were pinned before soldering. The plain reserves in the rim have had engraving removed from them, and the surface overall is brightly polished.

Although worn, this stand must once have belonged to a grand tureen. For a discussion of Sprimont, see cats. 91, 95, and 96. Also see cat. 281, which may share some history with this stand.

94

· 94 ·

CRUET STAND
Marked by Samuel Wood (ca. 1704–ca. 1794)
London, 1745/6
Silver, glass
38.1651a–f

MARKS: on underside of stand, and on underside of
each caster, maker's mark *SW* (repeated on handle
of stand, bezel of large caster cover, and bezel of one
small caster cover); date letter *k*; lion passant
(repeated on handle of stand, bezel of large caster
cover, and bezel of one small caster cover); leopard's
head crowned

ARMORIALS: engraved in cartouche on stand, and
on all three casters, the arms of Faneuil; engraved on
the silver cruet caps, the crest of Faneuil

38.1651a (frame): H. 20.6 cm (8⅛ in.); w. 17.1 cm
(6¾ in.); d. 17 cm (6¹¹⁄₁₆ in.)
38.1651b (large caster): H. 17.7 cm (6¹⁵⁄₁₆ in.); diam.
of base 5.1 cm (2 in.)
38.1651c (small caster): H. 12.6 cm (4¹⁵⁄₁₆ in.); diam.
of base 4.2 cm (1¹¹⁄₁₆ in.)
38.1651d (small caster): H. 12.6 cm (4¹⁵⁄₁₆ in.); diam.
of base 4.2 cm (1¹¹⁄₁₆ in.)
38.1651e (bottle): H. 16 cm (6⁵⁄₁₆ in.); diam. of base
5 cm (1¹⁵⁄₁₆ in.)
38.1651f (bottle): H. 16 cm (6⁵⁄₁₆ in.); diam. of base
5.2 cm (2¹⁄₁₆ in.)

WEIGHT: 1,111.33 gm (35 oz 15 dwt)

PROVENANCE: according to tradition, owned by
Benjamin Faneuil (1702–1785), by descent to his
great-grandson Dr. George Bethune who sold it at a
family sale (ca. 1890), purchased by Dr. Faneuil D.
Weisse, by descent to his son, Dr. Faneuil S. Weisse,
Gift of Faneuil Suydam Weisse and Henry Bethune
Weisse, November 10, 1938

EXHIBITED: Boston, Museum of Fine Arts, 1975,
p. 55, cat. 59

PUBLISHED: Kathryn C. Buhler, "Gifts of Faneuil
Silver," *Bulletin of the Museum of Fine Arts* 37, no. 221
(June 1939), pp. 51–53; Rita Feigenbaum, "A Faneuil
Family Silver Cruet Stand Rediscovered," *Antiques*
112 (July 1977), p. 121

DESCRIPTION: The cruet set consists of a large
caster, a pair of smaller casters, and two faceted glass
bottles that rest in a cinquefoil frame. The base of
the frame is formed from sheet, with wire circles
applied to the underside of the base outlining the
compartment for each caster. It rests on four cast
scrolled legs with shell feet. A frame of five molded
rings above contains the bottles, with two smaller

rings to hold the stoppers. At the front, attached to the base and the open frame, is a cartouche, formed from cut sheet and engraved with foliage, scrolls, and the arms of Faneuil. A tall cast handle with baluster stem and scrolled handle is threaded through the center of the frame. The casters are pear-shaped, resting on a spreading foot. Each is formed from two pieces of sheet, the lower section raised, the upper section seamed, and the join covered with a molded wire. The removable covers are raised, pierced, and engraved, with an interior bezel formed of sheet. The covers are surmounted by cast balusters. The faceted cut-glass cruet bottles have silver domed covers. The casters and the base have been extensively repaired and polished, and the shield bearing the arms appears to be a restoration.

Like the coffeepot bearing the Faneuil arms (see cat. 103), this set of casters descended in the Faneuil family. It is believed that the set was purchased by Benjamin Faneuil, younger brother of the prosperous merchant, Peter (1701-1743), who built Faneuil Hall. Benjamin inherited the vast fortune formed by his uncle, Andrew Faneuil, when Peter died without an heir. Benjamin married Mary Cutler, and the casters are believed to have descended to their daughter, Mary, who in 1754 married George Bethune, and thence to her son, George Bethune.[1]

This piece is one of countless surviving examples from Samuel Wood's shop, which specialized in cruet frames. Wood had apprenticed with another caster maker, Thomas Bamford, who in turn had trained under the caster maker Charles Adam.[2] This particular form, with a cinquefoil base reflecting the outline of the bases of the casters and bottles and a threaded baluster-stem handle, is the signature model of Wood's workshop.[3] In England by the 1750s, both in the provinces and in London, a cruet stand was essential to a properly outfitted table. The manufacture of such a specialized form was probably not cost efficient for colonial silversmiths, and London-made examples were imported regularly. Affluent colonists, including George Washington, had them sent from London,[4] and Lynford Lardner of Philadelphia bought one secondhand from his brother-in-law, Richard Penn.[5] (Also see cat. 97.) This cruet frame, in most respects an absolutely standard product of Wood's shop, has

the unusual feature of an engraved cartouche formed from sheet. Wood invariably used a shaped cartouche cast in low relief with scrolls and flowers surrounding a plain space for the engraved coat of arms. The tenuous engraving, on both the cartouche and the body of the casters, suggests that the set was extensively repaired at some point and the engraving refreshed. It might have happened in the mid-nineteenth century when a copy of the set was made by the Boston silversmith Newell Harding (active ca. 1821–60).[6] Two additional silver disks and rings were added to accommodate a second pair of bottles and have since been removed.

1. James H. Stark, *The Loyalists of Massachusetts* (Boston, 1910), pp. 229–33; Sargent 1856, pp. 495–544.

2. Grimwade 1990, p. 709.

3. Colonial Williamsburg has a set dated 1750 (Davis 1976, pp. 153–54, cat. 159). Also see Christie's, New York, April 11, 1995, lots 365 and 398; Christie's, New York, April 17, 1985, lot 386.

4. Davis 1976, p. 154.

5. Jack L. Lindsey, "Lynford Lardner's Silver: Early Rococo in Philadelphia," *Antiques* 143, no. 4 (April 1993), p. 612. My thanks to Jeanne Sloane for pointing this out to me.

6. Feigenbaum, "Faneuil Family," pp. 120–21.

95

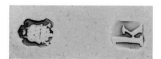

Fig. 1. *Design for a heart-shaped dish*, Nicholas Sprimont

· 95 ·

DISH

Marked by Nicholas Sprimont (1716–1770)
London, 1745/6, with later alterations
Silver
1988.1074

MARKS: on underside, lion passant; maker's mark *NS* (Grimwade 2102); leopard's head crowned; date letter *k*

INSCRIPTIONS: engraved on underside, *oz 8=15*

H. 4.2 cm (1⅝ in.); w. 19.9 cm (7¹⁵⁄₁₆ in.); d. 15.1 cm (5¹⁵⁄₁₆ in.)

WEIGHT: 283.5 gm (9 oz 2 dwt)

PROVENANCE: estate of Victor George Henry Francis, fifth marquess of Conyngham, sold Christie's, London, February 10, 1938, lot 10; Maj. W. M. Tapp; A. G. Lewis collection by 1951, New York; Lent by Mrs. Sigmund Katz, 1973, The Jessie and Sigmund Katz collection, November 30, 1988

EXHIBITED: Chelsea, The Royal Hospital, *Loan Exhibition of Chelsea China*, 1951, cat. 174

PUBLISHED: Gardner 1938, p. 208, fig. 5

DESCRIPTION: The heart-shaped dish, formed from sheet, has fluted edges and rests on three gadrooned ball feet. At the top of the heart, a cast cluster of encrusted shellwork is inset. The surface is buffed, and engraving has been removed from the underside.

Nicholas Sprimont's considerable reputation is based on sketchy biographical documentation and a very small number of surviving pieces of silver bearing his mark. However, two drawings survive that represent an aspect of his personal skill that, for nearly every other eighteenth-century goldsmith, is completely unknown. A drawing in the Society of Antiquaries, signed *N Sprimont in & del* (fig. 1), depicts a heart-shaped stand with a crimped border bearing two stemmed glasses.[1] The drawing was part of a collection formed by the antiquarian Jacob Schnebbelie (1760–1892) and was presented to the society in 1877.[2] It is related to a rather eccentric silver condiment frame by Sprimont that was published in 1933 soon after it was acquired by the ceramic historian Major W. H. Tapp.[3] The condiment frame rests on a heart-shaped stand with scrolled foliage along the border similar to that in the drawing. The vines rise from the base to form a three-lobed enclosure for glass bottles with silver caps. The quality and authenticity of the cruet stand are impossible to judge from the 1933 publication, and the object was apparently damaged or destroyed in the bombing of 1943.[4] This silver dish, extensively polished and restored, seems to be what remains of Major Tapp's cruet stand, although it was not identified as such when it was exhibited in 1951.

1. Mrs. A. Esdaile, "A Signed Drawing by Sprimont," *Apollo* 39, no. 232 (May–June 1944), p. 134. The second drawing is in the Victoria and Albert Museum, illus. Grimwade 1974, p. 5, pl. 96.

2. I acknowledge the kind assistance of Bernard Nurse, librarian, Society of Antiquaries, who allowed me to see the drawing and arranged for photography of it.

3. Gardner 1938, p. 208, figs. 5–6.

4. Gerald Pendred, "Major William H. Tapp, MC—Ceramic Researcher Extraordinary," *Derby Porcelain International Society Journal* 1 (1989), p. 35. I am grateful to Hilary Young, Ceramics Department, Victoria and Albert Museum, who was helpful to me with several questions regarding Sprimont, and who provided this reference.

· 96 ·

FOUR SAUCEBOATS, TWO SAUCE-
BOAT STANDS, TWO LADLES

Marked by, or attributed to, Nicholas Sprimont
(1716–1770)

London, ca. 1746 and 1746/7

Silver

69.1358, 1970.639, 1970.641, 1970.643, 1970.644,
1971.774, 1971.776–777

MARKS: 69.1358 (sauceboat stand): sponsor's mark
NS (similar to Grimwade 2102); lion passant; leopard's head crowned; date letter *l*. 1970.639, 1970.641,
1970.643, 1971.774 (sauceboats): unmarked. 1970.644
(sauceboat stand): on underside, maker's mark NS
(Grimwade 2102);¹ lion passant; leopard's head
crowned; date letter *l*. 1971.776–777 (ladles):
unmarked

ARMORIALS: 69.1358, 1970.644: engraved on center
of stand, the crest of Thomas Watson (1693– 1750),
first marquess of Rockingham, under a marquess's
coronet. 1970.639, 1970.641, 1970.643, 1971.774:
engraved on spout, the arms of Thomas Watson,
impaling the arms of his wife, Mary, daughter of the
earl of Winchelsea and Nottingham; earl's coronet;
motto of Order of Bath: *Tria Juncta In Uno*.
1971.776–777: in cartouche on back of handle, an
almost entirely obliterated crest

69.1358 (stand): H. 2.8 cm (1¹⁄₁₆ in.); w. 29.7 cm
(11¹¹⁄₁₆ in.); d. 22.7 cm (8 in.)
1970.639 (sauceboat): H. 16.3 cm (6⁷⁄₁₆ in.);
w. 9.7 cm (3¹³⁄₁₆ in.); d. 21.1 cm (8⁵⁄₁₆ in.)
1970.641 (sauceboat): H. 14.7 cm (5¾ in.);
w. 7.9 cm (3⅛ in.); d. 20.1 cm (7¹⁵⁄₁₆ in.)
1970.643 (sauceboat): H. 15.4 cm (6¹⁄₁₆ in.);
w. 9.5 cm (3¾ in.); d. 21.2 cm (8⁵⁄₁₆ in.)
1971.774 (sauceboat): H. 16.3 cm (6⁷⁄₁₆ in.);
w. 10.1 cm (4 in.); d. 21.1 cm (8⁵⁄₁₆ in.)
1971.776 (ladle): L. 21 cm (8¼ in.)
1971.777 (ladle): L. 21.6 cm (8½ in.)
1970.644 (stand): H. 2.7 cm (1¹⁄₁₆ in.); w. 29.4 cm
(11⁹⁄₁₆ in.); d. 22.5 cm (8⅞ in.)

WEIGHT: 69.1358: 558.5 gm (17 oz 19 dwt).
1970.639: 683.2 gm (21 oz 19 dwt). 1970.641:
626.5 gm (20 oz 3 dwt). 1970.643: 652 gm (20 oz
19 dwt). 1971.774: 690 gm (22 oz 4 dwt). 1971.776:
116.2 gm (3 oz 14 dwt). 1971.777: 121.9 gm (3 oz 18
dwt). 1970.644: 558.5 gm (17 oz 19 dwt)

PROVENANCE: 69.1358: Jessie and Sigmund Katz
collection, Gift of Mrs. S. J. Katz, December 30,
1969. 1970.639, 1970.641, 1970.643: Thomas Watson
of Wentworth Woodhouse, by descent through the
family to the Rt. Hon. the earl Fitzwilliam of

Wentworth Woodhouse, sold Christie's, London,
June 9, 1948, lot 81 or 82; The Jessie and Sigmund
Katz collection, Gift of Mrs. S. J. Katz, December
30, 1970. 1971.774, 1971.776–777: same as above,
made a gift December 28, 1971

EXHIBITED: 69.1358: Austin, Texas, University Art
Museum, *One Hundred Years of English Silver:
1660–1760*, 1969, cat. 83. 1970.639, 1970.644,
1971.776–777: New York, The Frick Collection,
English Silver, 1978, cat. 14. 1970.644, 1971.774,
1971.776: London, Victoria and Albert Museum,
Rococo: Art and Design in Hogarth's England, 1984,
cat. G19. 1970.644: Toronto, George R. Gardiner
Museum of Ceramic Art, *A Taste of Elegance*, 1986,
p. 12

PUBLISHED: 69.1358, 1970.639, 1970.641, 1970.643,
1971.776–777, 1970.644: Grimwade 1974, fig. 32B;
Gruber 1982, fig. 207; Elizabeth Adams, *Chelsea
Porcelain* (London, 1987), fig. 7

DESCRIPTION: Each sauceboat is in the form of a
shell with a fluted rim and spiraling ribs that are
alternately plain or modeled with shells against a
coral ground. It is cast in two halves and seamed in
the center. The panels of rockwork, coral, and shells
were cast separately and pinned to the body of the
boat before soldering. The cast double-scroll handle
is surmounted by a serpent. The boat rests on a cast
foot in the form of a shell, encrusted with coral and
smaller shells. The surface of all the sauceboats is
compromised by severe polishing and wear, and the
shell foot on many has been repaired. Each oblong
stand has a broad fluted rim filled with alternating
panels of finely modeled and chased shells against a
coral ground and plain panels. The stand is formed
from sheet and the coral panels were cast separately
and pinned to the rim before soldering. The ends of
the stand are chased with an abstracted shell form.
The ladles have heavy shell-shaped bowls and asym-
metrically curving handles that terminate in a scroll.
They are cast in two pieces, joined at the rim of the
bowl. The surface of each ladle is heavily worn.

This group of sauceboats and stands was sold in
1948 with other plate belonging to descendants
of Thomas Watson, earl of Malton and later first
marquess of Rockingham. The set was divided
into two lots and included seven sauceboats
(unmarked), four stands (fully marked by
Nicholas Sprimont for 1746/7), and four ladles
(unmarked).² Two boats, stands, and ladles were
deaccessioned by the Museum in 1990 and are
now in the Hartman collection.³ The engraved
arms on the sauceboats are surmounted by an

earl's coronet and have always been presumed to date before 1746 when Watson was created first marquess of Rockingham. Watson, a prominent Whig, inherited vast properties in Yorkshire from his wife's family as well as from his cousin. By the 1740s Henry Flitcroft's tremendously ambitious building project for him at Wentworth Woodhouse was well under way. Appropriately enough for such a vast residence, the house was furnished with a substantial display of plate, including a cistern[4] and a ewer and basin[5] by David Willaume and a pair of tureens by George Wickes.[6]

The sauceboats are all in considerably worse condition than the stands, having been extensively repaired, particularly on the feet, and having lost, through wear, much of the chased detail of the shell and coral ornament. It also appears that the coral panels on the stands are much finer and more sensitively modeled and chased than those on the sauceboats, condition notwithstanding. It is tempting to suggest that the original set was expanded with additional sauceboats in the early nineteenth century (when marine motifs in the rococo enjoyed a revival), but the engraved arms with the earl's coronet, which must date from before 1746, refute this. In addition, an account of the plate at Wentworth House taken by the executors of the first marquess (undated, but presumably after his death in 1750) lists twelve sauceboats and four "plates to set the boats on," so it appears that the numbers of boats and stands were always uneven.[7]

The extent of Nicholas Sprimont's business dealings with Paul Crespin has been the subject of much speculation.[8] At least six sauceboats similar in design to the present set but marked by Crespin exemplify the dilemma.[9] The design of the stands has always been strongly associated with Sprimont, largely because Chelsea produced a porcelain dish clearly based on the silver model that was listed in the 1755 sale as "silvershape."[10] In general, it is not possible to attribute a piece of silver securely to a single hand, but the sensibility of a workshop or the modeling style of an individual—almost always anonymous—can be characterized. This group of sauceboats and stands must have been designed and modeled by the same individual responsible for a teapot with swags formed of coral[11] and a coffeepot with similar decoration,[12] both marked by Crespin for 1740. The debate about the personal style of Crespin and Sprimont has focused on a group of centerpieces with naturalistically rendered creatures supporting a central vessel.[13] Charles Oman suggested that Nicholas Sprimont, newly arrived in London and without a registered mark, had entrusted his pieces to Crespin for marking at Goldsmiths' Hall. The relationship of the earlier centerpieces is perhaps not so close that they must be seen as the work of a single shop, but the sauceboats, teapot, and coffeepot are better candidates for such an explanation. If Sprimont was involved, the 1740 hallmarks on the tea- and coffeepots would place Sprimont in London earlier than any other evidence suggests.

1. Grimwade is without the pellet between.

2. The subsequent lot was a creamboat of the same design; see cat. 182.

3. Hartop 1996, pp. 216–19, cat. 45. The location of the seventh sauceboat is unknown, but it may be the piece illustrated in "Notable Works of Art on the Market," *Burlington Magazine*, supplement, 116, no. 861 (December 1974), pl. 32.

4. Sold Christie's, London, July 8, 1998, lot 60.

5. Sold Christie's, London, November 17, 1991, lot 121.

6. One is in the collection of Colonial Williamsburg, illus. Davis 1976, p. 120, cat. 123. Also see the tureen in this collection by Charles Kandler, cat. 74.

7. Northamptonshire Record Office, F (M) Misc. volume 82. I acknowledge gratefully the help of Rachel Watson, archivist.

8. Charles Oman, "The Exhibition of Royal Plate," *Connoisseur* 133 (January–June 1954), p. 151; Grimwade 1969, pp. 126–28; see the summary in Mallet 1996, vol. 29, p. 432.

9. Two are in the Clark Art Institute, illus. Wees 1997, p. 167, cat. 88; four were sold Christie's, London, March 26, 1975, lot 73.

10. Dr. Bellamy Gardner, "'Silvershape' in Chelsea Porcelain," *The Antique Collector* (August 1937), p. 213.

11. Hartman collection, illus. Hartop 1996, p. 311, cat. 76.

12. Photograph, credited to Spink's, in the Sotheby's, London, files.

13. The Ashburnham centerpiece in the Victoria and Albert Museum (marked by Sprimont for 1747); the Prince of Wales centerpiece, belonging to Her Majesty the Queen (marked by Crespin for 1741); the Somerset tureen in the Toledo Museum of Art (marked by Crespin for 1740); the Bolton centerpiece (marked by Parker and Wakelin), in the MFA, see cat. 115. See Oman, "Royal Plate," and Grimwade 1969.

97

· 97 ·

CRUET STAND
Marked by Samuel Wood (ca. 1704–ca. 1794)
London, 1747/8
Silver, glass
39.83a–f

MARKS: on underside of stand and on underside of each caster, maker's mark *SW* (Grimwade 2666) (repeated on bezel of each cover and on handle); lion passant (repeated on bezel of each cover and on handle); leopard's head crowned; date letter *m*

ARMORIALS: engraved in cartouche on stand and on each caster, the arms of Wheelwright impaling Apthorp, for Nathaniel Wheelwright (1704–1766) who married Ann (d. 1764), daughter of Charles Apthorp (1698–1758) of Boston; on covers of cruet bottles, an unidentified crest (a wolf's head)

INSCRIPTIONS: scratched on underside of stand, *oz/35–2, Mark b Young*; scratched under base of each caster, *38 " 10 " 0*

39.83a (frame): H. 23.4 cm (9³⁄₁₆ in.); w. 21.6 cm (8½ in.); d. 21.2 cm (8⅜ in.)
39.83b (large caster): H. 19 cm (7⁷⁄₁₆ in.); diam. of base 6 cm (2⅜ in.)
39.83c (small caster): H. 16 cm (6⁵⁄₁₆ in.); diam. of base 5 cm (1¹⁵⁄₁₆ in.)
39.83d (small caster): H. 16 cm (6⁵⁄₁₆ in.); diam. of base 5.2 cm (2¹⁄₁₆ in.)
39.83e (bottle): H. 18 cm (7¹⁄₁₆ in.); diam. of base 5.7 cm (2¼ in.)
39.83f (bottle): H. 18 cm (7¹⁄₁₆ in.); diam. of base 5.7 cm (2¼ in.)

WEIGHT: 2,480.6 gm (79 oz 15 dwt)

PROVENANCE: Gift of Mr. and Mrs. Maxim Karolik for The M. and M. Karolik Collection of Eighteenth-Century American Arts, January 19, 1939

EXHIBITED: Toronto, George R. Gardiner Museum of Ceramic Art, 1998

PUBLISHED: Hipkiss 1941, cat. 176

DESCRIPTION: The cruet set is composed of a frame that holds a large silver caster, two smaller casters, and two faceted glass bottles with removable silver stoppers. The base of the frame, formed from sheet and strengthened on the underside with five wire rings, rests on four scrolled legs with shell feet. Above is a series of five molded rings, with two smaller rings to hold the bottle stoppers. At the center is a cast baluster stem with scrolled handle, threaded through the flat base. A cast cartouche, engraved and chased, is applied to the front of the frame. The three silver casters are pear-shaped, resting on a cast molded foot. The lower section of the caster body is raised and joined at the midsection to a seamed upper half. The removable domed covers are raised, pierced, and engraved, with an applied wire flange. The pattern of the piercing is divided into vertical panels containing diaperwork and symmetrical scrolls. On the two smaller casters alternating panels have been made blind by the addition on the interior of silver sheet. The bottles are of faceted glass with a straight-sided lower half, tapering to a slender neck. They have cylindrical stoppers made from seamed sheet and a cast domed top.

Like the Samuel Wood cruet set in this collection bearing Faneuil arms (cat. 94), this object characterizes the taste and purchasing power of Boston's wealthy merchants in the mid-eighteenth century. The design, which was made in prodigious quantity by Samuel Wood's

shop, was also produced by silversmiths in New York and Philadelphia.[1] The form, with a cinquefoil base supported on scrolled legs with a central handle, is commonly called a "Warwick" cruet, named for an early set made for the earl of Warwick.[2] The casters were used for pepper, mustard, and sugar, and the bottles for oil and vinegar. James Lomax proposed that, instead of being passed at table, the cruet stands were intended to be placed on the sideboard.[3]

The engraved arms probably refer to Nathaniel Wheelwright[4] and his wife, Anne, a daughter of Charles Apthorp. Apthorp had established one of the largest mercantile fortunes in Boston, and the family was prominent among Boston's loyalist minority, profiting from contracts established to furnish supplies to the king's armies.[5] The arms appear to be engraved over a previous coat, but the engraving style is consistent with that used in the mid-eighteenth century. A pair of candlesticks bearing the same arms is recorded.[6]

1. New York, The Metropolitan Museum of Art, *American Rococo, 1750–1775: Elegance in Ornament*, 1992, pp. 124–26.

2. Sold Sotheby's, London, June 5, 1997, lot 134. Also see David Buttery, "Anthony Nelme's Masterpiece," *Country Life* 183 (1989), p. 142.

3. Lomax 1992, p. 95.

4. In 1763 Nathaniel Wheelwright testified in a case of fraud charged against two "notorious cheats" who had promised to reveal the location of a chest of money. Wheelwright and two others followed the defendants to the location, a tunnel under a mill, and were trapped there when the defendants closed the door and fled. They were rescued by a passerby, and the defendants were sentenced to prison for three months and to sit in the pillory for one hour wearing a sign inscribed, *A Cheat*. "Boyles Journal of Occurrences in Boston," *New England Historical and Genealogical Register* 84 (1930), pp. 160–61.

5. James H. Stark, *The Loyalists of Massachusetts* (Boston, 1910), pp. 351–52.

6. Charles Knowles Bolton, *Bolton's American Armory* (Boston, 1927), p. 178.

98

· 98 ·

SAUCEBOAT

Possibly by Joseph Sanders (first mark entered 1730)
London, 1747/8
Silver
57.59

MARKS: on underside, leopard's head crowned; date letter *m*; maker's mark *IS* (possibly Grimwade 1655); lion passant

ARMORIALS: engraved on side, the arms of Young, possibly for William Young (1725–1788), of Delaford in Iver, co. Buckinghamshire

INSCRIPTIONS: engraved on underside of body, *M.W.C.B./1894*

H. 14 cm (5½ in.); w. 17.9 cm (7¹/₁₆ in.); d. 12.9 cm (5¹/₁₆ in.)

WEIGHT: 558.5 gm (17 oz 19 dwt)

PROVENANCE: Lent by Dr. George Clymer, March 10, 1939, transferred to Mrs. George Clymer, Anonymous, August 28, 1956, Gift in Memory of Dr. George Clymer by his wife, Mrs. Clymer, January 10, 1957

DESCRIPTION: The large oval sauceboat has a wide pouring lip and an everted, fluted rim. Formed from sheet, it rests on cast scrolled legs with shell feet and a spirally fluted mount at the join to the body. A handle formed of two C-scrolls, cast in halves and seamed vertically, is mounted opposite the lip; it has been repaired at the join with a patch.

99 (Color Plate XI)

· 99 ·

PAIR OF TEA CANISTERS WITH SUGAR BOX

Marked by Peter Taylor (only known mark entered 1740)

London, 1747/8

Silver

1991.1–3

MARKS: on underside of each piece, maker's mark *PT* (Grimwade 2239); lion passant; date letter *m*; leopard's head crowned

1991.1: H. 12.4 cm (4⅞ in.); w. 7.7 cm (3 in.); d. 10.4 cm (4⅛ in.)

1991.2: H. 12.4 cm (4⅞ in.); w. 7.7 cm (3 in.); d. 10.3 cm (4⅟₁₆ in.)

1991.3: H. 12.4 cm (4⅞ in.); w. 10.2 cm (4 in.); d. 10.3 cm (4⅟₁₆ in.)

WEIGHT: 1991.1: 507.5 gm (16 oz 6 dwt). 1991.2: 487.6 gm (15 oz 14 dwt). 1991.3: 635 gm (20 oz 1 dwt)

PROVENANCE: purchased from Partridge Fine Arts, PLC, London,¹ January 23, 1991, Jessie and Sigmund Katz collection, Gift of Mrs. S. J. Katz, by exchange

EXHIBITED: Boston, Museum of Fine Arts, 1994

PUBLISHED: Hartop 1996, p. 322

DESCRIPTION: Each canister is rectangular in section, with bombé sides and an inset base with a molded wire rim. The sugar box is of a similar form, but square in section. The cast panels of the sides of the boxes are filled with complex architectural fantasies in low relief against a crisply matted ground. The arcades are occupied by figures in Chinese

dress, waterfalls, and foliage. On two sides of each box is centered an asymmetrical cartouche from which engraving has been removed. The cast hinged covers are modeled with coral and shells, and an applied cast figure of a lizard serves as a thumbpiece.

This set of tea canisters and sugar box is distinguished by the extreme complexity of its chinoiserie decoration. The side panels are filled with an elaborate architectural construct, reminiscent of a stage set, in which pillars, arcades, balconies, and steps are joined by cascading water, floral bouquets, and scrolls. Inhabiting these intricate spaces are figures in exotic dress; they gesture, as though to an audience, or pose with parasols. The surface, except for the removal of engraved armorials in the cartouche, is practically pristine. Even the delicately pounced dots on the silk costumes, the bright facets left by the burnishing, and the crisp matting of the background are clearly visible. Such details are ordinarily lost through use and polishing; these canisters must have been only rarely removed from their case.

Several other sets of canisters have similar, but not identical, decoration. A set marked by Eliza Godfrey for 1754 is clearly modeled after a related design.² Another, in the collection of Alan and Simone Hartman, marked by Peter Archambo for 1745, interprets a similar design on a larger scale and, interestingly, is formed of chased panels, not cast like the present examples.³ A fourth set, marked in 1748 by Thomas

Heming, who had apprenticed with Archambo, has a more exaggerated bombé profile but a similarly dense pattern of overlapping architecture.[4] The broad differences in style, design, and technique suggest that a number of London chasers and modelers were adapting printed designs according to their own needs. A precise source has not yet been identified, but the *Books of Ornament* published in 1741 by William de la Cour (fl. 1740s, d. 1767) shows similar scrolled architectural forms inhabited by delicately positioned chinoiserie figures.[5] Other related designs are the *Nouveau Cartouches chinois*, engraved by Huquier after Alexis Peyrotte (1699–1769), and *The Chinese Conversation*, engraved by Aveline after François-Thomas Mondon (1694–1770).[6]

Peter Taylor's mark is rare. The talented modeler-chaser responsible for these canisters certainly also participated in the making of a silver-gilt cup of 1746 at Anglesey Abbey.[7] The bombé cup is decorated with cast and chased grapevines, floral garlands, and shell scrolls finished, like those on the Boston canisters, to a very high level of detail. An applied lizard appears to be the same model used on the covers of the canisters. A pair of candlesticks of 1741 with unusual scrolls on the nozzle and stem[8] and a pair of sauceboats of 1751 with swags of shells and coral[9] may also be the work of the same talented individual.

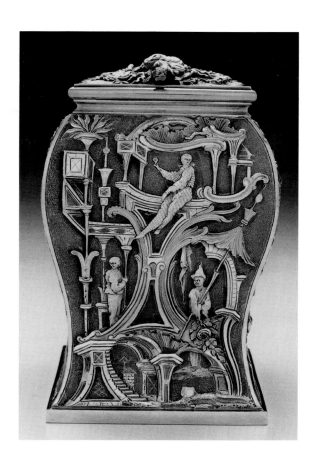

1. This group may be the same set sold (in a shagreen case) by Christie's, London, April 14, 1920, lot 41, which included a sugar ladle and a pair of sugar tongs and weighed 54 oz 6 dwt. The Museum's canisters were purchased in a shagreen case, with unmarked silver handles and lock plates, probably not contemporary with their manufacture.

2. Illus. Schroder 1988b, p. 204.

3. Hartop 1996, cat. 79. A related pair by the same maker marked for 1753 was sold by Christie's, London, February 25, 1970, lot 96.

4. Sold, Sotheby's, London, March 14, 1994, lot 131.

5. National Museum of Design, Cooper-Hewitt Museum, acc. no. 1962-126-1, William de la Cour, *First Book of Ornament* (London, 1742); *Second Book of Ornament* (London, 1742).

6. Illus. Alain Gruber, ed., *Classicism and the Baroque in Europe* (New York, 1992), pp. 308, 315.

7. Illus. Schroder 1988b, p. 189.

8. Sold Christie's, London, May 24, 1989, lot 252.

9. Sold Christie's, April 17, 1996, lot 180.

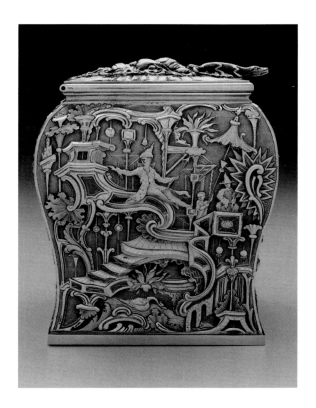

100

· 100 ·

SAUCEBOAT

Marked by William Grundy (first mark entered 1743)

London, 1748/9

Silver

1976.661

MARKS: on the underside, maker's mark *WG* (Grimwade 3147); date letter *n*; leopard's head crowned; lion passant

ARMORIALS: engraved on the side, the arms of Nealewell, Waff, Wass, or Waugh impaling an unidentified coat of arms (on a chevron sable three bezants impaling, per bend embattled gules and argent on a chief or a castle between two lions passant guardant)

H. 13.1 cm (5³⁄₁₆ in.); w. 20.6 cm (8⅛ in.); d. 11.6 cm (4⁹⁄₁₆ in.)

WEIGHT: 357.2 gm (11 oz 10 dwt)

PROVENANCE: Bequest of Barbara Boylston Bean, September 8, 1976

DESCRIPTION: The elliptical body of the sauceboat is raised, with a broad pouring spout and a shaped, cut rim. Three cast shell legs are applied. A double-scroll handle, cast in two halves and joined with a vertical seam, rises above the sauceboat.

· 101 ·

PAIR OF CHAFING DISHES

Marked by William Cripps (first mark entered 1743, d. 1767)

London, 1749/50

Silver, wood

65.263a–b

MARKS: on underside of each, maker's mark *WC* (Grimwade 3056); date letter *o*; leopard's head crowned; lion passant

INSCRIPTIONS: engraved on underside of each, *I/E★D*; *H/O★W* (twice); *M . I*

65.263a: H. 11 cm (4⁵⁄₁₆ in.); w. 24.1 cm (9½ in.); diam. of rim 13.5 cm (5⁵⁄₁₆ in.)

65.263b: H. 11.4 cm (4½ in.); w. 23.6 cm (9⁵⁄₁₆ in.); diam. of rim 13.4 cm (5⁵⁄₁₆ in.)

WEIGHT: 65.263a: 439.4 gm (14 oz 3 dwt). 65.263b: 456.4 gm (14 oz 13 dwt)

PROVENANCE: according to tradition, Edward Jackson (1707–1757) and his wife, Dorothy Quincy Jackson, by descent to their daughter, Mary Jackson (d. 1804), to her grandson, Dr. Oliver Wendell Holmes (1809–1894), to his grandson Edward Jackson Holmes, Bequest of Mrs. Edward Jackson Holmes, The Edward Jackson Holmes Collection, March 10, 1965

DESCRIPTION: Each bombé dish has a flaring rim that is pierced with quatrefoils and stylized foliage with an applied wire molding. The dish is raised, with a sunken center, and rests on four cast scrolled legs. A cylindrical socket supports the turned wooden handle. There is considerable wear to the surface and several breaks in the piercing.

This pair of chafing dishes was presented to the Museum by the widow of Edward Jackson Holmes, a former director and trustee, and the grandson of the eminent Boston physician and writer Dr. Oliver Wendell Holmes. The chafing dishes are believed to have descended in the family from Edward Jackson and his wife, Dorothy Quincy Jackson. The engraved initials for Edward and Dorothy Jackson, their daughter, Mary, and her grandson, Oliver Wendell Holmes, were apparently added by Holmes. Like many of his generation, he was fascinated with the colonial history of New England, and he romanticized the history of other pieces of family silver in a humorous verse of 1851.[1]

101

Unlike other wares bearing Cripp's mark, these dishes show a cautious use of rococo elements. They are lacking the pierced grate that would have held a cluster of burning charcoal to warm or cook a dish of food. In England by 1750 the form had been largely superseded by the dish cross, fueled by a spirit lamp, but in the colonies chafing dishes remained current, particularly, it seems, in Boston.[2]

1. Oliver Wendell Holmes, "On Lending a Punch Bowl," quoted in Kathryn C. Buhler, "Important Silver from the Edward Jackson Holmes Collection," *Boston Museum Bulletin* 65, no. 340 (1967), pp. 61–69. According to Buhler (see n. 2) the chafing dishes are not listed in the 1762 inventory of Dorothy Jackson's plate.

2. See examples in the Museum of Fine Arts, Boston, by John Coney, Jacob Hurd, Benjamin Burt, and Thomas Edwards, illus. Buhler 1972, pp. 70, 175–76, 188–89, 227–29, 284.

· 102 ·

KETTLE AND STAND
Marked by Henry Brind (first mark entered 1742)
London, 1750/1
Silver, rattan
33.153

MARKS: on underside of kettle and underside of lamp, maker's mark *HB* (Grimwade 950); leopard's head crowned; lion passant; date letter *p*

ARMORIALS: engraved on cover of lamp, an unidentified crest (a fish's tail erect)

H. 37.6 cm (14¹³⁄₁₆ in.); w. 24.3 cm (9⁹⁄₁₆ in.); d. 37.6 cm (14 ⁵⁄₁₆ in.)

WEIGHT: 2,024.2 gm (65 oz 1 dwt)

PROVENANCE: Anonymous Gift in Memory of Charlotte Beebe Wilbour (1833–1914), March 2, 1933

EXHIBITED: Boston, Museum of Fine Arts, 1933

PUBLISHED: Edward Wenham, "Georgian Silver in American Collections," *International Studio* 88 (1927), p. 42

DESCRIPTION: The inverted pear-shaped kettle, raised from sheet, rests on a stand. The kettle has a plain, highly polished body. The curved spout, cast

102

in two vertically seamed pieces, has a foliate base. The cover has a hidden hinge and a finial in the form of an inverted acorn. Two cast scallop shells support the hinged scrolled handle. The handle is cast and covered in the center with rattan. The stand is supported by three cast scrolled legs with acanthus leaves covering the knees and shell feet. A lamp is held by brackets and has a detachable cover with a crest engraved on it. A pierced apron composed of three panels extends below the rim of the stand. The hinge and upper rim of the kettle have been extensively damaged and repaired.

· 103 ·

COFFEEPOT

Marked by William Shaw (II) and William Preist
(entered into partnership 1749)
London, 1751/2
Silver, wood
13.2857

MARKS: to right of handle, lion passant; maker's mark *WS/WP* (Grimwade 3335); date letter *q*; leopard's head crowned

ARMORIALS: engraved on one side, the arms of Faneuil; engraved on other side, the crest of Faneuil

INSCRIPTIONS: engraved on underside, *Peter Faneuil Born June 20 1700 HIS POT*

H. 27.2 cm (10¹¹⁄₁₆ in.); w. 25 cm (9¹¹⁄₁₆ in.); diam. of foot 12.3 cm (4⅞ in.)

WEIGHT: 1,267.3 gm (40 oz 15 dwt)

PROVENANCE: according to tradition, Benjamin Faneuil (1702–1785), by descent to his daughter Mary Cutler who married George Bethune; by descent through Bethune family, Gift in the Name of Mrs. Jane Bethune Craig Hawkins, wife of General John P. Hawkins, November 4, 1913

EXHIBITED: Boston, Museum of Fine Arts, 1975, p. 54, cat. 58; Minneapolis, The Minneapolis Institute of Arts, *The American Craftsman and the European Tradition, 1620–1820*, 1989, p. 87, cat. 28

PUBLISHED: Bigelow 1917, pp. 374–77; Kathryn C. Buhler, "Gifts of Faneuil Silver," *Museum of Fine Arts Bulletin* 37, no. 221 (June 1939), pp. 51–53

DESCRIPTION: The pear-shaped body rests on a spreading circular foot. The body is formed of sheet, seamed vertically, with an inset base. The curved spout, cast in two pieces, has fluted, foliate scrolls at its base and an acathus leaf at its tip. The ear-shaped wooden handle is mounted from the top by a cast scrolled socket with a foliate base and at the base with a fluted scroll. The hinged, stepped, domed cover is raised and fitted with a wire rim and bezel. It is surmounted by a cast baluster finial.

By the 1750s a pear-shaped coffeepot such as this one was a standard model in London, produced by a number of specialized makers.[1] In a large shop, such a piece might have been fabricated entirely by journeymen who did not have their own mark registered at Goldsmiths' Hall. It would almost certainly have been available from a retailer readymade, with some clients choosing to add an engraved coat of arms, for which they would pay extra. The

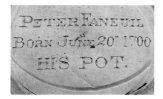

design and engraving style of this cartouche was also ubiquitous by the 1750s.

This pot bears the arms of Faneuil, a Huguenot family from La Rochelle that had come to the colonies through Holland.[2] According to tradition it had been ordered from London by Peter Faneuil (1700–1742/3), one of Boston's richest merchants and a philanthropist best known for his construction of the town hall and marketplace known as the Cradle of Liberty, Faneuil Hall. The coffeepot descended in the family until it was given to the Museum in 1913, and at some point, probably in the late nineteenth century, was embellished with the inscription under the foot: *Peter Faneuil Born June 20 1700 HIS POT*. As Peter Faneuil died in 1742, however, and the pot is hallmarked for 1751/2, it must be presumed that the arms refer to Peter's brother and heir, Benjamin (1701–1785). Benjamin inherited a large share of his brother's estate, which, excluding real estate, was valued at £44,451 and included 1,400 ounces of plate.[3] He added to his brother's business by establishing a paper mill in the town of Milton that had the sole privilege of making paper in the province. The family's overseas contacts were extensive, and the surviving papers from Peter Faneuil's tenure offer a good insight into the way a colonial merchant who aspired to live in the grand style might order his luxuries from abroad.[4] Porcelain, silks, glass, furniture, cutlery, books, reading glasses, as well as servants were sent for, often with explicit instructions about how the agent should negotiate the transaction. The family's agents in London, responsible for fulfilling a broad range of requests, probably made many of their purchases from a silversmith's secondhand goods or their retail stock. In this case, the pot was probably bought secondhand, since another coat of arms seems to have been removed before the Faneuil arms were added.

This pot has been cited as one of the earliest examples of rococo engraving to appear in Boston, one of a small number of imported "high style" London examples that would have had a direct influence on local smiths.[5] The Faneuil silver was certainly admired and emulated by visitors to their richly appointed house, but other similar coffeepots, so common

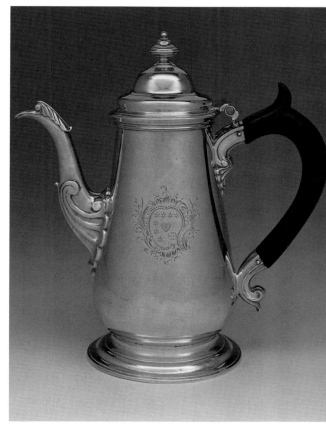

103

in London, must have been available. Peter Faneuil owned at least one silver coffeepot, left by bequest to his brother-in-law Gillam Phillips.[6]

1. Other examples of the form in the Folger's Coffee Collection are by Richard Bayley (1741), Thomas Whipham (1745), Richard Gurney & Co. (1747), exh. Boston, Museum of Fine Arts, 1968, cat. ed. by Ross Taggart, pp. 34, 38, 39. See also an example by Thomas Whipham and William Williams (1750) in Minneapolis, The Minneapolis Institute of Arts, *The American Craftsman and the European Tradition, 1620–1820*, 1989, p. 86, cat. 68.

2. Also see the cruet stand and cann in this collection with the arms of Faneuil (cats. 65, 94).

3. Abram English Brown, *Faneuil Hall and Faneuil Hall Market* (Boston, 1901), pp. 108–13. See also Sargent 1856, pp. 541–44.

4. Ibid., pp. 110–13.

5. Minneapolis, The Minneapolis Institute of Arts, *The American Craftsman and the European Tradition, 1620–1820*, 1989, p. 87.

6. Sargent 1856, p. 542.

PAIR OF CANDLESTICKS, SNUFFER TRAY, AND SNUFFERS

Marked by John Cafe (first mark entered 1740, d. ca. 1757)

London, 1751/2 and 1752/3

Silver, steel

58.377–378, 58.382, 58.381

MARKS: 58.377 (candlestick): on underside, maker's mark *IC* (Grimwade 1228); lion passant (repeated on nozzle); leopard's head crowned; date letter *r*. 58.378 (candlestick): on underside of base, maker's mark *IC* (Grimwade 1228) (repeated on nozzle); lion passant (repeated on nozzle); leopard's head crowned; date letter *q*. 58.382 (snuffer tray): on underside, maker's mark *IC* (Grimwade 1228); lion passant; leopard's head crowned; date letter *r*. 58.381 (snuffers): unmarked

ARMORIALS: engraved on the nozzle of each candlestick, on each waxpan, and on the handle of snuffer tray, the crest of Cary for Samuel Cary (1713–1769), of Charlestown, Massachusetts

INSCRIPTIONS: engraved around the base of each candlestick and on the tray, *The Gift of {Zachy. Bourrijan &/Hungerford Spooner/Esqrs.} to Captn. Saml. Cary 1726*

58.377 (candlestick): H. 21.9 cm (8⅝ in.); w. 13.8 cm (5⁷⁄₁₆ in.); d. 13.8 cm (5⁷⁄₁₆ in.)

58.378 (candlestick): H. 21.9 cm (8⅝ in.); w. 13.8 cm (5⁷⁄₁₆ in.); d. 13.8 cm (5⁷⁄₁₆ in.)

58.382 (snuffer tray): H. 6.1 cm (2⅜ in.); w. 20.9 cm (8¼ in.); d. 10.7 cm (4¼ in.)

58.381 (snuffers): L. 16.4 cm (6⁷⁄₁₆ in.); w. 5.3 cm (2¼ in.)

WEIGHT: 58.377: 569.8 gm (18 oz). 58.378: 555.7 gm (17 oz 17 dwt). 58.382: 328.9 gm (10 oz 11 dwt). 58.381: 90.7 gm (2 oz 18 dwt)

PROVENANCE: probably Samuel Cary, by descent to Richard Cary Curtis, Brookline, Mass., Gift of Mrs. Richard Cary Curtis, April 10, 1958

DESCRIPTION: Each candlestick has a fluted hexafoil base with a scallop shell on each corner. From a circle at the center of the base the baluster stem rises to a flattened knop and a flaring, fluted mid-

section. The nozzle is urn-shaped. The waxpan is hexagonal, with scallop shells at each corner. The bases are cast in a single piece. The stems are hollow-cast in two pieces and seamed vertically. 58.377 has been repaired on the midsection of the stem, possibly contemporary with manufacture. The snuffers are of scissors form, with silver handles and steel blades. The cast silver handles have flattened oval rings for grips and scrolled arms riveted to the steel blade just above the point of crossing. One part of the blade has a curved pan with a deep rim, and the other arm has a flat blade fitted to the pan. The snuffers are raised on three small feet. The bow-shaped tray rests on four trefoil feet and has a complex molded border cast with shells at intervals. A cast double-scroll handle is located at the center of one side. One of the legs has been repaired.

It is likely that this group of lighting implements—candlesticks, snuffers, and stand[1]—belonged to Captain Samuel Cary of Charlestown, Massachusetts, although the inscription, dated 1726 (twenty-three years before the London hallmarks) almost certainly refers to a presentation to his father, also Captain Samuel Cary (1683–1739). The senior Cary was a ship's captain descended from a Bristol family, at least two members of which had served as mayor of that city.[2] The inscription on the candlesticks and snuffer stand indicates that the gift in 1726 came from Zachary Bourryan and Hungerford Spooner, whose descendants seem to have remained in close touch with the Cary family. Whatever the form of the original silver gift, it must have been outdated or damaged and replaced in the 1750s by the son Samuel, also a ship's captain. The younger Cary married in 1741 Margaret Greaves (1719–1762), and he established a regular and lucrative route between London and the West Indies. In 1747 he was wounded when captured by a French privateer, and, although released only a few months later, he never fully recovered. Tradition records that he was presented with a piece of plate by the City of London for his bravery, although the circumstances of his valor are unclear.[3] The son of Samuel II and Margaret Greaves, Samuel Cary III (1742–1812) established himself in Grenada and became the manager of a plantation belonging to a Mr. Bourryan, presumably the descendant of his family's friend. On the death

104

of Mr. Bourryan in England, the property in Grenada fell to his five sisters, under the guardianship of a Mr. Charles Spooner.[4]

John Cafe's production of this candlestick model and matching snuffer stand must have been prodigious. The candlestick was executed in several sizes and also with variations in the base, which might be square rather than hexagonal.[5] Cafe was apprenticed to the candlestick maker James Gould (who also marked a similar model), and he, in turn, trained his brother, William Cafe.[6]

1. Two candlesticks from the set of four were sold by the Museum in 1979.

2. Thomas Bellows Wyman, *Genealogies and Estates of Charlestown, 1629–1818* (Boston, 1879), p. 179.

3. Clifford K. Shipton, *Sibley's Harvard Graduates* (Boston, 1956), vol. 9, pp. 30–32.

4. C. G. C., *The Cary Letters* (Cambridge, Mass., 1981), pp. 15, 21–22.

5. For example, see a stick of this model marked in 1750/1 at Colonial Williamsburg, illus. Davis 1976, p. 29, cat. 17; another with a square base of 1745 in the Huntington Collection, illus. Wark 1978, p. 148, cat. 378. For other examples of the snuffer stand, see Sotheby's, London, November 11, 1993, lot 412.

6. John P. Fallon, "The Goulds and Cafes, Candlestick Makers," *Proceedings of the Society of Silver Collectors* 2, nos. 9–10 (Autumn 1980) pp. 146–50.

• 105 •

TWO-HANDLED CUP AND COVER

Marked by John Berthellot (first mark entered 1738)

London, 1751/2

Silver gilt

61.656

MARKS: near rim and on bezel of cover, maker's mark *IB* (Grimwade 1179); lion passant; leopard's head crowned; date letter *q*

ARMORIALS: engraved on side, the arms of Warburton, co. Chester, quartering Dutton; on opposite side the arms of Grosvenor

INSCRIPTIONS: surrounding the cartouche, the inscription, *Sodalibus Pateram Hanc Donavit / Thoms Slaughter / 1751*; and the motto, *Je Vol le Droit Avoir*. On opposite side, surrounding cartouche: *Munera Laetitiam que dei / Sine Cerere et Baccho Friget Venus*

H. 26.9 cm (10⁹⁄₁₆ in.); w. 22.3 cm (8¾ in.); d. 11.7 cm (4⅝ in.)

WEIGHT: 1,298.4 gm (41 oz 15 dwt)

PROVENANCE: sold Christie's, London, November 30, 1960, lot 79, purchased by Thomas Lumley, Ltd., London, purchased September 20, 1961, Theodora Wilbour Fund in Memory of Charlotte Beebe Wilbour

PUBLISHED: Clayton 1971, pp. 94–96, fig. 213; Clayton 1985a, pp. 138, 144, fig. 213

DESCRIPTION: The inverted pear-shaped body rests on a circular domed foot that is richly chased with grapes, leaves, and two satyr's masks. The raised body of the cup is chased on all sides with sprays of flowers, and C-scrolls and flowers on either side form cartouches enclosing an engraved coat of arms. The cast double-scroll handles are surmounted by leaves and terminate in scrolls and leaves. The stepped, domed lid is chased with C-scrolls and flower sprays and surmounted by a finial in the form of the Warburton crest, a Saracen's head crowned with a wreath and three ostrich feathers. It is raised, with an applied rim and bezel. The heavy gilding is presumably a restoration.

John Berthelot, who marked this cup, is a little-known maker. His apprenticeship and freedom are unrecorded and his first mark as a watch case maker was entered in 1738.[1] His later marks (1739) were entered in the largeworkers' book, but, because the smallworkers' books from 1739–58 have not survived, it is not known whether he continued to enter marks as a smallworker. Watch cases bearing his mark have not survived.[2] The few pieces of hollow-ware that do bear his mark do not show the dense rococo chasing evident on this cup.[3] The rich overall decoration of flowers, grapes, and masks is unusual for a cup of this period, as is the distinctive small size. The masks on the foot, surrounded by clusters of grapes, suggest the cup's function as a loving cup, as does the engraved inscription taken from Terence, *Sine Cere et Baccho Frigere Venus* (Without Ceres and Bacchus, Venus grows cold). Ceres and Bacchus were often invoked in the seventeenth and eighteenth centuries as personifications of Abundance. The complex design of the handles is a variation of a model used on several of the grandest cups of the 1730s marked by Paul de Lamerie, George Wickes, Charles Kandler, and Benjamin Godfrey.[4] The decoration, however, which is entirely chased and without cast, applied elements, is not in keeping with the work of the circle of modelers sometimes called the "Lamerie group."[5]

The occasion for which this cup was commissioned remains obscure. On opposite sides of the cup are engraved two coats of arms. The arms of Warburton quartering Dutton are surrounded by an inscription naming the recipient of the cup, Thomas Slaughter, a prominent figure in the city of Chester, and the date, 1751. The Warburton crest, a Saracen's head, serves as the finial of the cup, and the Warburton motto is engraved beneath. Thomas Slaughter is recorded as having received the freedom of Chester in 1747. After 1739, he married Anne, daughter of Thomas Warburton (1676–1739), younger son of a baronet, George Warburton (1675–1743). He was elected councilman in the same year he received his freedom, served as sheriff in 1759, and alderman in 1767. Slaughter was a partner in a mining operation that proposed to draw lead from the lands bequeathed in 1658 to the Chester City Companies by a Chester butcher, Owen Jones. The modest bequest was intended to support the neediest members of the city's guilds, but the discovery of lead on the properties raised the value and desirability of the gift considerably.[6]

On the opposite side of the cup are engraved the arms of Grosvenor of Eaton. The Grosvenor family dominated the politics of the

105

city of Chester in the years after 1715, although not without some opposition.[7] The Grosvenors also apparently gave the gold cup each year for the Chester Races, although it seems unlikely that this cup, lacking an inscription, was offered as a prize.[8]

The connection between Thomas Slaughter and the Warburtons and the Grosvenors is somewhat complex. Robert Grosvenor (1695–1755), sixth baronet, served as member of Parliament for Chester from 1733 to 1755. His older brother, Richard (1689–1732), fourth baronet, had married in 1724 Anne, daughter of George Warburton, a cousin of Anne, who married Thomas Slaughter, recipient of this cup.[9]

When the cup was sold at Christie's in 1960, it was proposed that it was in some way associated with a meeting of a Jacobite group called the Cycle Club at the house of Thomas Slaughter.[10] The Cycle Club was founded by Sir Watkin Williams Wynn of Wynnstay and is perhaps the best known of the many secret societies devoted to the Jacobite cause. A complex series of regulations required that members must reside within a fifteen-mile radius of Wrexham, and meetings were held over dinner at each member's house in succession, explaining the club's name.[11] The meetings are also said to have been timed to coincide with the local races,[12] and to have evolved from a mainly political agenda to a bacchanalian one.[13] The decoration and inscriptions on the cup lack the traditional Jacobite motifs, but a Jacobite connection cannot be discounted completely. The three sons of Sir Thomas Grosvenor, third baronet, were raised by the Jacobite Francis Chomondeley of Vale Royal, and further research may prove that the Grosvenors and Thomas Slaughter were fellow members of the Cycle Club.

1. Grimwade 1990, p. 439.

2. I am grateful to Richard Edgcumbe, Metalwork Department, Victoria and Albert Museum, who kindly shared his thoughts on this question. The volumes in the Goldsmiths' Company record each maker's mark as required by the Plate Act of 1738. See Grimwade 1990, pp. 4–5.

3. See, for example, Sotheby's, London, July 4, 1989, lot 210.

4. See a cup in the Goldsmiths' Company marked by Lamerie for 1739, exh. London, Goldsmiths' Hall, 1990, p. 146, cat. 95; another cup supplied by Wickes to the Scrope family, illus. Barr 1980, p. 111; another supplied by Kandler to the ninth earl of Exeter, exh., Stamford, Burghley House, *Exhibition of Burghley Plate*, 1984, p. 33, cat. 34; another in the Gilbert collection marked by Godfrey and bearing the arms of the sixth earl of Anglesey, illus. Schroder 1988a, p. 235, cat. 59.

5. See Hartop 1996, pp. 48–53.

6. Maurice H. Ridgway, *Chester Silver, 1727–1837* (Chichester, 1985), pp. 12–13.

7. Howard Hodson, *Cheshire, 1660–1780: Restoration to Industrial Revolution* (Chester, 1978), pp. 24–27. I am grateful to Kristina Wilson for her tenacity in pursuing this subject.

8. For other Grovesnor race cups, see Christie's, London, March 10, 1965, lot 105; Christie's, London, October 4, 1950, lots 126–28; 148; also see Ridgway, *Chester Silver*, p. 53.

9. Mrs. L. Parker, archivist at the Cheshire Record Office, was helpful in establishing this relationship.

10. Correspondence in the curatorial files from Thomas Lumley, June 15, 1961.

11. Geoffrey B. Seddon, *The Jacobites and Their Drinking Glasses* (Woodbridge, 1995), pp. 64–68.

12. Hodson, *Cheshire*, p. 24.

13. Albert Hartshorne, *Antique Drinking Glasses* (New York, 1968), p. 368.

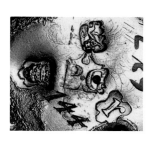

· 106 ·

COFFEEPOT

Marked by Phillips Garden (first mark entered 1738)
London, 1752/3
Silver, wood
63.7

MARKS: on underside of body, maker's mark *PG* (Grimwade 2179) (repeated on underside of cover); date letter *r*; leopard's head crowned; lion passant

ARMORIALS: chased below the spout, an unidentified crest (a winged sphinx)

INSCRIPTIONS: scratched on underside of foot, *45=7*; scratched next to marks, *144*

H. 30.3 cm (11¹⁵⁄₁₆ in.); w. 21.8 cm (8⁹⁄₁₆ in.); diam. of base 12.5 cm (4¹⁵⁄₁₆ in.)

WEIGHT: 1,434.5 gm (46 oz 2 dwt)

PROVENANCE: J. J. Klejman, New York, purchased January 9, 1960, Theodora Wilbour Fund in Memory of Charlotte Beebe Wilbour

DESCRIPTION: The elongated pear-shaped body is formed of a single raised and chased sheet. It rests on a cast circular spreading foot that is divided into three panels enclosing a cluster of cattails, a spray of flowers, and a winged dragon. The body is chased with flowers and C-scrolls against a scaled ground and, below the spout, a sphinx. The cast sockets for the scrolled wooden handle are formed of scallops, foliage, and, on the upper mount, a lion's mask and a cluster of grapes. The short spout, cast in two pieces and seamed, is fashioned as a cluster of coffee leaves and blossoms above a shell-shaped scroll. The raised domed cover, attached with a hinge, is chased with C-scrolls and flowers, and the cast finial is in the form of an opening bud.

This coffeepot exemplifies the complex associations within the London goldsmiths' trade in the mid-eighteenth century. The tall form on a spreading base with a short spout is uncommon, but not unique. The decoration on the body, consisting of conventional chased flowers and scrolls, is combined with a richly modeled and cast spout, foot, and handle sockets strongly reminiscent of work marked by Paul de Lamerie. Indeed, Phillips Garden is believed to have bought Lamerie's tools and models after his death in 1751. Most similar to Lamerie's work are the expressive lion's head cast into the support for the upper handle socket, possibly a "signature" of Lamerie's chief modeler, and the

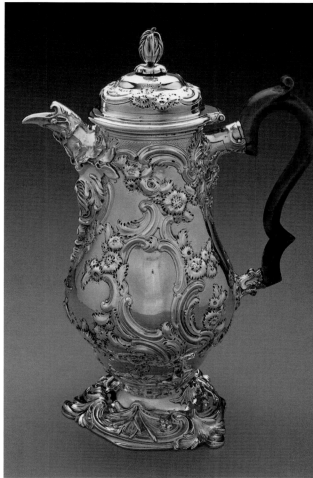

106

spout with its asymmetrical scrolls, shells, and naturalistically rendered coffee leaves. Garden's model for this spout had been used by Lamerie nearly ten years earlier, as shown on a coffeepot with stand in the Gilbert collection,[1] and it was later used in a pot marked by Thomas Gilpin of 1750.[2] The upper handle socket for Garden's coffeepot also follows the model of the Lamerie coffeepot. There are substantial differences in the finished design, however, suggesting that while Garden's shop may have had access to models from Lamerie's shop, they were adapted for each use. The foot used for the Garden coffeepot is thickly cast and divided into panels enclosing a cluster of cattails, a winged dragon, and a spray of flowers. A somewhat softer chased rendering of this same design appears on a coffeepot of 1755 marked by William Cripps in the Gilbert collection,[3] and the same lion's mask handle socket was used by Cripps on a pot of 1753 in the Folger's collection.[4] Other cast elements of the Cripps coffeepot may be seen on a pot marked by Samuel Courtauld.[5]

The explanation for the repetition of these cast elements on works marked by a range of makers over a broad span of years remains unclear. In some cases, it seems likely that objects with identical features were completed in a single shop and then sold to various gold-smiths for marking and sale. The pots in this group, however—marked by Lamerie, Garden, Cripps, Gilpin, and Courtauld—do not share a sensibility in overall design, proportion, or in the integration of the ornament and form. This may suggest that the head of each workshop was buying molds or even cast parts and adapt-ing them as desired.

Another unusual feature of this pot is the crest chased on the body under the spout. Unfortunately, it is unidentified, and the engraved arms have been removed.

1. Illus. Schroder 1988a, pp. 268–71, cat. 69.

2. Exh. Boston, Museum of Fine Arts, *The Folger's Coffee Collection of Antique English Silver Coffee Pots and Accessories*, 1968, p. 40. This pot has another fea-ture in common with the Garden pot—three-lobed leaves placed at intervals around the base where it is joined to the foot.

3. Schroder 1988a, pp. 301–3, cat. 79.

4. Exh. Boston, Museum of Fine Arts, *The Folger's Coffee Collection*, 1968, p. 41.

5. Schroder 1988a, pp. 298–300, cat. 78.

• 107 •

PAIR OF TEA CANISTERS AND A
SUGAR BOX IN A CASE
Marked by Samuel Taylor (first mark entered 1744)
London, 1753/4
Silver, shagreen, wood
1985.197, 1985.198a-b, 1985.199a-b, 1985.200a-b

MARKS: on underside of each canister, maker's mark *ST* (Grimwade 2645) (repeated on bezel of larger canister 1985.200b); lion passant (repeated on bezel of each cover); date letter *s*; leopard's head crowned. 1985.197 (box): on all silver sections of lock, hinges, and handle mount, maker's mark *CN* (unidentified); lion passant

INSCRIPTIONS: engraved in the cartouche on each canister, *SE*

1985.197: H. 20.4 cm (8⅛ in.); w. 30.9 cm (12⅕ in.); d. 12.8 cm (5½ in.)

1985.198a-b: H. 14.4 cm (5¹¹⁄₁₆ in.); d. 9.2 cm (3⅝ in.)
1985.199a-b: H. 12.8 cm (5½ in.); d. 7.7 cm (3 in.)
1985.200a-b: H. 12.9 cm (5⅛ in.); d. 7.8 cm (3¹⁄₁₆ in.)

WEIGHT: 1985.198a-b: 1,434.5 gm (46 oz 2 dwt). 1985.199a-b: 1,434.5 gm (46 oz 2 dwt). 1985.200a-b: 243.8 gm (7 oz 17 dwt)

PROVENANCE: according to tradition, given by William Shirley (1694–1771) to an ancestor of Andrew Montgomery Ritchie, by descent to Miss Janet Ritchie, Gift of the heirs of Miss Janet Ritchie, April 24, 1985

DESCRIPTION: The tea canisters are bombé in form, resting on a molded cast foot decorated with a band of cast and chased flowers. The body of the canister is raised and chased with spiraling flutes, with chased flowers filling the lobes. An asymmetri-cal cartouche is reserved at the front of each. The high rim is formed from seamed sheet and chased with flowers over the seam. The domed cover has a bezel, a tooled rim, and a finial in the form of a flower and stem. It is chased with spiraling flutes and flowers. The inverted pear-shaped sugar box is constructed and decorated in the same way. The canisters are identical in design; the sugar box is similar but has broader proportions. The inverted pear-shaped body rests on a circular domed foot with a band of flowers and foliage against a matted ground. The body is chased with spiral fluting alter-nating with bands of flowers. The domed cover is chased with similar spiral fluting and bands of flow-ers. There is a cast finial in the form of a flower and a tooled rim.

Samuel Taylor's workshop must have produced sets of tea and sugar canisters like this in enor-mous quantity, to judge by the number of sur-viving examples. They seem to have been made throughout the 1750s. The spiral fluting and chased flowers on this set are characteristic,[1] but there are some variations in design, includ-ing a set covered only with spiral scrolls,[2] and another straight-sided set, possibly made espe-cially to fit in their carved Chinese ivory box.[3] The shagreen box belonging to this set would have been supplied by a specialist box maker. The sponsor's mark on the simple silver mounts is unattributed.

107

The set, first lent to the Museum in 1927, is traditionally believed to have been given to an ancestor of the donor by William Shirley, governor of Massachusetts.[4] Shirley was born in England, educated in the law, and immigrated to America in 1731. He held the positions of judge of admiralty and then advocate general, and eventually, in 1741, with the support of the duke of Newcastle, he replaced the unpopular Governor Jonathan Belcher. Shirley successfully raised troops to recapture Louisburg on Cape Breton Island from the French, who had intended to use it as a naval base. Between 1749 and 1753 he was in England and France as part of a commission to determine the boundary between New England and the French territories to the north. When he returned to America, he assumed charge of all the fighting forces on the continent, but after the failure of his expedition to Niagara, he began to lose support. Suspected of treason and criticized for financial irresponsibility, he was ordered back to England in 1756. Seven years later he was appointed governor of the Bahama Islands, a position in which he was succeeded by his only surviving son, Thomas. He returned to Massachusetts in 1767, remaining there until his death.

1. For example, see Christie's, London, March 19, 1986, lots 216 and 222; Jackson 1911, vol. 2, p. 968; Christie's, New York, April 19, 1990, lot 359; Lauren Rogers Library and Museum of Art, *The Thomas and Harriet Gibbons Georgian Silver Collection* (Laurel, Miss., 1979), p. 14.

2. Grimwade 1974, pl. 68b.

3. Timothy Schroder, *The Francis E. Fowler, Jr., Collection of Silver* (Los Angeles, 1991), pp. 30–31, cat. 6.

4. The monogram, *SE*, has not been linked to a member of the Shirley or Ritchie families.

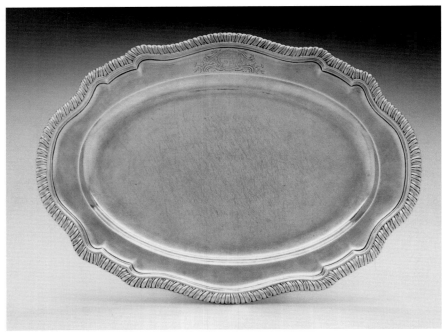

108

A pair to this dish was deaccessioned by the Museum in 1954 and is now in the collection of Colonial Williamsburg.[1]

1. Illus. Davis 1976, p. 140, cat. 143.

• 108 •

MEAT DISH
Marked by Magdalen Feline (first mark entered 1753)
London, 1754/5
Silver
33.158

MARKS: under rim, leopard's head crowned; date letter *t*; maker's mark *MF*; lion passant

ARMORIALS: engraved on rim, the arms of Trotter impaling Gordon for Sir Coutts Trotter of Westville, co. Lincolnshire (1767–1837), who married in 1802 Margaret, daughter of Alexander Gordon, lord Rockville

INSCRIPTIONS: engraved on underside, *No. 10/60–9*

H. 3 cm (1³⁄₁₆ in.); w. 41.7 cm (16⁷⁄₁₆ in.); d. 31.3 cm (12⁵⁄₁₆ in.)

WEIGHT: 1,808.7 gm (58 oz 3 dwt)

PROVENANCE: Anonymous Gift in Memory of Charlotte Beebe Wilbour (1833–1914), March 2, 1933

EXHIBITED: Boston, Museum of Fine Arts, 1933

PUBLISHED: Edward Wenham, "Women Recorded as Silversmiths," *The Antique Collector* 17 (March–April 1946), p. 64, fig. 6

DESCRIPTION: The raised oval dish has a broad rim and a shaped edge with an applied, cast gadrooned border.

• 109 •

MONTEITH
Marked by William Grundy (first mark entered 1743)
London, 1754/5
Silver
68.67

MARKS: on underside of bowl, maker's mark *WG* (Grimwade 3147); leopard's head crowned; date letter *t*; lion passant

ARMORIALS: engraved on the side, the arms, crest, and motto of Livingston quartering Hepburn and Callender, for Robert G. Livingston (1749–1787)

INSCRIPTIONS: engraved around inside of foot, *Robt. G. Livingston Junr*; scratched around inside of foot, *a present from his Grandmother To-.*; scratched on underside of bowl, *oz 64 = dwt 18*; scratched on underside of foot, *64=18 @ 8/o sterling*; scratched four times around underside of foot, *1755*

H. 22.2 cm (8³⁄₄ in.); w. 26.4 cm (10³⁄₈ in.); diam. of base 17.6 cm (6¹⁵⁄₁₆ in.)

WEIGHT: 2,012.9 gm (64 oz 14 dwt)

PROVENANCE: according to tradition, Robert Gilbert Livingston (1749–1787) who married Margaret Hude, to their daughter, Cornelia Beekman Livingston (d. 1847) who married John Crooke, to their son Philip Schuyler Crooke who married Margaret Caton, to their daughter Susanna who married John Henry Bergen, to their son Philip Crooke Bergen who married Helen Louisa Drowne, to their daughter Mary Helen who married Samuel St. John Morgan, Gift of Mrs. St. John Morgan, March 13, 1968

DESCRIPTION: The vessel has a bombé body and rests on a domed, spreading foot with a band of chased scrolls and flowers around the rim. The foot is formed of sheet, raised and chased, with an applied square wire around the rim. The body of the vessel is raised from sheet and has chased swags of flowers aligned with the shaped, notched rim. The rim is decorated with cast flowers, scrolls, and shells applied against a matted ground.

The monteith, a vessel for cooling glasses, was first produced in silver in the last decades of

109

the seventeenth century. Although the form enjoyed a revival in the neoclassical period, it is not generally associated with the rococo. The modest size of this monteith suggests that it may have been more important as part of a sideboard display than as a functional glass cooler, and because of the decorative nature of the rim it may have doubled as a punch bowl. The dense rococo ornament and broad chasing on the vessel are typical of the competent and somewhat dry work from Grundy's shop.[1]

The scratched inscription on the foot of this monteith records a tradition that it was given to Robert G. Livingston by his grandmother, Cornelia Beekman Livingston. She died, however, in 1742, so this must be discounted. The Livingstons, Scottish émigrés, were one of New York's preeminent families. The most distinguished member was Robert R. Livingston (1746–1813), a statesman and chancellor of New York for nearly twenty-five years.[2] For their properties in New York and estates along the Hudson River, the family acquired silver from predictably varied sources. Robert G.

Livingston, whose name is engraved on this monteith, was a second cousin of Robert R. Livingston, "the Chancellor," who purchased French tureens by Jacques Roettiers from his friend, Gouvernor Morris, ambassador to France.[3] The same arms, crest, and motto engraved on this monteith appear on a tankard by the New York maker Myer Myers.[4]

1. For example, see a coffeepot of 1764, illus. Grimwade 1974, pl. 63, another of 1759, exh. Boston, Museum of Fine Arts, *The Folger's Coffee Collection of Antique Silver Coffee Pots and Accessories*, 1968, p. 42. Also see cats. 100, 124, and 125 in this volume.

2. Clare Brandt, *An American Aristocracy: The Livingstons* (New York, 1986).

3. Clare Le Corbeiller, "Grace and Favor," *Metropolitan Museum of Art Bulletin* 27, no. 6 (February 1969), p. 294.

4. See a tankard in the Museum of the City of New York with the Livingston arms and an inscription for Robert and Mary Thong Livingston, a cousin of Robert Gilbert Livingston, illus. Jeanette W. Rosenbaum, *Myer Myers, Goldsmith 1723–1795* (Philadelphia, 1954), p. 132, pl. 26.

110

· IIO ·

PUNCH STRAINER

London, 1755/6

Silver

23.261

MARKS: in bowl of strainer, maker's mark illegible; leopard's head crowned; lion passant; date letter *u*

ARMORIALS: engraved on side, an unidentified crest (a lion sejant, dexter paw raised, murally collared and chained)

H. 3.5 cm (1⅜ in.); W. 17.6 cm (6¹⁵⁄₁₆ in.); d. 9.7 cm (3¹³⁄₁₆ in.)

WEIGHT: 99.2 gm (3 oz 4 dwt)

PROVENANCE: Gift of Miss Elizabeth Bartol, June 7, 1923

DESCRIPTION: The raised circular bowl is pierced overall in a rosette pattern. Two cast bracket-shaped handles are applied to the slightly everted rim.

· III ·

TWO DINNER PLATES

Marked by Peter Archambo (II) (1724–1768)

London, 1755/6

Silver

33.159–160

MARKS: on underside of each rim, date letter *u*; leopard's head crowned; lion passant; maker's mark *PA* with a *P* above and an *M* below (Grimwade 2129)

ARMORIALS: engraved on rim, the arms and crest of Curzon with Hanmer in pretence, for Asheton Curzon (1729–1820) who married Ester Hanmer (d. 1764), daughter of William Hanmer, Esq., of Hanmer Bettisfield and of Iscoyd, co. Flint

INSCRIPTIONS: 33.159: engraved on underside, *No 47/18-3*. 33.160: *No 23/17-17*

33.159: H. 1.9 cm (¾ in.); diam. 24.2 cm (9½ in.)

33.160: H. 2 cm (¹³⁄₁₆ in.); diam. 24.2 cm (9½ in.)

WEIGHT: 33.159: 518.8 gm (16 oz 13 dwt). 33.160: 501.8 gm (16 oz 3 dwt)

PROVENANCE: Anonymous Gift in Memory of Charlotte Beebe Wilbour (1833–1914), March 2, 1933

EXHIBITED: Boston, Museum of Fine Arts, 1933

DESCRIPTION: Each shaped circular plate has a broad rim with cast gadrooned borders.

Although Nathaniel Curzon purchased stylistically innovative neoclassical plate for Kedleston Hall as early as 1758, his younger brother, Asheton, seems to have chosen a more conventional design for this dinner service.[1] These plates date from the year of Asheton Curzon's marriage to Ester Hanmer, only daughter of William Hamner, Esq. Curzon was Tory member of Parliament for Clitheroe from 1754 to 1758 and again from 1792 to 1794. He was created baron Curzon of Penn in 1794 and in 1802 was created viscount Curzon; the crest, surmounted by a baron's coronet, must have been added between those dates. The engraved numbers on the reverse of these dinner plates, *23* and *47*, suggest that the original service included at least four dozen such plates, which would allow for several removes, or courses. Eight plates from the set, sold by the Museum

III

of Fine Arts in 1954, are now in Colonial Williams-burg,[2] and two more were sold in 1978.[3]

1. See the dinner service executed by Phillips Garden and retailed by William Cripps, sold Christie's, London, April 30, 1996, lots 107–18. Also see Cornforth 1996, pp. 128–31, cat. 132.

2. Illus. Davis 1976, p. 139, cat. 142.

3. Christie's, New York, March 8, 1978, lot 199.

· 112 ·

EPERGNE

Marked by Edward Wakelin (first mark entered 1747, d. 1784)
London, 1755/6
Silver
1986.241a–j

MARKS: on side of stand between branches, on underside of center dish, and on bezels of each small dish, date letter *u*; lion passant; maker's mark *EW* (Grimwade 656); leopard's head crowned

ARMORIALS: engraved in the well of central dish and in each smaller dish, the crest of Bouverie beneath a viscount's coronet, for Sir Jacob des Bouverie, third baronet, of Longford, co. Wiltshire (1694–1761)

INSCRIPTIONS: engraved on underside of central dish, *142=10*

H. 29.4 cm (11⁹⁄₁₆ in.); w. 49.6 cm (19½ in.); d. 47 cm (18½ in.)

WEIGHT: 4,507 gm (144 oz 18 dwt)

PROVENANCE: Firestone & Parson, Inc., Boston, purchased June 26, 1986, Theodora Wilbour Fund in Memory of Charlotte Beebe Wilbour

DESCRIPTION: The oval stand has four scrolled legs and foliate feet. The stand is chased and cast in an openwork design of leaves, flowers, scrolls, and two goat's heads. Four arms of coiling foliage support four shallow dishes of scroll and leaf pattern. Surmounting the stand is a pierced, boat-shaped basket with cast and chased scrolls and foliage.

By 1755, when this epergne was marked, Edward Wakelin had been working with George Wickes and Samuel Netherton for seven years. He is credited with having overseen the production of the workshop, leaving the retailing side of the business to Wickes and Netherton. It remains unclear precisely what was required to manage such a workshop. The design and modeling of an extraordinarily sophisticated epergne such as this may have been the work of several hands.

The epergne represents the full flowering of the English rococo style. Though it is of a relatively modest size, it is conceived as an abstract essay in three dimensions—the structure and the ornament are one. A small group of contemporary objects from the Wakelin

shop reflects this very distinctive aesthetic and incorporates some of the same motifs.[1] Two closely related epergnes were certainly designed and modeled by the same hand as the Bouverie epergne. One, bearing only a sponsor's mark, appeared on the London market in the 1950s.[2] A virtually identical example called the Burghley epergne with a matching plateau was made for the ninth earl of Exeter in 1755.[3] The frames for these two epergnes, like the Bouverie example, are composed of highly abstracted scrolls broken by guilloche patterning, intertwined with leaves and clusters of fruit. The stand for the Burghley epergne is an extraordinary conceit: the highly polished domed surface is torn away in irregular sections to reveal a matted subsurface. Naturalistic grapevines and leaves, raspberries, and clusters of fruit trail across the plateau, and goat's heads emerge above alternate feet. Simplified and more conservative versions of this design were also produced in the same year. A 1755 example shows the same structure and proportions and a similar apron of naturalistic fruit, but the rim of the basket and the legs are more restrained; the latter terminating in a simple scroll-and-shell.[4]

The present epergne is engraved with the crest of Bouverie beneath a viscount's coronet for Sir Jacob des Bouverie, third baronet of Longford, co. Wiltshire. After his succession in 1736, Sir Jacob moved to Clifford Street, St. James's; his principal country residence was at Longford Castle, where he made extensive changes to the gardens and the interiors. In 1747 Horace Walpole noted, "Sir Jacob Bouverie a considerable Jacobite who is made Viscount Folkestone bought his ermine at twelve thousand pounds a yard of the Duchess of Kendal (the King's mistress) d'aujourd'hui." Viscount Folkestone was an active patron of the arts; he was named president of the Society of Arts in 1753, and his private account books record the purchase of more than 109 pictures.[5] He was also a loyal client of George Wickes and his partners.[6] His first purchases recorded in the 1742/3 Gentlemen's Account Book were relatively small, totaling £39 10s. 12d.; they included two pairs of candlesticks and repairs

and engraving on several small items.[7] In 1747, the year of the creation of his viscountcy, he placed a substantial order that totaled £530 12s. 10d. Delivered in an iron-bound chest, the service included a pierced table, two pierced waiters, two pairs of candlesticks, four hand waiters, a bread basket, a teakettle and lamp, two coffeepots, four "nurled" sauceboats, four "nurled" salts and spoons, cutlery, tongs, casters, and so forth.[8] The order was placed on January 4, 1747/8, and delivered and paid for less than two months later on February 27, which suggests that it was composed of pieces in stock or bought in. The records pertaining to this epergne are somewhat unclear. In 1750 viscount Folkestone purchased a small epergne with four saucers and a basket weighing 134 oz 2 dwt for £63 14s., paying an additional £3 8s. for the engraving of five coats of arms. The present epergne, marked five years later, is more than ten ounces heavier (the scratch weight of 142 oz 10 dwt probably reflects the correct weight at the time of making, before substantial restorations, which seem to have added two oz to the total). In any case, viscount Folkestone returned the 1750 epergne, and was charged £5 "to taken out the Armes and altering the Epargne to make it more saleable."[9]

1. See a pair of candlesticks marked in 1755/6 by Wakelin in the Toledo Museum of Art, acc. no. 82.141–142, exh. Austin, Texas, University Art Museum, *One Hundred Years of English Silver*, 1969, cat. 89.

2. It was offered by a private seller to the Museum in 1956. A handwritten note records the mark as *IP* over *EW*, which would indicate a date sometime after 1758, the first year of the missing largeworkers' register. Grimwade 1990, p. 614. Clayton (1985a, p. 173, fig. 263) records it as engraved with the badge of the Prince of Wales.

3. Sold Christie's, London, December 18, 1997, lot 143.

4. Epergne, marked by Edward Wakelin for 1755 and 1756, sold Christie's, New York, October 5, 1983, lot 155.

5. The term *nurled* describes the gadrooned rims. Helen Matilda, countess of Radnor, and William Barklay Squire, *Catalogue of the Pictures: The Collection of the Earl of Radnor* (London, 1909), pp. 30–33, 45.

6. Other surviving objects include a pair of tureens
of 1739 sold Christie's, London, November 28, 1979,
lot 36, and a tankard of 1738 given by Bouverie to
the parish church of Stanton St. Quentin. See J. E.
Nightingale, *The Church Plate of the County of Wilts.*
(Salisbury, 1891), p. 207.

7. I am very grateful to Helen Clifford for kindly
providing a full summary of these references.
Victoria and Albert Museum, Garrard Ledgers,
Gentlemen's Account Book, VAM2, 1742/43, p. 104.

8. VAM3, p. 33.

9. Ibid., p. 118. There are apparently no pertinent
household papers that record the epergne among
the Bouverie possessions at the Northamptonshire
or Wiltshire Record Offices.

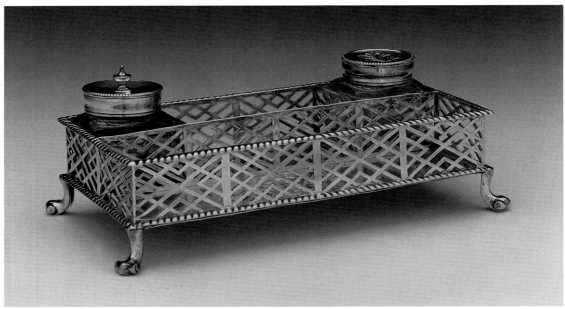

113

· 113 ·

INKSTAND

Marked by Edward Aldridge and John Stamper
(entered into partnership 1753)
London, 1756/7
Silver
1976.662a–c

MARKS: on underside, date letter *A*; leopard's head
crowned; lion passant; maker's mark *EA* with *I*
above and *S* below (Grimwade 528)

ARMORIALS: engraved on stand, the arms and
motto of Lyttleton quartering Westcote, Talbot, and
Beaufort, impaling Rich, for Sir George Lyttleton,
fifth baronet, as first baron Lyttleton of Frankley,
co. Worcester (1709–1773), and his second wife,
Elizabeth (1716–1795), daughter of Sir Robert Rich
of Roos Hall, co. Suffolk

H. 6.8 cm (2¹¹⁄₁₆ in.); w. 17 cm (6¹¹⁄₁₆ in.); d. 9.2 cm
(3⅝ in.)

WEIGHT: 388.4 gm (12 oz 10 dwt)

PROVENANCE: Bequest of Barbara Boylston Bean,
September 8, 1976

DESCRIPTION: The rectangular inkstand rests on
four cast scrolled feet. It has straight sides, formed
from rectangular sections of sheet, pierced with geometric fretwork. The flat base is secured by a hammered flange to the vertical sides of the inkstand.
Square compartments defined by similar pierced
panels contain small glass jars with silver covers for
ink and pounce.

This inkstand bears the arms of George
Lyttleton, who was created baron Lyttleton of
Frankley, co. Worcester, in 1756. Lyttleton was a
poet and author of considerable reputation, as
well as a generous patron of literature. Having
completed his grand tour, he joined the circle
centered on the Prince of Wales, whose secretary he became in 1737. When appointed a lord
of the treasury, however, in 1744, he was dismissed from the household of the prince. His
appointment as chancellor of the Exchecquer
severed his long friendship with William Pitt
and invited a long string of bitter observations
about his lack of aptitude for numbers. Walpole
referred to him as an "absent poet," who was
"strangely bewildered in the figures,"[1] and
Farington said he was unqualified for the
office, "being so deficient in knowledge of figures that He often made a jumble in his reports
to the House mistaking halfpence for guineas."[2]
Lyttleton must have purchased this inkstand
while Hagley Hall was being constructed, perhaps as a minor part of his overall refurnishing
scheme. The house, designed by Sanderson
Miller, is perhaps the last great Palladian mansion built, whose interiors are lavishly stuccoed
in the rococo style.

1. Lee 1909, vol. 12, p. 370.
2. Kenneth Garlick and Angus Macintyre, *The Diary
of Joseph Farington* (New Haven, 1978), vol. 2, p. 167.

· II4 ·

TANKARD

Marked by Thomas Moore (II) (first mark
entered 1750)
London, 1758/9
Silver
19.261

MARKS: to right of handle, maker's mark *TM*
(Grimwade 2845); lion passant; leopard's head
crowned; date letter *C*

INSCRIPTIONS: engraved on front tankard, *John
Hancock/to/L.B.Whitney./1770*; engraved on the handle, *D/I M*

H. 15 cm (5⅞ in.); w. 16.8 cm (6⅝ in.); d. 12.2 cm
(4¹³⁄₁₆ in.)

WEIGHT: 550 gm (17 oz 14 dwt)

PROVENANCE: according to tradition, given by
John Hancock (1737–1793) to Lydia Bowes Whitney
(1749–1805); Gift of Mr. and Mrs. W. de Forest
Thomson, June 26, 1919

DESCRIPTION: The cylindrical tapering tankard
is raised from sheet. It has a cast spreading foot, a
molded wire midband, and a wire rim. The scrolled
handle, formed from several pieces of sheet, has a
heart-shaped terminus. The piece has been badly
dented and torn and coarsely repaired.

The arresting engraving of John Hancock's
well-known signature as it appears on the
Declaration of Independence must have been
added to this tankard sometime in the late
nineteenth or early twentieth century.[1] It
records the tradition that the tankard was the
gift of the patriot to his first cousin, Lydia
Bowes, who in 1770 married Phineas Whitney
(1740–1819).[2] Whitney was the first minister
of the First Parish of Shirley, Massachusetts.
Through his wife's family, he became an intimate of the Hancocks and resided with the
president for a time in Philadelphia while
recovering from an illness.[3] A pair of Boston-
made salt spoons also in the collection of the
Museum of Fine Arts is traditionally said to
have been the wedding gift of John Hancock
to Lydia Bowes.[4]

1. See cats. 45 and 117, which are also associated
with John Hancock.
2. I am grateful to Nancy M. Wilson and Jeannine
Falino for sharing their research on the Hancock
genealogy.
3. Shipton 1968, p. 529.
4. Acc. no. 1973.735–736. See the forthcoming catalogue of American silver in the Museum of Fine
Arts by Jeannine Falino.

· 115 ·

EPERGNE

Marked by John Parker and Edward Wakelin
(entered into partnership 1760)
London, 1760
Silver
65.915

MARKS: on base under figural group, maker's mark
IP over *EW* (Grimwade 1602)

ARMORIALS: cast in cartouches on each side of the
base, beneath a duke's coronet, the arms of Powlett;
engraved on cover of bowl, beneath a duke's coronet, the crest of Powlett, for Charles, fifth duke of
Bolton (ca. 1718–1765); engraved on a banner surrounding the crest, the motto of the Order of Bath,
TRIA JUNTA IN UNUM

INSCRIPTIONS: engraved on underside of base,
636=17

H. 50.1 cm (19¾ in.); w. 95.5 cm (37⅝ in.); d. 50 cm
(19¹¹⁄₁₆ in.)

WEIGHT: 19,468 gm (624 oz 5 dwt)

PROVENANCE: lord Bolton, sold Christie's,
London, July 14, 1965, lot 145; S. J. Phillips, Ltd.,
London, purchased September 22, 1965, Theodora
Wilbour Fund in Memory of Charlotte Beebe
Wilbour

EXHIBITED: Boston, Museum of Fine Arts, 1994

PUBLISHED: Grimwade 1969, fig. 4; Clayton 1971,
p. 126, fig. 264; Grimwade 1974, pl. 51; Clayton
1985a, p. 175, fig. 264; Clayton 1985b, p. 165

DESCRIPTION: The oval plinth has an edge composed of scrolls and leaves, boldly modeled and cast
in sections. Four scrolled foliage feet are integrated
into the border and the half-figure of a goat
emerges at each end. Naturalistically rendered fruits
and nuts, cast in pieces and meticulously chased, are
attached to the plinth with nuts and bolts.
Projecting above each goat's head is an oak branch
bearing acorns and leaves, which forks into three
branches each terminating in a dish composed of
overlapping leaves. In the center of the plinth two
deer stand on the cast form of a forest floor with an
oak trunk between them. The figures are cast in sections, assembled, and finely chased and engraved.
Supported by the oak trunk and the backs of the
two deer is an oval bombé basket with pierced diaperwork and a cast scroll and foliate rim. The
domed cover is chased with foliage, surmounted by
a cast apple and pear.

The firm of Parker and Wakelin, successors to
George Wickes, has been well studied.[1] The
unique survival of many of the shop's ledgers,
day books, and accounts has permitted an
insight into the structure and economics of the
London silver trade. Edward Wakelin, who had
served under John Hugh Le Sage, joined
George Wickes's well-established business in
1747, the year he registered his first mark. He is
presumed to have taken over responsibility for
much of the production, leaving the business
side of the enterprise to Wickes and his partner, Samuel Netherton.[2] Wakelin was finally
able to raise the necessary cash to acquire part
of the business in 1760, when, on the retirement of Wickes and Netherton, he and John
Parker became partners.

Though the economics of the Wickes shop
and its successors have been analyzed extensively, the design process is less well understood. This monumental object, probably the
largest and latest of the rococo epergnes, is
marked on the base under the central figures
with only the sponsor's mark of Parker and
Wakelin, entered after 1758. Not long after it
appeared on the London market, Arthur
Grimwade published it in *Apollo*, relating its
design to that of the Ashburnham centerpiece,
marked by Nicholas Sprimont, and the
Somerset centerpiece, marked by Paul
Crespin.[3] The article was among the first to
address directly the complex issue of author-
ship and the possibility that large shops, such as
Wickes's, might have taken in commissions,
supplied a design, and contracted out the manufacture of the objects to working goldsmiths,
in this case Crespin and Sprimont. Grimwade
proposed that the three centerpieces were conceived by single designer, probably trained in
France. The three centerpieces, the only surviving monumental English examples of the form,
have in common a broad plateau for a base, a
central vessel supported by animals rendered in
highly naturalistic detail, and applied fruits and
nuts. In broad terms, the scale, choice of ornament, and high degree of finish reflect the
influence of French design of the late 1730s.
This epergne differs from the Somerset and
Ashburnham examples considerably. The large,

115 (Color Plate XII)

thick scrolls of the plateau border, the exaggerated bombé form of the vessel, and the attenuated branches represent a later interpretation of the French style. The modeling of the hinds is dry and almost rigid, unlike the animated figures of goats on the Somerset centerpiece, and the finishing is precise and relatively stiff, in keeping with its later date. Although the three objects are probably not the work of a single designer, they show the influence of French design over a period of twenty years.

The arms of the dukes of Bolton are cast into the panel at the center of the base, and the body of the central vessel is borne on the backs of two hinds, supporters of the Powlett arms. The cover is engraved with the Order of the Garter. While the arms might refer to any of the dukes, only Charles, fifth duke of Bolton, was elected a knight of Bath. He was styled the marquess of Winchester until his succession in 1759, served as lord lieutenant of Hampshire from 1758 to 1763, and was bearer of the crown of the queen consort at the coronation in 1761. Remarking on his suicide in 1765, Horace Walpole wrote:

> The Duke of Bolton the other morning—nobody knows why or wherefore, except that there is a good deal of madness in the blood—sat himself down upon the floor in his dressing room, and shot himself through the head. What is more remarkable is that it is the same house and the same chamber in which Lord Scarborough [Richard Lumley, earl of Scarborough, d. 1741] performed the same exploit. I do not believe that shooting oneself through the head is catching, or that any contagion lies in a wainscot that makes one pull a suicide trigger, but very possibly the idea might revert and operate on the brain of a splenetic man.[4]

The primary residence of the dukes of Bolton was Hackwood Park, near Basingstoke, Hampshire, built by the first duke in 1683–87. In the early 1760s, the fifth duke engaged John Vardy (d. 1765) for renovations at Hackwood and for the London house in Grosvenor Square. Because Hackwood was remodeled by Samuel Wyatt in the early nineteenth century, the nature and extent of the fifth duke's work at Hackwood is not well understood. A furnishing scheme for the great hall has been proposed.[5] Also surviving from this campaign are a pair of pier tables and glasses, the drawings for which are in the British Library.[6] The broad, thick leaves that compose the border of the epergne's stand share many qualities with the carved borders of the pier glasses, which may have been executed by John Vardy's brother, Thomas.[7] Numerous inventories of the Hackwood furnishings survive. The 1765 and 1795 inventories[8] include some plate but do not list the epergne, which is likely to have been kept in London. The 1807 and 1808 inventories mention a large epergne, without weights; in 1809 a large epergne is noted as being "now in London," and by 1810 it is recorded again at Hackwood.[9] Unfortunately, Parker and Wakelin's Gentlemen's Ledger for the years after 1760 has not survived, but in 1757 and 1758 the fifth duke bought several items.[10] An unmarked cup probably commemorating the fifth duke's role as bearer of the queen's crown at the coronation of George III was sold in 1969.[11]

The appearance of the piece is seriously compromised by its condition. The smooth surface of the plateau has been highly buffed, and the even, flat finish of the leaves on the branches suggests the possibility that it has been plated.

1. Barr 1980; Helen M. Clifford, "Parker and Wakelin: The Study of an Eighteenth-Century Goldsmithing Firm with Particular Reference to the Garrard Ledgers, ca. 1760-76," Ph.D. diss., Victoria and Albert, Royal College of Art, 1988.

2. Barr 1980, pp. 67–76.

3. Grimwade 1969, pp. 126–28.

4. Mrs. Paget Toynbee, ed., *The Letters of Horace Walpole* (Oxford, 1904), vol. 6, p. 267.

5. Christie's, Hackwood Park, April 20–22, 1998, pp. 10–15.

6. Anthony Coleridge, "John Vardy and the Hackwood Suite," *The Connoisseur* 149 (1962), pp. 12–17; exh. London, Victoria and Albert Museum, 1984, p. 46.

7. I am grateful to John Cornforth for this observation. Coleridge, "John Vardy," p. 16, fig. 5.

8. Hampshire Record Office, 11M49/204-5.

9. Hampshire Record Office, 11M49/206, 11M49/E/31/7, 11M49/E/B1/8.

10. The purchases included a ladle, orange strainer, and a mug (Victoria and Albert Museum, Garrard Ledgers, Gentlemen's Ledgers, VAM6). I thank Helen Clifford for offering this information.

11. Christie's, London, December 3, 1969, lot 28.

116

· 116 ·

CRUET STAND

Possibly by John Delmestre (only mark entered
1755)
London, 1760/1
Silver, glass
33.172

MARKS: on underside of stand, maker's mark *ID*
(Grimwade 3630) (repeated on each pierced cylinder); date letter *E*; lion passant (repeated on each
pierced cylinder); leopard's head crowned

INSCRIPTIONS: engraved on bottle covers,
Tarragon, Pepper, Elder, Soy, Cheroque; scratched on
underside of base, *13090*

H. 17.7 cm (6¹⁵⁄₁₆ in.); diam. of frame 17.5 cm
(6⅞ in.)

PROVENANCE: Anonymous Gift in Memory of
Charlotte Beebe Wilbour (1833–1914), March 2,
1933

EXHIBITED: Boston, Museum of Fine Arts, 1933

DESCRIPTION: The cruet stand rests on a cinquefoil base formed from sheet that stands on five claw-
and-ball feet. Ten cut-glass bottles and casters, each
with a silver cover, are contained in short cylinders
of various sizes, pierced with a trellis design and
with gadrooned edges. The cylinders, formed from
seamed, pierced sheet, are fitted with eyes that
extend through the base and are secured with small
hooks. From the center of the stand rises a baluster
stem surmounted by a shaped handle. The handle
has been torn and bent.

• 117 •

BASKET

Marked by William Plummer (first mark entered 1755)

London, 1760/1

Silver

66.286

MARKS: on side of pierced panel, maker's mark *WP* (Grimwade 3255); lion passant; leopard's head crowned; date letter *E*

INSCRIPTIONS: engraved on underside: *Madam Lydia Hancock/came in possession of this basket/ -1758-/John Hancock 1778/Mrs. Dorothy Hancock 1793/Mrs. Nancy Salisbury 1830/Mrs. Sarah Austin 1865/Elihu Chauncey 1887/Natalie Elizabeth Chauncey Pierrepont 1916/Heathcote M. Woolsey 1953*

H. 26.3 cm (10⅜ in.); w. 37.6 cm (14¹³⁄₁₆ in.); d. 30.3 cm (11¹⁵⁄₁₆ in.)

WEIGHT: 1,204.9 gm (38 oz 15 dwt)

PROVENANCE: according to tradition, Thomas Hancock (1703–1764), given in 1758 to his wife, Lydia Henchman Hancock (1714–1777), by descent to a nephew, John Hancock (1737–1793), to his wife, Dorothy Hancock Scott (1747–1830), to her niece Nancy Salisbury, to Mrs. Sarah Austin, to Elihu Chauncy, to Natalie Elizabeth Chauncy Pierrepont, to Heathcote M. Woolsey; purchased through Paul L. Fishman, Boston, May 6, 1966, Theodora Wilbour Fund in Memory of Charlotte Beebe Wilbour

EXHIBITED: Boston, Museum of Fine Arts, 1975, cat. 124; Boston, Museum of Fine Arts, *John Singleton Copley in America*, 1995 (not in catalogue)

PUBLISHED: Ian M. G. Quimby, "Silver: 1776—How America Really Looked," *American Art Journal* 7, no. 1 (May 1975), pp. 68–81

DESCRIPTION: The elliptical basket, formed from thin sheet, has flaring sides. It is supported by four cast foliate feet that extend from a ring of openwork foliage and scrolls. The sides of the basket are divided into vertical panels by bands of chased beading, and on each panel is a pierced pattern of either geometric, trellis, scroll, or curvilinear design. The rim of the basket is strengthened with a cast openwork band of foliage, scrolls, and beading. The cast and pierced bail handle is fastened with circular hinges and has beading on its lower sections and an open geometric pattern across the center.

Like the two-handled cup by George Wickes,[1] this basket is associated with Thomas Hancock, uncle of the patriot John Hancock. Thomas Hancock had amassed an enormous fortune in paper manufacturing and trade. At his death in 1764 he owned a fleet of vessels that supplied the Newfoundland fishing industry and had control over supplies of such contraband as French molasses, port, and tea. He had also inherited the fortune of the family of his wife, Lydia Henchman. The engraved inscription indicates that the basket came into Lydia Hancock's possession in 1758—clearly impossible since it bears London hallmarks for 1760. On Thomas Hancock's death in 1764, his estate was left to his wife and his nephew, John Hancock, and he indicated that there should be no inventory of his possessions. His silver and ten thousand pounds in cash or securities, the mansion on Beacon Hill and its furnishings, the carriages, and the slaves were left to his widow.[2] On Lydia Henchman Hancock's death in 1777, her estate passed to her mother. Her nephew, John Hancock, a co-executor of her late husband's will, received a silver bowl, a silver spout cup, and a large two-handled cup—a silver basket is not specified, although the inscription suggests that the basket was part of her bequest.[3]

John Hancock rose to prominence as a supporter of the patriot cause when in 1768 his ship *Liberty*, implicated in smuggling, was seized and burned. He went on to become president of the Congress and one of the most famous signers of the Declaration of Independence. The probate inventory taken on his death in 1793 records, in addition to a silver cruet stand, a bread basket.[4] His estate was divided between his widow, his mother, and his siblings. His widow, who remarried a shipmaster, Captain Scott, was widowed again in 1809. She returned to the Beacon Hill mansion but was forced to sell much of the property behind it, where the State House was constructed. Her will, proved in 1830, included the bequest of a silver basket to her niece Mrs. Nancy Salisbury (b. 1806), wife of Samuel Salisbury of Boston, and she requested her to "have it used at the weddings of my nieces and nephews as it has been heretofore."[5] According to the engraving on the underside of the basket, it descended in the family until 1953, and in 1966 it was offered for purchase to the Museum.

Thomas Hancock and other wealthy

117

Bostonians were sometimes very explicit when purchasing luxury goods from their agents in London.[6] In 1738 Hancock ordered a clock "of the newest fashion," further specifying, "on the Top instead of Balls let me have three handsome Carv'd figures Gilt with burnish'd Gold."[7] By 1760, when this basket was made, it was not, by London standards, "of the newest fashion." Not surprisingly, American silversmiths adopted the rococo style belatedly, but some high-style London silver, such as the Lamerie service bought for David Franks, was shipped to colonial clients in the 1740s.[8] Boston patrons and silversmiths resisted the rococo longer than their counterparts in New York or Philadelphia.[9]

William Plummer's workshop specialized in pierced bread baskets, sugar baskets, and strainers.[10] A second Plummer basket, nearly identical to the present one, and bearing hallmarks for 1762, was exported to Antwerp in 1779 and given in 1811 as a wedding gift to Mrs. Nicholas Biddle of Philadelphia.[11]

1. See cat. 45. Also see cat. 114.

2. Herbert S. Allan, *John Hancock, Patriot in Purple* (New York, 1948), p. 80.

3. Will of Lydia Hancock, 1777, Suffolk County Probate, vol. 76, pp. 512, 585. Typescript of Kathryn C. Buhler's notes in curatorial file.

4. Inventory of the estate of John Hancock, Suffolk County Probate, vol. 93, p. 11. Typescript of Kathryn C. Buhler's notes in curatorial file.

5. Suffolk County Probate, vol. 128, pp. 166–67. Typescript of Kathryn C. Buhler's notes in curatorial file. Also see Boston, Museum of Fine Arts, 1975, p. 99.

6. See cats. 94, 97, and 125.

7. Quoted in Boston, Museum of Fine Arts, 1975, p. 31.

8. London, Goldsmiths' Hall, 1990, pp. 162–63, cats. 109–10.

9. New York, The Metropolitan Museum of Art, *American Rococo, 1750–1775: Elegance in Ornament*, 1992, p. 75.

10. Grimwade 1990, p. 628. For similar baskets by Plummer, see Sotheby's, London, July 10, 1990, lot 359; Sotheby's, London, June 20, 1988, lot 177.

11. Letter from Nicholas Wainwright in the curatorial file. For references to other London baskets owned by colonists, see exh. New York, The Metropolitan Museum of Art, *American Rococo, 1750–1775*, 1992, p. 248 n. 164.

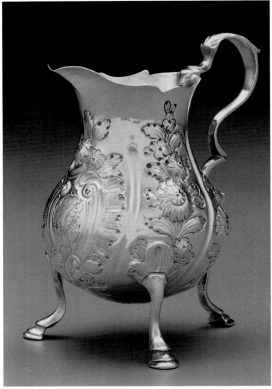

118

• 118 •

CREAM JUG
London, 1763/4
Silver
1984.512

MARKS: on underside, leopard's head crowned; lion passant; date letter *h*; maker's mark *M* (illegible)

INSCRIPTION: engraved on front, *MF*, possibly for Mary Fleet

H. 9.8 cm (3⅞ in.); w. 8.6 cm (3⅜ in.); d. 6.7 cm (2⅝ in.)

WEIGHT: 74.1 gm (2 oz 8 dwt)

PROVENANCE: descended in the Fleet family to Mrs. Franklin H. Williams, Gift of Mr. and Mrs. Franklin H. Williams in Memory of Louise Bodine Wallace, September 12, 1984

DESCRIPTION: The bulbous body, formed from thin sheet and chased with spiraling fluting and flowers, is supported by three scrolled legs with hoof feet. The flared rim is cut and shaped, and the handle is formed of a series of scrolls with a leaf-capped shoulder.

• 119 •

SALVER
Marked by Thomas Pitts (I) (first mark entered ca. 1758–d. after 1777)
London, 1763/4
Silver gilt
1989.311a-b

MARKS: date letter *h;* lion passant (repeated on border); leopard's head crowned; on underside, maker's mark *TP* (Grimwade 2875) (repeated on border)

ARMORIALS: engraved in the center, the arms of Portman impaling Wyndham for Henry William Portman, co. Somerset (1738–1796), and his wife, Anne, daughter of William Wyndham, co. Wiltshire

INSCRIPTIONS: engraved on back, *268=16*

H. 11 cm (4⁵⁄₁₆ in.); diam. 72.7 cm (28⅝ in.)

WEIGHT: 8,355 gm (268 oz 12 dwt)

PROVENANCE: purchased from Spink & Son, Ltd., London, November 29, 1989, European Decorative Arts Acquisitions Fund

EXHIBITED: Boston, Museum of Fine Arts, 1994; Boston, Museum of Fine Arts, *Chinoiserie: The Lure of the East*, 1997

DESCRIPTION: The round salver has a shaped openwork border filled with tea plants, flowers, C-scrolls, and four pagodas. It is assembled from many cast sections. At intervals in the border are four large seated chinoiserie figures wearing flowing robes and slippers, modeled in high relief. Two play sitarlike instruments and two hold tea bowls and saucers. The plateau is supported by four cast openwork feet, formed by C-scrolls and covered with tea plants and flowers. The center section of the plateau, formed from sheet, is set into a folded rim that is soldered onto the back of the border. The salver retains its iron-bound oak case.

The extraordinary modeling of the borders of this salver, composed of flowers and foliage intertwined with C-scrolls, Chinese figures, and pagodas, distinguishes it from the more conventional borders of the period. Weighing 268 ounces, it is also among the largest. The bunches of naturalistic flowers flowing through the C-scrolls to the edge of the plateau and the mannered postures of the chinoiserie figures suggest a modeler familiar with three-dimensional constructs. Thomas Pitts was a regular supplier of epergnes to Parker and Wakelin, and it is possible that this salver, with

119 (Color Plate XIII)

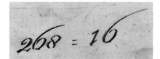

its massive oak case, was bought through them. Unfortunately the Gentlemen's Ledgers from the 1760s do not survive, and the second Workmen's Ledger begins with the year 1766.[1]

The most distinctive feature of the border, the Chinese figures, are modeled with a mannered grace in their cross-legged poses. Two are depicted holding teacups, while at opposite sides, two figures play sitarlike instruments, characteristically exotic subjects for a chinoiserie theme. They are likely to have been designed after one of the many printed pattern books available in London, but a precise source

has not been identified. In their graceful poses and flowing, flowered garments, there is some similarity to figures in the book of the Augsburg engraver J. E. Nilson (1721–1788), *Caffee, The und Tabac Zierathen*.[2] Closely related figures appear on the border of a large salver of the same year marked by William Cripps.[3] The rest of the Cripps border, where the design is much denser, with thick, complex C-scrolls and bunches of fruit, is not at all similar to the Pitts border, and in place of the pagodas are fierce dragons. It seems likely that the Cripps and Pitts

borders are the product of the same shop, since they share the same models for the chinoiserie figures; but the other discrepancies in style and general sensibility suggest not only a different design source but a different modeler. Other evidence of business dealings between Cripps and Pitts remains to be explored. Both specialized in epergnes with richly modeled pierced borders.[4] Cripps's mark also appears on a great many kettles and epergnes with distinctive large-scale chinoiserie figures amid flowers and C-scrolls.[5] These highly sophisticated designs and models must have been supplied by the small circle of specialists also associated with the circle of Paul de Lamerie.[6] The same modeler may have been responsible for a pair of candlesticks of 1761, marked by John Cafe.[7] They have high domed bases composed of scrolls and flowers, and a seated chinoiserie figure is positioned next to the stem.

The close connection between the design of this salver and the large group of epergnes invites the question as to whether it was intended as a plateau for such a centerpiece or for a mahogany tea table, such as that preserved at Dunham Massey.[8] A large oval plateau marked by Henry Dutton for 1755 is a rare example of a stand clearly intended for an epergne.[9] Though larger in scale than the present salver, it has swags of softly rendered flowers intertwined with scrolls and clusters of fruit on the border similar in feeling to the border of the Pitts salver.[10] On the other hand, the Pitts salver has ornament intended to be viewed from above, whereas the border of the Dutton plateau, seen from eye level, forms an apron.

Henry William Portman married Anne, daughter of William Wyndham, who bore him three sons and two daughters. The date of their marriage is uncertain, but as the first child was born in 1765 and their marriage settlement is dated 1766, it is possible that their marriage took place in 1763, and that this salver was a gift for the occasion.[11]

1. Barr 1980, p. 61.

2. Illus. Eva-Maria Hanebutt-Benz, *Ornament und Entwurf* (Frankfurt, 1983), p. 150, cat. 133.

3. Sold Christie's, London, March 28, 1984, lot 184. One of the female figures, who holds a teacup, appears to be identical to that on the Boston salver.

4. For Pitts, see Edith Gaines, "Powell? Potts? Pitts!—the TP Epergnes," *Antiques* 87 (April 1965), pp. 462–65; Edith Gaines, "More by—and about—Pitts of the Epergnes," *Antiques* 91 (June 1967), pp. 748–53.

5. See, for example, a kettle and stand of 1754, sold Sotheby's, London, October 22, 1979, lot 196, and another of 1749, sold Christie's, London, March 6, 1991, lot 125. An epergne of 1757 with some of the same motifs was sold by Christie's, London, November 25, 1966, lot 136.

6. In 1742 Cripps took over the shop once occupied by Christian Hillian, next door to Nicholas Sprimont. See the biographical data on Cripps, Sotheby's, London, October 17, 1985, lot 407; Christopher Hartop (Hartop 1996, p. 52) and Peter Kaellgren ("The Tea-Picker Design of English Rococo Silver Tea Caddies," *Antiques* 121 [February 1982], pp. 484–89) refer to the association of Cripps with Lamerie.

7. See Jackson 1911, vol. 1, p. 305, fig. 327.

8. Illus. Washington, D.C., National Gallery of Art, *The Treasure Houses of Britain: Five Hundred Years of Patronage and Art Collecting*, 1985, pp. 190–91.

9. Sold Christie's, London, March 17, 1999, lot 95.

10. Dutton's dealings with Cripps are also suggested by an epergne of 1754 bearing Dutton's mark. The boat-shaped basket is embellished on the rim with chinoiserie heads—apparently identical to a model marked by Cripps. See Sotheby's, New York, October 28, 1980, lot 541 (Dutton), and Christie's, London, November 25, 1966, lot 136 (Cripps).

11. I am grateful to Gale Glynn for this suggestion.

120

• 120 •

PAIR OF SALTS WITH LINERS
Marked by David Hennell (I) (1712–1785) and
Robert Hennell (I) (1741–1811)
London, 1764/5
Silver, glass
14.901a-b–902a-b

MARKS: on underside of each, maker's mark *DH*, an
R above and an *H* below (Grimwade 472); lion passant; date letter *I*; leopard's head crowned

INSCRIPTIONS: engraved on the side of each,
C. L. Rogers

14.901: H. 4.7 cm (1⅞ in.); diam. of rim 7 cm
(2¾ in.)

14.902: H. 4.8 cm (1⅞ in.); diam. of rim 6.5 cm
(2⁹⁄₁₆ in.)

WEIGHT: 14.901a: 82.2 gm (2 oz 13 dwt). 14.902a:
79.4 gm (2 oz 11 dwt)

PROVENANCE: Gift of the Misses Catharine
Langdon Rogers and Clara Bates Rogers,
November 5, 1914

PUBLISHED: Kathryn C. Buhler, *Philadelphia Silver
Given in Memory of Dr. George Clymer* (Boston, 1959),
pp. 25–26; Percy Hennell, *Silver Salt Cellars, 1736 to
1876* (East Grinstead, West Sussex, 1986), p. 56, fig. 33

DESCRIPTION: The compressed circular salts,
formed from sheet, rest on three cast legs, with
shells at the top and an applied cast shell forming
the foot. The salt has an applied, fluted rim. The two
glass inserts, one original, with a star cut into the
base, are chipped around the rim.

Though these plain tripod salts are not the
most ambitious model produced by the
Hennell workshops, they are distinguished by
the survival of one apparently original glass
liner.[1] The manufacture of salts, like casters and
many other domestic items, was the province
of specialists. David Hennell I had been
apprenticed to a maker of salts, Edward Wood,
and the business was carried on by subsequent
generations. The family supplied salts to
Wakelin and Taylor, whose records indicate that
glass liners were provided to the retailer with
the order and itemized separately in the
accounts.[2]

1. See Hennell, *Salt Cellars*, pp. 29-60.
2. Percy Hennell, "The Hennells'—a Continuity of
Craftsmanship," *Connoisseur* 182, no. 732
(February 1973), pp. 79–80.

· 121 ·

THE RICHMOND RACE CUP

Designed by Robert Adam (1728–1792)
Marked by Daniel Smith and Robert Sharp
(entered into partnership 1763)
London, 1764/5
Silver gilt
1987.488a–b

MARKS: on bezel of cover, maker's mark *DS* over
RS (Grimwade 3523); lion passant (repeated on
underside of base); leopard's head crowned (repeated
on underside of base); date letter *J* (repeated on
underside of base)

INSCRIPTIONS: along rim of cup, engraved
*Richmond Races 1764 Sir Marmyduke Wyvill Bart and
Thomas Dundas Esq. Stewards*

H. 48.6 cm (19⅛ in.); w. 39.8 cm (15¹¹⁄₁₆ in.);
d. 21 cm (8¼ in.)

WEIGHT: 4,408.5 gm (141 oz 15 dwt)

PROVENANCE: won by John Hutton, Esq., of
Marske Hall, Swaledale, Yorkshire, in September
1764, by descent to J. T. d'Arcy Hutton, Esq., sold
Christie's, London, October 4, 1950, lot 122; estate
of Mrs. Hilda d'Arcy Sykes, sold Sotheby's, London,
March 6, 1969, lot 186; property of the Hutton
Trustees; Christie's, London, July 8, 1987, lot 157,
purchased from E & CT Koopman & Sons,
London, October 28, 1987, Theodora Wilbour Fund
in Memory of Charlote Beebe Wilbour

EXHIBITED: London, The Royal Academy, *The 14th
Exhibition of the Council of Europe: The Age of Neo-
Classicism*, 1972, cat. 1746; Boston, Museum of Fine
Arts, 1994

PUBLISHED: Brett 1986, n. 1006; John Culme,
"Trophies of the Turf," *The Antique Collector* 61,
no. 6 (1990), pp. 112–17; Clifford 1993, pp. 102–6

DESCRIPTION: The vase-shaped cup rests on a
spreading, spiral-fluted foot with a border of
gadrooning and rosettes and is surmounted by a
knop with rosettes. The body of the cup is raised
from a single sheet, with a chased acanthus calyx
and water leaves on the lower section. At the center
of each side of the body, inside an applied border of
beading and bellflowers, are applied cast medallions
depicting the saddling-up and the race. A chased
garland of fruit and flowers hangs from the rim
between chased lion's masks. A low-relief frieze
depicting the race, formed of applied cast figures,
encircles the rim. The cast handles are in the form
of winged female caryatids with twisted termini.
The spool-shaped cover, formed from three raised
sections, is chased with water leaves. At the narrow-
est point a cast border of Greek key is applied. A
foliate finial on top of a fluted and gadrooned dome
surmounts the cover. The gilding has apparently been
renewed, and a repair to the juncture of the foot has
left a grainy surface.

Robert Adam's drawings for this cup are preserved in the Soane Museum, two of more than
ten thousand that were purchased by Sir John
Soane in 1833.[1] They are inscribed, *Vase for
Thomas Dundas Esqr. for a Prize* (fig. 2). Adam's
cups are among the earliest neoclassical designs
for silver, and the model became the standard
for race trophy design. The cup represents a
richly ornamented neoclassical taste that was
soon supplanted by a more austere aesthetic. As
Michael Snodin has pointed out, Adam relied
less on antique prototypes than is generally
assumed and drew heavily from Renaissance
and baroque compositions. The composition of
the vase is inspired by a design by Jacques Stella
(1596–1697), published in Paris in 1667.[2] Stella's
vase rests on a small foot with calyx, and the
oviform body rises to an acanthus-covered neck
with a flaring, fluted cover. In the first of the
Dundas drawings, Adam experimented with
standing lions (supporters for the Dundas arms)
for the handles (fig. 3). This motif seems to have
been borrowed from a mid-sixteenth-century
model for a ewer by Enea Vico.[3] In the second
drawing, Adam broadened the proportions of
the cup and altered the design for the handles,
adopting the winged female figures with twisting tails. This treatment had been used in the
Renaissance, on a Chinese porcelain bottle with
silver-gilt mounts,[4] for example, and revived in
the mid-eighteenth century.[5]

Sir Thomas Dundas (1741–1820), who commissioned the cup, was the son and heir of Sir
Lawrence Dundas (ca. 1710–1781), one of
Adam's important early patrons. Sir Lawrence,
a man of sophisticated tastes, had acquired an
immense fortune through his position as paymaster to the army. Adam worked for him at
Moor Park, Hertfordshire, and in London at
19 Arlington Street.[6] Thomas Dundas was born
in Edinburgh, and in 1764 he married Anne,
daughter of Thomas, first marquess of
Rockingham.

The Richmond Gold Cup,[7] a four-mile heat,
was first run in 1759, though there had been
races at Richmond since the late sixteenth cen-

121 (Color Plate XIV)

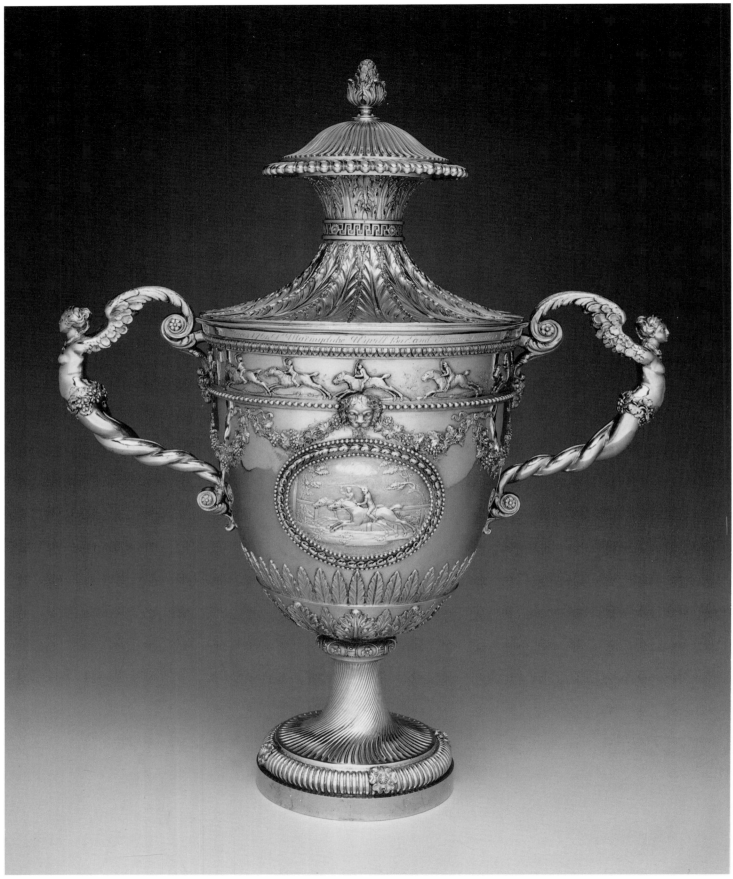

121

tury. The course was laid out at Aske Hall, a property in Yorkshire bought in 1763 by Sir Lawrence Dundas who brought in the architect John Carr (1723–1807) to design a luxurious stable in the Palladian style. Richmond became one of the most important breeding and training centers in the north, and the Richmond Cup, with the value of eighty pounds, became a coveted trophy. From 1760 to 1763 the race was won by the duke of Cleveland's bay, Dainty Davy.[8] In 1764, when Thomas Dundas commissioned this cup, Dainty Davy did not run, and the prize was taken by John Hutton's brown horse, Silvio, ridden by Charles Dawson.[9] Dawson had such success with Silvio that his training stable was renamed Silvio Hall, and in 1776 he retired to become a personal trainer for Sir Lawrence Dundas.[10]

Robert Adam's design was turned over to the prestigious goldsmiths Daniel Smith and Robert Sharp for execution. As Helen Clifford has demonstrated, the design then entered the mainstream and was reused, adapted, borrowed, and even revived for race cups for the next several decades.[11] Smith and Sharp used the design the same year for another client, Hugh Percy, earl of Northumberland, lord lieutenant in Ireland.[12]

1. Geoffrey Beard, "Robert Adam's 'Artificers,'" *Antiques* (June 1987), p. 1295.

2. Snodin 1997, p. 20, fig. 32.

3. Ibid., p. 20, fig. 33.

4. The Metropolitan Museum of Art, illus. Philippa Glanville, *Silver in Tudor and Early Stuart England* (London, 1990), fig. 100.

5. This observation was made by Rowe 1965, p. 36, referring to a Kandler kettle in the Victoria and Albert Museum, illus. Grimwade 1974, pl. 56A.

6. John Harris, "The Dundas Empire," *Apollo* 86 (1967), pp. 170–79.

7. See Clifford 1993, pp. 102–6.

8. John Fairfax-Blakeborough, *Northern Turf History* (London, 1948), p. 179. I am grateful to Dede Scott-Brown of the York Racing Museum for her assistance.

9. William Pick, *An Authentic Historical Racing Calendar* (York, 1805), p. 96.

10. Fairfax-Blakeborough, *Northern Turf*, p. 192.

11. Clifford 1993, pp. 104–6.

12. This cup is now in the Fairhaven collection at Anglesey Abbey, exh. Cambridge, Fitzwilliam Museum, *Cambridge Plate*, 1975, cat. 2H11.

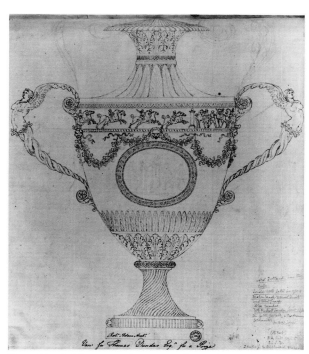

Fig. 2. *Vase for Thomas Dundas, Esq.*, Robert Adam

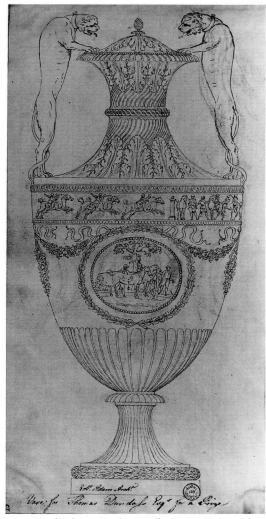

Fig. 3. *Vase for Thomas Dundas, Esq., first version*, Robert Adam

122

123

· 122 ·

TANKARD
Marked by G. S.
Probably London, ca. 1765–75
Silver
32.363

MARKS: to right of handle, maker's mark *GS* (unrecorded) (repeated on underside of cover)

INSCRIPTIONS: engraved on front of the tankard, *IAS* in monogram

H. 22 cm (8¹¹⁄₁₆ in.); w. 18.6 cm (7⁵⁄₁₆ in.); d. 12 cm (4¾ in.)

WEIGHT: 864.7 gm (27 oz 16 dwt)

PROVENANCE: Bequest of Charles Hitchcock Tyler, September 1, 1932

DESCRIPTION: The bulbous body, formed from sheet, has a molded wire applied to the midsection. It rests on a raised domed foot. The double-scroll handle, assembled from several fabricated pieces, has a heart-shaped terminus and an openwork thumbpiece. The hinged cover, raised with an applied bezel, is domed and stepped.

This tankard, a conventional London example of the 1760s or 1770s,[1] seems to have had its original marks removed and replaced by a single maker's mark, probably with intention to sell the tankard as American. The baluster tankard form was associated with Philadelphia silver in particular, and it may have been assumed that the mark *GS* would be interpreted as that of Godfrey Shiving.[2] The tankard was owned by Charles Hitchcock Tyler, who collected English and American brass, pottery, furniture, delftware, and silver. Also see cat. 123, which seems to have been altered in the same way.

1. For example, see a tankard marked by Fuller White for 1760/1, illus. Davis 1976, p. 66, cat. 53; another marked by Charles Wright for 1771/2, sold Sotheby's, London, July 19, 1982, lot 155; another marked by Joseph Lock for 1775/6, sold Sotheby's, London, November 21, 1985, lot 57; another marked by James Stamp for 1775/6, sold Sotheby's, London, October 25, 1984, lot 204; another marked by Samuel Godbehere, for 1785/6, sold Sotheby's, New York, October 23, 1984, lot 338.

2. Stephen Guernsey Cook Ensko, *American Silversmiths and Their Marks* (Boston, 1989), p. 270. For a Philadelphia example of the form, see exh. New York, The Metropolitan Museum of Art, *American Rococo, 1750–1775: Elegance in Ornament*, 1992, p. 107, fig. 68. I am grateful to Jeannine Falino for sharing her opinions about this.

· 123 ·

TANKARD

Marked by I. K.
Probably London, ca. 1765–75
Silver
32.364

MARKS: on underside, maker's mark *IK* (unrecorded) (repeated on underside of cover)

INSCRIPTIONS: engraved on the front of the tankard, monogram *RBH*

H. 20.6 cm (8⅛ in.); w. 17.4 cm (6⅞ in.); d. 12.3 cm (4¹³⁄₁₆ in.)

WEIGHT: 932.7 gm (30 oz)

PROVENANCE: Bequest of Charles Hitchcock Tyler, September 1, 1932

DESCRIPTION: The bulbous body formed from sheet rests on a cast domed foot. It has a molded wire applied to the midsection. The double-scroll handle, assembled from several fabricated pieces, has a scrolled terminus and an openwork thumbpiece. The hinged cover, raised with an applied bezel, is domed and stepped.

This tankard, like cat. 122, appears to have had its marks altered to make it saleable as American. There is evidence that marks on the base and inside the cover, the traditional location for marks on a London tankard, have been removed and replaced with a spurious maker's mark. The mark *IK* was perhaps intended to be read as the mark of James Kendall of Wilmington, Delaware.[1]

1. Stephen Guernsey Cook Ensko, *American Silversmiths and Their Marks* (Boston, 1989), p. 283.

· 124 ·

TEAPOT

Marked by William Grundy (first mark entered 1743)
London, 1765/6
Silver, wood
33.173

MARKS: on underside of foot, maker's mark *WG* (similar to Grimwade 3147)[1] (repeated inside cover); lion passant (repeated inside cover); leopard's head crowned; date letter *k*. Inside cover, maker's mark *WG* (possibly Grimwade 3148)

INSCRIPTIONS: engraved inside foot, *P★D/to/R★D 19=13*

H. 17.5 cm (6⅞ in.); w. 23.5 cm (9¼ in.); d. 12.6 cm (4¹⁵⁄₁₆ in.)

WEIGHT: 589.7 gm (18 oz 19 dwt)

PROVENANCE: Anonymous Gift in Memory of Charlotte Beebe Wilbour (1833–1914), March 2, 1933

EXHIBITED: Boston, Museum of Fine Arts, 1933

DESCRIPTION: The inverted pear-shaped body is raised and rests on a splayed, molded foot. The ear-shaped wooden scrolled handle is mounted on cast ornamented sockets. The curved, fluted spout has acanthus leaves at the tip and along the underside, and a scalloped base with a drop. It is cast in two pieces and seamed vertically. The domed, hinged cover is mounted on a hidden hinge. The cover is surmounted by a baluster gadrooned finial. The bright finish of the surface was probably a result of a large repair to the body near the spout, where a bruise was removed. The cover, which bears a different mark, was also probably repaired, as was the foot.

1. Grundy's mark here lacks the pellet shown by Grimwade.

124

125

· 125 ·

COFFEEPOT

Marked by William Grundy (first mark entered 1743)

London, 1767/8

Silver, wood

30.648

MARKS: on underside of base, maker's mark *WG* (Grimwade 3147) (repeated on bezel of cover); date letter *M*; leopard's head crowned; lion passant (repeated on bezel of cover)

INSCRIPTIONS: engraved in a cartouche on side, *IML* interlaced cipher

H. 40.8 cm (16⅛ in.); w. 25.9 cm (10³⁄₁₆ in.); diam. of base 14.2 cm (5⅝ in.)

WEIGHT: 2,089.4 gm (67 oz 4 dwt)

PROVENANCE: according to tradition, Harrison Gray Otis (1765–1836), by descent to his daughter Sophia (1798–1874) who married Andrew Ritchie (d. 1862), to their daughter Elizabeth (1830–1896) who married Dr. Edouard Duplessis Beylard, to their son Edouard Duplessis Beylard (1859–1925), Gift of E. Duplessis Beylard, September 4, 1930

PUBLISHED: *Museum of Fine Arts Bulletin* 28, no. 169 (October 1930), p. 102 (illus.)

DESCRIPTION: The inverted pear-shaped body rests on a domed, spreading circular foot. The foot is raised and chased, with a heavy square wire applied to the rim. The body of the vessel is raised from sheet and chased with spiraling flutes, interlocking C-scrolls, and trailing vines and flowers. The curved spout is cast with scrolling foliage, flowers, fluting, and an acanthus leaf at the tip. The double-scroll wooden handle is mounted on cast scrolled sockets. The stepped, domed cover is topped with a baluster-form finial of flaring scrolls and beadwork. It is raised and chased, and fitted with a bezel.

This monumental coffeepot, nearly twice the weight of an average example, represents the last and most mature flowering of rococo chasing. Workshops that specialized in such wares, such as those of Samuel Taylor (see cat. 107), William Cripps, and Samuel Courtauld, had used the spiraling scrolls that follow the bombé form of the body since the early 1750s. Although the rendering of the flowers is perfunctory, the trailing vines on the cast spout are integrated into the motifs on chased body with particular skill.[1]

According to a family tradition, the coffeepot had been the property of Harrison Gray Otis and descended in the family to the donor, E. Duplessis Beylard. Otis was a dynamic figure in federal Boston, renowned for his statesmanship, his successful business ventures, and his charming manner.[2] Trained in law, he became a leading representative of Boston in the national arena, until he was elected to Congress in 1797. After returning to Boston in 1800, he served as mayor for three terms. He hired the architect Charles Bulfinch (1763–1844) to build three houses for members of his family, which served as a social hub for Boston's political and intellectual elite. The coffeepot is not particularly in keeping with the austere neoclassicism favored by Otis. It may have been part of his inheritance, or it may have been inherited by his wife, Sally Foster, who in 1819 received a portion of the estate of her father, William Foster. Otis did buy a French mid-eighteenth-century silver tureen in Washington from the effects of the French minister.[3] The monogram, however, does not seem to align with any names of Otis's family, so the possibility remains that it was a later purchase.

1. Comparable designs are found on pieces marked by Smith and Sharp, 1761 (Boston, Museum of Fine Arts, 1968, p. 43); Whipham and Wright, 1766 (sold Sotheby's, London, April 28, 1988, lot 523); and Louisa Courtauld, 1764 (sold Christie's, New York, April 14, 1994, lot 443).

2. See Allen Johnson and Dumas Malone, eds., *Dictionary of American Biography* (New York, 1934), vol. 14, pp. 98–100.

3. A copy of William Foster's will and probate inventory (Harrison Gray Otis Papers, Massachusetts Historical Society, wf11241819/reel 7, p. 1/2) was furnished to me by Anne Grady, research historian, Society for the Preservation of New England Antiquities. I am grateful to her and to Richard Nylander, chief curator, for their thoughts about the possible origins of the coffeepot. Foster's silver is not itemized.

· 126 ·

COFFEEPOT

Marked by Benjamin Gignac (1713, first mark entered 1745)
London, 1767/8
Silver, wood
Res.65.27

MARKS: to right of handle, maker's mark *BG* (Grimwade 172) (repeated on bezel of cover); lion passant (repeated on bezel of cover); leopard's head crowned; date letter *m*

H. 25.9 cm (10³⁄₁₆ in.); w. 19.6 cm (7¾ in.); d. 11.8 cm (4⅝ in.)

WEIGHT: 791 gm (25 oz 8 dwt)

PROVENANCE: Bequest of Maxim Karolik, April 14, 1965

DESCRIPTION: The pear-shaped coffeepot, raised from sheet, rests on a spreading foot that is chased with scrolls and foliage. The body of the pot is chased along the lower and upper sections with scrolls and trailing flowers and vines. The curved spout, cast in halves and seamed vertically, is modeled at the base with sprigs of foliage. The domed cover, which is raised and chased, has an applied gadrooned border and an interior bezel. At the center of the spiraling chasing is an acorn knop. The wooden handle is mounded on cast scrolled sockets. The coffeepot has suffered considerable damage and has been buffed and repaired with lead.

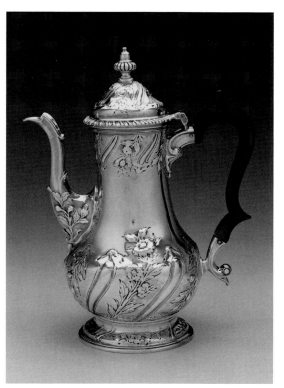

126

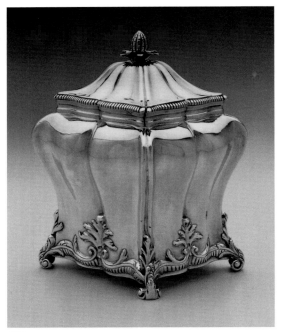

127

domed cover, raised from sheet and chased, has a gadrooned edge, eight undulating panels that correspond to the panels on the body, and is surmounted by a cast berry finial.

Pierre Gillois seems to have specialized in sets of tea canisters, often supplied in a silver-mounted shagreen box, sometimes including a sugar box. Variations on the rectangular bombé form include chased decoration of spiral fluting and floral garlands.[1] The gauge of the metal on the panels of this box is remarkably thin, but the ribbed structure provides rigidity.

1. See a pair sold Sotheby's, London, November 20, 1980, lot 336, and another pair sold Christie's, London, July 22, 1981, lot 170. A set of three of the same model as the Boston canister was sold Christie's, New York, September 17, 1990, lot 118.

· 127 ·

TEA CANISTER

Marked by Pierre Gillois (first mark entered 1754)
London, 1768/9
Silver
33.174

MARKS: on underside, date letter *n*; leopard's head crowned; lion passant (repeated on bezel of cover); maker's mark *PG* with an *I* above (Grimwade 2182)

INSCRIPTIONS: scratched on underside (twice), *No 9*

H. 14.9 cm (5⅞ in.); w. 10.3 cm (4¹/₁₆ in.); d. 9.2 cm (3⅝ in.)

WEIGHT: 323.2 gm (10 oz 8 dwt)

PROVENANCE: Anonymous Gift in Memory of Charlotte Beebe Wilbour (1833–1914), March 2, 1933

EXHIBITED: Boston, Museum of Fine Arts, 1933

PUBLISHED: Gruber 1982, fig. 250

DESCRIPTION: The rectangular canister has a bombé body with two vertical panels on each side and ribbed corners. The lower part of the body is chased with a foliate pattern, flowing into the four scrolled foliate feet. The body is assembled from five pieces of chased sheet, seamed on the corners, with a molded wire applied to the rim. The rectangular

· 128 ·

HOT WATER JUG AND STAND

Marked by Charles Wright (free 1754, d. 1815)
London, 1768/9
Silver, leather
33.175

MARKS: on underside of jug and underside of lamp, maker's mark *CW* (Grimwade 3511); leopard's head crowned; date letter *n*; lion passant (repeated on bezel of cover)

INSCRIPTIONS: scratched on underside of jug and lamp, *5616*

H. 35.1 cm (13¹³/₁₆ in.); w. 17.4 cm (6⅞ in.); d. 16 cm (6⁵/₁₆ in.)

WEIGHT: 1,136.8 gm (36 oz 11 dwt)

PROVENANCE: Anonymous Gift in Memory of Charlotte Beebe Wilbour (1833–1914), March 2, 1933

EXHIBITED: Boston, Museum of Fine Arts, 1933; Springfield, Massachusetts, Museum of Fine Arts, 1958

DESCRIPTION: The plain pear-shaped pot has an elongated neck and a short flaring spout decorated with fluting, beading, and a shell. The body is formed from sheet, seamed behind the handle, with an inset base. The ear-shaped handle is mounted directly to the body of the pot and is covered with

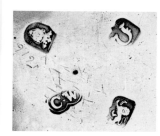

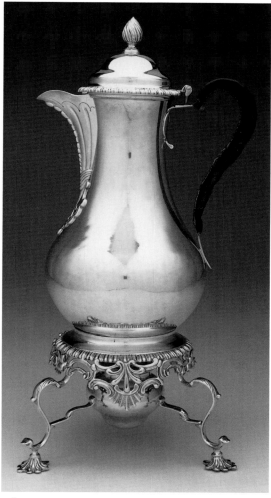

128

stitched leather. The high domed cover, raised from
sheet, has a gadrooned rim and a flame-shaped
finial. The plain circular foot of the pot fits into a
high stand resting on three splayed, scrolled feet. The
rim of the stand, cast from several pieces, is
gadrooned, with a pierced apron composed of scrolls
and shells. The braces for the legs are soldered to an
inverted pear-shaped heater, with detachable cover.

· 129 ·

PAIR OF CANDLESTICKS AND THREE-LIGHT BRANCH

Design by Robert Adam (1728-1792)
Marked by Sebastian (I) and James Crespell
(entered into partnership ca. 1760), Samuel
Whitford (II) (first mark entered 1800)
London, 1769/70 and 1825/6
Silver
1993.943.1a–b–.2a-d

MARKS: underside of each candlestick base, maker's
mark *SC* over *IC* (Grimwade 2497); date letter *O*;
leopard's head crowned; lion passant. On stem of
each waxpan, maker's mark *SW* (Grimwade 2663);
sovereign's head; lion passant; date letter *k*. On
underside of branch waxpans and on foot of each
end of nozzle, lion passant

ARMORIALS: on each pan and central waxpan, crest
of Sir Richard Phillips, seventh baronet of Picton
Castle, co. Pembroke (d. 1823), created baron Milford
1776

INSCRIPTION: engraved on corner of each, monogram *RMP* with crest in center; scratched underside
of each base *No1 42"11*; *No2 40"19*

1993.943.1a-b (candlestick): H. 35.3 cm (13¹⁵⁄₁₆ in.);
w. 15.2 cm (6 in.); d. 15.2 cm (6 in.)

1993.943.2a-b (candlestick): H. 35.3 cm (13¹⁵⁄₁₆ in.); w.
15.1 cm (5¹⁵⁄₁₆ in.); d. 15.1 cm (15¹⁵⁄₁₆ in.)

1993.943.2c-d (branch): H. 17.2 cm (6¾ in.);
w. 43.7 cm (17³⁄₁₆ in.); d. 8.9 cm (3½ in.)

WEIGHT: 1993.943.1a-b: 1,374.9 gm (44 oz 4 dwt).
1993.943.2a-b: 1,321 gm (42 oz 9 dwt).
1993.943.2c-d: 1,343.8 gm (43 oz 4 dwt)

PROVENANCE: by descent to Sir John Phillips, pur-
chased by Thomas Lumley, Ltd., London, 1945; with
Thomas Lumley, Ltd., London, 1982; sold Christie's,
London, May 13, 1992, lot 152, purchased by
Firestone & Parson, Boston, purchased January 26,
1994, Theodora Wilbour Fund in Memory of
Charlotte Beebe Wilbour, Gift of Mrs. Irving K.
Hall, Bequest of George Nixon Black, Estate of Mrs.
William Dorr Boardman through Gift of Mrs.
Bernard C. Weld, Gift of Mary W. Bartol, John W.
Bartol, and Abigail W. Clark, Gift of Mrs. Henry
Lyman, Anonymous Gift in Memory of Charlotte
Beebe Wilbour (1833–1914), Miss Grace W. Treadwell,
Gift of Miss M. H. Jewell, Gift in Memory of
Charlotte Beebe Wilbour, Gift of Hollis French, Gift
of Mrs. D. Wilmarth Cressey, Gift of Mr. and Mrs.
Stephen C. Greene, Bequest of Amelia Peabody, by
exchange, and Gift of Mrs. Stuart C. Welch

EXHIBITED: Boston, Museum of Fine Arts, 1994

DESCRIPTION: Each candlestick rests on a square plinth that is cast in one piece and bordered with a band of acanthus foliage. The two sections of the baluster stem, joined above the knop, are formed of cast halves, vertically seamed. The stem rises from a circular base with a guilloche border, beading, and acanthus fluting. Above a cluster of acanthus leaves, the stem is covered with spiral fluting, rising to a flared knop. A vase-shaped socket with an acanthus base, cast in two vertical halves, surmounts the stem. Two removable gadrooned waxpans, each engraved with a crest, fit into the sockets. The single three-light branch has a large central vase-shaped nozzle, scrolled, reeded arms, and one smaller nozzle on either side. The central socket is fitted with a detachable cone-shaped extinguisher with a fan of laurel leaves and a spherical finial.

Robert Adam's designs for these monumental candlesticks are preserved in the Soane Museum (figs. 4 and 5). Michael Snodin has pointed out the great originality of the form, which integrates elements of the Roman stone candelabrum and the ornament of some Renaissance bronzes. The proportions and motifs of this candlestick became standard, but Adam was working without precedent. The drawing is not inscribed with the name of a client, Adam's usual practice, and the possibility must be considered that the design was execut-

ed for a retail outlet.[1] It is clear that, as in the case of the Richmond Cup (cat. 121), once Adam's design was made available, it was passed from hand to hand and altered at will.[2] These later variations, though certainly based on Adam's design, have a simplified surface orna-mentation and lack the dense, tightly compact-ed foliage and fluting that are such distinctive features of the early models.

This pair of candlesticks is part of a set of four divided by the Toledo Museum of Art[3] and the Museum of Fine Arts, Boston in 1993. They are engraved on the waxpan with the crest of Phillips of Picton Castle, co. Pembroke, and on the bases with a monogram, possibly *RMP* for Sir Richard Phillips, seventh baronet, who, in 1764, married a cousin, Mary, daughter of James Phillips of Pontypark, co. Pembroke. The original set seems to have included at least twelve candlesticks by three different makers ranging in date from 1767 to 1796.[4] These are engraved with different crests and monograms, all, however, relating to the Phillips family. The branches belonging to the Boston pair are hall-marked 1825, and another set of branches in Toledo is marked for 1791, suggesting that additions to the set were being made continu-ously. The set is recorded as follows: 1. pair, marked by John Carter, 1767/8, Temple Newsam House;[5] 2. four, marked by D. Pontifex, 1796;[6] 3. six, including four marked by S. and J. Crespell, 1769/70,[7] and two marked by J. Carter, 1767/8.[8]

Sebastian and James Crespell were subcon-tractors for Parker and Wakelin, and their ledgers from 1778 to 1792 survive. These can-dlesticks cannot be identified in the accounts, nor is there a record of the Phillips family as clients in the Gentlemen's Ledgers of 1765–75 or 1770–76.[9]

There is evidence of previous gilding on the surface of the candlesticks. This may have been a nineteenth-century addition, but the more finished of Adam's designs have been given a delicate wash, suggesting that it may have been intended to be gilt.

1. Snodin 1997, p. 23. The earliest models of this design are a pair of unknown provenance marked by Whyte and Holmes in 1767/8, now in the Manchester City Art Gallery.

Fig. 4. *Design for a candlestick,*
Robert Adam

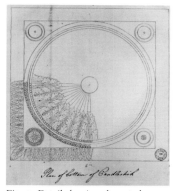

Fig. 5. *Detail showing alternate base,*
Robert Adam

129

2. For example, see four candlesticks marked by John Carter, 1774/5, sold Christie's, New York, October 17, 1996, lot 302; four candlesticks marked by Daniel Smith and Robert Sharp, 1775/6, sold Sotheby's, London, May 23, 1985, lot 108.

3. The Toledo Museum of Art, 1993.55a-f.

4. See Lomax 1992, pp. 159–60. James Lomax kindly shared with me his extensive research on this group of candlesticks.

5. Ibid., pp. 158–60.

6. Sold (with the pair by Carter, now at Temple Newsam), Christie's, London, June 19, 1963, lot 152.

7. The present pair, and The Toledo Museum of Art, acc. no. 1993.55a-f.

8. With Paul Smith, Ludlow, Shropshire, illus. John F. Hayward, "English and Foreign Silver and Gold at the International Art Treasures Exhibition," *Apollo* 76, no. 1 (March 1962), p. 34. These six candlesticks are said to have been purchased in Tenby, South Wales. Clayton 1985a, p. 62, fig. 80, illustrates a single stick from a set of six in a private collection marked by S. & J. Crespell in 1769/70. It is unclear if this set of six is yet another group or a reference to the present set. Another pair, marked by David Whyte and William Holmes in 1767/8, has only a slight variation on the base and may belong to the set; they are in the Manchester City Art Gallery (Lomax 1992, p. 159).

9. Victoria and Albert Museum, Garrard Ledgers, VAM 7, 8, 9, 40. I am very grateful to Helen Clifford for supplying this information. See Lomax 1992, p. 159, for the records of the Phillips family plate.

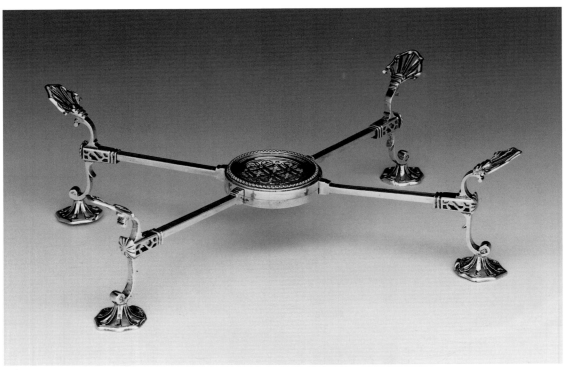

130

· 130 ·

DISH CROSS

Possibly marked by Richard Meach (first mark
entered 1765)
London, ca. 1770
Silver
63.198

MARKS: on two of the four arms, maker's mark *RM*
(possibly Grimwade 2364); lion passant (repeated on
each of the four feet)

H. 8.7 cm (3⁷⁄₁₆ in.); w. 29 cm (11⁷⁄₁₆ in.); d. 24.7 cm
(9¾ in.)

WEIGHT: 388.4 gm (12 oz 10 dwt)

PROVENANCE: Gift of Mrs. Joseph V. McMullan,
February 13, 1963

EXHIBITED: Toronto, George R. Gardiner Museum
of Ceramic Art, 1998

DESCRIPTION: The dish cross is constructed of a
central disk pierced with diaperwork securing two
heavy wire circles, each with two projecting arms.
The four arms, formed of square wire, have
adjustable sliding feet of cast scrolls and shells. The
angle of the cross can be changed by pivoting the
two central circles, and the position of the feet can
be adjusted by sliding the openwork bracket.

· 131 ·

HOT WATER URN

Marked by Charles Wright (free 1754, d. 1815)
London, 1771/2
Silver
1971.130

MARKS: on inner heat compartment and on upper
rim of base, date letter *Q*; leopard's head crowned;
lion passant (repeated on bezel of cover); maker's
mark *CW* (Grimwade 428)

ARMORIALS: engraved on front of urn, the arms of
Morteyn or Power quartering Bloen, Bloer, Kelston,
Little, Prydeux, Twichet, or Wotten, with Aldred in
pretence; engraved on cover, an unidentified coat of
arms and crest (quarterly 1 and 4, a fess embattled,
and in chief two five-pointed mullets sable, 2 and 3,
a sable a saltire engrailed, in pretence, gules a
chevron engrailed or, between three griffin's heads
erased; crest: a hand holding two serpents entwined)

INSCRIPTIONS: engraved under edge of urn, *100-8*

H. 57.8 cm (22¾ in.); w. 27.1 cm (10¹¹⁄₁₆ in.);
d. 31.8 cm (12½ in.)

WEIGHT: 3,161 gm (101 oz 12 dwt)

PROVENANCE: sold Parke-Bernet, New York,
March 16, 1971, lot 26, purchased April 14, 1971,

131

Theodora Wilbour Fund in Memory of Charlotte Beebe Wilbour

DESCRIPTION: The urn-shaped body rests on a shaped square plinth that has four leaf-capped scrolled feet and a cast openwork skirt. The raised base is chased with a band of guilloche along the edge of the plinth and panels of reeding emanating from an applied central collar of bead-and-reel. At the top of the base is a bezel, keyed to fit into the removable upper section of the urn and to enclose a cylindrical heating device (now missing). The body of the urn is formed of two raised and chased sections, joined at the midsection with an undulating line of bead-and-reel ornament with applied shells and scrolls. The bottom and top of the body are chased with broad fluting. A spout cast in the form of a serpent projects from the lower front of the urn. Cast openwork handles are joined to the body at the midsection. The fluted neck rises to a border of applied beading. The high domed cover is chased with fluting and surmounted with a coarsely formed pineapple finial. From the rim, the fluted neck of the urn tapers, then flares slightly to form another beaded rim.

Charles Wright's exuberant urns are a rather ungainly union of rococo motifs with a neo-classical carcass. Earlier examples of the 1760s, made in partnership with his former master, Thomas Whipham, have a pear-shaped body on a square base with openwork apron and are sometimes chased with chinoiserie themes.[1] The vase-shaped profile of the present example was well established by 1770, but the undulating lines of the handles are a characteristic peculiar to Wright.[2]

1. See an example at the Clark Art Institute, acc. no. 348, illus. Wees 1997, p. 365, cat. 252; another marked for 1767, sold Christie's, New York, September 17, 1990, lot 90; another marked for 1765, illus. Wark 1978, p. 45, cat. 104.

2. See an example in the Minneapolis Institute of Arts, acc. no. 77.1, illus. Puig 1989, p. 105, cat. 87.

132 (Color Plate xv)

· 132 ·

SET OF THREE CONDIMENT VASES

Marked by Louisa Courtauld and George Cowles
(entered into partnership ca. 1768)
London, 1771/2
Silver
1981.21–23

MARKS: on edge of base, maker's mark *LC* over
GC (Grimwade 1907) (repeated on underside of
cover); lion passant (repeated on underside of
cover); leopard's head crowned; date letter *Q*

ARMORIALS: engraved on side of each vase, the
arms of Curzon impaling Colyear for Nathaniel
Curzon, first baron Scarsdale (1726–1804) of
Kedleston Hall, co. Derbyshire, and Caroline
Colyear

1981.21: H. 19.1 cm (7½ in.); w. 10.1 cm (4 in.);
diam. of base 5.4 cm (2⅛ in.)

1981.22: H. 18.1 cm (7⅛ in.); w. 8.9 cm (3½ in.);
diam. of base 4.5 cm (1¾ in.)

1981.23: H. 18.1 cm (7⅛ in.); w. 8.1 cm (3³⁄₁₆ in.);
diam. of base: 4.8 cm (1⅞ in.)

WEIGHT: 1981.21: 379.9 gm (12 oz 4 dwt). 1981.22:
482 gm (15 oz 10 dwt). 1981.23: 377 gm (12 oz
2 dwt)

PROVENANCE: Nathaniel Curzon (1726–1804), first
baron Scarsdale, through the family by descent, sold
by order of the trustees of the Kedleston Estate,
Christie's, London, June 25, 1980, lot 87,
Museumpiece, Zurich, purchased February 11, 1981,
Theodora Wilbour Fund in Memory of Charlotte
Beebe Wilbour

PUBLISHED: Hatfield 1981, pp. 4–19; Philippa
Glanville, *Silver in England* (London, 1987), fig. 32,
pp. 84–85, 218–19; Schroder 1988b, p. 214; Truman
1993, p. 104

DESCRIPTION: The three vases are of identical
form, with two slightly smaller than the third. The
raised ovoid body rests on a spreading cast foot with
a chased gadrooned rim. The plain body is finely
engraved with mythological scenes in the style of
Greek vase painting, flowing continuously around
the object. The scenes are framed with an engraved
Greek key pattern below and above, along the
shoulder, circles of athemion. Two high arching handles, each cast in one piece, rise from the shoulder,

212

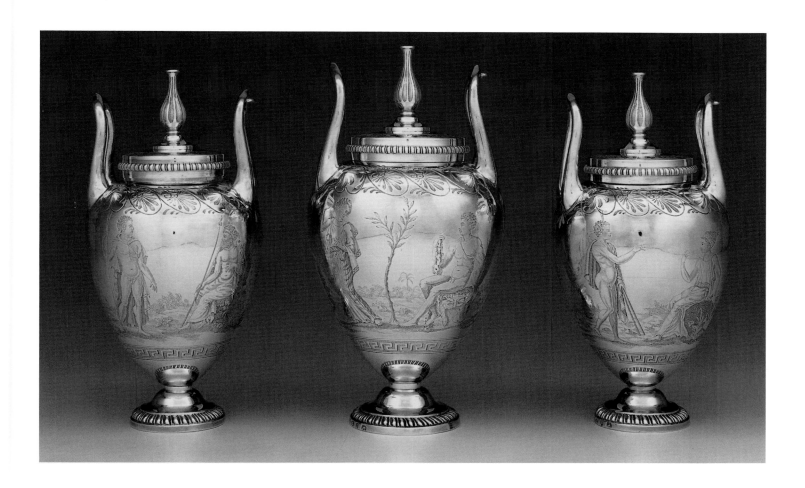

one with an attached loop to hold a ladle. The cover is formed from two pieces of sheet, one seamed to fit tightly over the bezel on the vase. Around the rim is a band of chased gadrooning and an engraved Greek key pattern. The tall flaring finial has engraved vertical fluting.

This set of condiment vases was made for Nathaniel Curzon, first baron Scarsdale, one of the great patrons of eighteenth-century neo-classicism.[1] His involvement with the design and furnishing of Kedleston Hall was intimate, and as Leslie Harris suggests, his accomplishment should be compared with that of lord Burlington at Chiswick or lord Leicester at Holkham.[2] Although he is not known to have made an extended grand tour, lord Scarsdale was committed to the classical idiom, and his library indicates that he was conversant with the considerable published material available. At Kedleston he first employed James "Athenian" Stuart (1713–1788), Matthew Brettingham (1699–1769), and James Paine (1717–1789),

eventually settling on Robert Adam, who shaped the architecture, gardens, and interiors including the furniture and the sideboard plate. Even before his inheritance in 1758 (the same year he was introduced to Robert Adam), lord Scarsdale was making every effort to update the family plate. In 1757 he bought and modi-fied a rococo epergne, and two years later he ordered a large and very eccentric service from Thomas Heming.[3] Adam's frequently illustrated design for a sideboard niche at Kedleston indi-cates the precision devoted to the design process, in which particular objects in the client's plate closet (such as the seventeenth-century cisterns and fountains) were accom-modated and new pieces proposed to integrate the whole.[4] The ensemble was the focal point of the house and drew admiring comments from Horace Walpole and the duchess of Northumberland.

By 1771, when these condiment vases were marked, Adam's interiors at Kedleston were

largely complete, and he had turned his attention to the landscaping. The architect's responsibility for the design of the vases cannot be confirmed, and indeed, the austerity of the design, relieved only by the finely engraved scenes, is unparalleled in Adam's designs for silver. Although the bills for these objects do not survive at Kedleston, Courtauld and Cowles supplied a quantity of plate (see the argyll, cat. 133). In 1776 the firm was paid £142 3s. 6d. for silver supplied for the country.[5] The vases are modeled in the form of a *lebes gamikos* (marriage bowl). Both the form and the decoration are based on illustrations in d'Hancarville's 1766 publication of the vases
in the collection of the great antiquarian Sir William Hamilton.[6] Lord Scarsdale had volumes one and two of the four-volume set in his library at Kedleston. The model for the decoration of the vases was one of Hamilton's most celebrated treasures, the Meidias Hydria (water jar), a fifth-century vase now in the British Museum.[7] The engraved scenes on the silver depict the eleventh of the Twelve Labors of Hercules in which Hercules takes the golden apples from the Garden of the Hesperides. The Hesperides, nymphs of the evening, were the seven beautiful daughters of Atlas and Hesperis, and the apples of their garden were guarded by the serpent Ladon.

D'Hancarville's publication of the Hamilton vases was intended to serve as a model for designers in many media, and indeed Josiah Wedgwood promptly rose to the opportunity. To commemorate the opening of the Etruria pottery in 1769 he and his partner, Thomas Bentley, produced a black basalt vase decorated with scenes of Hercules in the Garden of the Hesperides. Known as the First Day Vases since they marked the factory's first day of production, the vases were exhibited in London and subsequently manufactured in some quantity.[8]

Though often referred to as tea canisters, the silver vases were intended to contain condiments—dry mustard, sugar, and pepper.[9] A small loop on the upper edge of the handles is a fitting for a pierced ladle, now lost. Only one other set of silver vases of the same design is known, also marked by Courtauld and Cowles for 1771/2. Two, which appeared on the market in 1992, retain their ladles.[10] The sugar vase (the larger of the three) is in the collection of Courtaulds, Ltd.[11] They are engraved with the arms of Birch for Charles Birch (d. 1780) of Woodford, co. Essex, and his wife, Sarah Creed. Although the subjects of the engraved scenes have not yet been fully identified, they seem to have been engraved in the same shop as the Kedleston vases.

The engraving on the Kedleston vases fits into a distinct group of objects, all dated between 1770 and 1772, with narrative or dec-

orative scenes after printed sources. As Beth Wees has observed, the prevailing ornament for plain tea wares in the 1770s was bright-cut panels or borders.[12] Although the practices of silver engravers and the way they served the trade are not well understood, some light has been shed on the subject by the Garrard Ledgers.[13] Robert Barker has investigated one specialist engraver, Robert Clee (ca. 1710–1773), who worked for Parker and Wakelin in this period. The sale after his death of the prints and books in his possession included a broad range of images and suggests a sophisticated production.[14] Although there is no way to assess Clee's personal style accurately, it may not be a coincidence that the objects bearing this distinctive decoration are not found after 1773, the year of his death.

1. The condiment vases are discussed at length in Hatfield 1981, pp. 4–19.

2. Leslie Harris, *Robert Adam and Kedleston* (London, 1987), p. 9.

3. The epergne and part of the service have now been returned to Kedleston. See Cornforth 1996, pp. 128–31.

4. See Snodin 1997, pp. 17–19; Cornforth 1996, pp. 128–31; Hatfield 1981, pp. 14–15; Gillian Wilson, "The Kedleston Fountain: Its Development from a Seventeenth-Century Vase," *J. Paul Getty Museum Journal* 11 (1983), pp. 1–12.

5. Kedleston archives KB 26. I am very grateful to John Cornforth for providing this information.

6. Pierre François Hugues (called d'Hancarville), *Collection of Etruscan, Greek, and Roman Antiquities from the Cabinet of the Honorable William Hamilton*, 4 vols. (Naples, 1766–67). Also see Ian Jenkins and Kim Sloan, *Vases and Volcanoes: Sir William Hamilton and His Collection* (London, 1996), pp. 180–83.

7. See Lucilla Burn, *The Meidias Painter* (Oxford, 1987), pp. 15–21.

8. Hatfield 1981, pp. 16–17.

9. Michael Snodin, "Silver Vases and Their Purpose," *Connoisseur* 194 (1977), pp. 37–42.

10. Sold, Christie's, London, October 27, 1992, lot 341.

11. Illus. Hatfield 1981, p. 18, fig. 32.

12. Wees 1997, p. 340. In discussing an extraordinary engraved teapot in the Clark Art Institute, Wees (1997, p. 341 n. 21) lists six related objects. To these might be added a tea canister of 1772 engraved with scenes after Jean Baptiste Nicolas Pillement, sold Christie's, London, February 27, 1985, lot 185, and another by William Vincent, 1771, with chinoiserie scenes, sold Sotheby's, London, February 5, 1987, lot 129.

13. Helen M. Clifford, "Parker and Wakelin: The Study of an Eighteenth-Century Goldsmithing Firm with Particular Reference to the Garrard Ledgers ca. 1760–76," Ph.D. diss., Victoria and Albert, Royal College of Art, 1988, p. 260.

14. Unpublished paper by Robert Barker presented to the Silver Society, 1988.

· 133 ·

ARGYLL

Marked by Louisa Courtauld and George Cowles
(entered into partnership ca. 1768)
London, 1772/3
Silver
1985.807a–d

MARKS: inside rim, date letter *R*; leopard's head
crowned; lion passant (repeated on bezel of cover);
maker's mark *LC* over *GC* (Grimwade 1907)
(repeated on bezel of cover and on hot water vessel)

ARMORIALS: engraved on side of body, crest of
Curzon, beneath a baron's coronet, for Nathaniel
Curzon, first baron Scarsdale of Kedleston Hall,
co. Derbyshire (1726–1804)

H. 27.7 cm (10⅞ in.); W. 18.9 cm (7⁷⁄₁₆ in.);
D. 11.3 cm (4⁷⁄₁₆ in.)

WEIGHT: 952.6 gm (30 oz 12 dwt)

PROVENANCE: Nathaniel Curzon (1726–1804), first
baron Scarsdale, through family by descent, sold
Christie's, London, July 16, 1930, lot 65; Sotheby's,
New York, April 26, 1985, lot 78; Museumpiece,
Zurich, purchased November 27, 1985, Theodora
Wilbour Fund in Memory of Charlotte Beebe
Wilbour

EXHIBITED: London, Goldsmiths' Hall, *The
Courtauld Family: Huguenot Silversmiths*, 1985, cat. 30

PUBLISHED: Harold Newman, "Argylls: Silver and
Ceramic," *Apollo* 89, no. 84 (1969), pp. 98–103;
"Museum Acquisitions," *Decorative Arts Society
Newsletter* 12, no. 3 (1986), p. 7

DESCRIPTION: The vase-shaped body rests on a
trumpet foot. Around the foot rim there is applied
beading, and the stem is chased with vertical fluting.
The raised body is chased on the lower section with
acanthus leaves, and around the upper rim there is a
chased frieze of rosettes within panels, set off above
and below by two strings of applied beading. The
spout and handle, on opposite sides of the body, cast
in several pieces and finely chased, are formed from
two intertwining serpents, the open mouth of one
forming the spout, the mouth of the other biting
the tail of the first and forming the handle. The
raised, spool-shaped cover is chased with vertical
fluting, and rises to a dome bordered with a chased
laurel band and surmounted by a cast acorn finial.
The interior is fitted with a removable reservoir
formed by two conjoined cones.

Like the Kedleston condiment vases (cat. 132),
this argyll was made in 1771/2 by Courtauld
and Cowles for Nathaniel Curzon, first baron

Scarsdale.[1] The vases and the argyll were purchased after lord Curzon's first campaign of
plate purchases, which included a large service
by Thomas Heming, and well after the completion of the sideboard niche at Kedleston
designed by Robert Adam. Courtauld and
Cowles's bills from this period do not survive
at Kedleston, but there are records of substantial orders in 1776.[2]

The compact profile, fine chasing, and elegant proportions of this argyll are characteristic
of Courtauld and Cowles's best work in the
neoclassical style. After the death of Samuel
Courtauld in 1765, his widow, Louisa, took
over the business, and about 1768 she formed
a partnership with George Cowles, who had
been Courtauld's apprentice. The form of the
argyll, with its small foot, ovoid body, and high
flaring cover, echoes the proportions of the
Richmond Cup (see cat. 121), which in turn
reflects the influence of the seventeenth-
century designs of Jacques Stella (1596–1657).
Michael Snodin has suggested that the earliest
appearance of this form in English designs for
metalwork is recorded in a drawing of 1759–62
of a chestnut vase at Kedleston possibly
designed by James "Athenian" Stuart (1713–
1788).[3] Whoever provided a design of the argyll
to Courtauld and Cowles to be made up in silver is likely to have had the Kedleston sideboard firmly in mind. In England, as on the
Continent, the sources of many classicizing
vases were not the recently excavated and published antiquities from Herculaneum or
Pompeii but seventeenth-century designs by
such artists as Jacques Stella or Stefano della
Bella (1610–1664).[4] Courtauld and Cowles used
many of the same motifs on a two-handled cup
and cover of the same year now in the Victoria
and Albert Museum.[5] Some of their more
domestic productions from the same period
indicate that they had mastered the neoclassical
idiom, using acanthus leaves, beading, and
swags as restrained ornament on
a vase-shaped vessel.[6]

The argyll, traditionally believed to have been
invented by one of the dukes of Argyll, is a
sauceboat with an internal warmer.[7] Most silver
examples have double walls that could be filled
with hot water, but this example is fitted with
an interior vessel in the form of two conjoined

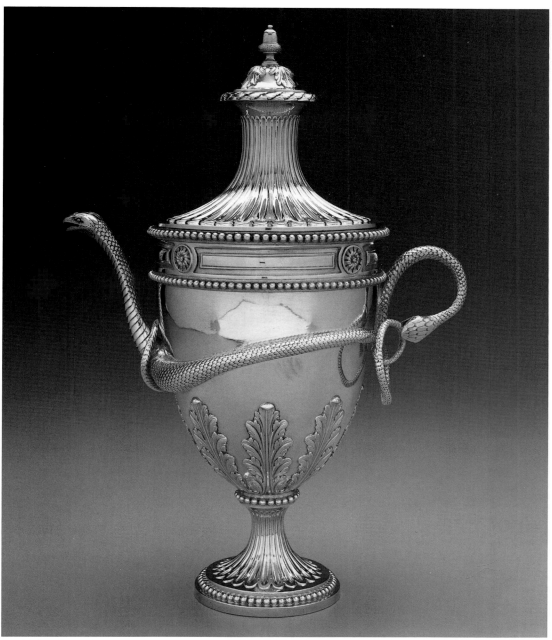

133 (Color Plate XVI)

cones that is screwed into the center of the base. Wakelin and Taylor used the design, with stouter proportions and a serpent spout but a wooden handle, in 1780.[8]

1. The engraved crest, a cockatrice, is associated with the Curzons, but the alternative crest, a popinjay rising, was more commonly used.

2. Kedleston archives KB 26. I am very grateful to John Cornforth for providing this information.

3. Snodin 1997, pp. 19–20.

4. Ibid., p. 21; Timothy Clifford, "Some English Ceramic Vases and Their Sources I," *English Ceramic*

Circle Transactions 10 (1978), pp. 159–73.

5. Acc. no. 804-1890, illus. Oman 1965, fig. 150.

6. See four sauceboats, 1776/7 in the Courtauld family, illus. E. Alfred Jones, *Some Silver Wrought by the Courtauld Family of London Goldsmiths in the Eighteenth Century* (Oxford, 1940), p. 120, pl. 62; and a set of three tea canisters, 1771, sold Parke-Bernet, New York, October 30, 1947, lot 424.

7. See Harold Newman, "Argylls: Silver and Ceramic," *Apollo* 89, no. 84 (1969), pp. 98–104.

8. Sold Parke-Bernet, New York, January 6, 1961, lot 79. Christopher Hartop kindly provided this reference.

134

• 134 •

PAIR OF WINE COASTERS

Marked by Richard Morton & Co.
Sheffield, 1773/4
Silver, wood
25.411–412

MARKS: on bottom rim of each, maker's mark *RM/&Co* (Jackson 1989, p. 441); lion passant; crown; date letter *E*

ARMORIALS: engraved on each, an unidentified crest (a greyhound courant)

25.411: H. 4.8 cm (1⅞ in.); diam. of rim 12.7 cm (5 in.)

25.412: H. 4.7 cm (1⅞ in.); diam. of rim 12.8 cm (5¹⁄₁₆ in.)

WEIGHT: 25.411: 178.6 gm (5 oz 15 dwt). 25.412: 175.8 gm (5 oz 13 dwt)

PROVENANCE: Bequest of Mrs. Thomas O. Richardson, July 16, 1925

DESCRIPTION: Each wine coaster has a pierced cylindrical gallery with a beaded border and applied laurel swags. At the center is a shield engraved with a crest. The piercing is apparently die-cut, and the swags are die-stamped. The base of the coaster is turned mahogany.

• 135 •

PAIR OF CANDLESTICKS

Marked by Matthew Boulton (1728–1809) and John Fothergill (d. 1782)
Birmingham, 1774/5
Silver
56.504–5

MARKS: on two sides of each base and on the bezel of one waxpan, maker's mark *IF* (Jones, p. 357) (repeated on bezel of other waxpan) and maker's mark *MB*; lion passant; anchor (repeated on bezel of other waxpan); date letter *B* (repeated on bezel of other waxpan)

INSCRIPTIONS: engraved on one corner of each base, *11..19..12*

56.504: H. 30.4 cm (11¹⁵⁄₁₆ in.); w. 11.6 cm (4⁹⁄₁₆ in.); d. 11.6 cm (4⁹⁄₁₆ in.)

56.505: H. 30.2 cm (11⅞ in.); w. 11.6 cm (4⁹⁄₁₆ in.); d. 11.6 cm (4⁹⁄₁₆ in.)

56.504: 618 gm (19 oz 17 dwt). 56.505: 652 gm (20 oz 19 dwt)

PROVENANCE: N. Bloom & Son, Inc., New York; purchased October 11, 1956, through Theodora Wilbour Fund in Memory of Charlotte Beebe Wilbour[1]

EXHIBITED: Washington, D.C., National Gallery of Art, *The Eye of Thomas Jefferson*, 1976, cat. 101; New York, Cooper-Hewitt Museum, *City Dwellings and Country Houses: Robert Adam and His Style*, 1982; Boston, Museum of Fine Arts, 1994

PUBLISHED: Rowe 1965, pl. 50

DESCRIPTION: Each candlestick has a square base with incurved, canted corners, with a guilloche and rosette pattern against a matted ground. The fluted terminal rises to a baluster stem with chased palmetto leaves and swags suspended from rosettes. The urn-shaped socket has chased palmetto leaves on a matted ground and a reeded rim. The removable waxpans have fluting and a rim of beading. The candlesticks are assembled from cast and chased components. The bases are apparently cast, while the stems are formed of seamed sheet, chased and molded over a solid core.

Matthew Boulton, one of the great enterprising forces of the Industrial Revolution, sought to transform his family's toy and button manufactory in Birmingham into a model of modern production. Boulton, in partnership with John Fothergill, concentrated his organizational

135

Fig. 6. *Design for a candlestick,* James Wyatt

efforts on the specialization of his workers and his technological efforts on such refinements as the manufacturing of better dies for stamping panels of ornament or making interchangeable components for hollowware.[2] His goal was to combine the best modern design with efficient and specialized production, and he pursued contacts with the leading neoclassical architects, including the Adam brothers, Sir William Chambers, and James Wyatt (1738–1814). Wyatt had emerged as a leading exponent of neoclassicism with the design of the Pantheon in Oxford Street, but it was with his innovations in the Gothic revival style that he proved more versatile than many architects of his generation. An album of drawings by Wyatt for silver wares from the collection of the late vicomte de Noailles shows some of Wyatt's inventions for Boulton.[3] His drawing for the present candlestick (fig. 6) shows a base resting on short acanthus feet, but when rendered for the factory's pattern book, the design had been altered to show the shaped square base used here. Several silver candlesticks after this pattern survive, executed with variations that indicate Boulton and Fothergill's resourcefulness in adapting patterns. The relative austerity of Wyatt's design included a slender stem with palm leaves at the base and swags above.[4] This model was also produced in fused silverplate.[5] A second version in sterling features the addition of vertical reeding on a slightly thicker stem, with acanthus leaves above and below.[6]

1. The Museum acquired a set of four; two were sold at Christie's, New York, October 21, 1993, lot 508.

2. The Matthew Boulton papers in the Birmingham Reference Library have been analyzed by several writers, notably Quickenden 1980, pp. 274–94; idem, "Boulton and Fothergill's Silversmiths," *Silver Society Journal* 7 (1995), pp. 342–56. Also see cat. 138.

3. Fergusson 1974, pp. 751–55.

4. Other examples of the same model are in the Birmingham Assay Office, illus. ibid., fig. 51.

5. See an example at Colonial Williamsburg, illus. Davis 1976, p. 226, cat. 254.

6. A pair of 1776 was sold Christie's, New York, October 18, 1995, lot 361, and another pair of 1778 was sold Christie's, Amsterdam, June 11, 1981, lot 55.

136

· 136 ·

BASKET

Marked by Thomas Daniell (free 1771)
London, 1775/6
Silver
33.177

MARKS: on rim, maker's mark *TD* (Grimwade 2728); lion passant; leopard's head crowned; date letter *u*

ARMORIALS: engraved on the interior of the basket in a floral medallion are the arms of Pattenson of Charry Burton, co. York, quartering Burton, Bodleigh, or Trethake

H. 27.5 cm (10¹³⁄₁₆ in.); w. 36.6 cm (14⅜ in.); d. 31.3 cm (12⁵⁄₁₆ in.)

WEIGHT: 961.1 gm (30 oz 18 dwt)

PROVENANCE: Anonymous Gift in Memory of Charlotte Beebe Wilbour (1833–1914), March 2, 1933

EXHIBITED: Boston, Museum of Fine Arts, 1933; Toronto, George R. Gardiner Museum of Ceramic Art, 1998

DESCRIPTION: The oval basket has flaring sides and rests on a low foot formed of seamed sheet and pierced with a vertical pattern. The rim is finished with twisted wire. The body of the basket, which is raised from sheet, is chased around the base with two sheaves of wheat. The sides are chased with a pattern of alternating rosettes and urns connected by drapery swags and pierced with panels containing a geometric pattern of rectangles and circles and scrolling foliage. A cast band of foliage and beads is applied to the rim. The swing handle is cast and pierced with ribbons and scrolls.

The chasing and piercing on this basket is competently, although dryly, executed, characteristic of the work bearing Thomas Daniell's mark. (Also see cat. 148.) Such a piece would doubtless have been available readymade, part of the "Twenty Thousand Ounces of every species of Silver Goods . . . always on hand" that Daniell advertised.[1]

1. Grimwade 1990, p. 744.

· 137 ·

CREAM PAIL

London, 1775/6
Silver, glass
Res.63.26a-b

MARKS: on underside of silver frame, date letter *U*; leopard's head crowned; lion passant

INSCRIPTIONS: engraved on underside of the silver frame, *A.L.L. 1877*

H. 9 cm (3⁹⁄₁₆ in.); diam. of rim 7.5 cm (2¹⁵⁄₁₆ in.)

WEIGHT: 68 gm (2 oz 4 dwt)

PROVENANCE: Bequest of Helen S. Coolidge; John Gardner Coolidge Collection, February 13, 1963

DESCRIPTION: The circular vessel, formed from two pieces of seamed sheet, has flaring sides, a beaded rim, and a beaded bail handle. The sides are pierced and engraved overall with a geometric floral pattern. There is a large broken section in the piercing, and the blue glass liner is a replacement.

Though pierced miniature pails of this form were made commonly to be used for clotted cream,[1] this example may have been part of a larger piece, perhaps a double salt. The incomplete hallmarks, the damage to one side of the piercing, and an apparently replaced handle suggest that it may originally have been joined to a second, identical vessel with interlocked handles to serve as a double salt.[2]

1. See an example in the Huntington collection, illus. Wark 1978, p. 93, cat. 227.
2. See an example illustrated in Judith Banister, *English Silver* (London, 1969), p. 116, pl. 55.

137

· 138 ·

EWER

Marked by Matthew Boulton (1728–1809) and John Fothergill (d. 1782)
Birmingham, 1776/7
Silver, parcel gilt
55.623

MARKS: to left of handle, maker's mark *MB* (Jones, p. 357) and *IF* (Jones, p. 357); to right of handle, lion passant; anchor; date letter *D* (all five marks repeated on underside of cover)

ARMORIALS: engraved on side, the coat of arms, crest, and motto of Cabbell of Cromer Hall, co. Norfolk

H. 34.5 cm (13⁹⁄₁₆ in.); w. 19.4 cm (7⅝ in.); d. 11.9 cm (4¹¹⁄₁₆ in.)

WEIGHT: 975.2 gm (31 oz 7 dwt)

PROVENANCE: Thomas Lumley, Ltd., London, purchased October 20, 1955, Theodora Wilbour Fund in Memory of Charlotte Beebe Wilbour

EXHIBITED: Washington, D.C., National Gallery of Art, *The Eye of Thomas Jefferson*, 1976, p. 53, cat. 100; New York, Cooper-Hewitt Museum, *City Dwellings and Country Houses: Robert Adam and His Style*, 1982

PUBLISHED: Rowe 1965, pl. 42; Gruber 1982, fig. 86; Schroder 1988b, p. 235; Truman 1993, p. 103

DESCRIPTION: The raised urn-shaped body rests on a spreading, fluted foot, raised in several sections. A braided wire encircles the stem, and at the juncture with the body there is a calyx of acanthus. The body is divided into three sections by an applied gilt band of chased Vitruvian scroll below and a milled gilt band of rosettes, with beading and laurel. Above and below the two bands the surface is faceted, and on the plain midsection there is an engraved coat of arms. The fluted rim flares to a high spout fitted with a raised cover and a hidden hinge. At the center of the cover is a gilt chased boss and cast pomegranate finial. The high curved handle is formed of sheet with edges of twisted wire and beading applied down the center.

By 1776, the year this ewer was marked, Matthew Boulton and John Fothergill's toy and button manufactory in Birmingham was running at full capacity. Having successfully lobbied to establish an assay office in Birmingham and failed to market ormolu with commercial success, the partnership turned to the manufacture of silver plate. Boulton paid close attention to the burgeoning interest in classical motifs

138

and chose to concentrate on ornamental wares instead of functional domestic plate.[1] Through his contacts with the leading neoclassical architects, among them James Wyatt,[2] and by making his factory a destination point for well-connected gentry, he received many of his best commissions. This jug was produced in several versions. In the pattern book preserved in the Birmingham Reference Library and an example marked for 1775, it is shown with a shaped square base identical to that used for the candlesticks in this collection (cat. 135) and with swags and paterae on the plain section of the body.[3] Another example of 1774 omits the swags on the body,[4] and a pair marked for 1776 is uncovered and lacks the chased acanthus at the base of the vessel.[5] The addition or subtraction of ornament from a standard design probably allowed Boulton some flexibility in the prices he charged, but in spite of his determination to streamline the production of plate, he was often asked to produce unique or customized wares, undercutting his profits.[6]

1. Quickenden 1980, p. 279. For other literature on Boulton and Fothergill, see cat. 135.
2. Fergusson 1974, pp. 751–55.
3. Rowe 1965, pls. 40–41.
4. Ibid., pl. 45.
5. Sold Phillips, New York, May 30, 1980, lot 193.
6. Quickenden 1980, p. 281.

139 (Color Plate XVII)

· 139 ·

NANNY

Marked by Charles Frederick Kandler (active after 1735, d. 1778)
London, 1777/8
Silver gilt
66.435

MARKS: on underside of pedestal, date letter *b*; leopard's head crowned; lion passant; maker's mark *FK* (Grimwade 3571)

H. 29.6 cm (11⅝ in.); w. 8.7 cm (3⁷⁄₁₆ in.); d. 8.2 cm (3¼ in.)

WEIGHT: 1,224.7 gm (39 oz 7 dwt)

PROVENANCE: Charles Howard, eleventh duke of Norfolk (1746–1815), sold Christie's, London, May 24, 1816, lot 70, purchased by the earl of Ducie, descended in the family, sold Christie's, London, October 7, 1959, lot 82; sold Christie's, London, June 15, 1966, lot 82; S. J. Phillips, Ltd., London, purchased September 21, 1966, Theodora Wilbour Fund in Memory of Charlotte Beebe Wilbour

PUBLISHED: Clayton 1971, p. 285, fig. 576, Clayton 1985a, p. 388, fig. 576

DESCRIPTION: The female figure stands on a shaped square plinth. Her right hand holds the edge of her upswept apron, and the left hand steadies a milk pail on her head. She wears a flowered dress with fitted bodice, an apron, and a small shawl. The figure is assembled from cast components and the skirt is chased. The figure's legs, with garters and stockings, are joined to the base and are exposed when the upper torso is lifted off. The base, formed from sections of sheet, is chased with ram's heads at the corners, joined by swags. The legs are cast.

The design of this unique figure is a variation on that of a wager, or marriage, cup. By twisting the torso, the upper section of the milk-maid can be lifted off the base, revealing her provocatively attired legs and allowing the inverted skirt to be used for drink. The traditional wager cup, examples of which survive from the late sixteenth century, is in the form of a female holding a chased, swiveling cup above her head. When inverted, the long skirt could be used as one cup, while the smaller cup was simultaneously filled. The challenge, for either a bridal couple or a wagering guest, was to drain both cups without spilling.[1] Wager cups seem to have been especially appropriate presentations to the London livery companies.

139

New members of the Vintners' were expected to drink from the company's seventeenth-century example.[2] A few late-eighteenth-century wager cups are known, though none comparable in size, weight, or quality to *Nanny*.[3] The form was revived in the nineteenth century when the Goldsmiths' Company received one from its prime warden, Francis Boone Thomas.[4] The removable torso and frank rendering of the undergarments put this cup in the category of *galanterie*: erotic objects for gentlemen's conversation or titillation.

Although not recorded in the Arundel Castle inventories,[5] this figure of *Nanny* was undoubtedly made for Charles Howard, eleventh duke of Norfolk, as it was sold with his collection in 1816. Howard was a colorful personality even against the backdrop of the lively circle surrounding the Prince of Wales and Charles James Fox (1794–1849). Born in

1746, he was known as "the Drunken Duke," or "the Jockey of Norfolk." "Nature which cast him in her coarsest mould, had not bestowed on him any of the external insignia of high descent. His person large, muscular, and clumsy, was destitute of grace or dignity. . . . He might indeed have been mistaken for a grazier or a butcher."[6] The discourse at his boisterous dinners was described as "in the first style: the subjects infinitely various, from bawdy to the depths of politics."[7] *Nanny* must have been conceived as a conversation piece for such raucous evenings. The duke conformed nominally to the established Church of England but was devoted nonetheless to his family's Catholic history. He was a voracious collector of books, pictures, and family memorabilia. At Arundel Castle he was responsible for extensive renovations, introducing, without the oversight of professional architects, an ambitious, if hybrid,

Gothic scheme that expressed his Whig principles.[8] The duke married twice. His first wife, Marian Coppinger, died in childbirth nine months after their marriage. His second wife, Frances Scudamore, fell victim to a hereditary psychological disorder and was confined to an asylum until her death. Although he had no legitimate offspring, he had numerous illegitimate children, six of them by his mistress, Mary Gibbon, daughter of the dean of Carlisle.

It has been proposed that the engraved inscription *Nanny* refers to "an actual portrait of a dairymaid of the family at the period," but there is nothing in the family documents to suggest this.[9] The milkmaid was often depicted as a figure of sexual fantasy,[10] and there are a few other objects that reflect this. A Chinese export porcelain saucer, for example, is enameled with a milkmaid on the front, her foot resting on a stile, revealing her leg and knee. The reverse is painted with a view of the milkmaid from the rear, her skirts lifted overhead, exposing her buttocks.[11] The fables of La Fontaine include the tale of the innocent milkmaid Perette who, eager to spend her earnings, hurries to the market and spills her precious milk along the way.[12] The milkmaid's broken pot and spilt milk, a symbol of lost virginity,

were adapted by John Gay (1685–1732) in his *Trivia* (published 1716) and would have been very familiar to an English audience; however, Gay's milkmaid is named Patty.[13] The graphic source for *Nanny* was a figure in Hogarth's engraving *The Enraged Musician*, which features a milkmaid at the center of an unruly street scene (fig. 7). The ragged woman with a crying babe in arms standing to the left of the open window is singing "The Ladies Fall." Hogarth's milkmaid, a pretty figure without overt sexual associations, follows the tradition of the "Cryes of the City of London," produced in many versions between 1687 and 1821.[14] The milkmaid is usually represented in the *Cries* with a headdress made of silver vessels and ribbons, reflecting the tradition that on May Day, milkmaids danced in the streets wearing such costumes. The silver figure is more stylishly dressed than Hogarth's milkmaid, with a string of pearls around her neck, a revealing neckline, and a stomacher decorated with ribbons and lacing. Hogarth's figure was produced in porcelain by the Longton Hall Factory and also served as a model for painted decoration on wares made at Worcester and Berlin.[15] Whether the eleventh duke had a role in the design of the object is not known, but he is recorded as having paid five hundred pounds for a collection of Hogarth's works.[16] He was satirized by James Gillray (1756–1815) in an etching entitled *Le Cochon et les deux petits*, showing him with two famously overweight courtesans.[17]

The association of the inscription *Nanny* with a milkmaid remains unclear. A "nanny house" or a "nanny shop" was a colloquial term for a brothel,[18] so it seems likely that the figure was understood to be a prostitute. Milkmaids were not typically associated with prostitution, which was more common among street vendors than household servants.[19] Erotic literature, ballads, broadsides, plays, and satirical engravings—the likely sources for such an association—do not seem to offer a direct link. One possibility is the Italian text *Ragionamenti*, by Pietro Aretino (1492–1556), which was first published in Rome in 1534 and later brought out in London. In it, Nanna explicitly recounts the story of her life as a nun, a wife, and a whore, while debating the future of her innocent daughter.[20] The book had a broad effect

Fig. 7. *The Enraged Musician,* William Hogarth

THE ENRAGED MUSICIAN.

on pornographic literature across Europe and might possibly have been the source of this figure's name.

The object bears the sponsor's mark of Charles Frederick Kandler, now believed to be a family member and successor to Charles Kandler, who emigrated from Dresden (see cat. 74). The Kandlers had supplied a great deal of silver to Catholic clients, among them the dukes of Norfolk, and the younger Kandler prepared an inventory of the Howard plate on the death of the ninth duke in 1777.[21] By the 1770s when this figure was made, Kandler's shop seems to have been primarily a retailer of high-quality, stylistically conservative wares. This figure, and a salver in the Birmingham Museum and Art Gallery with similar ram's heads,[22] are uncharacteristic of the late production of the shop.

1. Yvonne Hackenbroch, "Wager Cups," *Antiques* 95, no. 5 (May 1969), pp. 692–95; idem, "Wager Cups," *Bulletin of the Metropolitan Museum of Art* 26, no. 9 (May 1968), pp. 381–87.

2. George Russell French, *Description of the Plate and Tapestry of the Vintners' Company* (London, 1868), p. 481.

3. An example bearing London marks for 1770 and the sponsor's mark *AL* was sold at Christie's, London, March 3, 1982, lot 99. Also see Christie's, New York, October 18, 1995, lots 295–99.

4. London, 1829, marked by William Eaton, H. 26.7 cm; London, Worshipful Company of Goldsmiths, *The Goldsmith and the Grape*, 1983, p. 23, cat. 83.

5. Documents at Arundel Castle do not record the personal property of the eleventh duke. While examining the papers at Arundel Castle, Christopher Hartop very kindly searched the 1777 inventory of Norfolk House, and another list of silver at Worksop.

6. Sir Nathanial Wraxall, quoted in John Martin Robinson, *The Dukes of Norfolk* (Oxford, 1982), p. 171.

7. Ibid., p. 175.

8. Ibid., pp. 178–82.

9. See the entry for the sale, Christie's, London, October 7, 1959, lot 82. I am grateful to John Martin Robinson, librarian to the duke of Norfolk, for his opinion and advice about this.

10. For example, see the poem "The Maid of Tottenham" (ca. 1650), in E. J. Burford, ed., *Bawdy Verse* (Harmondsworth, 1982), pp. 104–6.

11. Illus. Michael Beurdeley, *Chinese Trade Porcelain* (Rutland, Vt., 1967), p. 62, figs. 39–40.

12. Henri Regnier, ed., *Oeuvres de J. de la Fontaine* (Paris, 1884), pp. 150–51.

13. Vinton A. Dearing, ed., *John Gay Poetry and Prose* (Oxford, 1974), vol. 1, pp. 141–42.

14. Sean Shesgreen, ed., *The Criers and Hawkers of London* (Stanford, 1990), p. 43.

15. Lars Tharp, *Hogarth's China* (London, 1997), figs. 67–69.

16. William Hogarth, *Anecdotes of William Hogarth Written by Himself* (London, 1833), p. 409.

17. E. J. Burford, *Wits, Wenchers, and Wantons: London's Low Life: Covent Garden in the Eighteenth Century* (London, 1986), p. 222. I am grateful to Ubaldo Vitali for this reference.

18. J. A. Simpson and E. S. C. Weiner, eds., *The Oxford English Dictionary* (Oxford, 1989), vol. 10, p. 209.

19. Natalie Zemon Devis and Arlette Farge, eds., *A History of Women in the West* (Cambridge, Mass., 1993), p. 471. I thank Nicola Shilliam and Lauren Whitley for their opinions about the costume.

20. Peter Wagner, *Eros Revived: Erotica of the Enlightenment in England and America* (London, 1988), p. 226.

21. Examples of plate supplied by the Kandlers for the dukes of Norfolk include a bowl and stand, ca. 1735–40, exh. London, Victoria and Albert Museum, *The British Antique Dealers' Association Golden Jubilee Exhibition*, 1968, cat. 34, pl. 16; a basket, 1734, illus. Brett 1986, p. 197, fig. 832; a holy water bucket, 1735, illus. Charles Oman, *English Church Plate, 597–1830* (London, 1957), pl. 184.

22. Illus. Rowe 1965, fig. 28.

140

· 140 ·

JUG

Marked by Charles Wright (free 1754, d. 1815)
London, 1778/9
Silver, wood
1991.251

MARKS: on underside, maker's mark *CW*
(Grimwade 428); lion passant (repeated inside
cover); leopard's head crowned; date letter *c*

ARMORIALS: engraved on front of jug, an unidentified crest (a broken dagger, the two parts in
chevron)

INSCRIPTIONS: scratched under foot, *29"5*

H. 34.3 cm (13½ in.); w. 20.1 cm (7¹⁵⁄₁₆ in.);
d. 12.5 cm (4¹⁵⁄₁₆ in.)

WEIGHT: 972.4 gm (31 oz 5 dwt)

PROVENANCE: Lent by Mrs. Henry Lyman, May 1,
1928, re-lent 1933, 1941, 1973, Gift of Charles P. and
Henry Lyman, and Richard Warren in Memory of
Cora Lyman Warren, March 27, 1991

DESCRIPTION: The urn-shaped jug rests on a
spreading, domed foot with a string of beading
around the edge and palmette leaves spreading
down from the base of the body. The foot is raised
in a single piece, with an applied wire on the interi-
or of the rim. The body of the vessel is raised in two
sections, its lower half chased with fluting and the
upper half chased with garlands of flowers and ribbons draped from roundels. The spool-shaped neck
is covered with vertical palmette leaves, and a string
of beading follows the rim of the jug. The raised
domed cover is chased with palmette leaves and has
an urn-shaped finial with a midband of beading.
The scroll-shaped wooden handle has foliate and
beaded mounts.

141

· 141 ·

SNUFFBOX
Possibly by James Perry (first mark entered 1763)
London, 1778/9
Silver, parcel gilt
39.182

MARKS: on inside of case, maker's mark *IP*
(Grimwade 1582) (repeated on underside of cover);
leopard's head crowned; lion passant (repeated on
underside of cover); date letter *c*

INSCRIPTIONS: engraved on cover, *HC* in monogram, for Hannah Cartwright

H. 2.1 cm (¹³⁄₁₆ in.); w. 8.8 cm (3⁷⁄₁₆ in.); d. 4 cm
(1⁹⁄₁₆ in.)

WEIGHT: 62.4 gm (2 oz)

PROVENANCE: Hannah Beasley Cartwright, of
Albany, to her daughter Elizabeth Robinson, by
descent to her grandson, Henry Codman, to his
granddaughter, Martha C. Codman (1858-1948),
The M. and M. Karolik Collection of Eighteenth-
Century American Arts, January 19, 1939

PUBLISHED: Hipkiss 1941, cat. 178

DESCRIPTION: The elliptical box, assembled from
sheet, has straight sides and a flat cover with a hidden hinge. The edges of the sides and cover are
ornamented with a pounced border, and the center
of the cover has an oval cartouche containing the
engraved monogram.

· 142 ·

TWO SECOND-COURSE DISHES
Marked by George Heming and William
Chawner (I) (entered into partnership 1774)
London, 1779/80
Silver
33.191–192

MARKS: on underside of each rim, maker's mark
GH with *W* above and *C* below (Grimwade 821);
lion passant; leopard's head crowned; date letter *d*

ARMORIALS: engraved on each rim, the arms of
Dixon of Rainshaw, co. Durham, impaling another

33.191: H. 2 cm (¾ in.); diam. 30.4 cm (11¹⁵⁄₁₆ in.)

33.192: H. 2.1 cm (¹³⁄₁₆ in.); diam. 30.6 cm (12¹⁄₁₆ in.)

WEIGHT: 33.191: 1,085.8 gm (34 oz 18 dwt). 33.192:
1,054.6 gm (33 oz 18 dwt)

PROVENANCE: Anonymous Gift in Memory of
Charlotte Beebe Wilbour (1833–1914), March 2,
1933

DESCRIPTION: Each shaped circular dish has a
broad rim with cast gadrooned borders.

The armorials on these dishes, which are
engraved over earlier armorials, were probably
added in the early nineteenth century.

· 143 ·

SNUFFBOX
Marked by John King (first mark entered 1775)
London, ca. 1780
Cowry shell, silver
80.507

MARKS: on inside of case, maker's mark *IK* (similar
to Grimwade 1446)

INSCRIPTIONS: engraved on cover, *CGS* in monogram

H. 4 cm (1⁹⁄₁₆ in.); w. 9.2 cm (3⅝ in.); d. 6.7 cm
(2¹¹⁄₁₆ in.)

PROVENANCE: given to Gilbert Stuart (1755–1828)
by the bishop of Ossory; Gift of Sydney Brooks,
April 15, 1880

PUBLISHED: Charles Merrill Mount, *Gilbert Stuart*
(New York, 1964), pp. 154, 346; Kenin 1979, p. 35

DESCRIPTION: The base of the box is formed of a
cut section of a cowry shell with a molded silver
rim. The flat silver cover, formed from sheet, has a
hidden hinge ornamented with wrigglework.

142

143

This box, engraved with the monogram of the portrait painter Gilbert Stuart, contains a note explaining its history: "This box was presented to the late Chas. Gilbert Stuart by the Lord Bishop of Ossory, whose portrait he had painted about 1790—Sometime before his death, Stuart gave this memento to Isaac P. Davis of Boston, whose widow, dying a few months since left it to Miss Jane Stuart of Newport R.I."

After beginning a modest career in America as a portraitist, Gilbert Stuart followed John Singleton Copley (1738–1815) and Benjamin West (1738–1820) to London in 1775 in search of recognition and patronage. He quickly established a reputation as gifted, outspoken, and profligate. In 1787 the magnitude of his debts forced him to flee to Ireland, prompting Sir Thomas Lawrence to remark, "the real cause of his leaving England was his having become tired of the inside of our prisons."[1] Jane Stuart, the painter's daughter, later contributed to a history of her father's life which explains the story of the snuffbox. Stuart painted a great many distinguished members of the Protestant ascendancy while in Ireland, but his health, his debts, and his temper continued to unsettle him. One of his sitters was the Honorable William Beresford, lord bishop of Ossory, who was aware of the artist's turmoil.[2] While the bishop was sitting, he "would give the conversation a religious turn, believing it to be a duty to improve every moment of his valueable time." Stuart, who was uninterested in religion and was struggling to fix this animated face, politely said, "Will your lordship please close your mouth?"[3] Chagrined, the bishop complied. He was pleased with the portrait, how-ever, and showed his esteem by presenting Stuart with this box. Stuart, whose father had built a snuff mill in Rhode Island, is said to have been a constant user of snuff, so it would have been an especially appropriate offering.[4] Mounted cowrie or tortoiseshell boxes were common presentation pieces.[5]

1. Kenin 1979, pp. 33–35.

2. Mount, *Gilbert Stuart*, p. 154.

3. George C. Mason, *The Life and Works of Gilbert Stuart* (New York, 1879), p. 234.

4. Kenin 1979, p. 35.

5. For a similar example at Williamsburg, see Davis 1976, p. 211, cat. 234. See also examples sold Sotheby's, London, May 20, 1982, lot 5, and Sotheby's, New York, October 28, 1992, lots 236–45.

144

· 144 ·

Seal matrix

Possibly marked by Hester Bateman (1708–1794)
London, ca. 1780
Silver
60.936

MARKS: on back, maker's mark, possibly *HB* (Grimwade 961)

H. 2.6 cm (1 1/16 in.); W. 2 cm (3/4 in.); D. 2.2 cm (7/8 in.)

WEIGHT: 25.5 gm (16 dwt)

ARMORIALS: on face of seal, the arms and crest of Southby, for Edward Southby (1712–1793) of Carswell, co. Berkshire

PROVENANCE: Claude Blair, co. Surrey, purchased September 21, 1960, Theodora Wilbour Fund in Memory of Charlotte Beebe Wilbour

DESCRIPTION: The seal is cut into an oval form and mounted with a cast openwork handle.

· 145 ·

Box, casket, tea canister, basket, and caddy spoon

Marked by James Perry (first mark entered 1763)
Silver
London, 1780/1
1976.607–609

MARKS: 1976.609 (tea canister), on underside, maker's mark *IP* (Grimwade 1582); lion passant; leopard's head crowned; date letter *e*

ARMORIALS: 1976.609, engraved on side, in a lozenge for a widow, an unidentified coat of arms (a saltire raguly sable between four nails, impaling argent a chevron sable between three buglehorns stringed, on chief of the second as many lions rampant) impaling Henchman or Hinchman

1976.607 (box): H. 19.5 cm (7 11/16 in.); W. 20.5 cm (8 1/16 in.); D. 16.1 cm (6 5/16 in.)

1976.608a (casket): H. 16.5 cm (6 1/2 in.); W. 18 cm (7 1/16 in.); D. 13.2 cm (5 3/16 in.)

1976.608b (basket): H. 2.7 cm (1 1/16 in.); W. 6.7 cm (2 5/8 in.); D. 4.6 cm (1 13/16 in.)

1976.608c (spoon): L. 9.1 cm (3 9/16 in.); W. 3.7 cm (1 7/16 in.)

1976.609 (tea canister): H. 7.9 cm (3 1/8 in.); W. 12.7 cm (5 in.); D. 8.3 cm (3 1/4 in.)

WEIGHT: 1976.608a (casket): 1,466 gm (47 oz 2 dwt). 1976.608b (basket): 25 gm (16 dwt). 1976.608c (spoon): 9 gm (6 dwt). 1976.609 (tea canister): 371 gm (11 oz 18 dwt)

PROVENANCE: purchased from Brand Inglis, Ltd., London, September 8, 1976, Theodora Wilbour Fund in Memory of Charlotte Beebe Wilbour

DESCRIPTION: The rectangular filigree chest is architectural in form. A shaped plinth rests on four ball feet. Four columns stand on the plinth framing the rectangular container. The cover is a rooflike structure, of shaped outline, with an interior compartment that may be accessed from a hidden sliding panel. A filigree caddy spoon and oval covered basket are concealed in the top compartment. The cover is hinged and opens to reveal the silver canister fitted inside. The chest is made of assembled filigree panels, each formed of tightly scrolled drawn and tooled wire. Broader strands of polished wire in the center of each panel form double scrolls, and the outer edges of each panel are framed in plain wire. The silver canister, formed from pieces of sheet, is rectangular with a hinged, shaped cover. The highly polished plain surface is engraved and

145

chased with a chain pattern along the borders, and the front and back panels have an engraved oval containing a gilt urn against a rayed ground. The side panels are filled with a gilt circle containing an engraved floral motif. The interior of the box is lead-lined.

As early as the 1740s, London retailers imported containers in exotic materials such as ivory, lacquer, or shell, which they fitted with silver tea canisters.[1] The origin of this silver filigree box remains uncertain. A group of closely related boxes is ascribed variously to Norway,[2] the Netherlands,[3] and Venice,[4] but perhaps the most likely source is the Portuguese colonies.[5] A closely related chest containing two canisters marked by Smith and Sharp suggests that importers may have been supplying several shops.[6]

1. See a chest mounted with panels of shell, exh. London, Victoria and Albert Museum, *Rococo: Art and Design in Hogarth's England*, 1984, p. 123, cat. G43, and an ivory chest illus. Partridge Fine Arts PLC, *Silver at Partridge* (London, 1998), p. 20, cat. 12.

2. Thale Riisøen, *Om filiigran: teknikk, historikk, filigran i norsk eie* (Oslo, 1959), p. 87, fig. 37.

3. Fries Museum, *Fries Zilver: Catalogus Fries Museum Leeuwarden* (Leeuwarden, 1968), fig. 215.

4. M. Postnekova-Loseva, *The Art of Filigree: Order of Lenin State History Museum* (Moscow, n.d.).

5. Lisbon, Museu Nacional de Arte Antiga, *Portugal na India, na China, e no Japao*, 1954, cat. 46.

6. Sold Christie's, London, June 15, 1983, lot 135.

146

147

· 146 ·

TEA CANISTER
Marked by WS, possibly William Stephenson (first mark entered 1775)
London, 1782/3
Silver
1976.659

MARKS: on underside, maker's mark *WS* (possibly Grimwade 3312); lion passant (repeated inside cover); leopard's head crowned; date letter *g*

ARMORIALS: engraved on front and back of canister, the arms of Nealewell, Waff, Wass, or Waugh impaling another unidentified coat of arms (on a chevron sable three bezants impaling, per bend embattled gules and argent on a chief or a castle between two lions passant guardant)

H. 10 cm (3¹⁵⁄₁₆ in.); w. 14 cm (5½ in.); d. 8.5 cm (3⅜ in.)

WEIGHT: 408 gm (13 oz 2 dwt)

PROVENANCE: Bequest of Barbara Boylston Bean, September 8, 1976

DESCRIPTION: The straight-sided tea canister is oval in section, with a hinged, flat cover with a lock. It is formed of sheet, seamed on one side, with an inset base. The upper and lower edges are decorated with a punched, cut, and engraved border, and on the plain body of the canister are engraved and cut swags and garlands. At the center of each side is a reserved ellipse containing a later engraved coat of arms. The finial, a flower, is broken from the leaves on the cover.

· 147 ·

TEA CANISTER
Marked by Hester Bateman (1708–1794)
London, 1785/6
Silver
33.189

MARKS: on underside, maker's mark *HB* (defaced) (Grimwade 960) (repeated on inside of cover); lion passant (repeated on inside of cover); leopard's head crowned; date letter *k*; sovereign's head

ARMORIALS: engraved on the front and back panel, an unidentified coat of arms and crest (quarterly 1 and 4, vert an endorse between two griffins segreant combatant; 2 and 3, per chevron gules and or two eagles displayed in chief; impaling, quarterly

1 and 4, azure three lozenges, 2 & 3, on a fess between two lions passant three crescents, and in pretence, a chevron gules between three swans; crest: a demi-griffen segreant)

H. 15.1 cm (5¹⁵⁄₁₆ in.); w. 10.5 cm (4⅛ in.); d. 10.5 cm (4⅛ in.)

WEIGHT: 413.9 gm (13 oz 6 dwt)

PROVENANCE: collection of viscount Henning; sold American Art Galleries, New York, March 10, 1922, lot 364; Anonymous Gift in Memory of Charlotte Beebe Wilbour (1833–1914), March 2, 1933

EXHIBITED: Boston, Museum of Fine Arts, 1933

PUBLISHED: Kurt M. Semon, *A Treasury of Old Silver* (New York, 1947), p. 19; Christopher Lever, *Goldsmiths and Silversmiths of England* (London, 1975), fig. 8

DESCRIPTION: The octagonal canister has straight sides and a hinged, peaked octagonal cover. The body is formed from seamed sheet with an inset base, and, around the interior of the rim, there is an applied wire that allows the cover to sit flush. The cover is formed from sheet and has a detachable urn-shaped finial. The upper and lower rims of the body are framed in borders of bright-cut geometric ornament, and the plain surface of the body is filled with engraved and chased swags, garlands, and ribbons.

Hester Bateman's sponsor's mark on the underside of this tea canister has been defaced, but not overstruck with another mark. The piece seems to be otherwise appropriately marked and unaltered. The Batemans did supply finished pieces to other silversmiths for retail sale,[1] and some may have had the Bateman mark overstruck. The defacement of the Bateman mark here is unexplained.

1. Wees 1997, p. 194, cat. 111.

· 148 ·

TEAPOT

Marked by Thomas Daniell (free 1771)
London, 1785/6
Silver, wood
1976.660

MARKS: on underside, maker's mark *TD* (Grimwade 2729) (repeated on cover); lion passant (repeated on cover); leopard's head crowned; date letter *k*; sovereign's head

ARMORIALS: engraved on one side, the arms and crest of Boylston; on the other, the initials *JAA* in cipher, both in bright-cut cartouches with bellflowers

INSCRIPTIONS: engraved around the Boylston armorial, *This was owned by Ex President John Adams and Presented to Ward Nichs. Boylston, by his Friend and Kinsman his Excellency John Quincy Adams, President of the United States. As a Memorial of his Father*; engraved on the underside of body, *T Daniell. No 20 Foster Lane London Maker*; on underside of body, scratched, *15=2*

H. 14.4 cm (5¹¹⁄₁₆ in.); w. 27.5 cm (10¹³⁄₁₆ in.); d. 9.9 cm (3⅞ in.)

WEIGHT: 490.5 gm (15 oz 15 dwt)

PROVENANCE: according to tradition, President John Adams (1735–1826), given by his son, John Quincy Adams (1767–1848) to Ward Nicholas Boylston (1749–1828), by descent to Barbara Boylston Bean, Bequest of Barbara Boylston Bean, September 8, 1976

DESCRIPTION: The body of the teapot is oval in section and has straight sides. It is formed of seamed sheet, with a band of fine beading marking the join of the inset base. The straight spout, applied to the exterior of the teapot, is seamed. The sides of the teapot are decorated with bright-cut swags and borders. At the center of each side is an elliptical cartouche. The ear-shaped wooden handle is mounted on cylindrical sockets. The stepped, domed cover has two rows of beading and bright-cut patterns, one at the rim along the body and one around the opening of the hinged section. The wooden baluster finial is oval-shaped and has a silver cap.

Though the engraved inscription on this teapot is clearly modern, it records the Boylston family tradition that the teapot was once owned by John Adams, second president of the United States. Trained as a lawyer, Adams first served as a delegate to the Continental Congress. In

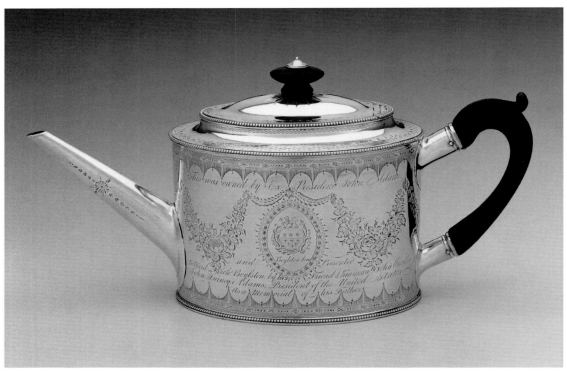

148

1776 he had the task of shepherding the passage of the Declaration of Independence through Congress, for which he was praised by Thomas Jefferson as "its ablest advocate and defender."[1] He was dispatched to France in 1778 to seek financial support for the cause of independence, from where he supplied Congress with bulletins on the state of European affairs. In 1785, the year this teapot was made, he was appointed envoy to the Court of St. James's and he remained in London until 1788. Returning to Boston, he was elected vice president under George Washington, a position he described as "the most insignificant office that ever the invention of man contrived."[2] In the election of 1796 he attained the presidency, in spite of the efforts of Alexander Hamilton, with Thomas Jefferson serving as his vice president.

According to the inscription, Adams's son, John Quincy Adams, presented the teapot to Ward Nicholas Boylston "as a memorial of his father," presumably referring to the late president. John Quincy Adams followed his father into public life after training to be a lawyer. As a young man he traveled abroad, both as a stu-

dent and as an assistant to his father. He served as secretary of state under President Munroe and was elected president in 1825, when he met continuous opposition from supporters of Andrew Jackson. Like his father, he tried to curb the influence of the old-school federalists, and he attracted bitter criticism. A skilled orator, he was dubbed "the old man eloquent."[3]

The recipient of this teapot was Ward Nicholas Boylston, a nephew of Nicholas Boylston (1716–1771), a wealthy importer in Boston. Ward Nicholas was a first cousin of the senior John Adams and the son of Benjamin Hallowell and Mary Boylston. He changed his name and was adopted by Nicholas Boylston, his mother's prosperous, unmarried brother.[4] Nicholas Boylston was a tremendously successful importer in Boston with loyalist tendencies who lived in grand style. Copley painted portraits of all the members of the family, and their house on School Street was richly furnished. John Adams was among Boylston's many guests, and he wrote in his diary in 1766: "Dined at Mr. Nick Boylstones. . . . An elegant dinner indeed! Went over the House to view the furniture, which alone cost a thousand

Pounds sterling. A seat it is for a noble Man, a Prince. The Turkey Carpets, the painted Hangings, the Marble Tables, the rich Beds with crimson Damask Curtains and Counterpins, the beautiful Chimney Clock, the Spacious Garden, are the most magnificent of anything I have ever seen."[5] The inscription suggests that the gift of the teapot commemorated that personal connection between the ex-president and his cousin.

With the rolling mill in wide use, a straight-sided teapot such as this could be made efficiently. This example has an unusual engraving on the base recording the silversmith's name and address, a feature that Grimwade noted on other pieces by Thomas Daniell.[6]

1. Quoted in Allen Johnson and Dumas Malone, eds., *Dictionary of American Biography* (New York, 1928), vol. 1, p. 74.

2. Ibid., p. 77.

3. Ibid., pp. 84–93.

4. I am grateful to Carol Troyen for her assistance with the Boylston family genealogy.

5. Quoted in Paul Staiti, "Character and Class," in *John Singleton Copley in America* (New York, 1995), p. 54.

6. Grimwade 1990, p. 484.

· 149 ·

URN

Marked by John Scofield (first mark entered 1776)
London, 1786/7
Silver, ivory
88.291

MARKS: on four corners under base, maker's mark *IS* (Grimwade 1670) (repeated on bezel of cover); lion passant (repeated on bezel of cover); sovereign's head (repeated on bezel of cover); leopard's head crowned; date letter *l*

ARMORIALS: engraved on one side, the arms of Whipple; on the other, *OAW* in monogram for Oliver (1744–1813) and Abigail Whipple (d. 1827)

H. 52 cm (20½ in.); w. 30.1 cm (11⅞ in.); d. 26.5 cm (10⁷⁄₁₆ in.)

WEIGHT: 2,835 gm (91 oz 3 dwt)

PROVENANCE: Oliver Whipple and his wife, Abigail, of Boston, by descent to their daughter Hannah, who married Frederic Allen of Portsmouth, New Hampshire, to their daughter, Margaret Allen Elton, Bequest of Mrs. M. A. Elton, February 14, 1888

DESCRIPTION: The plain vase-shaped urn has a spool-shaped stem and rests on a square base with four curved feet. The body of the vessel is raised from sheet and has a second incurved section applied to form the neck. Around the border of this join and at the rim is a milled beaded wire and beneath, a border of bright-cut ornament. The interior has a fitting at the base for a heater, now missing. The removable cover is spool-shaped, formed in two raised pieces, with a beaded flange at the join. It is surmounted by an urn-shaped finial. The edges are decorated with a narrow band of bright-cut ornament. At the base of the body is a fluted spout, cast in sections, with a rectangular tap and a bifurcated ivory spigot. The plain box-shaped base is assembled from panels of sheet with applied cast feet with scrolled borders.

This urn, along with the sugar basket marked by William Plummer (cat. 152) and the hot-water jug marked by John Scofield (cat. 151), bears the monogram and arms of Oliver and Abigail Whipple.[1] All marked in the same year, the pieces must have been assembled in London for retail sale as a service, for they are all decorated with the same bright-cut ornament. For most of the eighteenth century,

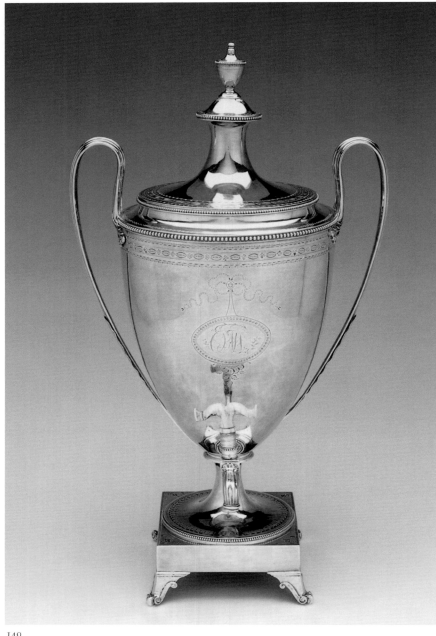

149

American clients buying English silver seem to have assembled their services piecemeal.[2] By the 1780s Paul Revere II, who made rolled plate a speciality, was producing tea wares comparable in design but lighter in weight than the present example. It is not known for what occasion the Whipples acquired the service. The market for English silver in America has not been studied in depth, but the traditional assumption has been that pieces such as this served as models for the native makers, such as Paul Revere.[3]

Colonel Oliver Whipple was born in Rhode Island and educated at Harvard. He practiced as a lawyer in Portsmouth, New Hampshire, and in 1774 he married Abigail, daughter of Dr. Silvester Gardiner of Boston. He served as a justice of the peace and assumed the title of colonel when he took over command of one of the Portsmouth alarm companies. He had a modest career, and when his wife's money was nearly gone, they divorced. Her affairs were then managed by a son, Silvester, who had been sent home from Harvard for his own good "as well as the comfort of this Society." Silvester's business acumen proved no better than his father's, however, and Oliver and Abigail remarried, although they lived apart after 1805. Whipple died in Washington, where he had established himself as a clerk.[4]

1. An American tankard of about 1735 also bears the Whipple arms. See Patricia E. Kane, *Colonial Massachusetts Silversmiths and Jewelers* (New Haven, 1998), p. 607.

2. A notable exception is the Franks service marked by Lamerie, probably sent to David Franks of Philadelphia as a wedding gift by his brother in London. London, Goldsmiths' Hall, 1990, pp. 162–63, cats. 9–10.

3. Boston, Museum of Fine Arts, 1975, p. 193.

4. Clifford K. Shipton, *Sibley's Harvard Graduates* (Boston, 1972), vol. 16, pp. 430–34.

150

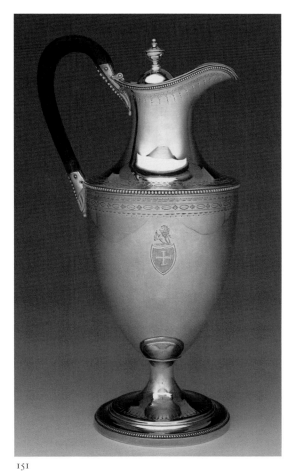

151

· 150 ·

CREAM JUG

Marked by Hester Bateman (1708–1794)
London, 1786/7
Silver
47.1355

MARKS: to right of handle, maker's mark *HB*
(Grimwade 961); lion passant; leopard's head
crowned; date letter *l*; sovereign's head

INSCRIPTIONS: engraved on front, *MB* in monogram; scratched on underside of foot, *216*

H. 16 cm (6⁵⁄₁₆ in.); w. 12.1 cm (4¾ in.); d. 5.5 cm
(2⅛ in.)

WEIGHT: 116.2 gm (3 oz 15 dwt)

PROVENANCE: Lent by Mrs. Adelaide J. Sargent,
April 24, 1915, transferred to Mrs. Mary Adelaide
Sargent Poor, December 10, 1931, Gift of Mary
Adelaide Sargent Poor in Memory of Adelaide
Joanna Sargent, September 18, 1947

DESCRIPTION: The helmet-shaped body, formed
from raised sheet, has a high, narrow pouring lip. It
rests on a circular spreading foot with a beaded rim
on a square base. A string of beading lines the rim
and spout. The high loop handle is reeded. The
body is engraved and chased along the borders with
bands of geometric ornament and on the plain surface of the body with swags of flowers and ribbons.

· 151 ·

HOT WATER JUG

Marked by John Scofield (first mark entered
1776)
London, 1786/7
Silver, wood
58.1193

MARKS: on side of foot, sovereign's head; date letter
l; leopard's head crowned; lion passant (repeated on
inside of cover); maker's mark *IS* (repeated on inside
of cover)

ARMORIALS: engraved on the side, the arms and
crest of Allen

INSCRIPTIONS: engraved on the front, *OAW*, in
monogram for Oliver (1744–1813) and Abigail
Whipple (d. 1827) of Boston

H. 30.6 cm (12¹⁄₁₆ in.); diam. of foot 10.4 cm (4⅛ in.)

WEIGHT: 768.3 gm (24 oz 14 dwt)

PROVENANCE: according to tradition, Oliver Whipple and his wife, Abigail, of Boston; Gebelein Silversmiths, Boston, purchased December 11, 1958, Theodora Wilbour Fund in Memory of Charlotte Beebe Wilbour

DESCRIPTION: The vase-shaped body, raised in two sections, rests on a spreading circular foot, with a string of beading applied to the edge, around the shoulder, and along the rim. Bands of bright-cut and wrigglework patterns outline the foot, shoulder, and rim. The hinged, shaped, and domed lid is raised and has an urn-shaped finial. The wooden handle is mounted on cast sockets decorated with applied beading and leaf-form drops.

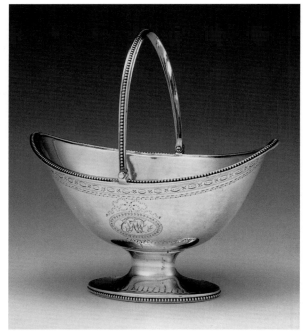

152

· 152 ·

SUGAR BASKET

Marked by William Plummer (first mark entered 1755)
London, 1786/7
Silver
58.1194

MARKS: on underside, maker's mark *WP* (Grimwade 3255) (struck twice); lion passant; leopard's head crowned; date letter *l*; sovereign's head

ARMORIALS: engraved on one side, the arms of Whipple; on the other, *OAW* in monogram for Oliver (1744–1813) and Abigail Whipple (d. 1827)

H. 17.9 cm (7¹⁄₁₆ in.); w. 16.8 cm (6⅝ in.); d. 11.7 cm (4⅝ in.)

WEIGHT: 243.8 gm (7 oz 17 dwt)

PROVENANCE: according to tradition, Oliver Whipple and his wife, Abigail, of Boston; Gebelein Silversmiths, Boston, purchased December 11, 1958, Theodora Wilbour Fund in Memory of Charlotte Beebe Wilbour

DESCRIPTION: The oval basket is boat-shaped with a dipped rim and rests on an oval spreading foot. The body and the foot are formed of sheet, and each has an applied beaded wire rim. The plain surface is ornamented with borders of bright-cut decoration. A high beaded bail handle is mounted on hinges on the long sides of the basket.

· 153 ·

STAND FOR A TEAPOT

Marked by Hester Bateman (1708–1794)
London, 1789/90
Silver
Res.33.122

MARKS: on underside, maker's mark *HB* (Grimwade 961); sovereign's head; date letter *o*; leopard's head crowned; lion passant

ARMORIALS: engraved in center, an unidentified crest (a demilion rampant, ducally crowned)

H. 2.2 cm (⅞ in.); w. 18.4 cm (7¼ in.); d. 14.7 cm (5¾ in.)

WEIGHT: 147.4 gm (4 oz 15 dwt)

PROVENANCE: Anonymous Gift in Memory of Charlotte Beebe Wilbour (1833–1914), March 2, 1933

EXHIBITED: Springfield, Massachusetts, Museum of Fine Arts, 1958

DESCRIPTION: The elliptical stand is formed from sheet with an applied molded border. It has a shaped outline and rests on short reeded feet. Around the perimeter of the molded border is a band of pounced and bright-cut ornament. An oval in the center encloses the engraved coat of arms.

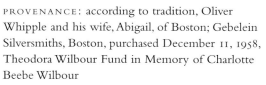

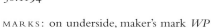

153

FOUR BOTTLE TICKETS

Marked by John Robins (first mark entered 1774, d. 1831)

London, ca. 1790

Silver

40.195–198

MARKS: on back of each, maker's mark *IR* (Grimwade 3678); sovereign's head (lacking on 40.196); lion passant

INSCRIPTIONS: engraved on front of each; 40.195, *ELDER*; 40.196, *SOY*; 40.197, *TARRAGON*; 40.198, *WALNUT*

40.195: H. 1.6 cm (⅝ in.); l. 2.7 cm (1¹⁄₁₆ in.)

40.196: H. 1.7 cm (¹¹⁄₁₆ in.); l. 2.7 cm (1¹⁄₁₆ in.)

40.197: H. 1.7 cm (¹¹⁄₁₆ in.); l. 2.7 cm (1¹⁄₁₆ in.)

40.198: H. 1.7 cm (¹¹⁄₁₆ in.); l. 2.8 cm (1⅛ in.)

WEIGHT: 40.195: 5.7 gm (4 dwt). 40.196: 5.8 gm (2 dwt). 40.197: 5.7 gm (4 dwt). 40.198: 2.8 gm (2 dwt)

PROVENANCE: Anonymous Gift in Memory of Charlotte Beebe Wilbour (1833–1914), April 11, 1940

EXHIBITED: Toronto, George R. Gardiner Museum of Ceramic Art, 1998

DESCRIPTION: Each ticket is a slightly curved oval piece of sheet, pierced with two holes so that it can hang from the plain chain. A bright-cut border defines the edge.

154

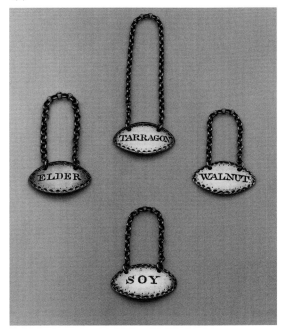

155

PUBLISHED: Kurt M. Semon, *A Treasury of Old Silver* (New York, 1947), p. 19

DESCRIPTION: The basket is boat-shaped, with fluted sides, and rests on a lozenge-shaped foot with a notched rim. Formed from sheet, it has a molded wire applied to the outer rim. The bail handle is reeded and fluted. The interior is gilt.

· 156 ·

PAIR OF BOTTLE TICKETS
Marked by Thomas Phipps and Edward Robinson (entered into partnership 1783)
London, ca. 1790
Silver
56.1320–1321

MARKS: on back of each, maker's mark *TP* over *ER* (Grimwade 2891); sovereign's head; lion passant

INSCRIPTIONS: on each, engraved in the front shield, *I/JEB* in monogram. 56.1320, *PORT*. 56.1321, *MADEIRA*

56.1320: ; H. 3.5 cm (1⅜ in.); l. 5.4 cm (2⅛ in.)

56.1321: ; H. 3.3 cm (1⁵⁄₁₆ in.); l. 5.4 cm (2⅛ in.)

WEIGHT: 56.1320: 11.3 gm (7 dwt). 56.1321: 11.3 gm (7 dwt)

PROVENANCE: Gift of Misses Rose and Elizabeth Townsend, October 11, 1956

DESCRIPTION: The slightly curved labels are crescent-shaped, with a shield at the center. The label hangs from a link chain. The edges are incised.

· 155 ·

SUGAR BASKET
Marked by Hester Bateman (1708–1794)
London, 1790/1
Silver gilt
33.195

MARKS: on underside, maker's mark *HB* (Grimwade 961); lion passant (repeated on handle); leopard's head crowned; date letter *p*; sovereign's head

ARMORIALS: engraved on one side, the arms of Eaglesfield, quartering another and impaling Tindall or Tindale; engraved on the other side, an unidentified crest (an eagle displayed) (probably that of Eaglesfield)

H. 19 cm (7½ in.); w. 18.5 cm (7⁵⁄₁₆ in.); d. 12.4 cm (4⅞ in.)

WEIGHT: 249.5 gm (8 oz)

PROVENANCE: Anonymous Gift in Memory of Charlotte Beebe Wilbour (1833–1914), March 2, 1933

EXHIBITED: Boston, Museum of Fine Arts, 1933

156

157

TEA CANISTER

Marked by Henry Chawner (1764–1851)

London, 1790/1

Silver

33.194

MARKS: on underside, maker's mark *HC* (Grimwade 972); lion passant (repeated on inside of cover); sovereign's head; leopard's head crowned; date letter *p*

ARMORIALS: engraved on side, an unidentified coat of arms, crest, and motto (sable on a bend between two cotises, three lions passant; crest: an eagle displayed; motto: *Spectemur Agendo*)

INSCRIPTIONS: scratched on underside, *12-3*

H. 14.6 cm (5¾ in.); w. 13.2 cm (5⁵⁄₁₆ in.); d. 9.9 cm (3⅞ in.)

WEIGHT: 357.2 gm (11 oz 10 dwt)

PROVENANCE: Anonymous Gift in Memory of Charlotte Beebe Wilbour (1833–1914), March 2, 1933

EXHIBITED: Boston, Museum of Fine Arts, 1933

DESCRIPTION: The oval fluted canister has straight sides and a hinged, domed cover. It is formed from seamed sheet, with an inset base. The upper and lower borders are chased and engraved with a pattern of medallions and stylized foliage, and the center and back panels of the body are filled with a cartouche.

Oval fluted tea canisters were a speciality of Henry Chawner,[1] who in 1786 took over the business of Charles Wright.[2] The arms engraved on this example are apparently a later addition, replacing an earlier engraving, traces of which may be seen on the back panel.

1. For other examples see Christie's, London, November 28, 1990, lot 92; Christie's, London, May 24, 1989, lot 186; Sotheby's, London, July 4, 1989, lot 200; Sotheby's, London, November 29, 1984, lot 191.

2. In addition to the biographical information recorded in Grimwade 1990, pp. 463, 741, see Culme 1987, p. 29.

158

· 158 ·

STAND FOR A TEAPOT

Marked by Thomas Watson (only mark entered 1784)

London, 1790/1

Silver

69.399

MARKS: on underside, maker's mark *TW* (possibly Grimwade 2967) overstriking another; lion passant; leopard's head crowned; date letter *p*; sovereign's head

INSCRIPTIONS: engraved in center, replacing earlier engraving, *ALR*

H. 2.3 cm (⅞ in.); w. 23 cm (9⁄16 in.); d. 15.4 cm (6¹⁄16 in.)

WEIGHT: 345.9 gm (11 oz 2 dwt)

PROVENANCE: Lent by Mrs. Horatio A. Lamb, July 11, 1916, re-lent 1922, 1924, 1926, 1935, transferred to Misses Aimee and Rosamond Lamb, December 3, 1952, Gift of the Misses Aimee and Rosamond Lamb, May 14, 1969

DESCRIPTION: The elliptical stand is formed from a single piece of sheet with an applied wire border. It rests on four reeded feet. The slightly flaring rim has a reeded edge and panels of piercing. A band of bright-cut and engraved lozenges follows the edge of the tray.

· 159 ·

HOT WATER URN

Marked by Hester Bateman (1708–1794)

London, 1790/1

Silver, jade

41.224

MARKS: on underside, sovereign's head (repeated inside cover); date letter *p*; leopard's head crowned; lion passant (repeated three times on heater and inside cover); maker's mark *HB* (Grimwade 961) (repeated three times on heater and inside cover)

INSCRIPTIONS: engraved on front, in monogram, *ALR*; engraved on back, in monogram, *HAL*

H. 62.1 cm (24⁷⁄16 in.); w. 34.1 cm (13⁷⁄16 in.); d. 30.8 cm (12⅛ in.)

WEIGHT: 3,472.9 gm (111 oz 13 dwt)

PROVENANCE: Gift of Mrs. Horatio A. Lamb, April 10, 1941

PUBLISHED: Rowe 1965, fig. 81; Truman 1993, p. 105

DESCRIPTION: The paneled vase-shaped body rests on a spreading, shaped square plinth, which is supported by four scrolled feet. The body and the foot are formed from raised sheet, with applied moldings and wires. The cast squared handles are harp-shaped with applied acanthus and palmette leaves and chased rosettes. The tapering spout, which is square in section, is joined to a shaped ellipse on the lower front of the body and has a jade spigot. The paneled trumpet-shaped cover is surmounted by an urn-shaped finial. Each panel—on the plinth, body, and cover—is ornamented with bright-cut bands and floral sprays. The interior of the urn is fitted with a removable cylinder to contain a heater that has a plain cap with handle and a shield in the form of a disk. These pieces are fabricated from sheet.

By 1790, when this urn was marked, the Bateman workshops were expanding to accommodate a massive steam-operated flatting mill, which would not only serve the needs of the Bateman shop but also supply sheet silver to other London manufacturers.[1] Hester Bateman, then eighty years old, was presumably retired, and under the direction of her sons, Peter and Jonathan Bateman, the shop continued to produce small items such as tongs, bottle tickets, sugar baskets, and tea canisters in large quantity. Larger pieces, such as this elegantly proportioned urn, are exceptional.

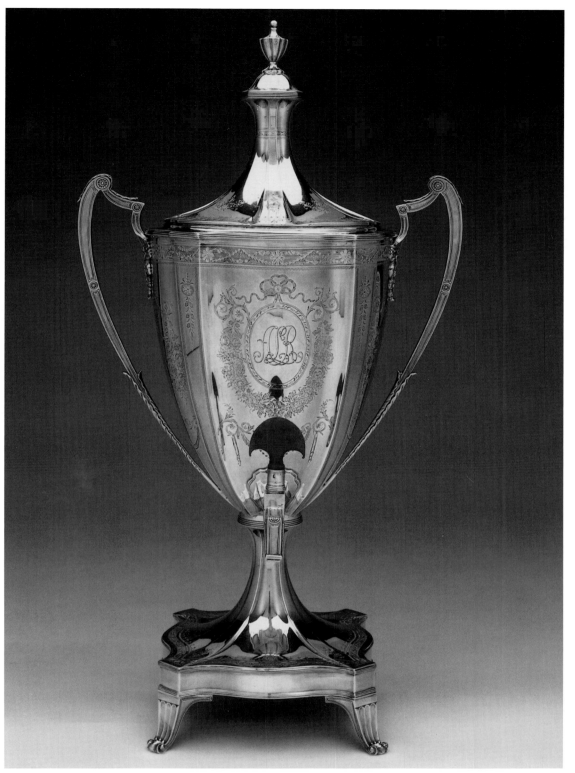

159

1. John Culme, "Beauty and the Beast: The Growth
of Mechanization in the Trade," *Proceedings of the Society
of Silver Collectors* 11, nos. 9–10 (1980), pp. 159–60.

160

· 160 ·

BASKET

Marked by Henry Chawner (1764–1851)

London, 1790/1

Silver

1983.398

MARKS: on underside of rim, maker's mark *HC* (Grimwade 972); lion passant; leopard's head crowned; date letter *p*; sovereign's head

ARMORIALS: engraved on the interior, an unidentified crest (a horse's head)

INSCRIPTIONS: engraved just below the crest, *RB* in script

H. 28.5 cm (11¼ in.); w. 41.5 cm (16⁵⁄₁₆ in.); d. 28.1 cm (11¹⁄₁₆ in.)

WEIGHT: 867.5 gm (27 oz 18 dwt)

PROVENANCE: Lent by Mr. and Mrs. Roger F. Hooper, March 18, 1925, Gift of Robert C. Hooper, Roger F. Hooper, Bayard Hooper and Justine V. R. Milliken, in Memory of their mother, October 12, 1983

DESCRIPTION: The boat-shaped elliptical basket is raised from sheet. It rests on an elliptical spreading foot, formed of seamed sheet with an applied reeded rim. The rim of the basket is thickened with a reeded wire below which is a wide band of floral bright-cut ornament and a band of geometric piercing. The reeded bail handle is attached to the basket with circular hinges.

· 161 ·

SCENT BOTTLE CASE

Marked by Samuel Penbeton (active ca. 1773–1801)
Birmingham, 1791/2
Silver
14.906

MARKS: on base, anchor; maker's mark *SP* (Jones, p. 364); date letter *T*. On cover, lion passant; maker's mark *SP;* sovereign's head

H. 4.5 cm (1¾ in.); w. 2.8 cm (1⅛ in.); d. 1.3 cm (½ in.)

WEIGHT: 11.3 gm (7 dwt)

PROVENANCE: Gift of the Misses Catherine Langdon Rogers and Clara Bates Rogers, November 5, 1914

DESCRIPTION: The case is oval in section, with a narrow base and straight sides flaring to a hinged, slightly domed cover. It is formed from seamed sheet, with an inset base and cover, and applied wire reinforcing the rim. The borders have bands of pouncing, and the cover and body have bright-cut shields and foliage.

161

· 162 ·

MUSTARD POT

Marked by Peter and Ann Bateman (entered into partnership 1791)
London, 1791/2
Silver
62.255

MARKS: on underside, leopard's head crowned; sovereign's head; lion passant (repeated inside cover); date letter *q*; maker's mark *PB* over *AB* (Grimwade 2140) (repeated inside cover)

H. 8.1 cm (3³⁄₁₆ in.); w. 10.5 cm (4⅛ in.); d. 5.4 cm (2⅛ in.)

WEIGHT: 102 gm (3 oz 6 dwt)

PROVENANCE: Gift of Miss Aimee Lamb, March 14, 1962

DESCRIPTION: The straight-sided oval body, formed from seamed sheet, has a reeded base and rim. The sides are pierced and engraved with a pattern of medallions and waves. The scrolled handle has an openwork scallop thumbpiece, and the oval domed lid has a square opening on the front edge to accommodate a spoon. The glass liner is lacking.

162

· 163 ·

TUREEN AND STAND

Marked by John Scofield (first mark entered
1776)

London, 1791/2

Silver

1975.665a–c

MARKS: on underside of stand, foot of tureen, and
bezel of cover, sovereign's head; date letter *q*; leopard's head crowned; lion passant; maker's mark *IS*
(Grimwade 1670)

ARMORIALS: engraved on stand, the coat of arms
and crest of the see of Westminster impaling
Vincent, surrounded by the motto and insignia of
the Order of the Bath, for Dr. William Vincent, C.B.
(1739–1815)

INSCRIPTIONS: engraved on stand, *Reverendo
Doctissmoque Viro GULIELMO VINCENT S.T.P.
Regiae Scholae Wesmonasteriensis paulo ante
Archididascalo hoc donum (animos ut testentur gratos)
Summa veneratione conferunt ALUMNI OPPIDANI.
A.D. 1802*; engraved on underside of base, *Rundell &
Bridge Fect.*

H. 32.7 cm (12⅞ in.); w. 58.7 cm (23⅛ in.);
d. 34.7 cm (13¹¹⁄₁₆ in.)

WEIGHT: 6,945 gm (223 oz 6 dwt)

PROVENANCE: sold Christie's, London, June 26,
1963, lot 166; Simon Kaye Ltd., London, November
1965; Thomas Lumley, Ltd., London, purchased
November 12, 1975, Theodora Wilbour Fund in
Memory of Charlotte Beebe Wilbour

EXHIBITED: New York, Cooper-Hewitt Museum,
*City Dwellings and Country Houses: Robert Adam and
His Style*, 1982; Boston, Museum of Fine Arts, 1994

PUBLISHED: Simon Kaye, Ltd., London advertisement, *Connoisseur* (November 1964), p. 36; Rowe
1965, pl. 93; Clayton 1971, p. 268, Clayton 1985a,
p. 364, fig. 540

DESCRIPTION: The oval body of the tureen rests
on a raised stepped foot with a rim of chased acanthus leaves and above, fluting. The body of the vessel
is raised from very heavy-gauge sheet, with chased
fluting decorating the lower third. Above, in the
midsection, is a band of foliate swags with pendants
that are cast and applied. The upper rim is edged
with rosettes, and beneath that, a border of acanthus
leaves cast in sets of two and applied. A large tear in
the rim near one of the handles has been repaired.
The handles are finely modeled and cast with reeded bases and a knop, and terminate in two snakes
joining the rim of the tureen. The raised cover has a
chased acanthus border beneath the dome, and its

fluted central panel has a finial in the form of a fruit
in a cluster of acanthus leaves. The boat-shaped
stand has a band of laurel along its rim and a raised
central section covered with palm leaves. The central
section creates a level platform with a molded rim,
on which rests the foot of the tureen. The stand is
formed of raised sheet. The scrolled handles with
acanthus leaf ornament are cast and applied, and the
lip at the center is also applied.

The inscription on the stand of this tureen
indicates that it was presented in 1802 to the
classical scholar William Vincent who had been
appointed that year dean of Westminster. The
tureen was the gift of the opiddan scholars of
Westminster School, where Vincent had served
as headmaster for fourteen years. A proportion
of the students at the school were scholars
sponsored by the abbey, and the remainder of
the student body was made up of pensioners,
peregrines, or oppidans (town boys), who paid
a fee and were either boarders or day students.[1]
Vincent had been educated at Westminster
himself as a town boy and afterward attended
Trinity College, Cambridge. He became a distinguished scholar of ancient geography with
an international reputation. In 1788 he was
appointed headmaster of Westminster, where
his tenure was marked by spirited debates and
disciplinary squabbles. His "plaguily severe" wig
was mocked by one student who threw paper
darts smeared with cheese into it to provoke
the headmaster to say in his nasal voice, "I
smell cheese." A more public scandal in 1771
involved the expulsion of Robert Southey, later
poet laureate, who had contributed to an
anonymous magazine attacking the headmaster's disciplinary measures.[2] As dean of
Westminster, Vincent presided over extensive
restorations, some of which were necessitated
by a fire in 1803. Presentations to the headmaster were not routine, so this gift is an indication of Vincent's preeminence in the history of
the school and the abbey. The arms, Vincent's
quartered with the see of Westminster, suggest
that the tureen was given to mark Vincent's
elevation to the deanery.

The tureen was retailed by Rundell and
Bridge, who had been in partnership for fourteen years but had not yet secured the royal
warrant. The maker, John Scofield, was among
the leading producers of neoclassical wares, and

163 (Color Plate XVIII)

this tureen exemplifies his most ambitious work.[3] The crisply cast and chased borders are meticulously applied, and great attention has been paid to the contrast between the highly polished surfaces and the textured areas.

Although by the 1790s this elongated urn shape was a well-established model, the delicate balance between the sculptural and the graphic role of the applied ornament is innovative. Boulton and Fothergill had produced tureens of this fundamental outline in the mid-1770s, possibly after designs by James Wyatt.[4] Indeed Wyatt's influence may be felt in another tureen marked by Scofield that is closely related to the Westminster tureen. The bodies and handles of the two tureens are identical, but the second

tureen rests on a high four-legged baluster base flanked by the figures of two grimacing satyrs.[5]

1. John Field, *The King's Nurseries* (London, 1987), p. 22. Tony Trowles, assistant librarian at Westminster School, kindly provided information and references on the history of the school.

2. Ibid., pp. 55–56.

3. For related works marked by Scofield, see a tureen of 1798, sold Sotheby's, London, October 31, 1974, lot 141; a cup and cover of 1787 in the Toledo Museum of Art; and a ewer of 1783 in Schroder 1988a, cat. 84.

4. See the sauce tureens by Boulton and Fothergill of 1773 and 1776 illus. Rowe 1965, pl. 56A–B. Fergusson 1974, p. 752, suggests that the Boulton and Fothergill forms derive from a Wyatt design.

5. The tureen was with S. J. Shrubsole, Corp., New York, in 1996. The complex figural base and proportions of the body are similar in conception to a sketch by Wyatt for a tureen on a tripod stand. See Fergusson 1974, fig. 56.

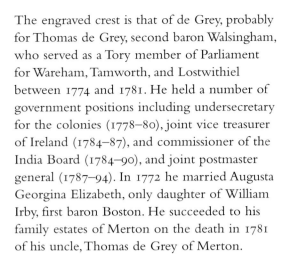

The engraved crest is that of de Grey, probably for Thomas de Grey, second baron Walsingham, who served as a Tory member of Parliament for Wareham, Tamworth, and Lostwithiel between 1774 and 1781. He held a number of government positions including undersecretary for the colonies (1778–80), joint vice treasurer of Ireland (1784–87), and commissioner of the India Board (1784–90), and joint postmaster general (1787–94). In 1772 he married Augusta Georgina Elizabeth, only daughter of William Irby, first baron Boston. He succeeded to his family estates of Merton on the death in 1781 of his uncle, Thomas de Grey of Merton.

1. The mark may also be interpreted as Grimwade 1149, for John Broughton.

164

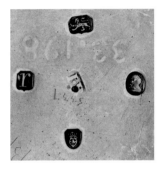

· 164 ·

COVERED SAUCEPAN

Possibly John Beldon (only mark entered 1784)
London, 1792/3
Silver, wood
33.198

MARKS: on underside, maker's mark *IB* (similar to Grimwade 1150)[1] (repeated on bezel of cover); lion passant (repeated on bezel of cover); sovereign's head (repeated on bezel of cover); leopard's head crowned; date letter *r* (repeated on bezel of cover)

ARMORIALS: engraved on front of bowl and on cover, crest of de Grey surmounted by a baron's coronet, probably for Thomas de Grey, second baron Walsingham (1748–1818)

INSCRIPTIONS: scratched on underside, *319, 13, 15/3/6, J[?]337*

H. 15.9 cm (6¼ in.); w. 20.4 cm (8 in.); d. 12 cm (4¾ in.)

WEIGHT: 459.3 gm (14 oz 15 dwt)

PROVENANCE: Anonymous Gift in Memory of Charlotte Beebe Wilbour (1833–1914), March 2, 1933

EXHIBITED: Boston, Museum of Fine Arts, 1933

DESCRIPTION: The baluster body has a slightly flaring, thickened rim and a large shaped pouring spout with a double drop. The body is raised from sheet, and the tapering cylindrical mount for the wooden handle, at a right angle to the spout, is formed from seamed sheet. The stepped, domed cover is formed from heavy sheet with an applied bezel and a wooden finial secured with a threaded nut and bolt.

· 165 ·

TEAPOT

Marked by Peter Bateman and Ann Bateman (entered into partnership 1791)
London, 1792/3
Silver, wood, ivory
55.683

MARKS: on underside, maker's mark *PB* over *AB* (Grimwade 2140) (repeated on underside of cover); date letter *r*; lion passant (repeated on underside of cover); sovereign's head; leopard's head crowned

H. 17.3 cm (6¹³⁄₁₆ in.); w. 27.3 cm (10¾ in.); d. 9.3 cm (3¹¹⁄₁₆ in.)

WEIGHT: 442.3 gm (14 oz 4 dwt)

PROVENANCE: Gift of Mrs. Edwin J. Hipkiss in Memory of her Husband, October 20, 1955

DESCRIPTION: The teapot has an elliptical body with straight sides formed from seamed sheet. A reeded wire strengthens the join of the inset base. The straight, tapered spout is formed of seamed sheet. The ear-shaped handle is wood, mounted on cylindrical sockets. The shoulder of the teapot has an applied reeded wire, as does the rim. The body is decorated with bands of bright-cut patterns along the base, shoulder, and rim, and bright-cut swags of flowers that frame an empty cartouche on both sides. The elliptical domed lid has a band of bright-cut design along its edge, and the elliptical baluster finial, broken and repaired, is made of ivory.

165

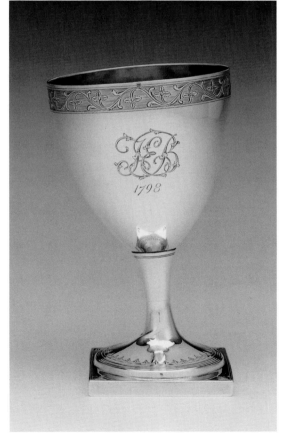

166

· 166 ·

GOBLET
Probably marked by Charles Chesterman (II)
(free 1774)
London, 1792/3
Silver, parcel gilt
56.677

MARKS: on base, in three corners, maker's mark *CC* (possibly Grimwade 282);[1] lion passant; leopard's head crowned; date letter *r*; sovereign's head

INSCRIPTIONS: engraved in monogram on side, *IEB/1798*; engraved in monogram on other side, *EHS/to/ET/1898*

H. 16.3 cm (6⁷⁄₁₆ in.); d. 7.1 cm (2¹³⁄₁₆ in.); diam. 8.8 cm (3⁷⁄₁₆ in.)

WEIGHT: 221 gm (7 oz 2 dwt)

PROVENANCE: Gift of the Misses Rose and Elizabeth Townsend, October 11, 1956

DESCRIPTION: The oviform cup rests on a trumpet-shaped stem with a square base. The cup is raised, and the stem is formed from two raised sections. The base is assembled from strips of sheet. The borders of the base and the rim of the cup are engraved with sprigs and scrolling foliage. The stem is bent.

1. Grimwade (1990, p. 464) raises the possibility that Charles Chesterman I's third mark, entered 1771, may have been used by his son. The date of this cup, well after the father's death, supports this suggestion.

167

· 167 ·

INKSTAND

Marked by John Robins (first mark entered 1774,
d. 1831)

London, 1792/3

Silver

57.60

MARKS: on underside, sovereign's head (repeated
twice on globe, interior near bottle); date letter *r*;
leopard's head crowned; lion passant (repeated twice
on globe, interior near bottle, and on frame); maker's
mark *IR* (Grimwade 1623) (repeated twice on
globe, interior near bottle, and on frame)

H. 15.7 cm (6³⁄₁₆ in.); diam. of frame 8.5 cm (3⅜ in.)

WEIGHT: 272.2 gm (8 oz 15 dwt)

PROVENANCE: Lent by Dr. George Clymer,
March 10, 1939, transferred to Mrs. George Clymer,
Anonymous, August 28, 1956, Gift in Memory of
Dr. George Clymer by his wife, Mrs. Clymer,
January 10, 1957

DESCRIPTION: The inkstand is in the form of a
globe and stand, resting on a spreading circular foot

with simple cast scallops, floral swags, and a string of
beading around the perimeter. It is assembled from
pieces of sheet and tooled wire. The finial serves as a
latch to unlock the two sides of the globe, which
split open to reveal a frame holding cut-glass bottles
for ink and for pounce. The finial of the globe stand
is egg-shaped with chased leaves on the lower half.

· 168 ·

SERVICE COMPRISING A TEAPOT
AND TWO JUGS

Marked by John Scofield (first mark entered
1776) and John Emes (first mark entered 1798)

London, 1792/3 and 1805/6

Silver, wood, parcel gilt

Res.65.29a–b–31

MARKS: Res.65.29 (teapot), on underside, in three
corners, maker's mark *IS* (Grimwade 1670) (repeated on bezel of cover); lion passant (repeated on

168

bezel of cover); leopard's head crowned; date letter *r;* sovereign's head (repeated on bezel of cover). Res.65.30 (cream jug), on side of base, maker's mark *IS* (Grimwade 1670); lion passant; leopard's head crowned; date letter *r;* sovereign's head. Res.65.31 (jug): on underside in three corners, maker's mark *JE* (Grimwade 1807); leopard's head crowned; lion passant; date letter *K;* sovereign's head.

INSCRIPTIONS: scratched on underside, *27=16*

Res.65.29: H. 19.6 cm (7¾ in.); w. 27.2 cm (10¹¹⁄₁₆ in.); d. 15.7 cm (6³⁄₁₆ in.)

Res.65.30: H. 14.3 cm (5⅝ in.); w. 13.9 cm (5½ in.); d. 10.3 cm (4¹⁄₁₆ in.)

Res.65.31: H. 12.5 cm (4¹⁵⁄₁₆ in.); w. 21.2 cm (8⅜ in.); d. 12.9 cm (5¹⁄₁₆ in.)

WEIGHT: Res.65.29: 907.2 gm (29 oz 3 dwt). Res.65.30: 348.7 gm (11 oz 4 dwt). Res.65.31: 464.9 gm (14 oz 19 dwt)

PROVENANCE: Bequest of Maxim Karolik, April 14, 1965

DESCRIPTION: Res.65.29 (teapot): The teapot is in the form of a low urn. The square base is assembled of flat sheet, joined to a spool-shaped stem with a border of laurel leaves. The body of the teapot is raised with chased fluting on the lower section and a laurel border at the shoulder. The long spout, cast in two pieces and seamed vertically, is fluted at the base. The silver ear-shaped handle probably replaces an original wooden handle. The domed cover is removable and has been considerably repaired. Surmounting the fluted dome is an acorn finial in a double coronet of feathers. Res.63.30 (cream jug): The urn-shaped jug rests on a square base assembled from strips of sheet. A laurel molding decorates the foot of the stem. The raised body is chased with fluting and has a laurel border on the rim. The open spout is worked separately and applied. The high flat handle is formed from sheet. Res.63.31 (jug): The form and decoration of the larger jug are similar to Res.63.30, but the proportions are broader. It was originally a waste bowl from the service and has been altered by the addition of a large spout, a handle, and the gilding of the interior.

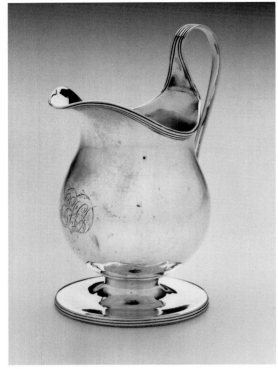

169

• 169 •

CREAM JUG

Marked by Abraham Peterson (first mark entered 1783)

London, 1792/3

Silver

1972.520

MARKS: under foot, maker's mark *AP* (Grimwade 78); sovereign's head; date letter *r*; leopard's head crowned; lion passant

INSCRIPTIONS: engraved on front in monogram, *EEHD*

H. 15.7 cm (6³⁄₁₆ in.); diam. of foot 8.1 cm (3³⁄₁₆ in.)

WEIGHT: 189 gm (6 oz 2 dwt)

PROVENANCE: according to tradition, Elizabeth Derby West (1762–1814), Salem, Massachusetts, by descent to Richard Edwards, Gift of Richard Edwards, June 7, 1972

PUBLISHED: Wendy Cooper, "The Furniture and Furnishings of the Farm at Danvers," *Bulletin of the Museum of Fine Arts, Boston* 81 (1983), p. 44, fig. 46

DESCRIPTION: The squat pear-shaped jug is raised from sheet and rests on a broad splayed foot. A high reeded handle is joined to the rim, which has a broad pouring lip.

• 170 •

HOT WATER JUG

Marked by Peter Bateman and Ann Bateman (entered into partnership 1791)

London, 1795/6

Silver, wood

41.623

MARKS: on underside of foot, sovereign's head; date letter *u;* leopard's head crowned; lion passant; maker's mark *PB* over *AB* (Grimwade 2140)

INSCRIPTIONS: engraved on side, *ED* in monogram/*1750*; on opposite side *Martha C. Codman 1870*

H. 36 cm (14³⁄₁₆ in.); w. 22.7 cm (8¹⁵⁄₁₆ in.); d. 11.7 cm (4⅝ in.)

WEIGHT: 854 gms (27 oz 9 dwt)

PROVENANCE: Elizabeth Derby, by descent to Martha C. Codman, Gift of Mr. and Mrs. Maxim Karolik for The M. and M. Karolik Collection of Eighteenth-Century American Arts, October 9, 1941

PUBLISHED: Hipkiss 1941, p. 244, cat. 172; Wendy Cooper, "The Furniture and Furnishings of the Farm at Danvers," *Bulletin of the Museum of Fine Arts* 81 (1983), p. 36, fig. 34

DESCRIPTION: The jug is vase-shaped and elliptical in section. The trumpet foot is raised and chased with panels of vertical fluting. The body of the vessel, raised from two pieces of sheet, has vertical panels of fluting alternating with plain panels. A band of reeding is applied to the midsection. The slender neck of the jug has a flaring lip and a hinged, domed cover with an urn-shaped finial. The high ear-shaped handle is mounted on foliate sockets. The rim of the foot and the panels on the body are chased and engraved with a geometric and floral border.

For a discussion of the Derby family silver, see cat. 174.

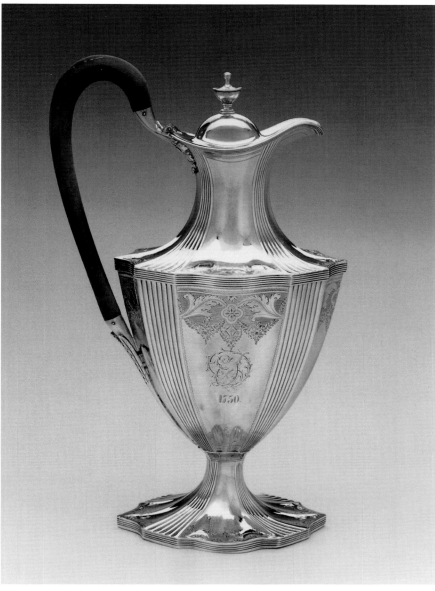

170

HOT WATER URN

Marked by Solomon Hougham (first mark
entered 1793)
London, 1795/6
Silver, wood
69.398

MARKS: on underside of urn and on side of lamp,
maker's mark *IR* (unrecorded); lion passant; leopard's
head crowned; date letter *u*; sovereign's head. On
bezel of cover, maker's mark *SH* (Grimwade 2536);
lion passant; sovereign's head; date letter *u*

INSCRIPTIONS: engraved on body, *AC* in monogram

H. 32.6 cm (12¹³⁄₁₆ in.); w. 16.95 cm (6¹¹⁄₁₆ in.);
d. 22.6 cm (8⅞ in.)

WEIGHT: 1,593.3 gm (51 oz 4 dwt)

PROVENANCE: Andrew Craigie (1743–1819) of
Cambridge, Massachusetts, by descent to his wife,
Elizabeth (d. 1841), purchased from her estate by
Mrs. Abott Lawrence, by descent to her grand-
daughter, Mrs. Horaitio Lamb, to her daughters,
Aimee and Rosamund Lamb, Gift of the Misses
Aimee and Rosamund Lamb, May 14, 1969

PUBLISHED: Bigelow 1917, p. 354, fig. 252

DESCRIPTION: The vase-shaped vessel rests on four
reeded legs on a shaped square base with ball feet.
The plain base is formed from sheet with an applied
wire rim. At the center of the base is a cup-shaped
spirit lamp with a dentiled rim, a removable cover,
and a fitting for a wick. The lamp may have been
added later to replace the original lamp. The body
of the vessel is formed from raised sheet with chased
fluting around the lower half. At the center of the
base, above the lamp, is an inset domed disk. The
rim is surrounded with a band of engraved and
bright-cut ornament between two applied wires. At
either side is an applied cast ram's head supporting a
silver hoop handle through the mouth. The
incurved neck of the body is formed from a second
shaped sheet, with a border of engraved and bright-
cut ornament. A cast spigot, with a fluted stem and a
rectangular tap, is centered at the base of the body.
The removable cover is domed and fluted around
the central ball finial. It has a border of engraved
and bright-cut ornament around the rim and a
bezel formed from sheet.

The low proportions and dense ornament of
this hot water urn are characteristic of late
neoclassical silver, although the diminutive size

171

is unusual.[1] The urn was owned by Andrew Craigie, a Boston apothecary, financier, and speculator. During the Revolution, he was entrusted with the medical stores of Massachusetts and later assumed the post of apothecary general, with the military ranking of lieutenant colonel. In 1791 Craigie bought the Vassall house in Cambridge (now known as the Craigie-Longfellow House), where General Washington had been based during the war.[2] After extensive refurbishment of the house and the gardens, Craigie and his wife, Elizabeth, staged lavish entertainments.[3] They later became estranged, and Craigie's speculations began to fail. Craigie, who died in 1819, was survived by his wife, from whose estate the urn was purchased in 1841. By 1916, when the urn was first lent to the Museum of Fine Arts, the story had evolved, inaccurately, that Mrs. Craigie had entertained George Washington.

1. Another example of the same model was sold by Christie's, New York, October 30, 1991, lot 206. For a comparable form by Chawner and Emes, see Christie's, London, March 4, 1992, lot 167.

2. Allen Johnson and Dumas Malone, eds., *Dictionary of American Biography* (New York, 1930), vol. 4, pp. 497–98. Also see Frederick Haven Pratt, "The Craigies," *Proceedings of the Cambridge Historical Society* 27 (1941), pp. 43–86.

3. Samuel Swett Green, "The Craigie House, Cambridge, during Its Occupancy by Andrew Craigie and His Widow," *Proceedings of the American Antiquarian Society* 13 (1901), pp. 312–52.

172

• 172 •

HOT WATER URN

Marked by Peter Bateman and Ann Bateman
(entered into partnership 1791)
London, 1795/6
Silver, ivory
1970.632

MARKS: on the underside, in corners, maker's mark
PB over *AB* (Grimwade 2140) (repeated on bezel of
cover and on spout); lion passant (repeated on bezel
of cover and on spout); leopard's head crowned; date
letter *u* (repeated on bezel of cover and on spout);
sovereign's head (repeated on bezel of cover and on
spout)

INSCRIPTIONS: engraved on front in monogram,
IMP

H. 52.5 cm (20¹¹⁄₁₆ in.); w. 32.4 cm (12¾ in.);
d. 28 cm (11 in.)

WEIGHT: 3,614.6 gm (116 oz 4 dwt)

PROVENANCE: Lent by Mrs. Charles E. Cotting,
1916, Gift of Mr. Charles E. Cotting, January 13,
1971

DESCRIPTION: The urn-shaped vessel rests on a
square molded base with four feet. The molded
lower section of the base is formed of seamed sheet,
with separately worked feet. The spool-shaped central section is raised and joined to the plinth with a
molded rib. At the four corners of the plinth are
bright-cut rosettes, and around the circular section is
a border of scrolled ornament. The body of the vessel is raised from a single sheet and chased with fluting at the base. Around the rim is a border of
bright-cut scrolls against a striated ground. The
spout is cast in two pieces and is reeded. It is fitted
with a spigot mounted with an ivory finial tinted
green. The high reeded handles have leaves at the
base and fan out into acanthus leaves at the juncture
with the body. The attachment of the spout to the
body has been reinforced with a disk soldered into
the interior, and there is solder at the base of the
interior suggesting that a mount for a heater has
been removed. The high domed cover is fitted with
a bezel and is decorated with fluting on the domed
section and bright-cut border around the reeded
rim. The finial is an elongated sphere, with acanthus
and fluting.

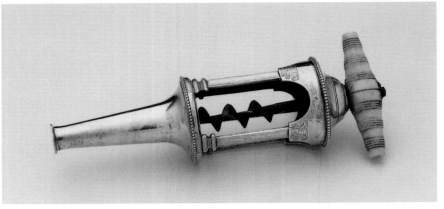

173

· 173 ·

CORKSCREW
Probably Birmingham, ca. 1800
Silver, steel, ivory
1979.503

UNMARKED

L. 11.5 cm (4⁹⁄₁₆ in.); w. 5 cm (2 in.)

WEIGHT: 56.7 gm (1 oz 16 dwt)

PROVENANCE: Anonymous Gift, October 17, 1979

DESCRIPTION: The corkscrew is formed of a piece
of sheet, seamed to form a cylinder and pierced
with a gallery supported by four columns, with
engraved fluting, capitals, and bases. Attached to the
ivory handle at the top is a steel helix, or "worm,"
in the center of the openwork sleeve. The tip of the
helix is covered with a removable tapering sheath
with a flat tip. It is assembled from three pieces of
sheet.

Until the eighteenth century, most wines were
intended to be drunk young (from the cask),
and glass bottles were generally used only for
transporting or serving. Straight-sided bottles
for maturing wine were eventually developed,
but corks were still tapered and did not require
a corkscrew until, with horizontally stacked
bottles, a straight-sided cork became necessary.[1]
The removable sheath protecting the iron
"worm" of this corkscrew is designed to be
used as a pipe tamper, a reminder that smoking
and drinking were inextricably linked. The
design of this corkscrew is based on a French
version, known as the "cage," first made in steel
in the late seventeenth century. The design

allowed the helix to be screwed into the cork
until the lip of the bottle reached the top of
the cage, or openwork sleeve. From that point,
further turning pulled against the lip of the
bottle, removing the cork from the neck.
Several specialist makers in Ireland, among
them Richard Singleton, John Fox, and John
Read, produced "cage"-style corkscrews in the
last decades of the eighteenth century, although
their marked pieces are generally in brass.[2] In
1795 the Reverend Samuel Henshaw, a fellow
at Brasenose College, Oxford, invited Matthew
Boulton to collaborate with him on a patented
corkscrew that used some of the principles of
the "cage" design but added a disk-shaped cap
at the top of the helix. No examples of the
patented corkscrew are known, but the tooling
and decoration of this unmarked corkscrew are
similar in character to Birmingham work.

1. I am grateful to Christopher Hartop for his sug-
gestions about this object. Bertrand B. Guilian,
Corkscrews of the Eighteenth Century (Yardley, Pa.,
1995), pp. 13–15; Penelope Mansell-Jones,
"Introducing Corkscrews," *The Antique Dealer
Collector's Guide* (December 1977), pp. 81–83.

2. Guilian, *Corkscrews*, pp. 137–50.

174

· 174 ·

TEA SERVICE COMPRISING TWO
TEAPOTS AND STANDS, A TEA
CANISTER, A COFFEEPOT, A
SUGAR BASIN, A WASTE BOWL, A
CREAM JUG, AND TWELVE TEA-
SPOONS

Marked by Richard Cooke (only mark entered
1799)

Silver, parcel gilt, wood

London, 1800/1

38.1832a-b, 38.1836, 38.1833, 52.1550, 38.1835,
38.1834, 38.1831a-b, 38.1837a-l

MARKS: 38.1832a-b (teapot and stand): on underside
of teapot and stand, maker's mark *RC* (Grimwade
2289); lion passant (repeated on inside of cover and
finial); leopard's head crowned; date letter *E*; sovereign's head (repeated on finial). 38.1836 (cream jug):
to right of handle, maker's mark *RC* (Grimwade
2289); lion passant; leopard's head crowned; date letter *E*; sovereign's head. 38.1833 (tea canister): on

underside, maker's mark *RC* (Grimwade 2289); lion
passant (repeated on underside of cover and finial);
leopard's head crowned; date letter *E*; sovereign's
head (repeated on finial). 52.1550 (coffeepot): on
side of base, maker's mark *RC* (Grimwade 2289);
lion passant (repeated on inside of cover and finial);
leopard's head crowned; date letter *E*; sovereign's
head. 38.1835 (waste bowl) and 38.1834 (sugar
bowl): below rim, maker's mark *RC* (Grimwade
2289); lion passant; leopard's head crowned; date letter *E*; sovereign's head. 38.1831a-b (large teapot and
stand): on underside of teapot and stand, maker's
mark *RC* (Grimwade 2289); lion passant (repeated
on inside of cover and finial); leopard's head
crowned; date letter *E*; sovereign's head (repeated on
finial). 38.1837a-l (12 teaspoons): on back of each
handle, maker's mark *RC* (Grimwade 2289); lion
passant; sovereign's head; date letter *E*

INSCRIPTIONS: 38.1832a-b, 38.1836, 38.1833,
52.1550, 38.1834, 38.1831a-b: engraved in monogram
on each side of body, *ED* for Elizabeth Derby.
38.1832a-b, 38.1833, 38.1831a-b: scratched on underside, a cursive letter. 38.1835: engraved in monogram

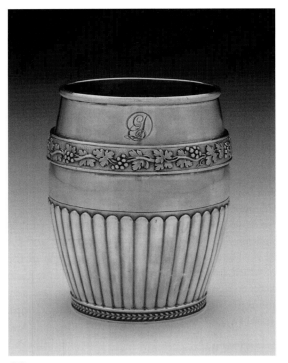

175

Elizabeth West of Salem, Massachusetts, at the time they bought the tea service by the same maker (cat. 174). Their household was well equipped with silver for the service of wine, for they had inherited from her father, Elias Hasket Derby, Salem's most prosperous merchant, a Sheffield plate monteith and a pair of bottle coolers. Like the beaker, the monteith and bottle coolers were ornamented with a band of grapevines, a motif that also was used on a mahogany stand in their dining room. The engraved initials *ED* may have been added after Elizabeth and Nathaniel's controversial divorce in 1806, since they represent Elizabeth's maiden name.[1]

1. Wendy Cooper, "Nathaniel and Elizabeth West and the Ownership of the Farm at Danvers," *Bulletin of the Museum of Fine Arts, Boston* 81 (1983), p. 15.

· 175 ·

BEAKER
Marked by Richard Cooke (only mark entered 1799)
London, 1800/1
Silver, parcel gilt
52.1551

MARKS: on underside, maker's mark *RC* (Grimwade 2289); lion passant; leopard's head crowned; date letter *E*; sovereign's head

INSCRIPTIONS: engraved in monogram on side, *ED* for Elizabeth Derby

H. 9.6 cm (3¾ in.); diam. of rim 6.5 cm (2⁹⁄₁₆ in.)

WEIGHT: 212.6 gm (6 oz 17 dwt)

PROVENANCE: Elizabeth Derby West (1762–1814), by descent to Allison Ellsworth Stuart, Gift of Mrs. Allison Ellsworth Stuart in Memory of her Husband, November 13, 1952

DESCRIPTION: The beaker is barrel-shaped, with chased fluting on the lower half. The plain section above has a cast band of grapes and vines. The vessel was raised or spun and has an applied wire at the rim and a foot rim of gilt wire cast with husks. The interior of the beaker is gilt.

This highly unusual form, a wine beaker, must have been purchased by Nathaniel and

· 176 ·

TWO TEAPOTS, CREAM JUG, SUGAR BOWL
Marked by Peter Bateman, Ann Bateman, and William Bateman (entered into partnership 1800)
London, 1800/1
Silver, wood
1985.62, 1985.63, 1985.64, 1985.65

MARKS: 1985.62, 1985.63, on underside, maker's mark *PB/AB/WB* (Grimwade 2141) (repeated on underside of cover); lion passant (repeated on underside of cover); leopard's head crowned; sovereign's head; date letter *E*. 1985.64, below spout, maker's mark *PB/AB/WB* (Grimwade 2141); lion passant; leopard's head crowned; sovereign's head; date letter *E*. 1985.65, near handle, maker's mark *PB/AB/WB* (Grimwade 2141); lion passant; leopard's head crowned; sovereign's head; date letter *E*

INSCRIPTIONS: 1985.62, 1985.63, 1985.64, 1985.65, engraved on side, *MD*; engraved on underside, *1802*

1985.62: H. 16.7 cm (6⁹⁄₁₆ in.); w. 27.9 cm (11 in.); d. 11.5 cm (4½ in.)

1985.63: H. 16.1 cm (6⁵⁄₁₆ in.); w. 27.4 cm (10¹³⁄₁₆ in.); d. 11.1 cm (4⅜ in.)

1985.64: H. 12.1 cm (4¾ in.); w. 12.5 cm (4¹⁵⁄₁₆ in.); d. 7.3 cm (2⅞ in.)

174

· 174 ·

TEA SERVICE COMPRISING TWO
TEAPOTS AND STANDS, A TEA
CANISTER, A COFFEEPOT, A
SUGAR BASIN, A WASTE BOWL, A
CREAM JUG, AND TWELVE TEA-
SPOONS

Marked by Richard Cooke (only mark entered
1799)

Silver, parcel gilt, wood

London, 1800/1

38.1832a–b, 38.1836, 38.1833, 52.1550, 38.1835,
38.1834, 38.1831a–b, 38.1837a–l

MARKS: 38.1832a–b (teapot and stand): on underside
of teapot and stand, maker's mark *RC* (Grimwade
2289); lion passant (repeated on inside of cover and
finial); leopard's head crowned; date letter *E*; sovereign's head (repeated on finial). 38.1836 (cream jug):
to right of handle, maker's mark *RC* (Grimwade
2289); lion passant; leopard's head crowned; date letter *E*; sovereign's head. 38.1833 (tea canister): on

underside, maker's mark *RC* (Grimwade 2289); lion
passant (repeated on underside of cover and finial);
leopard's head crowned; date letter *E*; sovereign's
head (repeated on finial). 52.1550 (coffeepot): on
side of base, maker's mark *RC* (Grimwade 2289);
lion passant (repeated on inside of cover and finial);
leopard's head crowned; date letter *E*; sovereign's
head. 38.1835 (waste bowl) and 38.1834 (sugar
bowl): below rim, maker's mark *RC* (Grimwade
2289); lion passant; leopard's head crowned; date letter *E*; sovereign's head. 38.1831a–b (large teapot and
stand): on underside of teapot and stand, maker's
mark *RC* (Grimwade 2289); lion passant (repeated
on inside of cover and finial); leopard's head
crowned; date letter *E*; sovereign's head (repeated on
finial). 38.1837a–l (12 teaspoons): on back of each
handle, maker's mark *RC* (Grimwade 2289); lion
passant; sovereign's head; date letter *E*

INSCRIPTIONS: 38.1832a–b, 38.1836, 38.1833,
52.1550, 38.1834, 38.1831a–b: engraved in monogram
on each side of body, *ED* for Elizabeth Derby.
38.1832a–b, 38.1833, 38.1831a–b: scratched on underside, a cursive letter. 38.1835: engraved in monogram

on front, *ED* for Elizabeth Derby. 38.1831a-b: scratched on underside of teapot, *9.* 38.1837 (12 teaspoons): for each, engraved in monogram on front, end of the handle, *ED*

38.1832a (teapot): H. 15.2 cm (6 in.); w. 26.2 cm (10⁵⁄₁₆ in.); d. 10.4 cm (4⅛ in.)

38.1832b (stand): H. 1.8 cm (¹¹⁄₁₆ in.); w. 15.2 cm (6 in.); d. 11.4 cm (4½ in.)

38.1836 (cream jug): H. 11.2 cm (4⁷⁄₁₆ in.); w. 13.5 cm (5⁵⁄₁₆ in.); d. 7.6 cm (3 in.)

38.1833 (tea canister): H. 17.6 cm (6¹⁵⁄₁₆ in.); w. 15.4 cm (6¹⁄₁₆ in.); d. 12.1 cm (4¾ in.)

52.1550 (coffeepot): H. 32.9 cm (12¹⁵⁄₁₆ in.); w. 30.3 cm (11¹⁵⁄₁₆ in.); d. 12.6 cm (4¹⁵⁄₁₆ in.)

38.1835 (waste bowl): H. 10 cm (3¹⁵⁄₁₆ in.); diam. of rim 15.2 cm (6 in.)

38.1834 (sugar bowl): H. 11.2 cm (4⁷⁄₁₆ in.); w. 16.4 cm (6⁷⁄₁₆ in.); d. 10 cm (3¹⁵⁄₁₆ in.)

38.1831a (teapot): H. 17.5 cm (6⅞ in.); w. 29.3 cm (11⁹⁄₁₆ in.); d. 12.1 cm (4¾ in.)

38.1831b (stand): H. 1.8 cm (¹¹⁄₁₆ in.); w. 16 cm (6⁵⁄₁₆ in.); d. 12.4 cm (4⅞ in.)

Spoons: 38.1837a: L. 13.6 cm (5⅜ in.); w. 2.6 cm (1 in.)

38.1837b: L. 13.5 cm (5⁵⁄₁₆ in.); w. 2.6 cm (1 in.)

38.1837c: L. 13.5 cm (5⁵⁄₁₆ in.); w. 2.7 cm (1¹⁄₁₆ in.)

38.1837d: L. 13.6 cm (5⅜ in.); w. 2.7 cm (1¹⁄₁₆ in.)

38.1837e: L. 13.4 cm (5¼ in.); w. 2.8 cm (1⅛ in.)

38.1837f: L. 13.5 cm (5⁵⁄₁₆ in.); w. 2.7 cm (1¹⁄₁₆ in.)

38.1837g: L. 13.5 cm (5⁵⁄₁₆ in.); w. 2.7 cm (1¹⁄₁₆ in.)

38.1837h: L. 13.6 cm (5⅜ in.); w. 2.7 cm (1¹⁄₁₆ in.)

38.1837i: L. 13.4 cm (5¼ in.); w. 2.7 cm (1¹⁄₁₆ in.)

38.1837j: L. 13.5 cm (5⁵⁄₁₆ in.); w. 2.7 cm (1¹⁄₁₆ in.)

38.1837k: L. 13.5 cm (5⁵⁄₁₆ in.); w. 2.7 cm (1¹⁄₁₆ in.)

38.1837l: L. 13.5 cm (5⁵⁄₁₆ in.); w. 2.7 cm (1¹⁄₁₆ in.)

WEIGHT: 38.1832a: 544 gm (17 oz 10 dwt). 38.1832b: 161.6 gm (5 oz 4 dwt). 38.1836: 255 gm (8 oz 4 dwt). 38.1833: 637 gm (20 oz 10 dwt). 52.1550: 1,598.9 gm (51 oz 8 dwt). 38.1835: 535.8 gm (17 oz 4 dwt). 38.1834: 348 gm (11 oz 4 dwt). 38.1831a: 722.9 gm (23 oz 4 dwt). 38.1831b: 192.8 gm (6 oz 4 dwt)

WEIGHT OF SPOONS: 38.1837a: 19.8 gm (13 dwt). 38.1837b: 19.8 gm (13 dwt). 38.1837c: 19.8 gm (13 dwt). 38.1837d: 19.8 gm (13 dwt). 38.1837e: 19.8 gm (13 dwt). 38.1837f: 22 gm (14 dwt). 38.1837g: 19.8 gm (13 dwt). 38.1837h: 17 gm

(10 dwt). 38.1837i: 19.8 gm (13 dwt). 38.1837j: 19.8 gm (13 dwt). 38.1837k: 19.8 gm (13 dwt). 38.1837l: 19.8 gm (13 dwt)

PROVENANCE: 38.1832a-b, 38.1836, 38.1833, 38.1835, 38.1834, 38.1831a-b, 38.1837a-l, Elizabeth Derby West (1762–1814), by descent to her granddaughter, Louisa Lander, purchased by her cousin Martha Codman Karolik (1858–1948), Gift of Martha C. Karolik, The M. and M. Karolik Collection of Eighteenth-Century American Arts, December 29, 1938. 52.1550, Elizabeth Derby West, by descent to Allison Ellsworth Stuart, Gift of Mrs. Allison Ellsworth Stuart in Memory of her Husband, November 13, 1952

PUBLISHED: Hipkiss 1941, cat. 173

DESCRIPTION: 38.1832a-b: The oval teapot is formed from raised sheet, with an inset base. Chased fluting decorates the lower half of the body and the spout, which is formed of seamed sheet. The upper and lower rims are bordered with an applied gilt wire cast with husks. The domed cover, formed from sheet, has a broad flat border and a hidden hinge and is gilt on the interior. At the top is a cast finial in the form of a reclining spaniel. The ear-shaped wooden handle is mounted on plain fabricated sockets. The oval stand rests on four low cast feet. It is formed of sheet, set into a cast rim, with a border of cast gilt wire, and bright-cut ornament on the stand. 38.1836: The helmet-shaped cream jug, oval in section, is formed from sheet, with an inset base and a gilt interior. Around the lower half of the body are chased flutes, and upper and lower rims are trimmed with a cast gilt wire. The handle, formed from sheet, is squared off at the top. 38.1833: The oval tea canister, raised from sheet, with an inset base, has fluting around the lower half of the body and tapers slightly at the foot. The domed cover, formed from a single piece of sheet, has a hidden hinge and a broad flat rim. A cast finial in the form of a reclining spaniel surmounts the cover. Around the foot and rim of the body is an applied cast gilt wire, and a border of bright-cut decoration decorates the upper rim. 52.1550: The tall, urn-shaped coffeepot rests on a flaring oval foot on a rectangular base. The base and stem are formed of several pieces of cast and fabricated sheet, with a gilt border and a bright-cut garland around the oval foot. The lower half of the plain raised body is chased with fluting. A curved spout with fluting is cast and seamed vertically. The hinged cover is spool-shaped with an oval domed top surmounted by a removable cast finial in the form of a reclining spaniel. The ear-shaped wooden handle is mounted on fabricated cylindrical sockets. 38.1835: The hemispherical waste bowl rests on a spool-shaped foot. Formed from sheet, with chased fluting around the lower half, it has a gilt interior. The rims of the bowl and foot are trimmed with a cast gilt wire, and a band of bright-cut engraving decorates the upper border of the bowl. 38.1834: The oval sugar bowl has a scooped rim and ring handles suspended from applied shells on either

side. The bowl, which has a gilt interior, is formed from sheet, with an inset base and chased fluting around the lower half. Around the upper and lower edges are applied gilt wires with finely cast husks. 38.1834: The larger teapot is of the same design and construction as the smaller example (38.1832). 38.1837a-l: The spoons, which are forged, have plain "Old English" ends, flattened stems, and a bowl chased with a shell pattern. The borders of the stem are engraved with a "feather edge."

Elizabeth Derby, daughter of the wealthiest merchant in Salem, Massachusetts, was married in 1783 to Nathaniel West (1756–1851), also the son of a successful mercantile family. The bride's father, Elias Hasket Derby (1739–1799), had reestablished and multiplied a shipping empire after the American Revolution, extending his range to St. Helena, the Cape of Good Hope, Mauritius, Ceylon, India, and Batavia, in favor of China.[1] Elizabeth and Nathaniel West had six children, and in 1801 they began construction of Oak Hill, a grand house in Danvers near Peabody. The house was conceived as a country seat rather than an income property, and they apparently also maintained a house in Salem. By all accounts, the furnishing of Oak Hill was meticulously supervised by Elizabeth Derby.[2]

The nature and quality of the interiors can be gauged by several contemporary inventories and, more tellingly, by a large group of furniture, porcelain, glass, and silver acquired by the Museum of Fine Arts between 1923 and 1972. The couple had inherited furnishings from each of their families, but the pieces they bought new for Oak Hill in the years around 1800, including this tea service, are handsome examples of neoclassical taste.[3] The unusual finials in the form of spaniels may be a special modification. The engraved monogram, *ED*, reflecting Mrs. West's maiden name, was per-

haps added slightly later, for Elizabeth and Nathaniel West separated in 1803, soon after the completion of the house. Mr. West moved into the Salem house, leaving the farm to his wife, and they were divorced in 1806. Elizabeth died eight years later, and a contemporary observed that she had "rendered herself unwelcome to any private family or boarding house. . . . Her last retirement was to her farm. . . . She had decorated it, furnished it, been sick in it, & died in it. Her hundred thousand pounds is to be divided among her children. Her plate was elegant and the pieces multiplied beyond example in this part of the Country."[4]

This tea service, like many pieces from the house, was acquired for the Museum by Martha Codman Karolik from her cousin Louisa Lander, a granddaughter of Nathaniel and Elizabeth West. A note from Mrs. Karolik indicates that the matching urn was separated from the set at some point and sold. Also see cats. 169, 170, and 176.

1. Richard H. McKey, "Elias Hasket Derby and the Founding of the Eastern Trade, Parts 1 and 2," *Essex Institute Historical Collections* 9, nos. 1–2 (January and April 1962).
2. Wendy Cooper, "Nathaniel and Elizabeth West and the Ownership of the Farm at Danvers," *Bulletin of the Museum of Fine Arts, Boston* 81 (1983), p. 15.
3. Wendy Cooper, "The Furniture and Furnishings of the Farm at Danvers," *Bulletin of the Museum of Fine Arts, Boston* 81 (1983), pp. 24–37.
4. Diary of William Bentley (1759–1819), quoted in Cooper, "Nathaniel and Elizabeth West and the Ownership of the Farm at Danvers," p. 16.

175

Elizabeth West of Salem, Massachusetts, at the time they bought the tea service by the same maker (cat. 174). Their household was well equipped with silver for the service of wine, for they had inherited from her father, Elias Hasket Derby, Salem's most prosperous merchant, a Sheffield plate monteith and a pair of bottle coolers. Like the beaker, the monteith and bottle coolers were ornamented with a band of grapevines, a motif that also was used on a mahogany stand in their dining room. The engraved initials *ED* may have been added after Elizabeth and Nathaniel's controversial divorce in 1806, since they represent Elizabeth's maiden name.[1]

1. Wendy Cooper, "Nathaniel and Elizabeth West and the Ownership of the Farm at Danvers," *Bulletin of the Museum of Fine Arts, Boston* 81 (1983), p. 15.

· 175 ·

BEAKER

Marked by Richard Cooke (only mark entered 1799)
London, 1800/1
Silver, parcel gilt
52.1551

MARKS: on underside, maker's mark *RC* (Grimwade 2289); lion passant; leopard's head crowned; date letter *E*; sovereign's head

INSCRIPTIONS: engraved in monogram on side, *ED* for Elizabeth Derby

H. 9.6 cm (3¾ in.); diam. of rim 6.5 cm (2⁹⁄₁₆ in.)

WEIGHT: 212.6 gm (6 oz 17 dwt)

PROVENANCE: Elizabeth Derby West (1762–1814), by descent to Allison Ellsworth Stuart, Gift of Mrs. Allison Ellsworth Stuart in Memory of her Husband, November 13, 1952

DESCRIPTION: The beaker is barrel-shaped, with chased fluting on the lower half. The plain section above has a cast band of grapes and vines. The vessel was raised or spun and has an applied wire at the rim and a foot rim of gilt wire cast with husks. The interior of the beaker is gilt.

This highly unusual form, a wine beaker, must have been purchased by Nathaniel and

· 176 ·

TWO TEAPOTS, CREAM JUG, SUGAR BOWL

Marked by Peter Bateman, Ann Bateman, and William Bateman (entered into partnership 1800)
London, 1800/1
Silver, wood
1985.62, 1985.63, 1985.64, 1985.65

MARKS: 1985.62, 1985.63, on underside, maker's mark *PB/AB/WB* (Grimwade 2141) (repeated on underside of cover); lion passant (repeated on underside of cover); leopard's head crowned; sovereign's head; date letter *E*. 1985.64, below spout, maker's mark *PB/AB/WB* (Grimwade 2141); lion passant; leopard's head crowned; sovereign's head; date letter *E*. 1985.65, near handle, maker's mark *PB/AB/WB* (Grimwade 2141); lion passant; leopard's head crowned; sovereign's head; date letter *E*

INSCRIPTIONS: 1985.62, 1985.63, 1985.64, 1985.65, engraved on side, *MD*; engraved on underside, *1802*

1985.62: H. 16.7 cm (6⁹⁄₁₆ in.); w. 27.9 cm (11 in.); d. 11.5 cm (4½ in.)

1985.63: H. 16.1 cm (6⁵⁄₁₆ in.); w. 27.4 cm (10¹³⁄₁₆ in.); d. 11.1 cm (4³⁄₈ in.)

1985.64: H. 12.1 cm (4¾ in.); w. 12.5 cm (4¹⁵⁄₁₆ in.); d. 7.3 cm (2⅞ in.)

176

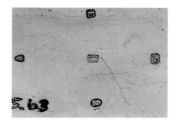

1985.65: H. 12.7 cm (5 in.); w. 17.5 cm (6⅞ in.);
d. 10.1 cm (4 in.)

WEIGHT: 1985.62: 476.3 gm (15 oz 6 dwt). 1985.63:
487.6 gm (15 oz 14 dwt). 1985.64: 144.6 gm (4 oz 13
dwt). 1985.65: 260.8 gm (8 oz 8 dwt)

PROVENANCE: Martha Coffin (1783–1832) of
Salem, Massachusetts, who married Richard
Derby, by descent through the family to her great-
great-granddaughter; Gift of Jeannie U. Dupee,
February 27, 1985

PUBLISHED: Jonathan Fairbanks, "Recent
Renovations to the Oak Hill Rooms at the
Museum," *Museum of Fine Arts Bulletin* 81 (1983),
p. 12, fig. 8

DESCRIPTION: 1985.62–63 (teapots): The two
teapots are identical in form; one is slightly smaller
than the other. The elliptical body is raised from
thin seamed sheet, with curved tapering sides and
panels of vertical fluting. The center panel of each
side is engraved with bright-cut floral sprays. The
base is inset. The scrolled handle is wood, mounted
on cylindrical sockets. The long curved spout is
formed of sheet and seamed. The elliptical domed
lid has a band of bright-cut around the rim and is
surmounted by a wooden baluster finial. A plate
has been applied to the hinge to strengthen the
cover. Both pieces have extensive surface wear.

1985.64 (cream jug): The elliptical body with curving sides has panels of fluting on either side of the
handle and spout. It is formed of seamed sheet, with
an inset base. The panel in the center of each side
and that below the spout is engraved with bright-
cut floral sprays, deeply worn. A band of bright-cut
follows the curved line of the molded rim. The
squared handle is formed of a reeded wire. The surface is extremely worn. 1985.65 (sugar bowl): The
elliptical body with curved tapering sides has panels
of fluting on either side of the handles. It is formed
of seamed sheet with an inset base. The panels in
the center of each side and behind the handles are
engraved with bright-cut floral sprays. The squared
handles are formed of reeded wire. The surface is
extremely worn.

This tea service belonged to Martha Coffin
Derby, whose husband, Richard, was one of
seven children of Elias Hasket Derby (1739–
1799), a tremendously successful Salem merchant. It is a typical production piece from the
Bateman shop and makes an interesting contrast to the contemporary service owned by
Martha Coffin Derby's fashion-conscious sister-
in-law, Elizabeth Derby West (cat. 174).

177

formed of seamed sheet, with an inset base. Joined at right angles to the spout, with a straight-sided socket, is a turned and faceted wooden handle. The slightly domed lid has a gadrooned rim and a wooden finial. The two beakers, one slightly smaller than the other, are identical. They are cylindrical in shape, with a wide band of matting in the middle.

This pot, probably part of a traveling service, contains two closely fitting beakers. The plain cylindrical form is traditional in French, but not in English, neoclassical silver. It may have been a coffeepot or a shaving jug included as part of an extensive *nécessaire de voyage* in a leather case. An example made for Marie Antoinette, now in the Musée International de la Parfumerie, Grasse, was fitted with silver vessels including a similar chocolate pot (similar in form to the present jug), a ewer and basin, candlesticks, a heater, and cutlery, and porcelain wares such as plates, cups, and a teapot.[1] A similar beaker forms the uppermost part of a French stacking set for making filtered coffee that includes a heater and a spouted vessel, surmounted by a cylindrical pot.[2]

The engraved arms on the side of the pot are those of Louis Philippe, king of France, who held successively the titles duc de Valois, duc de Chartres (from 1785), and duc d'Orléans (from 1793). Like his father, Louis Philippe Joseph (who was known during the Revolution as "Philippe Egalité"), he spoke at first in favor of the Revolution. However, he was later implicated in a plot to overthrow the Republic and fled France in 1793. After several years of travel, he settled in 1800 in Twickenham, where he lived quietly in exile with his brothers, Antoine, duc de Montpensier, and Louis Charles, comte de Beaujolais, and his sister, Adelaide.[3] The family lived modestly during this first exile, supported by the English crown. Louis Philippe was an avid gardener and an amateur heraldist, and he and his siblings entertained the local residents and occasional visitors "in a way that could give offence to no one."[4] On his later stays in Twickenham he lived more grandly, but he loved his "peaceful house in old Twick." This jug and beakers, hallmarked 1706/8, must have been given or purchased during this first period of exile in England. Louis Philippe married in 1809 Marie Amélie, daughter of the king of Sicily, and on the fall

· 177 ·

TRAVELING JUG AND TWO BEAKERS

Marked by Thomas Phipps and Edward Robinson (entered into partnership 1783) and John Cramer (first mark entered 1797)
London, 1806/8
Silver, wood
1977.110a–c

MARKS: 1977.110a (jug): on underside, maker's mark *TP* over *ER* (Grimwade 2891) (repeated on underside of cover); lion passant (repeated on underside of cover); date letter *L* (repeated on underside of cover); sovereign's head; leopard's head crowned. 1977.110b–c (beakers): below the rim, maker's mark *IC* (possibly Grimwade 1217); lion passant; leopard's head crowned; date letter *M*; sovereign's head

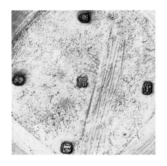

ARMORIALS: engraved on the jug, the arms of Louis Philippe, duc d'Orléans (1773–1850), and on the beakers *LC* in monogram beneath a crown of a prince of the blood

1977.110a: H. 12.7 cm (5 in.); diam. of rim 8.1 cm (3¼ in.)

1977.110b: H. 9 cm (3⁹⁄₁₆ in.); diam. of rim 7.6 cm (3 in.)

1977.110c: H. 9 cm (3⁹⁄₁₆ in.); diam. of rim 7.2 cm (2⅞ in.)

WEIGHT: 720.1 gm (23 oz 3 dwt)

PROVENANCE: sold Sotheby's, London, October 25, 1973, lot 54; purchased from Brand Inglis, Ltd., London, April 13, 1977, Theodora Wilbour Fund in Memory of Charlotte Beebe Wilbour

DESCRIPTION: The body of the jug is cylindrical with a molded wire rim and a small beak spout. It is

of Napoleon in 1814 he returned to France and the Orléans estates were restored to him. He was finally crowned king of the French after the Revolution of 1830, only to abdicate in 1848. He died in England in 1850. The engraved monogram, *LC*, on the beakers is difficult to explain. Louis Philippe's monogram, *LP*, survives on a variety of his possessions.[5] Perhaps the monogram *LC* beneath a crown of the prince of the blood was added by Louis Philippe's second son, Louis Charles d'Orléans, duc de Nemours (1814–1896).[6]

1. Illus. Véronique Alemany-Dessaint, *Orfèvrerie française* (Paris, 1988), p. 79, fig. 5.

2. Exh. New York, The Metropolitan Museum of Art, *Three Centuries of French Domestic Silver*, 1960, catalogue by Faith Dennis, p. 58, cat. 45.

3. T. H. R. Cashmore, "The Orleans Family in Twickenham 1800–1832," *Borough of Twickenham Local History Society Paper Number 49* (March 1982), pp. 1–10.

4. D. H. Simpson, "The Twickenham of Laetitia Hawkins, 1760–1835," *Borough of Twickenham Local History Society Paper Number 39* (April 1978), p. 31.

5. For example, see a bookbinding exh. Paris, Grand Palais, *Un Âge d'or des arts décoratifs, 1814–1848*, 1991, p. 242, cat. 114, and a silver tea service by J. V. Morel, sold Sotheby's, New York, October 19, 1994, lot 219.

6. I am grateful to Philippe Palasi, Paris, for his advice on the arms and monogram.

178

· 178 ·

TOAST RACK

Marked by Joseph William Story (first mark entered 1803)
London, 1808/9
Silver
Res.39.111

MARKS: on underside, sovereign's head; date letter *N*; leopard's head crowned; lion passant; maker's mark *IWS* (Grimwade 1761)

ARMORIALS: engraved on one end, the crest of Howard

INSCRIPTIONS: scratched on underside, *7000*

H. 15.5 cm (6 1/16 in.); w. 17.8 cm (7 in.); d. 11.6 cm (4 9/16 in.)

WEIGHT: 493.3 gm (15 oz 17 dwt)

PROVENANCE: Anonymous Gift in Memory of Charlotte Beebe Wilbour (1833–1914), December 14, 1939

DESCRIPTION: The rectangular toast rack has a frame with a gadroon and shell border resting on four feet in the form of flattened lotus pods. Secured to the cast frame are seven vertical brackets in the form of crocketted ogee arches. The brackets are assembled from drawn and cast parts.

This toast rack, an eccentric conflation of Gothic and Egyptian motifs,[1] was an uncharacteristic purchase for Miss Wilbour. In spite of her lifelong interest in Egypt, she seems not to have admired Regency silver with Egyptian motifs, favoring instead the austere lines of the early eighteenth century.

1. A variation on the design from the same shop offered a scrolled, rather than arched, arcade. See Sotheby's, London, February 5, 1987, lot 164.

· 179 ·

PAIR OF WINE COOLERS

Marked by Paul Storr (1771–1844)
London, 1808/9
Silver gilt
54.1798–1799

MARKS: on side of foot, maker's mark *PS*
(Grimwade 2235) (repeated on collar and liner); lion
passant (repeated on collar); leopard's head crowned
(repeated on liner); date letter *N* (repeated on collar
and liner); sovereign's head (repeated on liner)

INSCRIPTIONS: stamped on base, *RUNDELL
BRIDGE ET RUNDELL AURIFICES REGIS ET
PRINCIPIS WALLIAE LONDINI FECERUNT*;
scratched inside both bases, *3004/p849 pair/£ 101*;
scratched on both collars, *611 612 } 4 oz 670 £ hoo.*
54.1798, *168=2, 167-7*; stamped on base of body, *3*;
stamped on liner and collar, *2*. 54.1799, *167-12, 168-
12*; stamped on base of body, liner, and collar, *1*

54.1798: H. 28.2 cm (11⅛ in.); w. 26.3 cm (10⅜ in.)

54.1799: H. 28.2 cm (11⅛ in.); w. 26.7 cm (10½ in.)

WEIGHT: 54.1798: 5,202.2 gm (167 oz 5 dwt).
54.1799: 5,244.8 gm (168 oz 12 dwt)

PROVENANCE: Garrard and Co., London, purchased December 9, 1954, Theodora Wilbour Fund
in Memory of Charlotte Beebe Wilbour

EXHIBITED: Minneapolis, The Minneapolis
Institute of Arts, *French, English, and American Silver:
A Loan Exhibition in Honor of Russell A. Plimpton*,
1956, cat. 30; Cleveland, Ohio, The Cleveland
Museum of Art, *Neo-Classicism: Style and Motif*, 1964,
cat. 183; Indianapolis, Indiana, Indianapolis Museum
of Art, *Paul Storr Silver in American Collections*, 1972,
cat. 27; New York, The Frick Collection, *English
Silver*, 1978, cat. 17

PUBLISHED: Norman M. Penzer, "An Exhibition of
Silver at the Minneapolis Institute of Arts," *Apollo*
64, no. 381 (1956), pp. 133–36

DESCRIPTION: The wine cooler is campana-shaped
and rests on a fluted trumpet foot with a calyx. The
lower section of the vessel, which is cast in four sections, is covered with a pattern of acanthus leaves
and grapevines. Cast fluted handles, resting on two
satyr's heads, are joined to the lower section of the
body. The main section of the vessel, formed of
seamed sheet, is chased with the Triumph of
Bacchus against a matted ground. On one face,
Ariadne, supported by Bacchus, is shown in a chari-
ot drawn by lions and flanked by winged trum-
peters. On the other face, Bacchus, accompanied by
Ariadne, reclines in a triumphal car drawn by hors-

es. Above one handle is a figure of a satyr in human
guise, dressed in a goat skin and bearing a jug of
wine, and above the other is Silenus, carried by two
satyrs. A band of cast and fabricated grapevines is
applied to the upper edge above the figures. The
flared rim has a cast applied border of egg and dart.
The interior is fitted with a plain cylindrical sleeve,
formed of seamed sheet, that fits tightly into a wire
ring in the base. The interior rim is finished with a
removable raised flaring collar, with an applied guilloche border.

These wine coolers exemplify the muscular
classicism that Phillip Rundell and John Bridge
achieved in their collaboration with Paul Storr.
The story of their design and manufacture is
also representative of the complex business that
supplied a generation of aristocrats with grand
plate that signified England's economic and
military success.

In 1808 the firm of Rundell, Bridge &
Rundell was flourishing. They had secured the
appointment of goldsmith and jeweller to the
king in 1797 and turned the production over
to Paul Storr in 1807. The design for these
wine coolers may be the work of the sculptor
John Flaxman (1755–1826), who had spent
seven years in Rome, sponsored in part by
Wedgwood.[1] Another possibility is that they
were conceived by the artist William Theed
(1764–1817) who served as artistic director of
Rundell's and occasionally came into conflict
with Rundell & Bridge, as reported by the
diarist Joseph Farington: "He suffered from
their intruding their opinions in matters of
taste & design, & said He would always go one
better if He had access to the Nobleman or
Gentleman who gave them Commissions and
were easily led to adopt His opinions."[2]

The client for whom these wine coolers
were designed is not certain. At least a dozen
versions of the model are known; this 1808 pair
without armorials is the earliest.[3] The form of
the vessel is modeled on the Medici Krater in
the Uffizi. Rundell's had used this model in the
same year on a set of eight wine coolers made
for the Prince of Wales,[4] replacing the relief
decoration of the Medici Krater with a Dio-
nysian scene, probably after Piranesi's engraving
of the Borghese Krater. For the present wine
cooler, the designer introduced a new Bacchic

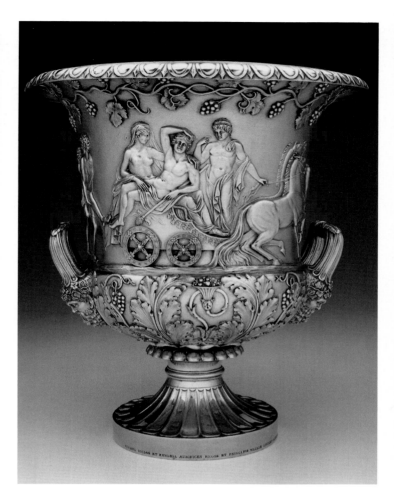

179 (see color plate XIX)

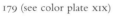

frieze, in this case borrowed from a marble relief of the late second century in the Vatican Museum.[5] While Flaxman might have recorded the relief while in Rome, it is more likely that, as David Udy suggests, his source was an engraving by E. Q. Visconti.[6] A drawing of the wine coolers, believed by Charles Oman to be a record by Theed of the model, rather than a design, survives in an album of drawings in the Victoria and Albert Museum.[7]

A key to Rundell's extraordinary success was their willingness to recycle designs, adding embellishments if the client was willing to pay for them, or leaving them off if not. Most of the other versions of this model are mounted on matching stands, some of which are circular and quite plain, resting on four feet,[8] while others are more sculptural.[9] Futhermore, Rundell's kept the patterns in circulation, adapting them as necessary to suit a new taste. Two tankards of 1820 and 1827 have sections of the same triumphal frieze, but it is integrated into a mannerist-revival design rather than an archaeological whole.[10]

1. David Udy, "Piranesi's 'Vasi,' the English Silversmith and His Patrons," *Burlington Magazine* 120, no. 909 (December 1978), p. 828.

2. Quoted in Norman M. Penzer, *Paul Storr: The Last of the Goldsmiths* (London, 1954), p. 75. Charles Oman (Oman 1966, p. 178) proposed Theed as the author of the design; Udy ("Piranesi," p. 829, pl. 30) suggests that Flaxman was responsible for the more prestigious commissions, and that Theed's complaints about Rundell & Bridge's interference indicates a secondary status.

3. Other examples include a pair made in 1809/10 for the marquess of Ormonde and now in the Victoria and Albert Museum, illus. in Oman 1966, fig. 9; a pair of the same year sold from the Burdett-Coutts collection, Christie's, London, March 9, 1943, lot 16; a pair of the same year with Rare Art (London), illus. *Antiques* 154, no. 4 (October 1998); a pair of the same year sold from the collection of Earl Howe, Christie's, London, July 1, 1953, lot 108, and a set of four sold in the same sale, lot 107, marked for 1811; a single example of 1814 mounted in 1817 on a plinth, in the Al-Tajiir collection, exh., London, Christie's, *The Glory of the Goldsmith: Magnificent Gold and Silver from the Al-Tajiir Collection*, 1989, cat. 142.

4. E. Alfred Jones, *The Gold and Silver of Windsor Castle* (Letchworth, 1911), p. 112, pl. 57.

5. Udy, "Piranesi," p. 827.

6. E. Q. Visconti, *Il Museo Pio-Clementino* (Rome, 1788), vol. 4, pl. 24.

7. Oman 1966, pp. 173–83.

8. The marquess of Ormonde's, for example, in the Victoria and Albert Museum, see n. 3.

9. Those made for the Prince of Wales, for example; see n. 4.

10. The tankard marked by Philip Rundell in 1820 was sold by Christie's, New York, October 22, 1984, lot 173; the second, marked in 1827, was sold by Christie's, London, October 17, 1962, lot 96.

· 180 ·

MEERSCHAUM PIPE

Marked by Joseph Ash (I) (first mark entered 1801)
London, 1812/3
Meerschaum with silver gilt mounts
65.1319

MARKS: on the mouthpiece and on the lip of the bowl, maker's mark *IA* (Grimwade 1105) (repeated on cover); date letter *R* (repeated on cover); lion passant (repeated on cover); sovereign's head

INSCRIPTIONS: in pierced work along the cap, *SALUS IN FUMO*

H. 20.2 cm (7^{15}/$_{16}$ in.); w. 12.5 cm (4^{15}/$_{16}$ in.); d. 7 cm (2¾ in.)

PROVENANCE: Ronald A. Lee, London, purchased November 10, 1965, Theodora Wilbour Fund in Memory of Charlotte Beebe Wilbour

DESCRIPTION: The pipe is carved from an elbow-shaped piece of meerschaum. It is mounted with a silver mouthpiece formed of a cast disk with concentric rings of acanthus and anthemion leaves. At the center is a cone-shaped fitting with a border of anthemion leaves and a ring-shaped handle. The bowl of the pipe is mounted with a silver collar formed of sheet that has a high hinged cover. The cover has a cast rim of anthemion leaves and a shaped midsection with saw-pierced lettering. The circular top of the cover is a cast medallion depicting men seated around a table, smoking pipes and drinking.

This pipe was very likely part of the vast collection formed by Augustus Frederick, duke of Sussex (1773–1843), sixth son of George III.[1] Among the property sold by Christie's after his death in 1843 was an "unrivalled collection of pipes," including more than fifty gold- and silver-mounted pipes decorated with heraldic, historic, and exotic subjects.[2] Also sold was the duke's enormous store of tobacco.

Augustus Frederick had suffered as a child with respiratory problems, but this seems not to have inhibited his passion for smoking as an adult. He was a large man, over six feet four inches tall and corpulent. His public image was that of a benevolent liberal, and he was devoted to many charitable causes, appearing at each fund-raising dinner. "His Royal Highness goes everywhere, from Houndsditch to Holland

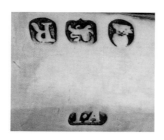

180

Adolphus wrote in 1838 that the duke had filled his meerschaum pipe, not with tobacco, but "with some fragrant herb."[5]

Meerschaum, a fine soft mineral found in Asia Minor, was exported to Vienna and other European centers for cutting and polishing. This pipe lacks the long flexible stem and mouthpiece with which it would have been fitted.[6] In the jovial scene depicted on the cover of the bowl, the Prince of Wales presides over a table of gentlemen, comfortably smoking and drinking wine, which they pour from bottles scattered on the table and stored in the cellarette on the floor.

1. I am very grateful to Christopher Hartop for this suggestion.

2. Christie's, London, July 10–11, 1843. The descriptions in the catalogue are insufficiently detailed to distinguish this pipe.

3. Mollie Gillen, *Royal Duke, Augustus Frederick, Duke of Sussex (1773–1843)* (London, 1976), p. 153.

4. Ibid., p. 177.

5. Ibid., p. 179.

6. For related examples, see Christie's, London, June 20, 1973, lot 63; Sotheby's, London, May 29, 1975, lot 167; Sotheby's, London, July 7, 1987, lot 261; Sotheby's, New York, October 28, 1987, lot 198; Sotheby's, London, February 9, 1988, lot 404; Christie's, London, October 25, 1989, lot 129.

House, where there is anything to eat," one writer complained.[3] He was a committed Whig, and his relations with his brothers, particularly the duke of Cumberland, were sometimes strained by politics. He was closest to the Prince of Wales, who is depicted, with feathered headdress, at the head of the table on the cover of this pipe. When named Prince Regent, however, his brother refused to endorse the Whig position, and the duke of Sussex fell from favor. He suffered financially when his brother became king and struggled hopelessly with debt. Smoking was clearly a large aspect of his persona. The *Morning Post* defined a miracle as a day when "His Royal Highness the Duke of Sussex, after a very short devotion, jumped nimbly out of bed, declined smoking and paid all his tradesmen."[4] The duke sat for a portrait by Solomon Alexander Hart, R.A., who wrote that he had difficulty rendering his subject's mouth because of the constant presence of a pipe, and the historian John

· 181 ·

TEAPOT

Marked by William Eley (I) (first mark entered 1778)
London, 1814/5
Silver
1977.117

MARKS: (defaced) on underside, maker's mark *WE* (Grimwade 3101); date letter *T* (repeated on bezel); sovereign's head; leopard's head crowned; lion passant (repeated on bezel)

H. 12.7 cm (5 in.); w. 10.8 cm (4¼ in.); d. 19.9 cm (7¹³⁄₁₆ in.)

WEIGHT: 739.9 gm (23 oz 16 dwt)

PROVENANCE: S. J. Shrubsole Ltd., London, purchased April 13, 1977, Theodora Wilbour Fund in Memory of Charlotte Beebe Wilbour

181

early pieces with Chinese scenes in low relief, some apparently made in China for export, others copied by London makers.[4]

The renewed enthusiasm in the early nineteenth century for Chinese subjects, epitomized by John Nash's (1752–1835) Brighton Pavilion, created a new market for the early forms. Many London goldsmiths, most notably Paul Storr, interpreted the paneled Chinese silver with interesting variations. A hexagonal sugar bowl marked in 1816 by John Edward Terrey[5] and a teapot marked in 1819 by James Pratt[6] have Chinese landscape scenes in low relief similar to those on the present teapot, while a plain hexagonal teapot marked by Storr in 1832 is a simplified version of the taste. Another characteristic example of the revival of the style is a gilt teapot with attenuated spout and handle marked in 1821 by John Edward Terrey.[7] The marks on the Boston teapot have been partially defaced, possibly with the intention of presenting it as a seventeenth-century example.

DESCRIPTION: The hexagonal globular body, assembled from heavily cast panels, seamed vertically, rests on a hexagonal foot. Each panel has a shaped oval reserve enclosing a roughly rendered landscape depicting a small figure on horseback, a bridge, and a pagoda against a matted ground. The cast angular, faceted spout and handle are similarly decorated. The teapot has a hexagonal neck and a flat hexagonal cover, joined by a chain to the handle, with a globe finial. The neck, cover, and finial all have cast landscape panels.

This heavily cast teapot is an early-nineteenth-century London version of a late-seventeenth-century model apparently made in China for export. The earliest hallmarked example of the form, now in the Peabody Essex Museum, Salem, Massachusetts, bears London marks for 1682/3 and the sponsor's mark *TA*.[1] It was traditionally held to be an early English copy of a Chinese piece.[2] However, the high standard of the silver and the fine rendering of the cast panels are considered by Crosby Forbes and others to be an indication that it was made in China and assayed and marked in London before retail sale, in keeping with English law.[3] The 1682/3 teapot belongs to a small group of

1. Acc. no. 25,031. Purchased by the Peabody Essex from the collection of Sam Wagstaff, at Christie's, New York, April 18, 1989, lot 589. Also see David S. Howard, *A Tale of Three Cities: Canton, Shanghai, and Hong Kong: Three Centuries of Sino-British Trade in the Decorative Arts* (London, 1997), pp. 204–5; H. A. Crosby Forbes, John Devereux Kernan, and Ruth S. Wilkins, *Chinese Export Silver, 1785–1885* (Milton, Mass., 1975), pp. 52–54.

2. Jackson 1911, vol. 2, p. 945. See Philippa Glanville, "Chinese Influences on English Silver, 1550–1720," *London International Jewellery and Silver Fair* (London, 1987), pp. 15–22 for further discussion on this group.

3. I am grateful to Crosby Forbes for sharing his insights on this group of objects and for offering many references from his files. I also benefited from discussions with Harriet Carlton Goldweitz.

4. See Glanville, "Chinese Influences." An unmarked example of the same design is in the Harriet Carlton Goldweitz collection. See Christie's, New York, October 20, 1998, lot 240.

5. Sold Sotheby's, London, March 6, 1969, lot 146.

6. Sold Sotheby's, New York, October 17, 1995, lot 56.

7. Sold Sotheby's, New York, April 12, 1994, lot 216.

182

This unmarked creamboat has traditionally been associated with Nicholas Sprimont, whose mark, along with Paul Crespin's, appears on a group of larger sauceboats and stands of related design. (See cat. 96.) There are some differences in the conception and rendering of the coral and shell panels, however, that suggest that this piece might tentatively be grouped with a number of early-nineteenth-century copies of Sprimont's "marine style."[1] The rather cursory, rigid modeling and chasing of the shells and, by contrast, the animated character of the serpent handle are not in keeping with the style of the sauceboats at the Clark Art Institute bearing Crespin's mark.[2] Several other small versions of this design, all unmarked, are known.[3]

This creamboat was sold in 1948 with others bearing the engraved arms of the first marquess of Rockingham. Several eighteenth-century inventories, without weights, in the Wentworth Woodhouse Muniments record sets of sauceboats, but it seems likely that these refer to sauceboats of the standard, larger size, rather than to this diminutive creamboat.[4]

· 182 ·

CREAM JUG

London, possibly ca. 1820
Silver
1988.1073

UNMARKED

INSCRIPTIONS: engraved on inside of base, *9=12*; on inside of spout, *6–6*

H. 10 cm (3¹⁵⁄₁₆ in.); w. 14 cm (5½ in.); d. 5.8 cm (2¼ in.)

WEIGHT: 292 gm (9 oz 8 dwt)

PUBLISHED: Grimwade 1974, fig. 32B

PROVENANCE: the Rt. Hon. the earl Fitzwilliam, D.S.C., sold Christie's, London, June 9, 1948, lot 83; Lent by Mrs. S. J. Katz, June 25, 1973, The Jessie and Sigmund Katz Collection, Gift of Mrs. S. J. Katz, November 30, 1988

DESCRIPTION: The shell-shaped jug has a fluted rim and spiraling ribs that are alternately plain or modeled with shells against a coral ground. It is cast in two halves and seamed in the center. The cast handle is in the form of a dotted serpent with a pointed tail. The boat rests on a cast foot modeled with shells, coral, and a watery border.

1. A copy of the Prince of Wales's centerpiece was made in 1780 by Robert Hennell and sold by the duke of Rutland in 1744. See Sotheby's, Monaco, June 20, 1992, lot 44. For other nineteenth-century versions of related models, see Joseph Bliss, *The Jerome and Rita Gans Collection of English Silver on Loan to the Virginia Museum of Fine Arts* (New York, 1992), p. 197, cat. 68.

2. Illus. Wees 1997, p. 167, cat. 88.

3. One is in the Royal Ontario Museum (acc. no. 939X45); I am grateful to Peter Kaellgren for providing a photograph. A second creamboat was with Asprey & Co., London, in 1988, illus. *Country Life* 182, no. 24 (June 16, 1988), p. 135.

4. Sheffield Archives, Wentworth Woodhouse Muniments. An inventory dated April 5, 1750, lists twelve sauceboats (M26/3), and another of the same year records twelve sauceboats and four plates (A1229, p. 15). After the death of the second marquis in 1782, the inventory of his Grosvenor Square house listed eight chased sauceboats and eight spoons weighing 211 oz 14 dwt and four stands weighing 74 oz 10 dwt (WWM A1204, p. 110). I am very grateful to Ruth Harman, senior archivist, Sheffield Archives, for her generous assistance.

183

· 183 ·

ENTREE DISH

Marked by Robert Hennell (II) (free 1785,
d. 1840)

London, 1820/1

Silver

1973.137a-b

MARKS: on side of dish, maker's mark *RH*
(Grimwade 2332) (repeated on underside of cover
and handle); lion passant (repeated on underside of
cover and handle); leopard's head crowned; date letter *e* (repeated on underside of cover); sovereign's
head (repeated on handle); on handle, possibly
maker's mark *WS*

ARMORIALS: engraved on each side of cover and
body, the arms and crest of Hurd

H. 18.5 cm (7⁵⁄₁₆ in.); w. 24.9 cm (9¹³⁄₁₅ in.); d. 33 cm
(13 in.)

WEIGHT: 1,981.7 gm (63 oz 14 dwt)

PROVENANCE: Lent by Mrs. Henry Lyman, May 1,
1928, Gift of Mrs. Henry Lyman, February 14, 1973

DESCRIPTION: The shallow rectangular dish has
rounded corners with an applied cast border of fluting and scallop shells. The stepped, domed cover,
raised from sheet, has a band of gadrooning and a
detachable cast loop handle rising from a foliate
rosette.

· 184 ·

CASKET

Marked by John Harris (VI) (first mark entered
1818)

London, 1820/1

Silver gilt, lined with wood and velvet

1994.89

MARKS: on lower edge of molding, maker's mark
IH (Grimwade 1819); lion passant; leopard's head
crowned; date letter *e*; sovereign's head

INSCRIPTIONS: incorporated into each of the
twelve panels of interior cover: *Le tems peut nous
detruire mais non pas nous detacher* surrounding initials
in cipher, possibly *FDM*

H. 15 cm (5⅞ in.); w. 32.2 cm (12¹¹⁄₁₆ in.); d. 25.3 cm
(9¹⁵⁄₁₆ in.)

WEIGHT: 5,769.3 gm (185 oz 10 dwt)

PROVENANCE: Chevalier Gregorio Franchi
(1770–1828), sold Christie's, London, May 16, 1827,
lot 99; sold Sotheby's, New York, April 16, 1989, lot
177; Spink & Son, London; Asprey & Co., London;
Titus Kendall, London, purchased May 25, 1994,
Theodora Wilbour Fund in Memory of Charlotte
Beebe Wilbour and Frank Brewer Bemis Fund

EXHIBITED: Lisbon, Gulbenkian Museum, *Portugal
e o Reino Unido: a Aliança Revisitada*, 1994, fig. 21

PUBLISHED: Eleanor H. Gustafson, "Museum
Accessions," *Antiques* 147, no. 3 (March 1995), p. 362

DESCRIPTION: The rectangular box rests on four
detachable lobed feet. The box has broad cast moldings above and below with a string of beads around
the top and bottom edges. The sides of the box are
formed of square panels of intricate geometric
ornament in low relief—four across the front of the
box and three along the sides. The box has two covers assembled on one hinge; the interior cover may
be concealed within the outer cover by a separate
lock. The square panels on the hidden cover are of a
different geometric design, incorporating an interlaced chain with an inscription and at the center
initials in cipher. The panels, separated by plain
moldings, are cast individually from a model that
was pierced and assembled. They are meticulously
finished.

This box was almost certainly a gift from the
great collector and antiquarian William
Beckford (1760–1844) to his agent and com-
panion, Gregorio Franchi. Beckford, who
inherited his father's vast sugar plantations in
the West Indies, was one of the richest men in

184 (see color plate xx)

England.[1] With boundless originality, he spent almost all of his inheritance, much of it on the construction and furnishing of Fonthill Abbey, a massive Gothic residence begun by James Wyatt in 1796. Beckford was a voracious collector, and his acquisitions and commissions reflect the breadth of his intellectual interests. He was among the first connoisseurs to appreciate the merits of antique plate,[2] and he bought French royal furnishings, Chinese and Islamic works of art, pictures, furniture, and books in prodigious quantity. His Gothic novel, *Vathek*, which he began in 1781 or 1782, reflects his taste for the exoticism of Islam, an interest also reflected in the decoration of this box. Because of a homosexual scandal in the 1780s, Beckford remained on the fringes of society, and he became increasingly reclusive

toward the end of his life. The eccentricity of his taste and his controversial lifestyle attracted memorable comment by his contemporaries. William Hazlitt, in a sweeping condemnation, wrote that Fonthill was "a cathedral turned into a toy-shop, an immense museum of all that is most curious and costly, and, at the same time, most worthless, in the production of art and nature."[3]

In 1787 Beckford was introduced to the young Gregorio Franchi, a music student at the Patriarchal Seminary, Lisbon, and the son of Italian immigrants to Portugal.[4] The following year Franchi returned with Beckford to England, and he became a close collaborator in all of Beckford's undertakings. Beckford's first silver acquisitions were French and English pieces in the neoclassical style which he

184

bought while redecorating his father's house, Fonthill Splendens. Soon after the completion of Fonthill Abbey, in about 1812, Beckford began to order modern silver.[5] Letters exchanged between Franchi and Beckford, discussing in detail their orders for plate, often illustrated with small sketches, reveal a deep involvement with the designs of these objects. These include some of the earliest examples of historicist silver known in England, and the group as a whole reveals the extraordinary originality of Beckford's interests. Most distinctive is a group of richly mounted agate, porcelain, and jade vessels, many marked by John Robins, James Aldridge, or John Harris, who marked this box. By 1820 the state of Beckford's finances had become unstable, though he continued to order silver for which he had to struggle to pay.[6]

Like other pieces commissioned by Beckford, this box is highly original in design. The hinged cover of the box hides a second cover on the interior, secured with a second lock. The square panels of the hidden cover are filled with interlacing ribbons surrounding a cipher and containing the motto "Le tems [*sic*] peut nous detruire mais non pas nous detacher" (Time may destroy us but cannot separate us). The panels of geometric tracery suggest the interlace patterns of Arabic calligraphy, a tradition that also had flourished in Renaissance Nuremberg. The interlaced knot, often used as a symbol of divine revelation, must have been chosen as an especially appropriate vehicle for the motto.[7] One possible source for the design of this box is Indo-Portuguese filigree work, which Beckford may have seen on one of his many periods of residence in Lisbon.[8]

The significance of the cipher at the center of the interlaced motto remains unclear. The initials might be read as *G*, *F*, *V*, in which case, as Clive Wainwright proposed, they might stand for Gregorio Franchi and Vathek or Viator, pseudonyms Beckford often used.[9] Although the *F* is clear enough, it seems more likely that the cipher includes the letters *D* and *M*. The interpretation of these initials remains obscure, and they may refer to any of a large number of pet names Beckford and Franchi used for each other, or even to characters in Beckford's writings. The motto itself may also have a literary source, but it is not an obvious one. The eccentric spelling of the word *tems* suggests an early French text, and the phrase may be derived from something obscure in Beckford's vast library of twenty thousand volumes.[10] Another possible source might be an epitaph collected by Beckford, who published a group of mostly amusing epitaphs that he claimed were recorded in local churchyards.[11]

In spite of the promise of the motto hidden in the box, Beckford did eventually abandon Franchi. Impoverished, Franchi withdrew to apartments in Baker Street and sold his collection in 1826. The auction included enamels, ivories, maiolica, and mounted jasper and lapis. This box was described as a jewel chest in the Moorish taste, and the inside of the outer cover was apparently fitted with a "delicately gilt frame for a portrait," now missing. It achieved the highest price in the sale, and the purchaser was recorded as "Fles," possibly a coded name indicating that Christie had bought it on behalf of Beckford, or for Franchi himself.[12]

1. The association of the box with Gregorio Franchi was made by Clive Wainwright, who identified it in the sale of Franchi's possessions. There are many histories of Beckford, some based on the voluminous writings that he left. See Boyd Alexander, *Life at Fonthill, 1807–1822* (London, 1957); Boyd Alexander, *England's Wealthiest Son: A Study of William Beckford* (London, 1962).

2. John F. Hayward, "Royal Plate at Fonthill," *Burlington Magazine* 10 (1959), p. 145.

3. William Hazlitt, *Criticisms on Art and Sketches of the Picture Galleries of England* (London, 1856), p. 284.

4. Boyd Alexander, *From Lisbon to Baker Street: The Story of the Chevalier Franchi, Beckford's Friend* (Lisbon, 1977), pp. 7–8.

5. Clive Wainwright, "Some Objects from William Beckford's Collection Now in the Victoria and Albert Museum," *Burlington Magazine* 113 (May 1971), pp. 254–64; Michael Snodin and Malcolm Baker, "William Beckford's Silver," parts 1 and 2, *Burlington Magazine* 122 (November 1980), pp. 735–48, and (December 1980), pp. 820–34. Also see the exh., London, Spink and Son, *Beckford and Hamilton Silver from Brodick Castle*, 1980.

6. In 1819 Beckford wrote to Franchi: "Cup, goblets, the Queen's salvers, harpsichord, china for sweet-meats, massive objects from Ceylon, Cuttel, Coulson, Aldridge and Fogg [jewelers and goldsmiths]—all are crying out 'Pay me! Pay me!' And how to pay I no longer know." Alexander, *Life at Fonthill*, p. 323.

7. See Alain Gruber, ed., *The Renaissance and Mannerism in Europe* (New York, 1993), pp. 29, 44–45.

8. This suggestion was made to me by Philip Hewat-Jaboor, who was extremely helpful to me on the subject. See *Ourivesaria Portuguesa no Museu de Arte Antiga* (Lisbon, 1984), fig. 15. A roughly similar basic design formula—a rectangular box resting on fluted bun feet and divided into panels filled with rich geometric ornament—is applied to a pair of gilt wood coffers, now in the Wallace Collection, that were ordered by Beckford at the same time as the silver box. See Peter Hughes, *The Wallace Collection: Catalogue of Furniture* (London, 1996), vol. 1, pp. 249–53. Though executed on a completely different scale, the diapered panels of the coffers are framed above and below with a border of simulated jewels, similar to that on the box.

9. Lisbon, Gulbenkian Museum, *Portugal e o Reino Unido: a Aliança Revisitada*, 1994, p. 96.

10. The library was sold by Phillips, London, September 9, 1823.

11. Signing his name Viator, Beckford submitted a collection of epitaphs to the *Literary Gazette*, published March 8 and April 5, 1823. He also published a small pamphlet of epitaphs, the manuscript draft for which is in the Bodleian Library, Oxford, MS Beckford d. 21 fol. 68. The verses, in English, are mainly humerous and naive, and not in keeping with the somber tone of the motto on the box.

12. Beckford, who had sold Fonthill and its contents to John Farquhar in 1822, removed some of his treasures to Lansdowne Tower, Bath. Farquhar, in 1823, sold off the contents of Fonthill, and Beckford bought some of them back. An inventory of possessions taken after Beckford's death in 1844 does not include the box.

· 185 ·

SALVER

Marked by Paul Storr (1771–1844)
London, 1823/4
Silver
55.918

MARKS: on underside of salver, maker's mark *PS* (Grimwade 2235) (repeated on border); lion passant (repeated on border); leopard's head; date letter *h* (repeated on border); sovereign's head (repeated on border)

ARMORIALS: arms of Ffarington quartering Benson, Rufine, Bradshaw, Bradshaw (ancient), Aspull, Fitton, Garden, Malvoisin, Brereton, Nowell, Merely, Fitton, Hargreaves, and Ffarington for William Ffarington, Esq., of Shaw Hall, co. Lancaster (1766–1837); motto: *Domat omnia virtus*

H. 6.9 cm (2¾ in.); diam. 66.3 cm (26 in.)

WEIGHT: 7,867.2 gm (252 oz 19 dwt)

PROVENANCE: purchased from Garrard & Co., London, September 15, 1955, Theodora Wilbour Fund in Memory of Charlotte Beebe Wilbour

EXHIBITED: New York, The Frick Collection, *English Silver*, 1978, cat. 19

DESCRIPTION: The circular salver has a broad, richly decorated rim with four cast scrolled feet. The rim, cast in sections and chased, is modeled with female masks at the feet that represent the Seasons. On the border between them, amid scrolls and shells, are fruits, flowers, foliage, and animals (birds, sheep, a rabbit, and a dog), also symbolizing the Seasons. The tray of the salver is chased with the signs of the zodiac enclosed by scrolls and flowers, at the center of which is engraved a coat of arms in a plain reserve. The edge of the tray is secured on the underside by a strip of sheet soldered onto the rim and hammered over the rim.

This salver and its mate in the Gans collection at the Virginia Museum of Fine Arts[1] are among the most exuberant examples of Paul Storr's work in the rococo-revival style. In an effort to suggest the riot of organic and abstract forms used by such mid-eighteenth-century makers as Paul de Lamerie, the modeler of this dense border has reduced the scrolls and leaves to surface ornament, misunderstanding the sculptural rhythm of the rococo. Storr, however, would have had easy access to superb examples of eighteenth-century plate, should he have wanted to produce a simple copy. The

rococo revival, like other historicizing styles, was intended to evoke and exceed the lavish prosperity of an earlier age, not to duplicate it.

Storr, having broken off his partnership with Rundell & Bridge in 1819, was nonetheless in charge of a large shop on Harrison Street, and he remained an integral part of the manufacturing trade. The classical designs provided by William Theed (1804–1891), John Flaxman (1755–1826), and Thomas Stothard (1755–1834) at Rundell's were no longer supplied to him, and during this period Storr began to produce rococo fantasies. The identities of his designers or modelers are not known, but it is clear that he had a steady supply of eighteenth-century plate from which to draw inspiration. In 1822 he entered into partnership with John Mortimer, who provided the retail outlet for his wares.[2]

Two other salvers, dated 1827 and presumably made as a pair, are known. One is in the Yale University Art Gallery and is engraved with an unidentified coat of arms.[3] The second, with a later monogram in the center, was sold from the Morgan collection in 1947.[4] Although the central panels follow the same design as the present salver, with small variations in the choice of ornament, the borders have been greatly simplified. The maker retained the four female heads representing the Seasons and the animals in cartouches between them, but eliminated the dense scrolls and shells.

The engraved arms are those of William Ffarington, Esq., of Shaw Hall. Ffarington served as lieutenant colonel of the first regiment of the Lancashire militia and in 1813 was appointed high sheriff of Lancashire. He married first Sybella Georgiana (d. 1799), daughter of Edward-Bootle Wilbraham, and in 1803 he married Hannah, daughter of John Mathews, Esq., of Tynemouth. As Joseph Bliss suggests, these salvers were certainly made as sideboard plate, not as part of a tea service, as their eighteenth-century prototypes would have been.[5]

1. Illus. Joseph Bliss, *The Jerome and Rita Gans Collection of English Silver on Loan to the Virginia Museum of Fine Arts* (New York, 1992), pp. 156–59, cat. 54.

2. Culme 1977, p. 79.

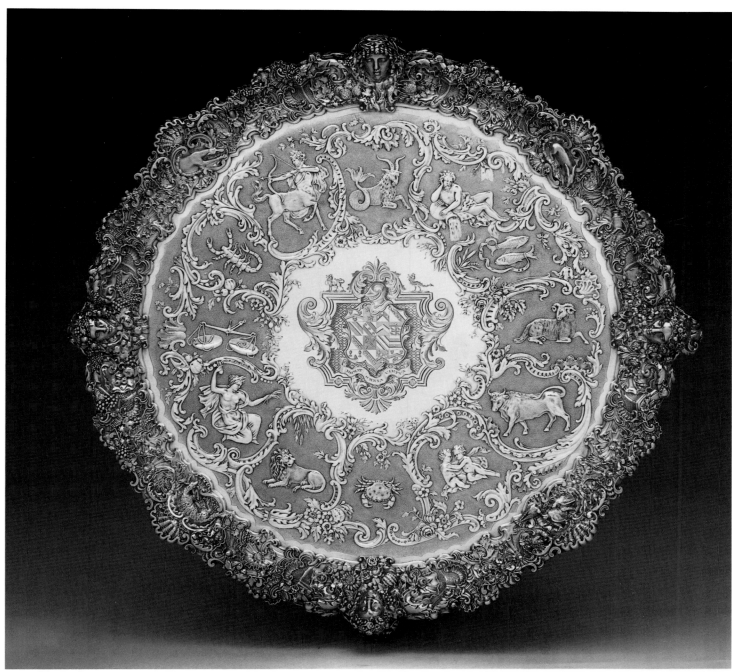

185 (see color plate XXI)

3. Acc. no. 1948.187, illus. Janine Ellen Skerry, "Paul Storr Silver in the Yale University Art Gallery," *Yale University Art Gallery Bulletin* 38, no. 1 (Fall 1980), p. 25. My thanks to Patricia Kane, curator of decorative arts at the Yale University Art Gallery, for making it available to me.

4. Parke-Bernet, New York, October 30, 1947, lot 166.

5. Bliss, *The Jerome and Rita Gans Collection*, p. 159.

· 186 ·

PAIR OF CANDLESTICKS
Marked by Paul Storr (1771–1844)
London, 1823/4
Silver gilt
66.436-437

MARKS: on underside of each base, maker's mark *PS* (Grimwade 2235) (repeated on bezel of each waxpan); lion passant (repeated on bezel of each waxpan); leopard's head; date letter *h* (repeated on bezel of each waxpan); sovereign's head (repeated on bezel of each waxpan)

ARMORIALS: engraved on the underside of one foot on each candlestick, *GB* in cipher with a duke's coronet above[1]

INSCRIPTIONS: 66.436: engraved on bezel of waxpan, *2*, engraved on nozzle where waxpan sits, *2*. 66.437: engraved on bezel of waxpan, *1*, engraved on nozzle where waxpan sits, *1*

66.436: H. 23.9 cm (9⁷⁄₁₆ in.); w. 12.8 cm (5¹⁄₁₆ in.)

66.437: H. 23.9 cm (9⁷⁄₁₆ in.); w. 12.7 cm (5 in.)

WEIGHT: 1966.436: 504.6 gm (16 oz 4 dwt). 1966.437: 504.6 gm (16 oz 4 dwt)

PROVENANCE: sold Sotheby's, March 31, 1966, lot 111; S. J. Phillips, Ltd., London, purchased September 16, 1966, Theodora Wilbour Fund in Memory of Charlotte Beebe Wilbour

EXHIBITED: Indianapolis, Indiana, Indianapolis Museum of Art, *Paul Storr Silver in American Collections*, 1972, cat. 62

PUBLISHED: Sarah B. Sherrill, "Current and Coming," *Antiques* (February 1972), illus. p. 278; Brett 1986, no. 1279

DESCRIPTION: Each candlestick rests on a base composed of three cast crouching lion's legs, with a cast palmette at the join. The shaft of the candlestick is modeled as a tree trunk, cast and chased, with a cast serpent coiled around the trunk. The cast urn-shaped nozzle is embellished with foliage and is fitted with a removable gadrooned waxpan.

Like many of Paul Storr's more successful works, this pair of candlesticks has a direct archaeological antecedent, in this case Etruscan bronze candelabra, produced from the fifth century B.C.[2] Storr took a particular interest in antique lamp and candelabra design, and most of the design elements of this model, such as the stylized crouching lion's paws in triangular

formation, the anthemion leaf at the join of each leg, and the collar of petals at the base of the column, are borrowed directly.[3] By 1823, the year these candlesticks were marked, Paul Storr had been independent of Phillip Rundell and John Bridge for four years. The conception may predate the breakup of the partnership. In 1811 the Prince Regent purchased a massive quantity of plate from Rundell, Bridge & Rundell for Carlton House including a pair of gilt bronze candelabra fundamentally similar to the present pair that are described in the invoice as "after those found in the ruins of Herculaneum."[4] The Prince Regent's models were monumental, like their Etruscan ancestors, standing nearly sixty inches high. As Geoffrey de Bellaigue has suggested, Rundell's most likely based their design on one published in a volume recording the excavated antiquities from Pompeii.[5] Storr's design for the present pair, which he seems not to have produced in large quantity, differs in its details, most strikingly in the treatment of the column as a tree and the addition of the snake. The latter may have been suggested by other antique designs for lamps or perfume burners,[6] but Rundell's in 1809 also supplied the Prince Regent with a pair of candelabra designed by John Flaxman (1755–1826) representing the Garden of the Hesperides, with a serpent descending the stem.[7]

The model was revived in the 1840s, when a set, marked by Thomas Smiley, was given by Josiah Wedgwood II, son of the founder of the manufactory, to a relative, the philosopher and lawyer Robert J. Mackintosh.[8]

1. These initials engraved on a spice box by Kandler, sold from the same property in 1966, were proposed by Michael Clayton to signify Georgina, wife of the sixth duke of Bedford. The spice box is now in the collection of Alan and Simone Hartman, illus. Hartop 1996, p. 187, cat. 34.

2. Eric Hostetter, *Bronzes from Spina* (Mainz am Rhein, 1986), vol. 1, fig. 21; Sybille Haynes, *Etruscan Bronzes* (London, 1985), p. 230, cat. 181. My thanks to John Hermann, curator of classical art at the MFA, for his assistance.

3. Vittorio Spinazzola, *Le Arti Decorative in Pompei* (Milan, 1928), p. 294.

186

4. Exh. London, Queen's Gallery, *Carlton House: The Past Glories of George IV's Palace*, 1991, p. 43, cat. 43.

5. Geoffrey de Bellaigue, *Delle Antichità di Ercolano*, vol. 8, . . . *delle Lucerne, delle Lanterne, e de' Candelabri* (1792), pls. 77, 92. Vuilliamy also published a design for one of the Herculaneum candelabra in 1825. See Lewis Vuilliamy, *Examples of Ornamental Sculpture in Architecture* (London, 1825), pl. 2.

6. Raffaele Gariulo, *Receuil des Monumens les plus intéressans du Musée National* (Naples, 1863), vol. 1, pl. 36.

7. Collection of Her Majesty the Queen, illus. Norman M. Penzer, *Paul Storr, the Last of the Goldsmiths* (London, 1954), pl. 28.

8. Sold Sotheby's, New York, April 12, 1995, lot 227.

· 187 ·

PAIR OF SALTS

Marked by Edward Farrell (first mark entered 1813)
London, 1824/5
Silver gilt
1989.313–314

MARKS: 1989.313: to right of handle, lion passant; leopard's head; date letter *i*; sovereign's head; to left of handle, maker's mark *EF* (Grimwade 585). 1989.314: to left of handle, lion passant; leopard's head; date letter *i*; sovereign's head; marker's mark *EF*

ARMORIALS: engraved on the lip of both salts to the right of the handle, the royal crest with the Garter motto, surmounted by a royal coronet, for the duke of York

1989.313: H. 22.2 cm (8¾ in.); w. 16.5 cm (6½ in.); d. 9.3 cm (3¹¹⁄₁₆ in.)

1989.314: H. 22.2 cm (8¾ in.); w. 16.5 cm (6½ in.); d. 9.3 cm (3¹¹⁄₁₆ in.)

WEIGHT: 1989.313: 1,077.3 gm (34 oz 13 dwt). 1989.314: 1,111.3 gm (35 oz 15 dwt)

PROVENANCE: Frederick Augustus, duke of York (1763–1827), sold Christie's, London, March 19, 1827, lots 85–86; the Rt. Hon. Earl Howe, sold Christie's, London, July 1, 1953, lot 109; collection of the late Villiers David, Esq., sold Christie's, London, November 27, 1985, lot 122; Museumpiece, Zurich, 1986, James Robinson, Inc., New York, purchased October 25, 1989, Theodora Wilbour Fund in Memory of Charlotte Beebe Wilbour

PUBLISHED: Richard Stone, "A Noble Imposture: The Fonthill Ewer and Early Nineteenth-Century Fakery," *The Metropolitan Museum Journal* 32 (1997), p. 192, fig. 40

DESCRIPTION: Each salt is composed of a spiral shell with a fluted lip on clawed legs. Beneath the lip of the salt is a bearded, turbaned demifigure. The whole rests on a base formed of a tortoise. The handle is formed from the serpent's tail of a fantastic winged creature who perches, as the thumbpiece of the salt, blowing a conch shell. The salt is assembled from heavily cast components, richly chased and thickly gilt.

These extraordinary mannerist-revival salts were made for Frederick Augustus, duke of York, second and favorite son of George III. Marked by the eclectic and unrestrained maker Edward Farrell, they were almost certainly

ordered from Kensington Lewis, a flamboyant retailer and pioneer of historicism. This triangle—patron, retailer, and maker—produced some of the most innovative and influential silver of the first half of the nineteenth century.

Soon after his birth, the duke of York was elected to the lucrative position of prince-bishop of Osnabrück.[1] At the age of seventeen he was sent to Germany and groomed for a military career. Although he did not distinguish himself in his first campaigns in the war with France, he was nonetheless appointed commander in chief of the army in 1798, and he eventually established a reputation as an inspired organizer of the troops. In spite of a scandal in 1809 involving his mistress, Mary Anne Clarke, who admitted receiving cash from officers whom she recommended to the duke for promotions, he was widely liked. His income as duke of York, £12,000, was supplemented by £40,000 on his marriage to Princess Frederica of Prussia in 1791, and by another £10,000 in 1818 when he was appointed guardian of the person of the king. As a reckless gambler, a devoted horseman, and renowned bon vivant, however, his expenses were enormous. In 1813, after a party celebrating the regent's birthday, Princess Charlotte wrote that the royal brothers were so drunk that they fell off their chairs, and the duke of York "fell over the back of his chair against a wine cooler and cut his head a good deal, and in recovering himself pulled the tablecloth and all the things upon him."[2] His debts had accrued to the point that in 1827, during his final, protracted illness, the *Times* wrote that he lay dying "with neither house, nor furniture, nor horses, nor tangible property of any kind incidental to the condition of a gentleman."[3] Estimations of his debt at the time of his death range from £200,000 to £500,000, and, with creditors competing for compensation, it was decided to sell the extensive collections of silver, furniture, pictures, and armor. In a four-day sale at Christie's[4] the duke's silver and silver gilt were sold for a total of £22,438 10s., with many pieces bringing only a fraction of what the duke had paid.[5] The sale attracted considerable public attention and fueled the growing fascination with antiquarian and historicist works of art.

187 (see color plate XXII)

The duke's tastes in silver were distinct and very new. Appreciation of antique silver was in its infancy, and the sale in 1816 of the collection of the duke of Norfolk contributed greatly to public enthusiasm.[6] In addition to a large group of French plate, the duke of York's collection included large holdings of buffet plate and table wares modeled with classical subjects and executed on a vast scale. Many of these were bought through Kensington Lewis, an enterprising retailer who built a lucrative business supplying antique plate, refurbished antique plate, and historicizing plate to the circle of collectors that included the duke of York and George IV.[7] Lewis's best client was certainly the duke of York, and of the objects sold by the duke's estate in 1827, eleven pieces marked by Farrell, including the present salts, have been identified.[8] The grandest of these is the candelabrum depicting Hercules Attacking the Hydra, now in the collection of Audrey Love.[9] The present pair of salts was part of a set of twelve, sold in two lots of six. The spoons,

"with vines in fruit, and figures" were sold separately.[10] Farrell used the same model for spoons that accompanied a related set of salts depicting Neptune, Amphitrite, Tritons, and Nereids astride dolphins and seahorses.[11]

Farrell's productions for Kensington Lewis reveal a liberal, almost indiscriminate use of diverse stylistic sources. The earliest date of their collaboration is uncertain, but it appears to have flourished for only about a decade, between about 1817 and 1827. Lewis sometimes bought antique pieces that were refitted by Farrell, exemplified by the pair of pilgrim bottles in the Gilbert collection made to incorporate seventeenth-century plaques.[12] As on the tureens and stands made for the duke of York,[13] they sometimes devised a dense conglomeration of rococo motifs. Their most successful works drew heavily on mannerist conceits. The present salts in the form of ewers combine elements from designs by Cornelius Floris (1514–1575) published in Antwerp in 1548.[14] From these, Lewis and Farrell borrowed the tortoise base, the shell-shaped vessel, and the ribbed lip. Floris's designs had some influence in England in the sixteenth century, as, for example, in the mounted agate ewer and basin at Belvoir Castle; Farrell may have had some familiarity with such objects.[15] Another single salt, apparently from the duke of York's set of twelve, but with the engraved crest removed, has appeared recently on the market,[16] and another example of the model, chased quite differently, has also come to light.[17]

1. Biographical material is from Sidney Lee, ed., *Dictionary of National Biography* (London, 1901), vol. 7, pp. 673–75, and Roger Fulford, *Royal Dukes: The Father and Uncles of Queen Victoria* (London, 1973), pp. 52–101.

2. Quoted in Clare Tomalin, *Mrs Jordan's Profession* (London, 1995), p. 276.

3. Quoted Fulford, *Royal Dukes*, p. 99.

4. Christie's, London, March 19–22, 1827.

5. Phillips and Sloane 1997, pp. 62–67.

6. See John Culme, *Attitudes to Old Plate, 1750–1900* (London, 1985).

7. See John Culme, "Kensington Lewis, a Nineteenth Century Businessman," *The Connoisseur* 190, no. 763 (1975), pp. 26–41.

8. See ibid., p. 31, and Phillips and Sloane 1997, p. 67 n. 10.

9. Phillips and Sloane 1997, pp. 62–67, cat. 12.

10. Christie's, London, March 19, 1827, lots 85–88.

11. The twelve from the duke of York's collection (lots 71–74) were subsequently bought by Victor Rothschild. Another set of twelve is in the Audrey Love collection, and a set of eight is at Burghley House. See Phillips and Sloane 1997, pp. 76–77, cat. 16.

12. See Schroder 1988a, pp. 452–58, cat. 122.

13. Sold Christie's, New York, October 15, 1985, lots 199–200.

14. See John F. Hayward, *Virtuoso Goldsmiths and the Triumph of Mannerism, 1540–1620* (London, 1976), p. 356, pls. 196–99. Floris's designs are inspired by Enea Vico (1523–1567).

15. Exh. Washington, D.C., National Gallery of Art, *The Treasure Houses of Britain: Five Hundred Years of Patronage and Art Collecting*, 1985, p. 104, cat. 27.

16. With James Robinson, Inc., New York. I am grateful to Edward Munves for allowing me to study it.

17. Sold Sotheby's, New York, October 12, 1990, lot 240.

· 188 ·

PAIR OF SALTS

Marked by Benjamin Smith (III) (1793–1850)
London, 1826/7
Silver gilt
69.1147–1148

MARKS: on base of each, maker's mark *BS* (similar to Grimwade 236)[1] (repeated on dolphin tail, side of shell, stem, and side of liner); sovereign's head (repeated on dolphin tail, coil of shell, and side of liner); lion passant (repeated on dolphin tail, coil of shell, side of liner, and on screw); date letter *l* (repeated on side of liner)

ARMORIALS: engraved on underside of each base and on outside of liners, an unidentified crest (an eagle's head ermine charged with a fountain and holding in the beak three ears of corn)

INSCRIPTIONS: 69.1147, stamped on base, underside of dolphin, stem of shell, and side of liner, *3*. 69.1148, stamped on base, underside of dolphin, stem of shell, and side of liner, *4*

69.1147: H. 6.4 cm (2½ in.); w. 10.4 cm (4⅛ in.); d. 7.3 cm (2⅞ in.)

69.1148: H. 6.5 cm (2⁹⁄₁₆ in.); w. 10.3 cm (4¹⁄₁₆ in.); d. 7.2 cm (2¹³⁄₁₆ in.)

WEIGHT: 69.1147: 323.2 gm (10 oz 8 dwt). 69.1148: 323.2 gm (10 oz 8 dwt)

PROVENANCE: Firestone and Parson, Inc., Boston, purchased October 15, 1969, Theodora Wilbour Fund in Memory of Charlotte Beebe Wilbour

DESCRIPTION: The vessel of each salt is in the form of a shell, cast in two pieces, seamed, and finely chased. A wrought liner slips into the open shell. The shell rests on the back of a cast dolphin, whose tail curls around the shell. The dolphin is pinned and bolted through the oval base, which is chased with stylized waves. The gilding appears to have been renewed.

The earliest salts of this model are marked for 1814 by Benjamin Smith II,[2] but the form was apparently renewed a decade later by his son, Benjamin III. Benjamin Smith II had worked for Rundell, Bridge & Rundell from 1802 or 1803 until 1814. His partner, Digby Scott, left the business in 1807. Smith ran a workshop in Greenwich, executing, like his counterpart Paul Storr, the massive commissions provided by the royal goldsmiths. Smith's son, Benjamin III, after completing his apprenticeship with his

188

father, worked with him for two years before entering his own mark.[3] The salts are thematically related to two huge groups of salts produced by Paul Storr for the Prince of Wales in 1811 and 1813.[4] Incorporating Tritons, they were probably designed by William Theed, one of several eminent members of the Royal Academy employed by Rundell's to raise the quality of design and modeling. Rundell's introduced a whole range of models with marine motifs, which show an awareness of the centerpiece made for Frederick, Prince of Wales,[5] as well as the mannerist sculpture from which it was derived.

1. The mark looks like the one entered by Benjamin Smith II in 1812, but given the date of the salts, 1826, it is ascribed to his son, Benjamin III. It may be the smaller mark not illustrated by Grimwade.

2. See a pair sold Sotheby's, New York, April 27, 1990, lot 342, and a set of four, sold Sotheby's, New York, April 23, 1993, lot 435.

3. Grimwade 1990, pp. 661–62.

4. Exh. London, Queen's Gallery, *Carlton House: The Past Glories of George IV's Palace*, 1991, pp. 124, 133, cats. 80, 95. Also see the discussion of the model in Phillips and Sloane 1997, pp. 47–49, cats. 6–7.

5. Exh. London, Queen's Gallery, *Treasures from the Royal Collection*, 1988, p. 119, cat. 114.

189

· 189 ·

CHAMBERLAIN'S KEY
London, 1833/4
Silver gilt
1975.317

MARKS: on shaft, maker's mark *RI* with a pellet between in a square shield (unrecorded); sovereign's head; lion passant; date letter *s*; leopard's head

L. 17.5 cm (6⅞ in.); w. 5.8 cm (2⁵⁄₁₆ in.)

WEIGHT: 161.6 gm (5 oz 4 dwt)

PROVENANCE: Nicolas E. Landau, Paris, purchased May 14, 1975, Theodora Wilbour Fund in Memory of Charlotte Beebe Wilbour

DESCRIPTION: The shaft of the key, which is cast in sections, is of baluster form, with horizontal bands of beading and a section of vertical fluting. The key tongue is a square, openwork foliate trellis pattern. The handle is in the form of a cartouche framing an openwork monogram for William IV, surmounted by the royal crown.

In the complex figural decoration of the bow this ceremonial key echoes French and English seventeenth-century designs, grander examples of which incorporated a monogram.[1] In this case, the monogram is that of William IV, surmounted by a crown. Such keys must have been made in some quantity for presentation. Two (marked for 1834/5) are in the royal collection,[2] and a third, set with diamonds, emeralds, and rubies, was sold in 1970.[3] A fourth key was on the market in 1988.[4]

It is likely that these objects are associated with the chamberlain's ceremonial duties. The lord great chamberlain and the lord chamberlain still wear keys to Westminster and Buckingham Palace, respectively, on a rosette on the back of their court dress. The keys are considered the personal possession of the office holders.[5] In the seventeenth century, the lord chamberlain wore the key on a girdle, as shown in Anthony van Dyck's portrait of Edward Sackville, fourth earl of Dorset (1590–1652), Charles I's lord chamberlain.[6]

These ceremonial keys might alternatively have been used to mark the presentation of the freedom of a city. At the opening of London Bridge in 1831, for example, William IV was presented with the sword, keys to the city, and commemorative medals by the lord mayor. The king invited the mayor to keep the sword and keys, and he later distributed to the spectators the commemorative medals with which he had been presented.[7]

1. Edgar B. Frank, *Old French Ironwork* (Cambridge, Mass., 1950), pls. 36–37.

2. Inventory reference 70442.1–2. I am grateful to Hugh Roberts, director of the royal collection, for having provided this information.

3. Sotheby's, London, November 12, 1970, lot 60.

4. Correspondence in the curatorial file.

5. I am grateful to David Rankin-Hunt, administrator of the royal collection, for offering this information. The lord great chamberlain is responsible for arranging royal occasions at Westminster, and the lord chamberlain is considered the senior member of the sovereign's household. Both offices are hereditary.

6. Illus. Emil Schaeffer, *Van Dyck* (Stuttgart, 1909), p. 403. The key itself is attached to the frame of the picture. This was pointed out to me by David Starkey, president, Society for Court Studies, who kindly pursued my inquiry.

7. John Ashton, *When William IV Was King* (New York, 1896), pp. 63–65.

190

· 190 ·

MUSTARD POT

Marked by John Figg (first mark entered 1834)
London, 1843/4
Silver, glass
1980.265

MARKS: on underside, maker's mark *IF* (Grimwade 1306) (repeated inside cover); lion passant (repeated inside cover); leopard's head; date letter *h* (repeated inside cover); sovereign's head

ARMORIALS: engraved on cover, an unidentified crest (a gloved hand holding a cross flory)

INSCRIPTIONS: scratched on underside, *No 39 CG, No 1*

H. 9.9 cm (3⅞ in.); w. 11.1 cm (4⅜ in.); d. 6.5 cm (2⁵⁄₁₆ in.)

WEIGHT: 133.2 gm (4 oz 6 dwt)

PROVENANCE: Gift of Mr. William O. Taylor, June 18, 1980

DESCRIPTION: The octagonal straight-sided body is pierced overall with geometric scrolls. Formed from seamed sheet, it has applied moldings on the foot and upper rim. The peaked octagonal cover is hinged to a double-scroll handle. Engraved on each panel of the cover is a stylized flower and at the center is an octagonal baluster finial. An octagonal blue glass liner fits inside the silver body.

· 191 ·

GAME DISH

Marked by John Samuel Hunt (d. 1865)
London, 1846/7
Silver, parcel gilt
1993.575

MARKS: on side of dish, lion passant (repeated on finial, underside of stand, one wing of each angel, heater, and all original nuts); leopard's head (repeated on heater); date letter *L* (repeated on underside of stand and heater); sovereign's head (repeated on finial, underside of stand, and heater); maker's mark *ISH* (Culme 8358) (repeated on finial, underside of stand, one wing of each angel, and underside of heater)

ARMORIALS: cast and engraved on a shield held by putti, the arms, crest, and motto of Hope, probably for John Alexander Hope, sixth earl of Hopetoun (1831–1873)

INSCRIPTIONS: stamped on underside of dish, *2959 HUNT & ROSKELL LATE STORR MORTIMER & HUNT*

H. 41.3 cm (16¼ in.); w. 49.4 cm (19½ in.); d. 28.5 cm (11¼ in.)

WEIGHT: 10,872.3 gm (349 oz 11 dwt)

PROVENANCE: sold Christie's, London, May 21, 1969, lot 162, purchased by Ferrara; estate of Scott Newhall, sold Christie's, New York, April 22, 1993, lot 296, purchased by Partridge Fine Arts, PLC, London, purchased September 22, 1993, John H. and Ernestine A. Payne Fund

PUBLISHED: Clayton 1985b, p. 295; Eleanor Gustafson, "Museum Accessions," *Antiques* (March 1995), p. 362

DESCRIPTION: The dish consists of three sections: a base supported on scrolled legs, a removable dish, and a domed cover. The base, formed from several panels of sheet, has a shaped oval stand, richly decorated with panels of chased strapwork and a border of palmettes with bosses in the form of masks. Bolted to the front and back edges of the stand are winged putti, cast in several sections, each holding a dove and a bow and wearing a quiver. Two bifurcated scrolled legs, cast in several pieces, rise to support the plateau. They are studded with quatrefoils, masks, diamonds, and beading. A cast snake encircles each leg, and small squirrels and lizards perch on the termini. Two projecting handles formed of a winged female figure and a scroll anchor the edge of the plateau. The base of the plateau, formed from sections of sheet and chased, has a heavy baluster pendant that hangs below the dish between the legs. It

is cast in two pieces. A plain oval heater rests on a wire rim within the plateau. It is formed of sheet and filled with sand. At the center of the underside is a shallow dome, possibly to accommodate an additional heating element stored in the pendant. The shaped oval dish has a broad molded border chased with scrolled foliage enclosing animal heads and a cast outer border of rosettes alternating with masks. Conjoined scrolls form a handle at each end. The domed bombé cover has an applied flaring rim with an ovolo border. The cover is chased overall with arabesques against a matted ground with an oval reserve at each side enclosing a monogram. The removable cast finial is modeled as a group of dead game birds.

The pair to this covered game dish is in the National Museum of Scotland. The removable plateau conceals a heater filled with sand, a practical feature that is unexpected in such a decorative form. The putti suspended from the sides bear shields with the arms of Hope, presumably for John Alexander, sixth earl of Hopetoun, who succeeded to the peerage on the death in 1843 of his father. In 1860 he married Etheldred Anne, daughter of Charles-Thomas Samuel Birch-Reynardson of Holywell Hall, co. Lincolnshire. He served as an officer in the 1st Life Guards and as lord lieutenant of Linlithgowshire in 1863. The game dishes were probably intended for use in the state dining room at Hopetoun House, the vast Palladian palace created by William and Robert Adam for the first earl. The state dining room, converted in about 1820 from a state bedchamber and a closet, was richly decorated in the late Regency taste, and George IV was received there in 1822.[1]

The flamboyant mannerist-revival style of this game dish is precocious. Only a few makers of the first half of the nineteenth century, most notably Edward Farrell,[2] exploited mannerist sources in favor of the antique. This game dish anticipates in its excess the Victorian exhibition pieces produced in the second half of the century, although the intricacy of the casting and degree of finish are up to the standard of Regency work. The inhabited scrolls that form the supports and the chased arabesque surface recall Nuremberg designs of

the sixteenth century. These would have been available to the London makers in prints,[3] but original works were also admired and their attributions discussed. The nautilus cup by Nicholas Schmidt (d. 1609), for example, bought by George IV from Rundell's in 1823, was thought by John Flaxman (1755–1826) to have been the work of Benvenuto Cellini (1500–1571).[4] The intertwined snakes, lizards, birds, and beading on the game dish suggest the influence of works by Christoph Jamnitzer (1563–1618).[5] In the originality of its conception and in the quality of its execution, this game dish can be compared with Hunt and Roskell's other extremely ambitious works, such as the shell coffee and tea service of 1849 in the Love collection.[6] Hunt and Roskell, successors to Storr, Mortimer, and Hunt, had retail premises on New Bond Street employing thirty-five people and a manufactory at 26 Harrison Street, where between eighty and one hundred people worked.[7] Descriptions of the extensive workshops recorded in 1865, and published by John Culme, reflect the romantic impressions of a visitor and suggest that Hunt and Roskell's productions had the desired impact: "[The chasing room] is a very interesting department, as every variety of chasing and finishing . . . are going on. Here is a stag's head, whereon every hair is being carefully and delicately made out; there an elaborate piece of arabesque tracery or floriated ornament is being perfected."[8]

1. Silver sold by the marquess of Linlithgow (Christie's, London, June 15, 1977) included only a few pieces of Victorian plate, so it is difficult to gain a sense of the mid-nineteenth-century furnishings.

2. See, for example, the duke of York's centerpiece, Phillips and Sloane 1997, cat. 12.

3. See the designs of Georg Wechter and Paulus Flindt II, for example, exh. Nuremberg, Germanisches Nationalmuseum, *Wenzel Jamnitzer und die Nürnberger Goldschmiedekunst, 1500–1700,* 1985, cats. 396, 419.

4. H. M. Queen Elizabeth II, exh. London, Queen's Gallery, *Carlton House: The Past Glories of George IV's Palace,* 1991, p. 187, cat. 162.

5. See the ewers by Christoph Jamnitzer in the

191 (see color plate XXIII)

Kunsthistorisches Museum, Vienna, and the Grünes Gewölbe, Dresden, for example, exh. Nuremberg, Germanisches Nationalmuseum, *Wenzel Jamnitzer und die Nürnberger Goldschmiedekunst 1500–1700*, 1985, cat. 89, fig. 26.

6. Phillips and Sloane 1997, cat. 23.

7. Culme 1987, vol. 1, p. 245.

8. Quoted by Culme 1977, p. 45.

192

· 192 ·

EPERGNE
Marked by John Samuel Hunt (d. 1865)
London, 1848/9
Silver, glass
64.128a–c

MARKS: on edge of rocky base, maker's mark *ISH* (Culme 8350) (repeated on underside of base), lion passant (repeated on underside of base and all original nuts); leopard's head; date letter *n;* sovereign's head (repeated on underside of base)

ARMORIALS: engraved in two cartouches on the base, arms, crest, and motto of Lowell

INSCRIPTIONS: engraved in cartouche on the base, the initials of John Amory Lowell in cipher; engraved on underside of base, *John Amory Lowell May 3rd 1848 from his grateful friend Mary Booth; John Amory Lowell/1798–1881/John Lowell/1824–1897/John Lowell/1856–1922*; stamped on rim of base, *HUNT & ROSKELL LATE STORR MORTIMER & HUNT*

H. 56 cm (22¹⁄₁₆ in.); w. 33 cm (13 in.); d. with dish 42.5 cm (16¾ in.)

WEIGHT: 4,862 gm (156 oz 6 dwt)

PROVENANCE: given in 1848 by Mary Boott to John Amory Lowell (1798–1881), who married Susan Cabot Lowell, to their son John Lowell (1824–1897), who married Lucy B. Emerson, to their son John Lowell (1856–1922), who married Mary Emlen Hale, to their son Ralph Lowell (1890–1978), who married Charlotte Loring (1897–1984), Gift of Mr. and Mrs. Ralph Lowell, February 12, 1964

EXHIBITED: New York, Cooper-Hewitt Museum, *Wine: Celebration and Ceremony*, 1985 (not in catalog)

PUBLISHED: Louise Belden, *The Festive Tradition, Table Decoration, 1650–1900: Two Hundred Years of American Party Tables* (New York, 1983), p. 87

DESCRIPTION: The centerpiece rests on a shaped triangular base with a pair of lion's feet at each corner. The base is assembled from sheet, and the lion's feet are thinly cast. An oval plaque with a chased scrolled frame is bolted to each side of the triangle. The stem of the epergne is modeled in the form of a complex rocky base supporting a twisted grapevine. The branches and leaves intertwine at the top to form a support for the fluted cut-glass bowl. The branches are cast in many sections and roughly assembled. Two putti are bolted to the rocky base, one standing, the other reclining and wearing a crown of grapes and raising a wine cup. A third putto leans down from the vines above, holding a cluster of grapes. The figures, each cast in several pieces, have an etched matte surface.

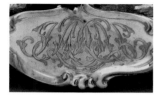

The epergne was a gift in 1848 from Mary
Boott to John Amory Lowell, a founding
trustee of the Museum of Fine Arts. Educated
at Harvard, Lowell helped to build his family's
already prosperous textile mills and with
Abbott Lawrence built the city of Lawrence, a
manufacturing hub. Among many philanthrop-
ic achievements, he was responsible for establishing the Lowell Institute, a foundation for
public education that had been generously
endowed by his cousin, John Lowell, Jr.[1] One
of Lowell's early business partners, John Wright
Boott, died in 1845 by his own hand, and
Lowell was named in his will as executor. The
Boott family, led by a daughter, contested the
will, and Lowell was embroiled in a bitter legal
dispute that lasted six years.[2] The gift of this
epergne in 1848 by Mary Boott must have
been in recognition of Lowell's efforts as
executor. The epergne was presented to the
Museum by Lowell's great-grandson, Ralph
Lowell, who served as president of the
Museum from 1951 to 1968.[3]

Figural presentation pieces were a speciality
of Hunt and Roskell. Their submissions to the
Great Exhibition of 1851 included about
twenty-five monumental centerpieces with literary, mythological, and allegorical themes.[4] As
successors to Storr & Co., the firm, which
employed about one hundred people, had not
only prototypes and designs at hand but also
modelers and chasers trained in the eighteenth-
century tradition. This centerpiece, with matted
and rather roughly chased figures, is perhaps
less ambitious than some of the firm's work. A
candelabrum dated 1845 is related in style and
suggests how the epergne might have been
conceived as part of an entire centerpiece.[5]

1. Edward Weeks, *The Lowells and Their Institute*
(Boston, 1966), pp. 37–54.

2. Ferris Greenslet, *The Lowells and Their Seven Worlds*
(Boston, 1946), p. 237.

3. Mark I. Gelfand, *Trustee for a City: Ralph Lowell of
Boston* (Boston, 1998), pp. 198–210.

4. Exh. London, Crystal Palace, *Great Exhibition of
the Works of Industry of All Nations*, 1851, pp. 686–88.

5. Sold Christie's, London, June 15, 1983, lot 41. For
other pieces in the same style, see a candelabrum
marked by Mortimer and Hunt for 1843, sold
Christie's, London, May 18, 1988, lot 137; an epergne
marked by Hunt for 1846/7 at Magdalene College,
Cambridge, exh., Cambridge, Fitzwilliam Museum,
Cambridge Plate, 1975, p. 46, cat. EPB5; another
marked by Hunt in 1858/9, sold Christie's, London,
March 6, 1991, lot 57.

· 193 ·

JUG

Marked by David Reid for Reid & Sons,
Newcastle (established 1788) overstriking another
London, 1850/1
Silver, ivory
1994.193

MARKS: on spout near rim, maker's mark *DR*
(Culme 2774); lion passant (repeated on handle);
leopard's head; date letter *P* (repeated on handle);
sovereign's head

ARMORIALS: engraved on upper body, an unidentified crest (a goose or duck holding in its beak a
flower slipped)

INSCRIPTIONS: on rim of foot, *REID & SONS,
Fecerunt*; inside foot rim, *REID & SONS NEW-
CASTLE UPON TYNE*; stamped, *474*; engraved in
panel on front, *Exhibited at the Great Exhibition in
Hyde Park/1851*; on underside of foot, *PRESENT-
ED/TO/FREDK. WM. REMNANT ESQR./BY
HIS SINCERE FRIEND/CHARLOTTE ANNAN*

H. 36.6 cm (14⁷⁄₁₆ in.); w. 16 cm (6⁵⁄₁₆ in.); d. 14.8 cm
(5¹³⁄₁₆ in.)

WEIGHT: 946.9 gm (30 oz 9 dwt)

PROVENANCE: gift from Charlotte Annan to
Frederick William Remnant; sold Sotheby's,
London, May 3, 1984, lot 154; sold Christie's,
London, March 2, 1994, lot 34; Wynard R. T.
Wilkinson, London, purchased June 22, 1994, The
John H. and Ernestine A. Payne Fund

193

Although monumental silver centerpieces with historical or allegorical scenes are perhaps the best-known products shown at the Great Exhibition of 1851, domestic silver wares, like the present jug, made up a large part of the display. This jug was exhibited at the Crystal Palace by the Newcastle retailers Reid & Sons, who were awarded an honorable mention for their submissions. The vertically fluted design with finely engraved oval panels was also applied to a tea service. The claret jug, shown in the *Illustrated London News*, was described as a "highly creditable specimen of silver work, being elegantly formed, and richly chased and engraved." Reid & Sons was established in 1788 by Christian Ker Reid, and the business was carried on by his three sons as a manufacturing and retailing operation. The firm handled silver and electroplated wares made in London and Sheffield. The connection by marriage of two senior partners to the Barnard family doubtless enhanced the firm's business relations with Edward Barnard & Sons, of London, which supplied them with a broad range of hollowware and flatware. The mark of David Reid on the cover is struck over another mark, which has been interpreted as that of Reily & Storer.[1] The jug, which exemplifies a large category of Victorian presentation plate, survives in many versions, ranging in date from 1850 to 1867 and bearing the marks or retailer's inscriptions of Charles Reily and George Storer,[2] Henry Wilkinson,[3] A. B. Savory & Sons,[4] Martin Hall & Co., Sheffield,[5] and Udney William Walker.[6]

EXHIBITED: London, Crystal Palace, *Great Exhibition of the Works of Industry of All Nations*, 1851 (not in catalogue)

PUBLISHED: *The Illustrated London News*, September 6, 1851

DESCRIPTION: The jug has a globular body with six vertical ribs and panels and a long neck with a shaped rim. It rests on a raised lobed foot. The body is raised from sheet, and the base is inset. Each panel has an oval reserve at the midsection of the jug that is engraved with flowers against a hatched ground. The oval is framed with rococo-style engraving that trails into the neck of the jug. The rim is reinforced with a cast scrolled border. The domed, lobed cover is hinged and surmounted with a cast scroll finial. The high handle, cast in two pieces and seamed vertically, terminates in scrolls. It is joined in two places with two pinned ivory spacers.

1. See Sotheby's, London, May 3, 1984, lot 34.

2. Marked for 1850, with inset plaques representing the Seasons, sold Sotheby's, New York, October 19, 1995, lot 309.

3. Marked for 1860, sold Christie's, New York, April 12, 1988, lot 120. Another marked by Wilkinson for 1867 is illus. Brett 1986, p. 290, fig. 1353.

4. Marked for 1862, maker's mark *WS*, sold Christie's, London, July 11, 1984, lot 569.

5. Marked for 1865, sold Sotheby's, London, November 11, 1993, lot 260.

6. Marked for 1867, sold Christie's East, New York, October 26, 1992, lot 444.

194

· 194 ·

TEA SERVICE COMPRISING
TEAPOT, SUGAR BASIN, CREAM
JUG, AND TRAY
Marked by Frederick Elkington, for Elkington &
Co. (1887–1963)
Birmingham, 1874/5
Parcel gilt, ivory
1991.539–542

MARKS: on each, sovereign's head; lion passant;
maker's mark *FE* (Culme 3876); anchor; date letter
Z

INSCRIPTIONS: 1991.539: on underside, stamped
pattern number *14130* and registration mark for
June 4, 1874, *ELKINGTON & CO.* 1991.541,
1991.540, 1991.542: on each, on underside, stamped
pattern number *15110*, registration stamp for July 10,
1875, *ELKINGTON & CO*

1991.539 (tray): H. 2.6 cm (1 in.); w. 44.1 cm
(17⅜ in.); d. 24.6 cm (9¹¹⁄₁₆ in.)

1991.541 (sugar basin): H. 7.9 cm (3⅛ in.);
w. 12.9 cm (5¹⁄₁₆ in.); d. 7.7 cm (3 in.)

1991.540 (teapot): H. 11.8 cm (4⅝ in.); w. 16.7 cm
(6⁹⁄₁₆ in.); d. 9.9 cm (3⅞ in.)

1991.542 (cream jug): H. 8.1 cm (3³⁄₁₆ in.); w. 8.3 cm
(3¼ in.); d. 4.9 cm (1¹⁵⁄₁₆ in.)

WEIGHT: 1991.539: 907.2 gm (29 oz 3 dwt).
1991.540: 394 gm (12 oz 13 dwt). 1991.541:
175.8 gm (5 oz 13 dwt). 1991.542: 45.5 gm
(1 oz 10 dwt)

PROVENANCE: Partridge Fine Arts, PLC, London,
Gift of Mrs. Frederick T. Bradbury, by exchange,
September 25, 1991

PUBLISHED: Timothy Schroder, *Silver at Partridge*
(London, 1991), pp. 46–47, cat. 34; "Museum
Acquisitions," *Decorative Arts Society Newsletter* 1,
no. 4 (1992), p. 8

DESCRIPTION: The oblong octagonal two-handled
tray (1991.539) has an applied border and handles of
bamboo, prunus blossoms, and leaves. It is engraved
and chased with butterflies, peonies, and circular
panels containing flowers on a diaper ground. The
surface overall is etched and gilt, with areas of the
bamboo and engraving left white. The teapot
(1991.450) is cylindrical and rests on a plain low
foot. The body is formed of seamed sheet, and the
base is inset. The cast handle is modeled as a prunus
branch and is separated from the body by ivory
spacers. The hinged cover flares over the mouth of

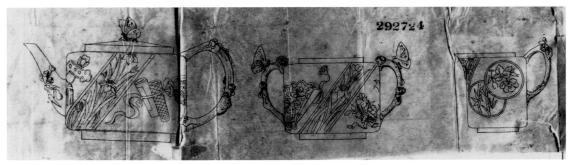

Fig. 8. *Design for a "Chinese" Tea Service,* Elkington & Co.

the teapot and is surmounted by a removable cast butterfly. The sugar bowl (1991.541) is cylindrical with a low molded foot. The handles are hollow-cast and are modeled as prunus branches, each with a butterfly on the top. The cream jug (1991.542) is also formed like a small cylinder, with a plain foot, a triangular spout, and a handle with blossoms. The cream jug and the sugar bowl were almost certainly formed of seamed sheet, but the thick gilding on the interior obscures any signs of solder. The teapot, sugar bowl, and cream jug are all etched, and engraved and chased with motifs in the Japanese style, including jars, fans, and scrolls. The surface is gilt, with areas of the engraved decoration left white.

By the 1870s Elkington & Co. dominated both the retail and manufacturing branches of the English silver industry. The firm was a key presence at all the great international exhibitions and responded quickly to the perception of a new taste, often with innovative techniques.[1] The displays of Japanese art at the International Exhibitions of 1862 and 1867 in London and Paris generated a tremendous response and had a broad influence on design in all media. The drawings for this service are preserved among the Elkington papers at the Victoria and Albert Museum's Archive of Art and Design, where the tea service is annotated "Chinese" and the tray is described as "Japanese."[2] A drawing for the service is dated July 13, 1875,[3] and records that the set should be spun and cast. The drawing for the tray is dated more than a year later, and it was apparently intended to produce an edition of fourteen in plated metal, fourteen in silver gilt, and fourteen described as "V. G. Frosted," presumably the surface used here.[4] The Registry Office symbols on the underside of the pieces show that the designs for the tray

and the tea service (fig. 8) were entered at the Patent Office Design Registry before the dates on the drawings in the Elkington archive, which must be late versions rendered as guides for the makers or as a record of the production.[5] The tea service is among the earliest designs in the Japanese taste recorded by Elkington & Co. The silver set was also retailed with Worcester porcelain cups and saucers in a fitted case.[6] The same year, Worcester supplied the same cups to be fitted in a case for a different silver service marked by Charles Favel for T., J., & N. Creswick, Sheffield.[7]

1. See Culme 1977, pp. 206–7.

2. I acknowledge with thanks the help of Amelia Fearn who undertook this research. Victoria and Albert Museum, Archive of Art and Design Number Book 1, AAD 3 1979PL 51.

3. Victoria and Albert Museum, AAD Drawing Book 9, fol. 126.

4. Victoria and Albert Museum, AAD Drawing Book 10, fol. 179.

5. June 4, 1874, and July 10, 1875, respectively. The designs are recorded in the Public Record Office, Representation Book BT 43/38 BC/3144.

6. See a set sold Sotheby's, London, July 10, 1990, lot 283, and another, with cups marked *Kutani,* sold Sotheby's Belgravia, London, December 11, 1980, lot 218.

7. Sotheby's, New York, April 16, 1996, lot 226.

· 195 ·

JUG

Marked by Frederick Elkington for Elkington &
Co. (1887–1963)

Birmingham, 1879/80

Silver, parcel gilt

1998.60

MARKS: on underside, maker's mark *FE* (Jones,
p. 335); anchor; date letter *e*; lion passant; sovereign's
head

H. 22 cm (8¹¹⁄₁₆ in.); w. 18.7 cm (7⅜ in.); d. 14.4 cm
(5¹¹⁄₁₆ in.)

WEIGHT: 930 gm (29 oz 18 dwt)

PROVENANCE: David Allan, Antiquaire, Paris, purchased June 24, 1998, Theodora Wilbour Fund in
Memory of Charotte Beebe Wilbour

DESCRIPTION: The raised pear-shaped jug has a
broad pouring lip and shaped rim and rests on a
splayed foot. It has a cast handle in the form of
bound sheaves of bamboo and bamboo borders
around the neck and foot rim. The body of the jug
has visible hammer marks and is applied with cast
bamboo canes and insects and a vase containing
flowers and plum branches. The insects and foliage
are picked out in gold, while the ground is left
white, and the interior of the jug is gilt.

195

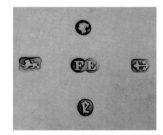

The restoration in 1853 of European trade with
Japan released a flood of Japanese art and decorative arts into Europe, where fascination with
the East had been simmering since the early
part of the century. At the International
Exhibition of 1862 in London the Japanese
exhibits were particularly admired, and by the
time of the 1878 Exposition Universelle in
Paris, Japonism had become a cult. One of the
most sensational exhibits in Paris was the display by Tiffany & Co. of silver in the Japanese
taste with various applied metals including
copper in several alloys, gold in several colors,
and bronze.[1] Samuel Bing (1838–1905), the
Parisian retailer, reported that "the borrowed
elements were so ingeniously transposed to
serve their new function as to become the
equivalent of new discoveries."[2] English hallmarking laws forbade the incorporation of base
metals into silver wares, but Elkington & Co.
resourcefully interpreted the technique with
chased ornament that was subsequently gilt in
various shades of gold. Though the firm was

admired for its chased work,[3] this style was not
widely produced. Engraved or flat-chased decoration against a matted or etched ground (see
cat. 194) is more characteristic of Elkington's
silver in the Japanese taste.

1. Frances Gruber Safford and Ruth Wilford
Caccavale, "Japanesque Silver by Tiffany and
Company in the Metropolitan Museum of Art,"
Antiques 132, no. 4 (October 1987), pp. 809–16.

2. Quoted in exh. New York, The Metropolitan
Museum of Art, *In Pursuit of Beauty: Americans and
the Aesthetic Movement*, 1986, p. 260.

3. Jones 1981, p. 159.

196

· 196 ·

SAUCEBOAT
London, possibly ca. 1880
Silver
1988.1078

MARKS: on edge of foot, traces of two marks, inde-cipherable

ARMORIALS: engraved below spout, a crest, possi-bly that of Trotter (a horse passant, saddled and bri-dled)

H. 12.1 cm (4¾ in.); w. 8.3 cm (3¼ in.); d. 17.2 cm (6¾ in.)

WEIGHT: 442.3 gm (14 oz 4 dwt)

PROVENANCE: Lent by Mrs. S. J. Katz, June 25, 1973; The Jessie and Sigmund Katz Collection, November 30, 1988

PUBLISHED: Gruber 1982, p. 155, fig. 205

DESCRIPTION: The boat-shaped body rests on an oval domed foot that is roughly modeled and cast with scrolls and shells enclosing two reserves con-taining a turtle and a lizard. The body is cast in two pieces and seamed along the middle. Scrolled car-touches on the side enclose a pastoral scene depict-ing a goat and a lamb leaping over a fence. A mold-ed foliate shell is applied just below the spout, and the panel behind the handle is flat-chased with foliage and scrolls. The cast double-scroll handle is capped by a goat's head.

The bizarre and unwieldy combination of motifs on this heavy sauceboat is difficult to analyze. There are at least eight sauceboats of this model known, of which only one has a full set of hall-marks.[1] Two bear the maker's mark of Edward Wakelin, and since several of the features on this sauceboat—the goat, the scale decoration, the lizard on the foot, and the tight scrolls—can be associated with Wakelin's shop, it is possible that there is an eighteenth-century prototype for this model. The figure of the prancing goat, a favorite rococo theme, appears on an epergne in the Museum's collection marked by Edward Wakelin (see cat. 112) and is a useful comparison. On the sauceboat, the opposite cartouche contains the figure of a lamb, but the rendering of both ani-mals is clumsy and unsure. The dating of this object to the third quarter of the nineteenth cen-tury must remain tentative, but its conception and manufacture are inconsistent with the output of a sophisticated shop like Wakelin's.

1. See a sauceboat marked only with the maker's mark of Edward Wakelin, sold Sotheby's, London, November 17, 1960, lot 61; another fully marked by the same maker for 1755, illus. Judith Banister, "Pottery and Porcelain of 'Silver-Shape,'" *Antique Dealer's and Collector's Guide* 36, no. 6 (January 1983), p. 26; another unmarked, illus. ibid., p. 26; another unmarked, with the arms of Cooper with Rickford in pretence, sold Christie's, London, May 12, 1993, lot 72; another with an indistinct maker's mark and hallmarks for 1809, sold in the same sale, lot 71; a pair, unmarked, sold Sotheby's, London, November 30, 1978, lot 71; another marked by John Chapman for 1736, sold Christie's, New York, April 29, 1987, lot 491; another, unmarked, sold Christie's, London, November 22, 1995, lot 121.

197

E (repeated on top of cover); sovereign's head

INSCRIPTIONS: engraved on underside, Design Office registration mark for August 9, 1880

H. 17.3 cm (6¹³⁄₁₆ in.); w. 9.5 cm (3¾ in.); d. 4.8 cm (1⅞ in.)

WEIGHT: 226.8 gm (7 oz 6 dwt)

PROVENANCE: Firestone & Parson, Inc., Boston, purchased November 20, 1991, Theodora Wilbour Fund in Memory of Charlotte Beebe Wilbour

DESCRIPTION: The flattened pear-shaped vessel is decorated overall with contorted grotesque faces. It is formed from two pieces of sheet, chased, and seamed along the narrow side. The globular stopper is chased with three bald heads and is attached to the body with a hinged bayonet closure.

About 1859 Louis Dee joined the firm that his father had established in 1827.[1] Described as jewelers and silversmiths, they produced an eclectic range of novelties, such as mounted agate, enamel, or glass vessels, vinaigrettes, and decanters. Such amusing conversation pieces were made by many Victorian firms, but Dee's creations of the 1880s were truly bizarre. A nip cup in the form of a lobster's claw,[2] a glass decanter with mounts in the form of an antelope,[3] and another with mounts in the form of the comic puppet Judy and a tomcat are characteristic.[4] More similar in spirit to the present flask is a pair of candlesticks modeled as three merging grotesque faces, based on a caricature of Louis Philippe.[5] The design for the flask is reminiscent of the inventions of Adam (ca. 1568–1627) and Christian (ca. 1600–1667) van Vianen, in which abstract organic motifs were rendered in a flowing style. These designs, called auricular, were greatly admired in the second half of the nineteenth century. In the South Kensington Museum Exhibition of 1862, three pieces of silver by Van Vianen belonging to the duke of Hamilton were exhibited,[6] and the ewer and basin sold from the duke of Sussex's collection in 1843 was exhibited in Amsterdam in 1881.[7] The association with seventeenth-century silver, however, is generic rather than specific, and the theme of contorted grotesque faces and figures was a recurring theme in Dee's designs. This design was registered at the Patent Office on August 9, 1880, part of a scheme initiated in 1842 to protect manufacturers' designs from piracy.[8]

· 197 ·

FLASK

Marked by Louis Dee (1832–1884)

London, 1880/1

Silver

1991.627

MARKS: on underside, maker's mark *LD* (Culme 10713) (repeated on top of cover); lion passant (repeated on top of cover); leopard's head; date letter

Other designs for flasks recorded by Dee in the same volume include a cloaked, tonsured figure, possibly a monk, a dwarf in a rocking chair, another of a squatting jockey, and a carp entangled with a frog.[9] None of these designs suggest that Dee was influenced by mannerist or auricular designs, and it may be that the faces on the present flask have another source.

1. See Culme 1987, pp. 116–17.

2. Sold Sotheby's, London, April 28, 1988, lot 484.

3. Sold, Sotheby's, London, November 17, 1988, lot 201.

4. Sold Sotheby's Belgravia, London, December 15, 1977, lots 371–72.

5. Sold Sotheby's, London, November 19, 1987, lot 187. Now in the Mitchell Wolfson Collection, Florida International University, exh. Miami Beach, Wolfsonian, *Designing Modernity*, 1995, p. 227, cat. 343.

6. London, South Kensington Museum, *Catalogue of the Special Exhibition of Works of Art*, 1862, cat. ed. by J. C. Robinson, p. 519, cats. 6, 232–34.

7. Exh. London, Christie's, *The Glory of the Goldsmith: Magnificent Gold and Silver from the Al-Tajiir Collection*, 1989, p. 15, cat. 5.

8. London, PRO, BT/44/4, Class 1, Parcel 1, no. 353405.

9. London, PRO, BT 43/47/353071; BT 43/54/334070, 344200, 343079.

· 198 ·

CLARET JUG

After a design by Christopher Dresser
(1834–1904)
Marked by Edward Hutton (joined William Hutton & Sons, 1880)
London, 1883/4
Glass, silver
1977.183

MARKS: near handle, maker's mark *EH* (Culme 332b) (repeated inside cover); lion passant (repeated inside cover); leopard's head; date letter *H* (repeated inside cover); sovereign's head

H. 21.4 cm (8⅜ in.); w. 14.8 cm (5¹³⁄₁₆ in.); d. 14 cm (5½ in.)

PROVENANCE: Thomas Lumley, Ltd., London, purchased May 11, 1977, Theodora Wilbour Fund in Memory of Charlotte Beebe Wilbour

EXHIBITED: Boston, Museum of Fine Arts, *This Is the Modern World: Furnishings of the 20th Century*, 1996

DESCRIPTION: The clear glass body of the vessel has a cylindrical neck and a flaring geometric base. The underside of the glass is cut with a geometric rosette. The neck is encased in a plain silver collar with a squared, angled spout surmounted by a hinged flat cover. The silver handle is formed of a vertical rod, supported on two horizontal struts that attach to the collar at the top and to a plain silver band at the base. The silver mounts are formed of assembled pieces of sheet. The handle is a seamed tube, attached with cast and fabricated mounts.

The radical simplicity of Christopher Dresser's designs reflects his admiration for the Japanese metalwork and pottery to which he was exposed at the Vienna International Exhibition of 1873.[1] Dresser was fascinated by the bold geometric forms of the Japanese objects and by the exposed structural elements, which made decorative use of such functional aspects as rivets and braces. His tour of Japan in 1876–77 was the first by a European designer, and Dresser's account of this journey, published in 1882, had a broad influence on the popularity of Japonism.[2]

Dresser designed several variations on this silver-mounted glass claret jug, which were first produced by the Birmingham manufacturers Hukin and Heath about 1880. In addition to the present design, other related models included a trapezoidal body on a silver foot, a tall glass form with tapering sides, and a tall jug with a trapezoidal base and extended neck.[3] The glass vessels, probably produced by the Tees Bottle Company, of Middlesbrough, were mounted by Hukin and Heath in both sterling and electroplate.[4] The mounts on the Museum's jug are marked by Edward Hutton, who joined the Sheffield manufactory established by his grandfather in 1800. All of the many examples of glass-mounted claret jugs appear to have been produced by Hukin and Heath, with the exception of the present jug, marked by Hutton & Sons.[5] In addition, the handle of the present jug is silver, whereas all the other examples appear to have handles in ebony.

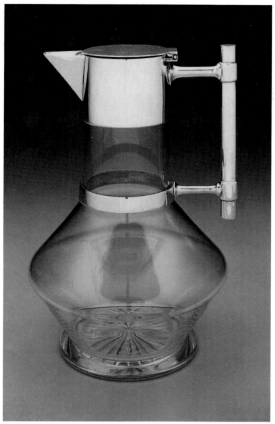

198

Hukin and Heath registered the design for the jug at the Patent Office in 1881;[6] whether the present jug by Hutton is an unauthorized use of Dresser's design remains unclear.[7]

1. For Dresser, see Halén 1990.

2. Ibid., p. 33.

3. Exh. New York, Historical Design Inc., *Truth, Beauty, Power: Dr Christopher Dresser, 1834–1904*, 1998, pp. 12, 49, 62.

4. Halén 1990, p. 158.

5. See, for example, a jug by Hukin and Heath, sold Christie's, London, February 5, 1992, lot 52; two jugs by Hukin and Heath and Heath and Middleton were exhibited New York, Historical Design Inc., *Truth, Beauty, Power: Dr Christopher Dresser 1834–1904*, 1998, p. 63.

6. See the electroplated example exh. London, Fine Arts Society, *Christopher Dresser, 1834–1904*, 1972, cat. 132.

7. Hutton & Sons are not included on the list of Dresser's manufacturers compiled by Halén 1990, appendix.

· 199 ·

PLAQUE

Executed by Leonard Morel-Ladeuil (1820–1888)
Elkington & Co., 1884
Silver, steel
1995.85

UNMARKED

INSCRIPTIONS: engraved on bottom edge of scene, *Morel-Ladeuil, Fécit 1884*; *Elkington co.*[1]

H. 45.7 cm (18 in.); w. 59 cm (23¼ in.); d. 1.5 cm (⅝ in.)

PUBLISHED: Leon Morel, *L'Oeuvre de Morel-Ladeuil, Sculpteur-Ciseleur, 1820–1888* (Paris, 1904), p. 45, pl. 10

PROVENANCE: Wynyard R. T. Wilkinson, London, purchased May 24, 1995, Theodora Wilbour Fund in Memory of Charlotte Beebe Wilbour and Gift of Wynyard R. T. Wilkinson, May 24, 1995[2]

DESCRIPTION: The shaped rectangular silver plaque is formed from sheet and chased with a scene depicting the richly decorated interior of a church. Hero, the swooning bride, is attended by Leonato and Benedick in the center, the priest steps toward her from the altar on the left, and Claudio gesticulates on the right. On the reverse, changes in the composition made during working are evident. The relief is mounted with decorative bolts onto a damascened iron frame of shaped rectangular form, with chased trophies and masks at each corner. The borders of the iron frame are decorated with applied burnished silver strapwork, and at each side is an applied silver plaque chased with a lyre. At the base of the scene is an applied plaque with the chased inscription *Much Ado About Nothing*, and above is an applied silver medallion with the head of Shakespeare in profile, flanked by putti bearing a laurel wreath. The iron frame is mounted on a shaped oak panel.

Leonard Morel-Ladeuil, born in Clermont-Ferrand, was apprenticed at a young age to Antoine Vecht (1799–1869), the famous French goldsmith and forger admired by his contemporaries as a modern Cellini. Vecht had revived silver chasing and damascening on iron in the Renaissance style. Morel-Ladeuil established himself as an expert chaser and was hired by Elkington & Co. in 1859 as a prestige artist to design their monumental exhibition pieces and to execute chased works for electrotype reproduction.[3] Among his most famous productions was the Milton shield and the silver table called *Sleep*, which was awarded a prize at the International Exhibition of 1862 in London and pre-

199

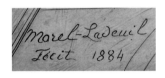

sented by the city of Birmingham as a wedding gift to the Prince and Princess of Wales.

In 1882 Sir Albert Sassoon commissioned as a wedding gift for the duke of Albany, Queen Victoria's youngest son, a plaque from Elkington & Co. depicting a scene from *The Merry Wives of Windsor*.[4] This suggested to the chaser a series of plaques with scenes from Shakespeare, whose plays were enjoying a tremendous revival in the London theater due to the successful productions of Henry Irving (1838–1905). This plaque, completed in February 1884, was presented to the queen at Windsor. He followed it with a plaque depicting a scene from *The Merchant of Venice*, one of the last works he executed for Elkington & Co. before returning to France.[5] The scene chosen for the present plaque represents the set of the Lyceum Theatre production of *Much Ado* produced in 1882 with Henry Irving as Benedick, Ellen Terry as Beatrice, and Johnston Forbes Robertson as Claudio. The set for the church scene was particularly admired, and it was recorded by Forbes Robinson on canvas

and later engraved.[6] Ellen Terry wrote that she had once suggested that Forbes Robinson was a far better painter than he was an actor, but his performance as Claudio convinced her to change her mind.[7]

1. Attached to the back of the wooden mount is a handwritten note with the following inscription: *We certify that this Placque, subject, the marriage scene from "Much ado about nothing," executed entirely by hand in repousse iron and silver by M. Morel-Ladeuil one of the principal artists of Elkington & Co. Ltd. in the year 1884 is the original work. / Elkington & Co. Ltd. / J. B. Read / Secretary.*

2. The plaque was offered by Sotheby's, London, March 2, 1995, lot 87, but withdrawn before the sale.

3. Culme 1977, p. 204.

4. Morel, *L'Oeuvre*, p. 27.

5. Lewis F. Day, "The Work of Morel-Ladeuil," *The Magazine of Art* (1890), pp. 271–75.

6. Percy Fitzgerald, *Henry Irving: A Record of Twenty Years at the Lyceum* (London, 1893), p. 193, frontispiece.

7. Ellen Terry, "The Story of My Life," *McClure's Magazine* 30, no. 5 (April 1908), p. 743.

200

• 200 •

BABY'S WHISTLE AND RATTLE
Marked by John Hilliard and John Thomason
(entered into partnership 1847)
Birmingham, 1889/90
Silver, coral
Res.43.2

MARKS: near handle, maker's mark *H&T* (Jones,
p. 346); date letter *p;* anchor*;* lion passant; sovereign's
head

L. 11 cm (4⅜ in.); w. 5 cm (2 in.)

WEIGHT: 34 gm (1 oz 2 dwt)

PROVENANCE: Gift of Miss Amelia Peabody, March
11, 1943

DESCRIPTION: The baluster whistle has a shaped
mouthpiece, a fluted central section, and a tapering
handle terminating in an irregularly shaped piece of
coral. The whistle is assembled from sheet and
chased overall with stylized geometric medallions
and foliage. Suspended on eyes around the circumference of the central section are six bells.

• 201 •

DISH
Marked by Walter Walker and Brownfield Tolhurst
(mark entered 1893)
Signed by Gilbert Leigh Marks (1861–1905)
London, 1895/6
Silver
1995.9

MARKS: in center of dish, maker's marks *WW/BT*
(Culme 16026); Britannia; lion's head erased; date
letter *U*

INSCRIPTIONS: engraved on underside, *Gilbert
Marks '96*

H. 3.2 cm (1¼ in.); diam. 41.3 cm (16¼ in.)

WEIGHT: 1,255.9 gm (40 oz 8 dwt)

PROVENANCE: with Nicholas Harris, London,
1990; Asprey Ltd., London, purchased January 25,
1995, Theodora Wilbour Fund in Memory of
Charlotte Beebe Wilbour

PUBLISHED: Frederick S. Robinson, "Silver Plate by
Mr. Gilbert Marks," *The Magazine of Art* (October
1896), pp. 437–40

DESCRIPTION: The circular dish, formed of sheet,
has a broad rim, a sunken center, and a thickened
rim. It is chased around the border with intertwining leaves and blossoms of sea holly (*eryngium*), and
at the center with a single blossom. A few areas of
high relief have been filled with solder from the
back, and there are several small details, such as leaf
tips, applied to the front.

In the early part of his career, Gilbert Marks
appears to have been on the periphery of the
goldsmiths' trade, and John Culme has specu-
lated that his early activity as a practicing goldsmith must have been in the capacity of an
amateur. As a young man he was a clerk for a
manufacturing goldsmith, and when he married in 1888 he was recorded as a wool broker's
manager. Whatever his training, he became a
skilled chaser and a passionate advocate of the
handwrought finish. He believed that mass-
produced silver had destroyed the craftsman's
inspiration. In 1895 he had an exhibition at
Johnson, Walker & Tolhurst that was well
received by the critics who congratulated the
firm for providing for the "few who have a
soul above Sheffield."[1] Marks held annual exhibitions until 1901. Usually working in
Britannia standard, he composed naturalistic

201

flowers around the borders of dishes, bowls, and vases. He also experimented with pewter, bronze, copper, and steel.[2] Before he registered his own mark in 1896, Marks signed and dated his pieces, which were marked by Johnson, Walker & Tolhurst as sponsors. His works range in date from 1895 to only 1902, when his health may have begun to fail.

This dish was dated by Marks in 1896 and was illustrated in the *Magazine of Art* after its exhibition, where it was praised as follows: "The mere preliminary tracing of the very intricate design of the sea holly salver would be a laborious task; and when we consider the loving patience and skill required to finish this important piece, and we are not surprised to learn that it was commenced fully two years before it was completed."[3]

1. "Notes on Recent Decorative Work," *The Art Journal* n.s., 47 (1895), p. 252.

2. Culme 1987, p. 312.

3. Robinson, "Silver Plate," p. 440.

Fig. 9. *Design for a jug,* Charles Herbert Thompson

• 202 •

CLARET JUG

Marked by Elkington & Company (1887–1963)
Birmingham, 1897/8
Silver, glass
1977.540a-b

MARKS: on mount to right of handle, maker's mark
E&CoLd (Culme 3092); anchor; date letter *x*
(repeated inside cover); lion passant (repeated inside
cover)

INSCRIPTIONS: engraved in cartouche on side,
Arthur Buckley Esq:/From/John & Gerald/Taylor;
scratched on lip of neck, *24255 cg/cg/-.*

H. 35.7 cm (14¹⁄₁₆ in.); w. 16.8 cm (6⅝ in.); diam. of
base 14.8 cm (5¹³⁄₁₆ in.)

PROVENANCE: Brand Inglis, Ltd., London, purchased June 8, 1977, Theodora Wilbour Fund in
Memory of Charlotte Beebe Wilbour

DESCRIPTION: The jug has a low broad base, rising
to a high cylindrical neck. It is formed of purple
glass mounted with electroformed silver that is
pierced and engraved with stylized Japanese ribbons,
flowers, and bamboo leaves. The heavy C-shaped
handle is undecorated. Just above the handle is a
band of pierced daffodils, a band of cast strapwork,
and a band of plain silver, surmounted at the rim
with a band of beading. The spout is cast and
scrolled. The domed lid has a gadrooned baluster
finial.

The elaborate sleeve of pierced decoration on
this glass jug was applied through an electrolyt-
ic deposit process, sometimes called silver overlay, that was developed in the 1880s.[1] Stevens
and Williams, the Stourbridge glasshouse that
supplied manufacturers and retailers such as
Elkington & Co., Hukin & Heath, and
Tiffany's, was among the first to have experimented with this process on a commercial
basis. The archives of Stevens and Williams
(now called Royal Breirley Crystal) suggest
that in the 1890s the firm worked with a local
metallurgist, Charles Herbert Thompson, to
develop a line of wares, including the present
jug, with silver deposit decoration in the
Japanese taste. The surviving design books
show a drawing for this jug (   ) and thirteen
other pieces with similar decoration.[2] These
include a hip flask and scent bottles and
decanters of various sizes and a white Coalport
china three-part service. Each drawing is anno-

202 (see color plate XXIV)

tated with the name *Thompson.* Thompson's
papers indicate that he experimented broadly
with formulas for colored enamels, glazes, and
gilding for the decoration of glass and ceramics.[3] In addition to Stevens and Williams,
Thompson worked for other manufacturers,
including Joseph Webb; Stuart & Sons;
Richardsons of Tutbury; Burtles, Tate & Co.;
Robinsons & Skinner & Co; and Thomas
Goode & Co. His notes record formulas for
many colors and shades of glass, including
amethyst (the color indicated in the design
book for this jug). Thompson may have begun
his experiments with the silver deposit process
as early as 1877, but the full recipe for the
treatment was properly recorded only in 1897.

The technique of silver overlay was patented

by another glass decorator who worked for Stevens and Williams, Oscar Pierre Erard. In partnership with Benjamin John Round, an electroplater and gilder, he developed a technique for silver deposit that called for the ornamentation of glass and pottery surfaces with silver by mixing a flux of calcined borax, sand, lead oxide, and potassium nitrate.[4] This flux was mixed with silver and turpentine and ground. The compound was applied to the glass or ceramic base in the required design. The object was then fired. The vessel could be immersed in a bath of silver in solution, and with the addition of a current of two volts for approximately six hours, the silver was deposited on the treated areas of the glass in a suitable thickness. The process was used by several English and American manufacturers, of which Gorham seems to have produced the largest share.[5]

1. I am extremely grateful to Amelia Fearn who enthusiastically undertook this research on the Stevens & Williams archives at Royal Breirley Crystal, Stourbridge, the Elkington Archive at the Archive of Art and Design, Victoria and Albert Museum, the Dudley Archives, Coseley, and at the Broadfield House Museum, Kingswinford. She is preparing an article that will treat her findings in greater depth. Robin Hillyard, Ceramics Department, Victoria and Albert Museum, was also generous with his knowledge.

2. Stevens & Williams Archive, Royal Breirley Crystal, Stourbridge, design no. 24255, description book no. 21, 1897. I am grateful to David Redman, designer at Royal Breirley Crystal, Stourbridge, who kindly assisted Amelia Fearn.

3. Charles Herbert Thompson Papers, Coseley Archive, Box 6i. I acknowledge gratefully the help of Hilary Atkins, archivist, Dudley Archive, and Roger Dodsworth of the Broadfield House Museum, who kindly assisted Amelia Fearn.

4. Charles R. Hajdamach, *British Glass, 1800–1914* (Woodbridge, 1991), pp. 287–89.

5. Jayne E. Stokes, *Sumptuous Surrounds: Silver Overlay on Ceramic and Glass* (Milwaukee, 1990), pp. 1–6.

· 203 ·

COVERED BOWL WITH SPOON

Designed by Charles Robert Ashbee (1863–1942)
Marked by the Guild of Handicraft Ltd. (active 1888–1908)
London, 1903/4
Silver, mother-of-pearl
1990.461a-b, 1992.181

MARKS: 1990.461a-b (bowl), below rim, maker's mark *GofHLtd* (Culme 6085) (repeated on bezel of cover); lion passant; leopard's head; date letter *h*. 1992.181 (spoon), on back of handle, maker's mark *GofHLtd* (Culme 6085); lion passant; leopard's head; date letter *h*

1990.461a-b: H. 10.7 cm (4³⁄₁₆ in.); w. 23.8 cm (9⅜ in.); diam. of cover 10.9 cm (4⁵⁄₁₆ in.)

1992.181: L. 1.4 cm (½ in.); w. 2.9 cm (1⅛ in.)

WEIGHT: 1990.461a-b: 311.9 gm (10 oz). 1992.181: 36.9 gm (1 oz 4 dwt)

PROVENANCE: (1990.461a-b): Historical Design Collection, Inc., New York, purchased September 18, 1990, Theodora Wilbour Fund in Memory of Charlotte Beebe Wilbour. (1992.181): Gift of Denis Gallion and Daniel Morris, Historical Design Collection, April 22, 1992

DESCRIPTION: The raised circular bowl has a trumpet foot. The wide looping handles on each side of the bowl are each formed of two wires. The circular detachable cover, formed from sheet, has a flat rim and a central disk of bright blue enamel set into a silver bezel. The finial is formed of six wires bent and soldered to form a cage that supports a piece of mother-of-pearl in a silver bezel. The forged spoon has a faceted stem and an elongated bowl. The openwork finial is formed from flat wires that support a piece of mother-of-pearl in a silver bezel.

Charles Robert Ashbee, one of the prime exponents of the Arts and Crafts movement, founded the Guild of Handicraft with four fellow socialists in 1888.[1] The membership of the guild, which numbered 175 in 1902, included woodworkers, goldsmiths, and decorative painters. Following the tenets of John Ruskin (1819–1900) and William Morris (1834–1896), Ashbee intended that the workshop provide education, skills, and pride in craftsmanship to the working classes. He summarized his idealistic goal with the declaration, "Humanity and

203

Crafts are inseparable." Ashbee himself was the chief designer for most of the workshop's production, including this two-handled bowl. However, he encouraged the craftsmen to interpret and vary the basic formula, so all of the many examples of this form have different details.[2] The design was also produced with only one handle and without a cover and is likely to have been intended as a jam or butter dish. Some examples are fitted with a glass liner.[3]

1. Alan Crawford, *C. R. Ashbee: Architect, Designer, and Romantic Socialist* (New Haven, 1985), p. 32.

2. See examples illus. Isabelle Anscombe and Charlotte Gere, *Arts and Crafts in Britain and America* (New York, 1978), fig. 131; Carl Benno Heller, ed., *Jugendstil: Kunst um 1900* (Darmstadt, 1982), p. 20, cat. 3; Truman 1993, p. 152; Christie's, New York, December 9, 1994, lot 102.

3. Philippe Garner, *The Encyclopedia of Decorative Arts* (New York, 1982), p. 168; Christie's, New York, June 11, 1994, lot 107.

• 204 •

BABY'S RATTLE AND WHISTLE
Marked by John Hilliard and John Thomason
(entered into partnership 1847)
Birmingham, 1904/5
Silver, ivory
1975.283

MARKS: near handle, maker's mark *H&T* (Jones, p. 346); anchor; lion passant; date letter *e*

L. 14.2 cm (5⁹⁄₁₆ in.); w. 6.3 cm (2½ in.)

WEIGHT: 493.3 gm (2 oz 7 dwt)

PROVENANCE: Gift of Mrs. Franklin A. Park, March 12, 1975

DESCRIPTION: The baluster whistle has a shaped mouthpiece, a spherical central section, and a tapering handle. It is assembled from sheet and chased overall with stylized geometric medallions and foliage. Suspended on eyes around the circumference of the central section are six bells. The handle terminates in a loop through which a ring of ivory is suspended.

204

205

• 205 •

DECANTER

Designed by Charles Robert Ashbee (1863–1942)
Marked by the Guild of Handicraft Ltd. (active
1888–1908)
London, 1904/5
Silver, blown glass, cork, crysophase
1998.400

MARKS: on base of handle, maker's mark
GofHLtd (repeated on neck mount and cover); lion
passant (repeated on neck mount and cover); leopard's head (repeated on neck mount and cover); date
letter *h*

H. 20 cm (7⅞ in.); w. 16.8 cm (6⅝ in.); d. 13.2 cm
(5³⁄₁₆ in.)

PROVENANCE: descended to Ann Symington,
Historical Design Inc., New York, purchased
December 18, 1998, Theodora Wilbour Fund in
Memory of Charlotte Beebe Wilbour

EXHIBITED: Rotterdam, Museum Boymans-van
Beuningen, *Silver of a New Era*, 1992, p. 32, cat. 14;
New York, Historical Design Inc., *Truth, Beauty,
Power: Dr. Christopher Dresser, 1834–1904*, 1998, p. 13

PUBLISHED: Alan Crawford, *C. R. Ashbee: Architect,
Designer, and Romantic Socialist* (New Haven, 1985),
p. 331, fig. 166

DESCRIPTION: The bulbous green glass bottle has a
tall tapering neck. A hammered silver collar, formed
from two hinged and pinned pieces, clasps the upper
part of the neck. A high looping handle, formed
from six joined wires, extends from the collar to an
oval mount below. An additional wire brace soldered
to the oval mount and the front of the collar follows
the curve of the body. The removable cover, set on a
cork stopper, is slightly domed with a flaring rim
and has a finial set with a chrysophase.

Among the romantic interests of the designer
C. R. Ashbee was the archaeology of his neigh-
borhood of Chelsea. About 1894 Ashbee built a
house at 37 Cheyne Walk on a site that his
mother had purchased when she left Ashbee's
father. The shell of a pub, the Magpie and
Stump, that had burned seven years earlier
stood on the lot, and while the excavations for
Ashbee's house were underway, he unearthed
several fragments of broken green glass.
Although the shards were probably Victorian,
Ashbee associated them with a more ancient
past, declaring, "it was doubtless bottles of that
shape, good solid glass, from which Falstaff and
his worthies drank their sack."[1] About 1897
Ashbee had the form copied in a thinner glass
by James Powell and Sons of Whitefriars and
designed the sinuous silver mounts. As was the
case with the small bowls (see cat. 203), the
makers were encouraged to improvise. One
example of 1901 in the Art Institute of
Chicago has a dramatic handle formed from
loosely intertwined wires and a chased collar at
the base of the neck with a slightly Gothic
feel. Another version of the model in the
Victoria and Albert Museum has a high finial
supported by spiraling wire.[2] A third jug has a
more simplified mount.[3]

1. Crawford, *C. R. Ashbee*, p. 331.
2. Ibid., p. 331.
3. Roderick Gradidge, Exhibition/Reviews, "C. R.
Ashbee in East London," *Crafts* (May 4, 1999),
pp. 57–58.

206 (see color plate xxv)

· 206 ·

ROSE BOWL

Marked by Bernard Cuzner (1877–1956)
Birmingham, 1911/2
Silver, mother-of-pearl, garnets
1991.536a–b

MARKS: just below the rim, maker's mark *B.C.*
(Jones, p. 325); anchor; lion passant (repeated on
each medallion with stones); date letter *m* (repeated
on each medallion with stones)

INSCRIPTIONS: engraved around bowl, *From Lord
Ilkeston to Sir Anthony Bowlby .C.M.G. And stand
indebted, over and above. In love and service to you ever-
more.*

H. 18.5 cm (7⁵⁄₁₆ in.); diam. of rim 25.7 cm (10⅛ in.)

WEIGHT: 1,505.4 gm (48 oz 8 dwt)

PROVENANCE: sold Christie's, London, February
20, 1991, lot 55; Historical Design Collection, Inc.,

New York, purchased September 25, 1991, Theodora
Wilbour Fund in Memory of Charlotte Beebe
Wilbour

EXHIBITED: Birmingham, City Museum and Art
Gallery, *Birmingham Gold and Silver, 1773–1973: An
Exhibition Celebrating the Bicentenary of the Assay
Office,* 1973, cat. F62

PUBLISHED: Jones 1981, p. 180, fig. 179; "Museum
Acquisitions," *Decorative Arts Society Newsletter* 1,
no. 4 (Fall 1992), p. 7

DESCRIPTION: The shallow bowl rests on five
columns rising from a stepped base. The foot is a
circular pedestal assembled from several pieces of
seamed sheet with bands of wire and twisted wire
along the rim, and above, a row of applied quatrefoils. Five spiraled columns, fabricated from cast and
wrought pieces, rest on the foot supporting the
bowl. In two borders above and below the columns
are horizontal bands of interlaced motifs. The raised
bowl has a wide band of chased stylized foliage just

below its rim. Overlapping this band and in line with the columns below are five applied medallions, each set with five pieces of mother-of-pearl forming a rosette pattern. The medallions are secured by a threaded post soldered to the bowl and a nut, decorated with five garnets mounted in a cinquefoil.

Bernard Cuzner had a long and influential career as head of the Department of Metalwork at the Birmingham School of Art. His 1935 text, *A Silversmith's Manual*, was for many years the standard practical guide for students of the craft. Cuzner's apprenticeship was begun under his father, a watchmaker, but he became interested in silversmithing after attending Redditch School of Art. He attended the Vittoria Street School for Jewelers and Silversmiths in Birmingham, where he was a student of Arthur Gaskin. About 1900 he began to design for Liberty's, where he contributed to the Cymric line.[1] This bowl, like others of his early period,[2] reflects the Celtic motifs of the Cymric designs and relies for its effect on the rich ornament of the applied mother-of-pearl bosses. These mounts are clearly influenced by the jewelry designs of Arthur and Georgie Gaskin. Cuzner recognized the shortcomings of the Arts and Crafts ideals. He acknowledged that most handwrought works could only be afforded by the rich, and that machines were a natural boon to the craftsman. However, Cuzner defended the intellectual values of the movement and called for craftsmen to embrace traditional methods of production to advance the trade.[3]

The bowl was given by the physician Sir Balthazar Walter Foster (1840–1913), created first baron Ilkeston in 1886, to Sir Anthony Alfred Bowlby (1855–1929), who was surgeon to King George V. Bowlby, through his work during the Boer War and World War I, became an expert in the treatment of wounds.[4]

1. Birmingham, City Museum and Art Gallery, *Birmingham Gold and Silver, 1773–1973: An Exhibition Celebrating the Bicentenary of the Assay Office*, 1973.
2. For example, see a bowl illus. Barbara Morris, *Liberty Design, 1874–1914* (Secaucus, N.J., 1989), p. 84; also a bowl of 1905/6, illus. Lionel Lambourne, *Utopian Craftsmen* (New York, 1980), fig. 96. For other works marked by Cuzner, see Jones 1981, pp. 213, 219, 225, 239.
3. Birmingham, City Museum and Art Gallery, *Birmingham Gold and Silver, 1773–1973: An Exhibition Celebrating the Bicentenary of the Assay Office*, 1973.
4. Some papers of Bowlby and Foster are preserved at the Wellcome Institute for the History of Medicine, London (RAMC 365; MS 2414), but they do not reveal the occasion for the gift of this bowl.

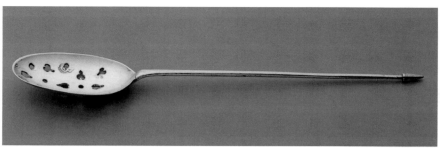

207

• 207 •

MOTE SPOON

London, 1703/4

Silver

33.217

MARKS: on inside of bowl, maker's mark possibly *L*; Britannia; lion's head erased; date letter *h*

L. 11.5 cm (4½ in.); w. 2.1 cm (¹³⁄₁₆ in.)

WEIGHT: 5.7 gm (2 dwt)

PROVENANCE: Anonymous Gift in Memory of Charlotte Beebe Wilbour (1833–1914), March 2, 1933

EXHIBITED: Boston, Museum of Fine Arts, 1933

DESCRIPTION: The spoon has an oval bowl that is pierced overall with heart-shaped openings in a geometric pattern. The slender stem tapers to a point. The spoon is forged from a single piece.

Mote spoons were used to skim stray tea leaves from a cup of tea. This is an unusually early example.

• 208 •

FOUR TABLESPOONS

Marked by John Smith (I) (free ca. 1690) and John Betts (first mark entered 1705)

London, 1704/5

Silver

35.1580, 35.1581, 35.1582, 35.1583

MARKS: 35.1580: on back of stem, maker's mark *SM* (Grimwade 2580); Britannia; lion's head erased; date letter *i*. 35.1581, 35.1582, 35.1583: on back of stem, maker's mark *B* (similar to Grimwade 154); Britannia; lion's head erased; date letter *i*

INSCRIPTIONS: 35.1580, 35.1581: engraved on back of handle, *Staple: Inn:*

35.1580: L. 20.4 cm (8 in.); w. 4.3 cm (1¹¹⁄₁₆ in.)

35.1581: L. 20.3 cm (8 in.); w. 4.5 cm (1¼ in.)

35.1582: L. 20.6 cm (8⅛ in.); w. 4.3 cm (1¹¹⁄₁₆ in.)

35.1583: L. 20.5 cm (8¹⁄₁₆ in.); w. 4.1 cm (1⅝ in.)

WEIGHT: 35.1580: 73.7 gm (2 oz 7 dwt). 35.1581: 76.5 gm (2 oz 9 dwt). 35.1582: 70.9 gm (2 oz 6 dwt). 35.1583: 70.9 gm (2 oz 6 dwt)

PROVENANCE: Bequest of Frank Brewer Bemis, November 7, 1935

DESCRIPTION: Each spoon is forged from a single piece of silver and has a deep oval bowl, a rat tail, a flattened stem, and a dog-nose terminus. On the back of the stem is an engraved cartouche containing a pillow and traces of obliterated initials.

Staple Inn, located on the east side of Chancery Lane, was one of the Inns of Chancery, a preliminary educational establishment for young lawyers. Like Barnard's Inn, Staple Inn was affiliated with Gray's Inn. The specialized legal needs of the wool trade were served there, giving the institution its name as well as the badge, engraved on the back of these spoons.[1]

1. Sir Robert Megarry, *Inns Ancient and Modern* (London, 1972), pp. 9–38.

208

209

210

· 209 ·

LADLE

Marked by John Fawdery (I) (free 1695, d. 1724)

London, 1704/5

Silver

35.1584

MARKS: on side of bowl, Britannia; maker's mark *FA* (Grimwade 662); lion's head erased (repeated on underside of stem); date letter *i*

INSCRIPTIONS: engraved on underside in monogram, *AGE*

L. 44.6 cm (17⁹⁄₁₆ in.); w. 7.7 cm (3 in.)

WEIGHT: 258 gm (8 oz 6 dwt)

PROVENANCE: Crichton Brothers, New York, purchased by Frank Brewer Bemis, February 2, 1920, Bequest of Frank Brewer Bemis, November 7, 1935

DESCRIPTION: The ladle has a deep oval bowl that is raised from sheet and joined to a long tapering cylindrical stem formed from seamed sheet.

· 210 ·

SPOON

Marked by Edward Sweet (d. 1737)

Exeter, 1710/1

Silver

41.227

MARKS: on back of stem, maker's mark *SW* (Jackson 1989, p. 292); Britannia; lion's head erased; castle; date letter *K*

INSCRIPTIONS: pricked on back of stem, *I.B/ M .S/1710*

L. 20.9 cm (8¼ in.); w. 4.8 cm (1⅞ in.)

WEIGHT: 51 gm (1 oz 13 dwt)

PROVENANCE: Bequest of Dr. George L. Walton, April 10, 1941

DESCRIPTION: The spoon has a deep oval bowl, a beaded rat tail, and a flattened stem with a trefid terminus. The bowl and stem are forged from a single piece.

211

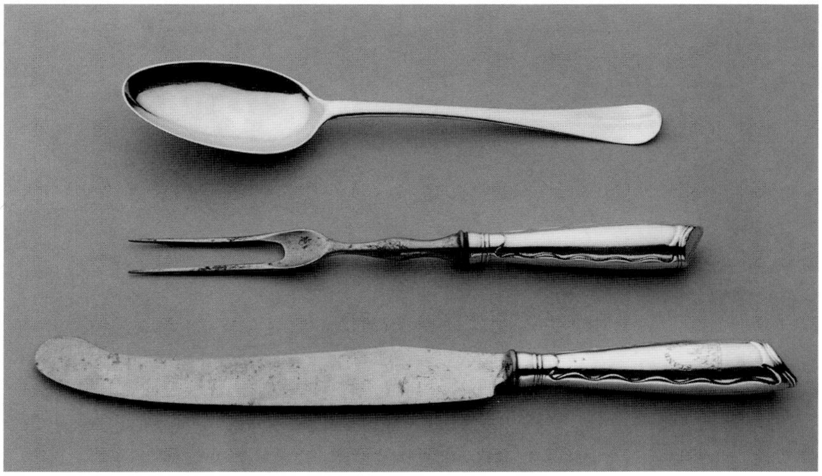

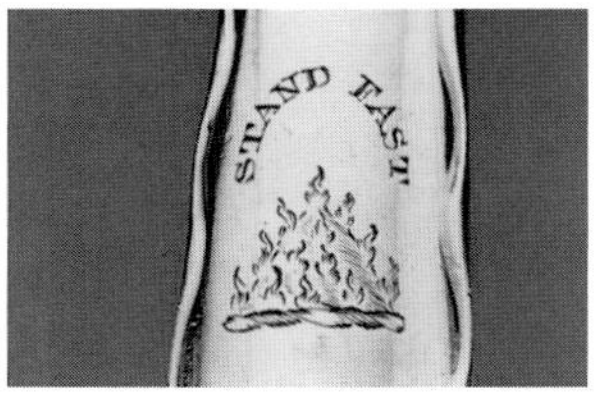

• 211 •

Set of knives, forks, spoons

London, ca. 1715

Silver, steel

32.368.1–.35

MARKS: 32.368.1–32.368.12 (knives) except 32.368.9 and 32.368.12 have an illegible maker's mark on the handle (possibly *IT* or *TI* or *II*). 32.368.13–32.368.24 (forks) have an illegible maker's mark on the stem (possibly *IT* or *TI* or *II*). 32.368.25, on stem, maker's mark *GR* with two pellets above; Britannia; lion's head erased; date letter *r* (1712). 32.368.26, on stem, maker's mark *AR* (possibly Grimwade 84 for Andrew Archer); Britannia; lion's head erased; date letter *t* (1714/5). 32.368.28, 32.368.31, on stem, maker's mark *HO* with a fleur-de-lys above and below in a shaped shield (Grimwade 1051 for John Holland I); Britannia; lion's head erased; date letter *B* (1717/8). 32.368.27, 32.368.29, 32.368.30, 32.368.32, 32.368.33, 32.368.34, 32.368.35, all marked on stem, all illegible

ARMORIALS: engraved on handles of all knives, except 32.368.9 and 32.368.12, the crest and motto of Grant

INSCRIPTIONS: 32.368.11: stamped on blade, *MOVES*

32.368.1: L. 27.8 cm ($10\frac{15}{16}$ in.); W. 2.1 cm ($\frac{13}{16}$ in.)
32.368.2: L. 27.5 cm ($10\frac{13}{16}$ in.); W. 2.1 cm ($\frac{13}{16}$ in.)
32.368.3: L. 27.3 cm ($10\frac{3}{4}$ in.);W. 2.2 cm ($\frac{7}{8}$ in.)
32.368.4: L. 27.4 cm ($10\frac{13}{16}$ in.); W. 2.2 cm ($\frac{7}{8}$ in.)
32.368.5: L. 27.2 cm ($10\frac{11}{16}$ in.); W. 2.1 cm ($\frac{13}{16}$ in.)
32.368.6: L. 27.4 cm ($10\frac{13}{16}$ in.); W. 2.1 cm ($\frac{13}{16}$ in.)
32.368.7: L. 27.2 cm ($10\frac{11}{16}$ in.); W. 2.1 cm ($\frac{13}{16}$ in.)
32.368.8: L. 27.4 cm ($10\frac{13}{16}$ in.); W. 2.2 cm ($\frac{7}{8}$ in.)
32.368.9: L. 27.1 cm ($10\frac{11}{16}$ in.); W. 2.1 cm ($\frac{13}{16}$ in.)
32.368.10: L. 27.3 cm ($10\frac{3}{4}$ in.); W. 2.1 cm ($\frac{13}{16}$ in.)
32.368.11: L. 27.3 cm ($10\frac{3}{4}$ in.); W. 2.1 cm ($\frac{13}{16}$ in.)
32.368.12: L. 27.4 cm ($10\frac{13}{16}$ in.); W. 2.1 cm ($\frac{13}{16}$ in.)
32.368.13: L. 21 cm ($8\frac{1}{4}$ in.); W. 2 cm ($\frac{13}{16}$ in.)
32.368.14: L. 21.1 cm ($8\frac{5}{16}$ in.); W. 2 cm ($\frac{13}{16}$ in.)
32.368.15: L. 21.2 cm ($8\frac{3}{8}$ in.); W. 2 cm ($\frac{13}{16}$ in.)
32.368.16: L. 21.1 cm ($8\frac{5}{16}$ in.); W. 1.9 cm ($\frac{3}{4}$ in.)
32.368.17: L. 21 cm ($8\frac{1}{4}$ in.); W. 2 cm ($\frac{13}{16}$ in.)
32.368.18: L. 21.2 cm ($8\frac{3}{8}$ in.); W. 2 cm ($\frac{13}{16}$ in.)
32.368.19: L. 21.2 cm ($8\frac{3}{8}$ in.); W. 2 cm ($\frac{13}{16}$ in.)
32.368.20: L. 21 cm ($8\frac{1}{4}$ in.); W. 1.9 cm ($\frac{3}{4}$ in.)
32.368.21: L. 21 cm ($8\frac{1}{4}$ in.); W. 2 cm ($\frac{13}{16}$ in.)
32.368.22: L. 21 cm ($8\frac{1}{4}$ in.); W. 2 cm ($\frac{13}{16}$ in.)
32.368.23: L. 21.5 cm ($8\frac{1}{2}$ in.); W. 2 cm ($\frac{13}{16}$ in.)
32.368.24: L. 21.2 cm ($8\frac{3}{8}$ in.); W. 1.9 cm ($\frac{3}{4}$ in.)
32.368.25: L. 19.4 cm ($7\frac{5}{8}$ in.); W. 4 cm ($1\frac{9}{16}$ in.)
32.368.26: L. 19.6 cm ($7\frac{3}{4}$ in.); W. 4.1 cm ($1\frac{5}{8}$ in.)

32.368.27: L. 20 cm (7⅞ in.); w. 4.3 cm (1¹¹⁄₁₆ in.)
32.368.28: L. 20.5 cm (8¹⁄₁₆ in.); w. 4.2 cm (1¹¹⁄₁₆ in.)
32.368.29: L. 19.9 cm (7⅞ in.); w. 4.1 cm (1⅝ in.)
32.368.30: L. 20.6 cm (8⅛ in.); w. 4.3 cm (1¹¹⁄₁₆ in.)
32.368.31: L. 20 cm (7⅞ in.); w. 4.2 cm (1¹¹⁄₁₆ in.)
32.368.32: L. 20.5 cm (8¹⁄₁₆ in.); w. 4.3 cm (1¹¹⁄₁₆ in.)
32.368.33: L. 19.6 cm (7¾ in.); w. 4.2 cm (1¹¹⁄₁₆ in.)
32.368.34: L. 19.9 cm (7⅞ in.); w. 4.2 cm (1¹¹⁄₁₆ in.)
32.368.35: L. 19.9 cm (7⅞ in.); w. 4.1 cm (1⅝ in.)

WEIGHT: (spoons) 32.368.25: 42.5 gm (1 oz 8 dwt).
32.368.26: 65 gm (2 oz). 32.368.27: 54 gm (1 oz
14 dwt). 32.368.28: 59.5 gm (1 oz 18 dwt).
32.368.29: 45 gm (1 oz 8 dwt). 32.368.30: 56 gm
(1 oz 16 dwt). 32.368.31: 59.5 gm (1 oz 18 dwt).
32.368.32: 56 gm (1 oz 16 dwt). 32.368.33: 48 gm
(1 oz 10 dwt). 32.368.34: 51 gm (1 oz 12 dwt).
32.368.35: 51 gm (1 oz 12 dwt)

PROVENANCE: Bequest of Charles Hitchcock Tyler,
September 1, 1932

DESCRIPTION: The knives and forks have a slightly
flaring decorated cylindrical handle, cast in two
pieces, with an angled terminus. The spoons have an
oval bowl, a rat tail, and a flattened stem with a
ridged, Hanoverian terminus.

· 212 ·

MARROW SPOON
Marked by Paul de Lamerie (1688–1751)
London, ca. 1715
Silver
33.231

MARKS: on back of handle, maker's mark *LA*
(Grimwade 1892)

ARMORIALS: engraved on back of larger end, the
crest of Frenband, Bedford, Brown, Cowmeadow,
Stoyt, or Western

L. 20.5 cm (8¹⁄₁₆ in.); w. 2 cm (¹³⁄₁₆ in.)

WEIGHT: 42.6 gm (1 oz 7 dwt)

PROVENANCE: Anonymous Gift in Memory of
Charlotte Beebe Wilbour (1833–1914), March 2,
1933

EXHIBITED: Boston, Museum of Fine Arts, 1933

DESCRIPTION: The spoon, forged from a single
piece, has a long shallow bowl with a rounded end.
The slightly tapering stem, semicircular in section,
forms a second narrow bowl.

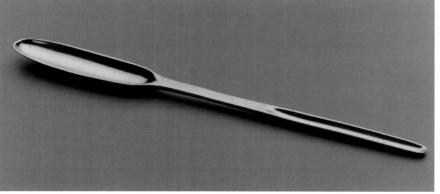

212

· 213 ·

SUGAR TONGS
Marked by John Gibbons (first mark entered
1700)
London, ca. 1720
Silver
38.984

MARKS: inside tongs, maker's mark *IG* (Grimwade
1321); lion passant

L. 13 cm (5⅛ in.); w. 3.4 cm (1⁵⁄₁₆ in.)

WEIGHT: 19.8 gm (13 dwt)

PROVENANCE: Walter H. Willson, Ltd., London,
purchased by Theodora Wilbour, August 1938,
Anonymous Gift in Memory of Charlotte Beebe
Wilbour (1833–1914), September 8, 1938

DESCRIPTION: The tongs are formed of two parallel fabricated balusters with shovel-shaped ends
joined to a lobed spring-activated terminus with a
baluster end formed of cast components.

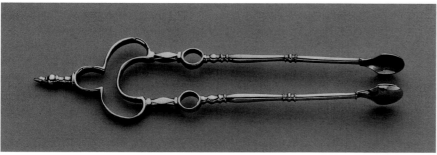

213

214

TABLESPOON
Marked by Andrew Archer (first mark entered
1703, d. 1725)
London, 1723/4
Silver
33.230

MARKS: on back of stem, maker's mark *A*
(Grimwade 1); lion passant; date letter *H*; leopard's
head crowned

ARMORIALS: engraved on back of stem, the crest
of Lewes

INSCRIPTIONS: engraved on back of bowl, *John
Goostrey Old Devil Temple Barr*

L. 20.2 cm (7¹⁵⁄₁₆ in.); w. 4.2 cm (1⅝ in.)

WEIGHT: 59.5 gm (1 oz 18 dwt)

PROVENANCE: Anonymous Gift in Memory of
Charlotte Beebe Wilbour (1833–1914), March 2,
1933

EXHIBITED: Boston, Museum of Fine Arts, 1933

DESCRIPTION: The spoon is forged from a single
piece of silver and has a deep oval bowl, a rat tail, a
flattened stem, and a ridged Hanoverian terminus.

The Old Devil Tavern, also known as the Devil
and St. Dunstan or the Noisy Devil, stood at
number 2 Fleet Street next door to a goldsmith's shop. It was made famous by Ben
Johnson who presided there over the Apollo,
one of London's earliest clubs. Other patrons
whose writings mention the site include
Samuel Pepys, John Evelyn, and Jonathan
Swift.[1]

1. Edward Callow, *Old London Taverns* (London,
1899), pp. 207–14; Henry C. Shelley, *Inns and Taverns
of Old London* (Boston, 1909), pp. 93–101. My thanks
to Taryn Zarrillo for contributing these references.

215

· 215 ·

PAIR OF FORKS

Marked by Paul Hanet (first mark entered 1716)

London, 1723/4

Silver

33.278-279

MARKS: on back of stem of each, maker's mark *HA* (Grimwade 942); lion's head erased; date letter *H*; Britannia

ARMORIALS: engraved on back of stem of each, an unidentified crest (a boar's head erased and erect)

INSCRIPTIONS: engraved on back of each, *SMG*

33.278: L. 20 cm (7⅞ in.); w. 2.3 cm (⅞ in.)

33.279: L. 19.9 cm (7⅞ in.); w. 2.3 cm (⅞ in.)

WEIGHT: 33.278: 70.9 gm (2 oz 6 dwt). 33.279: 73 gm (2 oz 3 dwt)

PROVENANCE: Anonymous Gift in Memory of Charlotte Beebe Wilbour (1833–1914), March 2, 1933

EXHIBITED: Boston, Museum of Fine Arts, 1933; Toronto, George R. Gardiner Museum of Ceramic Art, 1998

DESCRIPTION: Each three-pronged fork, forged from a single piece, has a flattened stem and a ridged, Hanoverian terminus.

216

· 216 ·

LARGE SPOON

Marked by Hugh Arnett and Edward Pocock (entered into partnership 1720)

London, 1723/4

Silver

42.9

MARKS: on back of stem, lion passant; date letter *H*; leopard's head crowned; maker's mark *HE* with an *A* above and a *P* below (Grimwade 993)

INSCRIPTIONS: engraved on back of stem, *M/T⋆D*

L. 36.8 cm (14½ in.); w. 6 cm (2⅜ in.)

WEIGHT: 226.8 gm (7 oz 6 dwt)

PROVENANCE: Anonymous Gift in Memory of Charlotte Beebe Wilbour (1833–1914), January 8, 1942

DESCRIPTION: The spoon, forged from a single piece, has a deep oval bowl, a rat tail, a flattened stem, and a ridged Hanoverian terminus.

217

218

· 217 ·

TABLESPOON

Probably by Philip Elston (d. 1755)

Exeter, 1725/6

Silver

33.253

MARKS: on back of stem, maker's mark *PE* (similar to Jackson 1989, p. 293); leopard's head crowned; lion passant; castle; date letter *a*

ARMORIALS: engraved on back of stem, the crest of Tatum; engraved on end of stem, the crest of Hall or Butts

INSCRIPTIONS: pricked on back of stem, *MW/Sept. ye 4th/1725*

L. 20.8 cm (8³⁄₁₆ in.); w. 4.2 cm (1⅝ in.)

WEIGHT: 76.5 gm (2 oz 9 dwt)

PROVENANCE: Anonymous Gift in Memory of Charlotte Beebe Wilbour (1833–1914), March 2, 1933

DESCRIPTION: The spoon, forged from a single piece, has a deep oval bowl, a rat tail, a flattened stem, and a ridged Hanoverian terminus.

· 218 ·

TABLESPOON

Marked by Edward Hall (free 1720)

London, 1726/7

Silver

12.40

MARKS: on back of stem, maker's mark *EH* (Grimwade 594); leopard's head crowned; lion passant; date letter *L*

INSCRIPTIONS: engraved on back of stem, *A★B/S : F*

L. 20 cm (7⅞ in.); w. 4 cm (1⁹⁄₁₆ in.)

WEIGHT: 68 gm (2 oz 4 dwt)

PROVENANCE: Anonymous Gift (Miss S. E. Hearsey), January 4, 1912

DESCRIPTION: The spoon is forged from a single piece of silver and has an oval bowl, a rat tail, a flattened stem, and a ribbed Hanoverian terminus. The bowl is worn and pitted.

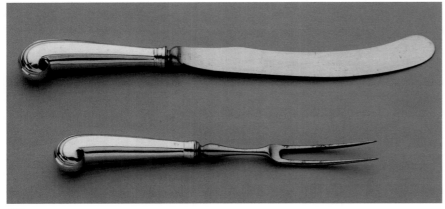

219

• 219 •

A PAIR OF KNIVES AND A PAIR OF FORKS

London, ca. 1740
Silver, steel
33.274–277

MARKS: 33.274 (knife): on side of handle, an illegible mark. 33.275 (fork), 33.277 (fork), 33.276 (knife): on side of handles, maker's mark *AB* incuse; on the other side, lion passant. 33.274, 33.276 (knives): on blade, cutler's mark, a dagger; cutler's personal devices (2 devices and *HOW*)

ARMORIALS: engraved on side of each handle, the crest of Kilmore or Tany

33.274 (knife): L. 26.8 cm (10⁹⁄₁₆ in.); w. 2.8 cm (1⅛ in.)

33.275 (fork): L. 18.7 cm (7⅜ in.); w. 2.5 cm (1 in.)

33.276 (knife): L. 26.5 cm (10⁷⁄₁₆ in.); w. 3 cm (1³⁄₁₆ in.)

33.277 (fork): L. 19.8 cm (7¹³⁄₁₆ in.); w. 2.6 cm (1¹⁄₁₆ in.)

WEIGHT: 33.275: 82 gm (2 oz 6 dwt). 33.277: 76.5 gm (2 oz 4 dwt)

PROVENANCE: Anonymous Gift in Memory of Charlotte Beebe Wilbour (1833–1914), March 2, 1933

EXHIBITED: 33.274, Boston, Museum of Fine Arts, 1933. 33.274, 33.275, Toronto, George R. Gardiner Museum of Ceramic Art, 1998

DESCRIPTION: Each knife and fork has a ribbed pistol handle cast in two vertically seamed pieces.

220

• 220 •

PAIR OF KNIVES

London, ca. 1740
Silver, steel
33.292–293

MARKS: 33.293: on blade, cutler's devices, a crown with *V* or *W* left and *R* right, over *GARRARD*

33.292: L. 21.3 cm (8⅜ in.); w. 2.8 cm (1⅛ in.)

33.293: L. 21.6 cm (8½ in.); w. 2.7 cm (1¹⁄₁₆ in.)

PROVENANCE: Anonymous Gift in Memory of Charlotte Beebe Wilbour (1833–1914), March 2, 1933

EXHIBITED: Boston, Museum of Fine Arts, 1933

DESCRIPTION: Each knife has a tapering octagonal pistol handle formed from two vertically seamed cast pieces.

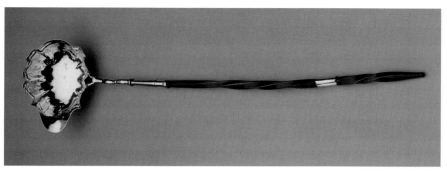

221

· 221 ·

PUNCH LADLE

Marked by Samuel Meriton (I) (first mark
entered 1739)
London, 1747/8
Silver, horn
18.31

MARKS: on inside of bowl, date letter *m*; lion passant; maker's mark *SM* (Grimwade 2590); leopard's
head crowned

L. 40 cm (15¾ in.); w. 8.7 cm (3⁷⁄₁₆ in.)

WEIGHT: 54 gm (1 oz 14 dwt)

PROVENANCE: Gift of Miss M. H. Jewell,
March 21, 1918

DESCRIPTION: The ladle has a long stem of twisted
horn that has been repaired near the end with a silver ferrule. The fluted silver bowl, formed from
raised sheet, has a shaped spout at one end and is
joined to the stem by a scrolled bracket.

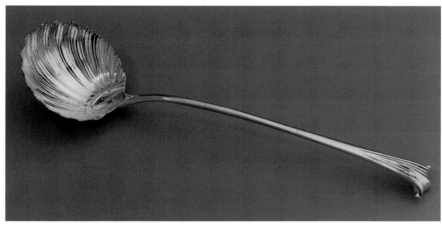

222

· 222 ·

LADLE

Marked by Isaac Callard (free 1726)
London, ca. 1750
Silver
20.1626

MARKS: on back of handle, maker's mark *IC*
(Grimwade 1224) (struck four times)

L. 27.7 cm (10⅞ in.); w. 7.6 cm (3 in.)

WEIGHT: 110 gm (3 oz 5 dwt)

PROVENANCE: Lent by Mrs. B. M. Jones, June 14,
1916, purchased October 7, 1920, Samuel Putnam
Avery Fund,

DESCRIPTION: The ladle, which is forged, has a
fluted, round bowl, a curving stem that is square in
section, and a ribbed Onslow end.

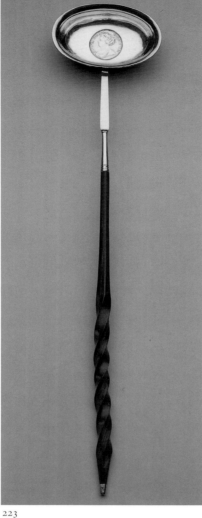

223

· 223 ·

PUNCH LADLE

England, ca. 1750

Silver, horn

Res.35.39

UNMARKED

INSCRIPTIONS: engraved in monogram on front of
bowl, *HAF*

L: 36.7 cm (14⁷⁄₁₆ in.); W. 7.8 cm (3¹⁄₁₆ in.)

WEIGHT: 48 gm (1 oz 10 dwt)

PROVENANCE: Bequest of Charles Hitchcock Tyler,
December 5, 1935

DESCRIPTION: The ladle has a long stem of twisted
horn with a faceted silver finial. The oval silver
bowl, formed from raised sheet, has a Queen Anne
shilling set into the center and is joined to the stem
by a plain silver ferrule.

· 224 ·

FOUR TABLESPOONS

Probably by James Tookey (first mark entered
1750, d. 1773)

London, 1752/3 and 1760

Silver

33.245, 33.246, 33.247, 33.248

MARKS: 33.245, 33.246: on back of stem, maker's
mark *IT* (Grimwade 1703); date letter *r*; lion passant;
leopard's head crowned. 33.247, 33.248: on back of
handle, maker's mark *IT* (Grimwade 1703); lion passant; leopard's head crowned; date letter *E*

ARMORIALS: engraved on each stem, the crest of
Hall or Butts

33.245: L. 20.3 cm (8 in.); W. 4.3 cm (1¹¹⁄₁₆ in.)

33.246: L. 20.2 cm (7¹⁵⁄₁₆ in.); W. 4.2 cm (1⅝ in.)

33.247: L. 20.3 cm (8 in.); W. 4.3 cm (1¹¹⁄₁₆ in.)

33.248: L. 20.1 cm (7⅞ in.); W. 4.3 cm (1¹¹⁄₁₆ in.)

WEIGHT: 33.245: 68 gm (2 oz 4 dwt). 33.246:
65.2 gm (2 oz 2 dwt). 33.247: 65 gm (2 oz). 33.248:
65 gm (2 oz)

PROVENANCE: Anonymous Gift in Memory of
Charlotte Beebe Wilbour (1833–1914), March 2,
1933

EXHIBITED: 33.247, Toronto, George R. Gardiner
Museum of Ceramic Art, 1998

DESCRIPTION: Each spoon is forged from a single
piece of silver and has a deep oval bowl, a rat tail, a
flattened stem, and a ridged Hanoverian terminus.

224

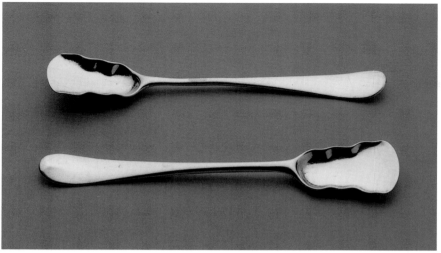

225

· 225 ·

PAIR OF SALT SPOONS
Probably London, ca. 1760
Silver
35.1628–1629

MARKS: on stem of each, illegible

35.1628: L. 8.9 cm (3½ in.); w. 1.7 cm (¹¹⁄₁₆ in.)

35.1629: L. 9 cm (3⁹⁄₁₆ in.); w. 1.7 cm (¹¹⁄₁₆ in.)

WEIGHT: 35.1628: 8.5 gm (2 dwt). 35.1629: 8.5 gm
(2 dwt)

PROVENANCE: Crichton Brothers, Inc., New York,
purchased by Frank Brewer Bemis, May 1, 1918,
Bequest of Frank Brewer Bemis, November 7, 1935

DESCRIPTION: Each forged spoon has a plain
upturned terminus and a shovel-shaped bowl with
rippled sides.

226

· 226 ·

SUGAR NIPPERS
Probably by Henry Plumpton (only mark entered
1761)
London, ca. 1760
Silver
Res.46.42

MARKS: lion passant (repeated on other handle
ring); on inside of one handle ring, maker's mark
HP (similar to Grimwade 1059) (struck twice on
other handle ring)

INSCRIPTIONS: scratched on side of hinge, RW

L. 11.7 cm (4⅝ in.); w. 5.2 cm (2¹⁄₁₆ in.)

WEIGHT: 36.8 gm (1 oz 4 dwt)

PROVENANCE: Anonymous Gift in Memory of
Charlotte Beebe Wilbour (1833–1914), November
14, 1946

DESCRIPTION: The scissor-style nippers have
shaped ring handles and scrolled stems terminating
in shells that are formed from cast components.

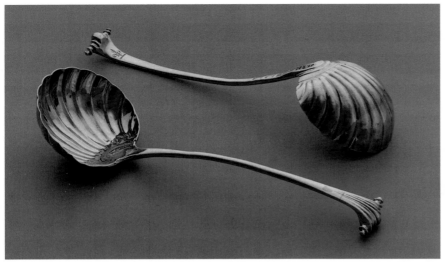

227

PAIR OF LADLES

Probably by George Baskerville (first mark entered 1738)

London, 1761/2

Silver

33.260–261

MARKS: on back of stem of each, date letter *F*; leopard's head crowned; lion passant; maker's mark *GB* (similar to Grimwade 750, 754)

ARMORIALS: engraved on back of stem of each, an unidentified crest (a fleur-de-lys)

33.260: L. 17.7 cm (6¹⁵⁄₁₆ in.); w. 5.5 cm (2³⁄₁₆ in.)

33.261: L. 17.7 cm (6¹⁵⁄₁₆ in.); w. 5.8 cm (2⁵⁄₁₆ in.)

WEIGHT: 33.260: 48.2 gm (1 oz 11 dwt). 33.261: 51 gm (1 oz 13 dwt)

PROVENANCE: Anonymous Gift in Memory of Charlotte Beebe Wilbour (1833–1914), March 2, 1933

EXHIBITED: Boston, Museum of Fine Arts, 1933; Toronto, George R. Gardiner Museum of Ceramic Art, 1998

DESCRIPTION: Each forged ladle has a fluted round bowl, a curving stem that is square in section, and a ribbed Onslow end.

228

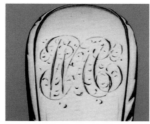

· 228 ·

SERVING SPOON

Probably by Thomas Chawner (1734–d. ca. 1802/11)

London, ca. 1765

Silver

33.255

MARKS: on back of stem, maker's mark *TC* with a *W* above and a *C* below (Grimwade 3817); lion passant; leopard's head crowned; date letter, possibly *k* or *p*

INSCRIPTIONS: engraved on end of stem in monogram, *WAC*; engraved on back of stem, *Prince of Wales Coffee House/61*

L. 27.8 cm (10¹⁵⁄₁₆ in.); w. 4.9 cm (1¹⁵⁄₁₆ in.)

WEIGHT: 88 gm (2 oz 16 dwt)

PROVENANCE: Anonymous Gift in Memory of Charlotte Beebe Wilbour (1833–1914), March 2, 1933

EXHIBITED: Boston, Museum of Fine Arts, 1933

DESCRIPTION: The forged spoon has a shallow oval bowl and a long plain stem with an engraved feather edge. The bowl has been crudely repaired and the stem has been broken and soldered at the midsection.

229

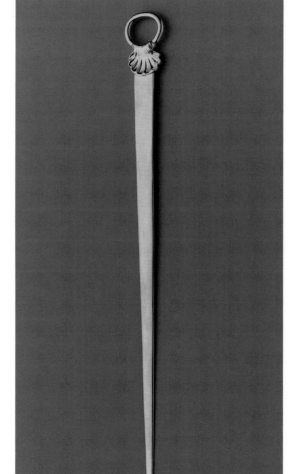

230

• 229 •

SIX MINIATURE SPOONS
Marked by Richard Richardson (II) or (III)
(first mark entered 1730)
Chester, ca. 1765–70
Silver
39.820–825

MARKS: on back of stem of each, maker's mark *RR*
(similar to Jackson 1989, p. 399 or p. 400)

39.820: L. 5.9 cm (2⁵⁄₁₆ in.); w. 1.1 cm (⁷⁄₁₆ in.)

39.821: L. 6 cm (2⅜ in.); w. 1.2 cm (½ in.)

39.822: L. 5.9 cm (2⁵⁄₁₆ in.); w. 1.2 cm (½ in.)

39.823: L. 5.9 cm (2⁵⁄₁₆ in.); w. 1.2 cm (½ in.)

39.824: L. 5.9 cm (2⁵⁄₁₆ in.); w. 1.2 cm (½ in.)

39.825: L. 5.9 cm (2⁵⁄₁₆ in.); w. 1.2 cm (½ in.)

WEIGHT: 39.820: 2.8 gm (2 dwt). 39.821: 2.8 gm
(2 dwt). 39.822: 2.8 gm (2 dwt). 39.823: 2.8 gm
(2 dwt). 39.824: 2.8 gm (2 dwt). 39.825: 2.8 gm
(2 dwt)

PROVENANCE: Anonymous Gift in Memory of
Charlotte Beebe Wilbour (1833–1914),
December 14, 1939

DESCRIPTION: Each fabricated spoon has a small
oval bowl and a plain stem with a Hanoverian terminus.

• 230 •

SKEWER
Marked by Samuel Herbert & Co. (first mark
entered 1747)
London, 1767/8
Silver
33.265

MARKS: below ring, maker's mark *SH* with an *H*
above and a *B* below (Grimwade 2545); lion passant;
leopard's head crowned; date letter *m*

L. 34.2 cm (13⁷⁄₁₀ in.); w. 3 cm (1³⁄₁₀ in.)

WEIGHT: 110 gm (3 oz 5 dwt)

PROVENANCE: Anonymous Gift in Memory of
Charlotte Beebe Wilbour (1833–1914), March 2,
1933

EXHIBITED: Boston, Museum of Fine Arts, 1933

DESCRIPTION: The skewer is forged, with a tapering flat blade and, at the terminus, a shell joined to a
flattened ring.

231

· 231 ·

SOUP LADLE

Marked by Thomas Ellis (mark entered as plate-
worker 1780)

London, ca. 1769/70

Silver

1980.264

MARKS: on back of stem, maker's mark *TE*
(Grimwade 2743); lion passant; leopard's head
crowned; date letter *O* or *D*

L. 34.7 cm (13¹¹⁄₁₆ in.); w. 9.3 cm (3¹¹⁄₁₆ in.)

WEIGHT: 155.9 gm (5 oz)

PROVENANCE: Gift of Mr. William Taylor, June 18,
1980

DESCRIPTION: The forged ladle has a broad fluted
bowl and a curved stem with a rounded end.

· 232 ·

MOTE SPOON

ca. 1770

Silver

35.1634

MARKS: on back of stem, maker's mark *B* in monogram (unrecorded) (struck twice)

L. 13.7 cm (5⅜ in.); w. 2.2 cm (⅞ in.)

WEIGHT: 8.5 gm (2 dwt)

PROVENANCE: Bequest of Frank Brewer Bemis,
November 7, 1935

DESCRIPTION: The spoon has an oval bowl with a
shell back pierced overall with crosses and scrolls in
a geometric pattern. The slender stem tapers to a
point. The spoon is forged from a single piece.

232

233

· 233 ·

TEASPOON
Possibly marked by John Scofield (first mark entered 1776)
London, ca. 1770
Silver
64.924

MARKS: on back of stem, maker's mark *JS* (Grimwade 3709); lion passant

INSCRIPTIONS: engraved on back, end of handle, *D/N A*

L. 12.1 cm (4¾ in.); w. 2.5 cm (1 in.)

WEIGHT: 14.2 gm (9 dwt)

PROVENANCE: Bequest of Maxim Karolik, June 8, 1964

DESCRIPTION: The forged teaspoon has a shallow oval bowl with a picture back depicting a ship in full sail and a plain stem with an upturned Hanoverian end.

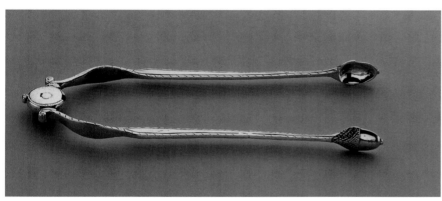

234

· 234 ·

TONGS
Possibly marked by James Harmar (only mark entered 1761)
London, ca. 1775
Silver
40.601

MARKS: on inside of one tong, lion passant; maker's mark *IH* (similar to Grimwade 1374); (repeated on inside of other tong) (struck twice)

L. 14.2 cm (5⁹⁄₁₆ in.); w. 4.6 cm (1¹³⁄₁₆ in.)

WEIGHT: 34 gm (1 oz)

PROVENANCE: Lent by Hollis French, February 2, 1915, Gift of Hollis French, October 10, 1940

DESCRIPTION: The tongs are formed from two shaped, fabricated pieces joined with a sprung end. The edges are engraved with a feather edge, and the grippers are in the shape of acorns.

235

236

· 235 ·

SIX TEASPOONS
Marked by William Sumner (I) and Richard Crossley
(entered into partnership 1775)
London, 1775–82
Silver
Res.33.99–104

MARKS: on back of stem of each, maker's mark *WS* over
RC (Grimwade 3334); lion passant; an unidentified mark,
H with part of a pellet to the right in a square

INSCRIPTIONS: engraved on front end of handle, *S/I★A*

Res.33.99: L. 11.2 cm (4⁷⁄₁₆ in.); w. 2.4 cm (¹⁵⁄₁₆ in.)

Res.33.100: L. 11.6 cm (4⁹⁄₁₆ in.); w. 2.4 cm (¹⁵⁄₁₆ in.)

Res.33.101: L. 11.5 cm (4½ in.); w. 2.4 cm (¹⁵⁄₁₆ in.)

Res.33.102: L. 11.7 cm (4⅝ in.); w. 2.4 cm (¹⁵⁄₁₆ in.)

Res.33.103: L. 11.6 cm (4⁹⁄₁₆ in.); w. 2.4 cm (¹⁵⁄₁₆ in.)

Res.33.104: L. 11.4 cm (4½ in.); w. 2.3 cm (¹⁵⁄₁₆ in.)

WEIGHT: Res.33.99: 11.3 gm (7 dwt). Res.33.100: 11.3
gm (7 dwt). Res.33.101: 11.3 gm (7 dwt). Res.33.102:
11.3 gm (7 dwt). Res.33.103: 11.3 gm (7 dwt).
Res.33.104: 11.3 gm (7 dwt)

PROVENANCE: Anonymous Gift in Memory of
Charlotte Beebe Wilbour (1833–1914), March 2, 1933

DESCRIPTION: Each forged teaspoon has a shallow oval
bowl with a plain drop and a flattened stem with a
ridged Hanoverian end.

· 236 ·

PAIR OF LADLES
Marked by Hester Bateman (1708–1794) and George
Smith (III) (first mark entered 1774)
London, 1779/80
Silver
33.258–259

MARKS: 33.258: on back of stem, date letter *d*; leopard's
head crowned; lion passant; maker's mark *HB* (Grimwade
960). 33.259: on back of stem, date letter *d*; leopard's
head crowned; lion passant; maker's mark *GS* (Grimwade 906)

33.258: L. 17.3 cm (6¹³⁄₁₆ in.); w. 5.4 cm (2⅛ in.)

33.259: L. 17.2 cm (6¾ in.); w. 5.3 cm (2¹⁄₁₆ in.)

WEIGHT: 33.258: 42.5 gm (1 oz 4 dwt). 33.259: 42.5 gm
(1 oz 4 dwt)

PROVENANCE: Anonymous Gift in Memory of
Charlotte Beebe Wilbour (1833–1914), March 2, 1933

EXHIBITED: Boston, Museum of Fine Arts, 1933

DESCRIPTION: Each forged ladle has a round fluted
bowl, a curved handle that is square in section, and a
ribbed Onslow terminus.

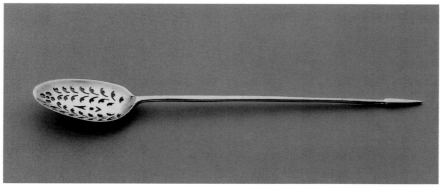

237

· 237 ·

Mote spoon

Marked by Hester Bateman (1708–1794)
London, ca. 1780
Silver
33.254

MARKS: on back of stem, lion passant; maker's mark *HB* (Grimwade 961)

L. 14.5 cm (5¹¹⁄₁₆ in.); w. 2.4 cm (¹⁵⁄₁₆ in.)

WEIGHT: 8 gm (5 dwt)

PROVENANCE: Anonymous Gift in Memory of Charlotte Beebe Wilbour (1833–1914), March 2, 1933

EXHIBITED: Boston, Museum of Fine Arts, 1933

DESCRIPTION: The spoon has an oval bowl that is pierced overall with garlands and flowers in a geometric pattern. The slender stem tapers to a point. The spoon is forged from a single piece. The stem has been repaired at the midsection, raising the possibility that the spoon was converted from a plain teaspoon into a mote spoon.

· 238 ·

Skewer

Marked by William Pearse (first mark entered 1774)
Exeter, 1783/4
Silver
33.263

MARKS: below ring handle, maker's mark *WP* (Jackson 1989, p. 295); lion passant; castle; date letter *K*

L. 36.5 cm (14⅜ in.); w. 2.6 cm (1 in.)

WEIGHT: 99 gm (3 oz 1 dwt)

PROVENANCE: Anonymous Gift in Memory of Charlotte Beebe Wilbour (1833–1914), March 2, 1933

EXHIBITED: Boston, Museum of Fine Arts, 1933

DESCRIPTION: The skewer is forged, with a tapering flat blade and, at the terminus, a shaped oval joined to a flattened ring. A garland is engraved around the oval.

238

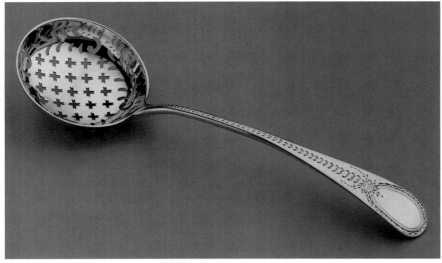

239

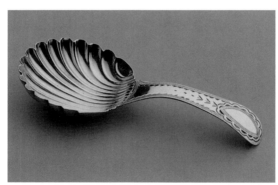

240

· 239 ·

SUGAR SIFTER SPOON
Marked by Thomas Wallis (II) (first mark entered
1778, d. 1836)
London, 1786/7
Silver
40.194

MARKS: on back of stem, maker's mark *TW*
(Grimwade 2975); lion passant; date letter *l*; sovereign's head

INSCRIPTIONS: scratched on handle, *11147*

L. 17.1 cm (6¾ in.); w. 5.1 cm (2 in.)

WEIGHT: 39 gm (1 oz 3 dwt)

PROVENANCE: Anonymous Gift in Memory of
Charlotte Beebe Wilbour (1833–1914), April 11, 1940

DESCRIPTION: The spoon, forged from one piece,
has a deep round bowl pierced with crosses and garlands in a geometric pattern. The curving stem has
an "Old English" end with a bright-cut medallion.

· 240 ·

CADDY SPOON
Marked by Hester Bateman (1708–1794)
London, 1789/90
Silver
33.190

MARKS: on back of stem, lion passant; date letter *o*;
sovereign's head; maker's mark *HB* (Grimwade 961)

L. 8 cm (3⅛ in.); diam. of bowl 3.7 cm (1⁷⁄₁₆ in.)

WEIGHT: 8.5 gm (2 dwt)

PROVENANCE: Anonymous Gift in Memory of
Charlotte Beebe Wilbour (1833–1914), March 2,
1933

EXHIBITED: Boston, Museum of Fine Arts, 1933

DESCRIPTION: The spoon, fabricated from sheet,
has a broad fluted bowl and a short curved stem
with a bright-cut border and medallion.

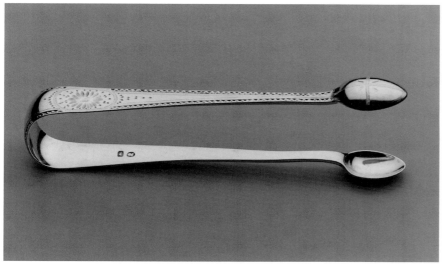

241

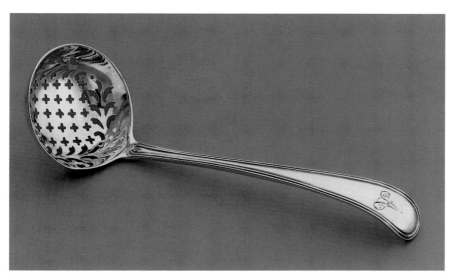

242

· 241 ·

SUGAR TONGS

Probably by Samuel Wintle (first mark entered
1778)
London, ca. 1790
Silver
47.1352

MARKS: on inside of one arm, maker's mark *SW*
(possibly Grimwade 2662). Inside other arm, lion
passant; sovereign's head

INSCRIPTIONS: engraved on top of tongs in
monogram, *MB*

L. 14 cm (5½ in.); w. 4.8 cm (1⅞ in.)

WEIGHT: 34 gm (1 oz)

PROVENANCE: Gift of Mary Adelaide Sargent Poor
in Memory of Adelaide Joanna Sargent,
September 18, 1947

DESCRIPTION: The U-shaped tongs are formed
from a single piece of silver, with shaped oval grippers, flat arms, and bright-cut ornament on the
outer edges enclosing a medallion.

· 242 ·

SUGAR SIFTER SPOON

Marked by George Smith (III) (first mark entered
1774)
London, 1792/3
Silver
41.624

MARKS: on back of stem, maker's mark *GS* over
WF (Grimwade 910); sovereign's head; date letter *r*;
leopard's head crowned; lion passant

INSCRIPTIONS: engraved on front end of stem, *A*

L. 14.9 cm (5¹³⁄₁₆ in.); w. 4.9 cm (1¹⁵⁄₁₆ in.)

WEIGHT: 34 gm (1 oz)

PROVENANCE: Amory family by descent to Martha
Codman Karolik (1858–1948), Gift of Mr. and Mrs.
Maxim Karolik for The M. & M. Karolik Collection
of Eighteenth-Century American Arts, October 9,
1941

PUBLISHED: Hipkiss 1941, cat. 179

DESCRIPTION: The spoon, forged from one piece,
has a deep round bowl pierced with crosses and garlands in a geometric pattern. The curving stem has
an Old English Thread end.

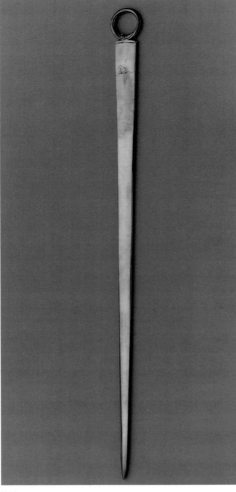

243

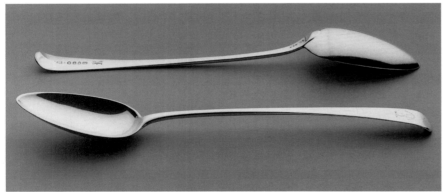

244

· 243 ·

SKEWER
Marked by Robert Jones (I) (first mark entered
1786)
Chester, 1793/4
Silver
33.264

MARKS: below ring, maker's mark *RI* (Jackson
1989, p. 401); sovereign's head; leopard's head
crowned; city arms for Chester; lion passant; date
letter *s*

ARMORIALS: engraved on side opposite marks,
below ring, the crest of Bagnall, Breach, Buggine,
Burgoigne, Eyre, Welch, or Welsh

INSCRIPTIONS: scratched below ring, *4079,
1570/SO1*

L. 35.7 cm (14¹⁄₁₆ in.); w. 2.3 cm (¹⁵⁄₁₆ in.)

WEIGHT: 104 gm (3 oz 3 dwt)

PROVENANCE: Anonymous Gift in Memory of
Charlotte Beebe Wilbour (1833–1914), March 2,
1933

EXHIBITED: Boston, Museum of Fine Arts, 1933

DESCRIPTION: The skewer is forged, with a tapering flat blade and, at the terminus, a ring.

· 244 ·

PAIR OF BASTING SPOONS
Marked by George Smith (III) (first mark entered
1774)
London, 1794/5
Silver
31.491–492

MARKS: on back of stem of each, lion passant; leopard's head crowned; date letter *t*; sovereign's head;
maker's mark *GS* over *WF* (Grimwade 910)

ARMORIALS: engraved on front of each, the crest
and motto of Campbell

INSCRIPTIONS: engraved on back of handle, *R*

31.491: L. 30.4 cm (11¹⁵⁄₁₆ in.); w. 5.3 cm (2¹⁄₁₆ in.)

31.492: L. 30.4 cm (11¹⁵⁄₁₆ in.); w. 5.4 cm (2⅛ in.)

WEIGHT: 31.491: 110.6 gm (3 oz 11 dwt). 31.492:
110.6 gm (3 oz 11 dwt)

PROVENANCE: Bequest of Miss O. M. E. Rowe,
July 16, 1931

DESCRIPTION: Each spoon, forged from a single
piece, has an oval bowl and a flattened stem with a
plain drop and a plain Hanoverian end.

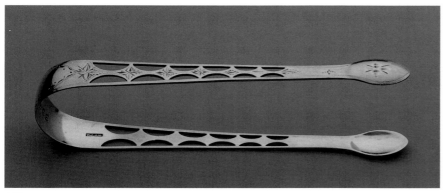

245

· 245 ·

SUGAR TONGS

Marked by Thomas Law (first mark entered 1773)
Sheffield, 1795/6
Silver
33.272

MARKS: on inside of one arm, maker's mark *T.LAW* (Jackson 1989, p. 441). Inside other arm, date letter *q*; sovereign's head; lion passant; maker's mark *TL* (Jackson 1989, p. 441)

INSCRIPTIONS: engraved on top of tongs, *EHL*

L. 14.2 cm (5⁹⁄₁₆ in.); w. 4.7 cm (1⅞ in.)

WEIGHT: 28 gm (9 dwt)

PROVENANCE: Anonymous Gift in Memory of Charlotte Beebe Wilbour (1833–1914), March 2, 1933

EXHIBITED: Boston, Museum of Fine Arts, 1933

DESCRIPTION: The U-shaped tongs are formed from a single piece of silver, with shaped oval grippers and flat arms that are pierced with semicircles in a geometric pattern and engraved with bright-cut medallions.

246

· 246 ·

MARROW SPOON

London, 1797/8
Silver
30.465

MARKS: on back of central section, sovereign's head; date letter *B*; leopard's head crowned; lion passant; maker's mark possibly *W*

ARMORIALS: engraved on underside of large bowl, the crest of Babcock

INSCRIPTIONS: engraved below crest in monogram, *AMB*

L. 23.1 cm (9¹⁄₁₆ in.); w. 1.9 cm (¾ in.)

WEIGHT: 51 gm (1 oz 13 dwt)

PROVENANCE: according to tradition, Adam Babcock of Boston (1740–1817); Gift of Miss Marian Lee Blake, June 19, 1930

DESCRIPTION: The spoon, forged from a single piece, has a long shallow bowl with a plain drop. The slightly tapering stem forms a second narrow bowl.

247

248

· 247 ·

CADDY SPOON

Chester, 1799/1800

Silver

55.970

MARKS: in cap, maker's mark *HA* in a rectangle (unrecorded); city mark for Chester; date letter *C*; lion passant; leopard's head crowned

L. 6 cm (2⅜ in.); w. 3.8 cm (1½ in.)

WEIGHT: 14.2 gm (9 dwt)

PROVENANCE: Shreve, Crump, and Low, Co., Boston, purchased December 8, 1955, Theodora Wilbour Fund in Memory of Charlotte Beebe Wilbour

DESCRIPTION: The caddy spoon is fabricated from sheet in the form of a jockey's cap with pounced and wrigglework ornament around the crown and brim.

· 248 ·

APOSTLE SPOON

Marked by Lionel Alfred Crichton (1866–1938)

London, 1934/5

Silver

36.154

MARKS: on back of handle, maker's mark *LAC* (Culme 10620–10647); date letter *t*; leopard's head; lion passant; sovereign's head

INSCRIPTIONS: engraved on front of handle, *SYNT.NYCOLAS.PRAY.FOR.VS*

L. 18.5 cm (7⅜ in.); w. 5.1 cm (2 in.)

WEIGHT: 90.7 gm (2 oz 18 dwt)

PROVENANCE: Anonymous Gift in Memory of Charlotte Beebe Wilbour (1833–1914), March 5, 1936

DESCRIPTION: The forged spoon has a fig-shaped bowl, a tapering hexagonal stem, and a cast finial depicting the bishop-saint Nicholas standing behind two boys emerging from a tub.

249

This simple cup, a characteristically Scottish form, has the flaring rim and applied ornament around the base that suggested its modern name, "thistle cup." The large number of surviving examples dating from the last decades of the seventeenth century suggest the popularity of the form.[1] James Penman marked this cup twice, once as its maker and the second time as assay master of the Edinburgh goldsmiths.

1. See an example marked by James Sympsone for 1693, illus. Wark 1978, p. 24, cat. 52; another marked for 1695, sold Christie's, London, March 19, 1934, lot 149; another marked by Alexander Forbes for 1696, illus. Finlay 1956, pl. 47; another marked by John Luke, Jr., Glasgow, ca. 1708, sold Christie's, London, January 31, 1979, lot 195.

· 249 ·

CUP

Marked by James Penman (first mark recorded 1673)
Edinburgh, 1700/1
Silver
32.407

MARKS: on underside, maker's mark *P* (Jackson, p. 544); castle; assay mark *P* for James Penman; date letter *u*

INSCRIPTIONS: engraved on underside, *IR*; *S*; scratched, *1722*

H. 8 cm (3³⁄₁₆ in.); w. 11.6 cm (4⁹⁄₁₆ in.); diam. of rim 8.5 cm (3⁵⁄₁₆ in.)

WEIGHT: 156 gm (5 oz)

PROVENANCE: Gift of the estate of Edith, Lady Playfair, October 18, 1932

DESCRIPTION: The raised cup has a flared rim and rests on a circular wire rim. The lower section of the cup is decorated with applied ribs formed of chased sheet. The midband is a reeded wire, and the flat scrolled handle is decorated with a string of applied beading.

· 250 ·

SUGAR CASTER

Marked by Walter Scott (first mark recorded 1701)
Edinburgh, 1700/1
Silver
1987.57

MARKS: on underside, maker's mark *WS* (Jackson, p. 545); castle; assay mark *P* for James Penman; date letter *u*

ARMORIALS: engraved on front, the crest and motto of Thomson of Charleston

H. 24 cm (9⁷⁄₁₆ in.); diam. of foot 8 cm (3³⁄₁₆ in.)

WEIGHT: 504.6 gm (16 oz 4 dwt)

PROVENANCE: Brand Inglis, Ltd., London, purchased January 21, 1987, Harry W. Anderson Fund

PUBLISHED: "Museum Acquisitions," *Decorative Arts Society Newsletter* (Fall 1988), p. 6

DESCRIPTION: The pear-shaped body rests on a circular stepped foot with gadrooning around its edge. The body is raised with an applied twisted wire midsection. A cut-card collar of complex outline design radiates from the foot. The foot is con-

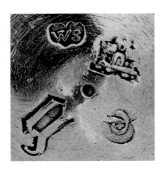

250

trade.[3] The complex profile of the cut-card work on this caster represented a challenge for the maker, who seems to have had difficulty controlling the flow of solder. The caster is engraved with the crest of John Thomson, a clerk of the Exchequer.

1. For a general discussion of the Edinburgh trade, see Finlay 1956, pp. 121–31.

2. There are several other monumental casters of the period. See a set of 1703, illus. Finlay 1956, pl. 68; another of 1702, exh. Glasgow, Scottish Historical Pavillion, *Old Scottish Silver*, 1938, pl. 11, cat. 50.

3. Finlay 1956, p. 124.

structed of two pieces: a cast, gadrooned rim soldered to a raised, molded section. The raised domed cover has a gadrooned rim and is pierced in a foliate and scroll design. A cut-card design, like that below the rim of the body, radiates from the gadrooned baluster finial. The finial has been repaired. The silver is etched around the cut-card work on the lower part of the body in vertical streaks.

In the years before the Act of Union in 1707, the goldsmiths of Edinburgh enjoyed a period of generous patronage. Their most ambitious work, like this caster, is distinguished by its simplicity of outline and its large scale.[1] Unlike London, where certain shops seem to have produced mainly casters or related forms, the Edinburgh goldsmith shops seem not to have been highly specialized.[2] The cut-card ornament shows an awareness of current English and ultimately French contemporary forms, and the piercing is executed with particular skill.

   Although Huguenots immigrated to Scotland in some numbers, there is little indication that they penetrated the goldsmiths'

· 251 ·

EWER AND SHAVING BASIN
Marked by Thomas Ker (first mark recorded 1694)
Edinburgh, 1702/4
Silver
62.4–5

MARKS: 62.4 (ewer): on underside, maker's mark *TK* (Jackson, p. 545); castle; assay mark *P* for James Penman; date letter *y*. 62.5 (basin): on underside of rim, maker's mark *TK* (Jackson, p. 545); castle; assay mark *P* for James Penman; date letter *r*

ARMORIALS: engraved on each, the arms and motto of Hamilton quartering Melrose for Thomas, sixth earl of Haddington (1680–1735)

INSCRIPTIONS: 62.5: scratched on underside of rim, *1/62*

62.4: H. 19.4 cm (7⅝ in.); w. 16.2 cm (6⅜ in.); d. 7.3 cm (2⅞ in.)

62.5: H. 6.5 cm (2⁹⁄₁₆ in.); w. 34.5 cm (13⁹⁄₁₆ in.); d. 24.5 cm (9⅝ in.)

WEIGHT: 62.4: 663.4 gm (21 oz 7 dwt). 62.5: 791 gm (25 oz 9 dwt)

PROVENANCE: sold Sotheby's, London, October 19, 1961, lot 156 [Garrard & Co., London], purchased January 10, 1962, Theodora Wilbour Fund in Memory of Charlotte Beebe Wilbour

PUBLISHED: Finlay 1956, p. 124, pl. 58; Brett 1986, p. 154, fig. 588

251

DESCRIPTION: The elliptical basin is raised from sheet and has a flared rim and a semicircle cut out of one of the long sides. The rim is strengthened on the underside with a half-round wire. The raised body of the elliptical ewer rests on a stepped foot. The triangular spout has a baluster drop. A reeded wire lines the rim of the ewer. The domed cover is attached by the scrolled thumbpiece, which is joined to the hinge on the handle. The ear-shaped handle is cast in two pieces and has a baluster drop at the top. The body has been rehammered, particularly at the base, and highly polished.

This shaving basin and ewer represent a category of well-made Scottish domestic plate that is substantial in weight and somewhat simpler in design than a London-made example of the same form.[1] Thomas Ker was apprenticed to James Penman, and for acceptance into the Incorporation of Goldsmiths he submitted as his essay (or trial piece) a posset pot and a gold buckle. In addition to noble clients, his patrons included the Edinburgh town council and several Edinburgh churches. He held several positions of distinction in the city, among them trades councillor (1698–1700), deacon of the goldsmiths (1708–10), and council deacon (1708–10). His son James, who was apprenticed to him in 1709, achieved even greater distinction and was elected member of Parliament for Edinburgh by the merchants of the city and assay master of the Scottish mint.[2]

Thomas Hamilton, sixth earl of Haddington, was an ardent Whig and a supporter of the house of Hanover. He and his brother, the earl of Rothes, helped to overcome the opposition of their peers to the Act of Union, and during the Rebellion of 1715 Hamilton served with the duke of Argyll at the Battle of Sherrifmuir, where he was wounded. The following year he was appointed lord lieutenant of the county of Haddington and was elected one of the sixteen representative peers of Scotland.

1. See a shaving set marked by William Fawdery for 1725, illus. Hackenbroch 1969, pl. 151, and another marked by Simon Pantin for 1717, sold Sotheby's, London, June 20, 1988, lot 154.

2. Glasgow, Royal Museum of Scotland, *The Loveable Craft, 1687–1987*, 1987, pp. 14–15.

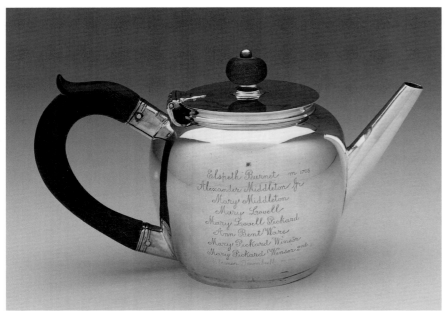

252

· 252 ·

TEAPOT

Marked by Robert Cruickshank (active
1697–1730)
Aberdeen, ca. 1710
Silver, wood
1991.686

MARKS: on underside, maker's mark *RC* in a rectangle (similar to Jackson 1989, p. 583); partially
obscured Gothic letter; *AB* in a shaped shield (for
Aberdeen)

INSCRIPTIONS: engraved on side, *Elspeth Burnet m
1705/Alexander Middleton Jr/Mary Middleton/Mary
Lovell/Mary Lovell Pickard/Ann Bent Ware/Mary
Pickard Winsor/Mary Pickard Winsor 2ⁿᵈ/Eleanor
Trumbull 1942*; engraved on underside in monogram,
A.B.W.; scratched on underside, *T43980*

H. 13.2 cm (5³⁄₁₆ in.); w. 22.5 cm (8⅞ in.); d. 12 cm
(4¾ in.)

PROVENANCE: according to tradition, Elspeth
Burnet, wife of Alexander Middleton, Sr., to their
son, Alexander Middleton, Jr. (d. 1750), who married
Ann Todd, to their daughter Mary Middleton
(1736–1817), who married James Lovell (1737–
1814/16), to their daughter Mary Lovell (1769–
1812), who married Mark Pickard (1751–1823), to
their daughter Mary Lovell Pickard (1798–1849),
who married Henry Ware, Jr. (1794–1843), to their
daughter Ann Bent Ware (1830–1907), who married

Frederick Winsor (1828–1889), to their daughter
Mary Pickard Winsor (1860–1950), to her niece,
Mary Pickard Winsor II (1896–1919), who married
Walter Henry Trumbull (1893–1976), to their
daughter, Eleanor Trumbull, who married John
Lowell II, Lent by Mrs. John Lowell, February 25,
1971, Gift of Mrs. John Lowell, November 20, 1991

DESCRIPTION: The apple-shaped body has a circular foot rim and a molded wire around the rim of
the pot. The spout is straight-sided and tapered, and
the mounts for the ear-shaped wooden handle are
cylindrical with molded edges. The flat, circular lid
is attached to the body with a molded triangular
hinge. The ball finial is wooden.

The engraved inscription on this teapot, added
in the twentieth century, records the tradition
that it was owned by Elspeth Burnet who in
1705 married Alexander Middleton, the son of
Robert Middleton, a customs collector in
Aberdeen. Their son, Alexander Jr., emigrated
from England to Boston, where he married in
1735.[1] The teapot descended in the family
matrilineally and was presented to the Museum
in 1991.

The maker, Robert Cruickshank, is one
of only a few silversmiths recorded in Old
Aberdeen, and there is no record that he
applied for membership to the Hammermen
of New Aberdeen, a separate burgh. It has been
proposed that the use of the town mark *AB*,
for New Aberdeen, used on this teapot and
on a jug at King's College, reflects the fact
that Cruickshank was apprenticed in New
Aberdeen, probably to George Walker.[2] Two
other early Scottish teapots of this shape are
recorded.[3]

1. I am very grateful to Jeannine Falino and Nancy
M. Wilson, who generously shared their research on
the family genealogy.

2. I. E. James, *The Goldsmiths of Aberdeen* (Aberdeen,
1981), pp. 53–54. David Dunbar and two Frenchmen
were also active in Old Aberdeen, but there is insuf-
ficient documentation to trace their careers.

3. See an example of 1714 illus. Finlay 1956, p. 125.
Another teapot with Edinburgh marks for 1716 was
sold Christie's, New York, October 20, 1998, lot 405.

253

· 253 ·

PATEN(?)
Marked by Charles Dickson (first mark recorded 1719)
Edinburgh, 1718/9
Silver
35.1598

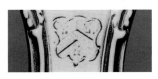

MARKS: on underside, maker's mark *CD* (Jackson, p. 545); castle; assay master mark *EP* for Edward Penman; date letter *O*

INSCRIPTIONS: engraved in center in cipher, *EL* with an earl's coronet above; engraved on underside, *Ex . Dono* with a cipher beneath; on rim, *1719*; *12 oz/15 d*

H. 3 cm (1¾₆ in.); diam. 18.6 cm (7⁵⁄₁₆ in.)

254

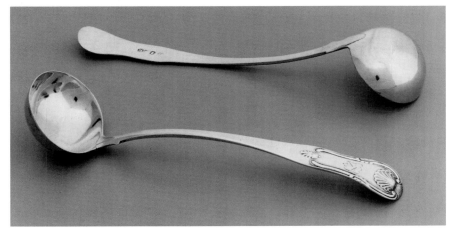

WEIGHT: 371.4 gm (11 oz 19 dwt)

PROVENANCE: William E. Godfrey, New York, purchased by Frank Brewer Bemis, April 1, 1922, Bequest of Frank Brewer Bemis, November 7, 1935

DESCRIPTION: The shallow circular dish is raised and has a plain flaring rim. It rests on a straight foot formed from sheet.

The forms of Scottish church plate are distinctive. Most familiar are the capacious communion cups that were sometimes made in sets.[1] The shape and size of this dish suggest that it may have been a paten,[2] although patens do not seem to have been a standard component of Scottish church fittings. Alms dishes, sometimes very plain, tend to be larger than this small dish, as are the basins that were used with matching lavers for the baptism. The earl's coronet engraved over the cipher *EL* cannot be associated with a Scottish earl of the period.

1. See Thomas Burns, *Old Scottish Communion Plate* (Edinburgh, 1892), pp. 180–434.
2. See English examples illustrated in Charles Oman, *English Church Plate, 597–1830* (London, 1957), pls. 101, 103.

· 254 ·

PAIR OF LADLES
Marked by IZ
Edinburgh, 1816/7
Silver gilt
40.202–203

MARKS: on back of each handle, maker's mark *I* (or *J* or *G*) *Z* in monogram; sovereign's head; thistle; date letter *k*

ARMORIALS: on each, engraved on front, end of handle, an unidentified coat of arms (three wheat sheafs between a chevron or)

INSCRIPTIONS: scratched on back of handle, *9138*; *S1495*

40.202: L. 15.6 cm (6⅛ in.); w. 4.5 cm (1¾ in.)

40.203: L. 15.7 cm (6³⁄₁₆ in.); w. 4.5 cm (1¾ in.)

WEIGHT: 40.202: 31 gm (1 oz). 40.203: 31 gm (1 oz)

PROVENANCE: Anonymous Gift in Memory of Charlotte Beebe Wilbour (1833–1914), April 11, 1940

DESCRIPTION: Each forged ladle has a deep oval bowl and a shaped stem with King's pattern terminus.

255 (Color Plate XXVI)

· 255 ·

TWO-HANDLED CUP

Marked by Thomas Bolton (free 1686, d. 1732)
Dublin, 1694/6
Silver
30.112

MARKS: on underside of cup and on top of cover,
maker's mark *TB* (Bennett, p. 176, no. 479);[1] harp
crowned; date letter K

ARMORIALS: engraved on side and cover, the crest
of Brodrick of Midleton, co. Cork

INSCRIPTIONS: engraved on underside, *95=00*

H. 30 cm (11¹³⁄₁₆ in.); W. 34.2 cm (13⁷⁄₁₆ in.); D. 22 cm
(8¹¹⁄₁₆ in.)

WEIGHT: 2,913 gm (93 oz 13 dwt)

PROVENANCE: Lady Mary Carbery, Castle Freke,
co. Cork, sold Sotheby's, London, March 2, 1921, lot
53; G. W. Panter, Esq., Dublin, sold Sotheby's,
London, July 18, 1929, lot 61, purchased by the
Goldsmiths and Silversmiths Company, London, sold

to Richard C. Paine, Boston, Gift of Richard C.
Paine, March 6, 1930

EXHIBITED: Boston, Museum of Fine Arts, 1994

PUBLISHED: "In the Sale Room," *Connoisseur* 60
(1921), p. 47 (mentioned); "In the Sale Room,"
Connoisseur 84 (1929), pp. 201–2 (mentioned);
Kathryn C. Buhler, "An Irish Silver Cup," *Bulletin of
the Museum of Fine Arts* 28, no. 166 (1930), pp. 36–38

DESCRIPTION: The cup, raised from heavy sheet, is
in the form of an inverted bell resting on a molded,
gadrooned foot that is assembled from three cast
sections. Around the lower section of the cup, a cut-
card border is applied, with eight foliate straps separated by trefoils. The two ear-shaped handles, cast in
halves and seamed vertically, are capped with a curl-
ing leaf above and beading below. At the juncture of
the handle to the body is a cut-card leaf and a tail
of beading. The raised domed cover has an applied
knurled flange and a bezel formed from sheet. A
calyx of eight cut-card leaves surrounds the
gadrooned baluster finial, which is cast in halves.

Thomas Bolton was the foremost goldsmith working in Dublin at the turn of the seventeenth century. He was apprenticed to Gerard Grace in Dublin in 1676 and was sworn a free brother of the Dublin Goldsmiths' Company in 1686. He was elected junior warden in 1690, master warden in 1692, and assay master from 1693 to June 1697. Following the Williamite Wars which culminated with the defeat of the Catholic James II by the Protestant William III at the Battle of the Boyne, Dublin's economy recovered quickly. This is reflected in an increase in the goldsmiths' work assayed at the Dublin Goldsmiths' Hall. From 1694 to 1699 the total ounces assayed at the hall rose steadily from 12,500 to 45,000. Thomas Bolton was responsible for close to a quarter of the total of 168,000 ounces submitted by about fifty goldsmiths.[2] As a result of his thriving business, he was in a position to act as a banker and loan money to clients such as the Goldsmiths' Hall. After resigning his post as assay master, he became active in the city of Dublin corporation. He was soon elected alderman and then in 1716, lord mayor of Dublin.[3] Despite his success, a comfortable retirement eluded the lord mayor.[4]

This cup is the earliest and one of the largest pieces of Irish silver showing strong Huguenot influence. Though the cup itself is executed to a high standard, the craftsmanship shows a slight provincial character where the maker struggled with the application of the complex cut-card work. He must have been working at the limits of his technical expertise and had difficulty controlling the flow of the solder on the fragile cut sheets, which twisted and broke in several places. On a similar but smaller cup in the Metropolitan Museum, the maker seems to have had less difficulty.[5]

The pattern of the cut-card work is almost identical to that on an ecuelle and cover of 1694 by Daniel Garnier in the Metropolitan Museum[6] and a two-handled cup and cover marked by *DG* at All Souls, Oxford.[7] Like the ewer in this collection (see cat. 257), this cup reflects Bolton's awareness of contemporary English models.

The engraved crest of Brodrick may have been used by three members of the family who were active in Ireland in the period. St. John Brodrick of Midleton (1627–1696) played an important part in the civil wars beginning in 1641 and received a large land grant in Cork in 1670. Under the Act of Settlement he obtained additional tracts, and the family wielded tremendous power. Of his six sons, two were in a position to have commissioned such a cup. The eldest, Thomas Brodrick of Ballyanan Castle, Midleton (1654–1730), served as member of Parliament for Cork in 1703 and joint comptroller of army accounts in 1708. His younger brother, Alan Brodrick (ca. 1656–1728), is perhaps the likeliest candidate to have owned the cup. He was an eminent lawyer and statesman, serving as solicitor general for Ireland in 1695 and speaker of the House of Commons in 1703. He pursued a distinguished career in politics, and in 1714 he was appointed lord chancellor of Ireland by George I. The following year he was raised to the peerage as baron Midleton, and in 1717 he was named first viscount Midleton of Midleton. One of Alan Broderick's granddaughters, Mary, married Sir John Redmond Freke, third baronet of Castle Freke in 1739.

1. The maker's mark on the cover is struck with a different punch (Bennett, p. 176, no. 478).

2. Sinsteden 1999, p. 153.

3. John McCormack, "The Sumptuous Silver of Thomas Bolton (1658–1736)," *Irish Arts Review* 11 (1995), pp. 112–16.

4. At a city council meeting on July 19, 1728, Thomas Bolton petitioned for support for the relief of himself and his family, having had many misfortunes and troubles which had left him in reduced circumstances. Thirty pounds were granted to John Bolton, the petitioner's son, and fifty pounds per annum paid quarterly for the support of his children. Sir John T. Gilbert, *Calendar of the Ancient Records of Dublin* (Dublin, 1898), vol. 7, pp. 424–25.

5. Hackenbroch 1969, p. 53, cat. 101.

6. Ibid., p. 45, cat. 83.

7. Exh. Oxford, Ashmolean Museum, *Catalogue of a Loan Exhibition of Silver Plate Belonging to the Colleges of the University of Oxford*, 1928, p. 34, cat. 149, fig. 53.

256

· 256 ·

FOOTED SALVER

Marked by Joseph Walker (free 1690, d. 1722)
Dublin, 1696/8
Silver
33.88

MARKS: on face of salver, makers mark *JW* (Bennett, p. 171, no. 325); harp crowned (repeated on underside of foot); date letter *L*

ARMORIALS: engraved in center, the crest of Brykes or Pigot[1]

INSCRIPTIONS: scratched on underside, *3112*

H. 6.8 cm (2¹¹⁄₁₆ in.); diam. of rim 20.8 cm (8³⁄₁₆ in.)

WEIGHT: 354 gm (11 oz 8 dwt)

PROVENANCE: Anonymous Gift in Memory of Charlotte Beebe Wilbour (1833–1914), March 2, 1933

DESCRIPTION: The circular salver, formed from sheet, has a chased gadrooned border. It rests on a raised trumpet foot with a similar gadrooned rim.

The Dublin assay records of 1694 list "servars," probably referring to footed salvers. Joseph Walker submitted four "servars" for assay in a six-month period that year.[2] Several similar Dublin salvers with gadrooned rims have survived.[3] Such footed salvers were used to hold glasses for serving drinks and to catch any spills, but they also may have been used as stands for display.[4] The early examples have gadrooned, or "knurled," rims, which by the early eighteenth century gave way to a plain molded border.

1. An identical crest appears on a caster (now in the Ulster Museum, Belfast) of 1699 by Anthony Stanley of Dublin, sold Sotheby's, London, July 18, 1929, lot 47.

2. Sinsteden 1999, p. 148.

3. Jackson (1989, p. 627) recorded a salver on foot with gadrooned edge by Joseph Walker of the same year as the present salver, and another pair of 1696 by Walker was sold Sotheby's, New York, June 6, 1980, lot 116. The earliest Irish examples of the form appear to be a pair by James Welding of Dublin, 1685, now in a private collection.

4. These salvers are sometimes referred to, inaccurately, as tazze, a shallow bowl on foot.

· 257 ·

EWER
Marked by Thomas Bolton (free 1686, d. 1732)
Dublin, 1699/1700
Silver
55.383

MARKS: to left of handle, date letter *M*; harp crowned; maker's mark *TB* (Bennett, p. 176, no. 479)

ARMORIALS: arms of Codrington impaling Bethell, for Sir William Codrington, first baronet of Dodington, co. Gloucester, who married in 1717/18, Elizabeth, daughter of William Bethell, of Swindon, co. York

H. 33 cm (13 in.); w. 24.7 cm (9¼ in.); d. 14 cm (5½ in.)

WEIGHT: 2,403 gm (77 oz 5 dwt)

PROVENANCE: by descent to Sir Gerald Codrington, Dodington Park, Chipping Sodbury, Gloucestershire, sold Christie's, London, July 18, 1923, lot 53; Wark estate, sold Parke-Bernet Galleries, Inc., New York, May 21, 1955, lot 270 [Stephen Ensko, Inc., New York], purchased June 9, 1955, Theodora Wilbour Fund in Memory of Charlotte Beebe Wilbour

EXHIBITED: Boston, Museum of Fine Arts, 1994

DESCRIPTION: The helmet-shaped ewer has a shaped rim and rests on a molded stepped foot assembled from cast and raised parts. The foot is spool-shaped, with a broad band of gadrooning and a flattened, fluted knop. The knop is cast in two parts and seamed horizontally. The lower part of the raised vessel has twenty-four applied moldings of ninepin shape. At the juncture of the foot with the body, there is a calyx of radiating laurel leaves. The plain surface of the body, engraved with a coat of arms within an elaborate cartouche, is divided by two horizontal bands (a square wire below and a cast gadrooned band above). The handle, in the form of a nude female demifigure, is cast in several parts. The figure is modeled with narrow facial features and hair swept back in a knot. Her armless shoulders terminate in volutes, and below the waist the figure merges into an acanthus bracket with a scroll above and a shell below. Centered under the lip against a shell is a mask of Diana with crescent above. The absence of a vent hole caused a smooth depression on the inside of the lip, when, after soldering, the silver cooled and contracted.

This remarkably fashionable ewer shows strong Huguenot influence, and in design, if not in execution, it is equal to the most ambitious London work of the period. Although Dublin welcomed many Huguenot refugees, even supporting them with pensions,[1] their inroads into the Dublin goldsmiths' trade in the early 1700s were weak.[2]

The design of the ewer is closely related to a model produced by Huguenot goldsmiths working in London for the most prestigious clients.[3] Though the details of proportion and modeling vary considerably, all of the London examples have in common the handle in the form of a half-length female figure and the female mask under the lip. The model, which was also used on the handles of several cisterns,[4] seems to have fallen from fashion after about 1705. This ewer is a powerful reminder that many English peers had vast estates and grand residences in Ireland, and similarly, that many Irish peers had fashionable residences and property in England. Thomas Bolton may have had English or French goldsmiths working in his shop, or perhaps he was provided with a London piece to reproduce. In any case, it is clear that there was a demand in Dublin for silver of very grand pretension.

The ewer is engraved with the arms of Codrington impaling Bethell for Sir William Codrington, first baronet of Doddington, co. Gloucester, and for his wife, Elizabeth, daughter of William Bethell of Swindon, co. York, whom he married in 1717/8. The baronetcy was created in 1721. The arms may have been engraved at the time of Sir William's marriage and probably replaced an earlier coat of arms on the ewer, which is hallmarked for 1699/1700. It is likely that the piece came to Sir William with the family estates at Dodington. Sir William was the heir of his cousin, Christopher Codrington (1668–1710), who succeeded his father as captain general and commander in chief of the Leeward Islands in the Caribbean in 1698. He seems not to have been active in Ireland in the years around 1700, though the ewer may have been bought in London as a secondhand piece. Christopher Codrington was a distinguished scholar and collector of books who was described by his contemporaries as the embodiment of a poet and a soldier. The success of his governership was mixed, but he spent his retirement in Barbados pursuing his interest in church history and

257 (Color Plate XXVII)

metaphysics. On his death in 1710 he left ten thousand pounds in cash and six thousand pounds' worth of books to All Souls College, Oxford, to endow a library.[5] His cousin and heir, Sir William Codrington, was a gentleman of the bedchamber and member of Parliament for Minehead until his death in 1738.

It is interesting that Sir William's arms also appear on an extraordinary dish made in Lille by Eli Pacot in about 1695, now the property of the city of Westminster, and on a punch-bowl of 1701 by Benjamin Pyne in the Nelson-Atkins Museum of Art.[6] Grimwade proposed that the engraved arms on the Lille dish may have been originally engraved for Christopher Codrington and updated when the dish passed to his cousin Sir William Codrington. This ewer may have a similar history.[7]

1. *Calendar of State Papers, Domestic Series 1702–1703* (London, 1916), vol. 1, p. 228.

2. The most successful were David Rummieu and Francis Girard who submitted a modest quantity of silver for assay. By midcentury the D'Olier family became prominent banker-goldsmiths and were among the founders of The Bank of Ireland. The LeBas family settled in Dublin in the late 1700s and established a preeminence in the goldsmiths' trade that continues to the present. Sinsteden 1999, p. 151. Also see Bennett 1972, p. 379, and Bennett 1984, p. 137.

3. See a ewer marked by Pierre Harrache(?) for 1702, the collection of the duke of Portland, illus. London, St. James Court, *Old Silver-work, Chiefly English, From the XVth to the XVIIIth Centuries*, 1902, pl. 98; another marked by Pierre Harrache for 1697 with Vintners' arms, at the Vintners' Hall, London, illus. Hayward 1959, no. 34a; another marked by Pierre Harrache for 1700 made for the earl of Ancaster, exh. London, Seaford House, *Queen Charlotte's Loan Exhibition of Old Silver*, 1929, no. 411, pl. 57; another marked by Pierre Harrache for 1705, engraved with the arms of Methuen, sold Christie's, London, February 25, 1920, lot 59, now in the Portland Art Museum, Portland, Oregon; another marked by Pierre Harrache for 1705 at the Wadsworth Atheneum, acc. no. 1977.78; a pair marked by Pierre Harrache engraved with the arms of the second earl of Chesterfield, sold Sotheby's, London, February 4, 1988, lot 76. For examples with a double shell rather than the head of Diana, see a ewer marked by David Willaume I for 1702/3,

engraved with the Wentworth arms, sold Sotheby's, London, June 27, 1963, lot 52; another marked by Phillip Rollos I for 1705 with a sideboard dish, engraved with the royal arms, sold Sotheby's, London, June 27, 1963, lot 49.

4. See an example marked by Pierre Harrache for 1697 in the Barber-Surgeons' Company, illus. Hayward 1959, pl. 21.

5. The surviving family papers do not include any inventories of personal possessions of the seventeenth or early eighteenth century. Peter Lewis, librarian, Codrington Library, All Souls College, and David Smith, county and diocesan archivist, Gloucestershire County Record Office, were most helpful in providing information about the records. See Vincent T. Harlow, *Christopher Codrington, 1668–1710* (Oxford, 1928).

6. Illus. Clayton 1985b, p. 105, fig. 2. Christina Nelson kindly provided photographs and information from the files on this piece.

7. Grimwade 1988, pp. 88–89. The elaborate surround on the Lille dish displays all the the features identified as Gentot's "signatures," the berried laurel leaves and the bracket or ledge on which the supporters rest.

· 258 ·

SIDEBOARD DISH
Marked by Thomas Bolton (free 1686, d. 1732)
Dublin, 1702/3
Silver
55.382

MARKS: on underside of rim, date letter *P*; harp crowned; maker's mark *TB* (Bennett, p. 176, no. 477)

ARMORIALS: engraved in center the royal arms and motto as borne by Queen Anne

INSCRIPTIONS: engraved on underside, *140=5*; *Melancholy-Septemb^r 16/-1703-*

H. 5.5 cm (2³⁄₁₆ in.); diam. 58 cm (22⅞ in.)

WEIGHT: 4,309 gm (138 oz 10 dwt)

PROVENANCE: Wark estate, sold Parke-Bernet Galleries, Inc., New York, May 21, 1955, lot 271, [Stephen Ensko, Inc., New York], purchased June 9, 1955, Theodora Wilbour Fund in Memory of Charlotte Beebe Wilbour

EXHIBITED: Boston, Museum of Fine Arts, 1994

DESCRIPTION: The circular dish is raised and has a broad rim with an applied gadrooned (or knurled) border that is cast in several sections. There are four vent holes on the underside of the rim. An applied molded wire runs inside the border.

Large sideboard dishes like this one were used for display and were usually accompanied by a ewer and two-handled cups, among other items.[1] This type of plate was issued as a loan by the Jewel House through a royal warrant to an ambassador while on service abroad. The royal arms engraved on these pieces indicated not only that the ambassador represented the sovereign but also that the plate was owned by the crown.[2] This charger is one of four items made by Thomas Bolton in 1702/3 bearing the arms of Queen Anne. In addition to this dish, there are a ewer[3] and two covered jugs.[4] (Ireland did not have an office equivalent to the Jewel House in England, which recorded the outgoing and incoming plate issued by a lord chamberlain's warrant. Nor do the English warrant books record this Irish silver.) It is possible that the warrant for this plate may have come through the Irish House of Lords, the House of Commons, or Dublin city corporation and that it was paid out by the receiver general in Ireland. Unfortunately the manuscript records of the receiver general of Ireland burnt in a fire at the Public Records Office during the 1922 rising. There is some record, however, that large sums were handed out by the receiver general of Ireland to a newly appointed lord justice or lord lieutenant analogous to the Jewel House disbursements for ambassadorial equipage and plate. Some of that money may have been used for plate.[5] On February 12, 1703, the receiver general was authorized to pay James Butler, second duke of Ormonde (1665–1745) who had just been appointed lord lieutenant of Ireland, the sum of three thousand pounds "for his equipage as Lord-Lieutenant and his voyage to Ireland."[6] Ormonde set out for Dublin in May, traveling in grand style and accompanied by a large retinue.[7] To welcome him in Dublin, the lord mayor and a committee of aldermen and commoners prepared a public entertainment to be held in the Tholsell (town hall) on August 12.[8]

Among the members of the committee was the silversmith Thomas Bolton, who held the position of master of the city works. It seems possible that due to his position as a member of the council and master of the city works, Bolton got a substantial order of plate for presentation to the duke. None of the four pieces of plate can be clearly identified in a 1705 inventory of the duke's plate at Dublin Castle and Kilkenny Castle.[9]

The ewer that was made as part of this service[10] is remarkably similar in nearly every design detail to a silver gilt example marked in London in 1702 by Pierre Platel that bears the arms of Henry Gorges of Eye and Mynde (ca. 1665–1719).[11] The Gorgeses had strong connections to Ireland,[12] and it is possible that Thomas Bolton, seeking the latest fashions for his Dublin clients, had an opportunity to copy the London ewer soon after it was made.

This sideboard dish and the ewer made to accompany it are both engraved with the curious inscription *Melancholy Septemb' 16 1703*. Although the significance of the inscription cannot be confirmed, the most likely possibility is that it commemorates a horse race run on the Curragh, the race course in Kildare, on September 16. Unfortunately there is no record of the winning horse or owner for the 1703 race, but it can be established that the King's Plate was run on September 16.[13] It was the duty of the lord lieutenant to attend, and it is possible that the duke of Ormonde offered up as a prize the sideboard dish and ewer. The King's Plate had been established in 1696 and was run yearly in September.[14] Prizes for these early races seem to have been offered up with a cash value, which the winner would then claim as a piece of plate.[15]

This group of sideboard plate bearing the royal arms ranks as one of the finest and grandest sets of Irish silver known. The pieces suggest the ambition of the Dublin goldsmiths to match the work of their London counterparts, but the high technical skill demanded in the manufacture of these pieces was a challenge. As is evident in the two-handled cup in this collection (cat. 255), there is a slight roughness in the assembly that suggests the relative inexperience of the maker.[16]

1. Hartop 1996, p. 68.

2. Often, on returning from a mission, an ambassador might make arrangements to keep the plate for personal use.

3. Sold Sotheby's, London, November 17, 1988, lot 69.

4. One was sold Sotheby's, London, November 17, 1988, lot 70 (previously sold Sotheby's, London, February 1, 1951, lot 115, and Sotheby's, London, June 8, 1972, lot 73). The second was sold Christie's, New York, April 28, 1992, lot 262. A fifth item, sold Sotheby's, London, July 18, 1968, lot 102, a two-handled cup marked by Bolton for 1701, is engraved with the royal arms with Queen Anne's earlier motto and probably does not belong to this group. This cup could have been made for a race of the previous year. Compare with a race cup of 1702, believed to be the earliest surviving Irish race cup, sold Sotheby's, London, July 14, 1960, lot 14, now in the Metropolitan Museum of Art.

5. One stray volume of the receiver general's accounts was found among the records of the corporation of Kilkenny. This volume shows accounts of disbursements made by the receiver general in the years 1715–17 and includes "3000 pounds to the Duke of Grafton, and Earl Gallway, Lord Justices of Ireland, for their Equipage, warrant dated 21 September 1715 and 3000 pounds to the Duke of Bolton for his Equipage as Lord Lieutenant of Ireland, warrant dated 5 June 1717." *Journal of the Royal Historical and Archaeological Association of Ireland* 1, 4th series (1878), pp. 274–77. A silver gilt ewer and dish marked by John Humphries for 1693/6 with the arms of Henry Sydney, earl of Romney, lord lieutenant of Ireland from 1692 to 1695 (sold Christie's, London, December 3, 1969, lot 102), may be another example of plate granted to the official as part of his equipage.

6. London, PRO, Treasury Out Books T 14/8, p. 262.

7. Historical Manuscripts Commission, *Calendar of the Manuscripts of the Marquess of Ormonde, K.P., Preserved at Kilkenny Castle* (London, 1920), vol. 8, p. 37.

8. Gilbert 1896, vol. 6, p. 289.

9. National Library of Ireland, MS 2521.

10. Sold Sotheby's, London, November 17, 1988, lot 69.

11. Sold Sotheby's, London, February 11, 1999, lot 26.

12. Dr. Robert Gorges of Kilbrew married Jane, daughter of Sir Arthur Loftus, vice-treasurer and

258 (Color Plate XXVIII)

decendant of Adam Loftus, archbishop of Armagh, and his son, Lieutenant General Richard Gorges, married Nichola Beresford (1667–1714), née Hamilton. Raymond Gorges, *The Story of a Family, History of the Family of Gorges* (Boston, 1944), p. 215.

13. A letter from Sir Thomas Keightly to Sir Donat O'Brien refers to the upcoming race. John Ainsworth, ed., *The Inchiquin Manuscripts* (Dublin, 1961), p. 76.

14. Lord Walter Fitzgerald, "The Curragh: Its History and Traditions," *Journal of the Kildare Archaeological Society* 3 (1902), p. 9. Lord Walter Fitzgerald copied three entries out of receiver general's papers (later destroyed) of which one records "Paid to John Phillips [a Dublin goldsmith] for a Piece of Plate run for on ye Curragh of Kildare the 16th inst., and of his Majesties bounty, given yearly for encouragement to breed horses, as by warrant dated the 13th of September, 1697, and acquittance appears £ 103 16 0."

15. An article drawn up by the Corporation of Horse Breeders of co. Down in February 1704 states, "It is agreed that there shall be Yearly for ever three Plates to be run for, the Greater Plate to be of the Value of Fifty Pounds *Sterling*, and the second Plate the value of Ten Pounds *Sterling*, the fashion of each included." This clearly states that the prize money was not only cash but also silver. *Articles and Orders Agreed upon by the Corporation of Horse Breeders in the County of Down* (Dublin, 1703/4), pp. 1–4.

16. A similar dish marked by Thomas Bolton for 1708/9 with the city of London arms and inscription, *London's Plantacion in Ulster*, within a roundel, is in the Ulster Museum, Belfast, advertised S. J. Shrubsole Corp., *Antiques* 135, no. 5 (May 1989), p. 1047. A slightly smaller dish with the arms of Foster marked by Thomas Bolton for 1708/9 was offered for sale, Sotheby's, London, May 21, 1999, lot 236.

259

· 259 ·

TEAPOT

Marked by William Archdall (free 1704, d. 1751)
Dublin, 1713/5
Silver, wood
33.103

MARKS: engraved on underside, maker's mark *WA* (Bennett, p. 178, no. 521) (repeated inside cover); date letter *x*; harp crowned

ARMORIALS: engraved on side, the arms and crest of Nesbitt

INSCRIPTIONS: engraved on underside, *AN*; *21:13*; scratched, *8455*

H. 19 cm (7½ in.); w. 22.5 cm (8⅞ in.); d. 13.4 cm (5¼ in.)

WEIGHT: 645 gm (20 oz 15 dwt)

PROVENANCE: Anonymous Gift in Memory of Charlotte Beebe Wilbour (1833–1914), March 2, 1933

PUBLISHED: Bennett 1972, p. 69, fig. 8

DESCRIPTION: The octagonal pear-shaped body is raised in two parts with a molded band applied to the seam. It rests on a plain foot formed from a scored and seamed length of sheet. The curved octagonal spout applied over a pierced section is cast in halves and seamed vertically and terminates in a stylized duck's head. The ebonized wooden handle is

pinned onto seamed octagonal handle sockets. A five-knuckle hinge is applied to the upper handle socket and to the molding of the raised octagonal domed cover. The turned wooden mushroom-shaped finial is attached to the cover by a silver bolt and nut with a cast baluster top.

It was not unusual for pear-shaped teapots like this to be accompanied by warming stands, and this example, with its plain foot, may once have had such a stand. The form was widely used in England.[1] Several Irish octagonal teapots survive from the first quarter of the eighteenth century, including another by the same maker marked for 1717.[2]

1. For an English example, see Schroder 1988a, p. 171.
2. Sold Sotheby's, London, November 17, 1988, lot 86. Also see a diminutive, seamed octagonal teapot, H. 4½ in., marked for 1714, sold Sotheby's, West Wycombe, June 22, 1989, lot 517, and another marked by Anthony Stanley for 1715/6, illus. Victoria and Albert Museum, *Irish Silver* (London, 1959), pl. 7. An octagonal pear-shaped teapot and stand with burner made by David King in 1712 is illustrated in the Clark Art Institute photographic and clippings archive, Williamstown, Mass.

260

WEIGHT: 3,449 gm (110 oz 18 dwt)

PROVENANCE: Anonymous Gift in Memory of Charlotte Beebe Wilbour (1833–1914), March 2, 1933

PUBLISHED: Bennett 1972, p. 70, fig 9.

DESCRIPTION: The flattened pear-shaped kettle rests on a three-legged stand. It is formed from two raised sections with an applied molded band at the neck and the rim. The faceted curved spout is cast in halves and seamed vertically. The cast octagonal bail handle, with baluster ivory insert, is supported on two cast brackets. The raised stepped, domed cover has an applied rim molding and bezel. The turned ivory finial is secured to the cover with a button-top bolt passing through it and a spool-shaped spacer with a square nut. The molded ring of the stand is cast in three parts. The three scrolled legs, cast in halves, terminate in hemispherical feet closed with pierced plates. The inverted pear-shaped lamp, fitted with a removable cover with a fitting for the wick, rests in a ring supported by three scrolls extending from the legs. On the rim of the stand are two drop handles, each cast in parts. The kettle is hinged to the frame and may be tilted by removing the pin on a chain mounted opposite the spout. A second pin below the spout may be removed from the hinge to lift the kettle from the stand. Part of one chain is plated.

Although many English examples of this form have survived,[1] this kettle is one of three known Irish examples. One is marked by Edward Workman for 1715/6,[2] and another by David King for 1714/5.[3] William Archdall obtained his freedom in 1704 having trained under David King and served as assay master from 1736 until 1751.

1. For example, see cat. 33.
2. Wees 1997, p. 354, cat. 246.
3. Sold Christie's, London, May 7, 1939, lot 94.

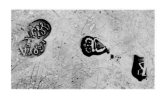

· 260 ·

KETTLE AND STAND

Marked by William Archdall (free 1704, d. 1751)
Dublin, 1717/8
Silver, ivory
33.106

MARKS: on underside of kettle and lamp, maker's mark *WA* (Bennett, p. 178, no. 521) (struck twice) overstriking another, possibly *TS* for Thomas Sutton (Bennett, p. 177, no. 503); harp crowned (repeated on side of stand ring, side of each foot, top of lamp cover, underside of both handles, and bezel of kettle cover); date letter *a*

INSCRIPTIONS: engraved on underside of kettle, *140=5*; scratched, *7590*

H. 32.7 cm (12⅞ in.); w. 31.5 cm (12⅜ in.); d. 23.7 cm (9⁵⁄₁₆ in.)

261

PUBLISHED: Helen Comstock, "A Dublin Tankard by a Huguenot Goldsmith," *Connoisseur* 103 (1939), pp. 152–55

DESCRIPTION: The tapering cylindrical vessel has an applied molded wire at the midsection, and above the heavy molded foot rim, an applied scalloped border. The tankard is raised, and the base is inset with coarsely applied solder. The lip has an applied wire molding. The double-scrolled handle is formed of two fabricated pieces, with a shield-shaped terminus engraved with stylized foliage. The upper part of the handle joins the body with a long tapering tail. A five-knuckle hinge with ribbed hinge plate joins handle and cover, surmounted by a cast fleur-de-lys thumbpiece. A raised stepped, domed cover has a button top and a broad shaped rim with flat-chased leaves and scrolls. Four acanthus leaves are engraved on the top of the handle underneath the hinge.

The maker's mark on this tankard is attributed to Abraham Barboult, goldsmith and clock maker, the only Dublin goldsmith with the initials *AB* active in this period. The mark also appears on a covered jug marked for 1717.[3] Abraham Barboult was a Huguenot and registered as a quarter brother of the Dublin Goldsmiths' guild before being sworn a free brother in 1710.[4] The curious deep double-scrolled handle, forming an almost complete circle at the lower scroll, can also be seen on a tankard by Thomas Bolton of 1718.[5] The scalloped band just above the foot does not appear on other Irish tankards but may be found on colonial American tankards by makers of Dutch descent.[6]

1. Barboult's mark (Bennett 12) is generally recorded in a rectangular shield.

2. The arms of Thomson impaling Wilmot also occur on a dressing mirror of 1698 by John Humphrey, sold Christie's, New York, April 18, 1991, lot 337.

3. Sold Sotheby's, London, February 5, 1987, lot 84.

4. As a quarter brother he was not permitted to employ journeymen or to keep a shop.

5. Sold Christie's, London, December 2, 1981, lot 64.

6. For American examples, see New Haven, Yale University Art Gallery, *Silver in American Life*, 1979, p. 126, cats. 130–31.

· 261 ·

TANKARD

Marked by Abraham Barboult (free 1710, d. 1751)
Dublin, 1717/8
Silver
42.80

MARKS: to right of handle, maker's mark *AB* in a shaped shield (unrecorded)[1] (repeated twice on top of rim of cover); date letter *a* (repeated on underside of rim of cover); harp crowned (repeated on underside of rim of cover)

ARMORIALS: engraved on side, the arms of Thompson impaling Wilmot[2]

INSCRIPTIONS: engraved on handle, *C/I*★*K*; scratched on underside, *8542*

H. 21 cm (8¼ in.); w. 20 cm (7⅞ in.); diam. of base 13.9 cm (5½ in.)

WEIGHT: 1,109 gm (35 oz 13 dwt)

PROVENANCE: Anonymous Gift in Memory of Charlotte Beebe Wilbour (1833–1914), February 12, 1942

262

· 262 ·

FREEDOM BOX

Probably Dublin, 1718
Gold
56.309

MARKS: on underside, *HA* incuse (unrecorded)

ARMORIALS: engraved on cover, the arms of Tighe with Bor in pretence and motto: *NON SIBI SED PATRIAE* and *SUMMUM NEC METUAM DIEM NEC OPTEM*, for the Rt. Hon. Richard Tighe (1678–1736), who married Barbara, daughter and co-heir of Christian Bor, Esq., of Drinagh, co. Wexford; engraved on underside, the arms of Kilkenny with motto: *INSIGNIA ARMORUM CIVITATIS KILKENNIENSIS*

INSCRIPTIONS: engraved on interior of cover, *Com/Civit Kilkensis/at an Assembly of ye Mayor/& Citizens of ye sd City held August/ye 2, 1718 John Desarroy Esq. Mayor/Ordered that Richard Tighe Esq. be/presented with his Freedom of/this City in a Gold Box of the Value/of twenty Guineas for his Singular/Service in the Chair of the Committee/of the House of Commons upon/the Bill for regulating this/Corporation & that Robert/Hacket do take care to/Get the same/Done*

H. 1.8 cm (¹¹⁄₁₆ in.); diam. 7.7 cm (3¹⁄₁₆ in.)

WEIGHT: 136 gm (4 oz 6 dwt)

PUBLISHED: Thomas Sinsteden, "A Freedom Box for 'a Hot Whiffling Puppy': Tighe Family Silver from Kilkenny," *Irish Arts Review* 16 (1999), pp. 139–41

PROVENANCE: Thomas Lumley, Ltd., London, purchased May 10, 1956, Theodora Wilbour Fund in Memory of Charlotte Beebe Wilbour

DESCRIPTION: The shallow, flat circular gold box has a removable cover that fits over the base. A thin wire molding at the perimeter of the cover and base joins them to the vertical sides.

The fine quality of engraving on this gold box exceeds that on all other known Irish freedom boxes.[1] The presentation of freedom boxes was well established in Ireland; this was the third gold box awarded by the Kilkenny corporation.[2] The earliest surviving Irish gold freedom box was made by Thomas Bolton in June 1707 and is now in the National Museum of Ireland.[3] Another finely engraved silver freedom box was awarded to Sir John Stanley on October 15, 1714, and is very similar in construction to the Tighe box.[4] It is thus tantalizing to attribute this box to a Dublin maker and the engraving to a foreigner brought to Dublin by an enlightened patron. Robert Hacket, recorded in the engraved inscription as the person responsible for executing the commission, did travel to Dublin frequently and had traveled to England the previous year in his capacity as clerk of the corporation (the legal adviser) to settle issues of incorporation for the city. Therefore the possibility remains that the box was ordered and made abroad. Incuse makers' marks are found frequently on Irish gold boxes made from the mid-eighteenth century on.

Richard Tighe (1678–1736), a man of short stature, was known as "Little Dick Tighe," and for his love of fashionable dress, as "Beau Tighe." His grandfather was twice mayor of

Dublin in the 1650s. He led a distinguished career, being elected member of Parliament for Balturbet in 1703, for Newtown in 1715, for Augher in 1727, and was then made Irish privy councillor under George I, gaining the title of the Right Honorable. He married Barbara Bor in 1708. Two years later, while in London, Dean Swift overheard an altercation between the newlyweds in the neighboring house. In his "Journal to Stella" he described Richard Tighe as "a hot whiffling puppy, very apt to resent."[5] This animosity to Richard did not relent throughout his career, with frequent derision appearing in print.

1. It may be compared in quality with the work of Blaise Gentot, called the "Master of George Vertue" who worked in England at the turn of the eighteenth century. Grimwade 1988, pp. 83–89.

2. Ida Delamer, "Irish Freedom Boxes," *Proceedings of the Silver Society* 3, nos. 1–2 (1983), pp. 18–23; Edward J. Law, "The Presentation Plate of the Corporation of the City of Kilkenny, 1684–1834," *Old Kilkenny Review* (1994), p. 57, no. 46.

3. Exh. Dublin, National Museum of Ireland, *The Company of Goldsmiths of Dublin 1637–1987*, 1987, p. 33. This gold box was awarded to Richard Freeman, lord high chancellor of Ireland, on June 24, 1707, and is recorded in Gilbert 1896, vol. 6, p. 368.

4. Ian Cameron and Elizabeth Kingsley-Rowe, eds., *Das Grosse Antiquitäten-Lexikon* (Freiburg, 1983), p. 129. The award is recorded in Gilbert 1896, vol. 6, p. 498.

5. Jonathan Swift, *Journal to Stella*, ed. Harold Williams (Oxford, 1948), p. 343.

· 263 ·

PAIR OF FOOTED SALVERS
Marked by William Newenham (d. 1739)
Cork, ca. 1720
Silver
35.1601–1602

MARKS: on face of each, maker's mark *WN* (Bennett, p. 193, no. 142);[1] *STERLING*

INSCRIPTIONS: 35.1601: engraved on underside *4 " 12*. 35.1602: engraved on underside *4 " 15*

35.1601: H. 3.8 cm (1½ in.); diam. of rim 12.3 cm (4¹³⁄₁₆ in.)

35.1602: H. 3.8 cm (1½ in.); diam. of rim 12.3 cm (4¹³⁄₁₆ in.)

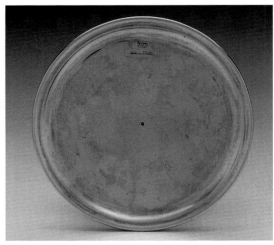

263

WEIGHT: 35.1601: 130 gm (4 oz 4 dwt). 35.1602: 136 gm (4 oz 8 dwt)

PROVENANCE: William E. Godfrey, New York, purchased by Frank Brewer Bemis, 1924, Bequest of Frank Brewer Bemis, November 7, 1935

DESCRIPTION: Each plain circular salver has a slightly shaped, molded rim. The applied trumpet-shaped foot with flaring rim is raised.

Plain circular salvers, most commonly five to six inches in diameter, were made throughout Ireland from the mid-seventeenth century until the mid-eighteenth century.[2] Though often made for domestic use and recorded in inventories and archives as "servers,"[3] many were made for or donated to churches for use as patens.[4]

The Master and Wardens and Company of the Society of Goldsmiths of Cork was founded during the Cromwellian protectorate and flourished until about 1730.[5] On several occasions in the early eighteenth century, the Dublin goldsmiths refused an application from goldsmiths in Cork to establish their own assay hall and insisted that silver made in Cork be sent to Dublin for assay.[6] According to the Dublin assay records, the first delivery was made in 1709.[7] Because of the risk of transport to Dublin, much of the silver produced in Cork and other Irish provincial towns continued to be locally marked *STERLING* and the maker's mark. By the 1780s, however, the Dublin wardens had prevailed, and most provincial silver was sent to Dublin for assay and hallmarking.

William Newenham came from a prominent Cork family and served the Cork Goldsmiths' Company in 1721 as warden and in 1726 as master. He was elected sheriff of the city in 1732. Other silver bearing his mark includes a coffeepot in the National Museum of Ireland.[8]

1. The mark is recorded with a V–shaped device above. The mark here lacks that device.

2. For a pair of similar salvers marked in Cork by William Clarke, see Sotheby's, London, November 24, 1977, lot 107.

3. See cat. 256, n. 2. The term was also used in church records in Williamsburg, Virginia, referring to a salver presented in 1694. See Davis 1976, p. 124, cat. 126.

4. Tony Sweeny, *Irish Stuart Silver* (Dublin, 1995), pp. 236–41, recorded eighty-five Stuart examples.

5. Robert Wyse Jackson, *Irish Silver* (Cork, 1972), p. 60.

6. Bennett 1972, p. 169.

7. Sinsteden 1999, p. 153.

8. John Tehan, *Irish Silver* (Dublin, 1979), p. 11, pl. 3.

· 264 ·

TEAPOT
Marked by John Moore (free 1724, d. 1767)
Dublin, 1726/7
Silver, wood
52.9

MARKS: on underside, harp crowned (repeated on underside of cover); date letter *G*; maker's mark *IM* (Jackson, p. 632) (repeated on underside of cover)

INSCRIPTIONS: engraved on underside, *7:17*

H. 9.5 cm (3¾ in.); w. 17.9 cm (7⁷⁄₁₆ in.); d. 9 cm (3⁹⁄₁₆ in.)

WEIGHT: 255 gm (8 oz 4 dwt)

PROVENANCE: S. J. Shrubsole, Corp., New York, purchased January 10, 1952, Theodora Wilbour Fund in Memory of Charlotte Beebe Wilbour

DESCRIPTION: The raised apple-shaped teapot has an inset foot with a narrow reeded rim. The straight tapered spout is seamed longitudinally. A wooden handle with scrolled thumbpiece is mounted on seamed sockets. The hinged flat circular cover, mounted on a three-knuckle hinge, sits flush with the body on an interior bezel. The cover and the opening of the body are circumscribed with chased concentric rings. The baluster finial of turned wood is mounted on the cover with a silver nut and bolt.

Plain apple- or bullet-shaped teapots were made in Ireland in a range of sizes from about 1700 to 1740. The smallest, sometimes called saffron pots, are hardly larger than toys and weigh three to five ounces.[1] This teapot, with a capacity of 325 milliliters, is an example of the next larger size group, weighing from nine to eleven ounces. More common are the largest category, weighing from twelve to seventeen ounces with a capacity of around 500 milliliters.

1. Bennett 1972, pp. 68, 79–80.

264

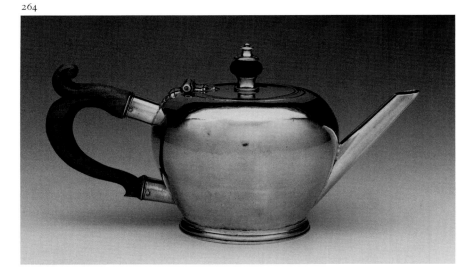

· 265 ·

BOWL
Marked by Robert Calderwood (free 1727,
d. 1766)
Dublin, 1728/9
Silver
42.13

MARKS: on underside, maker's mark *RC* (Bennett,
p. 174, no. 416); harp crowned; date letter *K*

ARMORIALS: engraved below rim, the arms and
crest, possibly for Moore

INSCRIPTIONS: on underside, *17 10*; scratched,
11749

H. 8.4 cm (3⁵⁄₁₆ in.); diam. of rim 18.8 cm (7⁷⁄₁₆ in.)

WEIGHT: 522 gm (16 oz 16 dwt)

PROVENANCE: Anonymous Gift in Memory of
Charlotte Beebe Wilbour (1833–1914), January 8,
1942

DESCRIPTION: The plain raised hemispherical
bowl has a caulked rim and rests on a molded,
seamed foot.

Chinese ceramic wares provided the model for
the form of silver bowls with slightly flaring
rims like this, as well as for other vessels used
for serving tea. Many of these bowls, in a range
of sizes, were made in Dublin during the first
half the eighteenth century. Small versions of
the shape were used as sugar bowls, larger
ones—perhaps including this example—as
waste or slop bowls, and the largest sizes served
as punch bowls. Five "beer bowls" were
brought to the Dublin Goldsmiths' Hall for
assay in the 1640s, but their size and appearance
are uncertain.[1]

The arms on this bowl appear on a bowl
marked by Thomas Sutton for 1717,[2] on a pair
of plain dinner plates marked by Joseph Walker
for 1708,[3] on a beer jug marked by Mathew
Walker for 1727,[4] and finally on a covered jug
marked by Thomas Sutton, Dublin, 1723.[5]

1. Sinsteden 1999, pp. 144, 146.

2. Sold, Christie's, New York, June 14, 1982, lot 119.

3. Exh. Grand Rapids, Michigan, Art Museum, *Irish
Silver*, 1982, p. 18, cat. 14.

4. Sold, Christie's, New York, December 10, 1986,
lot 110.

5. Jeffrey Munger et al., *The Forsyth Wickes Collection
in the Museum of Fine Arts, Boston* (Boston, 1992),
p. 303, cat. 276.

265

266

· 266 ·

PUNCH BOWL

Marked by William Williamson (II) (free 1740)
Dublin, 1751
Silver
1973.482

MARKS: below rim, maker's mark *WW* (Bennett, p. 180, no. 582); date letter *E*; harp crowned (repeated twice along outside rim of base); Hibernia

ARMORIALS: on either side the arms and crest of Gore, for Sir Ralph Gore (1725–1802) of Manor Gore, co. Donegal

INSCRIPTIONS: engraved in banner around side, *The Great match Run on the Curragh of Kildare Septr. 5th 1751 for 1000 Guineas by Black & all Black the property of Sr. Ralph Gore Bart. & Bajezet ye. Property of ye. Rt. Honble. y Earl of March won with ease by ye former;* scratched on underside, *124-10*

H. 21.9 cm (5⅝ in.); diam. of rim 36.2 cm (14¼ in.)

WEIGHT: 3,827.3 gm (123 oz)

PROVENANCE: Sir Ralph Gore, baronet, 1751; collection of Lord Wavertree; collection of the Hon. Mrs. Collins, sold at Christie's, London, June 27, 1973, lot 37, purchased by Firestone and Parson, Boston, purchased September 12, 1973, Theodora Wilbour Fund in Memory of Charlotte Beebe Wilbour

PUBLISHED: Anthony Phillips, "A Fine Trophy for a 'Great Match,'" *Christie's Review of the Season 1973* (New York, 1973), pp. 234–45

DESCRIPTION: The raised circular bowl has a caulked rim. It rests on a raised spreading domed foot constructed of two pieces with an applied wire rim.

The September 5, 1751, race on the Curragh recorded on this bowl became immediately famous in a period when the sport of horse racing was rapidly gaining popularity in Ireland. Sir Ralph Gore, owner of the winning mare, was educated at Trinity College, Dublin, and succeeded to the baronetcy in 1746. He

had a distinguished career in the army and was wounded at the Battle of Fontenoy in the war of the Austrian Succession. Gore seems to have come from a racing family.[1] One of his horses, Black and All Black, had captured the public attention several years earlier.[2] Gore had brought the horse from England, where he had been recorded as Othello. He was matched against a gray mare called Irish Lass owned by a Mr. Archibold and, contrary to expectation, had lost. This was attributed by many to the fact that Archibold had placed a rosary around Irish Lass's neck. Since 1695 it had been illegal for a Catholic to own a horse worth more than five pounds, so the loss, pitting Gore's heavily favored horse (and his landowning backers) against the Catholic underdogs, was symbolic. Irish Lass became known as Paddereen Mare after the Irish word for rosary, *paidirin*. A contemporary wrote, "We hear that there is a benevolent subscription on foot among the nobility and the gentry of this kingdom, who are great patrons of merit, in order to assist Black and All Black in his contest with the Paddereen Mare."[3]

Black and All Black's reputation was recovered in the race commemorated by this bowl. Black and All Black's opponent was Bajazet, the property of William Douglas, earl of March and duke of Queensbury (1724–1810), known as "Old Q." Lord March was a colorful bon vivant and a devoted supporter of racing. His attentions were focused not only on the breeding of horses, at which he was very successful, but on the outfitting of his jockeys and stablemen. The prize for the September 5 race was set at one thousand guineas, and, to discourage bribery, Gore did not choose a jockey until just before the race. His jockey was heavier than lord March's rider, and, to equal the challenge, lord March's jockey wore a belt filled with shot, as was customary. However, the rider was observed removing the belt during the race and discreetly replacing it at the end of the race, just before the jockeys were required to weigh in. Gore exposed the fraud and challenged lord March to a duel. On the appointed day, Gore arrived with a large oak coffin bearing a plaque inscribed with lord March's name and, as his date of death, the present day. Duly chastised, Lord March backed down and apologized for his lapse.[4] Gore went on to other racing victories and the following year presented a horse called Skuball, still known through popular songs.[5]

The fine engraving on the bowl depicts the two horses in their final furlong and, in the background, other riders and observers. The same scene, in reverse, appears in the borders of a map of the county of Kildare published in 1752.[6] Beneath the scene is an inscription identical to that on the bowl. The map is also embellished with a cartouche, very close in design and style to those on the bowl and, surrounding the list of symbols, a cluster of figures representing the prosperity of the county. The engraver, Daniel Pomerede, signed his work beneath the scale. Although the bowl is not signed, it is quite clear from similarities in design and style, as Anthony Phillips has pointed out, that Pomerede was responsible.[7] Little is known about the training of engravers and

their commercial relationship to the goldsmiths. It is remarkable to have a secure attribution for the engraving on a piece of plate. There were about twenty engravers recorded to have worked in Ireland in the eighteenth century and most were brothers of the Stationers' Guild.[8] Some like Pomerede were also registered with the Goldsmiths' Guild.[9]

William Williamson II most probably trained under his father, William. He was elected to the common council of the city of Dublin in 1752 and elected assay master by the goldsmiths in 1754, a post he held until 1770.[10]

1. A silver beer jug marked by John Williamson for 1734 bears the arms of Gore and is engraved, *This plate run for at Waterford and wone by Smileing Bald.* Sold Christie's, New York, October 28, 1986, lot 568, now in the National Museum of Ireland.

2. Watson 1969, pp. 10–13. Also see John Welcome, *Irish Horse-Racing, an Illustrated History* (New York, 1982), pp. 7–11.

3. Oliver Goldsmith, quoted in Watson 1969, *Between the Flags,* p. 11.

4. J. P. Hurstone, *The Picadilly Ambulator, or Old Q* (London, 1808), pp. 23–30.

5. Watson 1969, pp. 12–13.

6. British Museum Map 12170. A print of the scene was issued in London on September 5, 1751, by Henry Roberts, print seller. Walter George Strickland, *A Dictionary of Irish Artists* (Dublin, 1968), vol. 2, pp. 249–50.

7. Phillips, "A Fine Trophy," pp. 234–35.

8. Robert Munter, *A Dictionary of the Print Trade in Ireland, 1550–1775* (New York, 1988), pp. 211-12.

9. Pomerede was a quarter brother. Strickland, *A Dictionary of Irish Artists,* vol. 2, pp. 249–50.

10. There is another bowl of about 1750 with his mark, bearing the arms of Lowther, sold Christie's, New York, April 29, 1987, lot 336.

267

· 267 ·

DISH RING AND COVER

Cover marked by Samuel Walker (apprenticed
1726, d. 1769)
Dublin, ca. 1765 (cover) and 20th century, bearing
marks for 1781 (dish ring)
Silver, wood
40.726a–b

MARKS: 40.726a (dish ring): on outside of lower
foot band, *MS* (Jackson, p. 640); date letter *I*; harp
crowned; Hibernia. 40.726b (cover): on rim, harp
crowned; maker's mark *SW* (Bennett, p. 176, no.
471); Hibernia

ARMORIALS: 40.726b: engraved on cover, the arms,
crest, and motto of Seward

40.726a: H. 9.9 cm (3⅞ in.); diam. of base 20.5 cm
(8¹⁄₁₆ in.)

40.726b: H. 8.9 cm (3½ in.); diam. of rim 29.1 cm
(11⁷⁄₁₆ in.)

WEIGHT: 40.726a: 439 gm (14 oz 2 dwt). 40.726b:
448 gm (14 oz 8 dwt)

PROVENANCE: Janet Morse, New York, purchased
November 14, 1940, H. E. Bolles Fund

DESCRIPTION: The spool-shaped dish ring is
chased and pierced with scrolls, foliage, flower heads,
a figure of a Chinese man, a woman gathering flow-

ers, and a swan. The upper and lower edges are reinforced with a square wire rim. The domed circular
cover, formed from chased, pierced sheet of light
gauge, has an everted crimped rim. The chased work
represents scrolls, roses, sunflowers, grapevines, figs,
and pomegranates. A cast finial in the shape of an
eagle with splayed wings is attached to the cover
with a bolt and star-shaped nut.

This dish ring is a forgery probably made in
the twentieth century and later united with the
cover, which, although worn, is an unaltered
example of about 1765. It is unlikely that the
combination of silver dish ring, wooden bowl,
and pierced silver cover was used in the eighteenth century. Dish rings or ring stands served
to protect the tabletop and to elevate a dish—
probably silver or ceramic—for decorative
effect. They were made in England and Ireland
from at least the mid-seventeenth century. The
duke of Ormonde's 1684 inventory of Dublin
Castle records ten ring stands, weighing a total
of 199 ounces.[1] The pierced and chased spool-
shaped dish ring is a peculiarly Irish version
that became popular from about 1745.
Following changes in style, dish rings reflect
the taste for rococo, transitional, and neoclassical decoration.[2] In 1787 over twenty dish rings
and four dish stands were submitted for assay.[3]
The term *potato ring*, a reminder of the famine,
seems to have been attached to the form in the
early part of the twentieth century, when dish
rings, as uniquely Irish forms, became very
popular among collectors.[4] Many, like the present example which incorporates a full set of
marks from a spoon, were forged.

Pierced dish covers seem to have been made
mainly in Ireland to complement the popular
spool-shaped dish rings made from the 1740s.[5]
The rococo decoration on these objects, with
fanciful depictions of lush landscape inhabited
by fancifully dressed figures, has been identified
as a characteristically Irish style.[6]

Though produced in some quantity, only
few dish covers seem to have survived.[7] These
were made in both circular and oval shapes and
may have served as covers for pierced baskets of
similar construction.[8] A pair of oval Ch'ien
lung famille rose bowls with pierced covers
chased with flowers, fruit, and foliage and with
flower finials suggest that they may have been
used as potpourri containers.[9]

1. Historical Manuscripts Commission, *Calendar of Manuscripts of the Marquess of Ormonde, K.P., Preserved at Kilkenny Castle* (London, 1912), vol. 7, p. 510. Two are described as having "whole bottoms," possibly meaning that the base of the ring was closed.

2. M. S. D. Westropp, "Irish Silver Dish Rings," *Connoisseur* 98 (July–December 1936), pp. 213–15.

3. Sinsteden 1999, p. 155.

4. In the 1902 St. James's Court exhibition, very few Irish items were exhibited, but "Irish Potato Rings" were well represented. London, St. James's Court, *Old Silver Work, Chiefly English, from the XVth to the XVIIIth Centuries,* 1902, pl. 71.

5. Bennett 1972, p. 122.

6. Joseph McDonnell, "Irish Rococo Silver," *Irish Arts Review* 13 (1997), pp. 78–86.

7. Fourteen dish covers were submitted at the Dublin Goldsmiths' Hall for assay in 1787, Sinsteden 1999. Also see an oval pierced cover of about 1770 marked by William Townsend, illus. Bennett 1972, p. 125, fig. 32; also see advertisement, *Connoisseur* 140, no. 566 (January 1958), p. lv.

8. See an oval basket and cover of about 1770 marked by John Craig, illus. John Davis, "The Genius of Irish Silver," *Antiques* 141, no. 1 (January 1992), p. 197, pl. 15.

9. Sold Sotheby's, Slane Castle, November 20, 1978, lot 314.

· 268 ·

PAIR OF SALVERS

Marked by William Homer (d. 1773)
Dublin, 1768
Silver
Res.63.61–62

MARKS: on underside of each rim, Hibernia; maker's mark *WH* (Bennett p. 179, no. 546); harp crowned

ARMORIALS: engraved in center of each, the arms of Dromore impaling Newcombe, for the Most Rev. William Newcombe D.D., archbishop of Armagh and lord primate of All Ireland (1729–1800), who married first Maria, daughter of Sir Thomas D'Oyley, baronet, married second, Anna Maria, daughter and co-heir of Edward Smyth, Esq., of Callow Hill, co. Fermanagh

INSCRIPTIONS: Res.63.61: engraved on underside, *24=7 pr.* Res.63.62: engraved on underside, *24=7*

Res.63.61: H. 3.1 cm (1¼ in.); diam. of rim 21.3 cm (8⅜ in.)

Res.63.62: H. 3.1 cm (1¼ in.); diam. of rim 21.2 cm (8⁵⁄₁₆ in.)

WEIGHT: Res.63.61: 376 gm (12 oz 2 dwt). Res.63.62: 359 gm (11 oz 11 dwt)

PROVENANCE: Gift of the Trustees of the Reservation, estate of Mrs. John Gardner Coolidge, October 17, 1963

268

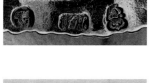

DESCRIPTION: The shaped circular salver is constructed from sheet with a raised rim and an applied cast gadrooned border. The salver rests on three hoof feet, each cast in two pieces. One foot has been repaired.

This pair of salvers, along with other surviving silver marked by William Homer, including salvers[1] and a set of four figural candlesticks,[2] suggests that he was a silversmith of considerable prominence, although he remained a quarter brother and never became a freeman of the city of Dublin.[3]

The engraved arms are those of William Newcome, who in 1766 left his post as vice principal of Hertford College, Oxford, to serve as chaplain to Frances Seymour Conway, earl of Hertford, when he was appointed lord lieutenant of Ireland. He was almost immediately appointed to the see of Dromore, and in 1775 he was transferred to Ossory. His elevation to the archbishopric in 1795 was said to have been the express act of George III. Newcome's arms are impaled with the see of Dromore, a convention that presents the bishop's see on the sinister, or "wife's," side.

1. See a pair of salvers marked for 1770, sold Christie's, London, November 9, 1994, lot 176, and a single salver advertised by S. J. Shrubsole, *Apollo* 87, no. 76 (June 1968), p. cxxix.
2. Sold Sotheby's, New York, June 6, 1980, lot 83.
3. G. Thrift, *Roll of Freemen, City of Dublin* (Dublin, 1919).

269

FISH OR PUDDING SERVER
Marked by Christopher Haines (II) (active ca. 1787–94)
Dublin, 1777
Silver
39.817

MARKS: on back of handle, date letter *E*; Hibernia; Paris mark for foreign work used 1819–38; maker's mark *CH* (Bennett, p. 161, no. 69); harp crowned

ARMORIALS: engraved on end of stem, an unidentified crest (out of a ducal coronet, a greyhound's head ermine)

L. 32.2 cm (12¹¹⁄₁₆ in.); w. 9.6 cm (3¾ in.)

WEIGHT: 107 gm (3 oz 10 dwt)

PROVENANCE: Anonymous Gift in Memory of Charlotte Beebe Wilbour (1833–1914), December 14, 1939

DESCRIPTION: The server, formed from two pieces of wrought sheet, has a broad triangular blade, slightly dished, that is pierced overall with a pattern of ovals with crosses surrounded by a border of reversed triangles. The rim of the blade and handle are edged with a narrow bright-cut border. The Old English–style handle, joined to the blade with a fan-shaped boss, is arched and curved like a scoop around its long axis. An oval cartouche of bright-cut work contains the crest.

Contemporary documents suggest that a serving implement of this form might have been called a trowel, a fish slice, or a fish trowel.[1] The broad range of pierced decoration on such servers included many with fish motifs, but those with geometric decoration such as this one were likely to have been used for serving all types of food. The design of the piercing on this example belongs to a category sometimes called "Chippendale Gothic." The handle curving on two axes appears to be an Irish style.[2]

1. In 1787 four trowels, three fish slices (including two by Christopher Haines), and eight fish trowels were submitted for assay in Dublin. Sinsteden 1999.
2. Benton Seymour Rabinovitch, *Antique Silver Servers for the Dining Table* (Concord, Mass., 1991), pp. 68–77.

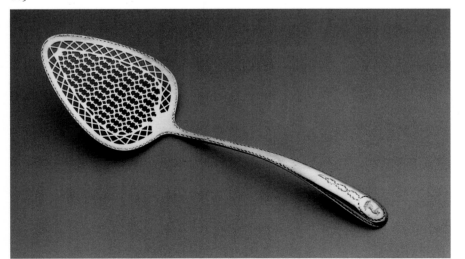

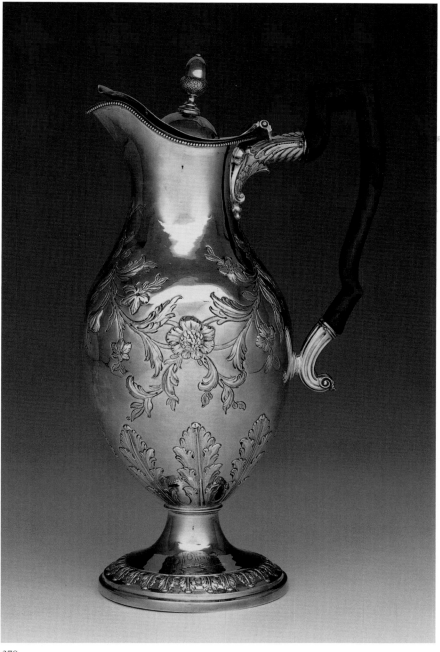

270

COVERED JUG

Marked by John Lloyd (free 1768, d. 1821)
Dublin, 1778
Silver, wood
Res.65.28

MARKS: to right of handle, date letter *F*; harp
crowned; Hibernia; maker's mark *JL* (Bennett p. 169,
no. 259)[1]

ARMORIALS: engraved below lip, an unidentified
coat of arms and crest (per chevron or and azure
three mullets counterchanged, overall a chevron
gules; crest: a lion passant guardant holding in the
dexter paw a mullet)

H. 31.6 cm (12⁷⁄₁₆ in.); w. 17.7 cm (6¹⁵⁄₁₆ in.);
d. 13.1 cm (5³⁄₁₆ in.)

WEIGHT: 742 gm (23 oz 18 dwt)

PROVENANCE: Bequest of Maxim Karolik,
April 14, 1965

DESCRIPTION: The raised ovoid jug has a narrow
neck and shaped rim with high pouring lip edged
with an applied beaded wire. The body is mounted
with a ring molding on a tall raised spreading foot
with a band of chased acanthus leaves above an
applied band foot. The domed cover with acorn
finial is attached to the top of the handle mount by
a five-knuckle hinge with an oval hinge plate. The
wooden handle is mounted on cast and chased
scroll-handle sockets. The body is chased around the
base with eight large vertical acanthus leaves and
above with scrolled branches and flower heads.

The ovoid outline of this jug is somewhat
unusual for Dublin examples of this period,
which were more commonly vase-shaped,[2] but
the conflation of rococo chasing on a neoclassical carcass is not unknown.[3] Tall jugs with
wooden handles and short spouts may have
been used for hot water, wine, or punch.
Dublin assay office records for 1787 list five
punch jugs and two water jugs, although the
term *wine jug* does not occur.[4]

1. This mark has also been attributed to John
Laughlin and John Locker. See Bennett 1984, p. 169.
2. Bennett 1972, p. 126.
3. See a jug illus. Bennett 1972, p. 146.
4. Sinsteden 1999, p. 155.

271

272

· 271 ·

LADLE
Marked by John Nicholson (free 1805, d. 1824)
Cork, ca. 1780
Silver
12.1157

MARKS: on back of handle, rectangular standard
mark *STERLING*; maker's mark *IN* (Bennett,
p. 189, no. 46) (struck twice)

INSCRIPTIONS: engraved on handle, *MAT Ware*

L. 37.8 cm (14⅞ in.); w. 9.6 cm (3¾ in.)

WEIGHT: 204 gm (6 oz 12 dwt)

PROVENANCE: Gift of Horace E. Ware, November
7, 1912

DESCRIPTION: The bowl of the ladle has a scalloped edge and is chased with spiral fluting inter-
spaced with punched dots radiating from a double-
drop handle joint. The long plain curved handle is
of the Old English style.

Flatware was produced in Ireland in great
quantities, not only in Dublin but also in such
provincial towns as Cork and Limerick. Soup
ladles are referred to as "tureen ladles" in
records of the Dublin assay office, where about
150 were submitted for assay in 1787.[1] The flat-
chased rococo decoration with hook-ended
handle is characteristically Irish and appears in
both Dublin and provincial examples.[2]

1. Sinsteden 1999, p. 155.
2. See an example marked in Dublin in 1765, illus.
John Graham et al., *The Campbell Museum Collection*
(Camden, N.J., 1972), cat. 8, and a Cork ladle sold
James Adam, Dublin, October 1, 1997, lot 146.

· 272 ·

STRAINER SPOON
Marked by John Stoyte (free 1789)
Dublin, 1787
Silver
47.206

MARKS: on back of handle, maker's mark *JS*
(Bennett, p. 170, no. 303); Hibernia; harp crowned;
date letter *P*

ARMORIALS: engraved on end of handle, an
unidentified crest (a right hand open)[1]

L. 30.7 cm (12¹⁄₁₆ in.); w. 5 cm (1¹⁵⁄₁₆ in.)

354

WEIGHT: 119 gm (3 oz 16 dwt)

PROVENANCE: Gift of Mrs. Gardiner M. Lane, February 13, 1947

DESCRIPTION: The oval bowl has a vertically pierced divider inserted along the long axis. The plain stem has a pointed terminus.

Strainer spoons were made in both England and Ireland, but a large proportion of those surviving are from Ireland. They appear to have been used for straining gravy.[2] The term *strainer spoon* does not appear in the 1787 records of the plate submitted for assay at the Dublin Goldsmiths' Hall,[3] but more than 200 "sauce spoons" and 500 "gravy spoons" were submitted. These numbers doubtless include the spoons now referred to as "strainer," "basting," or "stuffing" spoons. Bennett attributes the mark on this spoon to John Shields. However, since John Shields did not submit any silver for assay in 1787, whereas John Stoyte submitted more than 140 gravy spoons and 6 sauce spoons that year, the mark is here attributed to John Stoyte. John Stoyte ran a very productive shop producing around 8,800 ounces of flatware (and only flatware) in 1787, second only to John Pittar, who produced over 10,000 ounces.[4]

1. The crest is that of Ulster, but it was also used by several Irish families.

2. Ian Pickford, *Silver Flatware* (Woodbridge, 1983), pp. 194–95.

3. Sinsteden 1999, p. 155.

4. Ibid.

273

· 273 ·

SUGAR BOWL

Irish provincial, probably Cork, ca. 1790
Silver
58.1349

UNMARKED

INSCRIPTIONS: engraved on underside, *M/D★A*; scratched on underside, *oz 6=9*

H. 6 cm (2⅜ in.); diam. of rim 12.7 cm (5 in.)

WEIGHT: 200 gm (6 oz 9 dwt)

PROVENANCE: Gift of Misses Aimee and Rosamond Lamb, December 12, 1958

DESCRIPTION: The raised circular bowl has vertical sides and a wavy everted rim and rests on three mask and paw feet. The body is chased with spiral fluting and scattered punched foliage and flower swags between the flutes. The thickly cast and chased paw feet, soldered unevenly to the bowl, are surmounted by a chased scroll and a heavily cast and chased grotesque mask head.

The heavy gauge and simple design of this bowl are characteristic of provincial Irish work. The embossing and spiral fluting is heavyhanded, as are the unusual heavy cast supports. A bowl marked by Carden Terry of Cork using the same cast supports was recently on the Dublin market.[1]

1. Sold James Adam, Dublin, October 1, 1997, lot 115.

274, 275

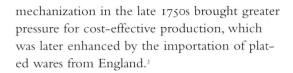

mechanization in the late 1750s brought greater pressure for cost-effective production, which was later enhanced by the importation of plated wares from England.[3]

1. An example similar to this was sold Sotheby's, New York, June 6, 1980, lot 90.

2. Sinsteden 1999, p. 155.

3. The minute books for May 1760–June 1779 (Book no. 21) in the Company of Goldsmiths, Dublin, record several meetings at which competition from cheap wares imported from England was discussed.

· 275 ·

SAUCEBOAT

Marked by G&PW
Dublin, 1800
Silver
30.670

MARKS: on underside, maker's mark *G&PW* (Jackson, p. 643); Hibernia; harp crowned; date letter *D*

INSCRIPTIONS: engraved in monogram on side, *ER*

H. 10.6 cm (4 3/16 in.); w. 17 cm (6 11/16 in.); d. 8 cm (3 1/8 in.)

WEIGHT: 176 gm (5 oz 14 dwt)

PROVENANCE: Gift of Mrs. Richard M. Saltonstall, October 16, 1930

DESCRIPTION: The plain oval boat has a slightly everted bead-punched rim and rests on three shell-headed scrolled hoof feet. The leaf-capped double-scrolled handle is mounted to the rim on a shell support. The lower handle mount is surrounded by radiating linear punching.

Simple sauceboats, both plain and decorated, were made in great quantities in Dublin from the 1770s to the early 1800s. Mathew West, for example, submitted over 250 boats for assay in 1787.[1] Smaller versions of this form were called "cream boats," and in 1787 approximately twenty cream boats were submitted for assay.

1. Sinsteden 1999.

· 274 ·

SUGAR BOWL

Marked by George West (free 1792, d. 1828)
Dublin, 1796
Silver
30.671

MARKS: on underside, maker's mark *GW* (Bennett, p. 166, no. 180); harp crowned; date letter *z*; Hibernia

INSCRIPTIONS: engraved on side in monogram, *ER*

H. 7.9 cm (3 1/8 in.); diam. of rim 12.7 cm (5 in.)

WEIGHT: 212 gm (6 oz 16 dwt)

PROVENANCE: Gift of Mrs. Richard M. Saltonstall, October 16, 1930

DESCRIPTION: The plain hemispherical raised bowl has a double row of punch beading around the everted rim and rests on three shell-headed scrolled hoof feet.

Sugar bowls, both plain and chased with flowers or genre scenes, were made in great quantities by the West family of Dublin.[1] In 1787 Mathew West submitted over 150 sugar dishes for assay.[2] With the production of certain forms like this, the Dublin silversmiths established a presence, and for a time even dominated, the increasingly competitive international market of mass-produced items. The onset of more

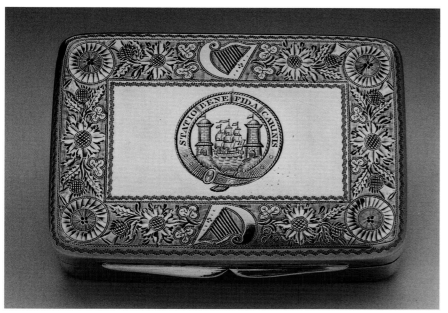

276

ing of flowers, thistles, shamrocks, and foliage. Engraved at each corner are a starburst and in the center of the band above and below the arms, a harp. The lid is mounted onto the rear wall of the base with a flush five-knuckle hinge. The sides of the box are plain and the base engraved with an inscription as noted above. The interior of the box is gilt.

A considerable number of freedom boxes were presented by the city of Cork to various dignitaries and to persons who distinguished themselves or did significant service for the local community.[2] The plain boxes were marked in either Cork or Dublin and apparently decorated by a Cork engraver.[3]

    William Pitt (1759–1806) was the second son of William Pitt, earl of Chatham. Pitt the Younger rose to great political eminence as a statesman and orator. He graduated from Pembroke College, Cambridge, and became member of Parliament for Appleby in 1781. He was appointed chancellor of the Exchequer in 1782. By 1784 he was elected with an overwhelming majority the youngest ever prime minister and remained in office for seventeen years. After Pitt's session in office Pitt Clubs were founded about 1808 in London, Leeds, and Scotland. Mr. Atcheson, to whom this box was presented, was the father and founder of the Pitt Club. He stated during one of the yearly meetings held in London that the seed was sown for the Pitt Club as far back as 1792. The annual meetings were held on May 27, Pitt's birthday, in a rented hall such as the Taylor Guild Hall. Minutes were kept, and six hundred or so members might attend each event. Speeches extolling Pitt and British politics were given by presidents of the clubs followed by many toasts. The evening concluded

· 276 ·

FREEDOM BOX

Marked by Carden Terry (1742–1821) and Jane Williams (d. 1845)
Cork, 1815
Silver
25.166

MARKS: on underside of cover, maker's mark *CT* over *IW* (Bennett, p. 188, no. 13); sovereign's head. On inside of box, date letter *T*; harp crowned; Hibernia; sovereign's head

ARMORIALS: engraved in center of top of box, the arms of the city of Cork surrounded by motto, *STATIO BENE FINA CARINIS*

INSCRIPTIONS: engraved on underside, *The Major Sheriffs & common Council of the/City of Cork unanimously voted the Freedom/at large of their City to be presented to/Nathl. Atcheson of London, Esq./Founder of the Pitt Club. As a public/Testimony of the opinion they entertain of his high Character./Henry Sadleir, Mayor./W. Waggett, Recorder./Thos. Deane,[1]/Wm. Lucas,/} Sheriffs./W. Jones, T. Clerk.*

H. 2.3 cm (⅞ in.); w. 7.5 cm (2¹⁵⁄₁₆ in.); d. 5.1 cm (2 in.)

WEIGHT: 99 gm (3 oz 4 dwt)

PROVENANCE: Gift of Miss M. H. Jewell, April 13, 1925

DESCRIPTION: The rectangular box features the arms of Cork engraved centrally within a plain rectangular cartouche surrounded by a band of engrav-

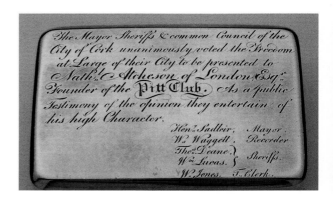

with an elaborate toast to their chairman, Mr. Atcheson, after which came his recognition speech and a final song composed for the occasion.[4] The clubs, of which the duke of Wellington was a prominent member, supported the Protestant ascendancy which had a strong following in Cork, although there is no evidence that there was a Pitt Club in Cork.

1. Thomas Deane, one of the sheriffs of Cork, was a founder of the prominent Cork architectural firm Deane Woodward Deane. This firm expanded under his son Thomas Newenham Deane and eventually moved to Dublin. The Museum Building in Trinity College, Dublin, is a fine example of their work. See Patrick Wyse Jackson, "A Victorian Landmark: Trinity College's Museum Building," *Irish Arts Review* 11 (1995), pp. 149–54.

2. For example, see Richard Caufield, *The Council Book of the Corporation of the City of Cork* (Guilford, 1876), pp. 729, 799. For a more detailed discussion of freedom boxes, see cat. 262.

3. For other Cork freedom boxes, see a Dublin-marked box sold Sotheby's, London, April 23, 1981, lot 203, and a Cork-marked box sold Sotheby's, London, April 24, 1986, lot 50.

4. The toast is described in the minutes as a "three times three toast" and the lyrics of the song are recorded. Yale University, Beinecke Rare Book and Manuscript Library, Pitt Papers, OSB MSS 13.

277

· 277 ·

COFFEEPOT

London, 20th century, bearing marks for 1699/1700
Silver, wood
33.90

MARKS: on underside, maker's mark *PE* for Edmund Pearce (first mark entered 1705) (Grimwade 2169) (struck twice); date letter *d*; lion's head erased; Britannia

INSCRIPTIONS: engraved on underside of foot, 27=5

H. 23.5 cm (9¼ in.); w. 23.5 cm (9¼ in.); d. 10.7 cm (4¼ in.)

WEIGHT: 884.5 gm (28 oz 9 dwt)

PROVENANCE: Anonymous Gift in Memory of Charlotte Beebe Wilbour (1833–1914), March 2, 1933

EXHIBITED: Boston, Museum of Fine Arts, 1933

DESCRIPTION: The body of the coffeepot is pear-shaped and formed of two pieces: a raised lower section with twelve faceted panels joined to a cylindrical upper section that is seamed. The domed foot is spun, with a molded rim. The curved faceted spout is cast in two pieces and seamed vertically. The wooden scrolled handle is attached to the body with two cylindrical sockets. It is broken across the middle and patched with a small silver square secured with nails. The raised domed cover is faceted and is surmounted by a round baluster finial. A hole once pierced near the finial has been patched.

This coffeepot must have been made in about 1920 perhaps by a firm such as Garrard's or Crichton Brothers as part of a "Queen Anne style" service and was doubtless properly marked.[1] Soon afterward, a disk bearing marks for 1699/1700 must have been let into the foot. The center punch on the disk is off-center, the cover is unmarked, and the interior of the vessel is blackened from the soldering. The form has no precedent in the early eighteenth century, and the coffeepot is a remarkably unambitious forgery.

1. See examples sold Christie's, London, May 24, 1989, lot 104; another sold Christie's, London, May 23, 1990, lot 71; another sold Christie's, London, October 25, 1989, lot 99.

278

278

· 278 ·

SUGAR BOWL AND CREAM JUG

London, 20th century, bearing marks for 1721/2

Silver

33.115, 33.116

MARKS: 33.115 (sugar bowl): on underside, maker's mark *G* with an *R* for Richard Green (first mark entered 1703) (Grimwade 876); date letter *F*; lion's head erased; Britannia. 33.116 (cream jug): on underside, maker's mark *NA* for Bowles Nash (first mark entered 1721) (Grimwade 2083); date letter *F*; lion's head erased; Britannia

ARMORIALS: 33.115: engraved on side, an unidentified crest (a boar's head erased). 33.116: engraved on side, an unidentified crest (a lion's head erased on a ducal coronet)

INSCRIPTIONS: 33.115: engraved on underside, *S*★*P*; *5=11*; scratched, *9659*. 33.116: engraved on underside, *LC*; *7=1*; scratched, *10452*

33.115: H. 7.2 cm (2¹³⁄₁₆ in.); w. 21.9 cm (8⅝ in.); d. 7.9 cm (3⅛ in.)

33.116: H. 11.6 cm (4⁹⁄₁₆ in.); w. 10.5 cm (4⅛ in.); d. 6.6 cm (2⁹⁄₁₆ in.)

WEIGHT: 33.115: 164.4 gm (5 oz 6 dwt). 33.116: 209.8 gm (6 oz 15 dwt)

PROVENANCE: Anonymous Gift in Memory of Charlotte Beebe Wilbour (1833–1914), March 2, 1933

EXHIBITED: Boston, Museum of Fine Arts, 1933

DESCRIPTION: The cream jug, raised from sheet, has a pear-shaped octagonal body and rests on a cast octagonal stepped foot. A molded wire is applied to the midsection. The scrolled handle is cast in two vertical pieces, set opposite a triangular spout with a rounded drop. The raised sugar bowl has a bulbous octagonal body and rests on a plain octagonal foot. It has a molded wire around its middle and rim, and two cast scrolled handles with rounded drops.

Like the coffeepot with let-in hallmarks (cat. 277), this cream jug and sugar bowl must have been altered to appeal to the perennially strong collector's market for plain Queen Anne silver of geometric form.[1] All the marks on the cream jug are struck from forged punches, while the fragmentary maker's mark on the sugar bowl may be authentic and enhanced by the addition of forged hallmarks.

1. For another example of spurious silver in this category, see Wees 1997, p. 387, cat. 277.

279

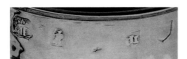

· 279 ·

WATER JUG
Marked by Micon Melun (1697–1757)
Exeter, 1701–20
Silver
35.1576

MARKS: to right of handle, maker's mark *ME* with a crown above in an octagon (repeated on handle); Britannia; obscured mark, probably lion's head erased; Exeter castle; illegible date letter

H. 14.5 cm (5¾ in.); w. 13.5 cm (5⁵⁄₁₆ in.); d. 11 cm (4⁵⁄₁₆ in.)

WEIGHT: 368.5 gm (11 oz 17 dwt)

PROVENANCE: Crichton Brothers, New York, purchased by Frank Brewer Bemis, March 28, 1921, Bequest of Mr. Frank Brewer Bemis, November 7, 1935

DESCRIPTION: The vase-shaped body rests on a molded wire foot. The lower half of the body is chased with fluting and punched with quatrefoils and pellets. The shoulder of the jug is similarly chased and punched. The neck of the jug is formed of a molded band and a spout; beneath the spout is a bellflower drop. The scrolled handle has a shaped flat terminus.

The straight neck of this jug, bearing Exeter hallmarks and the maker's mark of Micon Melun, was transposed from another object. The small handle, which is also marked, suggests that it may have been a mug. There is no precedent for a pouring vessel of this form, and the bulbous body with small neck must have been an invention of the forger.

Falmouth seems to have had a sizable Huguenot community. Micon Melun was one of seven children born to René Melun, a French-born surgeon who was granted the rights of citizenship in 1681. He apprenticed to the Plymouth goldsmith Henry Muston and entered marks for both sterling and Britannia standard.[1]

1. T. A. Kent, "Goldsmiths of Falmouth," *Proceedings of the Silver Society* 11, nos. 9–10 (1980), p. 156.

280

These problematic objects, bearing Paul de Lamerie's mark and hallmarks for 1745/6, are engraved with the arms of Sir William Clayton of Marden, fourth baronet, impaling those of East, for his wife, Mary, daughter of Sir William East. The salts are in the form of the family crest (out of a mural coronet, a gamb holding a bezant), a design formula common in the Regency period,[1] but completely inconsistent with the date of the hallmark. The objects cannot be dismissed as simple forgeries, however, since in the eighteenth century the family seems to have bought silver from Lamerie, and the salts remained in the family until the twentieth century.[2] A second pair is in the Indianapolis Museum of Art.[3]

One possible explanation is that the fourth baronet may have taken some of his inherited plate to be updated in a more current style. The bowls of these salts might have left Lamerie's shop in 1745 in the form of tumblers, small salvers, or soap boxes and were easily adapted by the addition of cast bases in the Regency taste. However, the Lamerie marks on the rims, though stretched, have been carefully preserved, suggesting that the "alterations" were made during a period when the value of the Lamerie mark was significant.

1. For example, see a pair of dish covers in the Minneapolis Institute of Arts, illus. Puig 1989, pp. 148–49, cat. 128.

2. Listed as having been sold by Sir Harold Dudley Clayton (b. 1877), tenth baronet, advertisement, S. J. Shrubsole, *Antiques* 63, no. 6 (June 1953), p. 483. See the rococo basket marked by Lamerie for 1745 with the arms of William Clayton, second son of the first baronet, sold Sotheby's, New York, October 21, 1998, lot 293.

3. Acc. no. 75.661–662. I thank Barry Shifman, curator of decorative arts, for sharing material from the Indianapolis Museum files.

· 280 ·

PAIR OF SALTS

Marked by Paul de Lamerie (1688–1751)
London, 1745/6
Silver gilt
63.485–486

MARKS: on side of each, maker's mark *PL* (Grimwade 2204); lion passant; leopard's head crowned; date letter *k*

ARMORIALS: engraved on side of each, the arms of Clayton impaling East, for Sir Harold Clayton, fourth baronet of Marden Park Godstone, co. Surrey, and Harleyford, co. Buckinghamshire (1762–1834), and Mary, only daughter of Sir William East, baronet of Hall Place, co. Berkshire

H. 9.9 cm (3⅞ in.); diam. of rim 7.2 cm (2¹³⁄₁₆ in.)

WEIGHT: 63.485: 343 gm (11 oz). 63.486: 440.2 gm (10 oz 19 dwt)

PROVENANCE: by descent to Sir Harold Dudley Clayton, tenth baronet of Marden, sold by S. J. Shrubsole, 1953; The Antique Porcelain Co., Inc., New York and London, purchased May 8, 1963, Theodora Wilbour Fund in Memory of Charlotte Beebe Wilbour

EXHIBITED: Houston, Texas, Museum of Fine Arts, 1956, ill. 62

DESCRIPTION: Each salt is in the form of a heavily cast and chased leopard's paw emerging from a crenelated turret and surmounted by a raised hemispherical bowl.

281

· 281 ·

BASKET AND LINER

Marked by Nicholas Sprimont (1726–1770)
London, 1745/6, with later alterations
Silver, silver plate
67.1191

MARKS: on underside, leopard's head crowned; date letter *k*; lion passant; maker's mark *NS* (Grimwade 2102)

INSCRIPTIONS: engraved on fluting of both sides, an illegible cipher; on underside, engraved, *Mae C. Plant 1917*

H. 19.4 cm (7⅝ in.); w. 42.3 cm (16¹¹⁄₁₆ in.); d. 27 cm (10⅝ in.)

WEIGHT: 4,224.2 gm (135 oz 16 dwt)

PROVENANCE: estate of Mrs. Frieda Wertheimer, sold Christie's, London, February 15, 1905, lot 41; estate of Mae C. Rovensky, sold Parke-Bernet Galleries, Inc., New York, January 15–19, 1957, lot 928; Mr. and Mrs. S. J. Katz, Gift of Mrs. Sigmund J. Katz, The Jessie and Sigmund Katz Collection, December 21, 1967

PUBLISHED: Grimwade 1974, ill. 42a; Schroder 1988a, p. 289, fig. 72

DESCRIPTION: The oval bombé body rests on four scrolled feet. The lower section of the body is raised

and chased with fluting. Four female busts draped with garlands of flowers are cast in pieces and applied above the feet. The upper section of the body has a pierced trellis pattern with chased rosettes on the intersections of the trellis work. Over the trellis pattern are chased large floral swags. The scrolled handles on either end are heavily cast and chased with similar floral patterns and secured to the body with nuts and bolts. The undulating rim of the basket is outlined with a twisted rope border that is cast in sections, large cast acanthus leaves on either end and smaller acanthus leaves in the center of each longer side. A plain plated liner fits inside the body.

It is difficult to say with certainty the degree to which this object has been reworked. The marks appear to be genuine. There is no eighteenth-century precedent for a two-handled basket of this weight or proportion.[1] Many features, however, are quite eccentric and characteristic of Sprimont's work and are therefore not likely to be the invention of a forger. Two unaltered swing-handled baskets marked by Sprimont, one in the Gilbert collection and the other in the Ashmolean Museum, show several related features including female heads on the border with upswept hair.[2] The coarsely chased floral swags on the bombé body of this basket, however, and the cursory pierced diaperwork are almost certainly later "enhancements." There is a second basket, slightly smaller in size and without handles, that appears to have been treated similarly.[3]

An unusual pair of tureens with the mark of John Romer and the arms of the fourth earl of Dyssart-Tollemache may represent the original composition of these baskets.[4] Distinctly French in design, the tureens rest on four scrolled feet, considerably taller than those on the basket, that emerge from applied cast female busts draped in flowering swags. The bombé body of each tureen has chased gadrooning at the base, similar to the baskets, and panels of engraved diaperwork. The tureens rest on an oval stand with scrolled feet and a broad rim that appear to be identical to the stand marked by Sprimont in this collection. (See cat. 93.) It seems possible that the baskets were adapted from tureens similar to this model, possibly in the 1880s when, because of the enthusiasm among ceramic collectors, Sprimont's silver became highly prized.

1. In the Victorian period, however, bombé baskets with pierced diaperwork and floral chasing were popular. For example, see a set of baskets marked by Carrington & Co., sold Christie's, London, May 21, 1986, lot 102.

2. Schroder 1988a, pp. 284–89, cat. 74.

3. Sold Christie's, London, March 26, 1980, lot 131.

4. Sold by Sir Lyonel Tollemache, J. Trevor & Sons, New York, May 12, 1955, lot 60.

SEAL-TOP SPOON

Probably London, 19th century, bearing marks for 1761/2
Silver gilt
95.1163

MARKS: on back of stem, maker's mark *WW* possibly for William Wooller (first mark entered 1750) (similar to Grimwade 3364); lion passant; leopard's head crowned; date letter *F*

L. 17.8 cm (7 in.); w. 4.8 cm (1⅞ in.)

WEIGHT: 56.7 gm (1 oz 16 dwt)

PROVENANCE: Bequest of Jas. W. Paige, April 16, 1895

DESCRIPTION: The spoon has a fig-shaped gilt bowl and a tapering stem with a lobed baluster terminus. The back of the bowl is engraved with a blank cartouche in a baroque surround. The bowl and stem are forged from a single piece, and the cast finial is applied.

This spoon is a naive alteration of an eighteenth-century tablespoon. The goal was to forge a typical early-seventeenth-century seal-top spoon, but the marks indicate clearly that the original was made in 1761/2. It must have been altered in the mid-nineteenth century, when the meaning of the hallmarks was still not widely understood.

282

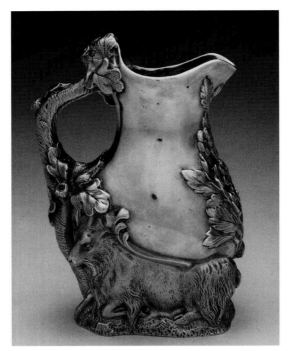

283

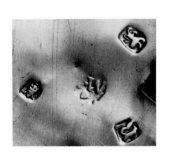

· 283 ·

CREAM JUG

London, 20th century bearing marks for 1772/3
Silver, parcel gilt
1988.1072

MARKS: on underside, maker's mark *IW* possibly for
James Waters (first mark entered 1769) (Grimwade
1743); lion passant; date letter *R*; leopard's head
crowned

H. 11.2 cm (4⅜ in.); w. 8 cm (3⅛ in.); d. 4.7 cm
(1⅞ in.)

WEIGHT: 241 gm (7 oz 15 dwt)

PROVENANCE: Lent by Mrs. S. J. Katz, June 25,
1973, The Jessie and Sigmund Katz Collection,
November 30, 1988

PUBLISHED: Harold Newman, "Silver 'Goat and
Bee' Jugs," *Antique Collector* 60, no. 7 (July 1989),
p. 67, fig. 3

DESCRIPTION: The jug has a pear-shaped body
that is modeled on the lower portion with two
goats, lying head to toe on a bed of grass. A floral
branch rises from a C-scroll at the front of the jug.
The handle is in the form of an oak branch with
leaves. The jug is cast in two halves and seamed
behind the handle and beneath the spout. The base
is inset and the handle is cast.

This jug is one of four silver versions of the
famous Chelsea porcelain model known as the
"goat and bee" jug.[1] The heavily cast sections
of the body contrast with the relatively light
gauge of the base, and the stiff chasing is
uncharacteristic of rococo work.

The jug must have been intended to be sold
as the work of Nicholas Sprimont, whose reputation as founder of the Chelsea porcelain
factory was well established by the late nineteenth century. Several examples of the porcelain jug bearing the inscription *1745 Chelsea*
were identified as the earliest known pieces of
English porcelain, ensuring a ready market for
any object associated with the factory's history.
The connection between Sprimont's porcelain
and his silver was not made until 1883, when
William Chaffers published his research on silver marks, *Gilda Aurifabrorum*.[2] The collecting of
Chelsea porcelain flourished by the 1880s and
created a market for forgeries such as this one,
as well as for altered objects, such as the
pierced basket bearing Sprimont's mark (see
cat. 281). It is interesting that although Morgan
and Chaffers had published the meaning of the
hallmarks, they were not sufficiently understood by the forger, who inserted hallmarks for
1772, much too late for the style of the jug.
Jessie and Sigmund Katz, important collectors
of English porcelain who presented the jug to
the Museum of Fine Arts, were aware, apparently, that it was not authentic, but admired the
piece for its documentary interest.

1. Two jugs are in the collection of the Goldsmiths'
Company, London, one bearing marks for 1724 and
the other bearing marks for 1762. See Newman,
"Silver 'Goat and Bee' Jugs," pp. 64–69. Based on
spectrographic analysis, the assay office has conclud-
ed that the marks on the first jug are probably
forged and those on the second are transposed from
an earlier piece. A third jug marked for 1737 is in
the Huntington Collection, illus. Wark 1978, p. 55,
cat. 128.

2. Tamara Rebanks examined the history of the
scholarship and collecting of works by Nicholas
Sprimont and the Chelsea factory in a paper presented to the American Ceramics Circle, November
1998. See William Chaffers, *Gilda Aurifabrorum: A
History of English Goldsmiths and Plateworkers and
Their Marks Stamped on Plate* (London, 1883).

Concordance

Accession Number	Catalogue Number
80.507	143
88.291	149
95.1163	282
12.40	218
12.1157	271
13.2857	103
14.901A–.902A	120
14.906	161
15.915	8
15.916	9
18.31	221
18.658	61
19.261	114
19.1384–.1385	80
20.1626	222
23.261	110
25.166	276
25.411–412	134
30.112	255
30.437A–B	45
30.465	246
30.648	125
30.670	275
30.671	274
31.491–492	244
32.363	122
32.364	123
32.368	211
32.407	249
33.82–.83	2
33.88	256
33.89	3
33.90	277
33.92–.93	12
33.95A–B	15
33.98	17
Res. 33.99–Res.33.104	235
33.102	27
33.103	259
33.106	260
33.107	34
33.115, 33.116	278
33.118	46
Res. 33.122	153
33.123	53
33.124	54
33.126	60
33.127	62
33.128	63
33.131–.132	64
33.133	69
33.134–.137	72
33.142	83
33.144, .146	85
33.153	102
33.158	108
33.159–.160	111
33.172	116
33.173	124
33.174	127
33.175	128
33.177	136
33.189	147
33.190	240
33.191–.192	142
33.194	156
33.195	157
33.198	164
33.217	207
33.230	214
33.231	212
33.245–33.248	224
33.253	217
33.254	237
33.255	228
33.258–259	236
33.260–261	227
33.263	238
33.264	243
33.265	230
33.272	245

33.274-277	219	40.193	33
33.278-279	215	40.194	239
33.292-293	220	40.195-.198	154
33.469	4	40.202-3	254
Res. 35.39	223	40.545	37
35.1546	13	40.601	234
35.1574	1	40.726A-B	267
35.1576	279	41.224	158
35.1577-.1578	5	41.227	210
35.1580-35.1583	208	41.623	170
35.1584	209	41.624	242
35.1585	16	42.8	23
35.1587	25	42.9	216
35.1589	31	42.10-.11	59
35.1598	253	42.12A-B	75
35.1599	41	42.13	265
35.1600	42	42.14	89
35.1601-.1602	263	42.80	261
35.1604	47	42.84-.87	11
35.1606-.1607	48	42.218	84
35.1612	49	Res. 43.2	200
35.1613	51	Res. 46.42	226
35.1614-.1615	52	47.206	272
35.1617	55	47.1352	241
35.1618	56	47.1355	150
35.1619-.1620	71	51.2	24
35.1626	78	52.9	264
35.1628-1629	225	52.1551	175
35.1630-.1631	88	53.2083	65
35.1634	232	54.1798-.1799	179
36.154	248	55.382	258
37.242	21	55.383	257
37.1166-.1167	14	55.460	57
37.1168	26	55.462A-B	73
37.1170	43	55.623	138
38.984	213	55.683	165
38.1651	94	55.918	185
38.1831-1837, 52.1550	174	55.970	247
39.20	10	55.975, 55.974, 55.973	38
39.83	97	55.976	6
Res. 39.111	178	55.977A,B, 55.972, 55.971,	
39.182	140	55.980	39
39.183	36	55.978A-C	67
39.817	269	55.979, 56.507	40
39.819	66	56.138	28
39.820-825	229	56.309	262
40.191	18	56.504-.505	135
40.192	22	56.677	166

56.1320–.1321	155	69.1358, 1970.639,	
57.59	98	.641, .643, .644,	
57.60	167	1971.774, .776–.777	96
57.101	58	1972.520	169
57.715	70	1973.137A–B	183
58.377–378, 58.381–382	104	1973.138–.139	87
58.1010	79	1973.482	266
58.1193	151	1974.564	29
58.1194	152	1975.19	92
58.1349	273	1975.283	204
60.936	144	1975.317	189
60.946	82	1975.361A–B	44
61.107	68	1975.665A–C	163
61.656	105	1975.733	90
62.4–5	251	1976..607A–C–.609	145
62.255	162	1976.659	146
63.7	106	1976.660	148
Res. 63.26A–B	137	1976.661	100
Res. 63.61–.62	268	1976.662A–C	113
63.198	130	1977.110A–C	177
63.485–486	280	1977.117	181
63.488	50	1977.183	198
63.784–.785	19	1977.540A–B	202
63.1419	32	1977.812–.813	30
64.128A–C	192	1978.177A–B	76
64.924	233	1979.503	173
Res. 65.27	126	1980.264	231
Res. 65.28	270	1980.265	190
Res. 65.29A–B–.31	168	1981.21–.23	132
Res. 65.32–.33	86	1983.398	160
65.263A–B	101	1984.185	35
65.397A–B	74	1984.512	118
65.915	115	1985.62–.65	176
65.1319	180	1985.198–.200A–B	107
66.286	117	1985.807A–D	133
66.435	139	1986.241A–J	112
66.436–.437	186	1987.57	250
67.1191	281	1987.488A–B	121
68.67	109	1988.282	77
69.398	171	1988.283	81
69.399	159	1988.1072	283
69.1147–.1148	188	1988.1073	182
1970.632	172	1988.1074	95
1970.641	96	1988.1075A–B–1077A–B	91
1970.644	96	1988.1078	196
1971.776–.777	96	1989.311A	119
1971.130	131	1989.313–.314	187

1990.461A–B, 1992.181	203
1991.1–3	99
1991.251	141
1991.536A–B	206
1991.539–.542	194
1991.627	197
1991.686	252
1992.433.1–3	7
1993.575	191
1993.943.1–2	129
1994.89	184
1994.193	193
1995.9	201
1995.85	199
1996.269	93
1998.60	195
1998.400	205
1999.98	20

Index

Numbers indicate page references. Page references for Museum objects are set in bold. The index includes all marks and makers represented in the Museum's collection. Works in other public collections are listed by city. All known former owners are indexed, as are amorials. For provincial plate, see town name.

A

Abbot crest, 76
Aberdeen silver, 330
AB in a shaped shield maker's mark, 342
AB incuse maker's mark, 312
AB (New Aberdeen) town mark, 330
Adam, Charles, 55–56, 158
Adam, Robert, 33, **198–201**, **207–209**, 212, 213, 284
Adams, John, 233
Adams, John Quincy, 136, 233
Alcott, Abigail May, 101, 102
Alcott, Louisa May, 10–11, 101, 102
Aldridge, Edward, **186**
Aldridge, James, 272
Allan, David, Antiquaire, 291
Allen, Frederic, 235
Allen arms and crest, 237
American Art Galleries, 233
ANe maker's mark, 65, 110
Annan, Charlotte, 287
Anne, Queen, 337
Annendale, marquess of, 109
Anson, Lord, 114
Antique Porcelain Co., Inc., 361
AP maker's mark, 252
Apollo club, 308
apostle spoon, 326
Apthorp, Ann, 165
Apthorp, Charles, 164, 165
Archambo, Peter, 125, 134, **138–39**, 166, **182–83**
Archdall, William, **340**, **341**
Archer, Andrew, **309**
Archer, Susanna, 141
Archer, William, 141
Aretino, Pietro, 225
argyll, 35, 216–17
Arnett, Hugh, **310**
Arts and Crafts movement, 13, 300–301, 304
art *vs.* artifact, 12–13
Arundel Castle, 224

Ash, Joseph, **267–68**
Ashbee, Charles Robert, **300–301**, **302**
Ashburnham, Bertram, fifth earl of, 107
Aske Hall, 201
Asprey & Co., 270
Asprey Ltd., 297
assaying, 13
Atcheson, Nathaniel, 357
Augustus Frederick, duke of Sussex, 266
August Wilhelm, duke of Brunswick-Wolfenbüttel, 75
Austin, Sarah, 192
Ayde arms and crest, 76, 85

B

Babcock, Adam, 325
Babcock crest, 325
baby's rattle and whistle, 297, 301
Bache, John, 90
Bagnall crest, 324
Bajazet, 348
Baltzell, Alice Cheney, 76
Baltzell, William Hewson, Dr., 76
Ba maker's mark, 64
Bamford, Thomas, 158
Barboult, Abraham, **342**
Barham arms, 116
Barnard, Edward, & Sons, 288
Barnard, Emma, 62
Barnard, John, **64**
Barnardston arms, 116
Barnet, John S., 54, 93, 94, 95, 121
Bartol, Elizabeth, 182
Bartol, John W., 207
Bartol, Mary W., 207
Baskerville, George, **316**
baskets, 28, 124–25, 138–39, 141–43, 192–93, 220, 230–31, 244, 362–63
  sugar, 238, 240
basting spoons, 324
Bateman, Ann, **245**, 249, **252**, **255**, 260
Bateman, Hester, **230**, **232–33**, **237**, **238**, **240**, **242–43**, **320**, **321**, **322**
Bateman, Jonathan, 242
Bateman, Peter, 242, **245**, 249, **252**, **255**, 260
Bateman, William, 260
Bayley, Richard, 82

B.C. maker's mark, 303
beakers, 260
    with traveling jug, 262–63
Bean, Barbara Boylston, 168, 186, 232, 233
Beckford, Susan, 104
Beckford, William, 104, 270–73
Bedford crest, 308
Behrens, Balthasar Friedrich, 75
Belcher, Jonathan, 178
Belcher, Thomas, 179
Beldon, John, **248**
Bell, Joseph, **82**
Belton House, 70, 122
BE maker's mark, 53
Bemis, Frank Brewer, 11, 50, 53, 62, 66, 78, 84, 96,
    104, 106, 108, 109, 111, 112, 126, 137, 148,
    306, 315, 318, 331, 344, 360
Bentley, Benjamin, **53**
Bentley, Thomas, 214
Beresford, William, lord bishop of Ossory, 229
Bergen, John Henry, 180
Bergen, Philip Crooke, 180
Bernoulli, Christophe, 138
Berthellot, John, **174–76**
Bethell, Elizabeth, 335
Bethell, William, 335
Bethune, George, 158, 170
Bethune, George (Dr.), 157
Bethune, George (son), 158
Bettisfield, Hammer, 182
Betts, John, **305**
BG maker's mark, 141
Biddle, Nicholas, Mrs., 193
Bi maker's mark, 65
Bing, Samuel, 291
Birch, Charles, 214
Birch-Reynardson, Charles-Thomas Samuel, 284
Birch-Reynardson, Etheldred Anne, 284
Bird, Joseph, 65–66
Birmingham silver, 218–19, 221–22, 244, 256,
    289–90, 291, 297, 299–300, 301, 303–304
Bishop, Ogden Mills, 133
Black, George Nixon, 207
Black and All Black (horse), 348
Blackwell, J. G., 128
Blackwell, Mary, 128
Blair, Claude, 230
Blake, Marian Lee, 325
Blakiston, Elizabeth, 90
Bloom, N., & Son, 218
B maker's mark, 305, 318
Boardman, William Dorr, Mrs., 207
Bodendick, Jacob, 90

Bolton, Thomas, 45, 46, 47, **332–33, 335–37,
    337–39,** 342, 344
Booth, George, earl of Warrington, 70, 97, 125, 138
Boott, John Wright, 287
Boott, Mary, 287
Bor, Barbara, 344
bottle tickets, 239, 240–41
Boucher, Elizabeth, 56, 57
Boucher, Louis, 56, 57
Boucher, Sarah, 56, 57
Boulton, Matthew, **218–19, 221–22,** 256
Boulton and Fothergill, 247
Bourryan, Zachary, 172
Bouverie, Sir Jacob de, 182, 183
Bowes, George, 90
Bowes, John, 92
Bowes, John, earl of Strathmore, 90, 92
Bowes, Lydia, 187
Bowes, Mary-Eleanor, 90
Bowes, Sir William, 90
Bowes, William Blakiston, 90
Bowes arms, 90
Bowlby, Sir Anthony Alfred, 304
bowls, 345
    covered, 52, 300–301
    marriage, 214
    punch, 347–49
    rose, 44, 303–304
    sugar, 52, 124, 260–61, 355, 356, 359
    waste, with tea service, 257–59
boxes, 230–31
    freedom, 343–44, 357–58
    pair, 61
    snuffboxes, 228–29
    sugar, 152–54
    sugar, with tea canisters, 166–67, 178–79
    tobacco, 84, 89
Boylston, Mary, 234
Boylston, Nicholas, 233
Boylston, Ward Nicholas, 233, 234
Boylston arms and crest, 233
Brabazon, Chambre, fifth earl of Meath, 72
Brabazon, Edward, fourth earl of Meath, 72
Bradbury, Frederick, 62
Brand Inglis, Ltd., 230, 262, 299, 327
braziers, 21, 147
Breach crest, 324
Brettingham, Matthew, 213
Bridge, John, 264, 276
Briggs, Anna R., 120
Brigham, Abigail, 56, 58
Brigham, Willard, 56, 58
Brighton Pavilion, 268

Brind, Henry, **169–70**
Brittania mark, 13
Brodick Castle, 104
Brodrick, Alan, 333
Brodrick, St. John, 333
Brodrick, Thomas, 333
Brodrick crest, 332
Brooklyn Museum, 11
Brooks, Sydney, 228
Brooks Reed Gallery, Inc., 50
Brown cresr, 308
Browne, Mary, 138
Browne, Thomas, 138
Brownlow, earl (John Cust), 122
Brownlow, Sir John (third baronet), 70
Brownlow, Richard, 70
Brunswick-Wolfenbüttel, duke of (August
        Wilhelm), 75
Brykes crest, 334
BS maker's mark, 280
Buggine crest, 324
Buhler, Kathryn C.(Mrs. Yves Henry), 62, 88
Bulfinch, Charles, 204
Burghley epergne, 184
Burgoigne crest, 324
Burnet, Elspeth, 330
Buteux, Abraham, 155
Buteux, Elizabeth, 142
Butler, James, second duke of Ormonde, 337
Butts crest, 311, 314

C
Cabbell arms, crest, and motto, 221
Cafe, John, **172–73**, 195, 196
Calderwood, Robert, **346**
Callard, Isaac, **313**
Campbell, John, 138
candlesticks, 50–51, 64, 104–105, 145–46, 172–73,
        207–209, 218–19, 276–77
    snuffers and, 65–66
canisters. *See* tea canisters
cann, 120–21
Carbery, Lady Mary, 332
Carlton House, 276
Carlyon, T. R. G., 82
Carlyon, Thomas, 82
Carr, John, 201
Carter, John, 208
Cartwright, Hannah Beasley, 228
Cary, Samuel, 172
caskets, 39, 230–31, 270–73
casters, 20, 54–56, 56–57, 96–97, 112, 327–28
Castle Freke, 332
Catherine the Great, Empress of Russia, 152

Caton, Margaret, 180
Caton, Susanna, 180
CC maker's mark, 249
CD maker's mark, 331
Cellini, Benvenuto, 284
Chaffers, William, 364
chafing dishes, 58–59, 148–49, 168–69
chamberlain's key, 282
Chambers, Sir William, 219
Charles, Archduke of Austria, 150
Charles, fifth duke of Bolton, 188, 190
Chauncy, Elihu, 192
Chawner, Henry, **241**, **244**
Chawner, Thomas, **316**
Chawner, William, I, 228
Chelsea porcelain, 364
Chester, 324, 326
Chesterman, Charles, III, **249**
Chester silver, 317, 324, 326
CH maker's mark, 352
Chomondeley, Francis, 176
Christie's, 70, 87, 107, 112, 119, 122, 128, 138, 150,
        160, 174, 188, 198, 207, 212, 216, 223, 246,
        269, 270, 278, 283, 287, 303, 335, 347, 362
cistern and fountain, 22–23, 72–75
CK maker's mark, 130
claret jugs, 43, 287–88, 294–95, 299–300
Clark, Abigail W., 207
Clarke, Mary Anne, 278
Clayton, David, **93**, **94**, **95**
Clayton, David, II, 93
Clayton, Sir Harold, 361
Clayton, Sir Harold Dudley, 361
Clayton, Sir William of Marden, 361
Clee, Robert, 215
Clymer, George, Dr., 165, 249
Clymer, George, Mrs., 165, 250
Cocks, Margaret, 113
Coddington, Sir William, 335
Codman, Henry, 228
Codman, John Amory, 89
Codman, Martha Catherine, 89, 228, 252
Codrington, Christopher, 335, 336
Codrington, Sir Gerald, 335
Codrington, Sir William, 335, 336
coffeepots, 66, 82, 116, 137, 144, 170–71, 177–79,
        204–205, 205, 358
    with tea service, 257–59
    toy, 94
Coffin, Martha, 260–61
Collier, Joseph, **116**
Collins, Hon. Mrs., 347
CO maker's mark, 50, 84, 89, 120
Combemale, Pamela J., 107

communion cup and paten/cover, 80–81
condiment vases, 34, 212–15
Conolly, William, 128
Cooke, Richard, **257–59**, **260**
Cooke arms and crest, 124
Coolidge, Helen S., 221
Coolidge, John Gardner, Collection, 221
Coolidge, John Gardner, Mrs., 351
Copley, John Singleton, 229, 234
Coppinger, Marian, 224
Cork Goldsmiths' Company, 344
corkscrew, 256
Cork silver, 344–45, 354, 355, 357–58
Cornock, Edward, **84**, **89**, **117**
Cory, John, **50**
Cotting, Charles E., Mrs., 255
Cour, William de la, 167
Courtauld, Augustine, 107, **120**
Courtauld, Louisa, 34, 35, **212–15**, **216–17**
Courtauld, Samuel, 178, 204, 216–17
Cowles, George, 35
Cowles, George, 34, **212–15**, **216–17**
Cowmeadow crest, 308
Craig, John, 141
Craigie, Andrew, 254, 263
Craigie, Elizabeth, 253, 254
Craigie-Longfellow House, 254
Cramer, John, 262
Craven, William, 66
cream boats, 356
cream jugs, 155, 194, 237, 252, 260–61, 269, 364
    sugar bowl and, 359
    with tea service, 257–59, 289–90
cream pail, 221
Creed, Sarah, 214
Crespell, James, 207, 208
Crespell, Sebastian I, 207, 208
Crespin, Paul, 27, 107, 125, 128, **133–35**, **148**, **148–49**, 153, 162, 188, 269
Cressey, D. Wilmarth, Mrs., 207
Crewe, Anne, 54
Crewe, John, 54
Crichton, Lionel Alfred, **326**
Crichton Brothers, 66, 87, 96, 104, 106, 108, 109, 111, 122, 126, 148, 306, 315, 358, 360
Cripps, William, **168–69**, 177, 195, 204
Crooke, John, 180
Crooke, Philip Schuyler, 180
Crossley, Richard, **320**
cruet stand, 157–58, 164–65, 191
Cruickshank, Robert, **330**
Crystal Palace, 288
CT over IW, 357
cups, 327

communion, and paten/cover, 80–81
marriage, 223
Richmond Race, 198–201
spout, 78
standing, 77
thistle, 327
tontine, 11, 62–63
two-handled, 50, 78–79, 88, 332–33
    with cover, 10–11, 24, 27, 45, 98–100, 100–102, 128–29, 133–35, 174–76
    toy, 53
    wager, 223
Currah (race course), 347
Curzon, Asheton, 182
Curzon, Nathaniel, 182, 212, 216
Cust, John (first earl of Brownlow), 122
Cutler, Mary, 158, 170
Cuzner, Bernard, 44, **303–304**
CW maker's mark, 206, 210, 227
Cycle Club, 176

D

Dainty Davy (horse), 201
Daniell, Thomas, **220**, **233–35**
d'Arcy Hutton, J. T., Esq., 198
d'Arcy Sykes, Hilda, 198
date letters, 13
Davis, Isaac P., 229
Dawson, Charles, 201
DC maker's mark, 93, 94, 95
decanter, 302
decorative arts, 12–13
Dee, Louis, **293–94**
della Bella, Stefano, 216
Delmestre, John, **191**
Derby, Anstiss, 89
Derby, Elias Hasket, 257–59, 260, 261
Derby, Elizabeth, 252, 257–59, 260
Derby, Martha Coffin, 261
Derby, Richard, 261
Devil and St. Dunstan, 308
DeYoung, S. Sydney, 136, 141
DG maker's mark, 115, 333
DH maker's mark, 197
Dickson, Charles, **331**
dimensions, 49
dish covers, 350–51
dish cross, 207
dishes, 47, 96, 112–14, 159, 297
    alms, 331
    chafing, 58–59, 148–49, 168–69
    dinner plates, 182–83
    entree, 270
    game, 42

meat, 180
   second-course, 228
   sideboard, 337–39
dish ring and cover, 350–51
Dixon arms, 228
D maker's mark, 54
Douglas, William, 348
dredgers, 79, 112, 120
Dresser, Christopher, 294
DR maker's mark, 287
Drowne, Helen Louisa, 180
Drowne, Mary Helen, 180
DS over RS, 198
Dublin Castle, 350
Dublin Goldsmiths' Company, 333
Dublin Goldsmiths' Hall, 333
Dublin silver, 332–33, 334, 335–37, 337–39, 340, 341,
   342, 343–44, 345, 346, 347–49, 350–51,
   351–52, 353, 354–55, 356
Dulcie, earl of, 223
Dundas, Anne, 198
Dundas, Sir Lawrence, 198, 201
Dundas, Sir Thomas, 198
Dunham Massey, 196
Dupee, Jeannie W., 261
Duplessis Beylard, Edouard, Dr., 204
Dutton, Henry, 196
DW maker's mark, 124
Dyck, Anthony van, 282

E

Eaglesfield, Tindall, 240
EA maker's mark, 78
East , John, **78**
East, Mary, 361
East, Sir William, 361
EA with I above and S below, 186
EC maker's mark, 117
E&CoLd maker's mark, 299
ecuelle, 119
Edgcumbe, George, 98
Edgcumbe, Mathilde, 98
Edgcumbe, Richard, baron, 98
Edinburgh silver, 327–29, 331
Edwards, Richard, 252
EF maker's mark, 144, 278
EG maker's mark, 155
EH maker's mark, 294, 311
Eley, William, **267–68**
Elkington, Frederick, **289–90, 291**
Elkington & Co., 43, 290, **291**, 295–96, **299–300**
Ellis, Thomas, **318**
Elston, Philip, **311**
Elton, Margaret Allen, 235

Emerson, Lucy B., 286
Emes, John, 250–52
Enraged Musician, The (Hogarth), 225
Ensko, Robert, 78, 81
EP assay master mark, 331
epergne, 12, 31, 183–85, 188–90, 286–87
Erand, Oscar Pierre, 300
Ernst August IV, 72
Evelyn, John, 309
ewers, 46, 221–22, 335–37
   shaving basin and, 328–29
Exeter silver, 306, 311, 321, 360
Eyre crest, 324

F

Falino, Jeannine, 10
FA maker's mark, 80, 306
Faneuil, Andrew, 158
Faneuil, Benjamin, 121, 157, 158, 170, 171
Faneuil, Peter, 121, 158, 170
Faneuil arms and crest, 170
Faneuil Hall, 158
Farington, Joseph, 264
Farrell, Edward, 41, **278–80**, 284
Farren, Thomas, 25, **116, 119, 120–21, 122–23**
Fawdery, John, **80–81, 306**
Feline, Edward, **107**, 134, **144**
Feline, Magdalen, **180**
Fellows crest, 119
FE maker's mark, 289
Fe maker's mark, 107
Fenwick, George, 104
Ffarington, William, Esq., 274
Figg, John, **283**
Firestone & Parson, Inc., 83, 120, 183, 207, 280,
   293, 347
Fishman, Paul L., 192
fish server, 352
Fithie (Fythie) arms, 146
Fitzroy, Charles, 148, 149
Fitzwilliam, earl, 160, 269
FK maker's mark, 223
flask, 293–94
flatware. *See also* forks; knives; ladles; spoons
Flaxman, John, 264, 274, 276, 284
Fleming, William, **79, 88, 109, 112**
Flitcroft, Henry, 113, 133, 134, 162
FL maker's mark, 79, 88, 110, 112
Floris, Cornelius, 279
Folkestone, Viscount, 184
Folkingham, Thomas, **76, 104–105**
FO maker's mark, 76, 104
Fontaine, 225
Fonthill Abbey, 271

Fonthill Splendens, 272
Fordham, William, **124**
forgeries
    coffeepot, 358
    cream jug, 364
    pair of salts, 361
    seal-top spoon, 363
    sugar bowl and cream jug, 359
forks, 310
    with knives, 312
    with knives and spoons, 307
Foster, Sir Balthazar Walter, 304
Foster, Sally, 205
Foster, William, 204
Fothergill, John, 218–19, 221–22
fountain, cistern and, 72–75
Fox, John, 22, 256
Foye, John, 56, 57
Franchi, Chevalier Gregorio, 270–73
Francis, Victor George Henry, 152, 159
Franks, David, 193
Frederica, Princess of Prussia, 278
Frederick, Prince of Wales, 281
Frederick Augustus, duke of York, 278
freedom boxes, 343–44, 357–58
Freke, Sir John Redmond, 333
Freke, Mary, 333
Frenband crest, 308
French, Hollis, 207, 319
FS over s maker's mark, 55
Furnese, Sir Henry, 98, 130
Furnese, Mathilde, 98

G

Galliyn, John, 102
GA maker's mark, 56, 85
Gamble, William, **56–57**
game dish, 42, 283–85
Gamon, John, **144–45**
Garden, Phillips, **140**, **177–79**
Gardiner, Abigail, 236
Gardiner, Silvester, 236
Garnier, Daniel, 333
Garrard and Co., Ltd., 115, 264, 358
Garrard Ledgers, 14, 215
Garthorne, Frances, 77
Garthorne, Francis, **85–86**
Gaskin, Arthur, 304
Gaskin, Georgie, 304
Gay, John, 225
GB maker's mark, 316
Gebelein Silversmiths, 238
Gentot, Blaise, 55, 90
George I, 98, 109, 122, 333, 344

George II, 72, 98
George III, 278, 352
George IV, 279
George V, 304
GH with W above and C below maker's mark, 228
Gibbon, Mary, 224
Gibbons, John, **308**
Gibbs, 113
Gignac, Benjamin, **205**
Gilda Aurifabrorum (Chaffers), 364
Gillois, Pierre, **206**
Gillray, James, 225
Gilpin, Thomas, 177
Glanville, Philippa, 142
Glynn, Gale, 62
"goat and bee" jub, 364
goblet, 249
Godfrey, Benjamin, 28, 134, **141–43**, 155, 174
Godfrey, Eliza, 142, **155**, 166
Godfrey, William E., 104, 331, 344
GofHLtd maker's mark, 300, 302
goldsmiths. *See also* silver
    specialization of, 14
    trade, 13
    use of term, 12
Goldsmiths and Silversmiths Company, 332
Goldsmith's Company. *See* Worshipful Company of
        Goldsmiths
Goode, Thomas, & Co., 299
Gordon, Alexander, 180
Gordon, Margaret, 180
Gore, Sir Ralph, 347–48
Gorges, Henry, 338
Gould, James, 66, 173
Gould, William, 66
G&PW maker's mark, 356
Grace, Gerard, 333
Graham, James, 126
Grant crest and motto, 307
Gray's Inn, 305
Greaves, Margaret, 172
Greaves, Samuel, II, 172
Greaves, Samuel Cary, III, 172
Green, Anna, 140
Green, David, 66, **115**
Green, Joshua, 140
Green, Richard, 359
Green, Samuel Abbott, 140
Green, William H., 112
Greene, Harding, Mrs., 83
Greene, Stephen C., Mr. and Mrs., 207
Grenville, Richard, 58
Grey, Thomas de, of Merton, 248
Grey, Thomas de, second baron of Walsingham, 248

Gribelin, Simon, 97
Grosvenor, Richard, 176
Grosvenor, Robert, 176
Grove, Sir Thomas-Fraser, 86, 87
Grundy, William, **168**, **180–81**, **203**, **204–205**
GR with two pellets above maker's mark, 307
GS maker's mark, 108, 118, 137, 202, 320
GS over WF maker's mark, 323, 324
Guild of Handicraft Ltd., 203, 300
Gurney, Richard, & Co., **147**
G with an R maker's mark, 359
G with W inside maker's mark, 100
GW maker's mark, 145, 356

H
Hacket, Robert, 343
Hackwood Park, 190
HA in a rectangle maker's mark, 326
HA incuse, 343
Haines, Christopher, 352
Haines, Christopher, II, **352**
Hale, Mary Emlen, 286
Hall, Edward, **311**
Hall, Irving K., 207
Hall, Martin, & Co., 287–88
Hall crest, 311, 314
hallmarks, 13–14, 15, 49
    forgeries and, 363, 364
Hallowell, Benjamin, 235
HA maker's mark, 62, 310
Hamilton, Alexander, 234
Hamilton, Alexander, tenth duke of, 104
Hamilton, ninth duke of, 104
Hamilton, Thomas, sixth earl of Haddington, 329
Hamilton, Sir William, 214
Hamilton arms and motto, 104, 328
Hancock, Dorothy, 102, 192
Hancock, John, 100, 101, 187, 192
Hancock, Lydia Henchman, 100, 101, 192
Hancock, Thomas, 100, 101, 102, 192–93
Hancock Cup, 10–11, 100–102
Hanet, Paul, **310**
Hanmer, Ester, 182
Hanmer, William, 182
Hanover, 72
Harache, Peter, 56, **62**
Harding, Newell, 158
Hardwicke, baron (Phillip Yorke), 142
Harley, Edward, 113, 141, 142
Harmar, James, **319**
Harris, John, 39
Harris, John, VI, **270–73**
Harris, Leslie, 213
Harris, Nicholas, 297–98

Hart, Solomon Alexander, R.A., 267
Hartman, Alan and Simone, Collection, 122, 156, 166
Hatfield, Charles, 134
Hawkins, Elizabeth, 82
Hawkins, Jane Bethune, 170
Hawkins, John P., General, 170
Hawkins, Philip, 82
Hazlitt, William, 271
HB maker's mark, 169, 230, 232, 237, 238, 240, 242, 320, 321, 322
HC maker's mark, 241, 244
Heming, George, **228**
Heming, Thomas, 152, 166–67, 213, 216
Henchman, Daniel, 102
Henchman, Elizabeth, 102
Henchman, Lydia, 100, 101, 192
Henley, Sir Robert, 136
Hennell, David, I, **197**
Hennell, Robert, **197**
Hennell, Robert, II, **270**
Henning, viscount, 233
Henshaw, Samuel, Rev., 256
Herbert, Samuel, & Co., **317**
Hervey, John, 98
Hesilrige, Sir Thomas, 50
HE with an A above and a P below, 310
hexafoil salver, 115
Hicks arms, 144
Hill, Abigail Brigham, 56, 58
Hill, Harriet A., 56, 58
Hill, Joseph, 58
Hilliard, John, **297**, **301**
Hipkiss, Edwin J., Mrs., 249
Historical Design Collection, Inc., 302, 303
Hobson crest, 61
Hogarth, William, 225
Holmes, Edward Jackson, 168
Holmes, Edward Jackson, Mrs., 168
Holmes, Oliver Wendell, Dr., 168
Homer, William, **351–52**
Hooker arms, 109
Hooper, Bayard, 244
Hooper, Robert C.., 244
Hooper, Roger F., 244
Hooper, Roger F., Mrs., 244
Hope, Lucy, 138
Hopetoun House, 284
Horn (Horne) arms, 110
horse racing, 198–201, 347–49
hot water jugs, 237–38, 252–53. *See also* water jug and stand, 205–206
hot water urns, 210–211, 242–43, 253–54, 255
Houghman, Solomon, **253–54**

Howard, Charles, 223, 224
Howard, Henry Charles, 130, 132
Howard crest, 262
HO with fleur-de-lys above and below in a shaped shield, 307
HP maker's mark, 315
H&T maker's mark, 297, 301
Hude, Margaret, 180
Hukin and Heath, 294–95, 299
Hunt, John Samuel, 42, **283–85**, **286–87**
Hunt, Mary, 124
Hunt, Thomas, 124, 125
Hunt and Roskell, 284, 287
Huquier, 167
Hurd arms and crest, 270
Hutchinson, Thomas, 101
Hutton, Edward, **294–95**
Hutton, John, 198, 201
Hutton, William, & Sons, 294
Hutton Trustees, 198

I

IA maker's mark, 267
IB maker's mark, 174, 248
IC maker's mark, 172, 313
ID maker's mark, 191
IF maker's mark, 218, 283
IG maker's mark, 121, 144, 308
IH maker's mark, 270, 319
II maker's mark, 307
IK maker's mark, 203, 228
IM maker's mark, 345
Incorporation of Goldsmith's, 329
inkstand, 186, 250
IN maker's mark, 354
IO maker's mark, 103
IP maker's mark, 146, 228, 230
IP over EW, 188
Irby, Augusta Georgina Elizabeth, 248
Irby, William, 248
Ireland
    flatware, 354, 355
    horse racing in, 347–49
Irish gold, 342, 343–44
Irish Lass (horse), 348
IR maker's mark, 109, 239, 250, 253
Irminger, Johann Jacob, 130
Irving, Henry, 296
ISH maker's mark, 283, 286
IS maker's mark, 127, 128, 130, 235, 237, 246, 250
IT maker's mark, 307, 314
Ivers, Hannah Trecothick, 85
Ivers, James, 65

IW maker's mark, 364
IWS maker's mark, 263
IZ maker's mark, 331

J

Jackson, Sir Charles James, 83
Jackson, Dorothy Quincy, 168
Jackson, Edward, 168
Jackson, John, **70–71**
Jackson, Mary, 168
Ja maker's mark, 70
Jamnitzer, Christoph, 284
Janssen, Abraham, 136
Janssen, Catherine, 141
Janssen, Henry, 136
Janssen, Robert, 136
Janssen, Stephen, 141
Janssen, Stephen Theodore, 136
Janssen, Sir Theodore, 136, 141
Janssen, Williamsa, 136
JC maker's mark, 116
Jefferson, Thomas, 234
Jewel House, 100, 122, 337
Jewell, M. H., Miss, 207, 313, 357
Jewel Office, 70
JL maker's mark, 353
John Alexander, sixth earl of Hopetoun, 284
Johnson, Ben, 309
Johnson, Glover, 120
Johnson, Walker & Tolhurst, 297–98
Jones, B.M., Mrs., 313
Jones, E. Alfred, 10
Jones, George Greenhill, **103**
Jones, Owens, 174
Jones, Robert, I, **324**
JS maker's mark, 319, 354
jugs, 227, 291. *See also* cream jugs
    claret, 43, 284–95, 287–88, 299–300
    covered, 353
    hot water, 205–206, 237–38, 252–53
    with teapot service, 250–51
    traveling, with two beakers, 262–63
    water, 360
JW maker's mark, 334

K

Kandler, Charles, 15, 26, **130–32**, 174
Kandler, Charles Frederick, 36, 130, **223–26**, 226
Kandler, Johann Joachim, 130
Karolik, M. and M., Collection of Eighteenth-Century American Arts, 164, 228, 252, 323
Karolik, Martha Codman, 259, 323
Karolik, Maxim, 89, 164, 205, 251, 252, 319, 353

Karolik, Maxim, Mrs., 164
Katz, Jessie and Sigmund, collection, 152, 159, 160, 166, 269, 292, 362, 364
Katz, Sigmund J., Mrs., 150, 152, 159, 160, 166, 269, 292, 362, 364
Kaye, Simon, Ltd., 246
Keatt, William, **52**
Kedleston Hall, 182, 213, 216
KE maker's mark, 52
Kendall, James, 203
Kendall, Titus, 270
Kent, William, 75, 134
Ker, James, 329
Ker, Thomas, **328–29**
kettles, 85–86, 86–87, 108, 118, 142, 169–70, 341
    toy, 94, 121
key, chamberlain's, 282
Kilmore crest, 312
King, David, 341
King, John, **228–29**
kitchen peppers, 120
Klejman, J. J., 177
knives, 312
    with forks, 312
    with forks and spoons, 307–308
Koopman, E & CT Koopman & Sons, 198

L
LAC maker's mark, 326
ladles, 160–63, 306, 313, 316, 320, 331, 354
    punch, 313, 314
    soup, 318, 354
    tureen, 354
Lajoüe, Jacques de, 142, 144
LA maker's mark, 57, 106, 112, 308
Lamb, Aimee, 242, 245, 253, 355
Lamb, Horatio A., Mrs., 117, 242, 253
Lamb, Rosamond, 242, 253, 355
Lamerie, Paul de, 15, **106**, **112–14**, 116, **126**, **136**, 138, **141**, 148, 174, 177, 196, 274, **308**, **361**, 398
Lamerie group, 174
Landau, Nicolas E., 282
Lander, Louisa, 259
Lane, Gardiner M., Mrs., 355
Lardner, Lynford, 158
Laughton, John, **II**, **57–58**
Law, Thomas, **325**
Lawrence, Abbott, 287
Lawrence, Abott, Mrs., 253
Lawrence, Eliza, 140
Lawrence, Sir Thomas, 229
LC over GC, 212, 216

LD maker's mark, 293
Leach, John, **68**
Lee, Ronald A., 267
LE maker's mark, 68
Lennox, Lady Louisa, 128
leopard's head crowned mark, 13
Le Roy, Henri, 55
Le Sage, John Hugh, **128–29**, 138, 188
Lewes crest, 309
Lewis, A. G., 152, 159
Lewis, Kensington, 278, 279
Liger, Isaac, **96–97**
LI maker's mark, 96
lion passsant mark, 13
lion's head erased mark, 13
Livingston, Cornelia Beckman, 180, 181
Livingston, Robert Gilbert, 180, 181
Livingston, Robert R., 181
Livingston arms, crest, and motto, 180
Lloyd, John, **353**
L maker's mark, 305
Lock, Nathaniel, **67**
LO maker's mark, 67
Lomax, James, 165
Loring, Charlotte, 286
Louis Charles, comte de Beaujolais, 262
Louis Charles d'Orléans, duc de Nemours, 263
Louis Philippe, duc d'Orleans (King of France), 262–63
Louis Philippe Joseph, king of France, 262
Lovell, James, 330
Lovell, Mary, 330
Lowell, John, 286–87
Lowell, John, II, 330
Lowell, John, Jr., 287
Lowell, John, Mrs., 330
Lowell, John Amory, 286–87
Lowell, Ralph, 287
Lowell, Ralph, Mrs., 286
Lowell, Susan Cabot, 286
Lowell arms and crest, 286
Lowell Institute, 287
Lucas crest, 84
Lumley, Thomas, Ltd., 124, 138, 141, 152, 174, 207, 221, 246, 294, 343
Lyman, Charles P., 227
Lyman, Henry, 227
Lyman, Henry, Mrs., 147, 207, 227, 270
Lyman, Theodore, Mrs., 147
Lynde, Sarah, 56, 57
Lynde, Simon, 56, 57
Lyttleton, Sir George, 186

M

Macclerfield, earl of (Thomas Parker), 74
Mackintosh, Robert J., 276
maker's marks, 13–14, 15, 49
    identification of, 49
MA maker's mark, 81
Manjoy, George, **81**
Margas, Jacob, 100
Margas, Samuel, 24, **98–100**
Marie Amélie, 262
Marie Antoinette, 262
Marks, Gilbert Leigh, 297–98
Marot, Daniel, 58, 68, 70, 98
marriage bowl, 214
marriage cup, 223
marrow spoons, 308, 325
Massey, Dunham, 125, 138
Mathews, Hannah, 274
Mathews, John, 274
Mathews (Matthews) arms, 110
May, Frederick Goddard, 100
May, Frederick Warren Goddard, 102
May, Joseph, 100
May, Samuel, 100
May, Samuel Joseph, 100
MB maker's mark, 218, 221
McMullan, Joseph V., Mrs., 210
Meach, Richard, **210**
meat dish, 180
Medici Krater, 264
meerschaum pipe, 266–67
Meidias Hydria (water jar), 214
Melun, Micon, **360**
Melun, René, 360
ME maker's mark, 360
Menshikov, Prince, 152
Meriton, Samuel, **I, 313**
ME with a crown above in an octagon, 360
MF maker's mark, 180
Middlecott, Sarah, 57
Middleton, Alexander, Jr., 330
Middleton, Alexander, Sr., 330
Middleton, Mary, 330
Middleton, Robert, 330
Miller, Sanderson, 186
Millikin, Justine V. R., 244
miniatures. *See* toys
Minneapolis Institute of Arts, 56
Minors, Thomas, 122
M maker's mark, 194
Mondon, François-Thomas, 167
Montagu, Samuel (lord Swathling), 112
monteiths, 68–69, 180–81

Montfichett arms, 110
Montford, lord, 96
Montpensier, Antoine, duc de, 262
Moore, John, **345**
Moore, Thomas II, **187**
Moore crest, 133
Morel-Ladeuil, Leonard, **295–96**
Morris, Gouvernor, 181
Morris, William, 300
Morse, Janet, 350
Morshead crest, 127
Morteyn arms, 210
Mortimer, John, 274
Morton, Richard, & Co., **218**
Moseley, David, 140
Moseley, Mary, 140
mote spoons, 305, 318, 321
MR maker's mark, 108
mugs, 67, 144–45
    cann, 120–21
    toy, 95
Munroe, Abigail, 56, 57
Munroe, David, 56, 57
Murray, James, 130
Museum of Fine Arts, 11, 12
mustard pots, 245, 283
Muston, Henry, 360
Myers, Myer, 181

N

NA maker's mark, 359
Nanny, 36, 223–26
Nash, Bowles, 107, 134, 359
Nash, John, 268
Nealewell arms, 168, 232
nécessaire de voyage, 262
Nelme, Anthony, **58–59**, **65–66**, 74, 82, 111
Nelme, Francis, **III**
Ne maker's mark, 58
Nesbitt arms, 340
Netherton, Samuel, 183, 188
New Aberdeen (AB) town mark, 330
Newcombe, Rev. William, 351
Newcome, Rev. William, 352
Newenham, William, **344–45**
Newhall, Scott, 283
Nicholson, John, **354**
Nilson, J. E., 195
Noisy Devil, 309
Norreys arms and crest, 150
Norris, John, 150, 152
Norris, Thomas, 150, 152
NS maker's mark, 150, 152, 156, 159, 160, 362

O

Offley, John, 54
O'Grady, Katherine-Grace, 86
Old Devil Tavern, 309
Oman, Charles, 163
Oranienbaum service, 152
Orchard House, 11
Orléans-Penthièvre service, 136
Ormonde, second duke of (James Butler), 337
Osborne crest, 111
Othello (horse), 348
Otis, Harrison Gray, 204–205
Otis, Sophia, 204

P

Pacot, Eli, 336
Paddereen Mare (horse), 349
Paige, Jas. W., 363
Paine, James, 213
Paine, Richard C., 332
PA maker's mark, 66, 138, 182
Panter, G. W., Esq., 332
Pantin, Simon, 66, 134
pap boat, 117
Pargeter, Richard, **140**
Park, Franklin A., Mrs., 301
Parke-Bernet Galleries, Inc., 210, 335, 337, 362
Parker, John, 31, **188–90**
Parker, Thomas, earl of Macclerfield, 74
Parker and Wakelin, 188, 194–95, 209
Partridge Fine Arts, 166, 283
paten, 331
Patterson arms, 220
Payne, Humphrey, 82
Payne, John H. and Ernestine A., Fund, 283, 287
Payne, Thomas, 142
PB/AB/WB maker's mark, 260
PB over AB, 245, 249, 252, 255
PC maker's mark, 133, 148
Peabody, Amelia, 207, 297
Peabody, James, 133
Peabody, James, Mrs., 133
Pearce, Edmund, **96**, 358, **358**
Pearse, William, **238**
Pearson, William, **77**
PE maker's mark, 85, 96, 104, 311, 358
Penbeton, Samuel, **245**
Penman, James, 327, **327**, 328, 331
Penn, Richard, 158
Penstone, Henry, 85
Pepys, Samuel, 309
Percy, Hugh, 201
Pero, John, **104**
Perry, James, **228**, **230–31**

Pert arms, 116
Peter III (Prince Peter Fedorovich), 152
Peterson, Abraham, **252**
Peter the Great, 152
Peyrotte, Alexis, 167
PG maker's mark, 140, 177
PG with an I above, 206
Philippe, Louis, 293
Phillips, Gillam, 171
Phillips, James, 208
Phillips, Sir John, 207
Phillips, Mary, 208
Phillips, Sir Richard, 207, 208
Phillips, S. J., Ltd., 86, 122, 223, 276
Phipps, Thomas, **240**, **262**
Pickard, Mark, 330
Pickard, Mary Lovell, 330
Pickman, Anstiss Derby, 89
Pickman, Benjamin, 89
Pickman, Benjamin, II, 89
Pierrepont, Natalie Elizabeth Chauncy, 192
Pigot crest, 334
PI maker's mark, 77
Pitt, George, 146
Pitt, William, 186
Pitt, William, earl of Chatham, 357
Pitt, William (Pitt the Younger), 357
Pittar, John, 355
Pitt Clubs, 357
Pitts, Thomas, 32, **194–96**
plaque, 295–96
Platel, Pierre, 74, 338
plate rack, toy, 95
plates. *See also* dishes
    dinner, 182–83
Playfair, Lady Edith, 327
PL maker's mark, 126, 136, 141, 361
Plummer, William, **192–93**, 235, **238**
Plumpton, Henry, **315**
P maker's mark, 327
Pocock, Edward, **310**
Polhill, Charles, 137
Pollock, John, **146**
Pomerede, Daniel, 349
Poor, Mary Adelaide Sargent, 237, 323
porcelain
    Chelsea, 364
porringer, 85
    toy, 54
Portman, Henry William, 194, 196
potato rings, 350
Powell, James, and Sons of Whitefriars, 302
Power arms, 210
Pratt, James, 268

Preist, William, **170–71**
provenance, 49
PS maker's mark, 264, 276
PT maker's mark, 166
pudding server, 352
punch bowl, 347–49
punch ladles, 313, 314
punch strainer, 182
PY maker's mark, 61
Pyne, Benjamin, **61**, 336

Q
Queen Anne style, 359

R
rattle, baby's, with whistle, 297, 301
RC in a rectangle maker's mark, 330
RC maker's mark, 257, 260, 346
Read, John, 256
Reden, Oberhofmarschall von, 75
Registry Office symbols, 290
Reid, Christian Ker, 288
Reid, David, **287–88**
Reid & Sons, 287–88
Reily, Charles, 288
Reily and Storer, 288
Remnant, Frederick William, 287
Revere, Paul, II, 236
RG maker's mark, 147
RH maker's mark, 270
Ribouleau, Isaac, **110**
Rich, Elizabeth, 186
Rich, Sir Robert, 186
Richardson, Richard, II or III, **317**
Richardson, Thomas O., Mrs., 218
Richardsons of Tutbury, 299
Richmond Race Cup, 33, 198–201, 208
RI maker's mark, 282, 324
ring stands, 350–51
Ritchie, Andrew, 204
Ritchie, Andrew Montgomery, 178
Ritchie, Elizabeth, 204
Ritchie, Janet, 178
RM&Co maker's mark, 218
RM maker's mark, 210
Robertson, Johnston Forbes, 296
Robins, John, **239**, **250**, 272
Robinson, Edward, **240**, **262**
Robinson, Elizabeth, 228
Robinson, Frederick S., 297
Robinson & Skinner & Co., 299
Rockingham, earls of, 130
Rockingham, marquess of, 198
Rockley arms, 93
Roe, Ebenezer, 83

Roettiers, Jacques, 181
Rogers, Catherine Langdon, 245
Rogers, Clara Bates, 245
Rogers, John W., 89
Rogers, Martha Pickman, 89
Rollos, Phillip, 56
RO maker's mark, 53, 83
Romer, John, 363
Rood, Mary, **108–109**
Roode, Alexander, **53**
rose bowl, 44, 303–304
Roubiliac, Louis-François, 138
Round, Benjamin John, 300
Rovensky, Mae C., 362
Rowe, O. M. E., Miss, 324
Royal Brierley Crystal, 299
RP maker's mark, 140
RR maker's mark, 317
Rundell, Phillip, 264, 276
Rundell, Bridge, & Rundell, 70, 122, 264, 276, 280
Rundell & Bridge, 246, 274
Ruskin, John, 300
Rysbrack, John Michael, 138

S
Sackville, Edward, 282
Salisbury, Nancy, 192
Salisbury, Samuel, 192
Saltonstall, Richard M., Mrs., 356
salts, 41, 53, 60, 108–109, 127, 133, 197, 278–80,
    280–81, 361
salt spoons, 315
salvers, 25, 32, 40, 90–92, 109, 122–23, 136, 150–52,
    194–96, 274–75. *See also* waiters
    footed, 334, 344–45
    hexafoil, 115, 351–52
Sanders, Joseph, **165**
Sargent, Adelaide J., 237
Sargent, Daniel, 117
Sargent, Henry, 117
Sargent, Winthrop, Mrs., 117
Sassoon, Sir Albert, 295
sauceboats, 140, 146, 148, 160–63, 165, 168, 292,
    356
sauceboat stands, 160–63
saucepans, 103, 110, 248
    toy, 93
sauce spoons, 354–55
Savory, A. B., & Sons, 288
scent bottle case, 245
Schmidt, Nicholas, 284
Schnebbelie, Jacob, 159
Schruder, James, 15
scissors
    sugar, toy, 121

Scofield, John, 37, **235–36**, 237–38, **246–47**, **250–51**, **319**
sconces, 70–71
Scott, Captain, 192
Scott, Digby, 280
Scott, Dorothy Hancock, 100
Scott, Walter, 327–28
SC over IC, 207
Scudamore, Frances, 224
seal matrix, 230
seal-top spoon, 363
second-course dishes, 228
Sekford arms, 115
serving spoon, 316
Seward arms, crest, and motto, 350
Sharp, Robert, 33, 198, 201
shaving basin, ewer and, 328–29
Shaw, William, II, **170**
Shaw Hall, 274
Sheffield silver, 218, 288, 325
Shelley, Sir John, 137
Shelley, Tryphena, 137
Shields, John, 355
Shirley, William, 85, 178, 179
SH maker's mark, 253
Shreve, Crump, and Low, Co., 93, 94, 95, 121, 326
Shriving, Godfrey, 202
Shrubsole, S. J., 361
Shrubsole, S. J., Corp., 98, 345
Shrubsole, S. J., Ltd., 267
SH with an H above and a B below, 317
sideboard dish, 337–39
silver. *See also* goldsmiths
    assaying, 13
    as a decorative art, 12–13
    deposit technique, 300
    marks, 13–14, 15, 49
Silvio (horse), 121
Singleton, Richard, 256
skewers, 317, 321, 324
Skuball (horse), 348
Slaughter, Thomas, 174
Sleath, Gabriel, 76, 86
Sleath, Gabriel, **78**, **108**, **118**, **137**
Sl maker's mark, 78
Smiley, Thomas, 276
Smith, Benjamin, II, 280
Smith, Benjamin, III, **280–81**
Smith, Mrs. Charles Gaston, Group, 53
Smith, Daniel, 33, 198–201
Smith, George, III, **320**, **323**, **324**
Smith, James, I, **127**, **133**
Smith, John, I, **305**
Smith and Sharp, 231

SM maker's mark, 98, 305, 313
Smythin, Samuel, 100
snuffboxes, 228–29
snuffers, 57–58, 65–66, 172–73
snuffer trays, 65–66, 172–73
Soane, Sir John, 198
Soane Museum, 208
Somerset, Charles, 149
Somerset, Henrietta, 149
Sotheby's, 98, 198, 216, 262, 276, 287, 328, 332
Soulgere, Catherine, 141
Soulgere, Col., 141
soup ladles, 318, 354
Southey, Robert, 246
Spalding, Hobart Ames, 145
Spalding, Katherine Ames, 144–45
Spalding, Oakes Ames, 145
Spalding, Philip, 145
Spalding, Philip Leffingwell, 145
Spalding, Philip Leffingwell, Collection, 144, 145
spice casters, 112
Spink & Son, Ltd., 194, 270
SP maker's mark, 245
sponsor's marks, 13, 15, 49
Spooner, Charles, 173
Spooner, Hungerford, 172
spoons, 306. *See also* tablespoons; teaspoons
    apostle, 326
    basting, 324
    caddy, 230–31, 322, 326
    with covered bowl, 300–301
    gravy, 354–55
    large, 310
    marrow, 308, 325
    miniature, 317
    mote, 305, 318, 321
    salt, pair, 315
    seal-top, 363
    serving, 316
    set, with knives and forks, 307–308
    strainer, 354–55
    sugar sifter, 322, 323
spout cup, 78
Sprimont, Nicholas, 29, **150–52**, **152–54**, **156**, **159**, **160–63**, 188, 269, **362–63**, 364
St. John Morgan, Mary Helen, 181
St. John Morgan, Samuel, 180
St. Owen arms, 110
Stamper, John, 186
standing cup, 77
stands. *See also* kettles and stands
    cruet, 157–58, 164–65, 191
    with hot water jug, 205–206
    ring, 350–51

sauceboat, 160–63
  for teapots, 238–39, 242, 257–59
  tureen, 156, 246–47
Stanley, Sir John, 343
Staple Inn, 305
Stationers' Guild, 348
Steinkopff, Edward, 128
Stella, Jacques, 198, 216
Stephenson, William, **232**
Stevens and Williams, 299
Stevenson, Ambrose, **86–87**
ST maker's mark, 178
St maker's mark, 86
Storer, George, 288
Storr, Paul, 38, 40, **264–66**, 267, **274–75**, **276–77**, 281
Storr & Co., 287
Storr, Mortimer, and Hunt, 284
Story, Joseph William, **263**
Stothard, Thomas, 274
Stourbridge glasshouse, 299
Stoyt crest, 308
Stoyte, John, **354–55**
strainer spoons, 354–55
Stuart, Allison Ellsworth, 260
Stuart, Charles Stuart, 229
Stuart, Gilbert, 228
Stuart, James "Athenian," 213, 216
Stuart, Jane, 229
Stuart & Sons, 299
sugar basins
  with tea service, 257–59, 289–90
sugar baskets, 238, 240
sugar bowls, 52, 124, 260–61, 355, 356
  cream jug and, 359
sugar boxes, 152–54
  with tea canisters, 29, 30, 166–67, 178–79
sugar caster, 327–28
sugar nippers, 315
sugar scissors, toy, 121
sugar sifter spoons, 322, 323
sugar tongs, 308, 323, 325
Sumner, William, I, **320**
Sutton, Thomas, 341, 346
Swathling, lord (Samuel Montagu), 112
Sweet, Edward, **306**
Swift, Dean, 344
Swift, Jonathan, 309
SW maker's mark, 157, 164, 306, 323, 350
Sylvestre (Sylvester) arms, 95
Sy makers mark, 50
Symington, Ann, 302
Syng, Richard, **50–51**

T

tablespoons, 305, 309, 311, 314. *See also* spoons
  seal-top, 363
tankards, 76, 107, 187, 202, 203, 342
  toy, 81
Tany crest, 312
taperstick, 106
Tapp, W. H., 159
Tapp, W. M., 159
Tate & Co., 299
Tatum crest, 311
Taylor, Peter, **166–67**
Taylor, Samuel, 30, **178–79**, 204
Taylor, William O., 283
TB maker's mark, 82, 332, 335, 337
TC with a W above and a C below, 316
TD maker's mark, 220, 233
tea canisters, 76–77, 83, 104, 152–54, 206, 230–31, 232–33, 241
  with sugar box, 29, 30, 166–67, 178–79
  with tea service, 257–59
tea kettle, 85
teapots, 204, 233–35, 248–49, 250–51, 260–61, 267–68, 330, 340, 345
  with tea service, 257–59, 289–90
  toy, 94
teapot stands, 238–39, 242, 257–59
tea services, 257–59, 289–90
teaspoons, 319, 320. *See also* spoons
  with tea service, 257–59
Tees Bottle Company, 294
TE maker's mark, 318
Temple, Eleanor, 58
Temple, Sir Peter, 58
Terrey, John Edward, 268
Terry, Carden, 355, **357–58**
Terry, Ellen, 296
TF maker's mark, 116, 119, 120, 122
Theed, William, 264, 274, 281
thistle cup, 327
Thomason, John, **297**, **301**
Thompson, Charles Herbert, 299
Thompson arms, 342
Thomson, John, 328
Thomson, W. de Forest, Mr. and Mrs., 187
Thomson crest, 327
Tiffany & Co., 291, 299
Tighe, Richard, 343–44
Tighe arms, 343
TI maker's mark, 307
Timbrell, Robert, **82**
Tirrell (Tyrell) arms, 93
Titus, Lady Katherine, 62, 63
TK maker's mark, 328

T.LAW maker's mark, 325
TL maker's mark, 325
toast rack, 263
tobacco box, 84, 89
Todd, Ann, 330
toilet services, 61
Tolhurst, Brownfield, **297–98**
tongs, 319
Tonti, Lorenzo, 62
tontine cup, 11, 62–63
Tookey, James, **314**
Toppan, Benjamin, III, 89
Toppan, Bezaleel, 89
Toppan, Mary, 89
town marks, 13
Townsend, Elizabeth, 240, 249
Townsend, Rose, 240, 249
toys
    coffeepot, 94
    kettles, 94, 121
    mug, 95
    plate rack, 95
    porringer, 54
    saucepans, 93
    sugar scissors, 121
    tankard, 81
    teapot, 94
    two-handled cup, 53
TP maker's mark, 194
TP over ER, 240, 262
traveling jug
    with two beakers, 262–63
trays
    snuffer, 65–66, 172–73
    with tea service, 289–90
Treadwell, Grace W., 207
Trecothick, Barlow, 85
Trecothick, Hannah, 85
Trecothick, Mark, 85
Trecothick de Silva, Mark, 85
Trecothick de Silva, Mark, Mrs., 85
trencher salts, 53, 108–109, 127, 133. *See also* salts
TR maker's mark, 83
Trotter, Sir Coutts, 180
trowel, 352
Trumbell, Eleanor, 330
Trumbell, Walter Henry, 330
Truss, William, **83**
Trustees of the Museum of Fine Arts, 10
TS maker's mark, 341
Tuite, John, 134
tumblers, 126
tureen ladles, 354
tureens, 26, 37, 130–32, 246–47
tureen stands, 37, 156, 246–47

TW maker's mark, 242, 322
two-handled cups, 50, 78–79, 88, 332–33
    with covers, 10–11, 24, 27, 45, 98–100, 100–102,
        128–29, 133–35, 174–76
    toy, 53
Tyler, Charles Hitchcock, 202, 308, 314
Tysoe, John, 122

U

urns, 210–211, 235–36, 242–43, 253–54, 255

V

van Vianen, Adam, 293
van Vianen, Christian, 293
Vardy, John, 190
Vardy, Thomas, 190
vases, condiment, set of three, 213–15
Vathek (Beckford), 271
Vecht, Antoine, 295
Vernay, Arthur S., Inc., 137
Videau, Aymé, 138
Vincent, William, 246
Vincent arms, 96

W

Waff arms, 168, 232
wager cup, 223
Wainwright, Clive, 272
waiters, 111, 115, 116, 136, 141. *See also* salvers
Wakelin, Edward, 31, **183–85**, **188–90**, 292
Wakelin and Taylor, 197, 217
Walker, George, 330
Walker, Joseph, **334**, 346
Walker, Mathew, 346
Walker, Samuel, **350–51**
Walker, Udney William, 288
Walker, Walter, **297–98**
Wallis, Thomas, II, **322**
Walpole, Horace, 98, 113, 184, 190, 213
Walpole, Robert, 98
Walton, George L., Dr., 306
WA maker's mark, 340, 341
Warburton, Anne, 174, 175
Warburton, Jane, 138
Warburton, Thomas, 138, 174
Warburton arms, 174
Ware, Ann Bent, 330
Ware, Henry, Jr., 330
Ware, Horace E., 354
Wark estate, 337
Warren, Richard, 227
Warrington, earl of. *See* Booth, George, earl of
        Warrington
Washington, George, 158, 234, 254
Wass arms, 168, 232

waste bowl with tea service, 257–59
water jug, 360. *See also* hot water jugs
Waters, James, 364
Watson, Lewis, 130
Watson, Mary, 160
Watson, Thomas, 160, **242**
Watson-Wentworth, Thomas, 130, 132, 160
Waugh arms, 168, 232
Wavertree, Lord, 347
WC maker's mark, 168
Webb, Joseph, 299
Wedgwood, Josiah, 214
Wedgwood, Josiah, II, 276
Weisse, Faneuil D., 157
Weisse, Faneuil S., 157
Weisse, Henry Bethune, 157
Welch, Stuart C., Mrs., 207
Welch or Welsh crest, 324
Weld, Bernard C., Mrs., 207
WE maker's mark, 267
Wendy, Letticia, 62, 63
Wendy, Sir Thomas, 62
Wenham, Edward, 122
Wentworth, Lady Anne, 128
Wertheimer, Frieda, 362
West, Benjamin, 117
West, Elizabeth Derby, 252, 259, 260, 261
West, George, **356**
West, Mathew, 356
West, Nathaniel, 259, 260
Western crest, 308
WF maker's mark, 124
WG maker's mark, 168, 180, 204
Wheelwright, Nathaniel, 164, 165
Whipham, Thomas, 211
Whipple, Abigail, 235, 236, 237, 238
Whipple, Oliver, 235, 236, 238
whistles, baby's, with rattle, 297, 301
White, Fuller, 152
White, John, 92, 107, 128
Whitford, Samuel, II, 207
Whitney, Lydia Bowes, 187
Whitney, Phineas, 187
WH maker's mark, 351
Wickes, George, 14, 96, **100–102**, 132, 141, **145–46**,
        162, 174, 184, 188, 192
Wilbour, Charles Edwin, 11
Wilbour, Theodora, 11, 58, 68, 76, 79, 85, 90, 96, 308
Wilbraham, Edward-Bootle, 274
Wilbraham, Sybella Georgiana, 274
Wilkinson, Henry, 288
Wilkinson, Wynyard R. T., 287, 295
Willaume, David, I, 22, 23, 55, 56, **60**, **72–75**, **90–92**,
        92, 96, 128, 138, 162

Willaume, David, II, 107, **124–25**, 138
William IV, 282
Williams, Colonel Rowland, 81
Williams, Franklin H., 194
Williams, Franklin H., Mrs., 194
Williamson, William, II, **347–49**
Willmott, Samuel, 116
Willoughby, Katherine, 62
Willoughby, Letticia, 62
Willoughby, Sir Francis, 62, 63
Willson, Walter H., Ltd., 53, 64, 78, 79, 84, 96, 308
Wilson arms, 83
WI maker's mark, 60, 72, 76, 90, 96
Wimpole Hall, 142
wine coasters, 218
wine coolers, 38, 264–66
Winslow, Anna, 140
Winslow, Joshua, 140
Winsor, Frederick, 330
Winsor, Mary Pickard, 330
Winsor, Mary Pickard, II, 330
Winstanley, Clement, 62, 63
Winstanley, James, 62, 63
Winstanley, Katherine, 62, 63
Winthrop, Elizabeth, 81
Winthrop, John, 81
Winthrop, Samuel, 81
Wintle, Samuel, **323**
Wisdome, John, **76–77**, 85
W maker's mark, 325
WN maker's mark, 344
Wood, Samuel, **157–58**, **164–65**
Wooler, William, 363
Woolsey, Heathcote M., 192
Workman, Edward, 341
Worshipful Company of Goldsmiths, 13, 14, 59
WP maker's mark, 192, 238, 321
Wright, Charles, 205, **210–211**, **227**, 241
WS maker's mark, 232, 270, 327
WS over RC, 320
WS/WP maker's mark, 170–71
WW/BT maker's mark, 297
WW maker's mark, 347, 363
Wyatt, James, 219, 222, 247, 271
Wyatt, Samuel, 190
Wyndham, Anne, 194, 196
Wyndham, William, 196
Wynn, Watkin, Williams, 175

Y

Yorke, Philip, first earl of Hardwicke, 112, 113
Yorke, Phillip, first earl of Hardwick, 142
Young, William, 165